# Politics and Constitutions in Southeast Asia



In recent years the constitutional landscape of Southeast Asia has changed tremendously. Against a worldwide background of liberalization, globalization, and democratization, states in the region have begun to alter their constitutions, reinforcing human rights provisions, and putting in place institutional safeguards, such as constitutional courts and human rights commissions. On closer examination, however, the picture is very complex, with constitutional developments differing greatly between states. This book explores a range of current constitutional developments in the different states of Southeast Asia. It considers various constitutional areas, including constitution drafting, human rights, legal safeguards and the continuing role of the military, sets constitutional developments in the wider political and historical context of each country, and makes comparisons both with Western democracies and with other developing regions. The book concludes by assessing overall how far constitutional practices and trajectories are converging toward a liberal Western model or toward a distinctly Southeast Asian model.

**Marco Bünte** is Associate Professor at the School of Arts and Social Science at Monash University, Malaysia Campus.

**Björn Dressel** is Senior Lecturer in the Crawford School of Public Policy at the Australian National University, Australia.

**Routledge Law in Asia**
Series editors: Randall Peerenboom and Pip Nicholson

3 **Support for Victims of Crime in Asia**
*Edited by Wing-Cheong Chan*

4 **Administrative Law and Governance in Asia**
Comparative perspectives
*Edited by Tom Ginsburg and Albert H.Y. Chen*

5 **Regulation in Asia**
*Edited by John Gillespie and Randall Peerenboom*

6 **New Courts in Asia**
*Edited by Andrew Harding and Penelope (Pip) Nicholson*

7 **Legal Education in Asia**
*Edited by Stacey Steele and Kathryn Taylor*

8 **Legal Reforms in China and Vietnam**
A comparison of Asian Communist regimes
*John Gillespie and Albert H.Y. Chen*

9 **Public Interest Litigation in Asia**
*Po Jen Yap and Holning Lau*

10 **Freedom of Information Reform in China**
Information flow analysis
*Weibing Xiao*

11 **Law and Development in Asia**
*Edited by Gerald Paul McAlinn and Caslav Pejovic*

12 **The Judicialization of Politics in Asia**
*Edited by Bjorn Dressel*

13 **Juries in the Japanese Legal System**
The continuing struggle for citizen participation and democracy
*Dimitri Vanoverbeke*

14 **Confucian Constitutionalism in East Asia**
*Bui Ngoc Son*

15 **Religion, Law and Intolerance in Indonesia**
*Tim Lindsey and Helen Pausacker*

16 **Constitutional Interpretation in Singapore**
Theory and practice
*Jaclyn L. Neo*

17 **Politics and Constitutions in Southeast Asia**
*Edited by Marco Bünte and Björn Dressel*

# Politics and Constitutions in Southeast Asia

**Edited by Marco Bünte and Björn Dressel**

Routledge
Taylor & Francis Group
LONDON AND NEW YORK

First published 2017 by Routledge

2 Park Square, Milton Park, Abingdon, Oxfordshire OX14 4RN
711 Third Avenue, New York, NY 10017

*Routledge is an imprint of the Taylor & Francis Group, an informa business*

First issued in paperback 2017



*British Library Cataloguing in Publication Data*
A catalogue record for this book is available from the British Library

*Library of Congress Cataloging in Publication Data*
Names: Dressel, Bjèorn, editor. | Bèunte, Marco, 1970– editor.
Title: Politics and constitutions in Southeast Asia / edited by
Marco Bèunte and Bjèorn Dressel.
Description: Abingdon, Oxon ; New York : Routledge, 2016. | Series:
Routledge law in Asia ; 17 | Includes bibliographical references and index.
Identifiers: LCCN 2016005449| ISBN 9781138847545 (hardback) |
ISBN 9781315726687 (ebook)
Subjects: LCSH: Constitutional law–Southeast Asia.
Classification: LCC KNC524 .P65 2016 | DDC 342.59–dc23
LC record available at http://lccn.loc.gov/2016005449

ISBN: 978-1-138-84754-5 (hbk)
ISBN: 978-0-8153-5604-2 (pbk)

Typeset in Times New Roman
by Wearset Ltd, Boldon, Tyne and Wear

# Contents

# Illustrations

## Figures



## Tables

# Contributors

**Bui Hai Thiem** is a Research Fellow and Deputy Director of the Department for General Affairs at the Institute for Legislative Studies, National Assembly Standing Committee of Vietnam in Hanoi. His research focuses on civil society, constitutional politics, human rights, and electoral governance in Vietnam and has been published in a number of scholarly peer-reviewed journals such as *Asian Journal of Social Science*, *Contemporary Southeast Asia*, *Journal of Vietnamese Studies*, and *Global Change, Peace and Security*.

**Marco Bünte** is an Associate Professor of Politics and International Relations and Deputy Head of School (Research) in the School of Arts and Social Sciences at Monash University, Malaysia Campus. His research interests include constitutionalism, governance, democratization, human rights, and civil–military relations. He is co-editor of *The Crisis of Democratic Governance in Southeast Asia* (Palgrave 2011) and *Democratization in Post Suharto Indonesia* (Routledge 2009). He has published in a number of international journals such as *Armed Forces and Society*, *Asian Survey*, *Contemporary Southeast Asia*, and *Journal of Current Southeast Asian Affairs*.

**Paul Chambers** serves as Professor and Researcher, Office of the University, Chiang Mai University. He is also concurrently Research Fellow at the Peace Research Institute Frankfurt (Germany), and the German Institute of Global and Area Studies, Hamburg (Germany). He has written extensively on democracy and civil–military relations in Southeast Asia and has published widely as the author of books, chapters and journal articles.

**Aurel Croissant** is Professor at the Institute of Political Science at the Ruprecht-Karls-Universität Heidelberg, Germany. His main areas of research include comparative politics of East and Southeast Asia, democratization studies, civil–military relations, and comparative authoritarianism. He is co-editor of the journal *Democratization* (Taylor & Francis) and has published about 200 books, edited volumes and articles in English, German, Korean, Russian, and Spanish.

**Imelda Deinla** is a Postdoctoral Research Fellow at the Regulatory Institutions Network, College of Asia and the Pacific of the Australian National University.

Her main area of research is in socio-legal studies looking at the intersection between law, society and justice, and dynamics of plural legal orders in national and transnational settings. She works on research on pluralist justice, women, and peacebuilding in Mindanao, the Philippines.

**Björn Dressel** is a Senior Lecturer in the Crawford School of Public Policy at the Australian National University (ANU), Australia, and also currently holds an Australian Research Council Early Career Research Award (2013–2016). His research is concerned with issues of comparative constitutionalism, judicial politics, and governance and public sector reform in Asia and sub-Saharan Africa. He has published in a range of international journals, including the *Journal of Democracy, Governance, Administration and Society*, *Contemporary Southeast Asia*, and *Pacific Review*. He is editor of *The Judicialization of Politics in Asia* (Routledge 2012).

**Renaud Egreteau** (PhD Sciences Po Paris, 2006) is a 2015 to 2016 Wilson Scholar at the Woodrow Wilson International Center for Scholars, Washington DC, where he researches the resurgence of parliamentary and legislative affairs in post-junta Myanmar. He previously taught comparative politics at Sciences Po Paris (2008–2009) and the University of Hong Kong (2009–2013), and held a visiting fellowship at the Institute of Southeast Asian Studies (ISEAS) of Singapore (2015). His latest monographs include *Caretaking Democratization: The Military and Political Change in Myanmar* (forthcoming 2016) and (with Larry Jagan) *Soldiers and Diplomacy in Burma* (2013).

**Rui Graça Feijó** (D.Phil, Oxon, 1984) is Assistant Researcher at the Centro de Estudos Sociais, University of Coimbra. He is the author of *Tropical Landscape with People Inside* (2006), *The Timorese Semi-presidentialism* (2014), and of a forthcoming volume, *Dynamics of Democracy in Timor-Leste – The Birth of a Democratic Nation* (2016) as well as several articles and book chapters on the construction of Timorese identity and its democratic process after 1999. His current research focuses on the dynamics of power at grassroots level, comprehending both *suco*s and *aldeia*s and the novel municipal institutions.

**Stephen McCarthy** is a Senior Lecturer in Southeast Asian politics and a member of the Griffith Asia Institute, Griffith University, Australia. He is the author of numerous articles and a book on politics in Singapore and Burma. His current research interests include the rule of law in Southeast Asia and the political economy of forestry governance in the Asia Pacific.

**Eugénie Mérieau** is currently pursuing a PhD in Political Science from the National Institute of Oriental Languages and Civilizations (INALCO), Paris, France. She holds a Master's degree in International Security from Sciences Po, Paris, and undergraduate degrees in political sciences, law, and Thai studies from Sciences-Po, Sorbonne and INALCO, respectively. She teaches political sciences and law at Sciences-Po, Paris, France and Thammasat

University, Bangkok, Thailand. Her research interests include constitutional law, political crisis, democratization, and the rule of law in Southeast Asia, and especially in Thailand. Her latest book publication is *Red-shirts in Thailand* (2013) (in French).

**Michael H. Nelson** is a Senior Research Fellow at the German-Southeast Asian Center of Excellence for Public Policy and Good Governance (CPG), Faculty of Law, Thammasat University. He published *Central Authority and Local Democratization in Thailand* (1998), and co-authored *Parliaments and Political Change in Asia* (2005). He edited *Thailand's New Politics* (2002) and *Thai Politics: Global and Local Perspectives* (2005). His research and publications concern the development and operation of Thailand's system of political representation (political parties, politicians, elections, and voting behavior), constitutionalism, varieties of contemporary Thai political culture, and provincial-level political and administrative structures.

**Huong Thi Nguyen** received her PhD in Law and Democracy at Indiana University Maurer School of Law in 2014, where she also served as a Research Fellow at the Center for Constitutional Democracy from 2008 to 2014. Her research focus includes Vietnamese constitutionalism, constitutional design from a multidisciplinary perspective, judicial review in new democracies, and gender and constitutions. She was educated in Vietnam and France before coming to the USA. She received a Bachelor of Law degree from the University of Rennes I, a Master's I degree in French Public Law and a Master's II degree in Common Law from the University of Paris II, France.

**Malik Imtiaz Sarwar** is a Malaysian lawyer recognized for having been at the forefront of efforts to promote the rule of law, civil liberties, and a rights discourse in Malaysian society both in and out of court. He is regularly engaged as counsel to argue cases in the superior courts and has vast experience in the areas of civil and commercial, and constitutional and public interest litigation. He is well known for his work in constitutional, administrative, and human rights law, having appeared as counsel in many of the key cases of the past two decades. He is an opinion leader whose views are regularly sought on matters pertaining to law and society, and the administration of justice.

**Eugene K.B. Tan** is Associate Professor of Law at the School of Law, Singapore Management University (SMU). His interdisciplinary research interests include constitutional and administrative law, law and public policy, the regulation of ethnic conflict, and the government and politics of Singapore.

**Andreas Ufen** (PD Dr. Phil.) is a Senior Research Fellow at the German Institute of Global and Area Studies (GIGA), Hamburg. His main research interests are politics in Southeast Asia, with a focus on democratization, political Islam, political finance, and political parties. Among his publications are books on politics in Malaysia and Indonesia, edited volumes on *Democratization in Post-Suharto Indonesia* (with Marco Bünte) and on *Party Politics in Southeast Asia* (with Dirk Tomsa), and articles in journals such as *Pacific Review, South East Asia Research, Democratization, Critical Asian Studies*, and *Asian Survey*.

**Kheang Un** is an Associate Professor of Political Science and an associate of the Center for Southeast Asian Studies at Northern Illinois University. His teaching and research interests include democratization, the rule of law, and political economy with a focus on Cambodia. He is co-editor of *Cambodia's Economic Transformation* (2011). His other publications appear in such journals as *Democratization, International Political Science Review, Journal of Asian Studies, Pacific Affairs*, and *Asian Survey*.

# Preface

Over the past 25 years, the constitutional landscape of Southeast Asia has changed tremendously. As liberalization, globalization, and democratization were emerging throughout the world, states in the region began to dramatically alter their constitutions, reinforce the human rights provisions, and establish institutional safeguards for those rights, such as constitutional courts and human rights commissions. Even regimes that are less than democratic have at least to some degree followed this trend, strengthening judiciaries and expanding provision for the rule of law.

Or so it seems. A closer look at individual states in Southeast Asia suggests that constitutional trajectories and realities are not all that clear-cut. The region is marked by unusual diversity in terms of colonial history (British, Spanish, French, Dutch); religion (Christianity, Islam, Buddhism, Hinduism), and above all political regimes (democratic, semi-authoritarian, authoritarian, monarchical); it should thus not be surprising that not only do constitutional practices still differ substantially, but in practice the very notion of liberal Western constitutionalism is deeply contested.

This volume draws attention to areas of constitutional politics that have become flashpoints in the region: constitutional drafting and design – an arena where interests have clashed over both drafting dynamics and content choices (the rules of the political game); individual, collective and religious rights – an area that critically shapes the nature of state–society relations; the role of the military, which raises questions about how to tame extra-constitutional actors; and the rule of law, especially the extent to which courts should be guardians of the constitutional order, ensuring the primacy of law over politics. How such conflicts are resolved will critically shape future constitutional practice in the region. In turning a distinctly political lens on the debate, we seek to provide new insights, both empirical and conceptual, into whether and how deeper notions of constitutionalism may emerge in Southeast Asia. It is thus our hope that this collection will make a seminal contribution to the study of law and politics in Asia.

This collection had its genesis in the presentations of a panel at the European Association of Southeast Asian Studies (EUROSEAS) in Lisbon in 2013. We owe a considerable debt to the participants in that conference for insights and lively discussions that propelled us to pursue this project and invite other scholars to reflect on constitutionalism in Southeast Asia from the distinctly political perspective highlighted here. We are also grateful to colleagues and friends who graciously shared their opinions and expertise on the book's structure and chapter outlines. In particular, Melissa Crouch, John Gillespie, Sue Ingram, Allen Hicken, Dominic Nardi, Haig Patapan, Fiona Yap, and a number of anonymous peer reviewers gave us their support and insights as the project unfolded.

The editors are also grateful to their institutions. Marco wants to thank the School of Arts and Social Sciences of Monash Malaysia. Björn is particularly grateful to the Australian National University's Crawford School of Public Policy and the Australian Research Council's Discover Early Career Researcher Award (DE 130101706) for giving him the intellectual space, time, and financial means to pursue this project.

It is always a real pleasure to work with Peter Sowden and his editorial team at Routledge, who encouraged our initial ideas from the start and have persevered throughout the process, which took much longer than expected.

Our greatest thanks, however, go to the contributors whose work follows, not only for their patience throughout the editing process but especially for their remarkable scholarly insights.

# Introduction

# 1 Contesting constitutionalism

## Constitutional politics in Southeast Asia

*Björn Dressel and Marco Bünte*

### Introduction

Over the past two and a half decades, Southeast Asian states have started to change their constitutions, strengthen human rights provisions, and put in place institutional safeguards for those rights, such as constitutional courts and human rights commissions (Tan 2002; Menzel 2009). Even less-than-democratic regimes have at least to some degree been reinforcing courts and expanding provision for the rule of law. No wonder Albert Chen claims that "constitutionalism has significantly broadened and deepened its reach in Asia in modern and contemporary times" (Chen 2010). But constitutional trajectories and realities in Southeast Asia are hardly that clear-cut. As one might expect, given the marked diversity within the region in terms of colonial history (British, Spanish, French, Dutch); religion (Christianity, Islam, Buddhism, Hinduism); and above all political regimes (democratic, semi-authoritarian, authoritarian), constitutional practices differ substantially. Although they may gradually be eroding, the barriers to a more intense constitutional practice in Southeast Asia are still immense. The military still regularly intervenes in politics, abuses of human rights and liberties continue, and citizens struggle with the extent of the rule of law, judicial review, and notions of justice (Hassall and Saunders 2007). What we are observing in Southeast Asia is that constitutional politics is generating social conflicts. In Thailand, the constitutional reform debates that dominate the political agenda often fuel the divisions in a polity that is not only increasingly polarized but also increasingly violent. In Malaysia, recent court decisions on religious freedom have tested the constitutional boundaries of the multi-ethnic religious state. In the Philippines and Indonesia there is growing tension between the executive and judicial branches as the political role of courts expands. Meanwhile, in Myanmar we are witnessing debates that revolve around the question of how the overtly powerful military elites can be sidelined in a constitutional order that gives them far-reaching autonomy (Bünte forthcoming) – similar to East Timorese efforts to accommodate diverse elite interests within the constitution. Less visibly, in Vietnam and Laos latent conflict over land as well as ethnic and religious minority rights has renewed calls to amend the constitution. Constitutional politics is increasingly the focal point for collective action by both elites and ordinary citizens.

This remarkable shift raises serious questions. For instance, who are the actors, and what are the real issues? How do the arguments affect constitutional practice and progress toward more normative constitutionalism? How are states in the region addressing the new constitutional fault lines? Finally, how can what has been happening in Southeast Asia inform the global scholarly debate about constitutions and politics?

Current scholarship has analyzed such questions predominantly through the lens of legal and socio-legal scholarship, though political scientists have also chipped in with some views. For instance, legal scholars have sought to identify typologies of constitutional patterns derived from previous scholarship (Chen 2014) while highlighting path dependencies (e.g., wars, revolutions, colonial legacies) that have made it harder for constitutionalism to gain traction in the region (Tan 2002; Chang *et al.* 2014: 1–7). Others have begun to apply standard constitutional theories to the region, contemplating socioeconomic preconditions for constitutionalism and defining trigger points that may enable courts to uphold the constitutional framework (Ramraj 2010). These studies have been complemented by socio-legal work on new courts (constitutional and administrative) throughout Asia (see, e.g., Ginsburg and Chen 2009, Harding and Nicholson 2010), the judicialization of politics in Southeast Asia (Dressel 2012), and reflections on such individual constitutional issues as emergency powers (Ramraj and Thiruvengadam 2009) and rule of law nuances (Peerenboom 2004). Meanwhile, political scientists have been talking about aspects of constitutional engineering for more than a decade, and about the consequences of constitutional design choices for such political regime features as stability, political representation, and party systems (Persson and Tabellini 2003). Most recently, scholars have expanded the discussion to authoritarian regimes; the constitutional nexus is that authoritarian rulers have a vital interest in writing constitutions because they can ensure survival of the regime by helping to control or coordinate the actions of diverse constitutional and administrative bodies (Ginsburg and Moustafa 2008; Ginsburg and Simpser 2014).

Taking all these studies together, there is beginning to emerge a comprehensive picture of the constitutional landscape in the region that has both empirical and theoretical dimensions. Yet, seen with these new perspectives, it is difficult to identify the specific dynamics that propel states toward deeper constitutional practice. It may be that commentators have shied away from an explicit focus on the underlying political dynamics, particularly the sometimes confrontational negotiations of social forces arguing over constitutional issues. We propose here to look at constitutional practice in Southeast Asia through the distinctly political lens of contestation in order to put the politics from which constitutions emerge at center-stage. By drawing attention to four areas where viewpoints regularly differ about what constitutions should stand for – constitutional drafting; individual and religious rights; where the military fit in; the rule of law, courts, and justice – we argue that how states in Southeast Asia resolve the related conflicts will be critical to the future of constitutionalism in the region. What is central to this effort is the dynamics of constitutional contestation itself – the process by which incumbent elites compete, bargain, and struggle with oppositional groups (e.g., students, members of civil society organizations, disenfranchised elites) about what state institutions and the broader political order should look like, what rights should be granted, how these should be enforced, and particularly by whom. For constitutionalism to take hold, it will clearly take more than institutional change on paper. Instead, elites and regular citizens alike must come to agreement to support such basic features as separation of powers, checks and balances, judicial review, and specified rights. Such "constitutional settlements," born out of contestation and struggles, are critical to whether constitutional principles are adhered to and enforced. By, drawing attention to continuing constitutional flashpoints and how some have been transformed, we seek to provide new insights, both empirical and conceptual, into the potential for deeper notions of constitutionalism in Southeast Asia to emerge.

To illustrate the argument, the chapter is structured as follows. First, as context for our argument, we briefly discuss some current debates about constitutional practice in Southeast Asia. We then turn attention to the four areas of contestation – constitutional drafting and design; individual and religious rights; the role of military in constitutional politics; and the rule of law, courts and justice – that we consider to be of critical importance to the future of constitutionalism. The case study chapters in this volume then explore these areas more fully. The chapter concludes with reflections on the future of constitutionalism in Southeast Asia and how current developments might inform that future.

## Constitutions and constitutionalism in Southeast Asia

Although all Southeast Asian states have constitutions in place, the very notion of constitutionalism is regularly and deeply embedded (Tan 2002; Saunders 2009). In the context of democratization, liberalization, and the growing integration of world economies, almost all Southeast Asian states have comprehensively altered their constitutions in the past two decades (see Table 1.1). For the most part, the new constitutions replaced those drafted as part of the colonial handover, or its revolutionary aftermath (Chang *et al.* 2014: 57–63). Even where it seems that the same constitutions have been in place since independence – as in Malaysia, Singapore, and Brunei – they have repeatedly been amended.[1] Despite the diversity of their features, scope, and ambition, constitutions have thus been both central to Southeast Asia's modern state-building and responsive to rapid change.

But has concern for the constitutional document actually deepened constitutional practice? Consider Thailand. Its volatile history of 18 constitutions since 1945 is a vivid reminder that constitutions in Southeast Asia have been used to legitimize a variety of regimes, some of them far from constitutional. Constitutions alone cannot constrain, control, and regulate the exercise of power, ensure protection of fundamental rights, or prevent the arbitrary use of power. Even

*Table 1.1* Constitutions in Southeast Asia

| *Country* | *Year of the first constitution* | *Number of constitutions 1898–2014* | *Latest revision or full redraft* |
|---|---|---|---|
| Brunei | 1959 | 1 | 2004 |
| Cambodia | 1947 | 5 | 1999 |
| East Timor | 2002 | 1 | – |
| Indonesia | 1945 | 4 | 1999, 2000, 2001, 2002 |
| Laos | 1947 | 2 | 2003 |
| Malaysia | 1957 | 1 | * |
| Myanmar | 1947 | 3 | 2008 |
| Philippines | 1898 | 6 | 1986 |
| Singapore | 1959 | 1 | * |
| Thailand | 1932 | 18 | 2007 |
| Vietnam | 1946 | 4 | 2001, 2013 |

Source: Tan (2002), Hassall and Saunders (2007), Hill and Menzel (2002).

Note
* Constant revision.

where a constitution was very thoughtfully drafted, features considered central to modern constitutionalism – separation of powers, checks and balances, the rule of law, and constitutional judicial review and human rights – are not always put into practice. Continuing patterns of executive dominance, military interventions, and human rights abuses, not to mention ideological challenges to liberal constitutionalism, remind us that changes in the governing document do not guarantee true constitutionalism.

It is unquestionably difficult for regional observers to make sense of current constitutional diversity and to capture the divergence between formal constitutions and actual practice (Menzel 2009; Chen 2014). Indeed, the region is deeply engulfed in legacies of what an African commentator has termed "constitutions without constitutionalism" (Okoth-Ogendo 1991). Other authors have turned to classic typologies to describe the constitutional landscape in Southeast Asia. Particularly dominant here has been Loewenstein's famous tripartite classification of normative, nominal, and semantic constitutions (Loewenstein 1957). For him, the first describes "a living constitution, one that is real and effective and faithfully observed, actually governing the dynamics of the power process" (Loewenstein 1957: 148) but a nominal constitution is one "not lived in practice because socio-economic conditions mitigate against it" and a semantic one may be "fully applied and activated, but its ontological reality is nothing but the formalization of the existing location of political power for the exclusive benefit of the actual power holders" (Loewenstein 1957: 149). Sartori expressed a very similar notion in describing "garantiste," "nominal," or "façade" constitutions (1962), as did Chen in his descriptions of "liberal," "communist/socialist," and "hybrid" constitutions in Asia (2014: 13–15).

Most constitutions (and states) in Southeast Asia may probably best be classified as hybrids. To be sure, there are absolutist states like sultanist Brunei, and until very recently the military-ruled Burma; their constitutions might be classified as semantic. At the other extreme, practices in Indonesia and the Philippines occasionally come close to the normative ideal. But for the most part Southeast Asian states are still deeply entrenched in hybrid-nominal constitutional practices (Chen 2014: 30–31). Sometimes this is for ideological reasons, as in socialist Laos and Vietnam; in others, practice falls short of consistently ensuring key features of the constitutional compact, as in Thailand, Malaysia, Singapore, East Timor, and Cambodia. The uneven track record of the courts in upholding the supremacy of law in the region is surely a critical factor in this, though hardly the only one (Ramraj 2010; Dressel 2015). In fact, over time there has been considerable movement from semantic (façade) constitutional practices to more hybrid types, if not the beginnings of true normative constitutional practice, but because these outcomes are fragile, they fall well short of Western liberal constitutional practice.[2]

Standard contemporary constitutional theories have rarely been debated to Southeast Asia. For instance, states in the region are rarely the subject of arguments between legal constitutionalists, who see courts as the principal guardians of the constitutional order, and political constitutionalists, who see political institutions, such as parliaments, as the proper locus of constitutional constraint.[3] The same holds true for debates about the potential for the transformation of existing constitutional patterns in the region – which have often been assigned to vague notions of political and social preconditions (Ramraj 2010: 214–215).

A notable exception here has been the attempt to identify constitutional "tipping points," such as popular dissatisfaction with the status quo, a solid legal infrastructure, and an alternative set of legal and political norms that are minimally threatening to the political elite (Ramraj 2010: 216–217); but the only application of this theoretical debate so far has been to the courts – an institution that can hardly be understood in isolation from the entire constitutional context.

What is needed for Southeast Asia is a more comprehensive view of transformative constitutional dynamics. Although international dynamics (e.g., diffusion of constitutional models and their convergence) may be a factor, ultimately the prevailing dynamics must be domestic, given the distinct relationship of a constitution to the state for which it was created (Saunders 2014). More importantly, constitutional dynamics are ultimately political – and intimately related to power struggles. This notion is embedded in Loewenstein's dictum that a "constitution is what power holders and power addresses make of it in practical application" (Loewenstein 1957: 148). Other scholars have similarly described constitutions as "power maps" embodying broad political settlements between elite groups (Duchacek 1973; Okoth-Ogendo 1991). And reflective of the experience of constitutionalism in Europe, scholars have also been quick to point out that if constitutionalism is to gain hold in the region, "political struggles will be needed to establish the conditions in which the legal order can flourish" (Ramraj 2010: 213). As Chen points out, in fact the dynamics of change are often linked to specific areas of contestation – areas that have the potential to be transformative for constitutional practice (Chen 2014: 15–16).

It is thus within this broader debate that we draw attention to areas of constitutional politics that have become flashpoints in the region: constitutional drafting and design – an arena where interests have clashed over both drafting dynamics and constitutional design choices (the rules of the political game); human rights (individual, collective, and religious) – an area that critically shapes the nature of state–society relations; the role of the military (part of the question of how to tame extra-constitutional actors); and judiciaries, courts, and the rule of law (to what extent should courts be guardians of the constitutional order and thus enforce the primacy of law over politics?). How conflict plays out in these areas, we argue, will critically shape constitutional practice in the region.

## Crafting constitutionalism: four arenas of contestation

Each of the four areas we have identified has become a flashpoint for growing contestation in the region as aspirations grow and struggles for constitutionalism deepen.

### *Constitutional drafting and design*

Since the 1980s, constitution-making has become one of the most visible arenas for contestation. Contested here have been both the process itself and the content of the constitutional document. The two are, of course, closely related: the process is critical to the legitimacy of the document, and the interests it represents influence the ultimate content (Ghai 2004; Brandt *et al.* 2011). In fact, when a constitution is redrafted, how to organize the process, from selection of drafters to final approval, has generally aroused considerable debate. For instance, the 1986 Philippines "Freedom Constitution," which was drafted by a commission of 46 drafters appointed by the president, was criticized early on for its elitist, if not conservative, content (Villacorta 1988). Similarly, Indonesia's incremental amendment process (1999–2002), dominated by Members of Parliament, was heavily criticized by civil society actors, who were only minimally consulted (Horowitz 2013). Even in Thailand, where the 1997 constitutional reform was undertaken by a group of 99 drafters, a mix of appointed academics and elected provincial delegates, and incorporated considerable public consultation and engagement with civil society, questions were raised about the composition of the drafting group, the sincerity of the public outreach, and the behind-the-scenes influence of monarchical networks (Connors 2002; McCargo 2002; Dressel 2009).

Not surprisingly, such questions have been put forward even more vigorously where the process was heavily orchestrated by the military, as in Thailand (2007) and Burma (2008), approval by public referendum notwithstanding (Dressel 2009; Nyein 2009). And while constitutional change has been less participatory and transparent in socialist (Laos 2003; Vietnam 2001, 2013), monarchical (Brunei 2004), and one-party-dominated states (Malaysia, Singapore) – in all of which change has been regular and incremental because amendments are easily passed – debate on social networks and in the blogosphere makes it clear that the change process can still be contested vigorously.

However, while the process can be critical to the legitimacy of the document, more often it is the content that triggers intense public debate and even social action. This is not surprising. Many of the new constitutions introduced comprehensive change, such as new agencies of horizontal accountability (e.g., constitutional courts, human rights commissions, ombudsman offices); expanded individual and collective rights; and restructured (decentralized) state functions and the electoral process. These are all matters at the heart of how political power is organized. In Indonesia, questions about the role of the military, the Jakarta Charter, direct election of the president, and the extent of the revisions to the 1945 constitution were all hotly contested, occasionally to the brink of deadlock (Indrayana 2005; Butt and Lindsey 2012; Horowitz 2013). During the 1997 drafting process in Thailand, debates about the composition of the Senate, qualifications for MPs, and the role of Buddhism all animated vociferous discussion and even public protest (Connors 2002); so did the quotas reserved for military in Burma's legislative assembly in 2008, and the executive-led efforts in the Philippines to change the constitution from a presidential to a parliamentary system (Rüland 2003). Public debate continues over the actual meaning of the "law-governed socialist state" phrasing in the 2001 amendments in Vietnam – debates fueled by growing discontent over both land issues and the state's treatment of ethnic and religious minorities (Gillespie 2009).

Perhaps above all it is the frequent mismatch in the region between ambitious constitutional wording and what happens after it is passed that has generated skepticism and thus debate about constitutional change. Again, consider the Philippines, where among the responses to liberal features and an ambitious socio-economic rights agenda in the constitution have been executive abuse, extra-constitutional threats, and lagging economic and social performance; constitutional reform debates have been alive there for almost 20 years (Rüland 2003; Abueva 2007). But, more than anywhere else in the region, it is surely in Thailand that constitutional debates have been central to social contestation in recent times. There, electoral promises by then Prime Minister Yingluck Shinawatra (2011–2014) to amend the military-imposed 2007 constitution (with the goal of returning more closely to the 1997 version) and put it to a public referendum have not only been met by challenges in the Constitutional Court but have also directly fueled violent public protests seeking to oust the Prime Minister, before prompting the military to orchestrate a very different model under the 2015 constitutional framework that is opposed equally strenuously by the red shirt movement still faithful to ousted Prime Minister Thaksin Shinawatra (Chairat Charoensin-o-larn 2013). The old pattern of intra-elite contestation between military and bureaucratic actors has disappeared beneath the battles between the new and old elites, and the confrontation outcome has become so polarized that it seems unbridgeable, despite military-led efforts for a new constitution.

Thailand is a particularly vivid illustration of the rapidly changing constitutional environment in Southeast Asia, where new social actors not only question previous elite arrangements but also seek to be accommodated by the constitution. And yet as highlighted by the 2015 framework and its emphasis on constitutional adjudication in "accordance with the constitutional convention in the democratic regime of government with the King as Head of State,"[4] a very different constitutional model is suggested here – one that complements positivist notions with a vaguely defined political order based on extra-constitutional principles and power centers that lend support to the current status quo (Glaser 2015a, 2015b). Combined with ever-more-detailed constitutional documents, some of which come with policy prescriptions and distributional ramifications, constitutional reform is thus likely to continue to be a contested issue in the region for the foreseeable future. How states manage this process will be critical to how constitutionalism evolves in the region.

### *The military and constitutional politics*

When we see constitutions as a social contract or a compromise between certain social groups, it is important to get the military on board. As the traditional political veto player in the region, the military is of critical importance for an emerging constitutionalism, because only if its members accept the supremacy of (elected) politicians and their constitutionally enshrined decision-making authority can constitutionalism really gain ground. It is surely not surprising that such settlements have been difficult to achieve in countries where the military was a major factor in gaining or maintaining independence or where prolonged periods of military rule have left the military far more powerful than civilian institutions, as in Burma, Indonesia, Vietnam, and Thailand. The point is underscored by the fact that where this has not been the case, militaries have not had much lasting impact on either the constitution or the regime (Alagappa 2001; Croissant *et al.* 2012).

At the moment, Thailand is the only country in Southeast Asia that is directly ruled by the military. But even after the military coup of May 22, 2015 against the elected government of Yingluck Shinawatra, the ruling military junta opted to draft a new constitution to legitimize its political power. This replicates an old pattern: constitutions follow coups and general elections, although one has to admit that in recent times coups have become relatively rare. Yet, the example of Thailand shows the destructive effects on constitutionalism to evolve (Croissant 2013). Even in Myanmar, although still dominating behind the scenes, the military has formally withdrawn from the apex of power after ruling by decree for nearly 20 years (Bünte 2014).

The situation is considerably more benign in Indonesia, where compromise between military and social forces has paved the way to a broadening of constitutionalism. Once a defining force in Indonesian politics and a pillar of the Soeharto regime that was granted significant prerogatives, since democratization in 1998, the military has gradually lost much of its hegemonic position. Since 2004, constitutional amendments have ended military representations in Parliaments and active military members may no longer hold cabinet positions, which has made space for civilian institutions to mature (Mietzner 2011). As a result, constitutionalism and democracy have deepened in Indonesia – though the military has still not been held accountable for human rights violations in West Papua (Bünte and Ufen 2008).

In a number of other states in the region, however, the military has taken on a distinct political role that has prevented constitutionalism from truly taking root. The Burmese military has only recently started to allow discussions on constitutional amendments that may eventually reduce the political role of the military. In March 2013, members of the military-backed Union Solidarity and Development Party (USDP) submitted a proposal that led to the establishment of the Joint Committee for Reviewing the Constitution (JCRC). The Committee, dominated by the USDP (52 members) and military representatives (25), may open up an opportunity for a constitutional settlement with the oppositional groups represented by the NLD (seven members) and 25 members of the ethnic parties.[5] This may be a remarkable breakthrough, considering that the former military regime spent 18 years drafting a constitution that totally reflected the military worldview and gave it a leading role in political affairs. The whole drafting process was "marred by a lack of inclusiveness, heavy restrictions on public debate and little input by the participants in the final product" (Pedersen 2011: 62). The constitution as not yet amended guarantees a military presence in local and national parliaments, reserves the most important ministries for military representatives, and gives them impunity for past human rights violations. Moreover, it allows them a veto over constitutional change, since the constitution can only be changed with a quorum of 75 percent and a public referendum. Thus, the process of military withdrawal and constitutional settlement is only in a very early stage; it may well be that the debate on constitutional reforms is only a ploy to appease the international community.

Then there is the Thai military. After staying in its barracks for more than ten years, it has chosen to re-enter politics – a move that has had considerable consequences for Thailand's nascent constitutionalism. In the first military coup since 1991, in 2006 the military ousted elected Prime Minister Thaksin Shinawatra, abrogated the constitution, and drafted an interim document to legitimize the coup. It also allowed them to heavily influence the Constitutional Drafting Assembly that put together the new 2007 constitution, a process limited to the elite and carefully selected representatives of civil society and the middle class (Hewison 2007; Dressel 2009). Not surprisingly, the 2007 constitution, which gave the military a guardian role over politics, was heavily criticized by opposition parties, the emerging red shirt movements, and academics and intellectuals; it succeeded only in creating divisions within Thai society between traditional power circles of the palace and bureaucracy and the new social forces that Thaksin had brought into play. The ensuing seven years of polarization, political maneuvers, and violent street politics make it obvious that there is as yet no viable constitutional settlement, despite renewed efforts under the 2015 constitutional framework.

### *Human rights*

Human rights, particularly the extent to which individual, collective, and religious rights are respected and enforced, are another substantial bone of contention. They are in fact critical to shaping the relationship of the individual to the state, and thus broader state–society relations, and it is here that progress has been particularly uneven.

To be sure, all the states in the region except Brunei have adopted constitutional rights "catalogs," many of which have greatly expanded political, social, and economic rights. All the ASEAN countries have also ratified at least two of the six major human rights treaties, which suggests a willingness to buy into the global human rights system (Rich 2010). And yet, as is too often illustrated by, for example, extrajudicial killings, constraints on political activities, and failure to ensure the rights of religious and ethnic minorities, the reality has often been starkly different from the constitutional ideals (Peerenboom 2006).

Authoritarian and semi-authoritarian regimes cite security and public order to justify the constraints on human rights. For instance, the regular use of Internal Security Acts has considerably suppressed the expression of human and political rights, as members of the opposition in Singapore and Malaysia well know (Jayasuriya 2001). Meanwhile, Thailand has increasingly used its *lèse-majesté* law to rein in critics of the arrangements of the old elites (Streckfuss 2011; Hewison 2013). And in Malaysia, with islamization growing, highly polarizing government and court decisions on religious rights have also highlighted heavier constraints on the right to choose, leave, and exercise a religion (Karean 2006; Sarwar 2012). Similarly, failures to protect religious minorities, such as the Ahmadiyya community in Indonesia or the Rohingyas in Burma, have illuminated practical constraints that religious minority groups face in exercising their faith (Schabas *et al.* 2010).

The broader human rights picture is hardly much better. For instance, as international human rights reports regularly stress, areas like Mindanao, West Papua, and parts of Burma are effectively beyond the reach of law and thus formal justice. There, extrajudicial killings, torture, and violence against minorities are widespread, often with the implicit support of the security forces, who illustrate the sense of impunity of those in power. Extrajudicial killings in the Philippines are well documented, particularly against members of the political Left (Dressel 2011: 532). In Indonesia, security forces have also been able to operate almost with impunity, as illustrated in the abuses committed in East Timor or Papua (International Commission of Inquiry 2000; Brundige *et al.* 2004). Similarly, during the "war on drugs" (2003) under the Thaksin government in Thailand, human rights abuses were far-reaching (though at times with the implicit support of the public), and abuses by the security apparatus also seem to have fueled violence in Thailand's South.[6]

Such failures to consistently uphold the rights regime, domestic or international, also illuminate the general weakness of the justice institutions that should be supporting it. Not unlike the formal courts themselves, new human rights commissions and ombudsman offices have generally been reluctant to hold the executive branch and its security apparatus accountable for human rights violations. It may also be that given authoritarian legacies in many developing states, citizens themselves are still somewhat ambivalent about how far rule of law principles and rights should prevail against state interests (Dressel 2014). However, growing networks of lawyers and civil society groups are increasingly challenging half-hearted rights enforcement. These not only lend critical support to judicial and quasi-judicial institutions but also help to constitutionalize public debate, and juridify state–society relations beyond the constitutional realm, particularly in areas of civil liberties (Chua 2012). The international community in tandem with transnational advocacy groups is pushing for an increased human rights compliance and Southeast Asian states have – at least rhetorically – supported the most important human rights treaties. Yet, the battle over rights is still ongoing and how it unfolds will be deeply important to the fate of constitutionalism in Southeast Asia.

### *Rule of law, courts, and justice*

Both the rule of law and the role of the judiciary have had a chequered history in Southeast Asia (Lindsey 2007; Chen 2009). Recent constitutional changes, many of which have greatly empowered courts, have returned them to center-stage, generally as part of a general process of "judicialization of politics" in Southeast Asia (Dressel 2015). Yet with conflict growing over the appropriate role of courts in political matters and persistent legacies of rule by law in support of political rule rather than rule of law that seeks to constraint it, both areas have become central to constitutional contestation in the region, with far-reaching consequences for constitutional practice.

Constitutional reforms have been a major impetus behind these developments. For instance, starting with the empowerment of the Philippines Supreme Court by the 1986 constitution, most reforms have reinforced the independence and powers of the judicial branch, such as the creation of high-profile constitutional courts in Thailand (1997) and Indonesia (2003), and the related Constitutional Council in Cambodia (1998) and Constitutional Tribunal in Burma (2011) (Harding and Leyland 2009). Combined with powers to uphold the new rights provisions and to intervene in high-level political conflict (e.g., impeachment, electoral disputes, and executive prerogatives), these new courts have become central players in the evolving constitutional landscape. Even in Vietnam, where the 1992/2001 constitutional reforms affirmed both property and human rights, there is now talk of creating a constitutional court that would replace the current constitutional council.[7] In short, within a dramatically transformed constitutional landscape, judicial actors have become critical to how constitutional practice is evolving in the region.

There are signs that judicial assertiveness has been growing, but courts in the region have highly uneven records. For instance, while the judicial activism of the Philippines Supreme Court has been well documented, practices of extra-constitutional ouster ("people power") and accusations of corruption and politicization of the court system indicate continuing weaknesses. And while the Indonesian Constitutional Court has actively intervened in electoral disputes and human rights cases, often supporting the deepening of democratic practice, the bold interventions of Thailand's Constitutional Court during the political crisis in 2006 to 2008 tell a far more cautionary tale – one that has raised questions about the independence of the court that have ultimately undermined its legitimacy (Dressel and Mietzner 2012). In other countries, meanwhile, the behavior of the courts has been far more muted, to the point that some have largely failed to consistently uphold the rule of law. This is certainly true of the socialist countries in the region, but also of Cambodia, Malaysia, and Singapore – states where executive and single-party dominance have in practice considerably constrained judicial behavior, particularly in terms of political cases (Khoo Boo Teik 1999; Worthington 2001). This has led to claims that justice mechanisms are absent (Armytage 2012).

In the wider political context, judicial attempts at greater assertiveness have occasionally been forcefully rebuffed by the executive, as was most obvious in the Malaysian constitutional crisis of 1988, which ended with the ousting of the Chief Justice and two of his colleagues. That event still has repercussions today, especially in high-profile political and religious cases, that raise troubling questions about the independence of the Malaysian court system (Lee 2010; Tey 2011). The 2012 impeachment of the Chief Justice of the Philippines for failing to report assets has been tainted by suggestions that the executive was trying to gain control over the court, which had been seen as hostile to him due to the close connections of the justices to his predecessor.[8]

Similar though perhaps more subtle interference is reported from Cambodia, and even in Singapore close relations with political elites have led to active judicial support for the state's communitarian values (political stability, interracial harmony, and economic development), which in turn severely limits the role of the courts in constitutional and political matters. And while thus far the Indonesian Constitutional Court has won much praise for its assertive and balanced views, the 2013 impeachment of its Chief Justice for corruption is a vivid reminder that perennial problems of capacity and corruption endemic to the region challenge public trust in judges and courts.[9] This is particularly so when courts are tested in high-profile political cases.

Newly empowered and critical to safeguarding the constitutional order, courts have become central actors in the region's search for viable justice mechanisms. Yet with a growing role in political matters, they have found it hard to avoid political interference and public criticism, particularly when mega-political cases can divide a whole nation. How courts navigate the demands upon them and whether they can resolve high-profile constitutional conflicts in a manner seen to be fair and consistent with rule of law principles will be critical to the future of constitutionalism in Southeast Asia.

## Conclusion and structure of the book

In this introduction, we have sought to draw attention to four arenas of continuing constitutional contestation (constitutional drafting and design; individual and religious rights; the role of the military in constitutional politics; and the rule of law and courts) that are of critical importance to how constitutional practice evolves in Southeast Asia. In doing so, we seek to supplement traditional legal scholarship with a distinctly political lens through which to view constitutional debates and the divergence between constitutional specifics and actual practice in the region.

With these parameters in mind, we now turn our attention to the specific contributions that follow. Organized in terms of the four arenas of contestation described, the chapters were selected for their instructive insights into those issues.

Part I brings together contributions on constitutional drafting and design. Drawing on developments in the region over the last quarter of a century, **Aurel Croissant** finds that the upstream, downstream, and procedural legitimacy that are often posited may be less relevant for the acceptance of constitutional documents than the day-to-day applications of the constitution in practice, thus opening up the possibility for a constitution which lacks procedural legitimacy to be transformed into a lasting and universally accepted law of the land. **Michael H. Nelson**'s contribution further explores drafting dynamics with an intensive study of the design of the electoral system and the Thai Senate during the 2007 constitution-making, highlighting how Thai traditional elites have used constitution-making to consolidate their power and ward off majoritarian challenges from new social forces. **Rui Graça Feijó** similarly looks closely at constitution-making in the often ignored case of East Timor, raising concerns that the traditional elite-driven approach taken in 2002 may have produced a legitimacy deficit that yet haunts the young nation and its evolving constitutional developments. Combined, these chapters thus illuminate the continuing contestation in the constitutional space in Southeast Asia – one that does not sit comfortably with propositions put forward in the literature.

Part II expands the analysis to a second area of contestation – the never-ending challenge of exerting civilian control over such extra-constitutional forces as the military. **Paul Chambers**, recognizing the diverse trajectories in Thailand, the Philippines and Myanmar, offers a cautionary tale here in pointing out that constitutional incorporation of security forces in many instances does not support a transition to civilian control. The chapter by **Renaud Egreteau** extends this critical analysis with an in-depth look at Myanmar – a country that according to the author has seen "constitutional praetorianism" emerge as a new model in the 2008 constitutional framework – thus raising the question of how it can move to a more liberal form of constitutionalism in the future. That this may not be easy task is also made clear by **Eugénie Mérieau** and her case study of developments in Thailand, in which she argues that increasingly intertwined networks between judges and military have consolidated the hold of traditional elites on power, despite liberal constitutional changes and a gradual retreat of the military under the 1997, 2007, and 2015 constitutions.

Part III turns the attention to contestation over human and individual rights in the region. **Marco Bünte** offers a panoramic overview of human rights developments, arguing that though the region has seen some minor improvements, the commitments have largely been rhetorical or tactical, leaving a wide gap between legal commitments and actual compliance. The more democratic states in Southeast Asia have established human rights institutions that bridge international and local institutions. The Indonesian and Philippine National Human Rights Institutions and (until 2006) their Thai counterpart enjoyed broad support and had considerable impact in the immediate post-authoritarian order. They helped to put human rights on the political agenda and socialize human rights among members of former military regimes. In the more authoritarian states, such as Malaysia, Thailand (after 2006), and to a limited extent Myanmar, national human rights institutions are important for challenging state power and raising human rights consciousness.

**Andreas Ufen** in his comparative study of Malaysia and Indonesia provides a compelling narrative on how differences in the composition and stability of elite structures have led to a gradual deterioration of religious minority rights in both, thus highlighting an often understudied nexus between political power and rights protection. Taking a close look at constitutional developments in Vietnam, **Bui Hai Thiem**'s chapter strikes a more optimistic note; he advances the argument that the changing discourse on human rights in Vietnam is likely to transcend the socialist-law-based-state concept and create a new human rights identity. Whether such a development indicates a trend unfolding throughout the region, or whether countries will be able to maintain their unique trajectories in the years to come is implicitly raised by **Eugene K.B. Tan**'s chapter on Singapore, in which he demonstrates how a statist discourse of interests, duties, and responsibilities – rather than rights and entitlements – has become the de facto language of citizenship, further consolidating Singapore's exceptional status in the region.

Finally, Part IV draws attention to the contested area of rule of law and courts. **Björn Dressel**'s contribution draws attention to the variety of constitutional politics patterns in the region, thus highlighting the need to pluralize the understanding of constitutionalism and drawing attention to variations in the role of the judiciary in sustaining such patterns as a result of the interplay between the dynamics of demand and supply. How these dynamics play out in detail is elaborated by the following chapters: **Huong Thi Nguyen**'s contribution provides evidence of the ongoing debates and power struggles over rule of law concepts in Vietnam as demonstrated in the 2013 constitutional amendment process. **Imelda Deinla**'s contribution focuses on the role of the Philippines Supreme Court in the post-Marcos democratic period. Drawing upon public opinion data, she argues that the court's behavior – particularly its assertive stance vis-à-vis contending political actors – is best understood as a direct outcome of the support the court has been able to generate within the wider public.

The last two contributions focus more narrowly on rule of law dynamics in semi-authoritarian, illiberal constitutional contexts. The chapter by **Stephen McCarthy** and **Kheang Un** points up the similarities and convergence of trajectories in Cambodia and Singapore, arguing that in both, political elites have come to use courts and legal proceedings as a subtle and legitimate strategy of social control. Similarly, the final chapter by **Malik Imtiaz Sarwar** discusses how the gradual erosion of the independence of the juridiciary in Malaysia since the late 1980s has gradually paved the way for the erosion of the constitutional protection of religious freedom, thus testing the very fabric of the nation's multiethnic and religious state in unprecedented ways.

In sum, as the articles selected for this volume highlight, Southeast Asia is certainly a challenging environment for constitutional theory and practice. Despite more than two decades of far-reaching constitutional and institutional changes, most states in the region are at best hybrids of tradition and Western constitutional practice, and features central to constitutionalism (separation of powers, checks and balances, judicial review, the rule of law) may be observed at best only partially. The diversity of political regimes in the region, from authoritarian through ideological counter-narratives (e.g., socialist, communitarian), and the traditional weakness of justice institutions that resulted from colonial practices and executive dominance are a partial explanation but are hardly sufficient to account for the current dynamics. A much better understanding may be gained by concentrating on the struggles, bargains, and contentious politics that take place among elites and between them and other citizens in the four constitutional areas treated here.

It is hoped that our approach will help to pave the way for a more nuanced understanding of Asian constitutional developments, one that views current outcomes not as simply lagging versions of Western constitutionalism but rather as distinctive models that directly reflect unique sociopolitical struggles, and bargains, among social forces. It should be clear from our description that constitutional trajectories are likely to remain diverse and far from certain, especially since the region lacks the cultural and political homogeneity of East Asia.[10]

By substituting for current legal and socio-legal approaches a distinctly political view of the contentious dynamics that underpin constitutional settlements in Southeast Asia, it is our hope to offer a new perspective on how the constitutional transformation is evolving there. It is also our hope that this entire volume will stimulate a new research agenda, one that is both theoretical and empirical, on constitutional politics in the region.

## Notes

1 Malaysia's constitution has been amended 50 times, and the Singaporean constitution 38 times.

2 Western constitutionalism is defined here by including both procedural and substantial notions; see, for instance, Louis Henkin, "A New Birth of Constitutionalism: Genetic Influence and Genetic Defects," in *Constitutionalism, Identity, Difference, and Legitimacy: Theoretical Perspectives*, edited by Michel Rosenfeldt (Durham, NC:

Duke University Press, 1994), pp. 39–54; Neville Johnson, "Constitutionalism: Procedural Limits and Political Ends," in *Constitutional Policy and Change in Europe*, edited by Jörg J. Hesse and Neville Johnson (Oxford: Oxford University Press, 1995), pp. 46–63.

3 See, for the broader law and politics debate: Martin Loughlin, *Swords and Scales. An Examination of the Relationship between Law and Politics* (Oxford, and Portland, OR: Hart Publishing, 2000); Adam Tomkin, "In Defence of the Political Constitution," *Oxford Journal of Legal Studies* 22, no. 1 (2002): 157–175; Tom Hickman, "In Defence of the Legal Constitution," *University of Toronto Law Journal* 55 (2005): 981–1022; Richard Bellamy, *Political Constitutionalism: A Republican Defense of the Constitutionality of Democracy* (Cambridge: Cambridge University Press, 2007).

4 Art 7, I of the 2015 constitution reads: "Whenever no provision under this Constitution is applicable to any case, it shall be decided in accordance with the constitutional convention in the democratic regime of government with the King as Head of State" (translation Pakorn Nilprapunt, Chintapun Dungsubutra, Vareerat Ratanaviboonsom and Natthanicha Aneksomboonphol, Office of the Council of State of Thailand).

5 Tim McLaughlin, "Pressure Mounts for Constitutional Reform," *Myanmar Times*, August 7, 2013.

6 See www.hrw.org/news/2013/03/08/thailand-justice-key-success-south-dialogue.

7 See http://english.vietnamnet.vn/fms/government/66904/vietnam-will-have-constitutional-council-or-constitutional-court-.html.

8 See www.eastasiaforum.org/2012/03/22/thrilla-in-manila-impeachment-of-the-philippine-s-chief-justice/.

9 See Top Indonesian "Anticorruption" Judge Is Arrested for Graft | TIME.com http://world.time.com/2013/10/04/arrest-of-antigraft-judge-shows-depth-of-indonesias-corruption-crisis/#ixzz2s3HZtvza.

10 Jiunn-Rong Yeh and Wen-Chen Chang, "The Emergence of East Asian Constitutionalism: Features in Comparison," *The American Journal of Comparative Law* 59, no. 3 (2011): 805–840.

## Bibliography


Abueva, J.B. (2007). "Proposed Constitutional Reforms for Good Governance and Nation Building." In *Whither the Philippines in the 21st Century?*, eds R.C. Severino and L.C. Salazar. Singapore, ISEAS, pp. 43–78.

Alagappa, M. (2001). *Coercion and Governance: The Declining Political Role of the Military in Asia.* Palo Alto, CA, Stanford University Press.

Armytage, L. (2012). *Reforming Justice. A Journey to Fairness in Asia.* Cambridge, Cambridge University Press.

Brandt, Michele, Jill Cottrell, Yash Ghai, and A. Regan (2011). *Constituton-making and Reform: Options for the Process.* Geneva, Interpeace.

Brundige, E., W. King, P. Vahali, S. Vladeck, and X. Yuan (2004). "Indonesian Human Rights Abuses in West Papua: Application of the Law of Genocide to the History of Indonesian Control." Paper prepared for the Indonesia Human Rights Network. New Haven, Allard K. Lowenstein International Human Rights Clinic Yale Law School.

Bünte, M. (2014). "Burma's Transition to Quasi-military Rule: From Rulers to Guardians." *Armed Forces and Society*, 40(2): 1–23.

Bünte, M. (forthcoming). "Myanmar's Protracted Transition: Actors, Arenas and Outcomes." *Asian Survey.*

Bünte, M. and A. Ufen, eds (2008). *Democratization in Post-Suharto Indonesia.* London, Routledge.

Butt, S. and T. Lindsey (2012). *The Constitution of Indonesia. A Contextual Analysis.* Oxford and Portland, Hart Publishing.

Chairat Charoensin-o-larn (2013). "Thailand in 2012: A Year of Truth, Reconciliation, and Continued Divide." In *Southeast Asian Affairs 2013*, eds D. Sing and L.C. Salazar. Singapore, ISEAS, pp. 285–304.

Chang, W.-C., L.-a. Thio, K.Y. Tan, and J-r. Yeh (2014). *Constitutionalism in Asia. Cases and Materials*. Oxford and Portland, OR, Hart Publishing.

Chen, A.H.Y. (2009). Conclusion: "Reflections on Administrative Law and Judicialized Governance in East and Southeast Asia." In *Administrative Law and Governance in Asia. Comparative Perspectives*, eds T. Ginsburg and A.H.Y. Chen. London and New York, Routledge, pp. 359–380.

Chen, A.H.Y. (2010). "Pathways of Western Liberal Constitutional Development in Asia: A Comparative Study of Five Major Nations." *I Con*, 8(4): 849–884.

Chen, A.H.Y. (2014). "The Achievement of Constitutionalism in Asia: Moving Beyond Constitutions without Constitutionalism." In *Constitutionalism in Asia in the Early Twenty-first Century*, ed. A.H.Y. Chen. Cambridge and New York, Cambridge University Press, pp. 1–24.

Chua, L.J. (2012). "Pragmatic Resistance, Law, and Social Movements in Authoritarian States: The Case of Gay Collective Action in Singapore." *Law and Society Review*, 46(4): 713–748.

Connors, M.K. (2002). "Framing the 'People's Constitution'." In *Reforming Thai Politics*, ed. D. McCargo. Copenhagen, NIAS, pp. 37–55.

Croissant, A. (2013). "Coups and Post-coup Politics in Southeast Asia and the Pacific – Conceptual and Comparative Perspectives." *Australian Journal of International Affairs*, 67(3): 264–280.

Croissant, A., D. Kuehn and P. Lorenz (2012). *Breaking with the Past? Civil–Military Relations in the Emerging Democracies of East Asia.* Honolulu, East–West Center.

Dressel, B. (2009). "Thailand's Elusive Quest for a Constitutional Equilibrium, 1997–2007." *Contemporary Southeast Asia*, 31(2): 296–325.

Dressel, B. (2011). "The Philippines: How Much Real Democracy?" *International Political Science Review*, 32(5): 529–545.

Dressel, B., ed. (2012). *The Judicialization of Politics in Asia*. Abingdon and New York, Routledge.

Dressel, B. (2014). "Public Administration and the Rule of Law in Asia: Breadth without Depth?" *The Asia Pacific Journal of Public Administration*, 36(1): 9–21.

Dressel, B. (2015). "Courts and Judicialization in Southeast Asia." In *Routledge Handbook of Southeast Asian Democratization*, ed. W. Case. Abingdon and New York, Routledge, pp. 268–282.

Dressel, B. and M. Mietzner (2012). "The Judicialization of Electoral Politics in Asia: A Tale of Two Courts." *Governance*, 25(3): 391–414.

Duchacek, I. (1973). *Power Maps: Comparative Politics of Constitutions.* Santa Barbara, A.B.C.-Clio.

Ghai, Y. (2004). *The Constitution Reform Process: Comparative Perspectives*. Conference, Toward Inclusive and Participatory Constitution Making. Kathmandu, IDEA.

Gillespie, J. (2009). "The Juridification of Administrative Complaints and Review in Vietnam." In *Administrative Law and Governance in Asia*, eds T. Ginsburg and A.H.Y. Chen. London and New York, Routledge, pp. 205–229.

Ginsburg, T. and A.H.Y. Chen, eds (2009). *Administrative Law and Governance in Asia. Comparative Perspectives*. New York, Routledge.

Ginsburg, T. and T. Moustafa (2008). *Rule by Law: The Politics of Courts in Authoritarian Regimes*. Cambridge and New York, Cambridge University Press.
Ginsburg, T. and A. Simpser (2014). *Constitutions in Authoritarian Regimes*. Cambridge, Cambridge University Press.
Glaser, H. (2015a). "Constitutional Conflict and Restatement: The Challenge and Transformation of the Hegemonic Basic Consent in Thailand." In *Norms, Interests, and Values. Conflict and Consent in the Constitutional Basic Order*, ed. H. Glaser. Baden Baden, Nomos, pp. 291–344.
Glaser, H. (2015b). "Weichenstellung fur den thailandischen Konstitutionalismus? Die Interimsverfassung 2014." *Die Offentliche Verwaltung*, January(Heft 2): 60–69.
Harding, A. and P. Leyland, eds (2009). *Constitutional Courts: A Comparative Study*. London, Wildy, Simmonds & Hill.
Harding, A. and P. Nicholson (2010). *New Courts in Asia*. Oxon and New York, Routledge, pp. 122–140.
Hassall, G. and C. Saunders (2007). *Asia Pacific Constitutional Systems*. Cambridge, Cambridge University Press.
Hewison, K. (2007). "Constitutions, Regimes and Power in Thailand." *Democratization*, 14(5): 928–945.
Hewison, K. (2013). "Thailand's Lèse-Majesté Erodes the Judiciary." *Asia Sentinel*.
Hill, Clauspeter and Jorg Menzel, eds (2009). *Constitutionalism in Southeast Asia*, vol. 3. Singapore, Konrad Adenauer Stiftung.
Horowitz, D. (2013). *Constitutional Change and Democracy in Indonesia*. Cambridge and New York, Cambridge University Press.
Indrayana, D. (2005). *Indonesian Constitutional Reform 1999–2002: An Evaluation of Constitution-making in Transition*. PhD thesis, The University of Melbourne.
International Commission of Inquiry (2000). *Report of the International Commission of Inquiry on East Timor to the Secretary-General*. New York, United Nations UN Doc. A/54/726-S/2000/59.
Jayasuriya, K. (2001). "The Exception Becomes the Norm: Law and Regimes of Exception in East Asia." *Asian-Pacific Law and Policy Journal*, 2(1): 108–124.
Karean, V.S. (2006). "The Malaysian Constitution and its Identity Crisis – Secular or Theocratic?" *LawAsia Journal*: 47–61.
Khoo Boo Teik (1999). "Between Law and Politics: The Malaysian Judiciary since Independence." In *Law, Capitalism and Power in Asia*, ed. K. Jayasuriya. London and New York, Routledge, pp. 205–232.
Lee, H.P. (2010). "Judiciaries in Crisis – Some Comparative Perspectives." *Federal Law Review*, 38(3): 371–389.
Lindsey, T., ed. (2007). *Law Reform in Developing and Transitional States*. London and New York, Routledge.
Loewenstein, K. (1957). *Political Power and the Government Process*. Chicago, IL, University of Chicago Press.
McCargo, D. (2002). "Introduction: Understanding Political Reform in Thailand." In *Reforming Thai Politics*, ed. D. McCargo. Copenhagen, NIAS, pp. 1–18.
Menzel, J. (2009). "Constitutionalism in Southeast Asia: Some Comparative Perspectives." In *Constitutionalism in Southeast Asia*, eds C. Hill and J. Menzel. Konrad Adenauer Stiftung 3, pp. 9–32.
Mietzner, M. (2011). "Overcoming Path Dependence: The Quality of Civilian Control of the Military in Post-authoritarian Indonesia." *Asian Journal of Political Science*, 19(3): 270–289.

Nyein, S.P. (2009). "Expanding Military, Shrinking Citizenry and the New Constitution in Burma." *Journal of Contemporary Asia*, 39(4): 638–648.

Okoth-Ogendo, H.W.O. (1991). "Constitutions without Constitutionalism: Reflections on an African Political Paradox." In *State and Constitutionalism. An African Debate on Democracy*, ed. I.G. Shivji. Harare, SAPES Trust, 1, pp. 3–27.

Pedersen, M. (2011). "The Politics of Burma's Democratic Transition. Prospects for Change and Options for Democrats." *Critical Asian Studies*, 40(1): 49–68.

Peerenboom, R. (2004). *Asian Discourses of Rule of Law*. London and New York, RoutledgeCurzon.

Peerenboom, R. (2006). *Human Rights in Asia*. London, Routledge.

Persson, T. and G. Tabellini (2003). *The Economic Effects of Constitutions*. Cambridge and London, MIT Press.

Ramraj, V.V. (2010). "Constitutional Tipping Points: Sustainable Constitutionalism in Theory and Practice." *Transnational Legal Theory*, 1(2): 191–220.

Ramraj, V.V. and A.K. Thiruvengadam, eds (2009). *Emergency Powers in Asia: Exploring the Limits of Legality*. Cambridge, Cambridge University Press.

Rich, R. (2010). "The Appreciation of the Human Rights Situation in Southeast Asia." In *The Crisis of Democratic Governance in Southeast Asia*, eds M. Bünte and A. Croissant. Basingstoke, Palgrave, pp. 236–260.

Rüland, J. (2003). "Constitutional Debates in the Philippines: From Presidentialism to Parliamentarianism?" *Asian Survey*, 43(3): 461–484.

Sartori, G. (1962). "Constitutionalism: A Preliminary Discussion." *American Political Science Review*, 56(4): 853–864.

Sarwar, M.I. (2012). "Freedom of Religion and Expression: A 'Rule of Law Perspective'." In *Islamic Law and International Human Rights Law. Searching for Common Ground?*, eds A.M. Emon, M.S. Ellis, and B. Glahn. Oxford, Oxford University Press, pp. 247–254.

Saunders, C. (2009). "Towards a Global Constitutional Gene Pool." *National Taiwan University Law Review*, 4(3): 1–38.

Saunders, C. (2014). "The Impact of Internationalisation on National Constitutions." In *Constitutionalism in Asia in the Early Twenty-first Century*, ed. A.H.Y. Chen. Cambridge and New York, Cambridge University Press, pp. 391–415.

Schabas, W.A., N. Prudhomme, and J. Powderly (2010). "Crimes against Humanity in Western Burma: The Situation of the Rohingyas." In *Project Report*. Galway, Irish Centre for Human Rights, National University of Ireland. Available at: http://burmacampaign.org.uk/images/uploads/ICHR_Rohingya_Report_2010.pdf.

Streckfuss, D. (2011). *Truth on Trial in Thailand: Defamation, Treason, and Lèse-majesté*. Abingdon and New York, Routledge.

Tan, K.Y. (2002). "The Making and Remaking of Constitutions in Southeast Asia: An Overview." *Singapore Journal of International and Comparative Law*, 6: 1–41.

Tey, T.H. (2011). "Malaysia. The Undermining of its Fundamental Institutions and the Prospects of Reform." In *Law and Legal Institutions of Asia: Traditions, Adaptations and Innovation*, eds A.E. Black and G.F. Bell. Cambridge and New York, Cambridge University Press, pp. 212–262.

Villacorta, W.V. (1988). "The Dynamics and Processes of Writing the 1987 Constitution." *Philippine Journal of Public Administration*, 32(3/4): 299–309.

Worthington, R. (2001). "Between Hermes and Themis: An Empirical Study of the Contemporary Judiciary in Singapore." *Journal of Law and Society*, 28(4): 490–519.

# Part I

# Constitution-making and constitutional design

# 2 Ways of constitution-making in Southeast Asia

## Actors, interests, dynamics

*Aurel Croissant*

### Introduction

This chapter presents a comparative analysis of constitution-making across the Southeast Asian region. The particular emphasis is on current episodes of constitution-building undertaken in the region since the late 1980s. The literature on the subject is still small, and while there is an important literature on constitutional systems in individual countries, few contributions discuss the topic from a comparative perspective (Tan 2002). This lacuna is striking since, for a long time, the constitutional design literature has noticed a causal link between the modes of constitution-making, the public acceptance of a constitution, and the democratic quality of a political regime (Elster 1993, 1997; Ginsburg *et al.* 2009; Samuels 2006). This is neither to say that representative democracy (the only viable organizational form of democracy for contemporary nation-states invented as of yet) is necessarily constitutional democracy; nor does it imply that constitution-making is only a relevant research topic in the context of democracy and democratization. First, representative and constitutional democracy share many common elements but are two distinct concepts. Representative democracy (or polyarchy) is defined as "public contestation and the right to participate" (Dahl 1971: 5); that is, free and open elections, freedom of speech and press, the right to freely form and join civic or political organizations, and the existence of "institutions for making government policies depend on votes and other expressions of preferences" (Dahl 1971: 3). Constitutional democracy requires additional institutional checks on public officials which assure that the democratically elected political institutions and authorities will govern according to the principles laid out in the constitution, and are bound by the constitutional text (Murphy 1993, 2009; Merkel and Croissant 2000; Morlino 2012; Holmes 2013). Second, the "new institutionalism in the study of authoritarian regimes" emphasizes the importance of formal political institutions such as constitutions, courts, elections, legislatures, and multiple political parties for the reproduction of authoritarian rule (Schedler 2009). Hence, authoritarian constitutions should not be dismissed as merely window dressing (Ginsburg and Simpser 2014: 2; Gandhi 2010). Certainly, many authoritarian constitutions serve this purpose. However, as Ginsburg and Simpser argue, dictators bother to create constitutions because it facilitates their objective of political survival by, among other things, enabling coordination among multiple institutional actors and eliciting cooperation from a dictator's subjects (Przeworski 2014; Elkins *et al.* 2014: 142f.).

Southeast Asia is particularly suited for drawing inferences from constitution-making in different types of political regimes. In the past three decades, the region has experienced a number of regime transformations as autocracies in the Philippines, Thailand, Cambodia, Indonesia, and East Timor have embraced more democratic forms of government. Yet, there is considerable diversity in the outcomes of these regime transitions (see, e.g., Croissant and Bünte 2011; Case 2015). For example, Cambodia's nascent democracy eroded into a new kind of electoral authoritarianism in the late 1990s, whereas Thai democracy has remained in a state of continued crisis since the mid-2000s. In contrast, democracy in the Philippines, Indonesia, and East Timor is perhaps "illiberal, hollow [and] poorly institutionalized" (Diamond 1999: 49) but has shown resilience despite hard challenges (Chu *et al.* 2008; Pongsudhirak 2013; Mietzner 2014). Meanwhile, the remaining autocracies in the region have also undergone important changes. Perhaps the most striking example is Myanmar. While the slow and controlled process of political liberalization that has taken place since 2008 "should not be understood simply as an exit strategy by the military to retreat from national politics" (Hung 2013; Croissant and Kamerling 2013; Bünte 2014; see also Egreteau, Chapter 6, this volume) the disbanding of the Burmese junta and the ratification of a new constitution is nevertheless an important development in the transition from military rule toward "something else" (O'Donnell and Schmitter 1986: 1).

This raises the questions of what the constitution-making designs in the region have been like since the late 1980s; which actors were involved and how their interests shaped the constitutional texts; and if there is a link between process designs and the legitimacy of the constitutional order. With these questions in mind, the rest of this chapter proceeds as follows. The next section introduces the analytical framework for this study. The following section locates contemporary episodes of constitution-making within the broader context of the region's constitutional history. The third section compares 12 cases of constitution-making in eight countries (i.e., the Philippines, Thailand, Cambodia, Indonesia, East Timor, Laos, Myanmar, and Vietnam). The fourth section investigates the relationship between process designs, the role of actors, and their interests. The final section provides some tentative conclusions regarding the regional dynamics of constitution-making and issues of constitutional legitimacy.

## The framework for analysis

The framework for the analysis of constitutional processes in Southeast Asia is based on the differentiation between "constitutional order" and "constitutional text" and reserves the use of the word "constitution" to the latter (Murphy 1993). Furthermore, the article adopts a narrow conceptualization of constitution-making as "state-supported, nationwide formal process of constitution drafting undertaken in the expectation that the resulting document will govern the country in the relative near term" (Williams 2009: 1657). Of course, constitutions can change over time through formal amendments to text as well as informal amendments that result from interpretative changes, and "no constitutional documents long remain coextensive with the constitutional order" as the "original words are soon overwritten by customs, usages, and interpretations" (Murphy 2009: 1304; see also Elkins *et al.* 2009: 55, 74). Nevertheless, this analysis is consciously limited to cases in which an existing constitution was replaced by a new one. Episodes of constitution-building through amendment and (re)interpretation are excluded from the analysis (with the exception of Indonesia in 2002; see below).

The following analysis applies and modifies an analytical framework developed by Kirsti Samuels. She examines constitution-building processes along four criteria (Samuels 2006: 8f.):

1 Whether the constitution was imposed from the top (by the incumbent regime, external actors, or a dominant national elite faction or polity party) or negotiated between competing elite factions.
2 The inclusiveness of the process; that is, the extent to which the composition of the institutional body that produced the constitutional text is inclusive or exclusive.
3 The representativeness of the process; that is, whether all the major interests in society were represented in the constitution-making process or if the processes was biased towards certain individual, group, or institutional interests that shaped the final document.
4 The participatory quality of the process; that is, the extent of involvement of the broader public in the process, either through direct consultation or dialogue with the public or representative groups at various stages before or during the drafting of the text, or afterwards through ratification of the document by free popular vote.

Related to these criteria is the issue of constitutional legitimacy; that is, whether a document produced during the constitution-making process can claim "upstream legitimacy," "process legitimacy," and "downstream legitimacy" (Elster 1993: 178f.; Böckenförde 1994: 67–69). As Elster observes, constitutional documents enjoy "upstream legitimacy" if the assembly that writes the document came into being in a legitimate way. Furthermore, constitutions possess "process legitimacy" if the internal decision-making procedures of the constitution-making body are not perceived to be a mere bargain among interest groups or dominated by extra-constitutional forces. Finally, a constitution enjoys "downstream legitimacy" if a constitution produced in a democratic process has been submitted to the people in a referendum; that is, some kind of plebiscitary approval in an act of free choice (which excludes rigged or shame referenda).

## Constitutional history and constitution-building in Southeast Asia

Since the end of World War II, "formal written constitutions have become ubiquitous features of modern nation-states" (Ginsburg and Simpser 2014: 1; Go 2003; Brown 2003). Southeast Asia is no exception to this development. While some countries had begun experiments with written constitutions prior to independence, constitutions became an essential part of proclaiming sovereignty in the 1940s and 1950s. A second rush of constitution-making occurred in the 1970s, when original constitutions were replaced in many countries. Finally, the downfall of the Marcos dictatorship in the Philippines and the passing of the provisional "Freedom Constitution" in 1986 ignited another outburst of constitutional activities in the region which resulted in the drafting of new constitutions or (in the case of Indonesia) a "total revision" (Indrayana 2008a: 101) of the constitutional text in eight countries (Table 2.1).

The constitutional histories of Southeast Asian countries are highly diverse. However, there are a number of cross-national patterns and trends. The first is the vicissitude of written constitutions. The average life expectancy of a constitution in Southeast Asia is about 13 years. Yet there are important differences between constitutions that were promulgated under authoritarian government, which endured for, on average, 13.5 years ($n$=45), and the average life span of the five constitutions promulgated under democratic government (10.1 years).

The shorter life span of democratic constitutions compared to authoritarian ones reflects the pre-eminence of authoritarianism in the region for most of the twentieth century. Nevertheless, this finding deviates from the statistical evidence provided in cross-regional studies which establishes that authoritarian regimes exhibit a higher probability for constitutional replacement than do democracies (Elkins *et al.* 2014: 145–147; 2009: 137). Yet, there are striking differences between individual countries (see Table 2.2). Brunei, Malaysia, and Singapore continue to utilize and augment constitutional structures inherited from the British colonial power (Tan 2002: 3), whereas the life expectancy of a Thai constitution for the period 1932 to 2013 (excluding the ridiculous post-coup constitution of May 2014), on average, is 4.5 years.

However, whether a country replaces or retains a constitution reveals little about the extent of constitutional change over time regarding basic constitutional provisions. For example, constitution-builders in Indonesia in 1999 to 2002 chose to revise the 1945 constitution that had been in force from 1945 to 1949, and again from 1959 to 1998 rather than redrafting a new constitution altogether. Yet, Indrayana observes that in Indonesia, "95% of the chapters, 89% of the Articles and 85% of the paragraphs" of the constitution "are either new or were alterations of the originals" as a result of constitutional amendments during the period 1999 to 2002 (Indrayana 2008a: 101). In the Philippines, the Constitutional Commission of 1986 basically revitalized the original constitutional model, invoked in the 1935 Commonwealth Constitution (Rebullida 2006a, 2006b). Further, taking into account the evolution of constitutions in Malaysia

*Table 2.1* Southeast Asian constitutions by decade*

| | *1890s* | *1900s* | *1910s* | *1920s* | *1930s* | *1940s* | *1950s* | *1960s* | *1970s* | *1980s* | *1990s* | *2000s* | *Total* |
|---|---|---|---|---|---|---|---|---|---|---|---|---|---|
| Brunei | | | | | | | 1959[2] | | | | | | 1 |
| Cambodia | | | | | | **1947** | | | **1972,**<br>**1976** | **1981**[3] | **1993** | | 5 |
| East Timor | | | | | | | | | | | | 2002 | 1 |
| Indonesia | | | | | | **1945,**<br>**1949** | **1950,**[1]<br>**1959**[5] | | | | | (2002)[11] | 4 |
| Laos | | | | | | **1947**[4] | | | | | **1991** | | 2 |
| Malaysia | | | | | | | 1957[6] | | | | | | 1 |
| Myanmar | | | | | | **1947** | | | **1974** | | | **2008** | 3 |
| Philippines | **1898** | | | | **1935** | **1943,**<br>**1945**[7] | | | **1973** | **1986,**[1]<br>1987 | | | 7 |
| Singapore | | | | | | | 1959[8] | | | | | | 1 |
| Thailand | | | | | **1932,**[1]<br>**1932** | **1946,**<br>1947,[1]<br>**1949** | **1952,**[9]<br>**1959**[1] | **1968** | **1972,**[1]<br>**1974,**<br>**1976,**<br>**1977,**[1]<br>**1978** | | **1991,**[1]<br>**1991,**<br>1997 | **2006,**[1]<br>**2007**<br>**2014**[1] | 18 |
| South Vietnam | | | | | | | **1956** | **1964,**[1]<br>**1967** | | | | | 3 |
| North Vietnam | | | | | | **1946** | **1959** | | | **1980** | **1992**[10] | | 4 |
| Total | 1 | | | | 3 | 11 | 9 | 3 | 9 | 4 | 6 | 4 | 50 |

Notes

* Cf. C. Hill and J. Menzel, *Constitutionalism in Southeast Asia*, vol. 2 (Singapore, KAS, 2008); Z. Elkins, T. Ginsburg and J. Melton, *Characteristics of National Constitutions, Version 1.0*. Comparative Constitutions Project. Last modified: May 14, 2010. Available at: www.comparativeconstitutionsproject.org/index.htm; and author's compilation.

1 interim constitution;
2 amended 2004–2006;
3 amended 1989;
4 excluding the 1945 provisional constitution ("Lao Issara" constitution);
5 reinstated the 1945 Constitution;
6 with several amendments;
7 reinstated the 1935 Constitution;
8 Constitution of Singapore with various amendments in 1965;
9 reinforced the 1932 Constitution;
10 amended 2001–2002 and in 2013;
11 amended the 1945 Constitution.

**Bold**: constitution promulgated during authoritarian regime.

*Table 2.2* Average life span and length of constitutions in Southeast Asia[1]

| | *Life span of constitutions (in years)*[2] | | *Length of constitutions (in words)* | |
|---|---|---|---|---|
| | *Current* | *Average* | *First* | *Current or with latest amendment* |
| Brunei | 54.3 | 54.3 | n/a | 13,869 |
| Cambodia | 20.2 | 13.3 | n/a | 8,936 |
| East Timor | 11.6 | 11.6 | – | 15,307 |
| Indonesia | 54.5 (11.4)[3] | 17.1 (13.7)[3] | 1,344 | 5,915 |
| Laos | 22.4 | 25.5 | 2,956 | 4,820 |
| Malaysia | 56.4 | 56.4 | n/a | 64,080 |
| Myanmar | 5.5 | 15.4 | 20,219 | 40,492 |
| Philippines | 26.9 | 13.8 | 5,259 | 21,954 |
| Singapore | 54.2 | 54.2 | n/a | 40,076 |
| Thailand | 6.3 | 4.5 | 2,013 | –[4] |
| South Vietnam | – | 7.0 | n/a | – |
| North Vietnam | 21.7 | 16.3 | 4,801 | 11,344 |

Notes
1 Author's calculations based on information from the same sources as Table 2.1.
2 From promulgation of first constitution until December 31, 2013.
3 numbers in brackets refer to the amended 1945 Constitution as the new "2002 Constitution".
4 No official translation of the 2014 Interim Constitution in English available.

and Singapore shows that both documents have been quite open for formal and informal amendments; hence, alterations have been numerous and substantial. In fact, Singapore's constitution had been changed so routinely at the whim of the People's Action Party's government through a submissive parliament that overriding the constitution in favor of individual pieces of legislation has become the normal order (Thio 2008, Thio and Tan 2009). Similarly, in Malaysia there have been over 50 Amendment Acts to the constitution since 1957 (Harding 2012). As a consequence, the current document runs to 64,080 words, the lengthiest constitutional text in the region. In contrast, Thailand's disregard for documentary constitutionalism contrasts with the stability and strength of the informal; that is, unwritten constitutional rules that have emerged gradually since the 1930s and relate primarily to the status of the monarchy and royal political prerogatives (Traimas and Hoerth 2008; Elkins *et al.* 2009: 189–190). In this regard it is telling that the only section of the 2007 constitution which was not abolished by the military junta (National Council for Peace and Order, NCPO) under Army Chief General Prayuth Chan-ocha in May 2014 was section two which regulates the prerogatives of His Majesty the King (The Manager, May 22, 2014; see also Chapter 7 by Mérieau, this volume).

Another trend is that constitutional texts have become more similar across countries and regime categories since the 1980s. Similar to developments in other regions (Elkins *et al.* 2009, 2014), constitutional documents have become more comprehensive regarding the topics incorporated into the text, and more detailed in the way they address these topics. Without going into detail, it is evident that in contrast to the brief "legalistic documents" (Tan 2002: 41) drafted just prior to or immediately after independence, constitutions from the 1980s onward manifest concern with, among other things, socioeconomic rights, the environment, human rights, rule of law, and the plebiscitarian involvement of citizens in the political process (Tan 2002: 41). This has contributed to a significant lengthening of constitutional documents (cf. Table 2.2). Third, the conventional wisdom in comparative politics suggests that region is associated with a number of theoretically important covariates such as colonial heritage, legal origin, religion, cultural and economic networks, and linkages to external actors (Go 2003; Gleditsch and Ward 2006; Brinks and Coppedge 2006: 466; Elkins *et al.* 2014: 153). However, the cases studied here are quite diverse. The sample includes former British, French, Portuguese, Dutch, and Hispanic-American colonies, predominantly Christian, Buddhist, and Muslim societies, and constitutions promulgated by authoritarian regimes and by democracies. This diversity explains the lack of a single foreign "reference model" in the region, in contrast to the prevalence of the "Gallic" constitutional model in West Africa, and the US model of presidential constitutions in most of Latin America (Elgie 2011; Cheibub *et al.* 2011; Stroh and Heyl 2015).

Of course, colonial legacies matter for constitutional choices in Southeast Asia: constitutional history in the Philippines is fundamentally shaped by American influence (Wenzel 2010: 409), whereas constitutions in Singapore and Malaysia as well as Burma's 1947 constitution are inspired by Britain's Westminster model. However, constitutional isomorphism tended to take place within the boundaries of colonial empires rather than across them (see also Go 2003; Menzel 2008b). Yet, while constitutional borrowing from the British and the Americans, and even the "Lusophone" model of semi-presidential government in East Timor (Neto and Costa Lobo 2014) remains influential until today, French-inspired constitutions were unceremoniously revoked by authoritarian rulers in South Vietnam and Cambodia (Tan 2002: 3), and communist parties in Laos, North Vietnam, and Cambodia adopted socialist constitutional models that were inspired by Soviet and Chinese experiences.

Finally, since 90 percent of all constitutions in Southeast Asia (46 out of 51 so far) were promulgated by authoritarian governments, most nations' constitutional history is shaped by a long tradition of what Okoth-Ogendo describes as "constitutions without constitutionalism" (Okoth-Ogendo 1993). With few exceptions, constitutional documents were designed to accommodate political rulers, and constitutional documents were usually drafted far from public scrutiny, ratified by a hand-picked assembly, and sometimes presented to "ritualistic plebiscites" (Brown 2003: 38). Only in Indonesia (1955) and in the Philippines (1934, 1970) was an independent constituent assembly popularly elected in free and fair elections (Santos 1994: 25). Insofar as constitutional referenda were organized in some countries, it was not to involve the broader public in the process but to legitimate the imposition of constitutions by autocratic rulers. Particular infamous examples include the 1974 referendum in Burma, and the 1973

Constitution of the Philippines that was drafted under martial law, adopted by a Constitutional Convention under duress, and "ratified" by voice vote in village assemblies where soldiers and policemen were in prominent attendance (Wurfel 1977; Taylor 1979; Rebullida 2006b).

## Ways of constitution-making in the recent wave of constitutional activity

In 1986, the overthrow of the Marcos regime in the Philippines signaled the beginning of a new era of constitution-making in Southeast Asia which includes 12 cases over a period of 28 years: The provisional "1986 Freedom Constitution" and the 1987 Constitution in the Philippines; the 1991 Constitution of Laos and Vietnam's 1992 Constitution (amended in 2001/2002 and, again, in 2013); the 1993 Constitution of Cambodia; Thailand's 1997 "People's Constitution," the 2006 and 2014 Interim Constitutions, and the 2007 "Post-Coup" Constitution; East Timor's 2002 Independence Constitution; the revision of the 1945 Constitution in Indonesia (1999–2002); and Myanmar's 2008 Constitution. These cases may be distinguished according to (1) political context and (2) type of constitutional change.

1 Cambodia and East Timor are categorized as transition countries from violent conflict to a post-conflict order which, as an explicit peace-negotiation element, included a transition toward representative democracy. Another three constitution-making processes took place during a largely non-violent transition from authoritarianism to democratic government (the Philippines, 1986/1987; Indonesia). Six constitutions were drafted under the watch of authoritarian governments, either military-dominated as in Thailand (2006, 2007, and 2014) and Myanmar (2008), or controlled by a communist party (Laos, Vietnam). Finally, Thailand's 1997 Constitution was drafted half a decade after the country had installed a democratic government.
2 Regarding the outcome, three of the processes led to the promulgation of an interim constitution (Thailand, 2006 and 2014; Philippines, 1986). In eight cases, the existing constitution was replaced by a new (permanent) constitution, whereas in Indonesia the charter was formally amended. These cases of constitution-building took place in an international environment characterized by the global diffusion of certain constitutional standards, such as written constitutional documents, constitutional review, greater awareness and acceptance of social and economic rights, human rights and environmental concerns, and a global trend toward greater interest in constitutional structures (Elkins *et al.* 2009: 36–65). This contributed to the homogenization of constitutional documents and, at the same time, "constitutional complexification and differentiation" (Go 2003: 71). In addition, the end of communist rule in Eastern Europe and the collapse of the Soviet Union contributed to a diminished attractiveness of the socialist constitutional model, and a (temporary) ideological hegemony of capitalist and democratic liberalism.

Table 2.3 summarizes the features of the 12 constitution-making processes from 1986 to 2014. As is evident from the table, there is much variation in the degree of representativeness, inclusiveness, and participatory quality of the process, and whether the constitution was negotiated between competing political and social forces or imposed by a single political actor. Nevertheless, three subregional clusters may be identified.

A first cluster comprises the 1987 Constitution in the Philippines and Thailand's 1997 People's Constitution. Here, the draft constitution was written by specially convened assemblies. While legislators (Thailand) and the executive (the Philippines) had a central say in calling these bodies into being and selecting the delegates, parliaments and political parties did not have a central place in the process, although the draft constitution had to be submitted to the National Assembly for approval. In addition, the cases fulfill at least two of Samuel's criteria of an inclusive, representative, and participatory constitution-building process.

In Thailand, the political process that culminated in the promulgation of the 1997 Constitution in Thailand began shortly after the transition to a democratic government in 1992. It involved, among others, the formation of an extra-parliamentary Democratic Development Committee in 1994, and the installation of a parliamentary Political Reform Committee in 1995. In 1996, the National Assembly allowed for the establishment of a Constitutional Drafting Assembly (CDA), whose members were selected from two different groups: 76 provincial representatives were selected by the National Assembly from lists prepared by provincial assemblies. Another 23 legal and academic experts were selected from nomination lists compiled by various government and private universities (Klein 1998: 10–12; Harding and Leyland 2011: 22–24; Uwanno and Burns 1998: 227–247). The exclusion of political parties from the CDA reflected the intention of the constitutional reform movement that had emerged in the early 1990s to act as an ideologically heterogeneous alliance of different social forces and political groupings. These included conservatives and liberals, academics, democracy activists, NGOs, and even military figures who shared a skeptical view of the existing parliamentary system, its political parties, and Thailand's "political class" (Connors 2007: 153–162). Much of the tension within the CDA resulted from the divergent interests of the provincial representatives and legal experts (Kuhonta 2008: 385f.).[1] The work of the CDA involved participation from various sectors of society and public debates over an eight-month period (Punyaratabandhu 1998: 165, Connors 2007: 153–182). As Harding and Leyland argue, the draft text that the CDA submitted to the National Assembly represented in many ways Thailand's "most imaginative, concerted and inclusive effort to settle its constitutional system" (Harding and Leyland 2011: 23). The Parliament had only an up or down vote over the whole draft and, against the backdrop of strong public sentiments in favor of the charter, the National Assembly approved the People's Constitution in October 1997 (Klein 1998; Munger 2007: 464; Ginsburg 2009; Leyland 2007).

In the Philippines, President Corazon Aquino had proclaimed an interim Freedom Constitution in March 1986 that gave her sweeping powers and was to

*Table 2.3* Modes of constitution-making processes in 12 Southeast Asian cases

| *Case* | *Negotiated or imposed* | *Inclusive or exclusive* | *Representative or non-representative* | *Participatory or closed* |
|---|---|---|---|---|
| East Timor (2001–2002) | Imposed by Fretilin | Exclusive | Representative | Closed |
| Indonesia (1999–2002) | Negotiated by MPR | Exclusive | Somewhat representative | Closed |
| Thailand (1997) | Negotiated by CDA | Inclusive | Somewhat representative | Participatory |
| Thailand (2006) | Imposed by CDR | Exclusive | Non-representative | Closed |
| Thailand (2007) | Imposed by CDR | Exclusive | Non-representative | Somewhat participatory |
| Thailand (2014) | Imposed by NCPO | Exclusive | Non-representative | Closed |
| Myanmar (1993–2008) | Imposed by SPDC | Exclusive | Non-representative | Closed |
| Cambodia (1993) | Negotiated by CA | Exclusive | Representative | Closed |
| Vietnam (1992) | Imposed by CPV | Exclusive | Non-representative | Somewhat participatory |
| Laos (1991) | Imposed by LPRP | Exclusive | Non-representative | Closed |
| Philippines (1986) | Imposed by President | Exclusive | Non-representative | Closed |
| Philippines (1986–1987) | Negotiated by CONCOM | Inclusive | Somewhat representative | Participatory |

remain in effect until a constitutional convention could write a new charter to be ratified by national plebiscite (Rebullida 2006c: 183). In May 1986, a Constitutional Commission was created by presidential proclamation. While the 48 members of that commission were selected by the president, they represented a range of different social groups and political stances. Some commissioners were leftists and some were ardent nationalists, but moderate conservatives held a majority (Villacorta 1988: 299–309). Among others, there were two former Supreme Court justices, three representatives of the Catholic Church of the Philippines, and five seats were reserved for members of Marcos's New Society Movement. To reduce the scope for personal interest, the commissioners were banned from running for office for one year after the constitution's ratification. The Commission involved the public through country-wide consultations, including public seminars and meetings, and coverage of its debates on national radio and television. While many proposals were controversial, a majority of the delegates favored a return to a US-style presidential system similar to the 1935 Constitution (Santos 1994: 37–41), with numerous new clauses pertaining to the demands of the many competing groups that tried to influence it, such as farmers, landlords, human rights groups, and the Catholic Church. In addition, the new constitution limits the president's ability to assume extraordinary powers which reflects the consensus among delegates to protect the constitution from any autocratic abuses of the Marcos era (Timberman 1991: 200–204; Rebullida 2006c: 189–195). The Commission approved the draft text by a vote of 44 to 2 in October 1986. A constitutional referendum was held on February 2, 1987 in which 89.3 percent of the electorate voted, with 77.1 percent of the votes in favor of the document (Nohlen *et al.* 2001: 209).

A second cluster comprises Indonesia, East Timor, and Cambodia, where competing political parties dominated the framing and adopting of the constitution. The process was representative as far as it concerns the representation of political parties in the constitution drafting body, but there was little participation of the broader public in the process, and no national referendum over the final document. In Cambodia and East Timor, constituent assemblies were elected while the countries were under administration by the United Nations (UN), which later also turned themselves into the first legislatures (Croissant 2008). In Indonesia, the People's Consultative Assembly (*Majelis Permusyawaratan Rakyat*, MPR) prepared and adopted four amendments to the 1945 Constitution over the course of three years. Of the 695 members of the MPR that carried out the amendments, 592 delegates were popularly elected members of the national legislature (*Dewan Perwakilan Rakyat*, DPR), or chosen by the elected Regional DPR (*Dewan Perwakilan Rakyat Daerah*, DPRD). Another 102 (non-elected) delegates came from the military and the police (38 appointed members of the DPR), or were representatives of designated functional groups (Indrayana 2008b: 2). The decision to revise the existing constitution was based on a compromise between the political parties who wanted to avoid the deadlock that arose in the 1955 Constituent Assembly over the issue of *Sharia* law (Butt and Lindsey 2012: 4). The process was largely elite-driven and elite-negotiated without much public participation. This reflected the concerns of party leaders that broader involvement of the public would have made constitutional change more difficult, especially on the contentious issue of the inclusion of Islamic law in the Constitution (Samuels 2006: 27).

In Cambodia, the constitutional process was guided by the UN's Transitional Authority in Cambodia (UNTAC), but sovereignty remained vested in the Cambodian representatives. The 1991 Paris Agreements required the election of a Constituent Assembly which was then to write a constitution. Following the 1993 election the Assembly appointed a Drafting Committee, with six members from FUNCINPEC, five from the Cambodian People's Party (CPP), and one from the Buddhist Liberal Democratic Party (BLDP); that is, approximately equal to each party's share of seats in the Assembly (Marks 2010; Brandt 2005: 11).[2] While the FUNCINPEC and CPP effectively controlled the process, efforts by the UN to engage the public in the constitutional process mainly consisted of providing information and education. In the end, however, there was little participation either of the NGOs or members of the Assembly in the formulation of the constitution (Marks 2010). Tellingly, the deliberations of the Committee were confidential and committee members were not allowed to talk about the drafting process in public (Menzel 2008a). When the Committee finally presented the UN administration with a draft it received harsh criticism due to the lack of provisions for an independent judiciary, or protections of human and civil rights, and far transversal prerogatives of the Head of State (Shawcross 1994: 32). As a result, CPP leader Hun Sen and FUNCINPEC chairman Prince Norodom Ranariddh presented their own drafts to Prince Norodom Sihanouk, the titular head of the Supreme National Council (a semi-sovereign power-sharing coalition of all four warring parties in Cambodia: Croissant 2008) for his approval. On that basis a compromise was mediated by Sihanouk, sidelining the Constituent Assembly's own drafting committee. After only five days of consultation, the Assembly finally adopted the text on September 21, 1993 by a vote of 113 in favor of ratification, five against, and two abstentions (Findlay 1997: 9).

While in Indonesia and Cambodia, no single political party or party leader was able to impose its draft and therefore the relevant political parties had to compromise; in East Timor the Fretilin (*Frente Revolucionária do Timor-Leste Independente*) controlled two-thirds of the seats in the Constituent Assembly. There were talks between Fretilin and the UNTAET (United Nations Transitional Administration in East Timor), but Fretilin ignored any efforts to render the process more participatory. Instead, the party pushed its own draft through the Constituent Assembly (Brandt 2005: 15; Samuels 2006: 19). After only ten days of debate and against a backdrop of objections by the opposition parties who felt sidelined, the assembly adopted Fretilin's draft (Brandt 2005: 20). The lack of consensus among the different political parties meant that the constitution was regarded by many as a "Fretilin Constitution," and only 65 out of 88 delegates voted for the draft, with 13 abstentions and 10 not casted votes (Aucoin and Brandt 2010; Shoesmith 2007: 224).

Finally, a third cluster comprises Vietnam, Laos, Myanmar, Thailand (2006, 2007, 2014), and the Philippines (1986). These cases are typified by government dominance over a process which was mostly non-participatory, exclusive, and non-representative in the sense that dissenting voices were de facto excluded from the process. Yet, there was some public consultation, including academic, legal officials, and party cadres, culminating in the release of a draft constitution to the general public in Vietnam in 1991 (Sidel 2010: 7). In Myanmar (2008) and Thailand (2007), constitutions were presented to the electorate in a referendum. Nevertheless, in all six cases the incumbent government imposed the constitution from the top, usually by controlling the creation and workings of the institution that drafted the constitution.

In Thailand and Myanmar, military juntas chose to write constitutions to facilitate their political objectives and to enhance their influence over post-transition civilian governments. However, it is worth mentioning that Thailand's 2007 Constitution, though deviating in important respects from the 1997 text, exhibits important elements of continuity with the prior document (Ginsburg 2009). Under the provisions of the 2006 Constitution proclaimed after the military coup against Prime Minister Thaksin Shinawatra in September 2006, the military council (Council for National Security, CNS) appointed a provisional National Assembly, which nominated 200 of its own members as candidates for a CDA. The CNS then selected 100 of these candidates to be appointed as actual members of the CDA (Traimas and Hoerth 2008). Against the backdrop of widespread criticism from opposition parties, politicians allied with exiled former Prime Minister Thaksin and the emerging social movement politically aligned to him. In addition, many academics and intellectuals perceived the whole process as utterly illegitimate and objected to many constitutional clauses as undemocratic and providing too much influence to extra-parliamentary forces (Jory 2012; Chambers 2010: 61f.). Finally, a constitutional referendum was held on August 19, 2007, in which a mere 57.6 percent of the electorate voted and only 56.9 percent of the votes approved the draft. Support for the constitution was quite strong in areas such as Bangkok and the South, but in the Northeast about 60 percent of the votes rejected the document (The Nation, August 25, 2007). In total, just 32 percent of the overall electorate was actually in favor of the new military-endorsed constitution.

In contrast, the military in Myanmar was significantly less constrained in writing a document that reflects its interests. After having convened 700 delegates for a National Convention to draft guidelines for a new constitution in 1992, the military junta (State Law and Order Restoration Council, SLORC) placed severe restrictions on the right of the convention to discuss constitutional issues, prohibited debate of the constitution outside the convention, and imposed a detailed set of non-debatable "constitutional principles that any constitution would be required to reflect and that would ensure that the military retained determinative power" (Diller 1993: 1167f.; Williams 2009: 1667f.). Frustrated by the military junta's unwillingness to compromise, Aung San Suu Kyi's National League for Democracy (NLD) boycotted the Convention. As a consequence, the military dismissed the NLD from the convention and halted the process in 1996. In 2004, the Convention was restarted without NLD participation. While the regime allowed ethnic ceasefire groups 10 percent of the total seats at the Convention, all their proposals were rejected (Min 2010: 97–99). There was a parallel process of deliberations among opposition groups and NGOs but the results did not make it into the official draft (Williams 2009). The draft constitution completed in 2007 was "more or less identical to the one proposed by the military junta in 1993" (Jones 2014). In May 2008, the junta held a national referendum. According to official statistics, the constitution was approved by 93.8 percent of the votes. However, the NLD and others claimed that the referendum had taken place under threat of force, with numerous allegations of intimidation and pre-marked ballots (Jones 2014). Nevertheless, the constitution was enacted with the inauguration of the newly elected Parliament in February 2011.

## Actors, interests, and the question of constitutional legitimacy

Building on the foregoing discussion we are able to identify different groups of actors and interests which have influenced the constitution-building in different ways. Elster differentiates three categories of potential interests (Elster 1993): (1) the "personal interests" of constitution-makers which refers to the private advantage that an individual expects to derive from a particular constitutional institution; (2) the "group interests" of political parties, territorial subunits, economic actors, social forces, or extra-constitutional forces such as the military and international actors (e.g., the UN); and (3) the self-interest of political institutions (e.g., of the executive or ordinary legislatures).

As is evident, the interests of political parties and political institutions played a particularly strong role in Indonesia, East Timor, and Cambodia. Here, established (or future) legislatures participated in the process of constituting a government; in fact, in Cambodia and East Timor, the constituent assemblies later transformed themselves into the regular Parliament. Partisan interests of political parties had a strong impact on the process that led to the adoption of four constitutional amendments in Indonesia, especially when the representatives of the Regional DPR were forced to join with other political parties' factions. Yet the two biggest party groups together held only 53 percent of the total MPR seats and therefore had to compromise with other factions (Indrayana 2008b: 116, 149–151). Regarding the dominant impact of political parties' interests in Cambodia, however, it is important to note that party leaders such as Hun Sen and Prince Ranariddh, together with Prince Norodom Sihanouk, were the decisive veto players rather than the political parties as such. Unsurprisingly, the text of the 1993 Constitution reflects the compromise reached between these three actors, resulting in a mixture of elements from the 1947 royalist constitution and the 1989 constitution of the CPP-led State of Cambodia (Menzel 2008a; Marks 2010).

In all three countries, participation by social organizations was limited and poorly organized. However, interest groups and civil society activists felt shut out from the process, particularly in East Timor and Cambodia (Brandt 2005: 11–14). International actors such as UN transitional administrations played a role in Cambodia and East Timor. For example, Annex 5 of the 1991 Paris Peace Agreement required the drafting of a new constitution for a "liberal democracy" in Cambodia, and it was the mandate of UNTAC to assist with the implementation of the peace accord (Croissant 2008). The scope of UNTAET's mandate was significantly broader and gave it full executive, legislative, and judicial authority over East Timor. However, concerned that it should not be seen as imposing a result, UNTAET chose to adopt a "hands-off" approach during the constitution-making process (Brandt 2005: 24). Other interests were a minor issue or did not play a role at all. For example, the interests of the armed forces, state bureaucracy, or subnational units were a non-issue in East Timor and Cambodia. In contrast, Indonesians were concerned that the military would utilize its access to the MPR through the 38 members of the combined military–police faction to impose its will on the delegates. Yet, with the (important) exception of Article 28I(1) that prohibits retrospective prosecution and makes it more difficult to prosecute military personnel responsible for past human rights abuses, there is no strong evidence that the military regularly intervened in the MPR's decision-making process (Indrayana 2008b: 164f.).

In contrast, in the Philippines and Thailand, the interests of political parties played a limited role in the constitution drafting. As previously described, this was mainly a result of the way in which the constitution-making bodies came into being. Although the Revolutionary Government of President Aquino held a strong interest in building constitutional legitimacy for the post-Marcos order (Bernas 1995: 2–4), there is little evidence that, other than this, its institutional self-interests played an important role. For example congressional powers were strengthened and, at the same time, presidential prerogatives were reduced, which reflects the constitutional commissioners' intention to firewall the constitutional order against future attempts to impose presidential autocracy rather than Parliament's self-interest (Rebullida 2006c).

In this regard, it is also important to mention that the adoption of the 1997 Constitution in Thailand was meant to regulate the role of political parties and to curtail the power of elected parliamentarians, as evidenced by the many clauses which aimed to regulate "dark influences" in electoral and party politics and to strengthen the Prime Minister vis-à-vis the House of Representatives. This also included the installation of a directly elected Senate, whose members were not to be allowed to join political parties (Hicken 2005: 105–107; Kuhonta 2008). In contrast, the 2006 interim Constitution aimed to legitimize the 2006 military *coup d'état* against Thaksin. Finally, the 2007 Constitution drafted by a selected group of delegates who owed their appointments to the military-composed CNS reflects the desire to prevent another "Thaksinization" of Thailand's political system by emphasizing the guardian role of the armed forces, and imposing further constraints on the executive branch of government and the functioning of the legislature (Muntarbhorn 2009: 80–89). The 2014 interim Constitution, promulgated by the NCPO on May 22, in contrast, seems to combine both aims, providing the legal legitimation for the exercise of government power by the military junta and, at the same time, imposing military control over the constitutional process in the future (Wall Street Journal 2014; Sayasombuth 2014).

Regarding Myanmar's 2008 Constitution, it is hard to deny that the constitutionally guaranteed presence of military officers in national and local parliaments, the granting of complete legal autonomy of the Defense Services (e.g., the military) over its own affairs as well as immunity for its past and future actions reflect the self-interest of the military. At the same time, the current constitution gives the military a non-negotiable veto on any potential future constitutional amendments. In fact, it is a prime example of a "military constitution" drafted by an assembly that was created and supervised by military rulers. This enables a military-dominated regime to demand obedience in the name of the law, to win legal recognition from the international community, and to regulate access to power within the ruling elite.

All of these strategies impose severe constraints on the functioning of the future political regime, "something which military rulers typically intend to do to preserve their reforms and protect their personal and corporate interests after leaving power" (Negretto 1999: 83).

A final glance at the constitution-making processes in Laos and Vietnam supports the idea that in authoritarian regimes, constitutional change serves mainly the interests of ruling elites to preserve their political clout. For example, when communist parties in Eastern Europe and the Soviet Union crumbled in 1989 to 1991, the Laotian Constitution, adopted in August 1991, reiterated the dominant role of the Lao People's Revolutionary Party as the leading nucleus of the political system (Constitution of the Lao People's Democratic Republic: Article 3). While Vietnam's 1992 Constitution also serves the purpose of maintaining the dominant political role of the Communist Party, the process of preparing constitutional change between 1990 and 1992 shows that there can also be debates and deliberations among government, party officials, and academics in authoritarian regimes, albeit this always has to take place within narrow limits. Moreover, as Sidel notes, since the adoption of the 1992 Constitution, "and partly as a result of the decisions taken by the party and demands from below, legislative, government and associational actors in Vietnam have a broader role to play now than at any time since the 1940s" (Sidel 2010: 7).

## Conclusions

At first glance, the relationship between the ways in which constitutions are made and the type of political regime seems straightforward. Democracies and regimes in transition to democracy employ more representative designs of constitution-building, whereas in authoritarian regimes not under pressure for democratic regime change, the design is utterly unrepresentative. However, at least in Southeast Asia, the link between the form of the political regime and the extent to which constitution-making is inclusive or participatory is less clear-cut. While we would expect better opportunities for public participation and broader inclusion of extra-parliamentary actors, especially from civil society, in constitution-making in democratic environments, the empirical evidence is mixed. In fact, as Elster observes, constitution-making in a transitional period comes out in conditions that are likely to work against a participatory and inclusive constitution-making process. Due to the difficult circumstances during a transition period which are characterized by uncertainty and the simultaneity of impending political crises, participatory and inclusive constitution-making through deliberation among many different social and political forces is unlikely to happen (Elster 1993). Here, constitution drafters have to carefully choose between the virtues of a democratically exemplary procedure and the perils of a long, potentially volatile interim phase without a legitimate constitution. While elected constituent assemblies do have a claim to democratic legitimacy, and ratification by free popular vote is an additional source of legitimacy, in a transitional environment the political actors (not only in Southeast Asia; see Merkel 1998) often opt for the completion of a constitution in a very short and effective way of constitution-making, accepting procedural and substantive deficiencies (cf. Table 2.4).

But does this matter for public support for a constitution and the social acceptance for the constitutional order? Elster, a leading experts in the field of comparative constitutional politics, generalizes that constitutions produced in a more democratic process (that is, with broader public participation and oversight) will tend to be more legitimate (Elster 1993: 125). Similarly, Samuels concludes from her study of 12 cases of constitution-making in Asia, Africa, Latin America, and post-communist Europe, that a more representative process of constitution-making results in constitutions that are free from provisions that undermine the quality of democracy. Moreover, constitutions that are drafted by representative bodies or that emerge in a process which involves consultation with a broad range of political and social forces are generally "perceived as more legitimate and hence received greater popular support" (Samuels 2006: 4). Yet, Ginsburg and co-authors note that broader participation may render constitutional change more difficult as it increases the number of potential veto points which have to be overcome and veto players who have to grant concessions before constitutional revisions can be adopted; it can also contribute to less contextual coherence of the constitution (Elkins *et al.* 2009: 216). An additional warrant regards the legitimizing consequences of referendums: "Approval by referendum may be an increasingly popular mode of public involvement, but it is clearly a limited one in that it involves only an up or down vote over a package of provisions" (Elkins *et al.* 2009a: 207–208). In addition, the extent of procedural legitimacy a plebiscite may provide for a constitutional order also depends on the political circumstances under which voters can cast their votes.

In fact, a glance at Elster's three sources of constitutional legitimacy discussed in the second section of this chapter and constitutional development in Southeast Asia seems to indicate that upstream, downstream, and procedural legitimacy may be less relevant for the acceptance of a constitution than the

*Table 2.4* Upstream, downstream, and procedural legitimacy of constitutions in Southeast Asia

| | *Upstream legitimacy (if that Assembly has come into being in a legitimate way)* | *Process legitimacy (internal decision-making procedure of the Assembly is perceived as democratic)* | *Downstream legitimacy (constitution ratified by free popular vote with no military force or blackmailing from spoilers)* |
|---|---|---|---|
| Philippines 1986 | – | No | No |
| Philippines 1987 | Yes | Yes | Yes |
| Laos 1991 | No | No | No |
| Vietnam 1992 | No | No | No |
| Cambodia 1993 | Yes (elected Constituent Assembly) | Somewhat | No |
| Thailand 1997 | Yes (semi-elected CDA with broad public consultation) | Yes | No |
| East Timor 2001 | Yes (elected Constituent Assembly) | No | No |
| Indonesia 2002 | Somewhat (mostly elected MPR) | Yes | No |
| Thailand 2006 | No (CNS promulgated interim constitution) | No | No |
| Thailand 2007 | No (CDA handpicked by CNS) | No | Somewhat (referendum, but military accused of interfering, low approval rate) |
| Thailand 2014 | No (NCPO promulgated interim constitution) | | No |
| Myanmar 2008 | No (members of the National Convention handpicked by military) | No | No (ritualistic plebiscite) |

legitimacy (see Table 2.4) of the "*plébiscite de tous les jours*" (Ernest Renan) by citizens and elites which can turn a constitution which lacks all procedural legitimacy into a lasting and universally accepted law of the land. For example, this seems to be the case in Indonesia (Mietzner 2014). Similarly, despite the recurring proposals for constitutional reform ("Charter Change") in the Philippines, it seems evident that the 1987 Constitution in the Philippines has also been able to gain empirical legitimacy in the eyes of the Filipino people and the political elite. But, although Thailand's 1997 Constitution enjoyed strong upstream and process legitimacy, it did not last long.[3] Yet, in East Timor, the final constitution was widely considered to be a Fretilin constitution. Unsurprisingly, "the public has grown increasingly critical of Fretilin's role in drafting it and of the flaws in the constitution itself," and as Aucoin and Brandt note, "the failings of the constitution have emerged as a favorite rallying point for whatever political forces are trying to gain favor among the population, and the charter appears to be sorely lacking in legitimacy" (Aucoin and Brandt 2010: 271).

In Myanmar and Thailand, the fact that the constitution was approved in a referendum did not lend legitimacy to a flawed process of constitution-making to which the opposition did not have equal access or from which it was completely excluded. Rather, the legitimacy of Thailand's 2007 referendum was negatively affected by a low approval rate which also laid bare the sharp divisions within the country.[4] Unsurprisingly, the question of constitutional change has been a contentious one since 2007. While the Puea Thai Party aligned with the deposed Prime Minister Thaksin Shinawatra, and the social movement allied with the party had made clear that they would not stop aiming for changes to the constitution, their opponents were not willing to accept any move to amend the constitution. Untamed constitutional conflict and contentious politics culminated in a political deadlock that was (temporarily) "solved" via another military coup.

Even though Myanmar's military has been more successful in creating and manipulating a constitution that grants it sweeping political powers, helps to elicit cooperation by societal groups and to coopt potential opposition and, hence, diminish the actual challenges they pose to the regime's interests, the 2008 charter grants minimal margins of power and autonomy to political institutions outside the military which contain seeds of subversion. This opens up arenas of contention in which opposition can test limits of the permissible and challenge the regime (Schedler 2013: 337f.). Certainly, the constitution was adopted because it would help the ruling military elite to ease their existential problems of governance and political survival. Yet, it has the potential to undermine autocratic rule. In fact, there are past examples of military regimes in Asia (i.e., South Korea) and Latin America (i.e., Chile) where authoritarian constitutions that are meant to preserve the power of forces associated with the military were inherently unstable and turned into institutional traps for authoritarian leaders (Negretto 2014; Przeworski 2014).

## Notes

1 While the experts proposed an indirectly elected Upper House, the provincial representatives were in favor of a directly elected Senate.
2 The 120 seats of the Constituent Assembly were distributed as follows: *Front Uni National pour un Cambodge Indépendant, Neutre, Pacifique, et Coopératif* (FUNCINPEC) 58 seats; Cambodian People's Party (CPP) 51 seats; Buddhist Liberal Democratic Party (BLDP) 10 seats; and MOLINAKA 1 seat (Croissant 2015: 176).
3 It is important to note, however, that in Cambodia three factors seem to have provided popular support for the 1993 Constitution: the endorsement by Sihanouk, the revered national leader; the recognition by the international community that the election was relatively free and fair, and the successful outcome of the transition process; and the intrinsic merit of the provisions on human rights and separation of powers in the constitutional text (see Marks 2010).
4 Moreover, as Vichit notes, the constitution introduced following the 2006 coup gave the CNS the authority to issue another constitution if the voters would have rejected the draft text of the 2007 Constitution (Muntarbhorn 2009. 82).

## Bibliography

Aucoin, L. and Brandt, M. (2010). "East Timor's Constitutional Passage to Independence." In *Framing the State in Times of Transition. Case Studies in Constitution Making*, ed. L.E. Miller. Washington, DC, United States Institute of Peace.

Bernas, J.G. (1995). *The Intent of the 1986 Constitution Writers*. Manila, Rex Book Store.

Böckenförde, E.-W. (1994). "Die verfassungsgebende Gewalt des Volkes – ein Grenzbegriff des Verfassungsrechts." In *Zum Begriff der Verfassung. Die Ordnung des Politischen*, ed. U.K. Preuß. Frankfurt am Main, Fischer.

Brandt, M. (2005). *Constitutional Assistance in Post-conflict Countries. The UN Experience: Cambodia, East Timor and Afghanistan*. UNDP Report, www.agora-parl.org/sites/default/files/Constitutional%20Assistance%20in%20Post-Conflict%20Countries.pdf.

Brinks, D. and Coppedge, M. (2006). "Diffusion Is No Illusion: Neighbor Emulation in the Third Wave of Democracy." *Comparative Political Studies*, 39: 463–489.

Brown, N.J. (2003). "Regimes Reinventing Themselves: Constitutional Development in Arab World." *International Sociology*, 18: 33–52.

Bünte, M. (2014). "Burma's Transition to Quasi-military Rule: From Rulers to Guardians?" *Armed Forces and Society*, 40: 742–764.

Butt, S. and Lindsey, T. (2012). *The Constitution of Indonesia. A Contextual Analysis*. Oxford and Portland, OH, Hart Publishing.

Case, W. (2015). "Democracy's Mixed Fortunes in Southeast Asia. Torpor, Change, and Trade-offs." In *Routledge Handbook of Southeast Asian Democratization*, ed. W. Case. London and New York, Routledge.

Chambers, P.W. (2010). "U-Turn to the Past? The Resurgence of the Military in Contemporary Thai Politics." In *Democracy under Stress: Civil–Military Relations in South and Southeast Asia*, eds P.W. Chambers and A. Croissant. Bangkok, ISIS.

Cheibub, J.A., Elkins, Z., and Ginsburg, T. (2011). "Latin American Presidentialism in Comparative and Historical Perspective." *Texas Law Review*, 89: 1707–1739.

Chu, Y-h., Diamond, L., and Nathan, A. (2008). "Conclusion: Values, Regime Performance and Democratic Consolidation," In *How East Asians View Democracy*, eds Y-h. Chu, L. Diamond, A. Nathan, and D.C. Shin. New York, Columbia University Press.

Connors, M. (2007). *Democracy and National Identity in Thailand.* London and New York, Routledge-Curzon.
Constitution of the Lao People's Democratic Republic (2003). In *Constitutionalism in Southeast Asia*, eds C. Hill and J. Menzel. Singapore, KAS.
Croissant, A. (2008). "The Perils and Promises of Democratization through United Nations Transitional Authority. Lessons from Cambodia and East Timor." *Democratization*, 15: 649–668.
Croissant, A. and Bünte, M. (2011). "Conclusion." In *The Crisis of Democratic Governance in Southeast Asia*, eds A. Croissant and M. Bünte. Basingstoke and New York, Palgrave.
Croissant, A. and Kamerling, J. (2013). "Why Do Military Regimes Institutionalize? Constitution-making and Elections as Political Survival Strategy in Myanmar." *Asian Journal of Political Science*, 21: 105–125.
Dahl, R. (1971). *Polyarchy*. New Haven, CT, Yale University Press.
Diamond, L.J. (1999). *Developing Democracy: Toward Consolidation.* Baltimore, MD, Johns Hopkins University Press.
Diller, J.M. (1993). "Constitutional Reform in a Repressive State: The Case of Burma." *Asian Survey*, 33: 399.
Elgie, R. (2011). "Exogenous Political Institutions? Constitutional Choice in Postindependence Francophone Sub-Saharan Africa." *Political Research Quarterly*, 65: 771–783.
Elkins, Z., Ginsburg, T., and Melton, J. (2009). *The Endurance of National Constitutions.* Cambridge, Cambridge University Press.
Elkins, Z., Melton, J. and Ginsburg, T. (2014). "The Content of Authoritarian Constitutions." In *Constitutions in Authoritarian Regimes*, eds T. Ginsburg and A. Simpser. New York, Cambridge University Press.
Elster, J. (1993). "Constitution-making in Eastern Europe: Rebuilding the Boat in the Open Sea." *Public Administration*, 71: 169–217.
Elster, J. (1997). "Ways of Constitution-making." In *Democracy's Victory and Crisis*, ed. A. Hadenius. New York, Cambridge University Press.
Findlay, T. (1997). *Cambodia: The Legacy and Lessons of UNTAC.* Oxford, Oxford University Press.
Gandhi, J. (2010). *Political Institutions Under Dictatorship.* Cambridge, Cambridge University Press.
Ginsburg, T. (2009). "Constitutional Afterlife: The Continuing Impact of Thailand's Post-political Constitution." *International Journal of Constitutional Law*, 7: 83–105.
Ginsburg, T. and Simpser, A. (2014). "Introduction: Constitutions in Authoritarian Regimes." In *Constitutions in Authoritarian Regimes*, eds T. Ginsburg and A. Simpser. New York, Cambridge University Press.
Ginsburg, T., Elkins, Z., and Blount, J. (2009). "Does the Process of Constitution-making Matter?" *Annual Review of Law and Social Sciences*, 5: 201–223.
Gleditsch, K.S. and Ward, M.D. (2006). "Diffusion and the International Context of Democratization." *International Organization*, 60: 911–933.
Go, J. (2003). "A Globalizing Constitutionalism? Views from the Postcolony, 1945–2000." *International Sociology*, 18: 7271–7295.
Harding, A. (2012). *The Constitution of Malaysia. A Contextual Analysis*. Oxford, and Portland, OH, Hart Publishing.
Harding, A. and Leyland, P. (2011). *The Constitutional System of Thailand. A Contextual Analysis*. Oxford and Portland, OH, Hart Publishing.

Hicken, A.D. (2005). "Thailand: Combating Corruption Through Electoral Reform." In *Electoral System Design: The New International IDEA Handbook*, ed. A. Hicken. New York, IDEA.

Holmes, S. (2013). "Constitutions and Constitutionalism." In *The Oxford Handbook of Comparative Constitutionalism*, eds M. Rosenfeld and A. Sajó. New York, Oxford University Press.

Hung, R.L. (2013). *Re-thinking Myanmar's Political Regime: Military Rule in Myanmar and Implications for Current Reforms*. Hong Kong, City University of Hong Kong.

Indrayana, D. (2008a). "Indonesia – In Search for a Democratic Constitution (1945–2008)." In *Constitutionalism in Southeast Asia*, eds C. Hill and J. Menzel. Singapore, KAS.

Indrayana, D. (2008b). *Indonesian Constitutional Reform 1999–2002. An Evaluation of Constitution-Making in Transition*. Jakarta, KOMPAS Book Publishing.

Jones, L. (2014). "Explaining Myanmar's Regime Transition: The Periphery is Central." *Democratization*, 21: 780–802.

Jory, P. (March 27, 2012). "Thailand's Constitutional Reform in Changing Times." In *EastASiaForum*, www.eastasiaforum.org/2012/03/27/thailand-s-constitutional-reform-in-changing-times/, March 27.

Klein, J.R. (1998). *The Constitution of the Kingdom of Thailand, 1997: A Blueprint for Participatory Democracy. Asia Foundation Working Paper #8.* Bangkok, Asia Foundation.

Kuhonta, E. (2008). "The Paradox of Thailand's 1997 'People's Constitution': Be Careful What You Wish For." *Asian Survey*, 48: 373–392.

Leyland, P. (2007). "Thailand's Constitutional Watchdogs: Dobermans, Bloodhounds or Lapdogs?" *The Journal of Comparative Law*, 2: 151–177.

Marks, S.P. (2010). "The Process of Creating a New Constitution in Cambodia." In *Framing the State in Times of Transition: Case Studies in Constitution-making*, ed. L.E. Miller. Washington, DC, United States Institute of Peace.

Menzel, J. (2008a). "Cambodia – From Civil War to a Constitution to Constitutionalism?" In *Constitutionalism in Southeast Asia*, eds C. Hill and J. Menzel. Singapore, KAS.

Menzel, J. (2008b). "Domestizierung des Leviathan?: Südostasiens Verfassungen und ASEAN's neues Homogenitätskriterium demokratischer Verfassungsstaatlichkeit." *Verfassung und Recht in Übersee*, 41: 534–559.

Merkel, W. (1998). "The Consolidation of Post-autocratic Regimes: A Multilevel Model." *Democratization*, 5: 33–65.

Merkel, W. and Croissant, A. (2000). "Formale und informale Institutionen in defekten Demokratien." *Politische Vierteljahresschrift*, 41: 3–31.

Mietzner, M. (2014). "How Jokowi Won and Democracy Survived." *Journal of Democracy*, 25: 111–125.

Min, W. (2010). "Under an Iron Heel. Civil–Military Relations in Burma/Myanmar." In *Democracy under Stress. Civil–Military Relations in South and Southeast Asia*, eds. P. Chambers and A. Croissant. Bangkok, Institute of Security and International Studies (ISIS).

Morlino, L. (2012). *Changes for Democracy: Actors, Structures, Processes.* Oxford, Oxford University Press.

Munger, F. (2007). "Constitutional Reform, Legal Consciousness, and Citizen Participation in Thailand." *Cornell International Law Journal*, 40: 455–475.

Muntarbhorn, V. (2009). "Deconstructing the 2007 Constitution." In *Divided over Thaksin: Thailand's Coup and Problematic Transition*, ed. J. Funston. Singapore, ISEAS.

Murphy, W.F. (1993). "Constitutions, Constitutionalism and Democracy." In *Constitutionalism and Democracy: Transitions in the Contemporary World*, eds D. Greenberg, S.N. Katz, M.B. Oliviero, and S.C. Wheatley. New York, Oxford University Press.

Murphy, W.F. (2009). "Designing a Constitution: Of Architects and Builders." *Texas Law Review*, 87: 1303–1338.

Negretto, G.L. (1999). "Constitution-making and Institutional Design: The Transformation of Presidentialism in Argentina." *European Journal of Sociology*, 40: 193–232.

Negretto, G.L. (2014). "Authoritarian Constitution Making: The Role the Military in Latin America." In *Constitutions in Authoritarian Regimes*, eds T. Ginsburg and A. Simpser. New York, Cambridge University Press.

Neto, O.A. and Costa Lobo, M. (2014). "Semi-presidentialism in Lusophone Countries: Diffusion and Operation." *Democratization*, 21: 434–457.

Nohlen, D., Grotz, F., and Hartmann, C. (2001). *Elections in Asia and the Pacific*, Vol. 2. Oxford, Oxford University Press.

O'Donnell, G.A. and Schmitter, P.C. (1986). *Tentative Conclusions about Uncertain Democracies.* London and Baltimore, MD, Johns Hopkins University Press.

Okoth-Ogendo, H.W.O. (1993). "Constitutions without Constitutionalism: Reflections on an African Political Paradox." In *Constitutionalism and Democracy: Transitions in the Contemporary World*, eds D. Greenberg, S.N. Katz, M.B. Oliviero, and S. Wheatley. Oxford, Oxford University Press.

Pongsudhirak, T. (2013). "Thailand's Uneasy Passage." In *Democracy in East Asia: A New Century*, eds L. Diamond, M.F. Plattner, and Y.-h. Chu. Baltimore, MD, Johns Hopkins University Press.

Przeworski, A. (2014). "Ruling against Rules." In *Constitutions in Authoritarian Regimes*, eds T. Ginsburg and A. Simpser. New York, Cambridge University Press.

Punyaratabandhu, S. (1998). "Thailand in 1997: Financial Crisis and Constitutional Reform." *Asian Survey*, 38: 161–167.

Rebullida, L.G.G. (2006a). "Executive Power and Presidential Leadership: Philippine Revolution to Independence." In *Philippine Politics and Governance, An Introduction*, eds N.M. Morada and T.S. Encarnacion Tadem. Quezon City, University of Philippines Press.

Rebullida, L.G.G. (2006b). "The Executive: Martial Law, Constitutional Authoritarianism, and the Marcos Administration." In *Philippine Politics and Governance, An Introduction*, eds N.M. Morada and T.S. Encarnacion Tadem. Quezon City, University of Philippines Press.

Rebullida, L.G.G. (2006c). "The Philippine Executive and Redemocratization." In *Philippine Politics and Governance: An Introduction*, eds N.M. Morada and T.S. Encarnacion Tadem. Quezon City, University of Philippines Press.

Samuels, K. (2006). *Constitution Building Processes and Democratization: A Discussion of Twelve Case Studies*. Geneva, IDEA.

Santos Jr., S.M. (1994). "History of the Debate: Parliamentary versus Presidential in the Philippines." In *Shift*, eds S.M. Santos Jr., F. Abad, J. Rocamora, and C. Florentino-Hofileña. Quezon City, Ateneo Center for Social Policy and Public Affairs.

Sayasombuth, S. (2014). "A First Look at Thailand's New Interim Constitution, 7-23-2014." In *Asian Correspondent*, http://asiancorrespondent.com/125027/a-first-look-at-thailands-new-interim-constitution/.

Schedler, A. (2009). "The New Institutionalism in the Study of Authoritarian Regimes." *Totalitarismus und Demokratie*, 6: 323–340.

Schedler, A. (2013). *The Politics of Uncertainty: Sustaining and Subverting Electoral Authoritarianism*. Oxford, Oxford University Press.

Shawcross, W. (1994). *Cambodia's New Deal*. Washington, DC, Carnegie Endowment for Peace.
Shoesmith, D. (2007). "Timor-Leste: Semi-presidentialism in a New, Small State." In *Semi-presidentialism Outside Europe*, eds R. Elgie and S. Moestrup. London and New York, Routledge.
Sidel, M. (2010). *The Constitution of Vietnam. A Contextual Analysis*. Oxford, Hart Publishing.
Stroh, A. and Heyl, C. (2015). "Institutional Diffusion, Strategic Insurance and the Creation of West African Constitutional Courts." *Comparative Politics*, 47: 169–187.
Tan, K.Y.L. (2002). "The Making and Remaking of Constitutions in Southeast Asia: An Overview." *Singapore Journal of International and Comparative Law*, 6: 1–41.
Taylor, R. (1979). "Burma's National Unity Problem and the 1974 Constitution." *Contemporary Southeast Asia*, 1: 88–102.
The Manager (2014). NPOMC Announces the Prime Minister Powers Belong to Prayuth, Repeals 2007, Charter, except Chapter 2 – Senate and Courts Remain in Office" (in Thai). *The Manager*, May 22, 2014, www.manager.co.th/Politics/ViewNews.aspx?NewsID=9570000057286 (accessed November 30, 2014).
Thio, L.-a. (2008). "Singapore – The Indigenisation of a Westminster Import." In *Constitutionalism in Southeast Asia*, eds C. Hill and J. Menzel. Singapore, KAS.
Thio, L.-a. and Tan, K. (2009). *Evolution of a Revolution: 40 Years of the Singapore Constitution*. London, Routledge-Curzon.
Timberman, D.G. (1991). *A Changeless Land: Continuity and Change in Philippine Politics*. Singapore, ISEAS.
Traimas, C. and Hoerth, J. (2008). "Thailand – Another New Constitution as a Way Out of the Vicious Cycle?" In *Constitutionalism in Southeast Asia*, eds C. Hill and J. Menzel. Singapore, KAS.
Uwanno, B. and Burns, W.D. (1998). "The Thai Constitution of 1997: Sources and Process." *University of British Columbia Law Review*: 227–247.
Villacorta, W.V. (1988). "The Dynamics and Processes of Writing the 1987 Constitution." *Philippine Journal of Public Administration*, 32: 299–309.
Wall Street Journal (2014). "Thai King Approves Interim Constitution Charter to Make Possible Legislature, Interim Government." *Wall Street Journal*, June 22.
Wenzel, N.G. (2010). "Constitutional Culture in Japan and the Philippines: Success and Failure in Post-war Constitutional Choice." *Pacific Focus*, 25: 396–416.
Williams, D. (2009). "Constitutionalism Before Constitutions: Burma's Struggle to Build a New Order." *Texas Law Review*, 87: 1658–1693.
Wurfel, D. (1977). "Martial Law: The Methods of Regime Survival." *Pacific Affairs*, 50: 5–30.

# 3 Delaying constitutionalism to protect establishment hegemony in Thailand

## Designing the election system and the Senate in the Constitution of 2007

*Michael H. Nelson*

### Official state ideology versus substantive constitutionalism

In Southeast Asia, Thailand is the country with by far the highest number of constitutions since they were first adopted as a means to structure the formal political order. After a group of civil servants and military officers had toppled the absolute monarchy, Siam (as Thailand was then called) received its first constitution in 1932. Since then, the country has had 19 constitutions (including interim charters issued following military coups). After the latest military *coup d'état* of May 22, 2014, yet another twist in Thailand's cycle of "permanent constitutionalism" (McCargo 1998: 5) or "hyper-constitution-making" (Harding and Leyland 2011: 1) began with the establishment of the National Reform Council (NRC) in October, and the Constitution Drafting Committee (CDC) in November 2014.[1] The CDC's draft was unexpectedly rejected by the NRC, and thus had to be abandoned. The military rulers established yet another Constitution Drafting Committee, which presented the final version of its draft on March 29, 2016. In order to become effective, it will have to pass a public referendum scheduled for August 7, 2016. If it is approved, a lengthy process of drafting subordinate laws mandated in the constitution will follow, with general elections anticipated to take place in the second half of 2017.

As with the 2007 Constitution, which resulted from the military coup of September 2006, the latest round will relate to the institutional innovations introduced with the 1997 Constitution, combined with assumptions of the ruling military and civilian cliques about undesirable political consequences of those innovations, in the context of the elite perceptions of politicians, political parties, elections, voters, and the political events since 2001, when Thaksin Shinawatra first became prime minister. It remains to be seen how much of an "afterlife" (Ginsburg 2009) of the 1997 Constitution will be found in the 2015 version, whether it will continue the "return to politics past" (Hicken 2007) of the 2007 document, or whether it will include new elements that important strata of the people will either accept or oppose.

Yet, this line of constitution-making from 1997 through 2007 to 2015 occurs in the context of a more fundamental contestation in the Thai polity between two main "notions of legitimacy" (Dressel 2010) or two contrasting models of the political order (Nelson 2012), in which the long-standing hierarchical nature of rule is challenged by more recent bottom-up ideas. This situation leads us back to the beginnings of Thai constitutionalism, meaning the attempt effectively to regulate the entire political order – its state apparatus, political organizations, and the public – by a written constitution. Notwithstanding earlier movements in 1885 and 1912, Thai constitutionalism seriously started in 1932, only after the royal elite's own considerations of a constitutional order, including the introduction of a parliamentary system, had stalled around 1926. It is important to note here that the 1932 revolt against the absolute monarchy was not a broad-based popular uprising aiming to establish a republic. Rather, middle-level members of the military and civil state apparatus realized their claim to participation in political decision-making against the royal elite. Moreover, they were satisfied with keeping the monarchy in place, though in its constitutional version. Decades of rule by the state apparatus followed, mostly in the form of military dictatorships. This was captured in the view that Thailand was a "bureaucratic polity" (Riggs 1966). Furthermore, it was of great importance that, from the late 1950s, military strongman and Prime Minister Sarit Thanarat revived the monarchy as an ideological support resource for his autocratic rule (Thak 2007: 205). Instead of positioning the constitution as the highest value in the political order, the pre-1932 trinity of "Nation, Religion, and Monarchy" (Murashima 1988) eventually became the key value of the paternalist polity, emphasizing the monarchy and the bureaucracy as key components, the good of the nation as its claim to legitimacy, a unity and control-oriented mode of operation, and obedient and conformist people. "Nation, Religion, and Monarchy" became the "three pillars," or the "fundamental institutions," that support the very existence of the eternal and sovereign Thai nation, while the foundation on which these three pillars rest is provided by the military and civilian state apparatus.

Until today, civil servants and the military do not legitimize their actions by reference to their constitutional positions, based on the stipulation that the people are the sovereign of the country, but by reference to the official state ideology of "Nation, Religion, and Monarchy." Since 1974, Thai constitutions stipulate that the people's first duty is "to protect and uphold Nation, Religion, and the Monarchy, and the democratic system of government that has the king as head of state according to this constitution" (section 70 in the 2007 Constitution). Democracy and constitutionalism in Thailand are thus sandwiched between a thick layer of state ideology and the strongly state-promoted remnant of an ancient institution, neither of which has a democratic or constitutional basis, thereby counteracting the formal constitutional stipulation that the people are the sovereign of Thailand (in fact, this stipulation, in section 3, also states that it is the king who exercises this sovereignty "through the National Assembly, the Council of Ministers and the Courts in accordance with the provisions of this constitution"). When Thailand's latest military dictator, General Prayuth Chan-ocha, announced what he thought the state apparatus should propagate as the 12 key values to which all Thai people should adhere, it was hardly surprising that the first value was "Nation, Religion, and Monarchy."[2] Thus, there is a perennial tension between this hierarchical, top-down ideological worldview and its increasingly vocal democratic-constitutional competitor that emphasizes equal citizens as the key components of this order, with popular sovereignty as its claim to legitimacy, a pluralistic mode of operation that stresses diversity, and an ideal of the people which relies on independent minds.

While the ideological and normative complex denoted by "Nation, Religion, and Monarchy" can hardly be challenged by citizens who see it as a relic of the past and who advocate a more people-centered political order in Thailand, constitutions are open to contestations. In principle, this can go in both directions. On the one hand, ascending new groups, such as politicians and newly politicized citizens, can try to expand their power and solidify it in constitutional changes. On the other hand, the state apparatus and its various support forces in the public sphere use constitutional engineering in reaction to political developments they see in a negative light to protect the establishment's hegemony in the political order. In practice, obviously, the state apparatus and its establishment allies are in a considerably stronger position to push through their ideas about the constitution than are extra-establishment politicians and citizens, simply because the latter two groups do not command any means of physical coercion.[3] This was manifest in the constitution-drafting following the military coups of 2006 and 2014.

Therefore, the hierarchical perspective does not altogether reject constitutions. Rather, within the restrictions described above, they have become an accepted component of a political order called Thai-style democracy. This order combines a (more or less) democratic constitution with effective supra-constitutional powers, in particular the monarchy and the military (Harding and Leyland 2011: 30; Kobkua 2003: 29; Anek 2007). There is little reason to believe that the idea of rule by pure coercive power still has significant currency (this is very different from the nearly ten years of military dictatorship between January 1959 and June 1968, when the exercise of state power was based on a 20-article "interim charter"). Consequently, the military coup of 2006 did not result in an attempt principally to replace constitutional rule with military power. The interim charter of 2006 stipulated a process and time frame for drafting a new document and for the return to electoral democracy. This chapter, then, provides two examples of how upper-level sociopolitical forces (members of the establishment, bureaucrats, technocrats, academics) joined the coup plotters in trying to write a new constitution that held the prospect of being more in line with the elitist forces' perception of the flaws of Thai politics. These flaws mainly concerned the Thai politicians, especially those representing the so-called Thaksin regime that had been in power between 2001 and 2006. Therefore, the country's representative system, being dominated by politicians since 2001, became an important target for trying to manage the influence of this group on the political order. In the following, it will be shown how this attempt worked out in the field of political recruitment (the election system to the House), and regarding the balancing of the fully elected House with an Upper House (Senate) that was originally supposed to comprise members of the establishment and would thus operate outside the political party logic of the lower chamber. In both cases, however, the underlying principle of establishment hegemony in the Thai-style democracy was maintained. Neither the drafting of the 2007 Constitution nor that of the 2015 document aimed to establish a political order free from supra-constitutional components.

## The 2007 Constitution: directed against the Thaksin regime

We will now turn to the substantive sections on the 2007 Constitution. Its drafting followed the pattern outlined in the preceding paragraphs. In concrete terms, the Democrat Party created a state crisis by using its near-absolute dominance in nine southern provinces to prevent Parliament from convening following the election of 2006. This action was part of a strong establishment movement against the Thaksin regime, the key components of which were seen by its adversaries as being authoritarianism, corruption, conflicts of interest, "parliamentary dictatorship" (meaning governments that use their majority in the House to govern without paying too much attention to opposition groups), and – of particular power – the accusation that Thaksin wanted to topple the monarchy. In September, the military staged a coup and tore up the 1997 Constitution, thereby necessitating the drafting of a new document. An ideologically relatively homogeneous group of 35 members, almost exclusively comprising members of the Bangkok-based bureaucratic and academic establishment (among them 19 legal bureaucrats, judges, and lecturers of law, but only one political scientist) (Ploy 2010: 13), was assigned this task.

This task seemed to be clear-cut enough: use this coup-generated exclusion from power of the Thaksin-aligned forces in order to redesign the rules of the game in a way that would reduce the election-based power of Thaksin Shinawatra, and increase the power of the establishment forces. This latter point was successful with the changed composition of the selection committees for the members of the "independent" accountability institutions which the 1997 Constitution had introduced as some sort of fence around the politicians in order to control their behavior that had often been seen as very questionable. The number of members was very considerably reduced, and high-level judges were given the majority of seats. This measure was to be complemented by eliminating the popular election of senators that had also been introduced with the 1997 charter. However, the initially strong intention of the drafting group to establish a privileged parliamentary representation for their fellow members of the establishment, designed to balance the politicians in the House, encountered public resistance that finally led to a compromise: the 2007 Constitution included a Senate with 76 elected and 74 selected members. The drafting committee felt the need to demonstrate sensitivity to public expectations, rather than pushing through its original intention unilaterally. Partly, this had to do with the fact that the interim constitution stipulated that the new document had to pass a public referendum, and the resultant perception of the CDC that unpopular stipulations could make it more difficult to get the constitution approved. In 2015, the situation was quite different in that the coup of 2014 was much more ideological than that in 2006, that the ideological orientation of the CDC was also much stronger, and that the interim charter did not require a referendum to put the new constitution into effect.

The third and final component in this redesign of the representative system was the attempt to introduce an election system – a German-style mixed-member proportional system (MMP) – that would have reduced the decidedly disproportionate share of House seats for the Thaksin parties, and given many more seats to the establishment's Democrat Party, thereby strengthening the balance of power in the House. Thus, this system would have corresponded to what most members on the CDC and the CDA wanted to achieve. In the end, it did not materialize. The time for drafting the constitution was insufficient for the more strongly anti-Thaksin faction on the CDC to overcome the concerns of more moderately conservative members, who thought that change should be gradual and not be as drastic as they thought MMP was. Moreover, most members of the CDC and CDA were not experts in institutional design, and certainly not well versed in election system design issues. Therefore, until the final vote, issues of simply understanding MMP and eliminating misunderstandings remained. In the following two sections, we will turn in more detail to how the Senate and the election system were designed, starting with the latter.

## The attempt to introduce a mixed-member proportional election system

From the first parliamentary elections in 1933, Thailand initially had a House with both elected and appointed members. Since the 1968 Constitution, Members of Parliament (MPs) were elected in single- and multi-member constituencies with multiple votes (notwithstanding prior attempts and subsequent interruptions by military coups). This system lasted for almost 30 years, until the 1997 Constitution introduced a mixed-member majoritarian system, namely 400 MPs elected in single-member districts, and 100 MPs elected from national party lists. When the drafters of the 2007 Constitution deliberated the election system they touched upon a number of issues that had been introduced by the 1997 document, such as whether the national party list should be abolished or perhaps changed to a number of regional party lists, whether they should return to multi-member constituencies with multiple vote, or whether they should return the counting of votes from central counting stations in the constituencies to the polling stations.

However, the systematically and politically most important proposal was inserted into the CDC's deliberations from the outside. Thammasat University lecturers with a background in German public law approached a CDC member, Krirkkiat Phipatseritham, who then became the most important advocate of MMP on the CDC. To this group, the major flaw of the election system was that it had led to the "parliamentary dictatorship" of the Thaksin regime. This was attributed to the MMM system, which had resulted in a vastly disproportionate seat share in the House for Thaksin's TRT. The introduction of MMP would have substantially reduced TRT's number of MPs, and at the same time increased the number of seats for TRT's main competitor, the establishment's Democrat Party. Yet, early in the drafting process, in mid-February 2007, the two main proposals concerning the election system on the CDC did not yet include MMP. The first promoted the return to the pre-1997 election system, meaning mainly the abolishment of the 100 party-list MPs, while the second represented a modified version of the 1997 system. When the CDC, at the beginning of April 2007, worked on producing a draft constitution to be put to public hearings, these were the main options. The first option was soon dropped, leaving as the main choice a split of 320 constituency MPs and 80 party-list MPs. That the MMP system proposed by Krirkkiat would become a serious competitor could hardly be expected when the CDC reached its preliminary electoral design decision for the revised MMM system by 21 votes in favor, with only nine votes for MMP.[4]

The struggle between what one might call the "conservatives" (anti-Thaksin, but pragmatic and thus against drastic changes) and the "reformers" (anti-Thaksin and ideological, and thus open to drastic changes) on the CDC was not without animosity. While the reformers insinuated that the conservatives, being against the introduction of MMP, somehow ignored the best interests of the country, the conservatives accused the reformers, insisting on MMP, of not properly understanding Thai political culture and structures, and had therefore proposed an election system that they thought was "inappropriate" for the country. While the reformers were proud to say that "This system will completely change the face of the election system,"[5] and considered sticking to a revised 1997 system as a major "blunder,"[6] the conservatives were worried that "Thais have not been used to this … it would be too complicated."[7] Thus, the "behavior of the Thais must be changed gradually. Sudden and strong change will lead to confusion."[8]

In fact, this confusion had already afflicted the CDC in its deliberations, because the meaning of the word "proportionality" with regard to the election system had become obscured. At one point, the chairperson of the CDC, Prasong Sunsiri, intervened in the discussions by saying, "As far as I have listened to everybody already, in principle, I think, the issue of proportionality is accepted by the meeting."[9] Only the number of MPs – 320 to 80 versus 200 to 200 – remained open. "Therefore, since the majority thinks that the proportional system should be used in the next elections, only the numbers have not yet been agreed upon."[10] These statements overlooked the fact that there were two fundamentally different proposals. One camp used the term "proportional system" by having in mind a revamped 1997 party-list system, thereby keeping the segmented system. The opposing camp also used the term "proportional system," but its members thought that this involved a fundamental restructuring of Thailand's election system along proportional lines by introducing a German-style compensatory system, in which the number of MPs a party could claim depended solely on the total number of votes that party received. In the revised 1997 system, proportionality was to be applied to only 80 out of 400 MPs, while the MMP system would have applied proportionality to all 400 MPs. This confusion even meant that the committee members, when entering into the post-public hearing deliberations, had to discuss what they had actually decided seven weeks earlier in Bang Saen (a seaside resort town). Krirkkiat insisted that "I was happy to an extent because the meeting at Bang Saen accepted the proportional system only that the numbers that I suggested lost"[11] (this referred to the formulas of 200 to 200 against 320 to 80). He apparently did not realize that the committee had not merely rejected his 200 to 200 formula, but with it his entire mixed-member proportional election system. For this reason, MMP was not included in the draft constitution, and the public hearings on this document could thus not touch on it. Woothisarn could then argue that it would be difficult to justify if the CDC suddenly came up with a new election system that would change what they had written in their original draft produced for the hearings. In addition, the CDC was now already close to the time of its final decision-making.[12] Of course, proponents of MMP were unhappy about such views. Whatever had been decided in April should not be used, in June, to "close our mouths."[13] In other words, they did not want to concede defeat easily, but to use the remaining time to recruit followers for their model both on the CDC and the CDA, which would have the last word on the content of the draft constitution. The CDC's chairperson, Prasong Sunsiri, had contributed to this approach by allowing further discussions that other members thought should have ended since their earlier decision in April. But he also clearly stated his skepticism of MMP by warning,

> This [MMP] is something new. It has been proposed, and we have talked about it. I believe that many committee members do not yet understand what this is all about. Even the political parties and politicians [do not yet understand]. It is true that we must always consider whether something new and better is appropriate for the nature of our country's politics, its economy, and society. How much has the people's knowledge foundation developed regarding what we want them to use, or what we determine what they must use?[14]

However, the proponents had two more opportunities to promote their MMP model. The first came on June 6, 2007, when members of the CDA presented their amendment motions (*prae yatti*) to the CDC, so that members could decide whether they wanted to make additional changes to their draft ahead of the final deliberation and vote on the CDA. Indeed, one of the groups that presented motions supported MMP. It was led by Chermsak Pinthong, a well-known anti-Thaksin crusader in the yellow shirt context. His key argument concerned a point that the MMP proponents had long made on the CDC – electoral justice, derived from the fact that all votes would be used to calculate a party's claim for their number of seats in the House. Political parties would receive a number of seats that was proportional to their vote total. For example, a party that gained 50 percent of the vote would get 250 MPs if the total number of MPs was 500.[15]

Overall, Chermsak's presentation looked very much like the German system of personalized proportional representation (*personalisiertes Verhältniswahlrecht*). Other groups proposing amendment motions, however, rejected any proportional element, even the 80 "proportional" MPs of the hearing draft. To them, those MPs did not only have no connection to the voters in the constituencies (without saying why all MPs needed such a direct connection). More importantly, proportional MPs would lead to calculating the national vote total of parties, and this could lead to a diminishing of the Thai monarchy by parties claiming that their

> party has gained 16 million votes, 14 million votes. This was like saying that they were already supreme in the country, although in reality we still have an institution that we have to respect, or that we have to admire and praise … [the king]. This [refers to the total number of votes that a party had received on the party list ballot] was similar to the presidential system.[16]

This quote expressed what a number of CDC members thought had happened when Thaksin Shinawatra was prime minister, and this was the reason why the CDC had resolved to replace the national party lists with regional "proportional" lists. The subsequent discussion on the CDC reflected the positions of the two main groups (MMM versus MMP). Reproducing concerns voiced in early meetings, Pairote Phromsan stated, "The country is not a tool for us to experiment with new things, while the time is so limited."[17] On the other hand, Krirkkiat repeated his group's concern about the "parliamentary dictatorship" that would prevail if they would not switch to MMP:

> The proportional election system is a means to prevent political dictatorship. It creates a balance between the political powers, because with this election system, political parties will have hardly any opportunity to win majorities and absolutely control the House, and form a single-party government.… We need a strong government to administer the country. But we do not need a dictatorial government.[18]

Following the lengthy debate about the future election system between CDC and CDA members, one of the latter concluded with some resignation that they were trying to change politics, and to eliminate vote-buying. Nevertheless, he felt that they sometimes went into a dead-end. From the rural perspective he wanted to say that "we can accept all systems, but we must understand them first.… At the same time, I think that many CDC members themselves do not yet understand the [MMP] system."[19] This assessment is certainly not inaccurate. It was reflected yet again when the CDC held its decisive meeting on June 7, 2007, with its secretary again framing the decision as one that merely concerned the number of MPs (that is, 320 to 80 versus 200 to 200), applying the term "proportional system" to both (though, later in the meeting, he referred to the alternative as "1997" versus "a new proportional system").[20] As so often already, even at this latest stage in the CDC's constitution-drafting procedure, the fundamental difference between a mixed-member *majoritarian* and a mixed-member *proportional* system was obscured, leading to much redundant and confusing debate. Perhaps surprisingly, the final vote on the CDC was very close. The proponents of MMP were defeated by only three votes – 15 members supported MMM, while 12 members supported MMP.[21] The latter camp, therefore, had made considerable progress since their retreat in Bang Saen two month earlier, when their proposal lost with 21 to nine votes.

The final step in deciding about the country's election system arrived on June 21, 2007 with the "special" 29th meeting of the CDA. In the minutes of this meeting, the debate about the election system is covered in nearly 200 pages, indicating the degree of contestation about this constitutional design decision. This contestation again included reflections of the persistent tension resulting from Thailand being embedded in global culture. One speaker, in his attack on MMP, warned, "Do not adopt too much foreign culture and values. Sometimes, they are not in harmony with the people who live in our present up-country Thailand."[22] Another speaker, also going against MMP, pointed out, "I think that the Thais must have Thai identity. Why do they have to copy things from other countries?"[23] Directly following on from this statement, Phairote Phromsan added that, for the future development of Thai politics, it was necessary and most important to have a constitution that was "appropriate" (*mosom*) to the conditions of Thailand; it should be "Thai style" (*baep thai*). Thus, it was not necessary to design the constitution according to models from this or that country.[24] Obviously, one could wonder whether Phairote intended to suggest that the proponents of MMP were somehow less Thai than Phairote considered himself to be, or that they simply did not adequately understood what "Thai style" implied, leading them to propose and push for an "inappropriate" election system, namely MMP. One could also wonder why some proponents of MMM thought that this system had not been an adoption of foreign culture.

Finally, the time for taking final votes on a number of issues had arrived. First, the CDA changed the CDC's proposal for single-member districts into multi-member districts with a vote of 48 to 28.[25] It should be noted here that the number of votes reached only 76, although the meeting was supposed to be attended by 95 members, according to the attendance list printed on pages 1 to 4 of the minutes. Since no abstentions were recorded, one might thus wonder what had happened to the remaining 19 members. Second, in a vote of 50 to 32, the CDA opted for 400 constituency MPs and 80 party-list MPs (the majority position on the CDC had been 320 to 80).[26] Third, there was no vote on the increase from the originally envisaged four electoral zones for party-list MPs to eight zones, because there were no dissenting voices.

Fourth, in the course of moving the election system issue to the vote, and in the course of some more explanations about MMM and MMP by key members of both camps, problems in understanding the issues were evident, delaying the vote again and again. As one member of the CDA exclaimed with frustration when the vote on the election system had already been urged to be taken, "The more I listen [to the explanations], the more I am confused about how I should decide."[27] Another CDA member added, "I have listened, and I am still confused."[28] After Winat Manmungsin had added that "If you allow the vote to take place, I am afraid that it will not be based on our shared understanding,"[29] Sunthorn Chanrangsi cautioned, "I confirm that the majority of CDA members does not yet understand [the election system issue]. Since we do not yet understand it, how can you force us to make a decision?"[30] Given the long, unsystematic, and confusing debate in this decisive CDA meeting, such statements were not surprising. Siva Saengmani suggested, "If there is somebody who really does not understand, he should abstain when voting."[31] Sakchai Unchittikul was concerned about the image of the CDA, saying, "Moreover, I think since there is still confusion, I do not want this confusion, and neither a decision based on a lack of understanding. This would make outsiders see us in a bad light."[32] After some more (but not very enlightening) explanations regarding the election system design, the chairperson of the meeting, Seri Suwanphanon, noted, "See, there are still members who do not understand [the proposed election systems]. Therefore, it is difficult to vote on them, right?... How can we decide when members do not yet understand [the issue]?"[33] Shortly afterwards, Seri followed up by asking, "Do you understand better now?" His own answer suggested that this was not the case: "Everybody makes a cloudy face."[34]

It took some more time until taking the vote was unavoidable. Only seven more votes, and Thailand would have introduced MMP: 45 votes for MMM, 39 votes for MMP, two abstentions, and one member who did not vote. Eight votes were missing, judging from the attendance list of this meeting. Perhaps the above account about how, in 2007, Thailand ended up with a revised version of the election system introduced with the 1997 Constitution – although this seemed to go against most CDC and CDA members' intentions substantially to reduce the power of the political camp led by Thaksin Shinawatra – illustrates the role which "mistakes" or "misconceptions" can play in determining "institutional outcomes" (Capoccia and Ziblatt 2010). We will now move to the second case: the design of the Senate in the 2007 Constitution.

## The decision-making process about the Senate

Before the Constitution of 1997 introduced a fully elected Senate, senators were chosen by the respective prime ministers, though the king had formally to appoint them. The Senate thus came to be seen by critics as a rubber stamp of the government, rather than fulfilling its ascribed role as an independent body tasked with inserting a non-political and corrective logic into the legislative process. Thus, when the provincial members of the CDA of 1997, with the help of some academic members, tried to push through a fully elected Senate, conservative members wondered whether, in that case, the categories of people making up the House and the Senate would not be the same, thereby rendering the Senate superfluous. In the end, the conservatives did not have the numbers to prevent the introduction of an elected Senate, though some elements were designed in an attempt to make the Senate a body not subject to the same political party logic that prevailed in the House (candidates could not be members of political parties; for example, they could not run election campaigns).

Before the first Senate election of 2000, the *Bangkok Post* expressed its skepticism that the Senate would take shape as designed, saying, "The first Senate election ... will not result in an Upper House free of the morally corrupt [meaning: most politicians] but instead bring in a 'proxy' body to protect the interests of politicians and state officials" (*Bangkok Post*, March 3, 2000). Some months earlier, *The Nation Weekend* had printed an article headlined "The siblings and husbands-and-wives assembly" (*The Nation Weekend*, December 16–22, 1999). After the Senate election, the *Thai Post* screamed in a front-page headline, "A bad joke! An assembly of slaves." Part of the subtitle read, "*Chao pho* [political mafia figures] and the children and wives of MPs come to reform politics and hold fathers, husbands, and bosses accountable" (*Thai Post*, March 5, 2000). Indeed, after about two years in operation, the Senate seemed to have changed from being a reasonably neutral body to being an organ of open support for the Thaksin Shinawatra government. After the second Senate election in April 2006, an editorial in *Thai Rath* must have left moralistic observers without hope:

> As expected, most of the newly elected senators in the provinces are related or linked to politicians, particularly those from the Thai Rak Thai party of caretaker Prime Minister Thaksin Shinawatra. Most of those elected in Bangkok are independent candidates, many of whom were involved in the recent mass rallies against Mr Thaksin.[35]

Given these experiences with an elected Senate, it did not come as a surprise that the establishment members filling the ranks of the CDC rejected the idea of an elected Senate full of members closely connected with the MPs in the House. The question, then, was how the Senate could be designed in a way that would correspond to the establishment's ideal of a counter-force to the MPs' political party logic. It was this logic of the proceedings in the House that led most CDC members to the view that the Senate with its supposedly technocratic logic should remain. Pisit Leeahtam doubted that the House had sufficiently matured to be the only representative body. For example, the Senate was still useful for the screening of laws, because the House had drafted many pieces of legislation in a hurry, and so the senators could serve as a balance in this respect.[36]

Consequently, the most important design issue regarding the Senate was how senators were to be recruited. There were three main options: direct elections by the people, appointment by the prime minister or another group of people, or indirect elections (better called "selection"). In the ninth meeting of the CDC, on February 15, 2007, Jaran Phakdithanakun reported the preliminary agreements which subcommittee two, on political institutions, had reached. Regarding the Senate there were five points. For the purposes of this chapter, the most interesting point was no. 5, which was about the recruitment method. Direct elections were to be abolished, partly because the CDC planned to deprive the Senate of the power to impeach elected officials.[37] The appointment by a single person (the prime minister) was also ruled out. Instead, Jaran's subcommittee had come up with the options of a search committee and indirect elections. The political logic of the previous Senate recruitment method was to be eliminated. In Jaran's words:

> We aim for representatives that do not come from localities but for representatives who originate from all the professional groups, or proportions of people who are experts, who are competent, at least one from every province ... in order to provide sense (*sati*) to the House of Representatives.[38]

The problem, then, was how an independent and neutral search committee could be devised that excluded any possibility of "Abuse" (Jaran used the English word here). Initially, they had two options. The first envisaged the existence of one national search committee and similar committees in every province. The second, as proposed in the draft prepared by the secretary, made provisions only for one single national-level committee. Jaran noted that he personally agreed with this second option. However, many members of the subcommittee still also wanted search committees in the provinces.[39] The national search committee was to have seven members:

1 The president of the Constitutional Court, and the chairpersons of four independent constitutional organizations: the Election Commission of Thailand (ECT), the Audit Commission, the National Counter Corruption Commission (NCCC), and the National Human Rights Commission (NGRC).
2 One judge appointed by the General Assembly of the Supreme Court.
3 One judge from the Supreme Administrative Court, as appointed by its meeting.[40]

According to Jaran, "We think that these seven people mostly will be pillars of the country in the sense of political neutrality, and they will be independent from political intervention. Moreover, they are seniors (*phulak phuyai*)."[41] "Political neutrality" here referred to political parties, while it was understood that the members of the search committee would share the establishment's political worldview. One is probably not mistaken in assuming that "pillars of the country" meant that the members would be firmly anchored in the state ideology of "Nation, Religion, and Monarchy."

At this point, then, the national-level search procedure for the 160 senators envisaged two elements.[42] First, there were to be applicants from the provinces, with one senator per province (76). Since there would be no limit to the number of applicants, the search committee would have to check their qualifications and then select one senator per province. Provincial senators were not to be permitted to have any connections with the usual provincial political circles, as was the case after the 1997 Constitution had introduced elected senators. They would have to be drawn from the non-political provincial elite, probably including businesspersons not involved in politics, members of religious organizations, and retired bureaucrats. Second, 84 more senators would pass an application process within their respective occupational organizations. These organizations would then name candidates to the search committee, which would check them and make its selection.

The CDC included the model described here when it submitted its draft constitution, issued on April 26, 2007, to the public hearings.[43] As it turned out, this model was unacceptable. In fact, Woothisarn Tanjai had earlier said that if the public hearings showed that the search approach was considered too much of a regression (given that senators had been popularly elected in 2000 and 2006), then he would opt for a mixed system, in which the people in each province would directly elect one senator, while there should be a search committee with indirect elections for another set of senators. The numbers of senators in each group should be different.[44] This was close to the final solution, namely 76 senators directly elected by the people in the provinces, and 74 senators selected by a Bangkok-based search committee. The decisive CDA meeting took place on June 22, 2007.[45] The long discussion included a major statement by one of the driving forces behind a mixed recruitment system, Jaran Phakdithanakun. He said,

> The majority in sub-committee two wanted a politically neutral Senate as a counter-balance to the strong political struggles in the House. If the Senate were not politically neutral, having a Senate would be useless. We could return to the unicameral system, as many members have suggested in their amendment motions.[46]

Moreover, they had to keep in mind that the Senate played an important role in the recruitment of the independent accountability organizations.

> If the independent accountability organizations are not politically neutral, the checking system will be destroyed, as we can currently see. This is the origin of the current constitution drafting assembly.... This was the point of death of the previous political system – the Senate was its bottleneck. If the Senate of 2000 had performed its duties in a politically neutral way, and if it had really been a pillar of support for the country, and if the independent accountability organizations had not become corrupt, then the various mechanisms that created the crisis would not have been as serious as they have been.[47]

However, they had to acknowledge that the pure search-and-selection method as written in the public hearing draft could not be kept, because, according to one of their opinion polls, 60 percent of the people wanted elections. Therefore, they suggested a mixed system. "This is what we have learned from the people. It is not that we do not listen to the people."[48] The 76 to 74 "compromise formula" was devised to create a "critical mass" (in English) of potentially independent senators (meaning senators who would share the political views of the establishment).[49]

When the CDA voted the result was very clear, with 50 votes for the CDC's draft principles, while 27 members voted against it.[50] Thereby, the most important design decision for a Senate comprising elected and appointed members had been reached. Yet there still needed to be a debate about the ratio of these two kinds of members, because some on the CDA preferred a 120 to 40 or a 76 to 84 formula, as opposed to the CDC's 76 to 74 version. In particular the 120 to 40 formula would obviously have tipped the balance in the Senate strongly in favor of the elected senators. The debate on these points went on for quite some time, until some members formally demanded an end to the debate. This time, the vote was quite narrow in that the CDC's version won by only two votes (37 in favor, 35 against, one abstention).[51] As noted earlier, the total number of votes did not reach the number of registered participants in the meeting. The attendance list that precedes the minutes said that six people missed the meeting, while 94 attended it. Yet, the first vote count only reached the number of 77, while the second stood at 73. Again, this seems unusual, given the importance of this design decision. Unfortunately, the reason for this phenomenon remains unknown.

## Conclusion

When Thaksin's Phuea Thai Party returned to power in the 2011 elections (Nelson, 2013), it tried to turn the tables of constitutional contestation on the establishment, countering the latter's basis in physical coercion through a military coup with the party's election-based legitimacy. At first, the party wanted to amend Article 291 of the constitution in order to set up another constitution-drafting assembly that would have been tasked with rewriting the entire document. This attempt was declared unconstitutional by the establishment's Constitutional Court in its verdict of July 13, 2013, arguing that the constitution had been approved in a public referendum, though this had been imposed upon the people and had been neither free nor fair in its conduct (Nelson, 2011). However, the House still had the authority to proceed with amending individual articles of the constitution.[52] The Phuea Thai Party then tried to use this approach to change the composition of the Senate. On September 28, 2013, the National Assembly, with the votes of the government parties and allied senators, passed a constitutional amendment that returned to the fully elected Senate of the 1997 Constitution. This prompted a group of mostly appointed senators and Democrat Party MPs to call on the Constitutional Court to decide whether this amendment violated Article 68 of the 2007 Constitution, which disallowed

> to overthrow the democratic regime of government with the King as Head of the State under this Constitution or to acquire the power to rule the country by any means which is not in accordance with the modes provided in this Constitution.
>
> (Constitution 2007)

Obviously, the constitutional amendment could by no stretch of the imagination be subsumed under Article 68. Nevertheless, when the Constitutional Court, which included three judges who had taken part in giving shape to the Senate-related stipulations of the 2007 Constitution while serving on the CDC, issued its verdict on November 20, 2013,[53] it annulled the constitutional amendment in a vote of 5 to 4. In what looked like an act of interpretative acrobatics intended to keep the upper hand in this round of contestation over the constitution, the Court claimed that the amendment constituted an attempt by "people or political parties" (the target of Article 68) to gain power outside the means stipulated in the constitution. In fact, it was a constitutional organ, namely the National Assembly, which had used its constitutional authority to change part of the institutional structure of the National Assembly – the composition of the Senate. Moreover, the Court's very brief reasoning entirely referred to the intentions of the majority on the CDC, of which Judge Jaran was a key person, such as using appointed senators to create some balance to the elected MPs and senators. The Court also repeated points mentioned above during the CDC deliberations, such as an elected Senate being a husbands-and-wives assembly, and that the Senate was supposed to provide "sense" or "intelligence" to the House.[54]

This contestation between establishment forces and the electoral elements of the Thai polity continued following the coup of 2014. By January 2015, it was clear that the drafters of the 2015 Constitution continued on the establishment's anti-Thaksin path by trying to limit the political weight of politicians and voters beyond what seemed to have been "achieved" with the coup-derived Constitution of 2007. It was often said that the coup plotters of 2014 had learned from the "mistakes" of their precursors in 2007, and that they did not want to "waste this opportunity"[55] (such as with the election system and the Senate as described in the case studies above) to establish an institutional order that would produce results in accordance with their views of the problems of Thai politics. Not surprisingly, a fully selected Senate comprising former senior civil servants and military commanders, members from civil society groups, and members from professional organizations was high on the agenda. The power of the Senate was also to be increased to vet ministerial appointments and to propose legislation. Moreover, the CDC adopted a proposal to set up so-called "citizens' assemblies," while another proposal suggested to further add a "national morality assembly," both intended as additional counterweights to the politicians in the House and in local administrative authorities.[56] The elected House of Representatives would thus not only be balanced by the independent constitutional organizations, but also by the Senate, the "citizens' assemblies," and the "morality assembly," all dominated by establishment and anti-politician forces. At the same time, the planned introduction of a German-style MMP would not only give the establishment's political party, the Democrats, more seats in the House, it would also reduce the number of seats of any Thaksin-based party still in operation in the post-coup election, and weaken the new government by making it harder for a party to gain the absolute majority. Significantly, the elected post-coup government would also face a constitutionally stipulated appointed "reform committee" designed to make sure that policies devised by the coup group would be continued after its demise. This reform committee would function like a parallel government with authority to draft laws in a wide range of policy areas. These laws would be passed through three readings by an equally appointed Senate before being transferred to the elected House for approval (*Bangkok Post*, February 18, 2015). This is another instance where supra-constitutional forces used their power, anchored plainly in their command of the means of physical coercion, to draft a new constitution that would undermine the key tenet of democratic constitutionalism – the sovereignty of the people, as expressed in an elected government that monopolizes the making and implementation of national policies.

In sum, the 2015 Constitution was apparently being designed to strengthen the establishment forces and to weaken those elements of the political order that rely on the will of the people. Constitutionalism based on popular sovereignty, and expressed in electoral democracy based on the equal political rights of individual citizens, would thereby be delayed far beyond what the constitutions of 1997 and 2007 had achieved. Importantly, this constitutional strengthening of establishment hegemony in Thailand will be complemented by an increased weight of the official state ideology, "Nation, Religion, and Monarchy," which started as a result of the 2014 military coup. It will further grow with the impending succession of King Bhumipol. Driven by the military and the civil bureaucracy, and supported by the conservative mass media, the succession will probably generate a new round of sustained promotion of the monarchy, combined with increased pressure for conformity with the role of the dominant supra-constitutional elements of the Thai political order. Under these circumstances, proponents of democratic constitutionalism, for the time being, will have little space to present their model as a viable option for structuring Thailand's political sphere. More importantly, they will lack both the political power and the constitutional opportunity structure successfully to challenge the establishment forces in a new round of counter-hegemonic constitutional contestation aimed at the equal Thai citizens taking center-stage in the country's political order.

## Notes

1 Both bodies were established based on the military coup-plotters' "Constitution of the Kingdom of Thailand (Interim), B.E. 2557 (2014)," which was issued on July 22, 2014.

2 The coup was followed by a wave of *lèse majesté* cases.

3 It is agony about this imbalance that has led to the creation of militant groups in the red shirt movement.

4 **รายงานการประชุมคณะกรรมาธิการยกร่างรัฐธรรมนูญ** [Meeting Minutes of the Constitution Drafting Committee], no. 26, April 10, 2007, p. 19.

5 Krirkkiat Phipatseritham, **รายงานการประชุมคณะกรรมาธิการยกร่างรัฐธรรมนูญ** [Meeting Minutes of the Constitution Drafting Committee], no. 20, April 3, 2007, p. 64.

6 Chuchai Suphawong, **รายงานการประชุมคณะกรรมาธิการยกร่างรัฐธรรมนูญ** [Meeting Minutes of the Constitution Drafting Committee], no. 35, June 1, 2007, p. 103.

7 Nakharin Mektrairat, รายงานการประชุมคณะกรรมาธิการยกร่างรัฐธรรมนูญ [Meeting Minutes of the Constitution Drafting Committee], no. 26, April 10, 2007, p. 11.
8 Woothisarn Tanjai, ibid., p. 17.
9 Ibid.
10 Ibid.
11 รายงานการประชุมคณะกรรมาธิการยกร่างรัฐธรรมนูญ [Meeting Minutes of the Constitution Drafting Committee], no. 38, June 6, 2007, p. 96.
12 รายงานการประชุมคณะกรรมาธิการยกร่างรัฐธรรมนูญ [Meeting Minutes of the Constitution Drafting Committee], no. 35, June 1, 2007, p. 78.
13 Krirkkiat, ibid., p. 104.
14 Ibid., p. 86f.
15 รายงานการประชุมคณะกรรมาธิการยกร่างรัฐธรรมนูญ [Meeting Minutes of the Constitution Drafting Committee], no. 38, June 6, 2007, p. 76.
16 Suraphon Phongthatsirikun, ibid., p. 82.
17 Ibid., p. 119. For the voters, the introduction of MMP would not have changed the procedure they had become used to since 2001. They would have had two ballots: one for the constituency candidates, and one for the party lists. However, voters would probably have been surprised at the outcome of the elections.
18 Ibid., p. 92. The claims made in the quote should be treated with caution. First, the governments led by Thaksin following the 2001 and 2005 elections would not have been less strong had MMP been employed. Second, even the highly fractious multiparty coalition government of Chartchai Choonhavan, in power from 1988 until the coup in 1991, had been accused of "parliamentary dictatorship," because his government claimed the right to make policy decisions without paying too much attention to the opinions of the "traditional" centers of power, namely the military and the civil service.
19 Withaya Khotchakhuean, ibid., p. 151.
20 Somkhit Lertpaithoon, รายงานการประชุมคณะกรรมาธิการยกร่างรัฐธรรมนูญ [Meeting Minutes of the Constitution Drafting Committee], no. 39, June 7, 2007, pp. 91 and 111, respectively.
21 Ibid., p. 111.
22 Seri Nimayu, สำนักรายงานการประชุมและชวเลข สำนักงานเลขาธิการสภาผู้แทนราษฎร. รายงานการประชุมสภาร่างรัฐธรรมนูญ วันพฤหัสบดีที่ ๒๑ เดือนมิถุนายน พุทธศักราช ๒๕๕๐ ครั้งที่ ๒๙/๒๕๕๐ เป็นพิเศษ [Minutes of the Meeting of the Constitution Drafting Assembly, no. 29, special, June 21, 2007], p. 85.
23 Montri Petcharakhum, ibid., p. 139.
24 Ibid., p. 141.
25 Ibid., p. 183.
26 Ibid., p. 186.
27 Chali Kangim, ibid., p. 206.
28 Akkharat Rattanachan, ibid., p. 207.
29 Ibid., p. 209.
30 Ibid., p. 210.
31 Ibid.
32 Ibid., p. 213.
33 Ibid., p. 216.
34 Ibid., p. 220.
35 *Thai Rath*, as printed in *Bangkok Post* (April 25, 2006). This second elected Senate did not start its work, because the military coup of September 2006 dissolved it.
36 รายงานการประชุมคณะกรรมาธิการยกร่างรัฐธรรมนูญ สภาร่างรัฐธรรมนูญ [Meeting Minutes of the Constitution Drafting Committee], no. 9, February 15, 2007, p. 61.
37 There was a strong sense that the degree of power given to the Senate depended on whether it was appointed or elected. As one speaker put it,

> If the Senate had only the power to screen laws or act as a *sapha liang* [foster assembly] for the lower House, or the House of Representatives, then stipulating that the Senate comes from appointment or from *sanha* was possible. However, since this draft constitution stipulates that the duties do not only include the power to screen laws, but also includes the power to appoint independent organizations, and the power to remove politicians from their positions, we think that the senators should be elected by the people.
>
> (รายงานการประชุมคณะกรรมาธิการยกร่างรัฐธรรมนูญ สภาร่างรัฐธรรมนูญ [Meeting Minutes of the Constitution Drafting Committee], no. 9, February 15, 2007, p. 66)

38 Ibid.
39 Ibid.
40 Ibid.
41 Ibid.
42 The figure of 160 seemed to have entered the discussion in the second meeting of subcommittee two on February 7, 2007, when Phairote Phromsan proposed that the National Assembly comprise no more than 500 members, namely 340 MPs and 160 Senators. รายงานการประชุมคณะอนุกรรมาธิการยกร่างรัฐธรรมนูญ กรอบที่ ๒ ว่าด้วยสถาบันการเมือง วันพุธที่ ๗ กุมภาพันธ์ ๒๕๕๐ [Meeting Minutes of the CDC's Sub-Committee 2 on Political Institutions], February 7, 2007, p. 4.
43 คณะกรรมาธิการยกร่างรัฐธรรมนูญ สภาร่างรัฐธรรมนูญ สำนักกรรมาธิการ ๓ สำนักงานเลขาธิการสภาผู้แทนราษฎร, *ร่างรัฐธรรมนูญแห่งราชอาณาจักรไทย พุทธศักร่าช … ฉบับรับฟังความคิดเห็น*. (กรุงเทพฯ: คณะกรรมาธิการยกร่างรัฐธรรมนูญ, 2550 [2007]) [Draft Constitution of the Kingdom of Thailand Buddhist Era … Edition for Receiving Opinions (Bangkok: Constitution Drafting Committee, Constitution Drafting Assembly, Committee Office 2, Office of the Secretary-General of the House of Representatives, 2007)].
44 รายงานการประชุมคณะกรรมาธิการยกร่างรัฐธรรมนูญ [Meeting Minutes of the Constitution Drafting Committee], no. 5, February 1, 2007, p. 40.
45 สภาร่างรัฐธรรมนูญ ครั้งที่ ๓๐/๒๕๕๐ เป็นพิเศษ วันศุกร์ที่ ๒๒ เดือนมิถุนายน พุทธศักราช ๒๕๕๐ [Constitution Drafting Assembly], no. 30, June 22, 2007.
46 Ibid., p. 80f.
47 Ibid.
48 Ibid., p. 83.
49 Ibid.
50 Ibid., p. 92.
51 Ibid., p. 145.
52 คำวินิจฉัยศาลรัฐธรรมนูญ ๑๘–๒๒/๒๕๕๕ [Verdict of the Constitutional Court 18–22/2012], July 13, 2013.
53 คำวินิจฉัยศาลรัฐธรรมนูญ ๑๕–๑๘/๒๕๕๖ [Verdict of the Constitutional Court 15–18/2013], November 20, 2013.
54 Ibid., p. 31f. In a convincing analysis, a well-known group of critical public law lecturers argued that the Court had no authority directly to accept the case from the plaintiffs, had no authority to rule on the amendment, and lacked legal and logical reason in rejecting the amendment. Therefore, the Constitutional Court's verdict was invalid and not legally binding (นิติราษฎร์, "แถลงการณ์คณะนิติราษฎร์ เรื่อง คำวินิจฉัยศาลรัฐธรรมนูญกรณีรัฐสภาแก้ไขเพิ่มเติมรัฐธรรมนูญเกี่ยวกับการได้มาซึ่งสมาชิกวุฒิสภา" [Nitirat, "Announcement of the Nitirat Group Sbout the Verdict of the Constitutional Court Regarding the Case of the National Assembly Amending the Constitution About the Origins of Senators"], November 23, 2013). Nevertheless, after the verdict had been issued, a number of groups, including mostly appointed anti-Thaksin senators, asked the National Anti-Corruption Commission (NACC) to initiate impeachment procedures against all those MPs and senators who had voted for the constitutional amendment. However, these procedures failed.

55 "Sia-khong" or "a waste" has become a buzzword in military political circles since the May 22 coup. It is a short version of, "Don't let the May 22 coup be a waste". The May 22 coup has often been compared with the Sept 19, 2006 seizure of power by Gen Sonthi Boonyaratglin, which has been described as "a waste" because it failed to fulfill its main objective, which was to neutralise the Thaksin regime and prevent its political comeback.

(*Bangkok Post*, July 29, 2014)

56 A summary of the initial design decisions may be found in *The Nation* (January 5, 2015). For the "national morality assembly," see *Post Today* (January 7, 2015). A proposal similar to the citizens' assembly was already included in the "new politics" proposals made by the People's Alliance for Democracy during their occupation of the Government House compound in 2008 (Nelson 2010: 141).

## Bibliography

Anek Laothamatas [อเนก เหล่าธรรมทัศน์] (2007). **สามสิบปี ประชาธิปไตยไทยไม่เปลี่ยนแปลง – เอกบุรุษ อภิชนาธิปไตย และประชาธิปไตย** [In 30 Years, Thai Democracy Has Not Changed: Great Men, Elitism, and Democracy]. Document no. 1154 of the Midnight University, posted on February 9, 2007 (accessed February 16, 2015 at http://v1.midnightuniv.org/midnight2544/0009999773.html).

Capoccia, G. and Ziblatt, D. (2010). "The Historical Turn in Democratization Studies: A New Research Agenda for Europe and Beyond." *Comparative Political Studies*, 43: 931–968.

Constitution of the Kingdom of Thailand, B.E. 2550 (2007). Translated by Pinai Nanakorn. Bangkok: Secretariat of the House of Representatives.

Constitution of the Kingdom of Thailand (Interim), B.E. 2557 (2014).

Dressel, B. (2010). "When Notions of Legitimacy Conflict: The Case of Thailand." *Politics and Policy*, 38: 445–469.

Ginsburg, T. (2009). "Constitutional Afterlife: The Continuing Impact of Thailand's Post-political Constitution." *International Journal of Constitutional Law*, 7: 83–105.

Harding, A. and Leyland, P. (2011). *The Constitutional System of Thailand: A Contextual Analysis*. Oxford and Portland, OR, Hart Publishing.

Hicken, A. (2007). "The 2007 Thai Constitution: A Return to Politics Past." *Crossroads*, 19: 128–160.

Kobkua Suwannathat-Pian (2003). *Kings, Country and Constitutions: Thailand's Political Development 1932–2000*. London and New York, RoutledgeCurzon.

McCargo, D. (1998). "Alternative Meanings of Political Reform in Contemporary Thailand." *The Copenhagen Journal of Asian Studies*, 13: 5–30.

Murashima, E. (1988). "The Origins of Modern Thai Official State Ideology in Thailand." *Journal of Southeast Asian Studies*, 19: 80–96.

Nelson, M.H. (2010). "Thailand's People's Alliance for Democracy: From 'New Politics' to a 'Real' Political Party?" In *Legitimacy Crisis and Political Conflict in Thailand*, ed. M. Askew. Chiang Mai. Silkworm Books.

Nelson, M.H. (2011). "Looking Back Before the Election of 2011: Thailand's Constitutional Referendum and the Election of 2007." *European-Asian Journal of Law and Governance*, 1(1): 49–74.

Nelson, M.H. (2012). "Some Observations on Democracy in Thailand." Hong Kong, Southeast Asia Research Centre, City University of Hong Kong. Working Paper Series No. 125.

Nelson, M.H. (2013). "The Democrat and Phuea Thai Parties in Thailand's 2011 Election: Thaksin Shinawatra Returns to Power." Hong Kong, Southeast Asia Research Centre, City University of Hong Kong. Working Paper Series No. 140.

Ploy Suebvises (2010). "Constitutional Policymaking by the Thai Elite: Designing the Election System for House and Senate in the 2007 Constitution." Hong Kong, Southeast Asia Research Centre, City University of Hong Kong. Working Paper Series No. 105.

Riggs, F.W. (1966). *Thailand: The Modernization of a Bureaucratic Polity*. Honolulu, Hawaii, East–West Center Press.

Thak Chaloemtiarana (2007). *Thailand: The Politics of Despotic Paternalism*. Chiang Mai, Silkworm Books.

# 4 Constitutionalism old and new in the "UN Kingdom of Timor-Leste"

*Rui Graça Feijó*

## Introduction

For the last quarter of a century, constitutionalism has been an important feature of the political landscape of Southeast Asia. The notion encompasses two different, although sometimes associated, meanings. In a narrow, mostly juridical, sense, constitutionalism may be thought of as the process through which formal constitutions are drafted. It has an institutional dimension most often supported in specifically designed state bodies, with the expectation that the charter which emerges will frame the future of the polity. However, it may also be understood as a significant step in the adoption of "constitutional policies" or the development of such political factors as separation of powers, rule of law, checks and balances, and human rights. Here constitutionalism is closely associated with the spread of democratic polities, a trend that Samuel P. Huntington (1991) dates to the Portuguese Carnations Revolution of 1974. It was then stimulated by the fall of the Berlin Wall in 1989 and is said to have reached Southeast Asia in the 1990s. True, some nations not considered democratic have constitutions, but practically all democracies elaborate fundamental charters that spell out the basic political structure. Linz (1997: 117) states that a fundamental condition for a democracy is the establishment of a formal state based on the rule of law – which is normally grounded in a constitution.

The organizers of this volume argue that the constitutional practices now sweeping Southeast Asia have had major impact in four critical areas: individual rights and religion; the role of the military; the rule of law, courts, and justice; and the process of constitutional drafting itself (Dressel and Bünte 2014: 4). In all these areas, much political contestation has been channelled into the emerging constitutional practice, laying a solid foundation on which democratic developments could be built. This chapter takes a close look at one of these areas, the process of drafting in Timor-Leste under the UN administration, since constitution-making is one of the most visible arenas for contestation. Of course, drafting a new constitution is a major step in the democratic process, but "[f]or constitutionalism to take hold, clearly it will take more than institutional change on paper. Instead, elites and regular citizens alike must come to agreement" to support the fundamental tenets of the new constitution (Dressel and Bünte 2014: 4). This chapter argues that there is a significant relationship between how the process of drafting the Timor-Leste Constitution was conducted and the ensuing difficulties in engaging both elites and regular citizens to adhere to it.

Two alternative models were put forward early in the process – what I call the "new" and the "old" constitutionalism. The old model emphasizes the need to craft a statement of fundamental issues of political organization that at least some ruling elites can share; it uses conventional means, such as the election of an assembly of democratically selected representatives, to accomplish that. However, other currents of thought call for a more broad approach in order to enable a novel constitution to emerge from a highly participative process of public consultation and effective engagement of significant numbers of the population at large; the goal is to guarantee that the legal prescriptions correspond to a socially relevant consensus so that the constitution will promptly root itself in everyday practice. Timor-Leste's choice of the more conservative approach may have alienated both significant groups of the elite and other sectors of the population in terms of how social and political life are organized. Although the Constitution of 2002 has been in force ever since independence was proclaimed, and there has been no attempt since to revise it, some major points of friction have emerged which suggest that the relationship between the constitution and the real state for which it was created is not fully established.

## The importance of process

On August 30, 1999 the people of Timor-Leste voted in a referendum to end the 24-year-long annexation to the Republic of Indonesia. This launched them on the path to statehood. Following the referendum, Timor-Leste engaged in two simultaneous political processes: the construction of the foundations of a new independent state and the definition of institutions and mechanisms for a democratic polity (Tansey 2009). A constitution was generally accepted as central to both. Recognition of a new political entity is contingent upon the existence of a legal framework which defines the main institutions and political mechanisms, and democracy cannot thrive without broad consensus on clear rules for the political game. These are elements which are normally enshrined in new constitutions that aspire to embody a real social contract.

As Croissant states (Chapter 2, this volume), there has long been a link between modes of constitution-making, acceptance of the constitutional provisions by the citizenry, and the democratic quality of the regime that emerges. It follows that one critical variable on which a positive outcome depends is how the institutional process is shaped. Samuels (2006) identified four questions that may be used to analyze the significance of the procedures: (1) Are constitutions imposed top down or do they derive from negotiations among a variety of actors? (2) Is the process inclusive or restricted to only some stakeholders? (3) How well does the process represent the citizenry? and (4) how were citizens allowed to participate in the constitution-drafting?

These considerations frame this attempt to evaluate how Timor-Leste's constitution was drafted. They also relate to the degree of legitimacy which the new constitution has achieved. Elster (1997) maintained that constitutional legitimacy may be sustained in three ways: "upstream legitimacy" if the body producing the charter was established in a legitimate way; "process legitimacy" if its deliberations were not subject to external pressure or limitation; and "downward legitimacy" if the end product was subject to a referendum or other form of public approval. Scrutinizing the constitution-drafting process in Timor-Leste against these benchmarks will illuminate how a democratic polity emerged in the first new nation of the twenty-first century.

Samuels' four issues stand out in studying the relationships between constitution-making and democracy. Two of them precede the drafting of a constitution, and are considered in detail in the survey of the roadmap to independence; the third, which pertains to the essence of that process, is only cursorily addressed here due to the dearth of sources available; and the last applies in assessing the importance of the new charter. This assessment also looks at another four dimensions of the constitution-making process that can only be evaluated ex post: the durability of the new constitution; temperance in the balance of powers it enshrines; how it affects performance of the new institutions; and the democratic nature not only of the constitution-making process itself but also of whether the rule of law is sustained. These will be considered in the final section of this chapter.

Fareed Zakaria (2013) considers the first issue, the timing of constitution drafting, to be critical to the success of democratization. Retrieving a historical argument which postulates that the rule of law developed before adult universal suffrage (although recent developments analyzed by Miller (2013) suggest that there are alternative paths), Zakaria puts "paper power" ahead of "people power," and adds:

> It's crucial that before the first elections, before politicians gain enormous legitimacy through the polls, a system is put in place that limits governmental power and protects individual liberty and the rights of minorities.... The focus should be more on constitutions, and less on elections.
>
> (Zakaria 2013: 33)

Thus, a central issue becomes the precise differentiation between a process that gains as much substance as it can to bring a plurality of actors to broad consensus and another, more competitive, process that stimulates confrontation, often verging on "winner takes all," that alienates some groups of stakeholders. Timor-Leste faced this dilemma, as may be seen from the main arguments in the debate discussed below.

The second issue relates to the institutional model that frames the decision-making process. As Garrison has noted,

> The degree of legitimacy and public support for a new constitution are critically affected by decisions about the time frame of the constitution building process, about who is to make key decisions, and about what the extent of the political participation will be.
>
> (Garrison 2005: 2–3)

Here there are two polarizing models: a classical process approach that is restricted to political elites in which formal institutions (constituent assembly, political parties, etc.) take full responsibility for writing and approval of a new constitution; and a model which Hart has called "new constitutionalism" (2003: 4) that considers it necessary to involve many more sectors of the citizenry through participatory processes. Mixed forms are possible (e.g., submitting the proposed text of a new constitution to a referendum or articulation of a constituent assembly with an institutionalized process of popular consultations). In fact scholars have identified no fewer than 18 alternative constitutional designs (Ginsburg *et al.* 2009: 205), and still more are conceivable. The relevance of analyzing how constitutions are elaborated has been stressed by Ginsburg and colleagues (2009: 202, 219): "the conditions under which founders write, deliberate and ratify are consequential" because they postulate the existence of links between processes and outcomes; the authors conclude that there is a close association between "processes that involve the public in the adoption of the constitution and the presence of rights and certain democratic institutions in the resulting document."

In relation to the third issue, Lijphart (e.g., 2004) has written extensively on "constitutional design for divided societies." He argues that it is possible to draw generic lessons from the myriad constitutional experiments the world has seen in recent times. Rather than copy models – often from former colonial powers – or delve into the extensive catalog of alternative models, critical elements from successful constitutions should be preferred. However, it may be easier to suggest fundamental principles, such as the establishment of power-sharing institutions and mechanisms, or group autonomy, than to pinpoint their precise morphology. Actual drafters are confronted with choices in critical areas, such as government systems or electoral models, or in relation to other institutions, such as the judiciary, the military, the police, or the civil service – and what they choose matters:

> The relative success of a power-sharing system is contingent upon the specific mechanisms devised to yield the broad representation that constitutes its core [because] it is naïve to expect that minorities condemned to permanent opposition [will] remain loyal, moderate and constructive.
>
> (Lijphart 2004: 98–99)

The constitution-drafting process of Timor-Leste addressed those issues, but space does not allow us to consider them in detail here.

The fourth issue pertains to what may be labeled "para-constitutional" provisions. It is common for constitutions to demand special treatment for certain political issues, such as imposing qualified majorities, which they do not directly provide for, and which must be considered as a special case straddling the constitution and ordinary legislation. On the other hand, as Sartori has noted, beyond the letter of constitutions there are often "material constitutions" that encompass established practices that offer a basis for political action not contemplated in the formal text – what he calls "the real configuration of the system" (Sartori 1997: 202). This issue will also be addressed in the framework of the Timorese political process, where a gap between the written constitutional word and the actual political frame has appeared in two distinct forms: (1) the constitutional text could not provide responses to all emerging difficulties, so that other sources of legitimation are required; and (2) the written norms required time and resources to be effectively deployed, delaying in practice the application of several constitutional provisions. Both cases call for a notion of "para-constitutional" provisions to fully enlighten the relationships between the constitutional process and the real politics of a living entity.

In brief, throughout the world how a constitution is drafted should be kept in mind in every investigation of the legitimacy and stability of the democratic polity that adopted it. If this process has managed to channel political contestation to the assembly and produce a charter that accommodates the aspirations of the vast majority of stakeholders, the regime that emerges is likely to have solid legitimacy that can keep the polity stable. Failure to produce those results would diminish the capacity of a new regime to sustain peaceful solutions when contestation occurs outside the realm of novel, narrowly defined institutions.

## Setting the frame

The United Nations had a double problem to solve in Timor-Leste: to provide humanitarian aid on a scale far beyond anyone's worst expectations, and to guarantee the country a way to transition to independence. Security Council (UNSC) Resolution 1272 (October 25) established the UN Transitional Administration of East Timor (UNTAET). Thus began the "UN Kingdom of East Timor" (Chopra 2000). Unlike other polities this one was not intended to last indefinitely, but simply to pave the way for Timorese independence relatively quickly. The main assumption of the UNSC Resolution was that "the East Timorese people expressed their clear wish to begin a process of transition under the authority of the United Nations towards independence," and thus UNTAET was created with the explicit goals of promoting the "development of local democratic institutions" and of "transfer[ring] to these institutions its administrative and public service functions."

The UNSC gave UNTAET "overall responsibility for the administration of East Timor and … empowered [it] to exercise all legislative and executive authority, including the administration of justice." The scope of responsibilities entrusted to the Transitional Authority, personalized in the Special Representative of the UN Secretary General, the Brazilian-born UN career official Sergio Vieira de Mello, was the broadest ever in a UN mission (Tansey 2009). For one thing, the collapse of public administration was much more profound than in any other circumstances, so that the definition of the UN role specified that providing the basic infrastructure of the state was a prerequisite for its operations. However, after acknowledging the collapse of public administration, many international actors drew a false conclusion: that all legitimate power had ceased to exist and that a power vacuum had replaced the ruins of the Indonesian governance. This view, which was to have pervasive effects in how the situation was handled, underestimated both the deep organizational roots of the resistance movement and the persistence of entrenched notions of political legitimacy that sustained a political hierarchy in the country (Hohe 2002).

How the UN's powers were configured raised two substantial problems. If the development of democratic governance was a major goal of the process, the method chosen ran contrary to the very essence of democracy: it amalgamated in a single individual the whole range of powers that are supposed to be separated and to provide checks and balances on the political system. This method was termed "benevolent autocracy" (Chesterman 2004), "benevolent despotism" (Beauvais 2001), and "benevolent dictatorship" (Powell 2008); the Transitional Administrator was compared to a "pre-constitutional monarch in a sovereign state" (Chopra 2002).

The stated goal of the intervention was to "support capacity building for self-government." But the initial approach entrusted governance to international personnel. UNSC Resolution 1272 called for setting up a structure with at least two components: "a governance and public administration component, including an international police element, with a strength of up to 1,640 officers," and "a military component with a strength of up to 8,950 troops and up to 200 military observers." This seems to have left little room for the Timorese in the transitional administration. Because some of the goals ascribed to this force derived from the international community's own political agenda and were to be enforced though a strong bureaucratic apparatus mainly composed of foreigners that would retain the reins of the process, Damien Kingsbury labeled the exercise "benign colonialism" (2009: 77).

To resolve the paradox and deal with the contradiction between ends and means, the UN mission was given two independent goals: in the short term, to build a state apparatus and a public administration that could deliver basic services and prefigure the future independent state's own structure but be operated by international personnel; and in the medium term to help the Timorese build their own organization to take over from the UN mission at the time of independence. The two self-contained goals had little in common. Vieira de Mello promulgated Regulation 1999/2 establishing a 15-member National Consultative Council, but in spite of references to "decision-making," section 1.1 stipulates that the Council was to "provide advice to the Transitional Administrator." It was conceived as "a joint consultative forum of representatives of the East Timorese people and UNTAET" that could not "prejudice the final authority of the Transitional Administrator" (section 1.3). The clear distinction between executive capacity, merged with legislative and judicial powers and reserved for UN personnel, and the consultative functions of representatives of Timorese organizations was thus enshrined in the founding regulation of UNTAET.

In this distinction of functions the Timorese leadership felt it had been relegated to a mere "advisory" capacity. Vieira de Mello conceded that the increasingly vociferous frustration was firmly grounded and required an evolution in the political structures he had created (Powell 2008). In July 2000 he redesigned the original council – which had been "a genuine, if largely failed attempt to engage the local population" (Kingsbury 2009: 84) – as the National Council (NC) "established to act as a forum for all legislative matters" (UNTAET Regulation 2000/24, section 1), with extended responsibilities. He also created "the Cabinet of the Transitional Government" aimed at "effectively governing and administering East Timor during the transitional period, leading to the adoption of a constitution and the establishment of a democratically elected government for East Timor" (UNTAET Regulation 2000/23). The "timorization" process reduced but did not eliminate frustrations and tensions, which were to endure until independence day. Voices from the CNRT (*Conselho Nacional da Resistencia Timorense*/National Council of the Timorese Resistance), the umbrella organization established in 1998 to unify all elements seeking political change, openly criticized the approach.

Pursuing that approach, based on a distinction between current governance and the preparation for independence, Vieira de Mello spelled out the two main tasks of the transitional administration regarding the latter: prepare a constitution, and organize an electoral process whose result would give the new government legitimacy to govern the new country.

## A controversial roadmap to independence

The UNSC Resolutions did not specify how the shift to an independent new nation would occur; nor was there any agreement like those in Cambodia or Afghanistan that defined the basis for the state-building effort (Aucoin and Brandt 2010). It was necessary to find "a delicate balance between imposing international standards and acknowledging the local historical and political context" (Charlesworth 2003). The rationale that framed Vieira de Mello's decisions bears the marks of a major decision behind the scenes in New York: transfer of the Timorese file from the UN Department of Political Affairs to the UN Department of Peace Keeping Operations (Suhrke 2001; Garrison 2005; Kingsbury 2009). The former had extensive knowledge of the political landscape and relationships with the major figures of the resistance; the latter advocated a standardized blueprint based on neutrality principles to be deployed in post-conflict situations in which rival parts face each other – which was difficult to justify in the case of Timor-Leste. Some do not seem to have realized that the conflict was actually over and that there was a legitimate winner

Meanwhile, Timorese organizations were active. CNRT convened a conference at Tibar in May 2000 to analyze prospects for the future, and reaffirmed its commitment to a strategic plan for drafting a constitution through a "constitutional convention" with ample public consultation, as had been agreed in April 1999 in Melbourne. According to Aucoin and Brandt (2010), at the Tibar conference the UNTAET Department of Political Affairs under Peter Galbraith proposed an alternative: "Elections will choose a Constituent Assembly which in turn will write, debate and adopt a constitution." Vieira de Mello was careful to keep the doors open at the CNRT Congress in August, when he stated that both options were legitimate. But when in September he addressed the UNSC, he presented only the plan to hold elections for a Constituent Assembly without reference to an eventual "constitutional convention" or any form of public consultation.

Despite a marked improvement in the engagement of Timorese leaders in matters pertaining to the transition, the sentiment was still that ownership of the process was in foreign hands. A substantial number of political actors could not understand why the results of the popular consultation were not translated into actual transfer of power. As relations with UNTAET grew strained, proclamation of independence emerged as the only way out.

At the end of 2000, the NC discussed a roadmap to full independence. The Timorese leadership was torn between two conflicting considerations. They recognized the immense difficulty of the tasks ahead and the need for time to lay the foundations of the new state, and were bound by earlier decisions pointing to a transitional period of ten or more years; on the other hand, they felt marginalized by the domineering presence of UNTAET and aspired to assume rapid control over the destiny of their country. Given the limitations that would continue as long as the UN retained control of the situation, designing a roadmap to full independence was thus a major opportunity to take matters into their own hands by (1) assuming a key role in defining those steps and their timing, and (2) making sure that local actors would subsequently take center-stage in crafting the tools required for independence. The lively debate engaged Timorese stakeholders and prominent representatives of the UN apparatus.

Not surprisingly, two major lines of argument were presented. The first favored a protracted period of transition to independence that could be associated with an increased role for the Timorese in the process, coupled with an approach centered on a constitutional convention as the instrument to craft the fundamental laws of the new nation. The second supported a rapid move and adopted the view that setting up formal democratic institutions and staging competitive elections for a Constituent Assembly were a prerequisite for independence. The contrast was pronounced.

The first vision was rooted in the history of the Timorese Resistance. Ramos-Horta's speech in Oslo when he accepted the Nobel Peace Prize (1996) proposed a three-stage transitional period from Indonesian rule lasting ten years or more. This was based on the proposal put forward by Gusmão before his arrest in 1992, which received scant public attention but was widely accepted by the Resistance. A similar lengthy period was agreed upon when various branches of the opposition to Indonesian rule met in Peniche, Portugal, in April 1998 and formed the new CNRT. The rationale was twofold. First, it gave Indonesia time to organize eventual withdrawal without turbulence, there by safeguarding its interests; second, it offered the Timorese time to heal the scars of past disputes that had only recently been overcome by the political elites represented in the CNRT. The first argument was overturned by the events that followed the agreement of May 5, 1999, but had remained a central concern of a sizable number of the Timorese leaders. This view was not unanimous.

The most outspoken voice proposing an alternative path was not of any Timorese but rather that of Peter Galbraith, Cabinet Officer in charge of Political Affairs and Timor Sea. He could hardly have been more explicit:

> The final phase of Political Transition begins with the election of a Constituent Assembly with a mandate to prepare the constitution for an independent Timor-Leste. UNTAET has an obligation to hold free and fair elections that meet the highest international standards and are open to all political parties and viewpoints. Only in this way can UNTAET be certain that it is turning power over to bona fide representatives of the Timorese people. The Constituent Assembly will have full plenary power. It can decide on the type of constitution, the method of drafting the constitution, the extent of debate on its adoption, and the method of ratification. Both theoretically and practically, it will be impossible for an un-elected National Council and Cabinet to limit the scope of the Constituent Assembly writing authority.
>
> (ETTA 2001: 27)

Contrary to those who believed that the process of constitution-drafting should be organized in such a way that it allowed for ample popular participation, Galbraith's view was that there had to be formal guaranteed conditions to facilitate the delegation of power from the people to a handful of members of the elite who would assume the burden of preparing and voting on the new Constitution. All other considerations were overridden by a procedural notion that competitive elections must be organized at all costs because they are prerequisite to the attribution of legitimate status to any sort of polity.

Galbraith and the Timorese who sided with him, such as Fretilin, were the winners. Realizing that a price had to be paid to advance self-rule, the NC agreed that elections for a constituent assembly would be held by mid-2001. However, it also took note of objections about the short time allowed for its preparation, the need to foster popular participation in the process, and the call for gradual methods leading up to the final election of that assembly, and issued two further statements. (1) It took upon itself "the responsibility of organizing a National Convention for the purpose of drafting, debating and adopting a Pact of National Unity" (ETTA 2001: Recommendations, B.1). The pact was drafted and all but two parties running in the August 2001 election subscribed to it. (2) The NC also decided to "establish a National Constitutional Commission to facilitate the process of consultation throughout the 13 districts of Timor-Leste" (ETTA 2001: Recommendations, C.1), the results of which were to be given to the constituent assembly upon its election.

It seemed that there had been a compromise on a multi-layered approach that would combine the two methodologies. However, the timetable established actually reduced the chances of the National Constitutional Commission carrying out significant work because so little time was allowed for that. And though through the Pact of National Unity the NC had imposed guidelines that the Constituent Assembly was to respect, these actually limited its powers. Because Gusmão felt uncomfortable with the apparent compromise, which amounted to a substantial defeat of the "new constitutionalism" approach, he resigned as NC chairman in March 2001 because of the limitations to the consultation process.

By late February 2001 the roadmap was complete and it became time to move along the path. For UNTAET, "early adoption of a new constitution would be a benchmark of success for the mission which needed to illustrate results to justify its huge expense" (Aucoin and Brandt 2010). At the time the success of UN missions in Indochina and the Balkans was being questioned; the chance of obtaining a result that vindicated the general UN approach was too tempting to be allowed to fail. For the Timorese, the coveted prize of independence overshadowed any shortcomings. Just as the elections for the constituent assembly were set in motion, Vieira de Mello disbanded the National Council (UNTAET Directive 2001/8, July 14) to prevent the co-existence of two bodies vested with legislative powers.

## On the Constituent Assembly

Elections for the Constituent Assembly were scheduled for August 30, 2001. The Assembly was given three months, later extended to another three, to complete its gigantic task. This compares with an average of 16 months and a mode of ten months for a large sample of constitutions (Elkins *et al.* 2009: 207). The severe time constraints placed on the assembly would have significant effects on the way it was to discharge its function.

Elections were preceded by a few months during which political parties had to register and offer proof of a modicum of support – a period also widely criticized for its brevity, which was deemed to unduly favor the long-established Fretilin and to generate substantial obstacles to other currents of opinion that had emerged late in Indonesian domination and were represented informally in CNRT. In brief, the way political parties were to be formalized undermined the likelihood of a wider franchise.

To counteract those effects, UNTAET adopted two devices (Resolution 2001/2): (1) 75 of the 88 seats would be allocated through proportional representation in a "national constituency" (thus allowing minorities who succeeded in forming a party to be represented in the Assembly) – a response to the academic consensus on the virtues of proportionality and power-sharing in institutions (Lijphart 2004). (2) The other 13 seats were to be fought on a first-past-the-post system in every district, with candidatures limited to persons who resided in the district where they were candidates (section 32.2). These special seats would facilitate the election of individuals without party affiliation, in an effort to enlarge the franchise beyond the reaches of political parties. Although "independent" candidates could present themselves in the national constituency, they were unlikely to secure enough votes to win a seat; the district seats would compensate for this bias in favor of established parties. The result was an assembly in which Fretilin secured 12 of the 13 district seats and 43 of the other 75 and thus dominated the process. However, it fell short of the 60 seats necessary for approval of the constitution, and was thus compelled to negotiate – albeit from a very strong position – with 11 other parties.

A feature that needs to be stressed is that this assembly offered the elected representatives of the Timorese elite an opportunity to conduct business their own way. In fact, in spite of voicing concerns about some aspects of the Assembly's work and making a number of suggestions, UNTAET and its officials mostly distanced themselves from the substance of the drafting process (Charlesworth 2003: 328). International advisors made their presence felt in Dili, but they kept a low profile and refrained from actively interfering. Thus the work of the Constituent Assembly reflected as much as possible local ownership of the process. In brief, "Once the constituent assembly model was adopted for drafting and adopting a constitution, political parties became the key decision-makers" (Garrison 2005: 12). This guaranteed that the process would be controlled by the Timorese elite. However, there were three contentious issues.

First, political parties were far from being effective social actors when the decision was made to move ahead with elections. The time allowed to register officially was short, and beyond bureaucratic compliance with the regulations, parties lacked the capacity to fully express the wealth of public opinion that still generally equated political parties with the "divisionism" reminiscent of the traumatic events of 1975. Several key figures, not least Xanana Gusmão, José Ramos-Horta, and influential personalities close to the Catholic Church, preferred to stay out of the fray. As a consequence, the Constituent Assembly, in spite of having allowed for "independent" candidates, suffered from the absence of major stakeholders.

The difference between Fretilin and all the other "parties" was enormous. The historical party had deep roots which the more recent currents of opinion that emerged in the latter years of the resistance did not have. It was not surprising that Fretilin supported early elections; the results vindicated its stance. However, the number of votes required in the House to approve the Constitution had been fixed at 60 out of 88 seats. Fretilin had only 55. But it only had to negotiate with one of the other parties represented in the Assembly. In the end, the constitution was approved with the votes of Fretilin and ASDT; the majority of the other parties voted against it. In terms of inclusiveness and consensus, the Constituent Assembly fell short of expectations.

Finally, the Constituent Assembly had the option of extending its own mandate and transforming itself into the first national parliament for five years without fresh elections. A substantial number of important stakeholders outside the House expressed the view that it was "illegitimate" for an assembly elected for a precise purpose to extend its own mandate without any kind of broad consensus, which was obviously missing (although the possibility was contemplated in the regulation governing the elections). In effect, then, the open political competition for elected posts prescribed in the constitution would not happen until 2007; in the meantime, political choices were distorted.

## Popular consultations pre-constitution

As had been generally recommended, and for "the purpose of soliciting the views of the people of East Timor on the future Constitution of an independent and democratic East Timor, in coordination with civil society initiatives," through UNTAET Directive 2001/3 Vieira de Mello established Constitutional Commissions in all 13 districts (Constitutional Affairs Branch 2001). Each Commission was required to present a report to the CA "reflecting the consolidated views expressed in those hearings." Only one month was allowed for this enormous task – earlier proposals had contemplated a full year. Yet 205 public meetings were held between June 18 and July 14, and reports of the proceedings were ceremoniously presented to Vieira de Mello on August 16. He presented them to the Constituent Assembly on September 17, the first day it sat.

The citizens had made epic efforts. "They did wish to participate, and they had plenty of things that they wanted to say" (Lutz 2003: 3). But the actual process was little more than a mockery of what people like Ramos-Horta had actually suggested. Gathering a crowd of several hundred to discuss in one day more than two dozen topics ranging from the national flag to public health and the organization of social services, religion and the police, official languages and the environment, may be adequate for disseminating the value of having a charter covering all those issues, but it is hardly a sound method to forge consensus or even to capture the views of the people on the basic constitutional text. In fact, many "felt that the consultation process had been United Nations-dominated, too short, and not representative of a genuinely East Timorese process" (Carter Center 2004: 44).

The reports are detailed as far as "the community's suggestions or desires to be included in the Constitution" go. However, the Constituent Assembly did not treat them as working documents, and in some cases of great symbolic nature (references to the 1975 proclamation of Independence, the flag, use of the crocodile as a symbol of the nation) it openly contradicted them. A few of the issues raised by citizens may have undermined the international standards expected of a modern constitution, but many others expressed views it would have been possible to accommodate, such as the desire to give the president a strong mandate.

## Consultations post-constitution

After the Assembly had completed its draft of the Timorese Constitution (February 9, 2002), another process of "consultation and socialization of the constitutional text" was organized. Teams of deputies were constituted with representatives of different parties and dispatched to the districts with directives to complete the hearings within one week (Baltazar 2004: 5).

It appears from a survey of the minutes of those meetings that two sorts of interventions were made. Political parties which had presented proposals that the Constituent Assembly rejected appealed to local militants to come before the Commission and defend their views. Meanwhile, several issues raised spontaneously were mostly concerned with symbolic matters. The Commission for Systematization and Harmonization selected proposals that, among other criteria, did not call into question "the unity and internal coherence of the draft constitution." Recommendations from the popular consultations were merged with those received from organizations of "civil society" whose advice had also been sought. Eight recommendations produced by the district consultation process were among the 21 amendment proposals the Commission presented to the plenary. The Constituent Assembly adopted only four of the 21 proposals (Baltazar 2004: 6).

The popular consultation process, both before and after the drafting of the constitutional text, is important not for the results it eventually yielded but for the tensions it revealed. Those opposed a dominant discourse on the virtues of participatory democracy to the pragmatic options of UNTAET and one Timorese political force, Fretilin, that emphasized the superior legitimacy of the electoral procedures over the "new constitutionalism." According to Lutz, "many national and international political advisors felt that public consultations … would be the most effective tool for integrating East Timorese people in the political and constitutional process" and "were seen as critical for public awareness and public 'ownership' of the new nation's constitution" – but in "neither the first nor the second set of consultations were the suggestions compiled at the village and sub-district level ever seriously considered by the Constituent Assembly" (Lutz 2003: 3). Keep in mind that Chesterman had asserted that "local ownership is the intended end of any state-building operation." However, the Carter Center noticed that the "energetic participation of citizens underscores the fact that the people of East Timor are deeply concerned that their voices be heard in their government bodies" (Carter Center 2004: 45)

Ultimately, the consultation process that supposedly permitted wide participation in how constitutional provisions were defined and offered a mechanism for the elected deputies to entertain a dialogue with the society at large was at best perfunctory. Critical decisions and political bargaining were made almost exclusively by the elected members of the CA. According to Aucoin and Brandt (2010), "If constitutions are to serve as a social contract, it is critical that the process be as inclusive as possible." However, the local elite who were involved in the process were undoubtedly not as frustrated as the rest of the East Timorese.

## The impact of the constitution-making process

In assessing the impact of the constitution-making process on the political life of Timor-Leste over the next ten years, expanding on Carey (2009: 156–159), four dimensions are considered: durability, temperance, stability, and democracy – the main goals a constitution may aspire to achieve.

### *Durability*

The CDRTL became effective on Independence Day (May 20, 2002) and has remained in force without amendment. Two presidential and two parliamentary elections have adhered to its requirements, and no candidate has ever run a campaign proposing that it be substantially altered, much less replaced. It appears from interviews with important institutional players (Gusmão, Ramos-Horta, Mari Alkatiri) that the country's leaders generally accept the constitutional text and have deferred substantial revision to a time when its long-term effects can be assessed (Feijó 2014b). Constitutional revisions of an "extraordinary" nature are permitted at any moment if supported by four-fifths of the Members of Parliament (CRDTL section 154-4), and "ordinary" ones requiring only the support of two-thirds could have been made after it had been in force for six years (CRDTL sections 154-2 and 155-1). Neither has happened. This puts the Timorese Constitution's survival above the mode of one year and the median eight years and on the path to the average life span of 17 for all the constitutions in the world since 1789, having surpassed the barrier of ten years at which over half the constitutions have perished (Elkins *et al.* 2009). Regionally, Timor-Leste has now reached the average Southeast Asian constitutional life span of 13 years and surpassed the 10.1-year average for democratic polities (see Croissant, Chapter 2, this volume). In these terms, it appears that the CRDTL has managed to rise above the troublesome process of its inception to wide acceptance, at least by the political elite.

### *Temperance*

If constitutional provisions vary from limited and institutional to very broad, encompassing a philosophy of social behavior, an underlying issue relates to the organization and division of power that in democratic contexts implies the setting up of checks and balances. Beyond assuring the formal tripartite division of power posited by Montesquieu, such mechanisms guarantee – in the classical formulation of Madison – that no political actor can unilaterally make and enforce decisions. Timor-Leste adopted a model that embodies the division of judicial, legislative, and executive powers and further divided those of the executive in terms of provisions for a semi-presidential regime. Although the exact terms in which presidential powers were crafted may have diverged substantially in the Constituent Assembly, the overarching design of the political institutions provided incentives for inclusive governance (Feijó 2014a).

The historical pace of development for each of the institutions that are considered to participate in the checks-and-balances system and to exercise horizontal accountability has been highly variable. As may be expected from the legacy of UNTAET, which had concentrated legislative, executive, and judicial functions in the hands of a single person, the executive branch was far better developed than either of the others and received much more international attention and support. Understandable as this may be, considering the dire necessities of the

Timorese people at the time, it made the construction of a democratic polity quite difficult. The critical feature of democratic rule is the limited function and power of individual entities, which means that there must be other bodies capable of exercising different types of mutual control. In this case those entities were severely underdeveloped. As Smith remarked, a strong government can be the sign of a weak state (Smith 2004). Here an active presidency for the Republic, endowed with the institutional and material means to discharge its functions and capable of exercising some control over the executive branch, seemed to be the pragmatic route to accountability of some sort. Constructing such a presidency was not made easy by a restricted view of the presidential powers inscribed in the CRDTL; but neither of the other branches opposed it. The repeated choice by Timorese citizens of independent presidents allowed the presidency to articulate political agendas far beyond those of any political parties, actively engaging Timorese civil society and prominent figures who had found it difficult to express their views through parties. Although there may have been temptations to reinforce the legal responsibilities attributed to presidents, the constitutional provisions have persisted unaltered. The main political actors have adapted their agendas to the constitutional provisions, and these have performed their function with the necessary limitation of individual powers.

### *Stability*

Stability is taken here not to signify the endurance of the constitution but rather its impact on how political institutions perform. Did the constitution provide incentives for a stable political environment, or is it responsible for the problems that marked the first few years after independence? Here it appears that there is scope for a less sunny view of the virtues of the constitutional process.

Timor-Leste suffered a severe political crisis in 2006, when leaders escalated a long-term political rivalry into open confrontation that was only overcome by the resignation of the Prime Minister. From a more institutional point of view, the first National Parliament supported three different governments (Alkatiri, 2002–2006; Ramos-Horta, 2006–2007; Estanislau Aleixo da Silva, 2007). Political instability thus characterized the first five years following independence. After the 2007 elections stability was further challenged on February 11, 2008, when the President of the Republic was shot and the Prime Minister ambushed. The constitutional provisions for dealing with presidential impediments, however, were deployed successfully. The second legislature also proved to be more stable than its predecessor, since there was only one government and it lasted out its full term. However, the political scenario was only stabilized when some para-constitutional restrictions were abolished and a new configuration emerged that allowed for significant changes in individual roles.

In fact, the decision of the Constituent Assembly to skip fresh elections at the end of its mandate and transform itself into a National Parliament for a full five-year term deserves critical attention. This option accorded with the rules under which the assembly was elected, but there was widespread criticism both in the

House (the majority of the parties voted against it) and outside (vociferous dissatisfaction was voiced by, among others, Gusmão, Ramos-Horta, and the Roman Catholic bishops). The Fretilin party managed to freeze its hold on executive power for five years, avoiding a fresh election that might have produced a National Parliament with a different composition. On the other hand, the only possibility for the charismatic Xanana Gusmão to play an institutional role – for which he was pressured by most international stakeholders – was to engage and control his popular support and discharge the function of President of the Republic, which had been very narrowly defined.

As soon as the para-constitutional constraints on political competition were dismantled in 2007, the political scenario moved significantly forward. The charismatic legitimacy of the Timorese leader was now superimposed with the electoral legitimacy of the executive power as Xanana became Prime Minister, while the new President was also politically tuned with the new situation. To conserve the constitutional text there had to be a substantial reconfiguration of the party system if the model was to operate smoothly. Thereafter, stability could take root – as it has done.

## *Democracy*

The goal of a constitution in a democratic polity is somewhat tautological: to ensure that democracy drives politics and is supported by specific institutional formulations. Here two main issues must be considered: Did the process of constitution-making respect democratic procedures and generate appropriate effects? Did the process actually produce a charter capable of sustaining a democratic state?

The second question is easier to answer. The CRDTL has been consistently judged to meet the requirements of international standards of democracy: separation of powers, limitations on individual power through checks and balances, defense of human rights and civil liberties, an enlarged franchise, and the rule of law. Timor-Leste has consistently been rated as a democracy by such international institutions as Freedom House, Polity IV, and The Economist Intelligence Unit Index of Democracy. Thus, the results of the constitutional process contributed positively to its democratic goal.

However, it would be hasty to conclude that the constitutional process explained political developments and that democracy actually derives from the charter. In many transitions from authoritarian regimes to democracy, negotiations between representatives of the old order and those who challenged it centered on the drafting of a new constitution, which then became the fulcrum of the bargaining process. This did not happen in Timor-Leste. The main bone of contention – independence – was resolved through a referendum, and those who had opposed the move vanished: thenceforth the political scenario was dominated by a pluralistic nationalism. The constitution-making process stemmed from a consensus favoring independence and democracy that was enshrined in a Pact of National Unity incorporating all sectors of the nationalist movement. This very broad consensus did not extend to other aspects of the process, but the hard bargaining dealt mostly with what were then considered secondary issues that did not affect the claim to independence. The importance of the constitution resides not so much in the choice of democracy as an unchallenged abstract concept but rather in the specific institutions that embody it. However, it would not be advisable to minimize the investment all stakeholders made in order to conform the final charter to visions and interests that were naturally divergent and even contradictory. There was considerable potential for acrimony from the use of majority rule to impose solutions that defied consensus.

The issue of the procedures used requires detailed analysis because it impinges upon the very notion of democracy. The choice of a constituent assembly elected by universal suffrage may be legitimately claimed to be considered a democratic procedure, although this seems to have been the chosen way in only 12 percent of all cases (Elkins *et al.* 2009: 205). There are alternative methods which base their claims to satisfy democratic principles on involvement of wider sectors of the elite and the population at large through participatory devices.

Assuming the method chosen meets basic democratic credentials, two problems must be addressed. Considering that "the content of constitutions depends on who sits at the table to hammer out their provisions" and that "more inclusive constitutional moments instil a widespread sense of ownership in, and commitment to new constitutions" among citizens and political actors alike (Carey, 2009: 176–177), were all the necessary steps taken to ensure that the main actors among the Timorese political elite were present in the Constituent Assembly?

The answer is no. Emphasizing formal political parties at a time when major independent political figures like Gusmão and Ramos-Horta refused to enter the race, and some significant currents of opinion found it very difficult to register a party and run successful campaigns, Vieira de Mello (assisted by Peter Galbraith) designed a model that was formally impeccable but far from inclusive. Contrary to the lessons of classical political theorists from Rousseau to Hegel, who were skeptical about attempting to implant constitutions in newly formed states by adopting models tested elsewhere and who stressed the need to conceive of them as institutions that need to grow locally in dialogue with the people, their assumption seems to have been that constitutions should be judged by their internal coherence and adhesion to universal values. Thus, some of the main actors were left out of the assembly. In addition, one should recall that the majority of the political parties in the CA actually voted against the final constitutional text. For this reason doubts may be raised about the end result, since "consensus among the political elites at the moment new political pacts are established are essential to their effectiveness and longevity" (Carey 2009: 157). In this case, formal procedures were paralleled by the restricted composition of the Assembly and rules about the minimum number of votes required for approval of the constitution that in turn limited consensus among the elite. The ensuing result could not help being rendered fragile by lack of the inclusiveness that should have fostered shared expectations about how politics should function.

Enfranchising the population at large is a positive and necessary step in empowering citizens to exert their rights – and the Timorese responded *en masse* to the opportunity to participate in the decisional process. But the right to participate is not limited to voting. Many international organizations have expressed the view that constitution-making should be a process that engages the largest possible majority of the population so as to ensure that the result is seen as legitimate and the property of all the people (Commonwealth Human Rights Initiative 1999), and that "participatory processes seem to have empowered the people" (International Institute for Democracy and Electoral Assistance). Carey summarized the argument by stating that more inclusive constitutional moments generate more democratic politics, more constraints upon government authority, and stronger and more durable constitutions (2009: 159–160). Similarly, Ginsburg and colleagues (2009) identified an association between processes that involve the public and strong democratic credentials in the final charter. A process along these lines, consisting of a combination of elections with a participatory model, was put forward in Timor-Leste but failed to attract the sympathy of UNTAET, which nevertheless accepted the need to pay some tribute to its virtues. However, this was a mere formality that failed to introduce real external inputs in the process of constitution-drafting, thus reducing the ownership factor to a fraction of the elite. By limiting the scope of inclusiveness and reducing participation to a marginal exercise that failed to generate external contributions to the writing of the constitution, the model which UNTAET adopted contributed to an unnecessarily fragile end result. Formally, the CRDTL responds positively to procedural and substantive claims to democracy. However, the elite consensus embodied in the charter was shallow, and the limited popular participation reduced the sense of ownership on which legitimacy at large is based.

## Conclusion

How a constitution is drafted assumes critical importance not only in the application of what has been termed "constitutional policies" to different domains, ranging from human rights to the place of the military in political life, but also – and primarily – in ensuring that the rules set down on paper actually permeate the workings of the polity and mobilize all the citizens so as to establish sound agreement on the rule of law. Based on this assumption, the UN-supervised process of drafting the Timor-Leste Constitution in 2001/2002, based on rules that could easily be recognized as offering formal legitimacy to the actors in the process, deserves a more balanced appraisal than the unqualified eulogy of official propaganda.

The Timorese Constitution does enshrine important elements that represent basic tenets of a democratic polity and were in consonance with the consensus that had emerged among the resistance and its several branches about the desirable regime following independence. Ramos-Horta's Nobel Peace Prize acceptance speech in 1996 prefigured what the Constitution actually accommodated in terms of human rights, civil liberties, and respect for pluralism and diversity.

The fact that the main tenets of the constitution are aligned with the political consensus of the resistance movement before the August 1999 Referendum is central to explaining the degree of its success. The efforts of the parliamentarians in those days went far beyond the need to have a minimal document responding to the immediate needs of a country rising literally from the ashes; they adopted measures that offered the country a horizon for institutional development over the next few decades. This may be seen in the provisions for the judicial system or the development of a decentralized form of state, which have constitutional weight but currently in Timor-Leste still lack important basic grounding. The Timorese Constitution of 2002 has a utopian element which is a driving force and an inspiration for current policies. It is also a check against some dubious initiatives that governments have been tempted to take. It thus contributes to the formulation of democratic policies (and is sometimes called to curb non-democratic proposals for new legislation, as is evidenced by interventions of the Court of Appeals serving as a Constitutional Court) – even if some might regard it as setting too high a threshold for a country that still lacks elementary building blocks. The Timorese Constitution is thus central to the process of rooting constitutional policies in a much wider sense.

However, setting aside the failure to mobilize and respond to wider social groups, as was advocated at the time by many who were not heard, the constitutional process was not inclusive even of local elites. The absence of such central political figures as Gusmão and Ramos-Horta is surely evidence that the elected body lacked participation by leading actors and was thus in danger of alienating the allegiance of significant segments of local elites. This negative element was discernible in detailed constitutional provisions determined primarily by the overwhelming predominance of a single party in the CA, causing the majority of the parties which had won seats to vote against acceptance of the constitution. In spite of the formalities followed in the election of the CA, the Assembly would have benefited from a subtle approach that was clearly lacking. One example is the definition of the powers of the President of the Republic, an area where Fretilin's desire to curb the influence of the first president who escaped their control determined its final shape, in contrast to other voices who claimed that more substantial responsibilities should be vested in the Chief of State. Later, the issue of presidential powers proved to be a theme for contention, and one that is not yet resolved. In addition, the decision of the Constituent Assembly to defer elections for Parliament to 2007, a power play heavily opposed by public opinion, created a para-constitutional barrier to the spread of a consensus on the rules of the political game, which were also postponed. Some of the decisions taken before the CA was elected and others implemented during its mandate are responsible for some of the difficulties the young Timorese democracy faced, such as the dangerous escalation of conflict that eventually led to the crisis of 2006.

Viewed in this light, the Timorese constitution-drafting process fell short of best practices, and was less than a clear demonstration of the recognition of Samuels's critical criteria: the basic document was provided by a single party without significant inclination to negotiate, it excluded important stakeholders from the process, and it was mainly insulated from the citizens' desire to contribute, paying little more than lip-service to the proponents of a new constitutionalism." The fact that the CA was conceived in formally democratic terms (and thus had "upstream legitimacy") and was reasonably free to take decisions (= "process legitimacy") must not conceal the critical fact that its contents were to a great extent devoid of "downstream legitimacy," since no substantial effort was made to include citizens in their ratification. The Timorese Constitution of 2002 was born unnecessarily fragile.

In this context, the fundamental role of a constitution – to lay a solid foundation for an overarching agreement that brings together elites and other citizens – has emerged more slowly than it would have done if certain approaches that were actually spelled out in the critical months preceding the drafting process had been given a chance to leave their imprint. The cost of this course was the disjunction between "constitutional order" and the expression of legitimate dissenting views in the period which culminated in the crisis of 2006 that threatened the survival of the constitutional republic.

On the other hand, the Timorese Constitution of 2002 is still in force, having outlived the average life span of identical charters in the region. Its endurance is to a large extent a paradox, given that the conditions in which it was drafted would have predicted that it would sooner rather than later be deeply contested. In general, this has not been the case. Although Aucoin and Brandt (2010) stressed that criticism of the constitution has been a rallying point for those who seek to gain favor with the population, which would militate to reduce the legitimacy of the charter, in my opinion it has functioned mostly as a cult object. In fact, even when the constitution seems to operate against the wishes of those in power (or aspiring to be), no serious attempt has been made to revise it, even though it actually anticipates that possibility. Take, for instance, the fact that when Gusmão was unhappy with the powers granted to the President, instead of taking advantage of his official position and his immense popularity to press for modification of the constitution to grant him more power, he adapted himself to its prescriptions and decided to gain power by seeking the job of prime minister. More recently, when Prime Minister Gusmão's resignation was being discussed and the idea of a non-elected Council of Elders was floated as a possibility to accommodate him and other members of the old guard, the fact that such a council was not in the spirit of the constitution (which reserves formal legislative and executive power to elected officers, as is proper for a democracy) determined a different solution rather than a challenge to the constitution.

The explanation for this paradox has two elements: the fact that the Timorese Constitution enshrines basic elements of a modern democratic polity subscribed to by the citizenry, and the fact that Timorese leaders – above all, the still vastly popular and charismatic Gusmão – opted to accept its terms in spite of the turbulence of the process and the persistence of contentious issues. In addition, the fact that para-constitutional measures were put aside in 2007, allowing for open political competition for all the social players, helped to keep the constitutional text at the center of Timorese political life.

The fact that the Timorese Constitution has been in force since May 20, 2002 without a single amendment should not obfuscate the difficulties that the consolidation of democracy – one of its major goals – still suffers at the hands of critical choices made under the UN transitional administration. The decision of Gusmão to resign from his position as Prime Minister in order to secure the transition to a younger generation may also allow for a recomposition of the parliamentary basis of the government, which now embodies the sort of "national unity" platform that, following the Referendum, key political figures proposed, unsuccessfully, as a medium-term alternative to open political competition. Perhaps this means a fresh start to the political game – one that may include revision of certain questionable sections of the Timorese Constitution of 2002.

## Bibliography


Aucoin, L. and Brandt, M. (2010). "East Timor Constitutional Passage to Independence." In *Framing the State in Times of Transition. Case Studies in Constitution Making*, eds L.E. Miller and L. Aucoin. Washington, DC, United States Institute of Peace, pp. 245–274.

Baltazar, A. (2004). "An Overview of the Constitutional Drafting Process in East Timor." *East Timor Law Journal*, 9, available at: http://easttimorlawjournal.wordpress.com/2012/05/19an-overview-of-the-constitution-drafting-process-in-east-timor/.

Beauvais (2001). "Benevolent Despotism: A Critique of UN State-building in East Timor." *International Law and Politics*, 33: 1101–1178.

Carey, J.M. (2009). "Does it Matter How a Constitution is Created?" In *Is Democracy Exportable?*, eds Z. Barany amd R.G. Moser. Cambridge, Cambridge University Press, pp. 155–178.

Carter Center (2004). *The East Timor Political and Electoral Observation Project*. Atlanta, GA, The Carter Center/The Democracy Program.

Charlesworth, H. (2003). "The Constitution of East Timor, May 20, 2002." *International Journal of Constitutional Law*, 1(2): 325–344.

Chesterman, S. (2004). "Building Democracy through Benevolent Autocracy." In *The UN Role in Promoting Democracy: Between Ideals and Realities*, eds E. Newman and R. Rich. New York, New York University Press, pp. 86–112.

Chopra, J. (2000). "The UN Kingdom of East Timor." *Survival*, 42 (3): 27–39.

Chopra, J. (2002). "Building State Failure in East Timor." *Development and Change*, 33(5): 979–1000.

Dressel, B. and Bünte, M. (2014). "Constitutional Politics in Southeast Asia: From Contestation to Constitutionalism?" *Contemporary Southeast Asia*, 36(1): 1–22.

East Timor Transitional Authority (ETTA). Standing Committee on Political Affairs (2001). *Report on the Political Transition Calendar*.

Elkins, Z., Ginsburg, T., and Melton, J. (2009). *The Endurance of National Constitutions*. Cambridge, Cambridge University Press.

Elster, J. (1997). "Ways of Constitution Making." In *Democracy's Victory and Crisis*, ed. A. Hadenius. Cambridge, Cambridge University Press, pp. 123–142.

Feijó, R.G. (2014a). "Semi-presidentialism, Moderating Power and Inclusive Governance. The Experience of Timor-Leste in Consolidating Democracy." *Democratization*, 21(2): 268–288.

Feijó, R.G. (2014b). *O Semi-presidencialismo Timorense. História, Politica e Desenho Institucional. Depoimentos e análises*. Coimbra, Almedina/CES.

Hadenius, A. (1997). *Democracy's Victory and Crisis*. Cambridge, Cambridge University Press.

Hohe, T. (2002). "The Clash of Paradigms: International Administration and Local Political Legitimacy in East Timor." *Contemporary Southeast Asia*, 24(3): 569–589.

Garrison, R. (2005). *The Role of Constitution-building Processes in Democratization*. Stockholm, International IDEA.

Ginsburg, T., Elkins, Z., and Blount, J. (2009). "Does the Process of Constitution Making Matter?" *Annual Review of Law and Social Sciences*, 5(5): 201–223.

Hart, V. (2003). *Democratic Constitution Making*. UN Institute of Peace Special Report, online at www.usip.org.

Huntington, S.P. (1991). *The Third Wave: Democratization in the Late Twentieth Century*. Norman, OK, University of Oklahoma Press.

Kingsbury, D. (2009). *East Timor: The Price of Liberty*. Basingstoke, Palgrave Macmillan.

Lijphart, A. (2004). "Constitutional Design for Divided Societies." *Journal of Democracy*, 15(2): 96–109.

Linz, J.J. (1997). "Democracy Today: An Agenda for Students of Democracy." *Scandinavian Political Studies*, 20(2): 115–134.

Lutz, N.M. (2003). "Constitutionalism as Public Culture in East Timor." Paper presented at the Law and Society Association Meeting, Pittsburgh, PA, June 7.

Miller, L.E. and Aucoin, L., eds (2010). *Framing the State in Times of Transition. Case Studies in Constitution Making*. Washington, DC, United States Institute of Peace.

Miller, M.K. (2013). "Democratic Pieces: Autocratic Elections and Democratic Development since 1815." *British Journal of Political Science*, 45(3): 501–530.

Newman, E. and Rich, R. (2004). *The UN Role in Promoting Democracy. Between Ideals and Reality*. Tokyo, New York and Paris, United Nations University Press.

Powell, S. (2008). *Chasing the Flame. Sergio Vieira de Mello and the Fight to Save the World*. London, Allen Lane.

Samuels, K. (2006). *Constitution Building Processes and Democratization: A Discussion of Twelve Cases*. Stockholm, International IDEA.

Sartori, G. (1997). *Comparative Constitutional Engineering. An Inquiry into Structures, Incentives and Outcomes* [1994]. New York, New York University Press. First published 1994.

Smith, Anthony L. (2004)."Timor-Leste: Strong Government, Weak State." *Southeast Asian Affairs*: 277–294.

Suhrke, A. (2001). "Peacekeepers as National Builders: Dilemmas of the UN in East Timor." *International Peacekeeping*, 8(4): 1–20.

Tansey, O. (2009). *Regime Building: Democratization and International Administration*. Oxford, Oxford University Press.

Zakaria, F. (2013). "Write a Constitution." *Time* magazine, March 2.

# Part II

# Constitutional change and the military

# Part II

# Constitutional change and the military

# 5 Constitutional change and security forces in Southeast Asia

## Lessons from Thailand, the Philippines, and Myanmar

*Paul Chambers*

## Introduction

Taming security forces through constitutional reform has been a major challenge for young democracies of Southeast Asia. In some cases. security sector reform has been successful, with certain studies predicting a bright future for the region (Beeson and Bellamy 2008). In other cases, governments seeking to establish or consolidate civilian control have been faced with *coups d'état* or the threat of coups. On other occasions, the successful enshrinement of laws regulating security forces has accompanied compromises which provide militaries/police with considerable latitude in areas of decision-making. Ultimately, this study examines three country cases of young democracies where security forces have evolved toward becoming more integrated under the constitutional charters of civilian-led regimes. Yet, such moves have not led to civilianization but have instead mostly camouflaged continuing khaki clout – insulating security forces from civilian monitoring. As such, the study asks four questions with regard to each of the cases. First, how did the institutionalization of security services under civilian-led constitutions historically occur? Second, how did these experiences vary? Third, to what extent do security forces in different countries today possess differing degrees of enshrined powers? Based on these experiences, how might the constitutionalization of "true" civilian control eventually become sustained? Using a variant of historical institutionalism, the study argues that constitutional change acceded to by security forces results more often than not from sequences of transformative bargains – informal negotiations and concessions – between civilians and security officials.

## Historical institutionalism and security forces

An abundance of literature exists on the distribution of decision-making power between civilians and security officials, particularly regarding civil–military relations (see Agüero 2001; Trinkunas 2000: 77–109; Croissant *et al.* 2013). As part of the security sector, this study conceives of security forces (following the OECD definition) as "core security actors: armed forces; police service; gendarmeries; paramilitary forces; presidential guards; intelligence and security services (both military and civilian); coast guards; border guards; customs authorities; and reserve or local security units (civil defence forces, national guards, militias)" (OECD DAC 2007: 22). The study defines the relations between civilians and security forces as those interactions that in some way relate to the power to make political decisions (Welche 1976: 2). Civilians are defined as non-military state employees who are either elected or appointed by elected civilians. While retired military are technically civilians, they often identify with and share the same interests as active-duty soldiers. Kohn (1997) vaguely described civilian control as a situation where "civilians make all the rules and can change them at any time" (1997: 142). In young democracies, given that security forces possess the legal monopoly of violence,

> they may be tempted to act in a partisan or praetorian manner in relation to domestic politics.... [Alternatively,] they may be the subject of attempts by partisan factions within the civilian sector to ... disrupt democratic processes. Thus, effective and democratic civilian control of the security sector is a key component of any process of democratization.
>
> (Edmunds 2003: 13)

Constitutionally entrenched civilian supremacy implies that the arrangements of civilian control over security forces must be enshrined into law. Nevertheless, security officials sometimes engage in informal behavior outside the purview of law which helps them resist civilian control (Pion-Berlin 2010: 527–530). Moreover, civilians are sometimes unwilling to enforce constitutionally embedded civilian control.

Constitutions are important institutions for civilian control, as they represent rule-governed arenas that formally mediate between civilian and security force actors which must act within constitutional parameters. Such institutions are "collections of interrelated rules and routines that define appropriate action in terms of relations between roles and situations" (March and Olsen 1984: 160). Constitutions can also bolster democracy by enshrining liberal rule of law with the objective of achieving a liberal, embedded democracy, defined as consisting of "a democratic electoral regime, political rights of participation, civil rights, horizontal accountability, and the guarantee that the effective power to govern lies in the hands of democratically elected representatives" (Merkel 2004: 36)."[R]ule of law binds a state to uphold its laws effectively and ... act according to clearly defined prerogatives" (Merkel 2004: 39).

Ultimately, this study examines constitutions – as well as decrees within countries where embedded democracy and liberal rule of law have not been fully achieved. Historical institutionalism is useful in explaining the evolution of security sector reform as well as civil–military relations (see Croissant *et al.* 2013). Historical institutionalism offers explanations about how events in history either constrained or offered opportunities which affected institutional resilience or change (see Pierson 2000; Mahoney and Rueschemeyer 2003; Pierson and Skocpol 2002). Historical institutionalism points to patterns reflecting gradual institutional change. In young democracies, changes in constitutions across an historical period represent critical junctures which help define the parameters of the overall, gradual transformation. Such institutional change is generally of four types. Where the change is of a radical type, the charter will be fundamentally altered. This study views such a constitutional transition as *displacement.* Alternatively, where change-agents do not absolutely transform the charter but simply build upon what is already written in a previous one, such an alteration is referred to as *layering.* Moreover, if previously written rules continue to be applied, despite the fact that the environment surrounding these laws has abruptly changed, this legal phenomenon is called *drift.* Finally, where previously enacted rules (or the ambiguities surrounding these rules) are reinterpreted to fit the vested interests of newly dominant actors, such a situation is known as *conversion.* A fifth form of change – *exhaustion* – does not fit within this typology (Mahoney and Thelen 2010).

Elected civilians and security officials can each initiate institutional change toward a new constitution. Elected civilians are change-agents where, once they come to lead a regime, they initiate attempts to change constitutions toward greater civilian power vis-à-vis security forces. Where security forces resist these attempts, they become status quo agents. Meanwhile, security officials can be change-agents in two instances. First, if, following a military coup, the new ruling junta attempts to alter constitutions to either protect or extend its influence vis-à-vis civilians. Second, where regimes are led by weak elected civilians amidst very powerful security forces, those security forces may attempt to make rule alterations to their benefit. But if civilians leading an already democratic regime attempt to counter moves by security forces to increase their power, the civilians become status quo agents. Sometimes, both sides gain benefits from constitutional changes at the same time. In such cases, it becomes necessary to look more closely at the historical context surrounding the enactment of the constitution. Furthermore, certain civilians will sometimes resist greater civilian power, or some security officials will resist more clout for security officials.

Understanding the four modes of constitutional change as well as the behavior of civilians and security officials with regard to initiating or resisting such transformations demonstrates the importance of agency. It can also contribute to comprehending why one form of transition occurs as opposed to another (Mahoney and Thelen 2010). Table 5.1 matches different modes of rule alteration with the change-agent initiating change.

Structure is also significant as a factor which stimulates the abilities or decisions of actors to effect change. Indeed, whether constitutional change occurs at all, how often it happens, and which mode of alteration is selected depends upon three conditioning variables: (1) the heritage of authoritarianism; (2) the unity of elected civilians versus security forces; and (3) changing environments.

*Table 5.1* Change-agents and modes of constitutional change

| *Change-agent* | *Status quo agent* | *Regime* | *Mode of constitutional change* | *Displacement* | *Layering* | *Drift* | *Conversion* |
|---|---|---|---|---|---|---|---|
| Security forces | Civilians | Junta | Removal of more democratic rules; introduction of less democratic rules | Yes | Yes | No | No |
| Security forces | Civilians | Weak elected government amidst semi-autonomous security forces | Neglect of old rules which emphasize civilian control of security forces/reinterpretation of old rules to prevent civilian control of security forces | No | No | Yes | Yes |
| Civilians; security forces | Civilians; security forces | Strong elected government amidst semi-autonomous security forces | Attempts by civilians and security forces to displace, layer, drift, or convert | Yes | Yes | Yes | Yes |
| Civilians | Security forces | Strong elected government amidst weak security sector | Introduction of more democratic rules/removal of less democratic rules | Yes | Yes | No | No |

Source: Mahoni and Telen (2010).

### *The heritage of authoritarianism*

The heritage of authoritarianism denotes historical legacies of autocracy. Legacies of autocracy are ideational, social constructions based around political culture, history, and group psychology over time. With regard to security forces, such legacies reflect how security officials think about themselves in terms of legitimate behavior toward civilian actors. Regarding civil–military relations, Croissant *et al.* (2013) refer to this factor as the "military mindset" (54). The emphasis on this heritage illustrates to what extent sociocultural legacies in society influence the majority of people to resist, remain apathetic to, or encourage incisions by security forces against civilian decision-making (Croissant *et al.* 2013: 54; Parsons 2007: 94–104; Pion-Berlin 2001: 19–20).

### *Unity of civilians versus security forces*

The degree of agents' cohesion is crucial to the success of institutional change. If civilians (elected civilians and civil society) are more united than security forces in pressuring for greater civilian control via changes in law, they are more likely to succeed in their objective. Meanwhile, where security forces are more united than civilians, then security forces will be able to resist attempts by civilians to press for more control or even extend their martial/police power vis-à-vis civilians (see Croissant *et al.* 2013: 53; Avant 1994; Agüero 2001). Finally, where civilians and security forces are each united against the other, then success may depend upon the ability of one to remain united longer than the other across time. Relative heritage of authoritarianism or the changing environment may contribute to one side trumping the other.

### *Changing environments*

This condition includes both external and/or internal security threats such as interstate war or insurgency; external or internal economic changes; or alterations in the international political situation. Croissant and colleagues refer to such factors as "structure" (Croissant *et al.* 2013: 52–53). In unstable security, political, or economic situations, security forces can obtain greater legitimacy to engage in coercion, increase their powers, or overthrow civilian regimes (see Huntington 1968; Sundhaussen 1998: 329–349). Sometimes (e.g., external threats), however, security forces may be less inclined to challenge civilian authority (Desch 2001). Alternatively, at times of peace and prosperity, security forces find less reason to rationalize taking action. Regimes in power can be damaged by or benefit from changing environments. If civilians are in power amidst negative environments, security forces opposed to the regime can gain public support. However, if, under a military junta, the environment worsens (e.g., the economy plummets), civilian unity against the junta may grow.

## Three emerging democracies in Southeast Asia

In three fledgling democracies of Southeast Asia today, transformative bargains have contributed to differing and changing patterns of constitutional entrenchment of control over security forces. In Thailand, security forces tended to be insulated from most controls by elected civilians but then putsched the government in 2014. In the Philippines, constitutional control has been most successful, although there continues to be enormous informal autonomy of security forces. In Myanmar, constitutionalism has turned civilian control on its head, allowing civilians to superficially preside over politics while the military/police continue to exert enormous formal influence in the shadows.

### *Thailand's security forces: slight civilian control interrupted*

Thailand's security bureaucracy has a lengthy history of constitutionally granted authority. The country has experienced military coups partially for purposes of overthrowing one constitution and replacing it with another (Pinai 2002: 93). Prior to 1932, the country was effectively dominated by an asymmetrical partnership of an absolute monarch, with military as junior partner. The Criminal Code of 1908 first insinuated military enforcement for royal directives. However, Section 2 of this Code made the penalty for coup attempts death or lengthy imprisonment (Kingdom of Siam 1908). Perhaps, because of this Section, almost all constitutions or charters implemented following coups since 1947 included clauses granting amnesty to the coup-makers (Somchai 2013: 16). The Martial Law Act of 1914 allowed military commanders the authority to declare martial law in their area (Section 4), and granted the military near autonomy and control over civilians in situations where martial law was declared. The Martial Law Act represents one of the clearest examples of *drift* and *conversion*, whereby a decree originally meant to bolster the power of the military under absolute monarchy has come to be used to simply entrench the military's security powers over a certain area of control.

Post-1932 Thailand saw the military take power away from the king, an event which occurred through the passage of two constitutions in 1932. The leaders of the coup established a *Khana Ratsadon* (Assembly of the People), as led by a Council of the People. The first charter facilitated military dominance given Section 3's requirement that all 70 Assembly members be appointed and that all 15 Council ministers be appointed from this Assembly (Section 4). This first constitution marked a *displacement* from absolute monarchy to military domination. This displacement was due to three factors: the early 1930s environment of economic depression; increasing cohesion of an anti-royalist security bureaucracy; and growing perceptions among soldiers and civilians alike that the strength of security forces made them legitimate change-agents (Stowe 1991: 13). Thailand's second constitution (December 10, 1932) made permanent most of the provisions of the first temporary charter. Throughout the 1930s and early 1940s, military political dominance continued. The 1946 constitution represented the apex of elected civilian control in Thailand. As such, a new transformative bargain was reached between weakened security officers and strengthened elected civilians (led by Prime Minister Pridi Panomyong) that gave heightened powers to the latter. Only elected civilians could serve as legislative representatives, a situation which destroyed the power of any cabal such as *Khana Ratsadon* to return to power. This constitution represented the *displacement* of those charters enacted during the pro-military era (1932–1944). Nevertheless, this constitution was *displaced* by the constitution of 1947, which was enacted in the aftermath of a coup against Pridi in November of that year. This coup, led by the Soi Rajakru coup group, occurred as result of three factors: (1) growing anti-Pridi unity in the army; (2) changing security conditions, reflected in the new Cold War between the United States and the Soviet Union; (3) the assassination of King Ananda (implicitly blamed on the civilian leadership) helped the military emerge as the traditional protector of the kingdom, a situation which enabled its return to the political stage (Chambers 2013: 137–138). The 1947 charter was promulgated as the result of a transformative bargain between the Thai military and the monarchy – with civilians unconnected to soldiers or royalists forced to accept it. Among the provisions favored by the armed forces was the removal of the clause preventing permanent bureaucrats (i.e., soldiers) from serving in Parliament.

From 1949 until 1976, seven constitutions were consecutively enacted and *displaced*. The 1949 charter legitimized a co-monopoly on power between the military and the monarchy. The 1952 constitution (revised 1932 constitution), which followed the "radio" coup, re-established the political monopoly of security forces over Thailand. The charter of 1959, following an army putsch, re-established the power partnership between the military and the monarchy. The 1968 constitution institutionalized the beginning of representative democracy – as controlled by the military and the monarchy. The charter of 1972 rationalized a self-coup by the military in 1971. The 1974 constitution weakened the power of a tainted military, improved the rights of civilians, and escalated the power of the king. Finally, the constitution of 1976 and the charter of 1977 – slightly different documents implemented following military coups – resurrected the power partnership between the military and the monarchy.

Following the 1977 coup, the palace came to oppose the new military leadership of General Kriangsak (Handley 2006: 267). To sustain his regime, Kriangsak enacted a more inclusive constitution in 1978 – representing a bargain between his moderate military faction and pro-democracy civilians. The constitution banned active-duty soldiers from sitting in the Lower House. However, the Senate – still stronger than the Lower House – came under the virtual control of the armed forces, since the far majority of the Upper House was composed of active duty security officials. Furthermore, Section 167 proscribed active-duty security personnel from serving as cabinet ministers or prime minister, though this condition was not to take effect until the beginning of the next parliamentary term. As a result, Kriangsak's successor as prime minister, General Prem Tinsulanonda, when faced in 1983 with the end of the parliamentary term and the need to return to power through elections, used legal manipulation to continue as unelected prime minister. In 1991, a further coup *displaced* the 1978 constitution and brought about the temporary charter of February 1991. Similar to the aftermath of previous coups, this charter banned political parties and reduced the legislature once again to a unicameral body of appointees dominated by security forces. Moreover, the infamous clauses allowing for the prime minister to ensure authoritarian order was brought back under Section 27. In December 1991, a permanent constitution was implemented. This document maintained the power of the military-controlled Senate, as it could censure the prime minister (Kingdom of Thailand 1991b). In addition, the constitution did not state whether the prime minister needed to be elected or could not be an active-duty military official.

However, 1992 marked a critical juncture in Thai history. For the first time, previous bargains between security forces and the monarch, which had earlier ushered in constitutions not favored by the civilian majority, were henceforth null and void. Civilians suddenly united in favor of greater democracy and the global environment was, in general, becoming more conducive to civilian control. Indeed, growing public consternation against the enshrinement of security sector powers in the 1991 constitution, the manipulative manner in which Army Commander General Suchinda Kraprayoon rose to become prime minister in April 1992, and finally extreme negative reactions against security forces following their repression of demonstrators in May of that year, all helped facilitate changes which diminished the constitutional powers of Thailand's security forces. First, the military regime, led by Prime Minister Suchinda, was felled after pressure from the king. His successor, appointed Prime Minister Anand Panyarachun, *layered* the Government Administration in a Crisis Act of 1952 and the Martial Law Act of 1914, and abolished the Internal Security Act of 1976, "so that the use of armed forces in riot control now [required] authorization by the cabinet" (Surachart 1999: 150). Meanwhile, Anand *layered* the charter itself. In June 1992, an amendment to the 1991 constitution prevented the military-controlled Senate from being able to censure a sitting government. This helped ensure the dominance of the Lower House. Second, another 1992 amendment to the 1991 constitution required that the prime minister be a member of the elected Lower House (Dorman 1993: 7). Many members of Thai civil society now began to move toward constitutionally capping the authority of security forces once and for all.

In fact, the 1990s was an important period of elected civilian control. Civilians during this time were ever cohesive, while the security forces were divided. In terms of environmental factors, the country was at peace and (until 1997) quite prosperous. Finally, Thailand's heritage of military authoritarianism seemed to have hit a low while more Thais appeared to be in favor of greater democracy and many Thai security officials seemed willing to accept this. As such, the 1997 constitution marked a crucial formal *displacement* – a watershed event. As with the transformative bargain leading to the 1974 constitution, a debilitated military was compelled to accept most of the decisions of strengthened and united civilians as well as an already powerful monarchy. Under its provisions, the legislature was henceforth to be entirely elected, bicameral, and devoid of active-duty bureaucrats. After the document's implementation, and the end of the senatorial term in 2000, elections were held for all Senate seats, in the same way that elections were held for seats in the Lower House. Reflecting the earlier amendment to the 1991 constitution, Sections 187 and 221 mandated that prime ministers be elected and come from the Lower House (Kingdom of Thailand 1997), whereupon the political party of tycoon Thaksin Shinawatra won the 2001 election and came to exert overwhelming influence over most members of the Lower and Upper Houses of Parliament. Thaksin also sought to exert sway over the police and armed forces. In early 2004, following a sudden exacerbation of insurgency in Thailand's far south, Thaksin enacted the Emergency Decree on Public Administration in Emergency Situations on July 16, 2005 (Kingdom of Thailand 2005). This law gives overriding powers to a civilian prime minister or camouflaged clout for a military commander acting in the prime minister's stead to resolve an "emergency situation" (Section 4). In September 2006, the king endorsed a successful military coup against Thaksin (BBC News 2006). The 1997 "people's constitution" was *displaced* and a new temporary charter was substituted in its place (Kingdom of Thailand 2006). This document of 2006 once again banned political parties and created an appointed unicameral assembly to oversee the writing of a new constitution along with several other laws (Articles 5, 19). In addition, the coup leader's overthrow of the prime minister was legitimized (Article 14), while the coup group's use of authoritarianism was accepted (Article 36). Finally, as with all charters written in Thailand following a coup, a coup amnesty was *layered* onto the document (Article 37).

By 2007, a new permanent constitution had been implemented (Kingdom of Thailand 2007). Prior to its enactment, a referendum on the constitution was approved by a majority of Thais, and proponents used this as a form of popular consent to the charter, itself representing a bargain among royalists, the security sector, and civilians opposed to Thaksin. Large, anti-Thaksin demonstrations in 2005, 2008, and 2013 seemed to reflect popular support for this bargain. Nevertheless, as evidenced by pro-Thaksin electoral victories in the general elections of 2007 and 2011, as well as massive pro-Thaksin Red Shirt demonstrations in 2009 and 2010, the apparent popularity of the bargain emasculated a tremendous amount of pluralist opposition.

Although the 2007 constitution retained many of the provisions of the 1997 charter, some new key sections were *layered in*, a few of which assisted the security sector. Indeed, the new document mandated that half of the Senators were to be elected and the other half appointed, following a selection process (Part 3). The appointees included a 9.3 to 10.6 percent quota of guaranteed nominations from retired members of the security forces (Chambers 2013: 299). Aside from the constitution, Thailand's military junta ensured the enactment of a new Internal Security Act (ISA), which was implemented on February 19, 2008 (Kingdom of Thailand 2008a). The new law was similar to Thailand's other existing security laws (e.g., the 2005 emergency decree and the 1914 Martial Law Act) in that it allowed military action to be taken to ensure "the maintenance of internal security" (Section 3). The major difference between the Emergency Decree and the Internal Security Act is that, under the Internal Security Act, although the prime minister is officially in charge when the Act is enforced, effective power rests with the army. The 2008 ISA thus helped enhance the enshrinement of military influence. A final increase in military power was the Defense Act of 2008, which establishes a new senior military vetting committee, overseeing high-level military reshuffles above the rank of brigadier general (Kingdom of Thailand 2008b). According to Section 25 of this Act, any military promotion from the rank of brigadier general and higher who works either under the office of the permanent secretary of defense or the RTARF will be considered and approved by a committee of seven, comprising the defense minister, deputy defense minister (optional member), supreme commander, chiefs of the army, air force, and navy, and the permanent secretary of defense. The first two officials are from the elected government, while the final five belong to the active-duty military. If the latter group maintains unity, the elected government will in no way be able to formally influence senior military reshuffles.

In 2013, the legal equilibrium between security forces and elected civilians allowed the military to maintain insularity away from elected civilian control. Under Thaksin's sister Yingluck Shinawatra (2011–2014), the government succeeded in exerting personal control over the police, with the leadership of the armed forces remaining mostly independent (Chambers 2013: 375–376). On May 22, 2014, the army seized power and deposed the elected civilian regime of Yingluck Shinawatra. From the day of the coup until April 1, 2015, the new ruling National Council for Peace and Order (NCPO) junta ruled Thailand via the 1914 Martial Law Act – yet another illustration of *drift*. Then, at the end of March 2015, it replaced martial law with a set of draconian decrees called Article 44. Article 44, referred to a section of a new, junta-imposed constitution of July 2014. It mandated that whenever the junta leader believed it was necessary to deal with "any act," he could issue "any order ... regardless of the legislative, executive or judicial force of that order." The said order would be considered "legal, constitutional and conclusive." According to Section 47, all acts issued by the junta were and would be "deemed to be legal, constitutional and conclusive." Article 48 gave a legal amnesty to all 2014 junta members or anyone involved in leading or facilitating the coup (Kingdom of Thailand 2014). Articles 44, 47, and 48 represented yet another case of *displacement*, as the junta resurrected laws used in previous military constitutions.

Ultimately, throughout Thailand's history, while civilians and security forces have jousted for power, it has mostly been security forces which have acted as change-agents to increase their clout vis-à-vis royal or elected civilian opponents. Since 1932, there have been 19 constitutions or charters that have reflected attempts by the military to grow their power. Meanwhile, there have been far fewer attempts by opponents of security forces to keep the latter under constitutional civilian control. In Thailand, *displacement* has been the most common method of institutional change, as constitutions have regularly been substituted for other ones. In other cases (e.g., the 1914 Martial Law Act), *drift* was used. As such, security laws previously meant to benefit the absolute monarchy came to be used to simply protect the military or civilian-led government. In sum, though civilians have, since 1992, increased their power at the expense of security forces, the latter today (especially the military) finds itself both formally and informally insulated from any attempts at control by elected civilians.

### *The Philippines' security forces: clients to personalized civilian control*

Unlike in Thailand, security forces in the Philippines have been characterized by a constitutionally formalized commitment to civilian control simultaneous to informal incisions across it. Under Spanish and US colonialism, soldiers were granted *carte blanche* authority over internal security. Weakly embedded democratic institutions only emerged in 1907 – under strong, executive authority. Yet it was constitutionalism which facilitated the entrenchment of a powerful security sector, albeit formally in support of an oligarchic democracy. This situation led to ineffectual effective civilian control, as it provided the civilian actors with a reason to accept military prerogatives and, simultaneously, encouraged soldiers to acknowledge civilian elites as patrons, a situation which contributed to the erosion of democratic quality. The link between constitutions and security forces in the Philippines emerged during American colonial rule (1898–1946). During this period, seven lasting legacies developed which had an enormous impact upon the Philippine security sector later on. First, under Spanish colonialism (1565–1898) and later the US-commonwealth period, military officials tended to govern the Philippines directly and autocratically (Berlin 2008: 12–15). Second, with the assumption of US control, Washington promoted the emergence of a fledgling democracy in the colonial Philippines, though it was dominated by local elites (Anderson 1988: 11; Morada and Collier 1998: 551). The result was a military bureaucracy which was unstable, decentralized, and dependent upon the patronage of civilian elites (Hutchcroft 2000: 289). Third, as this Commonwealth military evolved, it developed a close affinity with the US armed forces (Pobre 2000: 267). As such, early generations of officers graduating from the Philippine Military Academy were inculcated in the principles of military professionalism and civilian supremacy (McCoy 1999: 25, Miranda 1985: 91). Fourth, civilian elites came to understand that the US supported civilian supremacy. Since soldiers relied on connections with civilian patrons to gain promotions, the elites were able to obtain influence in the military bureaucracy (Hutchcroft 2000: 289). Such influence carried over to military support for political candidates in the post-independence Philippines (Berlin 2008: 31). Fifth, under US colonialism, the main objective of the Philippine security forces was internal security. It was the task of US forces to provide external security for the islands (Berlin 2008: 11–26). Sixth, given that the Philippines never did engage in armed struggle to achieve independence (but instead was decolonized peacefully), the Philippine military had no legitimate claim to an autonomous role in the creation of the Philippine nation and state. This quality differentiated the country from other newly decolonized states such as Burma, where the armed forces spearheaded the achievement of independence, also legitimizing itself as a national rescuer. Seventh, under the 1935 Commonwealth Constitution, security forces were placed under formalized civilian control while enormous power was granted to a civilian president. The enactment of this charter *displaced* the use of the United States' own constitution, under which the Philippines had been governed until 1935. Although this constitution was promulgated under colonialism, it was implemented as the result of a transformative bargain between the United States (which directed Philippine security forces) and local elites. Still, it did not mark a critical juncture, as colonialism continued in the Philippines for 11 more years. In this sense, sections existing within the US constitution were simply *layered* onto the Philippines' 1935 charter. At the same time, it differed from Burma's 1935 constitution, the object of which was simply to facilitate more effective colonial administration.

During the Japanese occupation of the Philippines (1943–1945), a 1943 charter was enacted which continued the pattern of a strong executive in charge of powerful security forces. Although the enactment of this constitution *displaced* the 1935 charter, it *layered* the words from the aforementioned Article VII, Section 10 and placed them in Article 2, Section 9 to legitimize the physical application of order during this period. With the end of World War II, the 1943 constitution was itself *displaced*. For the first 26 years following the Philippines' decolonization (1946–1972), Filipinos engaged in *drift* and *conversion*, resurrecting the 1935 constitution and allowing it legitimize formalized civilian control. Four factors contributed to this state of affairs. First, there was a continuing economic and military dependence on the US, with the Philippines focusing upon internal security. The Philippines needed only to supply bases for US troops whose capabilities were relatively massive. Internal security thus became the prime objective of the AFP – as was the case during most of the colonial period. Yet, even with regard to internal order, Washington provided the weaponry, established the order of battle, and determined the AFP's troop strength (McCoy 1999: 26–27). Second, there was the perseverance of constitutionally granted democratic control by elites reliant upon the military but divided among themselves (Anderson 1988: 14). Third, security forces grew to become increasingly partisan and dependent upon elites. The competition among officers for partisan patronage from different elite civilian cliques spawned divisions within the military, and such factionalism sometimes allowed a particular elite clique to dominate (Selochan 2004: 61–62). Fourth, security officials became by and large committed to formalized civilian control, with most of them aware that both Philippine elites as well as US policy-makers preferred civilian supremacy. The persistence of these factors contributed to a power-sharing arrangement between oligarchs and security officials under the auspices of civilian supremacy, whereby soldiers were highly partisan, clientelistic, and generally supportive of civilian control but informally prone to intervention across areas of civilian decision-making. Constitutionalism during this period acted as a legal veneer for this power-sharing bargain.

In 1972, civilian President Ferdinand Marcos, with the assistance of several partisan generals of which he was patron, declared martial law and, from 1972 to 1986, ruled autocratically through his control over the presidency and influence across the military. As such, he became the "supreme cacique" (Anderson 1988: 13). Marcos, through his personalist control of the military, growing economic clout, and rationalization of a dictatorial national security state, established a single personal fiefdom across the entire country. Nevertheless, the parasitic, reciprocal, power-sharing arrangement between civilian elites and the military establishment continued (Miranda 1985: 91–93). To legitimize his dictatorship, Marcos proclaimed martial law. Using the aforementioned Article VII, Section 10, Paragraph (2) of the 1935 constitution, he enacted Proclamation 1081, which placed the Philippines under the direct control of the executive (Proclamation No. 1081, 1972). He then *displaced* the 1935 constitution and enacted the 1973 charter. There was, of course, barely any bargaining which brought this new constitution into existence. Instead, the new Marcos dictatorship forced the country to accept it – though the emergence of a national emergency was used as a pretext. Article IV, Section 12 of the new charter repeated verbatim the language of Article VII, Section 10 under the previous constitution pertaining to give the elected civilian leader the authority to declare martial law. Despite the 1973 constitution, Proclamation No. 1081 continued in force until 1981. Ultimately, the growth of Marcos' constitutional powers meant an equivalent increase in powers of the Philippines' security forces as they became the physical levers of Marcos' personalist clout. Although Marcos *displaced* the 1935 charter for the 1973 constitution, the latter represented a form of *layering*, given that Marcos only made certain changes to the previous 1935 document. Indeed, he simply moved the same sections relating to national security, which had been in the 1935 and 1943 constitutions, into the 1973 constitution. Ultimately, the pre-Marcos and Marcos period left lasting legacies which cast long shadows upon relations between civilians and security forces in the post-Marcos era. Marcos' success in establishing martial law, with security forces as a junior partner, contributed to a legacy of government toleration for military/police partisanship, factionalism, cronyism, corruption, authoritarianism, lack of civilian oversight, and the committing of extra-judicial human rights violations (Morada and Collier 1998: 552).

In 1987, following the fall of Marcos and the establishment of elected civilian rule (which had generally united in favor of democratic change), President Corazon Aquino led civilian change-agents, united in favor of democratic reform, to *displace* the 1973 charter and substitute it for a much more progressive constitution. This represented a critical juncture in the history of the Philippines, as the global environment was supportive of democracy and security forces were factionalized at the time. Thus, in the transformative bargain between civilians and security officials which resulted in charter change, there was little the latter could do to retain strong powers for themselves. Indeed, the new 1987 constitution curtailed many military prerogatives. First, it annulled the right of active-duty soldiers to hold civilian postings, insulating them from active-duty politics except for the right to vote (Article XVI, Section 5). Second, Article II, Section 17 established that the nation would give priority to education and four other sectors, with the remaining ones (including defense) considered peripheral (with military spending being diminished) (Biazon 2009: 2). In addition, the legislature was given supremacy over all budgetary appropriations, including that of the military (Article VI, Section 24). Meanwhile, the police were delinked from the military (Article 16, Section 6). Simultaneously, only the president, as military commander-in-chief, could use the military for purposes of suppression, while instituting martial law and/or suspending the writ of habeas corpus (Article VII, Section 18). A president could also temporarily rule by decree during a national emergency (thus expanding military authority), but again, only when Congress authorized it (Article VI, Section 23). Moreover, a Human Rights Commission and ombudsman were established to investigate cases, including those of the military (Article XIII, Sections 17–18; Article XI, Sections 5–13). Meanwhile, Congress was granted the sole power to declare war (Article VI, Section 23). War was renounced as an instrument of national policy (Article II, Section 1). During war or other national emergencies, Congress could, by law, authorize the president to temporarily rule by decree (Article VI, Section 23). Furthermore, with regard to senior military reshuffles, only the president could nominate potential candidates, whereupon members of Congress, comprising a Commission on Appointments, must agree to the president's military appointments for soldiers ranked colonel/naval captain and higher (Article VI, Section 18; Article VII, Sections 15–16). As for military retirements, the compulsory age is 56, except in certain cases (Thompson 1995: 173). Nevertheless, the armed forces continued to exert a more informal level of influence over civilians. Indeed, active-duty military officers were informally allowed to participate in decision-making bodies and Corazon Aquino became dependent on one military faction for her survival.

Although the 1987 constitution opened up more political space for Filipinos, the country's security forces continued to wield enormous power, though this was partially checked by the appearance of civilian control. In addition, the reforms embedded in the 1987 charter represented enormous strides in terms of greater political space. Yet these transformations did not rein in the security forces. Rather, it made factions of them more determined to safeguard or intensify their clout. Under the Corazon Aquino administration (1986–1992), there were no fewer than nine coup attempts (Thompson 1995: 168–169). While her successor, retired General Fidel Ramos (1992–1998) suffered no coup attempts (perhaps because he was a retired soldier himself and commanded respect), his successor, Joseph Estrada (1998–2001), was forced from office when civilian elites pressured active-duty military officers to withdraw support from Estrada in what amounted to a de facto *coup d'état* (Abinales 2010: 227). Estrada's successor, Gloria Macapagal Arroyo, sought to co-opt security forces, which assisted her even when she engaged in electoral irregularities to win the 2004 election

(CCTA 2006). There were, however, three coup attempts during her term (Hernandez 2007: 89). Moreover, Arroyo enhanced military insulation from civilian control by ensuring Congress's passage of the Human Security Act of 2007 (Dalangin-Fernandez 2007). This law, *layered* into the Philippines legal codes, codified crimes of terrorism, but was criticized as vague and intrusive: suspects could be detained and arrested without warrant by security forces (Lyew 2010). By 2013, no security sector official had ever served time for any human rights violations. Also in 2013, a group of rebel military officers challenged the administration of Arroyo's successor, Benigno Aquino III, and there were once again rumors of a possible coup (Military: "No Coup" 2013). Ultimately, though security officials may have formally agreed to place themselves under civilian supremacy through officially accepting civilian control as enacted in the country's constitutions, informally, security forces have sometimes tended to ignore civilian control in certain issue areas or to rebel against it in others.

Transformative bargains leading to constitutional *displacement* have been uncommon events in Philippine history. Political leaders have relied on *drift* and *conversion* from colonial rule as well as the *layering* in of laws from old constitutions into new ones. Elected civilian elites have always managed to lead the country while soldiers and police have acted as their clients. Today, the Philippines is a country where civilians are united in favor of democracy; security officials have generally accepted standing under civilian control; the threat environment is mixed (given the continuation of low-intensity insurgency in the south); and a tradition perseveres where society allows security officials to play a major political role (though it is second to that of elected civilian elites). Thus, regarding constitutional legitimacy for security forces, they remain formally under the control of elected civilians and the laws the latter make. Yet informally, Philippine security forces remain somewhat outside of civilian control and during internal security situations sometimes run roughshod over the law.

### *Myanmar's security forces: dominant in the background*

In Myanmar, the armed forces have been the dominant political institution since independence in 1948. Such clout has paralleled Burmese constitutionalism in which Burmese charters placed enormous power in the hands of Burma's security forces, even before the end of British colonialism (1824–1948). Four lasting legacies emerged during this period. First, Britain's colonial administration of Burma was highly centralized. It took three wars (1824–1826, 1852–1853, 1885–1886) for the British to eventually incorporate Burma as a colonial possession. Because of constant instability, the Governor General was granted enormous powers. In Burma's 1935 colonial constitution, the Governor General was given unlimited authority to guarantee the following: the prevention of any grave menace to the peace or tranquility of Burma or any part thereof (Part II, 1935 constitution). Previous to this 1935 constitution, British Governors General exercised carte blanche powers of authority over Burma, using colonial codes, including the Criminal Procedure Code (1898); the Unlawful Associations Act (1908); the

Official Secrets Act (1923); and the Burma Wireless Telegraphy Act (1933). These codes continued to be utilized by the state following independence (Article 19, 2011). In this way, earlier legal interpretations *drifted*, and were *converted* to protect the interests, not of British colonial authorities but instead of military elites. Second, strong security forces were created which focused upon internal security. The British Burma Army (BBA) was ruthless in its countless attempts to pacify and unite Burma under British colonial rule. As time wore on, the need for such internal security offered a rationale for a higher security budget, the expansion of the BBA, and more authority for it in "frontier" areas of the colony (Callahan 2002: 534). Third, a Burman-dominated force (originally called the Burma Independence Army or BIA) evolved from its creation in 1941 to become, first, a guerrilla army, and by 1945 the principal security body in Burma. It originally fought with the Imperial Japanese but then changed sides and helped the Allies defeat the Japanese. By 1947, the newly renamed Burmese Armed Forces was the strongest institution in the country with founder, General Aung San, having been appointed by the British as Deputy Chairman of the Executive Council of Burma. Most Burmese respected and feared the military for its physical power. Civilians and soldiers also perceived the military as the institution (as controlled by Aung San) which had spearheaded independence (Fink 2009: 21). Fourth, Burma's civilian elites were always less powerful than the security forces in colonial Burma. The Burma Act of 1923 first granted semi-elections to the colony, but as part of British India. The colony witnessed four partial elections (1922, 1925, 1928, and 1932). Following promulgation of the 1935 constitution, colonial Burma was divided from India, and elections were held in 1936. However, World War II intervened. In 1943, the Japanese brought independence to Burma and enacted a constitution which *displaced* the 1935 charter and *layered* in many parts of Japan's own 1889 constitution. Henceforth, the war minister became an active-duty military officer. This charter initiated "a pattern of political equality between the head of state and head of the army in the state which … is reasserted in the 2008 constitution" (Taylor 2009: 228). By Burma's independence from Britain in 1948, Burma had experienced only 15 years of superficial, interrupted, colonial democracy. Moreover, weakly embedded colonial democracy emerged only after the creation of Burma's coercive security forces, established in 1917/1918 (Callahan 2002).

In 1947, as independence approached, the 1943 charter was *displaced* and a new constitution was enacted as a result of a transformative bargain between British civilians representing the British government and BNA security forces, as dominated by General Aung San. After Aung San had (1) mollified the British by expelling communists, and (2) threatened to lead violent revolution, he succeeded in brokering with them the implementation of the 1947 constitution and eventual independence (Kyi 1984: 1–44). The new charter was preceded by the Panglong Agreement, negotiated between Aung San and the leaders of several Burmese nationalities. Thus, Aung San, former BNA head and leading politician, personally pushed the bargain which granted Burma its most progressive constitution while also maintaining a powerful executive. To some extent, the enactment of this 1947 constitution represented a critical juncture, as change-agents succeeded in moving Burma onto the path of democracy and civilian control. The new charter formally curbed the clout of security forces in that new laws "enshrined civilian control over military expenditures, security policy and senior promotions" (Min 2010: 103). Nevertheless, power remained centralized in the government. Section 25 (3) allowed the executive branch to suspend civil liberties "in times of war, invasion, rebellion, insurrection or grave emergency, if the public safety may so require." In addition, Section 27 stated that "in times of invasion, rebellion, insurrection or grave emergency," citizens can "be denied redress by due process of law for any actionable wrong done to or suffered." Finally, Section 116 created the possibility for a military official to temporarily assume power in the government. It was this section which allowed then-Prime Minister U Nu to invite Armed Forces Commander General Ne Win to assume the post of caretaker government prime minister in 1958. Moreover, the caretaker government amended Section 116 to abolish the six-month limit (Charney 2009: 99). Ultimately, the 1947 constitution was in many ways a compromise between advocates of democracy and champions of military security. However, this compromise of 1947 was not to be. Aung San's 1947 assassination, only a month before the constitution's passage, emboldened military hardliners to ignore much of the charter.

In 1950, a new decree was enacted which strengthened the security sector even further. This Emergency Provisions Act criminalized the spreading of false information; speaking with disrespect about the military; or engaging in any act that might lessen security in Burma. Although Prime Minister U Nu eventually suspended this law, General Ne Win staged a coup in 1962 which established dictatorship for the next 48 years. The 1947 charter was never formally *displaced*, but its provisions were effectively *layered* given that Ne Win's regime ruled by decree. It established the Burma Socialist Programme Party (BSPP) in July 1962. In 1964, the Law Protecting National Unity was implemented. It banned all political parties save for the military-dominated BSPP and established Burma as a single party-state (Fink 2009: 29, 33). In 1974, Ne Win and his military associates retired, and he established indirect, constitutional military rule as chairman of the BSPP. The new regime *displaced* the 1947 constitution and in its stead promulgated a new constitution for the country. Under this charter, 75 percent of the ruling committee was composed of active duty officers (Min 2010: 106). Other laws gave the Cabinet, led by the prime minister, the right to declare martial law, even without legislative approval (Articles 75, 76, 78). Finally, the constitution legitimized the denial of civil liberties if citizens undermined such ambiguous notions as "security of the state" and "public peace and tranquillity" (Articles 166, 167).

The fall of Ne Win in 1988 fractionalized Myanmar's armed forces for perhaps the first time since the early 1960s. Economic and political hardship in Myanmar amidst global moves toward democracy also contributed to changes in the country. Moreover, during that year, civilians were increasingly united in demanding reform. However, authoritarianism by a somewhat factionalized military remained entrenched. Thus, no transformative bargain toward a new, more democratic constitution could occur. Instead, in September 1988, following the August 8, 1988 uprising, security forces brutally re-established direct military rule, and a new junta, calling itself the State Law and Order Restoration Council (SLORC), led by General Saw Maung, began administering Myanmar (Fink 2009: 58). Nevertheless, the SLORC felt it necessarily to issue a series of decrees in order to formally legitimize its actions. Thus, after the September 1988 coup, the 1974 constitution was *displaced* and the entire country was placed under martial law.

Ironically, however, it was the SLORC which enacted the Political Parties Registration Law (1988) and the People's Assembly Election Law (1989), both of which allowed for a generally free election to be held in Burma in 1990. However, when pro-SLORC political parties failed to win this election, the regime immediately rejected the results and claimed that the elections were for drawing up an assembly to create a new constitution. Indeed, following the election, the Political Parties Registration Law experienced *conversion*, as the SLORC reinterpreted it so as to de-register any political party viewed as hostile by the regime (Article 19, 1996). In 1992, General Saw Maung (whose power within the SLORC was undermined following the election results) was replaced by General Than Shwe as SLORC chairman.

To legally govern, the SLORC issued several repressive laws and decrees while intentionally working very slowly toward completion of a new constitution in order to formalize its power and hinder democratic civilian opponents. These decrees included the Television and Video Act (1996), the Motion Picture Law (1996), the Computer Science Development Law (1996), the Internet Law (2004), and the Electronic Transactions Act (2004). The issuing of these orders amounted to *displacement* pure and simple. The regime also made use of laws from earlier periods of history, including all of the aforementioned colonial codes which had earlier been used by the British to quell insurgency, but under the SLORC, *drift* and *conversion* allowed these laws to simply legitimize different forms of martial law. In 1997, the SLORC was transformed into the State Peace and Development Council (SPDC), though dictatorship continued (Charney 2009: 180). The SPDC was only dissolved in 2011, the same day that General Thein Sein became Burma's semi-elected president.

Following 18 years of martial law, a few hollow constitutional conventions, and regime foot-dragging, the SPDC in 2008 finally enacted Burma's latest constitution. The drafting process – which involved military and civilian representatives – produced a transformative bargain highly skewed toward the military, a constitution establishing a regime to be led mostly by civilians, though the military retained power behind the scenes. The military (with Than Shwe supporting its pragmatic faction) enacted partial reforms to placate Burma's weak but growing democracy movement but the former remained politically dominant (Min 2010: 117–121). In May 2008, the military held a popular referendum (widely seen as fraudulent) on the constitution, the results of which, they claimed, demonstrated that over 90 percent of Burmese consented to the bargain. Aung San Suu Kyi's 2012 decision to participate in the new system further legitimized it.

The charter is progressive in that it allows for a mostly elected legislature and indirectly elected president while mandating some increases in civil liberties, among other changes (Myanmar, Constitution of 2008). However, it requires that 25 percent of the members of the Lower and Upper Houses of the national legislature be active-duty military personnel (Sections 109, 141). Regional and state legislatures are likewise required to include security personnel (Section 14, 17, 161, 170). In addition, legislative committees pertaining to defense are to comprise a majority of parliamentarians who are active-duty military personnel (Sections 115, 147). Meanwhile, the president can only be selected by a Presidential College formed from members of the legislature, including the 25 percent active-duty component of the security forces (Section 60). Furthermore, the president must be well acquainted with military affairs, which implies a military background (Section 59). Meanwhile, as with constitutions enacted by Thai military juntas, Burma's 2008 charter renders a blanket amnesty to all leaders of the SPDC regime for any prosecutions against them for previous crimes (Section 445). Moreover, the constitution establishes the creation of the National Defense and Security Council (NDSC), an enormously powerful civilian–military national security committee chaired by the president. Seven of its 11 members must be retired or active-duty security officials (Sections 59, 201, 232). This proportion allows the majority necessary such that military interests always trump those of elected civilians. However, an extra-constitutional State Supreme Council, chaired by retired General Than Shwe, is more powerful. Meanwhile, the charter denies due process of law during times of insurrection or national emergency (Section 381). Furthermore, the constitution grants the president extremely broad powers to declare a state of emergency (Section 410, 417) or military administrative order (Section 413). In so doing, the president may transfer all executive, legislative, and judicial powers to the commander of the armed forces (Section 418), effectively creating a formalized military dictatorship. Finally, amending this military-dominated constitution requires the approval of over 75 percent of all representatives in the legislature followed by a referendum in which over half of Burma's population supports the changes (Section 436). This is quite a hefty feat when 25 percent of the legislature is composed of active-duty defense personnel. In sum, the 2008 constitution formally enhances political space in Burma. However, the security forces, through the charter, have guaranteed for themselves a monopoly on formalized political power (Htoo 2010).

As President (2011 to the present), retired General Thein Sein, viewed as pragmatic, has been saddled with factional struggles by military hardliners (Zaw 2012). To placate civilians and the international community, he has modified certain laws to allow for slightly more freedom in Burma. He has eased media censorship (though old laws remain, thus producing self-censorship); improved labor rights; allowed the registration of non-governmental organizations (NGOs); relaxed restrictions on dissidents; freed political prisoners; removed people's names from lists forbidding entry into Burma; and allowed, in some cases, for the right to peaceable assembly. In late 2011, Thein Sein made slight amendments to the Political Party Registration Law which allowed opposition leader Aung San Suu Kyi and her political party to compete in by-elections held in 2012 (Associated Press 2011). With all of these reforms, the 2008 constitution remains untouched. Amendments to it have thus far yet to succeed (Associated Press 2013). Although Myanmar, since 2010, has moved toward greater political pluralism, the security forces remain dominant, having institutionalized themselves in the new regime (Bünte 2014). By using to a greater extent *drift* and *conversion*, and, to a lesser extent, *displacement*, as well as acting as change-agents (in implementing the 2008 constitution) before any actions by civilian change-agents toward civilian control, military leaders have retained much of their status quo monopoly on power. Today, despite some progressive changes in law, Myanmar remains, at its core, a quasi-democracy in which the dominance of the security forces has been constitutionally enshrined and sustained.

## Conclusion

In the emerging democracies of Southeast Asia, constitutions and decrees have either only sometimes reined in security forces or served merely to legitimize their dominance in politics. Such have been the lessons of Thailand, the Philippines and Myanmar. In answer to the questions initially presented, this study has argued, first, that all three countries saw their security forces become institutionalized under charters as a result of transitions through transformative bargains between civilians and security officials, with each new constitution created being the result of whether, at the time of charter formulation, either civilians or security officials were more cohesive; the security environment was conducive to the particular modification; and finally whether soldiers and non-soldiers alike were willing, because of historical legacies, to allow security officials to have more constitutional privileges. Second, security forces have become institutionalized under civilian-led constitutions, albeit in different ways. Thailand has been punctuated by numerous coups and constitutions, perhaps because of the more factionalized and fluid nature of Thai politics relative to the Philippines and Myanmar. Meanwhile, in the Philippines, security forces evolved even before independence to become the parasitic clients of civilian ruling elites. Finally, in Myanmar, security bureaucrats evolved to become the dominant class in the country. Third, in comparison, security forces in Myanmar have traditionally possessed the most enshrined constitutional powers, followed by Thailand and then finally the Philippines. Thailand's 2014 coup has now notoriously put it in first place. However, it must be acknowledged that in all countries, security personnel sometimes engage in informal actions despite the law. Fourth and finally, where active-duty defense personnel retire but are then appointed to civilian positions, thus continuing to exercise constitutionally enshrined powers, such individuals simply help sustain the power of security forces in politics. Indeed, perhaps the greatest challenge to achieving constitutionally formalized control over security forces today revolves around the issue of how to establish and sustain true civilian control which is verifiably institutionalized by oversight mechanisms. Achieving this objective in Thailand, the Philippines, and Myanmar will be not be easy.

Ultimately, both security officials and civilians, acting as change-agents or status quo defenders, have utilized the various forms of constitutional change – *displacement*, *layering*, *drift*, and *conversion* – in Thailand, the Philippines, and Myanmar. Such types of modifications are sometimes meant to enshrine greater civilian control, and at other times meant to help enhance or sustain the influence of security officials. Thus, the constitutional incorporation of security forces does not necessarily go hand in hand with a transition to civilian control. In sum, each of the country cases examined in this chapter reflects the serious challenges in achieving constitutionally enshrined civilian supremacy.

## Bibliography

Abinales, P. (2010). "The Philippines in 2009: The Blustery Day of August." *Asian Survey*, January/February, 50(1): 218–227.

Agüero, F. (2001). "Institutions, Transitions and Bargaining: Civilians and the Military in Shaping Post-Authoritarian Regimes." In *Civil–Military Relations in Latin America: New Analytical Perspectives*, ed. D. Pion-Berlin. Chapel Hill, NC, University of North Carolina Press, pp. 194–222.

Anderson, B. (1988). "Cacique Democracy in the Philippines: Origins and Dreams." *New Left Review*, 169(May–June): 3–33.

Article 19 (1996). "Global Campaign for Free Expression." *Burma Beyond the Law*, August. Available at: www.article19.org/pdfs/publications/burma-beyond-law.pdf.

Article 19 (2011). "Global Campaign for Free Expression, Union of Myanmar Article 19 Submission to the United Nations, Universal Periodic Review." Tenth Session of the Working Group of the Human Rights Council, February. Available at: http://lib.ohchr.org/HRBodies/UPR/Documents/Session10/MM/Article19_eng.pdf.

Associated Press (2011). "Burma Eases Limits on Party Membership." *Irrawaddy*, November 5. Available at: www2.irrawaddy.org/article.php?art_id=22394.

Associated Press (2013). "Suu Kyi Vows to Keep Pushing for Constitutional Amendments." *Democratic Voice of Burma*, September 24. Available at: www.dvb.no/news/suu-kyi-vows-to-keep-pushing-for-constitutional-amendments-burma-myanmar/32769.

Avant, D. (1994). *Political Institutions and Military Change: Lessons from Peripheral Wars*. Ithaca, NY, Cornell University Press.

BBC News (2006). "Thai King 'Endorses Coup Leader'," September 20. Available at: http://news.bbc.co.th/2/hi/asia-pacific/5365362.stm.

Beeson, M. and Bellamy, A.J. (2008). *Securing Southeast Asia*: *The Politics of Security Sector Reform*. London, Routledge.

Berlin, D. (2008). *Before Gringo: History of the Philippine Military 1830 to 1972*. Manila, Anvil.

Biazon, Hon. R.R. (2009). "Defence Spending in the Philippines." House of Representatives, Policy Paper, Manila.

Bünte, M. (2014). "Burma's Transition to Quasi-Military Rule: From Rulers to Guardians?" *Armed Forces and Society*, 4: 442–464.

Chambers, P. (2013). "A Short History of Military Influence in Thailand," in *Knights of the Realm: Thailand's Military and Police: Then and Now*, ed. P. Chambers. Bangkok, White Lotus Press.
Charney, M.W. (2009). *A History of Modern Burma*. London, Cambridge University Press.
Citizens' Congress for Truth and Accountability (CCTA) (2006). "Findings and Recommendations." In *Fraud: Gloria M. Arroyo and the May 2004 Election*, ed. B. Tuazon. Manila, Philippines, CenPEG Books, pp. 59–251.
Constitution, Burma (Government of Burma Act, 1935).
Constitution, Burma (1943).
Croissant, A., Kuehn, L.P., and Chambers, P.W. (2013). *Democratization and Civilian Control in Asia*. London, Palgrave Macmillan.
Dalangin-Fernandez, L. (2007). "Arroyo to Sign Anti-Terror Bill Tuesday." *Philippine Daily Inquirer*, March 5. Available at: http://newsinfo.inquirer.net.
Desch, M. (2001). *Civilian Control of the Military: The Changing Security Environment*. Baltimore, MD, Johns Hopkins University Press.
Dorman, T.L. (1993). "The 1991 Constitution of Thailand." Faculty of Law, University of Victoria. Victoria, BC, Canada. Occasional Paper #4.
Edmunds, T. (2003). *Security Sector Reform: Concepts and Implementation*. Geneva, Geneva Centre for the Democratic Control of the Armed Forces (DCAF).
Fink, C. (2009). *Living Silence in Burma: Surviving Under Military Rule*. New York, Zed Books.
Handley, P. (2006). *The King Never Smiles*. New Haven, CT, Yale University Press.
Hernandez, C. (2007). "The Military in Philippine Politics: Retrospect and Prospects." In *Whither the Philippines in the 21st Century*, eds R. Severino and L.C. Salazar. Singapore, Institute for Southeast Asian Studies, pp. 78–99.
Htoo, Aung (2010). "Major Flaws in the 2008 Constitution." *Democratic Voice of Burma*, March 6. Available at: www.dvb.no/about-elections/major-flaws-in-the-2008-constitution/7964.
Huntington, S. (1968). *Political Order in Changing Societies*. New Haven, CT, Yale University Press.
Hutchcroft, P. (2000). "Colonial Masters, National Politicos, and Provincial Lords: Central Authority and Local Autonomy in the American Philippines, 1900–1913." *The Journal of Asian Studies*, 59(2): 277–306.
Kingdom of Siam, Constitution, 1932b.
Kingdom of Siam, Criminal Code, 1908.
Kingdom of Siam, Martial Law Act, 1914.
Kingdom of Siam, Temporary Charter for the Administration of Siam Act, 1932a.
Kingdom of Thailand, Charter for Administration of the Kingdom, 1991a.
Kingdom of Thailand, Constitution, 1946.
Kingdom of Thailand, Constitution, 1978.
Kingdom of Thailand, Constitution, 1991b.
Kingdom of Thailand, Constitution, 1997.
Kingdom of Thailand, Constitution, 2007.
Kingdom of Thailand, Constitution (Interim), 2014.
Kingdom of Thailand, Emergency Decree Act, 1942.
Kingdom of Thailand, Emergency Decree on Public Administration in Emergency Situations, 2005.
Kingdom of Thailand, Interim Charter, 2006.
Kingdom of Thailand, Internal Security Act, 2008a.

Kingdom of Thailand, Organization of Ministry of Defense Act, 2008b.
Kingdom of Thailand, Temporary Charter, 1947.
Kohn, R.H. (1997). "How Democracies Control the Military." *Journal of Democracy*, 8(4): 140–153.
Kyi, A.S.S. (1984). *Aung San of Burma*. Edinburgh, Kiscadale.
Lyew, B.H. (2010). "An Examination of The Philippines' Anti-Terror Law – Suaviter in Modo, Fortiter in *Re*." *Pacific Rim Law and Policy Journal*, 19(1): 187–216.
Mahoney, J. and Rueschmeyer, D. (2003). *Comparative Historical Analysis in the Social Sciences*. Cambridge, Cambridge University Press.
Mahoney, J. and Thelen, K. (2010). "A Theory of Gradual Institutional Change." In *Explaining Institutional Change: Ambiguity, Agency and Power*, eds J. Mahoney and K. Thelen. Cambridge, Cambridge University Press, pp. 1–37.
March, J.G. and Olsen, J.P. (1984). "The New Institutionalism: Organizational Factors in Political Life." *American Political Science Review*, 78(3): 734–749.
Martial Law Act, Siam, 1914.
McCoy, A. (1999). *Closer than Brothers*. New Haven, CT, Yale University Press.
Merkel, W. (2004): "Embedded and Defective Democracies." *Democratization*, 11(5): 33–58.
"Military: 'No Coup'" (2013). *Sun Star*, September 25. Available at: www.sunstar.com.ph/breaking-news/2013/09/20/military-no-coup-detat-304322.
Min, W. (2010). "Under an Iron Heel: Civil–Military Relations in Burma/Myanmar." In *Democracy under Stress: Civil–Military Relations in South and Southeast Asia*, eds P. Chambers and A. Croissant. Bangkok, ISIS and FES, pp. 102–125.
Miranda, F.B. (1985). "The Military." In *The Philippines after Marcos*, eds R.J. May and F. Nemenzo. New York, St. Martin's Press.
Morada, N. and Collier, C. (1998). "The Philippines: State Versus Society?" In *Asian Security Practice: Material and Ideational Influences*, ed. M. Alagappa. Stanford, CA, Stanford University Press.
Myanmar, Constitution of the Republic of the Union, 2008.
OECD DAC (2007). "OECD DAC Handbook on Security System Reform: Supporting Security and Justice." Organization for Economic Cooperation and Development – Development Assistance Committee. Organization for Economic Cooperation and Development (OECD). DAC Guidelines and Reference Series, Security System Reform and Governance.
Parsons, C. (2007). *How to Map Arguments in Political Science*. Oxford and New York, Oxford University Press.
Pierson, P. (2000). "Increasing Returns, Path Dependence, and the Study of Politics." *American Political Science Review*, 94(2): 251–267.
Pierson, P. and Skocpol, T. (2002). "Historical Institutionalism in Contemporary Political Science." In *Political Science: The State of the Discipline*, eds I. Katznelson and H. Milner. New York, Norton.
Pinai Nanakorn (2002). "Re-Making of the Constitution in Thailand." *Singapore Journal of International and Comparative Law*, 6: 93.
Pion-Berlin, D. (2001). "Introduction." In *Civil–Military Relations in Latin America: New Analytical Perspectives*, ed. D. Pion-Berlin. Chapel Hill, NC, University of North Carolina Press, pp. 1–35.
Pion-Berlin, D. (2010). "Informal Civil–Military Relations in Latin American: Why Politicians and Soldiers Choose Informal Venues." *Armed Forces and Society*, 36(3): 526–544.

Pobre, C.P. (2000). *History of the Armed Forces of the Filipino People*. Quezon City, Philippines, New Day Publishers.

Selochan, V. (2004). "The Military and the Fragile Democracy of the Philippines." In *The Military and Democracy in Asia and the Pacific*, eds R.J. May and V. Selochan. Canberra, Australian National University, pp. 59–68.

Somchai Preechasinlapakun (2013). "Dynamics and Institutionalization of Coups in the Thai Constiution." V.R.F. Series, no. 483. Institute of Developing Economies, Japan External Trade Organization.

Stowe, J. (1991). *Siam Becomes Thailand: A Story of Intrigue*. London, C. Hurst.

Sundhaussen, U. (1998). "The Military: A Threat to Democracy?" *Australian Journal of Politics and History*, 44(3): 329–349.

Surachart Bamrungsuk (1999). "From Dominance to Power Sharing: The Military and Politics in Thailand, 1973–1992." PhD dissertation, Columbia University.

Taylor, R.H. (2009). *The State in Myanmar*. Singapore, NUS Press.

Thompson, M. (1995). *The Anti-Marcos Struggle*. New Haven, CT: Yale University Press.

Trinkunas, H. (2000). "Crafting Civilian Control in Emerging Democracies: Argentina and Venezuela." *Journal of Interamerican Studies and World Affairs*, 42(3): 77–109.

Union of Burma, Constitution, 1947.

Union of Burma, Constitution of the Socialist Republic, 1974.

Welche, C. (1976). "Civilian Control of the Military: Myth and Reality." In *Civilian Control of the Military: Theory and Cases from Developing Countries*, ed. C. Welche. Albany, State University of New York Press, pp. 1–42.

Zaw, A. (2012). "Thein Sein: Reformist or Caretaker?" *Irrawaddy*, February 21. Available at: www2.irrawaddy.org/article.php?art_id=23073&page=2.

# 6 Embedding praetorianism

## Soldiers, state, and constitutions in postcolonial Myanmar

*Renaud Egreteau*[1]

### Introduction

Non-democratic regimes often – but not always – seek to institutionalize their political domination and immunity through the enactment of a specifically designed constitutional document (Ginsburg and Simpser 2014). Military regimes, in particular, can use constitutional texts to strengthen the foundations of the political intervention of the armed forces (Feit 1972; Finer 1975; Stepan 1988). Likewise, when military juntas ultimately set in motion a transition from direct military rule to a civilian one, the armed forces are often tempted to control the constitution-drafting process and secure key legal prerogatives for the military institution under a new hybrid "post-junta" regime (Barros 2002, Croissant and Kamerling 2013; Chambers 2014; Negretto 2014). Myanmar[2] offers a case of a dominant military institution using a constitutional drafting process and a new supreme law for its own corporate interests. Indeed, the constitution adopted in 2008 confers high levels of policy prerogatives upon the Burmese armed forces – or *Tatmadaw* – and embeds "praetorianism"[3] in Myanmar's polity in a way that the country's two previous post-independence constitutions had not. Since it won its freedom from the British in 1948, Myanmar has produced three constitutions. The first postcolonial constitutional text was adopted in 1947, but its provisions were suspended after the *coup d'état* staged by General Ne Win in March 1962. A second constitution drafted by Ne Win's military administration was passed in 1974, but was abrogated in September 1988 following a further *coup d'état* orchestrated by the Tatmadaw leadership. The third and latest constitutional document was promulgated in 2008 after a controversial drafting process that lasted 15 years. All three constitutional texts which Myanmar adopted in 1947, 1974, and 2008 were quite different in content and spirit. They were framed in different political contexts and under the supervision of different leaderships with divergent political agendas. Above all, they made very different references (if at all) to the role of the Tatmadaw as a major state institution and potential policy-maker. The texts adopted in 1947 and 1974 indeed aimed to neither entrench military rule nor institutionalize the political intervention of the armed forces.

This chapter seeks to understand how and why the Tatmadaw has chosen to formulate its own constitutional vision in the early 1990s and thereafter establish a legal political system, which I define as "constitutional praetorianism." Drawing on the extant literature on postcolonial Myanmar politics, this chapter first provides a comparative overview of the first two postcolonial constitutions of the country and examines why both documents bestowed a marginal role upon the Burmese military. The study then focuses on the country's third constitution, which was adopted following a controversial referendum in 2008. It argues that the constitutional text embeds and institutionalizes praetorianism. As the literature on civil–military relations demonstrates, there are different levels of political intervention by the armed forces: they range from direct military rule to hybrid systems led by civilians, but in which the armed forces remain a powerful lobby (Egreteau and Jagan 2013; Bünte 2014). Building on this scholarship as well as on a series of interviews with Burmese parliamentarians and party leaders carried out in both Yangon and Naypyitaw (2013–2014), this chapter argues that the 2008 constitution serves three clear purposes for the Burmese armed forces. First, it manifests the Tatmadaw's view of itself as a legitimate political and policy-making state actor following 60 years of regular and pervasive intrusion into Burmese postcolonial politics and public affairs.

Second, it provides the military with legal instruments for a long-term policy intervention and influence. Third, it offers the armed forces and their personnel a form of self-insurance protecting soldiers from any form of prosecution and securing a much sought-after immunity for the leaders of the 1988 *coup d'état*. As long as this unhealthy policy influence of the army institution prevails, constitutionalism will not emerge in Myanmar. A thorough revision of the 2008 constitution remains highly unlikely. Despite the formation of a joint parliamentary committee tasked specifically to propose potential amendments, the first-ever attempt at reviewing the constitutional text was vetoed by the military-appointed representatives in June 2015. Given the country's historical and political legacies of military intervention, ethnic separatist insurgency, and political instability, I conclude this chapter with the bleak prospects for swift constitutional reform unless the Tatmadaw decides otherwise.

## Army and constitutions in Myanmar: a background

### *A civilian supremacy in the 1947 constitution*

The 1947 constitution[4] was designed to ensure a smooth – but quick – transfer of power from British colonial rule to an independent and, above all, legitimate Burmese civilian administration (Steinberg 2006: 199). Despite flaws, the constitution envisioned a federal state structure and a multi-party parliamentary system with competitive and regular elections to be held once independence was granted on January 4, 1948 (Inlow 1948; Maung Maung 1959). There were no non-military functions assigned to the Burmese armed forces, nor any specific prerogative for the wider security forces enshrined in the document. The weakness of the Burmese military forces in the last months of colonial rule may explain this lack of involvement in constitutional drafting. Since the early 1940s, the driving force behind the Burmese independence struggle had been the Burma Independence (and, from 1943, National) Army (BIA/BNA) under the aegis of a young military officer, Aung San. Yet, despite the glory inherited from several years of anti-colonial and then anti-Japanese fighting, it was not the nascent Tatmadaw that was asked to frame the first charter of the country after the end of the war in 1945. Rather, the Anti-Fascist People's Freedom League (AFPFL) – a loose coalition of political parties, charismatic politicians, and pre-war student activists – took up the task. At that time, the Tatmadaw was a fragile body, ill-equipped to form a powerful policy lobby. It also had to face myriad rival private armies and ethnic militias operating throughout the country (Callahan 2003: 115–116). Therefore, its senior officers, themselves bogged down in inter-ethnic dissension, could not ensure a crucial role for the military in shaping the new state structures.

A civilian committee of legal, political, and academic experts gathered in 1946 to draft a new constitution. A constituent assembly was elected in April 1947. It discussed several drafts prepared by the committee. The final one was eventually adopted on September 24, 1947 – two months after Aung San's assassination. Despite shortcomings and flaws, the constitutional text provided legitimacy to the newly created state, but interestingly not to the actors who participated in the independence struggle – the Tatmadaw in particular. This underscored some initial efforts by the AFPFL to keep the military out of politics. Aung San himself had relinquished his own military positions early on. This was not without debate, though. As highlighted by Maung Maung (1959: 146–147), in one of the first constitutional drafts submitted to the Constituent Assembly in June 1947, one article proposed the creation of a special "Defence Council." Through this non-elected body the President of the Union would have exercised "the supreme command of the armed forces." But the proposal was dropped at Aung San's own suggestion. Thus, in the final text, the Burmese armed forces were not granted any special place: they had to remain subordinate to the post-independence elected civilian authorities. Besides, to avoid the maintenance of competing private armies, the right to raise and maintain national military forces was then vested exclusively in the elected Parliament seated in Rangoon (Article 97 of the 1947 constitution).

The first post-independence constitutional framework lasted less than 15 years. During the 1950s, the raging civil war between Myanmar's central government and myriad ethnic and communist insurgencies propelled a more cohesive Tatmadaw into broader non-military policy roles. Under the charismatic leadership of General Ne Win, uncontested army chief from 1949, the Tatmadaw soon transformed itself into a disciplined and unified corporate institution, increasingly willing to discuss policy issues and civilian affairs (Callahan 2003). Above all, it started to openly highlight its legitimate role as guardian of the nation and its institutions against an array of centrifugal insurgencies, but also external threats – a common trend observed among coup-prone armed forces in the rapidly decolonizing world at that time. A mere decade after the country's independence, Maung Maung indeed noted: "the role of the [Defense] Services as a guardian of the constitution and servant of the people has [now] been clearly defined and deeply impressed on all officers and men by General Ne Win" (Maung Maung 1959: 146).

### *The 1974 constitution: drafted by, but not for, the Tatmadaw*

A first political intervention of the *Tatmadaw* was staged in September 1958. General Ne Win then formed a caretaker military administration at the invitation of U Nu, leader of the civilian government since February 1957. Sanctioned by Parliament a month later, this caretaker government – a perfect example of a short-lived praetorian intrusion into politics – lasted a year and a half. The military hierarchy kept its initial promises to hold national elections, and then withdrew to its barracks in April 1960 (Butwell 1961). However, a full-fledged military coup was ultimately staged by Ne Win on March 2, 1962. Less than two years after the caretaker administration was disbanded, the Tatmadaw clearly stepped in – this time without any invitation from the civilian authorities. The 1947 constitution was not abrogated per se, but gradually all its fundamentals were nullified. Unlike in 1958, Parliament was dissolved a day after the coup, and the Supreme Court and the High Courts of the country were disbanded. A socialist revolution was then imposed, one that could not be defined by a constitution, but rather by well-oiled propaganda and ad hoc legislation enacted by the military rulers (Badgley 1962; Cady 1965). The 17-member Revolutionary Council formed by Ne Win in March 1962 began to shape the new state institutions and ideology through the release of various official documents and policy statements.[5] These included the "Burmese Way to Socialism" (April 1962) and the "The System of Correlation of Man and His Environment" (January 1963), which both outlined the official ideology of the Burma Socialist Programme Party (BSPP). The core objective of this newly formed legitimate political party was to mobilize and educate the Burmese population about the revolution and to pave the way for a socialist democracy under the monitoring of the Revolutionary Council (BSPP 1963; Taylor 2009: 298–300). According to the original Revolutionary Council's statements this had to be fulfilled during a "transitional period." Once the socialist revolution was deemed secure, the civilianization of the regime, installed in 1962, could be initiated, and the disbanding of the Revolutionary Council prepared – but not before.

For that, conditions were deemed more favorable by Ne Win – then Chair of the BSPP – in the late 1960s. An observer of the time, Jon A. Wiant, argued that the BSPP could not long remain the sole instrument of the Tatmadaw or of its core leadership gathered in the Revolutionary Council (Wiant 1973: 182). Progressively, the need for the institutionalization of a civilian power and the withdrawal of the armed forces from the front scene – and therefore a new constitution – appeared obvious to the military top brass and to Ne Win himself. During a BSPP party meeting in 1965, Ne Win made his first public speech about the need for transition to civilian rule (Nakanishi 2013: 112). Therefore, a constitution-making process which claimed to involve the Burmese people was gradually initiated. In 1969, Ne Win asked a panel of civilian experts to make recommendations on new state institutions. For the first time since the 1962 coup, the regime openly hinted at a possible termination of the revolutionary moment imposed by the army seven years before.

In September 1971, a 97-member committee convened. Its aim was to draft the new constitutional text (Moscotti 1977: 7). The process, however, was still heavily influenced by the military leadership. Indeed, one-third of the committee comprised high-ranking officers. Fifteen subcommittees were formed but all were headed by a member of the still active Revolutionary Council. Yet, the latter was openly looking for a way to bestow some sort of legitimacy upon the whole process. Ne Win, as well as the members of the 15 subcommittees, toured the country for months between 1971 and 1973, coordinating thousands of meetings with representatives of the people, the peasantry, the workers, and the armed forces in their barracks (Arumugam 1975: 41). The well-orchestrated organization of mass meetings and public consultations aimed to enlist people's suggestions on each successive constitutional draft which had been prepared by the committee. In fact, it was a ritualistic and theatrical exercise purported to confer upon the document the necessary popular legitimacy that Ne Win was seeking for the post-Revolutionary Council regime (Steinberg 2006: 183). Ne Win and other army leaders had long considered the 1947 constitution to be the product of a handful of elite lawyers, foreign legal experts, and Burmese politicians (Moscotti 1977: 4). By involving mass consultations of the people or at least giving the impression that the Burmese population had been involved in the constitutional process, Ne Win sought a broader legitimacy for the new state institutions.

The fourth constitutional draft was eventually submitted to a national referendum in December 1973. It was claimed that over 90 percent of Burma's eligible voters approved the constitutional draft in a tightly controlled vote. The new constitution[6] was then promulgated on the twenty-sixth anniversary of the country's independence, namely January 4, 1974. A month later national elections were held, as the new constitutional text envisioned a (single-party) parliamentary system. Once the unicameral People's Assembly (or *Pyithu Hluttaw*) was convened, a few weeks after the elections the transfer of power from the military-run Revolutionary Council to a civilian government dominated by the sole BSPP became effective. Ne Win was elected president, and on March 4 he nominated the new members of his Cabinet, all civilians.[7] As long-time Burma watcher Josef Silverstein then noted, Burma entered a new phase of "*constitutional dictatorship*" (Silverstein 1977: 35). The 1974 constitution indeed offered the military-run Revolutionary Council and the armed forces a tool to withdraw from the direct policy-making process by institutionalizing the authoritarian rule of a single and trusted political party, the BSPP (Silverstein 1974). The text allowed the concentration of power in the sole hands of party members and their local representatives. Nonetheless, in the late 1970s, most of them happened to be active Tatmadaw officers seconded to the party bureaucracy or retired military officers (Nakanishi 2013: 108–109).

Although the constitutional drafting exercise had been upheld since the early 1970s by the Tatmadaw, the 1974 constitution was by no means a praetorian document. It neither aimed at legalizing nor entrenching military rule. It did not secure any specific prerogatives for the armed forces, save for the mention of a separate military justice for defense services personnel (Article 99) and the creation of a "National Defence and Security Committee," gathering members of the Council of State and the Council of Ministers (Article 54b). However, the committee's advising role was not clearly defined. Article 87 even stated that the Council of Ministers (which was to be responsible to Parliament) was the only governing body responsible for the management of foreign affairs and, more importantly, national defense. In theory, the second constitutional text intended the armed forces to remain subordinate to civilians (Maung Maung 1993: 199).

### *The 2008 Constitution: embedding praetorianism*

With the *coup d'état* staged on September 18, 1988, the 1974 constitution was abrogated. After a decade and a half of "re-civilianization" the Tatmadaw stepped in once more. A new generation of senior officers loyal to their old mentor Ne Win, who resigned from the BSPP chairmanship in July 1988, formed the State Law and Order Restoration Council (SLORC). The new junta, under the aegis of General Saw Maung, immediately exercised control over all branches of government. This was another example of a direct praetorian rule imposed in Myanmar, as it had been observed directly after the 1962 coup, but, this time, there was no ideological revolution dictated by the Tatmadaw. Rather, the junta abandoned the autarkical socialist agenda of the single legitimate party (which was disbanded) and promised to hold multi-party elections in order to give power back to civilians – as soon as the sociopolitical order was restored. Once again the Tatmadaw was asserting itself as the savior of the nation, forced to seize power to bring back political stability when the old Ne Win regime seemed about to collapse (Prager Nyein 2011). However, it would, take the army two decades to produce a new constitution and initiate another transition from direct military to quasi-civilian rule in 2011 (Taylor 2012; Bünte 2014; Egreteau 2014a; Maung Aung Myoe 2014).

### *Military control over the constitutional process (1993–2008)*

Not only has the Burmese military institution been able to control the entire constitution-drafting process following the 1988 coup, but it also managed to impose its views on how the transitional regime should be shaped once it eventually withdraws from politics and secured a constitutional immunity for its personnel. It has also directed the pace of its gradual retreat in the 2010s – similar to Chile in the 1980s, where the 1980 constitution entrenched army rule for another decade (Barros 2002; Negretto 2014). While it took four years to draft and promulgate Myanmar's 1974 constitution, more than 15 years were necessary to prepare the country's third constitutional text between 1993 and 2008.

The drafting process, however, echoed that of the early 1970s. The armed forces hierarchy was again at the core of the process from its very inception. But, unlike in the previous constitutional documents, the main objective of the military leadership was clearly to frame a new constitution according to a series of basic principles that would legally secure a military tutelage over national politics – or as I define it, a "constitutional praetorianism." Much to the despair of the rising Burmese opposition forces in the 1990s the military's corporate interests and continuing role in public affairs finally became enshrined in the new constitution. The process was therefore political, if not bluntly praetorian, rather than constitutional.

Just like during the early 1960s, the SLORC initially produced a series of documents and declarations to outline its idea of what the new constitutional order should be after the 1988 *coup d'état* (Mya Win 1992; Min Maung Maung 1993). Instead of touring the country, far more at war with itself in the late 1980s than in the early 1970s, the Tatmadaw leadership opted for the convening of a constituent assembly in order to offer the constitution-making process a façade of consultative approach. Following the electoral route it faced during the May 27, 1990 elections, which it had nonetheless decided to hold, the SLORC announced the transformation of the 485-member body then elected into a constituent assembly, or "National Convention" (SLORC Declaration 1/90, July 27, 1990). Two years later, in July 1992, after General Saw Maung was deposed by his deputy, General Than Shwe, 702 representatives were appointed and asked to join this National Convention. Only 99 of them were MPs elected in the May 1990 elections (Diller 1993: 398–399).

The assembly convened its first session on January 9, 1993. A senior member of the SLORC, Major-General Myo Nyunt, was appointed as its chairman. The first meeting officially set in motion the slow process of constitution-making, but six major policy objectives and 104 "basic principles" had already been put forward by the Tatmadaw. Spelled out during the first session, they were ratified in September 1993 (*The New Light of Myanmar*, September 10, 1993: 1). Non-negotiable, they laid down the policy and judiciary prerogatives the military intended to secure in the new constitution. Among them, the leading political role of the armed forces had to be acknowledged, as well as an extensive legal immunity for its members (active or retired). This plunged the non-elected assembly into a series of stalemates. In November 1995, the main opposition forces led by Aung San Suu Kyi, who had been released from her first house arrest in July 1995, eventually walked out. The assembly was adjourned in March 1996. The drafting process was heavily criticized from its inception, especially by opposition and ethnic movements, as well as by external observers (Diller 1993; Sarkin 2001; Williams 2009).

The National Convention was thereafter postponed for eight years. Constitutional debates were revived only in 2003. In the aftermath of the Depayin incident – which saw Aung San Suu Kyi and her supporters being attacked by rogue sympathizers of the junta – the regime unveiled a "roadmap towards a flourishing-disciplined democracy" on August 30, 2003. Proposed by General

Khin Nyunt, the newly appointed prime minister, the roadmap consisted of seven steps (Taylor 2006). The first was the reconvening of the National Convention. Thus, in May 2004, 1,076 new non-elected delegates were gathered under the aegis of Lt-General Thein Sein, the new chairman of the revived constituent assembly. The purge in October 2004 of the core thinker of the roadmap, Khin Nyunt, did not greatly alter the process (Taylor 2006). A draft was eventually presented during the last session of this second National Convention, which was concluded on September 3, 2007 (step 3 of the roadmap). It would then come into force as the official constitutional text following its adoption through a nationwide referendum[8] (step 4), echoing the referendum held in December 1973 by the previous military regime just before the 1974 constitution was adopted. The referendum was set for May 10, 2008 and the vote was eventually held, despite the tragic passage of Cyclone Nargis through the Irrawaddy Delta and the former capital Yangon a week earlier (Tin Maung Maung Than 2009). Approved by 92.48 percent, the new constitution was ratified and promulgated by the junta on May 29, 2008.[9]

### *A praetorian constitution*

While the previous constitutions did not insist on any key military prerogatives, the one ratified in 2008 does so bluntly.[10] Praetorianism – a situation where armed forces exercise a quasi-monopoly over policy-making processes and a strong influence over political power within a society by virtue of its military might (Finer 1975; Nordlinger 1977) – is embedded in the document. The 2008 constitution greatly distorts Myanmar's political system in favor of the Tatmadaw.[11] A full chapter is even devoted to the defense services (Chapter 7). In the introductory chapter detailing the basic principles of the Union, Article 20 outlines the complete autonomy of the Tatmadaw and defines its core objectives. The armed forces are indeed recognized as "mainly responsible for safeguarding the non-disintegration of the Union, the non-disintegration of National solidarity and the perpetuation of sovereignty" (Article 20e), they have the "right to independently administer and adjudicate" their internal affairs, especially in terms of budget allocation and nominations of senior army officers (Article 20b), and above all they are "responsible for safeguarding the Constitution" (Article 20f).

Furthermore, the military institution is charged with a key policy role as well as a check-and-balance function in each of the new institutions. Thanks to a permanent presence in every branch of government, the military can still exert considerable sway over state affairs. The 2008 constitution provides key positions for military officers in the executive power. It also reserves seats for military appointees in the newly formed provincial and national legislative bodies. With a quarter of the seats of each assembly reserved for men in uniform,[12] the armed forces were constitutionally designed to exercise a strong influence over the legislature (Tin Maung Maung Than 2011; Egreteau 2015). Extraordinary emergency powers for the armed forces are also legalized (Crouch 2013). Their commander-in-chief is indeed conferred "the right to take over and exercise State sovereign power" if a state of national emergency arises (Article 40c). Furthermore, civilian control of the armed forces seems out of place: the hierarchy of the armed forces is indeed not subordinated to the Ministry of Defense; it is the opposite. According to Article 232b(ii), the defense minister is not a civilian, but a man in uniform selected by the military chief himself – and thus a subordinate to the latter.

Lastly, the 2008 constitution also guarantees full immunity for army officers and former officials from the two governing bodies that were formed after the September 1988 *coup d'état*, the SLORC (1988–1997) and State Peace and Development Council (SPDC) (1997–2011). Article 445, labeled the immunity clause by pro-democracy activists, indeed stipulates that "no proceeding shall be instituted against the said Councils or any member thereof or any member of the Government, in respect of any act done in the execution of their respective duties." This pledges a continuing political intervention of the Burmese armed forces in the coming post-junta years, albeit in more sophisticated ways (Farrelly 2013, Maug Aung Myoe 2014, Egreteau 2014a). The provisions of the 2008 constitution are essentially extending – and legalizing – the prerogatives, political interventionism, and legal immunity of the Burmese army in a very praetorian – yet constitutionally legal – way (Prager Nyein 2011; Taylor 2012; Bünte 2014). Echoing Josef Silverstein's "constitutional dictatorship," as Myanmar was described following the 1974 constitution, one may thus argue that the 2008 constitution has shaped in Myanmar a new form of "constitutional praetorianism" that ensures the continuing political salience of the Burmese military.

## Negotiating the post-junta transition (2008–2011)

With the third constitution of the country adopted in May 2008, the transition from direct military rule (the SLORC-SPDC era) to a quasi-civilian one could be initiated. It echoed the process once tested by Ne Win and his Revolutionary Council associates immediately after the 1974 constitution came into force. The military regime was still in control of the whole transitional process in the late 2000s and in a position to decide about its pace, in particular, when to pass on the torch to the successor regime. This has been a key element of the roadmap to a "disciplined democracy" since 2003. The latter was not terminated with the mere adoption of the constitution. National and provincial elections had to be held (the fifth step of the roadmap), a national parliament had to be convened (sixth step), and a government led by a newly elected president of the Union was to be formed out of the parliamentary elections, before the successor hybrid regime could emerge (the seventh and last step).

In 2009, parliamentary elections were announced in order to choose people's representatives for the new bicameral Union Parliament (or *Pyidaungsu Hluttaw*) as well as in each of the 14 regional assemblies (Region and State *Hluttaws*) that were framed by the 2008 constitution. These national and provincial elected bodies were intended to become the backbone of the legislative branch of the new post-junta state structure. The date of the nationwide elections was set for

November 7, 2010 – a week before Aung San Suu Kyi was released from her third house arrest.[13] The vote was lambasted as a sham by many activist groups and foreign diplomats (Englehart 2012). Following a resounding victory (three-quarters of the seats were up for grabs), the allegedly pro-junta political party, or Union Solidarity and Development Party (USDP), rose as the main beneficiary of the soon-to-be-engaged transition. Most senior officials of the SPDC as well as high-ranking officers of the Tatmadaw had indeed retired to join its ranks. The Union Parliament convened for the first time on January 30, 2011. Four days later, it elected the former prime minister of the SPDC (2007–2010), ex-General Thein Sein, as president of the Union.[14] Thein Sein was sworn in two months later, on March 30, 2011, the day the SPDC was officially disbanded. The junta borne out of the 1988 coup was no more, its old pillars Senior-General Than Shwe and Vice Senior-General Maung Aye officially retired, and a new political era was to be opened according to the framework established by the 2008 constitution.

## Why a constitution? The view from the Tatmadaw

As Ivo Duchacek stated in the inaugural issue of *Comparative Politics*, "every constitution combines into one body a declaration of political intent, a commitment to an ideology, and an assertion of national purpose" (Duchacek 1968: 93). In that respect, Myanmar's 2008 constitution clearly embodies the political aspirations and ideology of the hierarchy of the Burmese armed forces. In particular, it serves three clear purposes for the Tatmadaw. First, it manifests the army's view of itself as a legitimate political actor in Myanmar's post-independence public affairs. Next, it provides the military with a legal instrument for policy intervention, and therefore rationalizes its presence in the newly shaped executive and legislative branches of the post-junta structure. Lastly, it offers a form of self-insurance to the armed forces and their personnel, protecting soldiers from any form of prosecution and securing a much sought-after immunity for the leaders (and their clientele) of the 1988 *coup d'état*.

## The constitution as an instrument of legitimacy

The SLORC and the SPDC have long sought constitutional legitimacy sanctioned by popular approval – however dubious the latter may be. This was meant to blot out the ignominious shadow of the 1990 elections, whose results the regime failed to recognize. Ginsburg and Simpser have argued that in some authoritarian regimes the process of constitution-making itself is more valued than the political system the new constitution, once ratified, aims to create (Ginsburg and Simpser 2014: 3). In the case of Myanmar in the 1990s, the drafting and enactment of a new constitutional text was construed by the post-coup leadership as the cornerstone of a strategy to reconstruct a basis for both domestic and international legitimacy for the armed forces (Steinberg 2006). Despite its absolute dominance of politics following the 1988 coup, the

Tatmadaw has obviously not succeeded in forging a broader legitimacy, either at home or abroad. Drafting a new constitution was therefore understood as a way to get this much sought-after acceptability, and therefore to bring the country back into the concert of nations during the 1990s and 2000s.

Military institutions can see constitutions as a key tool to drain legitimacy. As armed forces with a praetorian ethos tend to position themselves as the last defender of the state (and, above all, its institutions), they can seek to manipulate and rewrite these constitutional texts (Negretto 2014). Scholars have emphasized the legalism which many authoritarian regimes – including military ones – have boasted. The institutionalization of power, which can start with the drafting or amendment of existing constitutions in favor of the new ruling authority, serves as a key distinction between a mere dictatorship and an authoritarian-bureaucratic rule or a "sultanistic regime" (Feit 1972; Linz 1975; Chehabi and Linz 1998). Armed forces hoping to decrease the scale of praetorianism and gradually withdraw from politics need a specifically calibrated constitution to codify their new form of indirect political intervention while at the same time formalizing their relations with civilians if they want their policy role to remain relevant (Finer 1975; Nordlinger 1977; Egreteau and Jagan 2013: 25–29). For example, many constitutions which Brazil has adopted since the late nineteenth century have permitted the military to perform key political roles, yet allowing civilians to govern (Stepan 1971: 75–76). The armed forces of Chile have also regularly attempted to give institutional and legal structure to their rule, as demonstrated in the constitution written under military pen and ratified in 1980 (Barros 2002: 38–39).

Following the 1988 coup, the Tatmadaw early on expressed its willingness to participate in, if not simply lead, the constitution-making process. In 1993, an army ideologue wrote:

> neither the 1947 Constitution nor the 1974 Constitution had given a definite role to the Tatmadaw in national political leadership ... the country has now inescapably come to a stage where a definite role would have to be given to the Tatmadaw in the nation's political leadership ... all those who have the welfare of the country at heart should concentrate their attention on providing the Tatmadaw with a leading role in national politics in writing a new constitution.
>
> (Min Maung Maung 1993: 293 and 299)

If the political intervention of the Burmese armed forces was to be enshrined in the new constitution, it was said, the main task of the Tatmadaw would then be the protection of this highly symbolic document. In July 1997, Senior-General Than Shwe, then supreme commander of the Tatmadaw, delivered a speech to senior commanders, in which he detailed his understanding of the military's core missions. Among them, the Tatmadaw was to "abide by the provisions of the state constitution and ... safeguard the new nation that will emerge according to that constitution for sustained development."[15] The army has thus steadily presented itself as the sole legitimate institution which will bring a new constitution to the Burmese people and then safeguard it for the betterment of the nation, and it wanted this to be inked into the new supreme law of the Burmese nation.

## The constitution as a tool for policy intervention

Through the new 2008 constitution, the Tatmadaw has secured enough policy instruments to ensure a military tutelage over policy-making in the post-SPDC polity. Clearly, the Burmese armed forces still did not feel secure enough in the 2010s to completely disengage from politics (Callahan 2012; Egreteau 2014a). Historical legacies and decades of propaganda praising the Tatmadaw's traditional role as guardian of the country since its independence explain this reluctance to trust civilians and let them solely rule the country (Mya Win 1992; Farrelly 2013). According to the scholarship on civil–military relations, praetorian armies retain some form of political power as long as they consider it to be their legitimate duty (Finer 1975; Nordlinger 1977). The Tatmadaw, as an autonomous institution, therefore considers itself as relevant to the global policy decision in the post-junta era (2011 onward), although it appears to tolerate a certain degree of involvement of civilians in the overall decision-making process. The 2008 constitution indeed guarantees it. Article 6(f) of the constitution states that one of the consistent objectives of the Union of Myanmar is to enable the defense services "to be able to participate in the national political leadership role of the State." On each Armed Forces Day (March 27) he has supervised since succeeding Senior-General Than Shwe as Tatmadaw's supreme commander in March 2011, Vice Senior-General Min Aung Hlaing confirmed by letter this core mission of the army.[16] The armed forces will continue to intervene in public affairs beyond the mere realm of military matters as long as the political situation of Myanmar imposes it.

The 2008 constitution therefore stipulates that active-duty military officers (and not only retired ones, who have turned politicians and bureaucrats) have to populate key policy-making positions in the new hybrid political system. This is to ensure that the vested interests of the Tatmadaw (and beyond, of the nation) are not jeopardized by "unruly" civilians. For instance, three core ministries of the central government are left under the sole authority of the Tatmadaw: Home Affairs (Interior), Defense, and Border Affairs (Articles 232b and 234b). In addition, the Security and Border Affairs ministers to be nominated in the provincial government of each of the 14 decentralized states and regions will be active senior officers (Article 262a). As a matter of fact, in 2011, all of them were army colonels appointed by the Tatmadaw commander-in-chief.[17] These army ministers, both at the central and local level, can influence policy-making in various ways, including in ethnic issues and matters of foreign policy.

In the legislative branch, the armed forces have secured a quarter of the seats at both the national and provincial levels: 110 seats in the Lower House (*Pyithu Hluttaw*, Article 109b), 56 seats in the Upper House (*Amyotha Hluttaw*, Article 141b), and a total of 222 seats in the 14 state and region legislatures (Article

161d). All military delegates are nominated by the commander-in-chief without any oversight from civilians – including the president's office (Egreteau 2015). As guarding the constitution is one of the major tasks assigned to the Tatmadaw (Article 20f), military appointees have to make sure that all reform proposals introduced into Parliament – including constitutional amendments – are formulated according to the basic principles already enshrined in the text. A vote by 75 percent of all legislators is indeed required to pass any amendment, and with its 25 percent seat allocation the Tatmadaw effectively acts as a veto force. For instance, this was observed in June 2015 when the military bloc voted out the first amendment bills submitted to the *Pyidaungsu Hluttaw*.

Yet the military delegates have an absolute veto only in matters of constitutional amendments. This is not the case in the regular legislative process, where Tatmadaw representatives represent only a quarter of the assemblies, in which just a simple majority is needed to adopt a new piece of legislation or approve a budget. Since the first session of Parliament in January 2011, military appointees have not only regularly approved bills drafted by their civilian and elected colleagues (including from the opposition groups led by the National League for Democracy), but they have also voted against drafts prepared by the dominant (and supposedly pro-army) USDP (ICG 2013; Egreteau 2014b). However, they have never been in a position to veto any new legislation and have even proved rather supportive of the reforms inspired by President Thein Sein since 2011.

Finally, echoing the 1974 constitution Article 201 of the 2008 constitution creates a key decision-making body, the National Defense and Security Council (NDSC). Headed by the president of the Union, it is dominated by active senior officers. However, its functions and assignments are not defined by the text. Therein may lay a powerful decision center, where most policies are to be formulated, checked, and bargained among military men and their civilian counterparts in the new executive branch (Kyaw Yin Hlaing 2012: 211). In any case, the armed forces view the 2008 constitution as a critical instrument to provide them with key legal channels for policy influence and intervention in the polity that emerged out of the disbanding of the military junta in 2011.

## The constitution as a form of self-insurance

Finally, the 2008 constitution was construed as a way to grant the armed forces some sort of legal immunity against civilians or any emerging opposition force that could threaten the institutional survival of the military or erode its political influence. Using the case study of the Brazilian military, Alfred Stepan has examined the causes that commonly contribute to making the armed forces more insecure – and therefore more authoritarian – institutions (Stepan 1971: 153–156). The belief that civilians are systematically unruly rulers not competent enough to govern, the fear of centrifugal rival forces (e.g., ideological competitors to the military or separatist movements) and the apprehension of a successful mobilization of a new civilian elite that would rise against the traditional officer corps all drive military institutions into praetorianism, and thus broader autocratic behavior and policy intervention. As a consequence, the armed forces feel the need, in times of transition, for a certain degree of constitutional protection against retroactive justice and potential prosecution (David and Holliday 2012). They also seek tools to be in position to veto any new legislation that would undermine the military's authority and immunity. Senior officers and ex-members of military juntas commonly fear staunch reprisals from civilians once the latter are able to form better organized, legitimate, and cohesive institutions that openly rival the armed forces, as in Turkey or Argentina in the 1960s and 1970s, noted early on by military expert Samuel Finer (1975: 112).

In that respect, the 2008 constitution guaranteed the non-accountability of all Myanmar's defense services and their immunity on all matters deemed military related (Article 20b). Thus, Burmese soldiers cannot be trialed by civilians. The Supreme Court can boast no jurisdiction over the Tatmadaw and its personnel; only ad hoc martial courts have authority over the military (Articles 293, 319, and 343). Since 2008, local and international lawyers have relentlessly denounced the culture of impunity which the constitution de facto legalized (ICTJ 2009: 34–35). Above all, its Article 445 states that "no proceeding shall be instituted against the said Councils or any member thereof or any member of the Government, in respect of any act done in the execution of their respective duties." Heavily criticized, the "immunity clause" has consequently ensured that no former senior officials of the SLORC (1988–1997) and the SPDC (1997–2011) can be prosecuted for whatever policy they have formulated or implemented between 1988 and 2011 (ICTJ 2009: 32–33). No transitional justice can therefore be envisioned as long as the constitution is not amended. Neither can any local tribunal looking at human rights abuses conducted during the SLORC-SPDC rule be set up inside the country (Quintana 2013: 16).

## Prospects for amending the 2008 constitution

### *The procedure*

Since its enactment in 2008, the constitution has fostered a steady legal concentration of power in military hands. This has prompted strong criticism from the international community and Burmese opposition groups alike – including from Aung San Suu Kyi, who has long refused to play by the military-written rule.[18] The possibilities of amending the constitution – and not bluntly rejecting it – have nonetheless received a lot of attention among opposition circles and outside observers alike. A full chapter (Chapter XII) of the constitution details the amendment procedure. A proposed amendment begins as a bill in the national Parliament in Naypyitaw. The bill should be drafted and submitted by at least 20 percent of all representatives of both houses – including military delegates – to be considered (Articles 433 to 435). To be adopted, a vote of more than 75 percent of all elected and nominated delegates from both chambers of the bicameral Parliament should be obtained (Article 436a). Given the 25 percent seat allocation which the armed forces have constitutionally secured, no amendment can consequently be passed without military approval – or the defection of a few military appointees. For some specifically mentioned articles or sections of the constitution (as a matter of fact, for the most controversial and sensitive ones), a nationwide referendum must also be held after the vote approval by the parliamentarians, and more than half of the Burmese eligible voters should support the amendment(s) proposed (Article 436b).

Since Aung San Suu Kyi and the NLD eventually decided to accept the constitutional framework in 2012 and participated in the subsequent April 1 by-elections – which they euphorically won[19] – a great deal has been debated about how to amend the constitutional document and which clauses to focus on first. One highly symbolic article has caught the world's attention and overshadowed other major constitutional flaws. The "Suu Kyi Clause" (as Article 59f has now been labeled by local and transnational activist circles) indeed prevents Aung San Suu Kyi – and, in fact, any Burmese citizen having a parent with a foreign allegiance – from becoming a presidential nominee and being chosen as one of the two vice presidents or the president of the Union.[20]

However, many other provisions in the main body of the constitution also pose considerable challenges and thwart democratization prospects (ICTJ 2009; Williams 2014). Among them stands the non-civilian control of the fully independent military institution (Article 20) and of the opaque National Defense and Security Council (Article 201) as well as the unchecked army representation in all national and local legislative bodies (Articles 74, 109, and 141). Military appointees in parliaments as well as army ministers and their deputies in the executive cabinet are indeed removed on a very regular basis without any oversight. As observed in many other postcolonial societies, the constitution also grants through Article 40 and the full Chapter XI (Articles 410 to 432) some extraordinary emergency powers to both the executive (the president) and the military (Crouch 2013). Basic civil rights, although otherwise recognized, can also be summarily restricted (Articles 354 and 420). The immunity clause, which safeguards army officers and former junta officials against any form of civilian prosecution (Article 445) as well as the unchecked amnesty prerogatives of the president (Article 204), are also controversial. Finally, ethnic grievances have not been adequately addressed in Myanmar's latest constitutional document. Despite a major improvement upon the two previous constitutions (as a form of extensive decentralization it has been legally framed with 14 provincial legislative bodies), there is still a lack of proper devolution of power in the post-SPDC "federal" system. As a matter of fact, region and state chief ministers remain nominated by the central executive power in Naypyitaw and are not elected by the representatives of the 14 local assemblies (Nilsen and Tønnesson 2012).

### *Where to begin?*

Quite logically, the different forces of the emerging post-SPDC landscape have a different take on where to begin constitutional reforms and which amendments to examine and promote first. The NLD has openly been pushing for the removal of the clause prohibiting Aung San Suu Kyi from being nominated as presidential candidate (Article 59f).[21] The party also vocally militates for a full withdrawal of military representatives from the legislative and executive branches of government.[22] Aung San Suu Kyi herself, although often cautious about not openly deriding the very institution that her father founded, has repeatedly declared that the armed forces should promptly disengage from all public non-military-related affairs.[23] However, a few other Burmese or ethnic-based political movements have adopted more balanced views. For instance, the National Democratic Force (NDF), formed in 2010 by defecting senior leaders of the NLD, rather promotes a gradual withdrawal of the military from the legislative bodies. "Why not reducing the proportion of seats reserved to the military to 20 percent or 10 percent, before envisioning a full removal of the military appointees?" asks Khin Maung Swe, one of the party's founders.[24] According to the NDF leadership the relationship between the commander-in-chief and the Minister of Defense has also to be reframed. The ministry should be under civilian monitoring and have control over the nomination of the military top brass, not the other way round, paving the way for effective civilian control of the armed forces. NDF party leaders also openly push for greater autonomy to be granted to local and regional assemblies, therefore enshrining more federalism in the main body of the constitution.[25]

Besides, a few legislators outside the NLD realm have recently argued that the clause on the foreign allegiance of presidential nominees (Article 59f) should indeed be revised, but not fully removed. If the foreign allegiance of children should not be included as a factor impeding a Burmese citizen to become president, many a Burmese politician reckons, the case of the spouse has to be scrutinized. Indeed, given the highly emotional and sensitive ethnic issue, nobody seems to want a Burmese president with a Chinese or Bengali wife, to name just two nationalities receiving considerable (and negative) attention in Myanmar these days.[26] Beside the NDF official party line and the opinions of a few individual ethnic legislators, the Democratic Party (Myanmar) – founded, among others, by the daughter of former Prime Minister U Nu – has also developed similar arguments.[27] As the NDF, the DP(M) also insists on an electoral reform (Chapter IX of the constitution), to move away from the first-past-the-post system that favors powerful parties with nationwide political bases such as the USDP or the NLD.[28]

A few ethnic political parties have also taken a similar approach, arguing for a progressive withdrawal of the military presence from the executive and legislative powers. For instance, the Kayin People's Party (KPP) – a small party comprising former Burmese army and police officers of Karen origin which has won half a dozen seats in local and national assemblies in 2010 – maintains that it is not the right time to focus on reducing the constitutional powers of the military, but rather for civilians to consolidate what they have gained since 2010.[29] Others, like representatives of the Rakhine, Shan, and Chin communities, openly claimed that this should not be the focus of the first constitutional amendments to be discussed. Rather, more devolution of power and a broader federalist constitutional text should be the aim.[30] A Kachin parliamentarian developed the same line of argument: incremental change and broader capacity-building for local parliaments is needed before envisioning a full revision of the constitution.[31] Finally, the dominant USDP has long appeared to be divided over the constitutional controversies.[32] The speaker of the Upper House, ex-General Khin Aung Myint, asserted in a recent interview that only a few "technicalities" may be revised, as no provisions in the main body of the 2008 constitution were per se deemed "problematic."[33] But it was the speaker of the Lower House, Thura U Shwe Mann, who in July 2013 announced the formation of a parliamentary committee tasked to discuss amendment proposals.

### *The establishment of a committee for a constitutional review*

In March 2013, during the sixth parliamentary session of the Union Parliament, a motion was passed to discuss the formation of a parliamentary committee to start a potential review of the constitution. The 109-member committee was officially created in July 2013.[34] It gathered representatives of all political parties having parliamentary seats either in the *Pyithu Hluttaw* or the *Amyotha Hluttaw*. After collecting hundreds of thousands of public submissions throughout the second half of 2013, the committee eventually submitted a first report on January 31, 2014.[35] Overwhelmingly descriptive, the latter merely listed all amendment proposals without either drawing any conclusions or outlining any recommendations – except the blunt suggestion not to focus on the most sensitive articles: the military's political role (Article 59f), and the amendment procedure itself. A second joint parliamentary committee was thereafter convened, with this time only 31 appointed national legislators. Ordered to further the constitutional discussion, it was chaired by the deputy speaker of the Lower House, Nanda Kyaw Zwa.[36] Concomitantly, however, and in reaction to the lack of progress, the National League for Democracy opted for the organization of a mass campaign to rally public support for a prompt constitutional change. To do so, Aung San Suu Kyi's party even teamed with former student activists-turned-politicians, known as Generation 88, a party that does not boast any legislators. The campaign eventually collected about five million signatures nationwide.[37]

A first amendment bill was eventually put to Parliament in June 2015. Startlingly, the initiative came from USDP elected representatives. On June 25, the Bill Committee of the USDP-dominated *Pyidaungsu Hluttaw* announced that six proposed changes to the 2008 constitution were to be put forward. Five of them were rejected by the military legislators, included one seeking to lower the voting threshold for constitutional reform and one attempting to repeal Article 59f. A week later, amendments to 21 other Articles of the Constitution – including proposals that would have enhanced the prerogatives of the provincial assemblies and expanded a still fragile decentralization – met the same fate.[38] More than 50 addendums to the constitutional text were however approved by the parliamentarians gathered in Congress.

Given the number of years (15) that were needed to watchfully draft the constitutional text adopted in 2008 and given the fact that the initial principles laid down in 1993 were almost all reproduced (with only minor rephrasing) 15 years later in the final document, there should not be any misplaced optimism. Any constitutional reform will depend on the wills and whims of the Tatmadaw as well as on the stability of the relationship which its rejuvenated hierarchy (under the aegis of Senior-General Min Aung Hlaing since 2011) will maintain with the former commanders-turned-politicians of the post-SPDC political and legislative scene. As long as it perceives the political scene as unruly and divisive, the Tatmadaw will certainly wish to maintain its presence in all parliaments as well as its grip over key ministries and executive posts.[39] Therefore, any successful constitutional amendment in the near future should be minor – not directly affecting the military dominance.

## Conclusion: beyond constitutional praetorianism?

The 2008 constitution has embedded praetorianism in Myanmar's polity in a way the two previous constitutions (1947 and 1974) had not. As long as no other supreme laws or constitutional amendments circumscribe it, the political and legislative intervention of the armed forces is now fully institutionalized. But at the same time, the 2008 constitution has encouraged the historically dominant institution of the country – the Tatmadaw – to team up with the civilian bureaucracy and the emerging (and tolerated) civilian political and parliamentary class. Some of the constitutional provisions were indeed intended to facilitate a first step toward military disengagement and to smooth the transition from direct military rule (as observed between 1988 and 2011) to a quasi-civilian one, expecting another step toward full civilianization to be taken either through constitutional amendments or with a comprehensive constitutional change at a later stage of Myanmar's political future.

The question that now remains is how to move beyond this form constitutional praetorianism – or the sanctioning of the Burmese military's policy intervention by the Constitution, and to gradually frame a full military withdrawal from politics in order to impose an advanced form of constitutionalism in Myanmar (Bünte and Dressel 2014). As other neighboring authoritarian polities have long showed (e.g., China), a written constitution does not necessarily shape constitutionalism, just as the enactment of laws does not systematically mean that the rule of law is fully guaranteed (Zhang 2010). In order to reinforce the post-junta state institutions in Myanmar – such as the governments, the local and national parliaments, and the judiciary system (all in search of a wider autonomy from the Burmese armed forces) – political behavior has to fundamentally change in the country, especially among the ruling elites, including civilian ones. This may take one generation or more. A thorough revolution in the way Burmese military officers are socialized is expected – for the officer corps to move away from the entrenched idea that only the Tatmadaw can embody the Myanmar state. Beyond the Tatmadaw, all other state institutions – including the emerging legislative bodies – appear too weak to stand on their own (and even successfully complete a proper constitutional review), while often remaining too dependent on the charisma and activism of only a few prominent figures. Judicial review should also be independent and strong – it is far from being credible in Myanmar today. Above all, active and mature Burmese citizens need to be trained, educated, and encouraged to constructively intervene in politics and to be more broadly involved in state policy-making.

## Notes

1 The author wishes to thank the editors and the anonymous reviewer for their sharp comments on earlier drafts of this chapter.
2 For linguistic simplicity and without any political connotation, this article uses the vernacular name of the country Myanmar when appropriate (usually for post-1989 events), but retains the English adjective "Burmese."
3 In modern polities, "praetorianism" refers to the unchecked political influence of the military upon elected governing bodies and a democratic civil society, and the control that soldiers seek to exert over state policy-making and civilian affairs.
4 A scan of the original document in its English version may be found online at www.burmalibrary.org/docs07/1947Constitution-facsimile-red.pdf (accessed October 16, 2015).
5 Immediately after seizing power, armed forces and juntas commonly produce extensive legal documents and decrees aimed at detailing their political vision and agendas, but not necessarily a constitution. This has been observed in other places and other times, including during General Pinochet's military rule in Chile in the 1970s (Barros 2002).
6 An English version may be read online at www.burmalibrary.org/docs07/1974Constitution.pdf (accessed October 16, 2015).
7 Earlier, in April 1972, Ne Win and his military associates in the Revolutionary Council resigned from their positions in the armed forces. General Ne Win was from then on to be called "U" Ne Win.
8 *The New Light of Myanmar*, September 3, 2007, p. 5.
9 SPDC Announcement No. 7/2008 (May 29, 2008), in *The New Light of Myanmar*, May 30, 2008, p. 1.
10 A bilingual English-Burmese version is available online at www.president-office.gov.mm/en/sites/default/files/books/07–2012/ConRepubMyanmEng.pdf (accessed October 16, 2015).
11 For academic critiques of the document, see Williams (2009, 2014) and Prager Nyein (2009). For an activist view, read ICTJ (2009).
12 In both the Lower House (Article 109b) and the Upper House (Article 141b) of the national Parliament, a quarter of the seats are reserved for military appointees nominated by the sole commander-in-chief of the armed forces. In the 14 local assemblies (Article 161d), the number of military delegates will be equal to one-third of the total number of elected representatives – which mathematically corresponds to approximately 25 percent as well.
13 Her party, the National League for Democracy (NLD), opted for a boycott of the 2010 elections.
14 *The New Light of Myanmar*, January 31, 2001, p. 1; *The New Light of Myanmar*, February 5, 2011, p. 1.
15 The text was made public two years later (Maung Aung Myoe 2009: 4).
16 *Irrawaddy-on-Line*, "Burma Army Chief Defends Political Role," March 27, 2012; Reuters, "Myanmar's General Lauds Army Democratic Role," March 27, 2013.

17 *The New Light of Myanmar*, March 31, 2011, pp. 11–12.
18 Reuters, "Dissidents Line Up to Fight Myanmar Constitution," February 11, 2008. The NLD would then boycott the 2010 elections and hesitate in joining the regime's "legal fold" afterwards (see *The Myanmar Times*, "Why the NLD Should Register," November 14–20, 2011). Even when the party and Aung San Suu Kyi eventually decided to participate in the 2012 by-elections, and subsequently to win a landslide victory, the NLD MPs refused to take an oath to safeguard the constitution before joining the national Parliament in April 2012 (see Min Zin, "Picking the Wrong Battle." *Foreign Policy*, April 20, 2012).
19 *The Economist*, "The Lady of All Landslides," April 7, 2012.
20 Reuters, "Myanmar Constitution Likely to Dash Suu Kyi's Presidential Hopes," June 19, 2013.
21 Interview with NLD parliamentarians, Naypyitaw, January 2014.
22 Interview with NLD legislators from both houses, Naypyitaw, January and July 2014. It seems nevertheless that some NLD senior members increasingly favor a gradual disengagement of military MPs. See, for instance, *Southeast Asia Globe Magazine*, "From Prison to Parliament," May 1, 2013, available online at http://sea-globe.com/phyo-min-thein (accessed October 16, 2015).
23 Reuters, "Suu Kyi Says Army Has to Give Up Excessive Power," June 15, 2012.
24 Interview with NDF founder U Khin Maung Swe and other party leaders, Yangon, May 2013.
25 Radio Free Asia, "Myanmar Ethnic Alliance Mulls Constitutional Amendments," July 8, 2013.
26 Interview with a Shan MP from *Pyithu Hluttaw*, Naypyitaw, August 2013.
27 Interview with DP(M) party members, Yangon, May 2013.
28 *Irrawaddy-on-Line*, "Amyotha Votes to Change Electoral System," June 13, 2014.
29 Interview with the Vice Chairman of KPP, Shwe Pyi Tha (Yangon), May 2013.
30 Interviews with MPs from the Shan Nationalities Democratic Party (SNDP), the Chin Progressive Party (CPP), and the Rakhine Nationalities Development Party (RNDP), Naypyitaw, January and June 2014.
31 Interview with a legislator from the Unity and Democratic Party, Kachin State (UDPKS), Naypyitaw, January 2014.
32 Interview with a USDP legislator from Rakhine State, Yangon, May 2013.
33 Interview with author, Naypyitaw, August 2013.
34 AP, "Parliament Form Committee to Review Constitution," July 26, 2013. One of its members passed away in November 2013.
35 Interview with three members of the committee (from the USDP, the Chin Progressive Party, and the UDPKS), Naypyitaw, January 2014.
36 Interview with author, Naypyitaw, July 2014.
37 Interview with NLD legislators, Naypyitaw, July 2014.
38 *Irrawaddy-on-Line*, "Charter Push for Decentralization, Stronger Parliament Falters," July 9, 2015.
39 AFP, "Myanmar Army Bristles against Constitutional Change," November 18, 2014.

## Bibliography

Arumugam, R.S. (1975). "Burma: A Political and Economic Background." *Southeast Asian Affairs*, 1975: 41–48.

Badgley, J.H. (1962). "Burma's Military Government: A Political Analysis." *Asian Survey*, 2(6): 24–31.

Barros, R. (2002). *Constitutionalism and Dictatorship: Pinochet, the Junta, and the 1980 Constitution*. Cambridge, Cambridge University Press.

Bünte, M. (2014). "Burma's Transition to Quasi-Military Rule: From Rulers to Guardians?" *Armed Forces and Society*, 40(4): 742–764.

Bünte, M. and Dressel, B. (2014). "Constitutional Politics in Southeast Asia: From Contestation to Constitutionalism?" *Contemporary Southeast Asia* 36(1): 1–22.

Burma Socialist Programme Party (BSPP) (1963). *The System of Correlation of Man and His Environment*. Rangoon, BSPP Publications.

Butwell, R. (1961). "Civilians and Soldiers in Burma." *Studies in Asia*, 1(2): 74–85.

Cady, J.F. (1965). "Burma's Military Dictatorship." *Asian Studies*, 3(3): 490–516.

Callahan, M.P. (2003). *Making Enemies: War and State-Building in Burma*. Ithaca, NY, Cornell University Press.

Callahan, M. (2012). "The Generals Loosen their Grip." *Journal of Democracy*, 23(4): 120–131.

Chambers, P. (2014). "Constitutional Change and Security Forces in Southeast Asia: Lessons from Thailand and Myanmar." *Contemporary Southeast Asia*, 36(1): 101–127.

Chehabi, H.E. and Linz, J.J. (1998). *Sultanistic Regimes*. Baltimore, MD, Johns Hopkins University Press.

Croissant, A. and Kamerling, J. (2013). "Why Do Military Regimes Institutionalize? Constitution-Making and Elections as Political Survival Strategy in Myanmar." *Asian Journal of Political Science*, 21(2): 105–125.

Crouch, M. (2013). "The Constitution, Emergency Powers and the Rule of Law in Myanmar." In *Myanmar in Transition: Polity, People and Processes*, ed. K. Duell. Singapore, Select Books, pp. 45–55.

David, R. and Holliday, I. (2012). "International Sanctions or International Justice? Shaping Political Development in Myanmar." *Australian Journal of International Affairs*, 66(2): 121–138.

Diller, J.M. (1993). "Constitutional Reforms in a Repressive State: The Case of Burma." *Asian Survey*, 33(4): 393–407.

Duchacek, I.D. (1968). "National Constitutions: A Functional Approach." *Comparative Politics*, 1(1): 91–102.

Egreteau, R. (2014a). "The Continuing Political Salience of the Military in Post-SPDC Myanmar." In *Debating Myanmar's Democratization*, eds N. Cheesman, N. Farrelly and T. Wilson. Singapore, ISEAS Publications, pp. 259–284.

Egreteau, R. (2014b). "Emerging Patterns of Parliamentary Politics." In *Myanmar: The Dynamics of an Evolving Politics*, ed. D.I. Steinberg. Boulder, CO, Lynne Rienner, pp. 59–88.

Egreteau, R. (2015). "Soldiers as Lawmakers? Assessing the Legislative Role of the Burmese Armed Forces." In *Metamorphosis: Studies in Social and Political Change in Myanmar*, eds R. Egreteau and F. Robinne. Singapore, NUS Press, pp. 15–42.

Egreteau, R. and Jagan, L. (2013). *Soldiers and Diplomacy in Burma: Understanding the Foreign Policies of the Burmese Praetorian State*. Singapore, NUS Press.

Englehart, N.A. (2012). "Two Cheers for Burma's Rigged Elections." *Asian Survey*, 52(4): 666–686.

Farrelly, N. (2013). "Discipline without Democracy: Military Dominance in Post-colonial Burma." *Australian Journal of International Affairs*, 67(3): 312–326.

Feit, E. (1972). *The Armed Bureaucrats: Military-Administrative Regimes and Political Development*. New York, Houghton Mifflin.

Finer, S.E. (1975). *The Man on Horseback: The Role of the Military in Politics* (revised and enlarged edition). Harmondsworth, Penguin Books.

Ginsburg, T. and Simpser, A. (2014). *Constitutions in Authoritarian Regimes*. Cambridge, Cambridge University Press.
Inlow, E.B. (1948). "The Constitution of Burma." *Far Eastern Survey*, 17(22): 264–267.
International Center for Transitional Justice (ICTJ) (2009). *Impunity Prolonged: Burma and its 2008 Constitution*. New York, ICTJ.
International Crisis Group (ICG) (2013). *Not a Rubber Stamp: Myanmar's Legislature in a Time of Transition*. Brussels/Yangon, Asia Briefing No. 142.
Kyaw Yin Hlaing (2012). "Understanding Recent Political Changes in Myanmar." *Contemporary Southeast Asia*, 34(2): 197–216.
Linz, J.J. (1975). *Totalitarian and Authoritarian Regimes* (revised edition 2000). Boulder, CO, Lynne Rienner.
Maung Aung Myoe (2009). *Building the Tatmadaw: Myanmar Armed Forces since 1948*. Singapore, ISEAS Publications.
Maung Aung Myoe (2014). "The Soldier and the State: The *Tatmadaw* and Political Liberalization in Myanmar since 2011." *South Asia Research*, 22(2): 233–249.
Maung Maung (1959). *Burma's Constitution*. The Hague, Martinus Nijhoff.
Min Maung Maung (1993). *The Tatmadaw and its Leadership Role in National Politics*. Yangon, News and Periodicals Enterprise, Ministry of Information.
Mya Win (1992). *Tatmadaw's Traditional Role in National Politics*. Yangon, News and Periodicals Enterprise.
Moscotti, A.D. (1977). *Burma's Constitution and Elections of 1974*. Singapore, ISEAS Research Notes and Discussions, No. 5.
Nakanishi, Y. (2013). *Strong Soldiers, Failed Revolution: The State and Military in Burma, 1962–88*. Singapore, NUS Press.
Negretto, G.L. (2014). "Authoritarian Constitution Making: The Role of the Military in Latin America." In *Constitutions in Authoritarian Regimes*, eds T. Ginsburg and A. Simpser. Cambridge, Cambridge University Press, pp. 83–110.
Nilsen, M. and Tønnesson, S. (2012). *Can Myanmar's 2008 Constitution Be Made to Satisfy Ethnic Aspirations?* Oslo, PRIO Policy Brief No. 11.
Nordlinger, E.A. (1977). *Soldiers in Politics: Military Coups and Governments*. London, Prentice Hall.
Prager Nyein, S. (2009). "Expanding Military, Shrinking Citizenry, and the New Constitution in Burma." *Journal of Contemporary Asia*, 39(4): 638–648.
Prager Nyein, S. (2011). "The Armed Forces of Burma: The Constant Sentinel." In *The Political Resurgence of the Military in Southeast Asia: Conflict and Leadership*, ed. M. Mietzner. London, Routledge, pp. 24–44.
Quintana, T.O. (2013). *Report of the Special Rapporteur on the Situation of Human Rights in Myanmar*. Geneva, United National Human Rights Council A/HRC/22/58.
Sarkin, J. (2001). "Examining the Competing Constitutional Process in Burma/Myanmar from a Comparative and International Democratic and Human Rights Perspective." *Asia-Pacific Journal on Human Rights and the Law*, 2(2): 42–68.
Silverstein, J. (1974). "From Soldiers to Civilians: The New Constitution of Burma in Action." In *The Future of Burma in Perspective: A Symposium*, ed. J. Silverstein. University of Ohio, Centre of International Studies, pp. 80–92.
Silverstein, J. (1977). *Burma: Military Rule and Politics of Stagnation*. Ithaca, NY, Cornell University Press.
Steinberg, D. (2006). *Turmoil in Burma: Contested Legitimacies in Myanmar*. Norwalk, EastBridge.

Stepan, A.C. (1971). *The Military in Politics: Changing Patterns in Brazil.* Princeton, NJ, Princeton University Press.

Stepan, A.C. (1988). *Rethinking Military Politics: Brazil and the Southern Cone*. Princeton, NJ, Princeton University Press.

Taylor, R.H. (2006). "One Day, One Fathom, Bagan Won't Move: On the Myanmar Road to Constitution." In *Myanmar's Long Road to National Reconciliation*, ed. T. Wilson. Singapore, Institute of Southeast Asian Studies, pp. 3–28.

Taylor, R.H. (2009). *The State in Myanmar*. Singapore, NUS Press.

Taylor, R.H. (2012). "Myanmar: From Army Rule to Constitutional Rule?" *Asian Affairs*, 43(2): 221–236.

Tin Maung Maung Than (2009). "Myanmar in 2008: Weathering the Storm." *Southeast Asian Affairs*, 2009: 195–222.

Tin Maung Maung Than (2011). "Myanmar's 2010 Elections: Continuity and Change." *Southeast Asian Affairs*, 2011: 190–207.

Wiant, J.A. (1973). "Burma: Loosening Up On the Tiger's Tail." *Asian Survey*, 13(2): 179–186.

Williams, D. (2009). "Constitutionalism before Constitutions: Burma's Struggle to Build a New Order." *Texas Law Review*, 87: 1657–1693.

Williams, D. (2014). "What's So Bad about Burma's 2008 Constitution? A Guide for the Perplexed." In *Law, Society and Transition in Myanmar*, eds M. Crouch and T. Lindsey. Oxford, Hart Publishing, pp. 117–140.

Zhang, Q. (2010). "A Constitution without Constitutionalism? The Paths of Constitutional Development in China." *International Journal of Constitutional Law*, 8(4): 950–976.

# 7 The legal–military alliance for illiberal constitutionalism in Thailand

*Eugénie Mérieau*

## Introduction

Thailand is the only country in Southeast Asia that still regularly experiences *coups d'état* and direct military rule. Since the absolute monarchy ended in 1932, civilians have never fully achieved control of the army. Even during civilian-led governments, the army remained largely autonomous and insulated from government control (Chambers 2010, 2014b). Yet, notwithstanding its long tradition of military rule,[1] Thailand has never been governed by decree (without a constitution) for more than a few months at a time.[2] Military leaders seem to have always favored the adoption of constitutions: *coups d'état* followed by constitution-making are a common way to seize and consolidate power. Once in power, the new power-holders seek to entrench their preferences and interests in a new constitution.

Constitution-making under military rule has resulted in two types of constitution: fully authoritarian, with political parties and elections banned altogether,[3] and semi-authoritarian, allowing some degree of political representation through elections, but balanced by giving wide-ranging powers to appointed military and civilian bureaucrats.[4] After seizing power, the military leaders would usually enact a fully authoritarian temporary charter providing for the drafting of a "permanent" semi-authoritarian constitution. Thailand has had only three democratic constitutional experiments with non-elected individuals prohibited from becoming prime minister and providing for election of the legislature and limited government.[5] Following the most recent coups in 2006 and 2014, the army enacted two temporary charters (2006 and 2014) and two permanent constitutions (2007 and draft 2015). Both provided for a return to civilian rule through direct elections but gave broad powers to a Senate wholly or partly appointed.[6] They also gave courts and independent organizations much power over the government and the legislature.

In that, they resemble the 1997 constitution, which at the time was heralded as one of the most democratic in Asia. The 1997 constitution was the outcome of popular calls for political reform which had their roots in a massive uprising against military rule in May 1992.[7] The process of drafting the 1997 constitution was truly inclusive and incorporated nationwide public hearings (see McCargo

1998). The resulting constitution adopted many of the features of democratic "third-wave constitutionalism," most notably a powerful Constitutional Court tasked to guarantee the supremacy of the constitution. Ginsburg (2009: 83) defined it as a "post-political constitution":

> The post-political constitution involves enhanced efforts to structure and channel democratic power and to limit the role of partisanship, encompassing not only constitutional courts but myriad other institutions that effect a highly refined separation of powers.

Among those "other institutions" are such independent organizations as the Election, National Anti-Corruption, and State Audit Commissions and the Ombudsman. The 1997 constitution opened the way for judicial empowerment: judges, career and non-career, sitting in new independent bodies and courts were entrusted with wide-ranging powers of control and sanction over the elected branch of the state.[8] The Senate, traditionally an anti-politician stronghold, was placed in charge of appointing and removing the members of independent organizations, including the Constitutional Court,[9] which topped the whole post-political framework. Thailand seemed to have embarked on a path of democratic consolidation free from military influence.

The 2006 military coup leaders abolished the 1997 post-political constitution. They supervised the drafting of an even more post-political constitution, which reintroduced appointment for half of the Senate and sustained the powers of the independent organizations and the Constitutional Court. The 2014 military coup leaders in turn abolished the 2007 constitution; they oversaw the drafting of an even more post-political constitution. As of April 2015, the draft constitution had reintroduced a fully appointed Senate and created new, appointed, independent organizations and merged others.[10] What the 1997, 2007, and 2015 constitutions had in common, despite their quite different origins, was a mistrust of elected politicians. The introduction of post-political institutions helped maintain bureaucratic control over Thai politicians, and consequently the entire Thai political system.

Authoritarian constitutions are usually defined as having "the form of a constitution, but without fully articulated institutions of limited government" (Ginsburg and Simpser 2005). However, the 2007 post-coup constitution installed a highly limited government. The 2015 draft adds even more limits. Rather than empowering the executive, both post-coup semi-authoritarian constitutions have disempowered to the widest extent possible the executive and the legislature. Using modern constitutional techniques, they recreate a regime in which elected representatives are hemmed in by appointed bureaucrats in the well-known "bureaucratic polity" (Riggs 1966).

The Thai bureaucratic polity is composed of the civilian and military bureaucracies. Between them there is a necessary synergy: the military needs civilian bureaucrats to administer the country following *coups d'état*. This chapter therefore argues that after 1992, in order to preserve their status, which was threatened by the rise of elected politicians, Thai bureaucratic elites, both civilian and military, chose to reinvent bureaucratic rule by relying on post-political constitutions. At least two factors converged to lead to the embrace of post-political institutions: the domestic discredit of the military after the 1992 bloodshed,[11] and international norm diffusion. Post-political constitutions that adopt mechanisms of constitutional review may thus give the courts the power to veto political decisions made by the elected branch – a process which Hirschl (2004) has called the "judicialization of politics." The post-political constitutions of 2007 and 2015 may be understood as attempts at what Hirschl defined as "self-interested hegemonic preservation."

> [The creation of Constitutional Courts with wide-ranging powers] is best understood as a product of a strategic interplay between threatened political elites, who seek to preserve or enhance their political hegemony by insulating policy making in general and their policy preferences in particular from the vicissitudes of democratic politics while they profess support for democracy.... When their policy preferences have been, or are likely to be, increasingly challenged in majoritarian decision-making arenas, elites that possess disproportionate access to, and influence over, the legal arena may initiate a constitutional entrenchment of rights and judicial review in order to transfer power to supreme courts.
>
> (Hirschl 2004: 12)

This chapter seeks to analyze how, in the post-1992 context, post-coup contestation has led constitutional drafters to adopt post-political constitutions under both civilian (1997) and military (2007, draft 2015) rule. Elite bureaucrats, civilian and military, have preferred this type of constitution because it gives them the means for advanced bureaucratic cooperation against elected politicians. It therefore makes it possible to retain an illiberal status quo despite a seemingly democratic constitution.

Legal experts have been at the center of cooperation between civilian and military elites. They have integrated the preferences of civilian and military bureaucrats at three levels: (1) as producers of legal doctrines to justify *coups d'état*; (2) as constitution-drafters entrenching coups in the very text of the constitution; and (3) as appointed or career judges in courts and independent watchdog institutions dismissing elected governments. The legal–military alliance was essential in staging the 2006 and 2014 coups, drafting the post-political and semi-authoritarian 2007 and 2015 constitutions, and legalizing post-coup order. This chapter sheds light on the role of jurists mobilized to draft post-coup constitutions that empower the judiciary. Even though it was often observed that this subject demanded detailed analysis (see Kasetsiri Charnvit (2007) and Kasien Tejapira (2012), among others), it does not appear that any such study has yet been published. In the late 1970s Thai studies scholars laid the foundations for research on military involvement in Thai politics (Elliott 1978; Chaloemtiarana 2007; Samudavaniija 1982). Critical studies of Thai constitutionalism emerged at the end of the 1980s, especially with the drafting of the 1997 constitution (see, e.g., Saneh Chamarik 1986; McCargo 1998; Ginsburg 2009; Harding and Leyland 2011). Before that, Thai constitutions were considered either "nominal"[12] or "semantic"[13]: as a country that had "constitutions without constitutionalism", Thailand was not worth studying.

Recently, notable efforts have been made to link the study of constitutionalism with military rule in Thailand (Chambers 2014), reflecting a broader trend in comparative constitutional studies of recent interest in the study of authoritarian constitutions (Ginsburg and Simpser 2005). This chapter is intended to contribute to this emerging field by bringing empirical evidence to the fore: the Thai case illustrates how bureaucracies can divert post-political constitutions from their liberal and democratic spirit in order to use them against representative governments. This phenomenon is particularly likely to occur when the civilian and military bureaucratic elites are coordinated, allied with renowned legal experts, and free from government control. This chapter first examines how the Thai state has historically encouraged the legal–military alliance. It then turns to an analysis of how military rule has been constitutionalized. Finally, it explores the legal doctrines and jurisprudence developed to legalize military *coups d'état* and military rule. It concludes with a few remarks on the state of the political crisis industry that sustains the legal–military alliance.

## The legal–military alliance

The legal–military alliance is a network within the Thai bureaucracy which is both institutionalized as part of the bureaucratic polity and personalized at the highest levels of the state. Legal and military elites share common values and are highly interdependent – a situation shaped by a shared sense of community and destiny. The legal–military alliance is the most influential elite network within the bureaucracy because it combines normative with coercive power. Legal and military elites share many characteristics. Under Rama V (1868–1910), the emerging civilian and military bureaucracy was to function as a Westernization agent to avoid colonial occupation in the nineteenth century. The king wanted to modernize the state by Westernizing it in two stages. First, to hire foreign councilors while sending civilian bureaucrats and military officers abroad to study; second, to replace foreign councilors by the Thai bureaucrats who had been educated abroad. Both military officers and jurists were sent to Western countries to learn about the latest techniques in defense and law.

Together, the two fields were indeed instrumental in maintaining and preserving Thai independence. Weak military power on the one hand and archaism of the legal system on the other made Thailand very vulnerable to colonial powers and undermined its attempts to appear as a "civilized" country. Jurists had to find ways to reform Siam in order to make the legal system acceptable to Western countries which had been granted extraterritorial privileges.[14] In 1897 the military academy was created and the first law academy for high civil servants was established inside the Ministry of Justice. Both were to enroll members of the royal family and the nobility to form a bureaucratic elite (see Kollada Kesboochoo 2004: 66–82). Thanks to scholarships, students studied part of their curriculum in Thailand and part abroad. When they returned to Thailand, they were expected to occupy high positions in the civilian and military bureaucracies. Most law students were sent to England; military students were sent to France and Germany.

In the mid-1920s, the association of Thai students in France launched a plot to overthrow the monarchy. Two of them became leaders of the 1932 revolution: Pridi Banomyong, who was studying law at the University of Paris, and Plaek Khittasangkha (later known as Luang Phibun Songkhram), a student at the Military School in Paris. In 1927, together with two other students from the Military School, a London-based Thai lawyer, a science student, and a member of the Thai embassy in Paris, they planned a revolution in Siam. They recruited about 100 men to stage a coup against the monarch Rama VII (1925–1935) and succeeded in imposing Thailand's first written constitution. The People's Party (*khana rassadon*) consisted of equal numbers of military officers and civilians. In the successful 1932 revolution the Pridi/Phibun alliance was instrumental in bringing together force (the military) and legitimacy (the constitution). This legal–military strategic alliance imprinted itself on the modern Thai state. It was replicated under the leadership of King Rama IX (1946 to the present) in its choice and handling of men in the Privy Council.[15] The Privy Council is central to the "network monarchy" (McCargo 2005), comprising high-ranking members

*Table 7.1* Members of the Privy Council (the organizing principle is the one used by the Privy Council)

| *Name* | *Background* | *Date of appointment* | *Date of birth* |
|---|---|---|---|
| Prem Tinsulanond (President) | Army | 8/23/1988 | 8/26/1920 |
| Thanin Kraivichien | Judiciary | 12/15/1977 | 4/5/1927 |
| Surayud Chulanont | Army | 11/24/2003<br>4/8/2007 | 8/28/1943 |
| Chaovana Nasylvanta | Engineer | 12/19/1975 | 8/7/1948 |
| Siddhi Savetsila | Army | 12/24/1991 | 1/7/1919 |
| Khamthon Sindhvananda | Army | 8/1987 | 3/20/1926 |
| Pichit Khullawanit | Army | 7/13/1993 | 7/6/1932 |
| Ampon Sennanarong | Agriculture | 9/9/1994 | 10/30/1931 |
| Chamrat Khemacharu | Judiciary | 11/15/1994 | 8/11/1929 |
| M.L. Asni Pramoj | Law degrees and army titles | 3/3/1984 | 7/1/1934 |
| M.R. Thepkamol Thevakul | Ambassador | 8/7/1997 | 4/12/1936 |
| Kasem Wattanachai | Doctor/health | 7/18/2001 | 4/18/1941 |
| Palakorn Suwannarat | Civil servant/governor | 7/18/2001 | 7/14/1947 |
| Chumphon Pacchusanon | Army | 3/15/2005 | 6/30/1944 |
| Antanithi Disatha-amnart | Judiciary | 8/16/2007 | 8/24/1944 |
| Supachai Phungam | Judiciary | 4/8/2007 | 6/4/1945 |
| Chanchai Likhitchitta | Judiciary | 4/8/2007 | 4/25/1946 |
| Chalit Phukphasuk | Army | 11/18/2011 | 4/5/1948 |

of the palace, the military, and the bureaucracy. Members of the network monarchy enjoy a degree of proximity with the monarch which allows them to wield power within both the state and Thai society at large. The 2015 Privy Council is mainly composed of legal and military elites.

Of the 18 current Privy Councilors, sevren are army officers and five are judges. The two most influential figures on the council are its current president Prem Tinsulanond, retired general and former appointed prime minister (1980–1988),[16] and Thanin Kraivichien, former supreme court judge and appointed prime minister (1976–1977).[17] They both command great deference, being presented as role models to law and military students and new recruits. Because they have personal ties to high-ranking bureaucrats who owe them loyalty, within the Privy Council they can act as coordinators between the military and such legal bodies as the courts, independent constitutional organizations, the Council of State, state-appointed legal commissions, and to some extent law faculties. In the past, other powerful figures have played similar roles.[18]

Besides the Privy Council, other institutions create legal–military integration and foster consensus between the two status groups. The National Defense College is the most emblematic of these. Most Privy Councillors, whether judges or career military, have studied at the College, which was created in 1955 by Phibunsongkhram to establish a unitary *esprit de corps* among military and civilian bureaucrats.

> By the process of subjecting bureaucrats to a common institution of learning government propaganda, and personal contacts in a congenial setting, the Sarit regime was able to achieve a high level of elite bureaucratic solidarity.... Their experience at the prestigious National Defense College raised the morale and sense of efficacy of the participants, as well as allowing them to establish personal contacts which could be used later to facilitate intra-bureaucratic cooperation and efficiency. Through socialization at the Defense College, Sarit was able to persuade most top echelons civilian bureaucrats of the urgency of national development and the linked problem of national security, which had to be handled primarily by the armed forces, supported by a loyal civil service. In the final analysis, it is clear that a major purpose of the socialization programme was to try to convince civilian bureaucrats of the legitimacy of military supremacy in government.
>
> (Tak Chaloemtiarana 2007: 188)

The elite socialization process is the root of the alliance between jurists and the military. Recruitment into military schools and legal studies is highly competitive and strives to build both a feeling of gratitude toward the bureaucratic regime and a strong sense of comradeship and solidarity among graduates. Both the military and the judiciary have fostered the development of systems of recruitment, training, evaluation, promotion, and discipline that encourage conformity with the expectations of the bureaucratic regime.

## Constitution-drafting and constitutional practice

Legal–military integration has also been fostered by the pattern of coup constitution-making that has long characterized Thai politics. Since the end of the absolute monarchy in 1932, Thailand has had 20 constitutions and 13 successful coups: thus a Thai constitution lasts on average 4.5 years and there is a coup every 6.8 years. Samudavanija (1982) called this the "vicious cycle of Thai politics": there is a coup, a new constitution, elections, political crisis, and another coup. Within this cycle, there is another cycle in which the previous constitution is abolished, a temporary constitution is drafted that sets conditions for the drafting of a permanent constitution, and the permanent constitution is drafted. A prominent Thai studies scholar (McCargo 1998) has called this frenetic constitution-making "the disease of permanent constitutionalism."

In this coup–constitution sequence, drafters of the temporary constitution are likely to be associated with those who made the coup because they must provide a constitution within a few days or weeks after they take over (except following the 1958 and 1971 coups). By contrast, the drafting of the permanent constitution tends to be a more inclusive process that involves constitution-drafting committees and assemblies.[19] Before 1992, legal experts, usually from the courts and the Council of State,[20] were asked to draft the temporary document; constitution-drafting assemblies were mostly composed of military men and legal experts, usually from the courts, the Council of State, and law faculties.[21] As might be expected, the permanent document was usually more liberal than the temporary one, but in both cases the processes were supervised by the faction of the army that had staged the coup. This process resulted mainly in two types of constitution: authoritarian – giving the military unlimited power; and semi-authoritarian – providing for institutional power-sharing, which often featured an elected Lower House and an appointed Upper House (mainly filled with senior civilian and military bureaucrats). Both types were "preservative": they sought to embed the traditional pillars of the Thai state ("monarchy, religion, and nation") into constitutional practice in order to preserve the military-bureaucratic regime.

After 1992, demands for democratization were to some extent successful: for the first time in Thai constitutional history, the 1997 constitution specified a fully elected Senate and there was an absolute ban on having an unelected prime minister. Thus, the military, which had relied on an appointed Senate and the possibility of one of its members becoming the appointed prime minister, faded from the political scene. Most aspects of the 1997 constitution were transformative, especially in terms of individual and collective rights and liberties, and the building of a strong civilian government. As the military influence ebbed, the civilian bureaucracy, in particular legal elites comprising the top layers of the judiciary, rose to prominence.

A thorough examination of the minutes of the 1997 and 2007 constitution-drafting process shows that for both, the drafters envisioned judicial empowerment as a strategy to keep the bureaucracy in control of the political system by giving the judiciary a special role in times of crisis. For the 1997 drafting committee, the following article, dealing with crisis, gave unlimited powers to the Constitutional Court:

> Whenever no provision under this Constitution is applicable to any case, the Constitutional Court shall decide in accordance with the constitutional practice in the democratic regime of government with the King as Head of the State.[22]

It was later decided to incorporate this into Article 7 of the constitution and to drop any reference to the Constitutional Court.[23] It became:

> Whenever no provision under this Constitution is applicable to any case, it shall be decided in accordance with the constitutional practice in the democratic regime of government with the King as Head of the State.

Such wording is a traditional feature of post-coup constitutions. It first appeared in the constitution in 1959 following Sarit Thanarat's *coup d'état* to allow authorities discretionary powers as to how to interpret what was at the time a short constitution. In the 1972, 1976, 1977, and 1991a constitutions, it referred only to "the constitutional practice in the democratic regime of government," but, starting with the 1997 constitution, the expression "with the King as Head of State" was added. In 2007, Article 7, which had been used to call for the royal appointment of the prime minister in the lead-up to the 2006 coup, was left untouched.

In 2007, constitution drafters once again attempted to make judges actors of crisis resolution. According to the first draft of Article 68, judges were to meet and appoint a caretaker government if the office of prime minister became vacant. In March 2007, the constitution-drafting subcommittee on political institutions adopted the following principle, applicable in situations where the office of prime minister became vacant:

> The Constitutional Court President, the President of the Supreme Court and the Supreme Administrative Court choose the interim cabinet, which should be comprised of people with experience in administration.[24]

The committee also proposed to add the commanders of the three branches of the army,[25] but this proposal was discarded and the fourth paragraph of Article 68 softened: it no longer gave judges the authority to select a prime minister but instead mandated that they meet to "consider ways to solve the problem." By March 2007, this had become:

> If there is a national crisis or a political situation where it is necessary, there shall be a meeting of the following, the PM, President of House of

> Representatives, President of the Senate, Leader of the Opposition, President of the Constitution Court, President of the Supreme Court, President of the Supreme Administrative Court, and President(s) of Independent Agencies under the Constitution, to consider ways to solve the problem.

When this chapter was included in the draft constitution published for public hearings in April 2007, it met with strong opposition and was finally removed under popular pressure. Notwithstanding the failed attempts at constitutionalizing the crisis resolution role of the highest justices, judges did become involved in times of crisis. This began to unfold from 2006 onward, following the king's speech to the judges on April 25, 2006 in which he urged the justices to step in to solve the political crisis related to the legitimacy of Prime Minister Thaksin Shinawatra.[26] A few days after the royal speech, the Constitutional Court ruled that the elections were unconstitutional, which meant that Parliament could not reconvene to elect a new prime minister. The situation thus created was ripe for a *coup d'état*. The elections scheduled for October never took place because the army staged a coup on September 19, 2006.

The 2007 constitution was in force when the younger sister of Thaksin, Yingluck Shinawatra, was elected in July 2011. Facing mass protests, she dissolved the House in December 2013. The opposition boycotted the elections in February 2014 and the Election Commission refused to certify the results. A few months later, on May 7, 2014, the Constitutional Court dismissed Yingluck for the transfer of an official to an inactive post. The resultant political vacuum again created conditions for a coup, which was staged on May 22, 2014.[27] In both cases, coordinated court decisions paved the way for the military *coup d'état*.[28] After seizing power, the first move by the military was to appoint assemblies and constitution-drafting committees to distribute the spoils and thus build support.

## Building the constitutionality of *coups d'état*

Two related measures are emblematic of the entrenchment of military interests in Thai constitutions: amnesties for coup-makers and constitutionalization of the legality of *coups d'état*.

First, in 1932, following their revolution/coup, the People's Party, led by jurist Pridi Panomyong and military officer Plaek Phibunsongkhram, proposed simultaneously a constitution and an amnesty bill, which were sent to the king for endorsement. Later, coup-makers always used amnesties, sometimes as a separate bill, sometimes as an article in the constitution. Since 1972, post-coup (temporary) constitutions have included an amnesty for coup-makers and an article legalizing the coup.[29] Finally, starting in 2007, permanent constitutions have included a clause legitimizing temporary post-coup constitutions – thus giving constitutional status to the coup.

In 2006, the amnesty for coup-makers was written into Article 37 of the 2006 interim constitution:

> **Article 37 (2006).** All acts done by the Chairman of the Council for Democratic Reform which related to the seizure and control of the State administrative power on 19th September B.E. 2549 as well as any act done by persons involved in such seizure or of persons being assigned by the Chairman of the Council for Democratic Reform or of persons being commanded by the Chairman of the Council for Democratic Reform ... done for such above act. All these acts, whether done for the enforcement in legislative, executive or judicial force as well as the punishment and other acts on administration of the State affairs whether done as principals, supporters, instigators or persons being commanded to do so and whether done on such date or prior to such date or after such date which if such acts may be unlawful, the actors shall be absolutely exempted from any wrongdoing, responsibility and liabilities.

In 2014 the amnesty clause for coup-makers was written into Article 48 of the constitution.

> **Article 48 (2014).** All acts which have been done in relation to the seizure and control of the administration of State affairs on the 22nd Day of May B.E. 2557 (2014) of the Head of the National Council for Peace and Order and the National Council for Peace and Order, including all acts which have been done by any person in connection with the aforesaid acts, or by the person who has been entrusted or ordered by the Head of the National Council for Peace and Order or the National Council for Peace and Order, for the fulfilment of such purposes, regardless of their legislative, executive or judicial force, as well as any punishment and other acts performed in relation to the administration of State affairs and whether the actors of those act are principals, accessories, persons who employ another to commit those acts or the employed persons and whether those acts done before or after the date mentioned above, if the aforesaid acts were illegal, all related person shall be exempted from being offenders and shall be exempted from all liabilities.

In constitutionalizing the legality of coups, drafters used Article 36 of the 2006 constitution and Article 47 of the 2014 constitution.

> **Article 36 (2006).** All announcements or orders of the Council for Democratic Reform or the orders of the Chairman of the Council for Democratic Reform which announced or ordered during 19th September B.E. 2549 until the promulgated date of this Constitution whether done in any form and any announcement or commanded for the enforcement in legislative, executive or judicial force shall continue to be enforced and shall consider that announcements or orders as well as acts done upon such announcements or orders whether the acts of such announcements or orders were done prior to or after the promulgated date of this Constitution shall be announcements or orders which are considered lawful and constitutional.

> **Article 47 (2014).** All notifications and orders of the National Council for Peace and Order as well as orders of the Head of the National Council for Peace and Order which were notified or made between the 22nd Day of May B.E. 2557 (2014) until the date the Council of Ministers takes office under this Constitution, regardless of their legislative, executive or judicial force, as well as all acts performed in compliance therewith before or after this Constitution comes into force shall be deemed to be legal, constitutional and conclusive. Any Notification or Order that is still in force prior to the date this Constitution comes into force shall be in force until it is amended or repealed by law, rule, regulation, resolution of the Council of Ministers or order, as the case may be. In the case where the National Council for Peace and Order has ordered any person to hold or vacate any official position as prescribed by section 24 prior to the date this Constitution comes into force, the Prime Minister shall present the order to the King for appointment or removal.

Articles 36 and 37 of the temporary 2006 constitution were endorsed by the 2007 permanent constitution in Article 309. As of April 2015, Articles 47 and 48 of the temporary 2014 constitution are endorsed in Article 315 of the 2015 draft of the permanent constitution.

> **Article 309 (2007).** All acts recognised in the Constitution of the Kingdom of Thailand (Interim), B.E. 2549 (2006) as lawful and constitutional, including acts incidental thereto whether performed prior to or subsequent to the date of the promulgation of this Constitution, shall be deemed constitutional under this Constitution.

With these constitutional dispositions, coup-makers and their allies are protected from prosecution for past and future actions. Examining jurisprudence, these extensive protections against prosecution may be largely superfluous, given the traditional pro-military stance of Thai courts. Indeed, despite the fact that abolishing the constitution is a criminal offense punishable by the death penalty (Article 113 of the Thai Criminal Code), the Supreme Court has created a jurisprudential rule making *coups d'état* legally valid in Thailand once they are successful. According to Supreme Court Decision 45/2496 (1953), "The military coup council has the power to govern the country by changing, revising, abolishing or enacting laws because of their successful coup in 1947."[30] Similarly, in Supreme Court Decision 1167/2505 (1962), the court ruled that:

> In 1958 the Revolutionary Party successfully seized the power to administer Thailand and the Revolutionary Party can therefore exercise the powers to administer the country by such power. Any text that the Revolutionary Party enforces on the public is therefore deemed to be a law, even though the King may not have promulgated it with the advice and consent of the members of the National Assembly or the Legislative Assembly.[31]

Court decisions also strictly enforced amnesty for coup-makers. In May 1997, the Criminal Court dismissed assault charges brought by a victim of Black May 1992 against the coup leaders, arguing that they were covered by the amnesty decree validated by the Constitutional Tribunal.[32]

Now let us examine the construction of legal doctrines governing the drafting of the post-1992 constitutions – those of 1997, 2006, 2007, 2014, and 2015. Academic Bowornsak Uwanno – a role model for many law students and future legal elites – led the drafting of the 1997 and 2015 constitutions.[33] Interestingly, as a legal expert he also formulated the doctrines justifying military rule. He notably produced the doctrine of "shared sovereignty" whereby sovereignty reverts to the monarch whenever there is a *coup d'état*.

> In the Thai system of democracy, sovereignty resides in the monarchy and the people. It differs from other countries in which the people are the sole bearer of sovereignty. There are two reasons for this. The first one is related to customs. The Thai monarchy has been one with the people and this has become tradition. The second one is related to law. From time immemorial, sovereignty belonged to the monarchy. When the People's Party changed the system of government, the monarchy who had sovereignty, bestowed it onto the people by giving them the Constitution. It accepted to be put under the Constitution but still held sovereign power on behalf of the people. That is why whenever there is a *coup d'état* that abolishes the Constitution, we should consider that the power that was given with the Constitution comes back to the monarchy, the sovereign before 24 June 1932.
>
> (Bowornsak Uwanno 2007)

Thus, according to Bowornsak Uwanno, when the monarch signs the interim constitution following a *coup d'état*, the act is deemed legal and sovereignty reverts to being "shared" with the people. Other legal experts who participated in drafting constitutions after 1992, such as Vishnu Khruangam and Meechai Reechupan, have become the proponents of theories legalizing *coups d'état*, usually by reference to the continuity of the Thai state as embodied by the king.

However, the legality of coups has not gone without challenge. The Nittirat group – seven law lecturers from Thammasat University[34] – have become known for their critical attitude toward the legal–military alliance. On the fifth anniversary of the September 2006 coup, they issued a set of proposals contesting the legality of the coup. They notably recommended annulment of its legal consequences and cancellation of acts and laws based on its legality and of amnesties for coup-makers, which would have paved the way for their prosecution. They referred to similar processes in Germany after the fall of the Third Reich, in France after the Vichy Regime, in Turkey, and in Greece (Nittirat 2010). They insisted that the process of automatically legalizing successful *coups d'état* was the very cause of the vicious cycle of Thai politics. Outlawing such coups would put an end to that vicious cycle (Nittirat 2010: 15). Earlier, they had criticized the closing down of the Thai Rak Thai Party and several other controversial

Constitutional Court rulings. In 2011, the Nittirat group also launched a campaign against the *lèse-majesté* law.[35] This launched a wave of hatred against the informal leader of the group, Vorajet Pakeerat. Because he had formerly received the Ananda Mahidol scholarship,[36] he was criticized for being "ungrateful" to the monarchy which had given him the opportunity to study abroad. Among jurists, his behavior was considered deviant. In his case, however, cooptation by the military-bureaucratic regime had clearly failed. On September 30, 2012, Nittirat organized a seminar on the role of Thai jurists in sustaining military rule. Prominent intellectual Kasien Tejapira was invited to talk about "Jurists and *Coups d'État*." Comparing the relationship between jurists and coups to a rotten coffin and a rotten ghost, he pointed to the responsibility of jurists in making coups a "natural" feature of Thai politics by endorsing them.[37]

## Conclusion

Military rulers resort to constitutions for several reasons but mainly because constitutions act as operating manuals for subordinates and because they serve as window-dressing for both citizens and the international community. Constitutions allow leaders to reinforce their power by legitimizing their rule. As authoritarian constitutions, they ensure regime survival by neutralizing possible threats.

The Thai 1997, 2007, and draft 2015 constitutions embrace constitutionalism to the extent that they create the conditions for limited government, separation of powers, and some protection of individual rights. However, this constitutionalism is illiberal in that it does not rest on the idea of a neutral state, which is necessary to support liberal constitutionalism. The idea of the national good, enshrined in the country's "Nation, Religion, King" ideology, calls for actively militant citizens and state institutions. The military in the 1950s assumed this militant role of promoting the country's ideology through a form of despotic paternalism (*Tak Chaloemtiarana*); supported by legal elites, it lasted for almost half a century. Since 1992, when the military became discredited, the leading role has passed to jurists sitting in post-political institutions, with the military now the junior partner in the alliance.

The use of academics to lay the legal foundations for Thai authoritarianism is not a new phenomenon, but in the past decade it has taken on new, more sophisticated, forms. The word *nettiborikorn*, initially crafted in the 2000s to refer to legal experts advising politicians, now seems to refer specifically to Meechai Reechupan, Vishnu Khruangam, and Bowornsak Uwanno – academics involved in drafting pro-military constitutions following the 2006 and 2014 coups. Elite socialization processes in Thailand make legal–military cooperation easy. There is no doubt that the Thai state has planned for such connections between legal elites and military officers, from the formal education system (the National Defense College) through to the highest level (the Privy Council). As members of the bureaucratic elite, the two groups share preferences and values derived from the nationalist-royalist ideology (Thongchai Winnichakul 2001).

Occurring in times of crisis, constitution-making is driven by the passions and interests of those doing the drafting (Elster 1995). One passion which legal and military elites share is distrust of elected politicians and fear that "parliamentary dictactorship" would endanger the status quo. Both elites need a constitution that entrenches the status quo behind a democratic façade which will make it acceptable to the public and to the international community.

Because law is an applied science it is subject to conflict of interests, especially, when boundaries between the academic and professional fields are permeable. Law is being taught in an absolutely pro-regime manner because professors live off the jobs offered by a regime sustained by the theories the academics have built. There are now chains of legitimization between producers of normative legal discourse (legal academics) and practitioners (justices, high-level civil servants, members of independent organizations, appointed senators). Jurists are core agents of the interplay, involved as they are in both norms production and application. Their shared interests and preferences have created a fluid system for developing norms and their use. As a result, there is now considerable coordination between legal norms producers and practitioners in independent organizations. Legal committees for political reform, constitution-drafting committees, and assemblies have "bought" academics into the Thai system for sustained crisis.

Similarly, frequent constitutional change has fostered high levels of legal–military integration cemented in a common "business of political crisis." The business of staging *coups d'état* has produced a division of labor between jurists and military officers. Indeed, those staging coups need legal services to be successful both at the stage of constitution-making and in later constitutional practice. In exchange, military coups bypass the judiciary – rare attempts to affect the courts were unsuccessful – and inversely, judges do not rule against military coups. Thus is the status quo preserved and the resilience of the military-bureaucratic regime reinforced. As the history of Thailand demonstrates, military rulers can succeed in entrenching their interests through "real" constitutionalism, namely by constitutionalizing limited government.

## Acknowledgments

This chapter is based on research partially funded by the German-Southeast Asian Center of Excellence for Public Policy and Good Governance, Faculty of Law, Thammasat University, Bangkok. I thank Piyabutr Saengkanokkul for his invaluable comments, and Bjoern Dressel and Marco Bünte for their review of earlier drafts.

## Notes

1 The following is a list of military prime ministers and how they came to power. 1933–1937: Colonel Phraya Pahon Phonpayuhasena, appointed; 1938–1944: Marshal Plaek Phibulsongkhram, appointed; 1946–1947: Admiral Tawan Thamrongnawasawat, elected; 1948–1957: Marshal Plaek Phibulsongkhram; 1958: Genral Thanom

Kittikachorn, coup; 1959–1963: Marshal Sarit Thanarat, coup; 1963–1973: Marshal Thanom Kittikachorn, coup; 1976: Admiral Sangat Chaloryu, coup; 1977–1980: General Kriangsak Chomanan, coup; 1980–1988: General Prem Tinsulanond, elected; 1988–1991: General Chatichai Choonhavan, elected; 1991: General Sunthorn Kongsompong, coup; 1992: General Suchinda Kraprayoon, coup; 1996–1997: General Chavalit Yongchaiyuth, elected; 2006: General Sonthi Boonyaratglin, coup; 2006–2008: General Surayud Chulanont, appointed; 2014 to present: General Prayuth Chan-ocha, coup.

2 The longest period between a coup and promulgation of a constitution occurred in 1971. The coup by Thanom Kittikachorn was staged on November 17, 1971 and the 1972 constitution was promulgated on December 15, 1972. In addition, in 1958 Thailand lived without any constitution for three months. The coup by Sarit Thanarat was staged on October 20, 1958 and the temporary charter was promulgated on January 28, 1959. In 2006, the coup by Sonthi Boonyaratglin was staged on September 19 and the 2006 constitution was promulgated on October 1, 2006. Lastly, in 2014, Prayuth Chan-Ocha seized power on May 22, 2014, and the interim constitution was promulgated on July 22, 2014.

3 The following constitutions provide for neither elections nor political parties: 1947, 1959, 1972, 1976, 1977, 1991a, 2006, 2014.

4 The following constitutions allowed limited popular representation: 1932a, 1932b, 1949, 1968, 1978, 1991b, 2007, draft 2015.

5 The following constitutions were fully democratic: 1946, 1974, 1997.

6 Under the 2007 constitution, 74 members of the 150-member Senate were appointed by a seven-member committee consisting of the President of the Constitutional Court, the Chairman of the Election Commission, the Chairman of the Ombudsmen, the President of the National Counter Corruption Commission, the Chairman of the State Audit Commission, one judge from the Administrative Court, and one judge from the Supreme Administrative Court (Article 113 of the constitution). As of April 2015, the draft 2015 constitution provides for a fully appointed Senate.

7 In May 1992, a mass protest against the government of General Suchinda Kraprayoon took place in central Bangkok. Repression left more than 50 dead and hundreds injured. Thousands were arrested. Following a royal intervention, Sunchinda issued an amnesty for protesters and resigned as prime minister.

8 Independent organizations were given quasi-judicial powers over politicians and bureaucrats. The 1997 constitution also created a system of administrative courts (Klein 1998).

9 See Article 257 of the 1997 constitution.

10 The 2015 draft constitution notably proposes the creation of a National Ethics Committee and the merging of the Ombudsman and the National Human Rights Commission.

11 See note 8.

12 According to Karl Loewenstein, there are three types of constitution: nominal, semantic, and normative. The nominal constitution does not correspond to reality: it is nothing more than a window-dressing attempt. The semantic constitution is used to legalize dictatorial power. The normative constitution is the only "real" constitution: it is enforced and severely limits government power.

13 See note 15.

14 Extraterritoriality is the state of being exempted from the jurisdiction of local law. In 1855, Siam conceded extraterritoriality rights to British subjects as part of the Bowring Treaty. Nationals of other countries were progressively granted similar rights in bilateral treaties with Siam. For most of the second half of the nineteenth century up until World War I, Siam conceded extraterritoriality rights to colonial powers and Japan on its soil.

15 Appointment as Privy Councilor can be revoked at the discretion of the monarch. In practice, they serve for life. Privy Councilor is the most secure, prestigious position in the Thai system. The Privy Council and its members stay when the regime changes and constitutions are overthrown. That is why the Privy Council has become the horizon for bureaucrats, whether they are military or civilian.

16 Born in Songkhla in the South of Thailand, he entered the Royal Thai Military Academy in 1941. He became a member of the constitution-drafting committee in 1959. He served as appointed prime minister in 1980 to 1988 and was later appointed to the Privy Council. He became its president in 1998, a post he still held in 2015. His progression through the military, constitution-drafting, premiership, and the Privy Council enabled him to build connections not only within the military but also with legal elites.

17 Thanin Kraivichien studied law at Thammasat University and graduated in 1948. He continued his legal studies at the London School of Economics before returning to Thailand to become a judge. While he was a judge on the Supreme Court, he taught law at Chulalongkorn and Thammasat Universities in Bangkok. Following the October 1976 massacre at Thammasat University, the king appointed him prime minister (1976–1977). In 1977, he was toppled by a coup staged by Sangad Chaloryu. The same year, the king appointed him to the Privy Council. As a Privy Councilor, he held a concurrent position in the Office of the Judiciary, responsible for supervising the careers of judges, for seven years (1978–1985). Thus, throughout his life, he simultaneously held multiple positions that made him a keystone of judicial elite–legal academic integration on the one hand and legal–military integration on the other.

18 One could mention one of the fathers of legal theory in Thailand, Sanya Thammasak, who was also appointed to the Privy Council. Sanya served as president of the Supreme Court (1968–1973). He was also dean of the Faculty of Law and chancellor of Thammasat University (1971–1973). After the October 1973 democracy movement at Thammasat, the king appointed Sanya prime minister. In 1974 he served as vice-president of the Constitutional Drafting Committee. In 1975 the king appointed him president of the Privy Council; he was replaced as president by Prem Tinsulanond in 1998. He died in 2002 as a very respected legal scholar elite and Privy Councilor whose law manuals have been used by thousands of law students. Sanya Thammasak was a role model whose career through legal academia, the judiciary, prime ministership, up until the Privy Council was emulated by others, especially young law students – among them the future Thai legal elite.

19 As in the permanent constitutions of 1932, 1948, 1959, 1997, and 2007.

20 Prior to 1992, among prominent post-coup constitution-drafters were Sompop Hotrakit from the Council of State and Phraya Attakareeniphon from the Courts of Justice.

21 For a list of drafters by constitution until 1977, see Bandit Chantarochanakit, **ชีวประวัติธรรมนูญการปกครอง และรัฐธรรรมนูญแห่งราชอาณาจักรไทย พ.ศ.** 2475–2520 [Constitutional and Charter History, 1932–77], 2007. Academic paper 607, Thailand Research Fund.

22 It was initially a paragraph of Article 264/265. See **รายงานการประชุมคณะกรรมาธิการพิจารณาร่างรัฐธรรมนูญ วันอังคารที่** 24 **มิถุนายน** 2540 [Report on the [2nd] CDC meeting on Tuesday, June 24, 1997].

23 This paragraph was opposed by many CDC members, notably CDC Secretary-General Bowornsak Uwanno, who feared it would give too much power to the Constitutional Court. For more details see Mérieau (2014).

24 **รายงานการดำเนินงานของคณะกรรมาธิการยกร่างรัฐธรรมนูญ สภาร่างรัฐธรรมนูญ, สำนักกรรมธิการ** 3 [Report on the Proceedings of the Constitution-drafting Committee of the Constitution-drafting Assembly, Third Committee], March 9, 2007.

25 The proposal was made on June 18, 2006 by Sewot Thinkul. See **รายงานการประชุมสภาร่างรัฐธรรมนูญ ครั้งที่** 27/2550 [Constitution-drafting Assembly Minutes, 27th Session], June 18, 2007.
26 For details on the 2006 crisis, see Nelson (2006, 2007); see also Dressel (2010).
27 The army first declared martial law on May 20, 2014. On May 22, 2014, it announced on national television that it was a military *coup d'état*. On the 2014 coup, see International Crisis Group (2014).
28 See Mérieau (2014).
29 According to Vishnu Khruangam and Bowornsak Uwanno, this was prompted by the fact that politicians had sought to sue the coup-makers for treason (*kabot*). See Bowornsak Uwanno and Vishnu Khruangam (1977).
30 Quoted in Preechasinlapakun (2013).
31 Quoted in Varayudej (2014).
32 Ibid.
33 Bowornsak Uwanno, law professor at Chulalongkorn University, was the Secretary-General of the 1997 Constitution-Drafting Committee. He was, with Meechai Reechupan and Vishnu Khruangam, one of the drafters of the 2006 temporary charter. In 2014 he was appointed president of the 2015 Constitution-Drafting Commission.
34 Nittirat ("enlightened jurists") is composed of Vorajet Pakeerat, Piyabutr Saengkanokkul, Sawatree Suki, Jantajira Iammyura, Teera Suthiwarangkun, Thapanan Nipithakul, and Poonthep Sirinupong. Nittirat critics would say they are still prisoners of a culture of "hyperlegalism" (McCargo 1998) that prevails in Thai society, since they advocate for constitution-making as a cure to Thailand's problems. On Nittirat, see McCargo and Tanruangporn (2015).
35 The *lèse-majesté* law punishes insults to the monarchy. According to Article 112 of the Thai Penal Code: "Whoever defames, insults or threatens the King, Queen, the Heir-apparent or the Regent, shall be punished with imprisonment of three to fifteen years."
36 One of the institutions building gratitude toward the bureaucratic regime is the state scholarship system in Thailand. The best students in all fields can take examinations to win a scholarship to study abroad. Once their studies are completed, they must come back to Thailand and work for the state. One of the scholarships is provided by the Ananda Mahidol Foundation, created in 1955 by King Rama IX. It sends numerous students to further their studies in Europe and the United States. Through the system of scholarships, socialization, and training, legal-military elites are coopted by the regime. As a result, the legal-military elites share a high degree of regime support that in turn reinforces their integration and degree of consensus.
37 See a summary of the speech on the Prachatai website, "Summarizing Kasien Tejapira's Keynote Speech on Thai Lawyers and Coups d'Etat", **สรุปปาฐกถาเกษียร เตชะพีระ**: **นักกฎหมายไทยกับการรัฐประหาร** available at: www.prachatai.com/journal/2012/09/42903 (accessed April 15, 2015).

## Bibliography


Boonmee Thirayuth (2006). **ตุลาการภิวัฒน์** [Judicial Review]. Bangkok, Winyuchon.

Chaloemtiarana, T. (2007). *Thailand: The Politics of Despotic Paternalism*. Chiang Mai, Silkworm. First published Bangkok, Thammasat University, 1979.

Chamarik Saneh (1986). **การเมืองไทยกับการพัฒนาการรัฐธรรมนูญ** [Thai Politics and Constitutional Development]. Bangkok, Textbook Project.

Chambers, P. (2010). "U Turn to the Past? The Resurgence of the Military in Contemporary Thai Politics." In *Democracy under Stress, Civil–Military Relations in South and Southeast Asia*, eds P. Chambers and A. Croissant. Bangkok, ISIS, pp. 63–101.

Chambers, P. (2014a). "Constitutional Changes and Security Forces in Southeast Asia: Lessons from Thailand and Myanmar." *Contemporary Southeast Asia*, 36(1): 101–128.

Chambers, P. (2014b). "Obstacles to Civilian Control of the Security Sector in Thailand." *Middle East Institute*, online, March 18, 2014, available at: www.mei.edu/content/obstacles-civilian-control-security-sector-thailand (accessed April 15, 2015).

Chantarochanakit Bandit (2007). **ชีวประวัติธรรมนูญการปกครอง และรัฐธรรมนูญแห ?missing character?งราชอาณาจักรไทย พ.ศ.** 2475–2520 [Constitutional and Charter History, 1932–1977]. Academic paper 607, Thailand Research Fund.

Connors, M.K. (2008). "Article of Faith: The Failure of Royal Liberalism in Thailand." *Journal of Contemporary Asia*, 38(1): 143–165.

Dressel, B. (2010). "Judicialization of Politics or Politicization of the Judiciary? Considerations from Recent Events in Thailand." *The Pacific Review*, 23(5): 671–691.

Dressel, B. and Bünte, M. (2014). "Constitutional Politics in Southeast Asia: From Contestation to Constitutionalism?" *Contemporary Southeast Asia*, 36(1): 1–23.

Elliott, D. (1978). *Thailand: Origins of Military Rule*. London, Zed Books.

Elster, J. (1995). "Forces and Mechanisms in the Constitution-Making Process." *Duke Law Journal*, 45: 364–396.

Ginsburg, T. (2003). *Judicial Review in New Democracies, Constitutional Courts in Asian Cases*. Cambridge, Cambridge University Press.

Ginsburg, T. (2009). "Constitutional Afterlife, The Continuing Impact of Thailand's Post-political Constitution." *International Journal of Constitutional Law*, January, University of Chicago, Public Law Working Paper No. 252, Center on Law and Globalization Research Paper No. 09–04.

Ginsburg, T. and Moustafa, T. (2008). *Rule by Law. The Politics of Courts in Authoritarian Regimes*. Cambridge, Cambridge University Press.

Ginsburg, T. and Simpser, A. (2013). *Constitutions in Authoritarian Regimes*. Cambridge, Cambridge University Press.

Harding, A. and Bureekul, T. (2008). *Constitution Reform, Comparative Perspectives*. Nonthaburi, KPI.

Harding, A. and Leyland, P. (2011). *The Constitutional System of Thailand*. New York, Hart Publishing.

Harding, A. and Nicholas, P. (2010). *New Courts in Asia*. London, Routledge.

Hewison, K. (2010). "Thailand's Conservative Democratization." In *East Asia's New Democracies, Deepening, Reversal, Non-Liberal Alternatives*, eds Chu Yin-Wah and Wong Siu-lun. New York, Routledge.

Hirschl, R. (2004). *Towards Juristocracy, The Origins and Consequences of the New Constitutionalism*. Cambridge, MA, Harvard University Press.

Hirschl, R. (2008). "The Judicialization of Mega-Politics and the Rise of Political Courts." *Annual Review of Political Science*, 11: 93–118.

Huntington, S. (1957). *The Soldier and the State: The Theory and Politics of Civil–Military Relations*. Cambridge, Cambridge University Press.

Huntington, S. (1968). *Political Order in Changing Societies*. New Haven, CT: Yale University Press.

International Crisis Group (2014). "A Coup Ordained, Thailand's Prospects for Stability." Asia Report no. 63, December 3, 2014, available at: www.crisisgroup.org/~/media/Files/asia/south-east-asia/thailand/263-a-coup-ordained-thailand-s-prospects-for-stability.pdf (accessed April 15, 2015).

Ivarsson, S. and Isager, L. (2010). *Saying the Unsayable, Monarchy and Democracy in Thailand*. Copenhagen, NIAS.

Kasetsiri Charnvit (2007). 1 ศตวรรษทหารกับการเมืองไทย [One Ccntury of the Military and Thai Politics]. In ทหารกับการเมืองในอุษาคเนย์ [The Military and Politics in Southeast Asia]. Bangkok, Textbooks Project, pp. 31–42.

King Prajadhipok's Institute (2006). *Anniversary of 60th Year of Accession to the Throne Years of Thai Politics*. Nonthaburi, KPI.

Klein, J. (1998). "The Constitution of the Kingdom of Thailand, 1997: A Blueprint for Participatory Democracy." The Asia Foundation Working Paper Series, available at: http://aceproject.org/ero-en/regions/asia/TH/AsiaFoundationThailand.pdf (accessed April 15, 2015).

Klein, J. and Raksasataya, A. (2003). *The Constitutional Court of Thailand, The Provisions and the Working of the Court*. Bangkok.

Kullada Kesboochoo Mead (2004). *The Rise and Decline of Thai Absolutism*. New York, Routledge.

McCargo, D. (1998). "Alternative Meanings of Political Reform in Contemporary Thailand." *Copenhagen Journal of Asian Studies*, 13: 5–30.

McCargo, D. (2005). "Network Monarchy and Legitimacy Crisis in Thailand." *The Pacific Review*, 18(4): 499–518.

McCargo, D. (2008). "State of Anxiety." *Southeast Asian Affairs*, 2008: 333–356.

McCargo, D. and Tanruangporn, P. (2015). "Branding Dissent: Nittirat, Thailand's Enlightened Jurists." *Journal of Contemporary Asia*, 45(2): 419–442.

Mérieau, E. (2014a). "Thai Juristocracy." *New Mandala*, May.

Mérieau E. (2014b). "Hegemonic Self-Preservation Attempt by the Thai Military, the Agony of the Thai Deep State." *Perspectives Internationales*, available at: http://perspectivesinternationales.com/?p=1131 (accessed April 15, 2015).

Nelson, M. (2006). "Political Turmoil in Thailand: Thaksin, Protests, Elections, and the King." *eastasia.at*, 5(1): 1–22.

Nelson, M. (2007). "Thaksin Overthrown: Thailand's 'Well-intentioned' Coup of September 19, 2006." *eastasia.at*, 6(1): 1–16.

Nittirat (2010). คูมือประชาชนล้มรประหาร [Popular Guide for the Annulment of the Coup d'Etat].

Office of the Ombudsmen (2007). บทบาทขององค์กรตามรัฐธรรมนูญในการพัฒนาประเทศ [The Role of Constitutional Organizations in Developing the Country]. Bangkok, Office of the Ombudsmen.

Preechasinlapakun, S. (2013). "Dynamics and Institutionalization of Coups in the Thai Constitution." VRF Series, no. 483, July.

Rathamarit, N. (2006). *Eyes on Thai Democracy, KPI Yearbook 3*. Nonthaburi, KPI.

Riggs, F. (1966). *Thailand: The Modernization of a Bureaucratic Polity*. Honolulu, East-West Center Press.

Saengkanokkul, P. (2007). พระราชอำนาจ องคมนตรีและผู้มีบรมีนอกรัฐธรรมนูญ [Royal Power, Privy Council, and "Charismatic Persons Outside the Constitution]. Bangkok, Openbooks.

Saengkanokkul, P. (2009). ในพระปรมาภิไธย ประชาธิปไตยและตุลาการ [In the Name of the King, Democracy and the Judiciary]. Bangkok, Openbooks.

Samudavanija, C-A. (1982). *The Thai Young Turks*. Singapore, Institute of Southeast Asian Studies.

Tanchai, W. (2007). *Exploring the 2007 Constitution, KPI Yearbook 4*. Nonthaburi, KPI.

Tate, N.C. and Vallinder, T. (2005). *The Global Expansion of Judicial Power*. New York, New York University Press.

Uwanno, B. (2006). *Principles of a Righteous King and the King of Thailand*. Bangkok, Chulalongkorn University.

Uwanno, B. (2007). **กฎหมายมหาชน** [Public Law], vol. 2. Bangkok, Chulalongkorn University.

Uwanno, B. (2009). *Economic Crisis and Political Crisis in Thailand: Past and Present*. Nonthaburi, KPI.

Uwanno, B. and Vishnu, K. (1977). **ธรรมนูญการปกครองราชอาณาจักร** 2520 [The 1977 Charter]. Bangkok.

Varayudej, S. (2014). "The Quest for Constitutionalism, the Rule of Law and Democracy in Thailand." In *Comparative Constitutionalism, 82 Years of Constitutional Reform and Democratic Developments in Thailand*, ed. S. Varyudej and J. Brohmer. Bangkok, P. Press.

Winnichakul, T. (2001). **ประวัติศาสตร์ไทยแบบราชาชาตินิยม** [Thai Nationalist-Royalist History]. *Arts and Culture*, 23, no. 1, November.

## Primary sources

- **รายงานการประชุมคณะกรรมาธิการยกร่างรัฐธรรมนูญ วันอังคารที่** 11 **กุมภาพันธ์** 2540 [Report on the CDC Meeting on Tuesday, February 11, 1997].
- **รายงานการประชุมคณะกรรมาธิการพิจารณาร่างรัฐธรรมนูญ วันอังคารที่** 24 **มิถุนายน** 2540 [Report on the [2nd] CDC Meeting on Tuesday, June 24, 1997].
- **รายงานการดำเนินงานของคณะกรรมาธิการยกร่างรัฐธรรมนูญ สภาร่างรัฐธรรมนูญ, สำนักกรรมธิการ** 3 [Report on the Proceedings of the Constitution-Drafting Committee of the Constitution-Drafting Assembly, Third Committee].
- **รายงานการประชุมสภาร่างรัฐธรรมนูญ ครั้งที่** 15/2550 (**เป็นพิเศษ**) **วันพฤหัสบดีที่** 30 **เมษายน** 2550 [Report on the Meeting of the Constitution-Drafting Assembly, 16th Session (Special Session) on Thursday, April 30, 2007].
- **รายงานการประชุมสภาร่างรัฐธรรมนูญ ครั้งที่** 27/2550 [Report on the Meeting of the Constitution-Drafting Assembly, 27th Session on June 18, 2007].

## Speeches

Kasien Tejapira, **นักกฎหมายไทยกับการรัฐประหาร** [Thai Jurists and *Coups d'Etat*]. Faculty of Law, Thammasat University, Bangkok, September 30, 2012.

Piyabutr Saengkanokkul, "The Rise of Royalist Jurists in Thailand." Paper presented at the GRIPS Conference held in Tokyo on November 26, 2014.

# Part III

# Constitutions and human rights

# 8 Human rights in Southeast Asia

## From contestation to compliance?

*Marco Bünte*

### Introduction

In the late 1980s and 1990s, Southeast Asian state leaders were not only reluctant to acknowledge the universality of human rights; they also criticized the West for imposing its conceptions of rights onto Asia. Malaysian Prime Minister Mahathir Mohamad, Indonesian President Suharto, Singaporean Prime Minister Lee Kuan Yew, among others, argued that human rights are culturally specific and Asian societies have a "unique," "special" set of values that does not fit with Western human rights ideals (Christie 1995; Mauzy 1997; Thompson 2001, Peerenboom 2003). They also accused the West of embarking on a new form of colonialism. In what finally became known as the "Asian values debate" they argued that Asian societies place much greater emphasis on the community than on the individual and privilege order, and on social harmony over personal freedom. They also claimed that stability and economic development are necessary preconditions for political rights and democratization – thus reversing the notion of "first-generation" and "second-generation" rights often used in Western discourses, which put civil and political rights in the first place. Accordingly, the Asian values debate – though often descending into blunt culturalist assumptions and self-serving rhetoric – has revealed a genuine normative contestation over rights in the region (Christie 1995; Mauzy 1997; Eldridge 2002; Thompson 2001; Kingsbury 2009).

Although the Asian values debate slipped off the public agenda during the Asian financial crisis in 1997/1998, controversies over human rights remained. Political struggles played out as a multilayered contest over state and regime authority between numerous actors. While civil societies in the region have shown a strong commitment to universalism and began to advocate for human rights as early as the late 1980s and early 1990s (Gomez and Ramcharan 2012), most authoritarian states only reluctantly addressed human rights issues.

Yet much has changed since the late 1990s. While human rights issues became much more important, particularly in light of growing state abuses, the discourse became more standardized, reflecting an increasingly globalized norm. In the first decade of the new millennium, Southeast Asian states seem to have taken substantial steps toward human rights. A number of states have established

National Human Rights Institutions (NRHI). Regionally, the new ASEAN Charter of 2007 listed human rights as a fundamental goal of the organization and called for the establishment of a regional human rights body. In 2009, Southeast Asian states created the ASEAN Intergovernmental Commission on Human Rights and, in 2012, they released the ASEAN Human Rights Declaration (Renshaw 2013; Ciorciari 2012). All these developments seem to indicate that human rights are now firmly embedded in the political discourse of the region, and human rights are on the political agenda of Southeast Asian states. Have these developments also improved the human rights situation in the region?

This chapter aims to give a more nuanced view of human rights compliance in Southeast Asia. I argue that the commitment of most Southeast Asian states to human rights is still rhetorical or tactical, and there continues to be a deep divide between ratified standards and actual rights practice. Compliance is conceptualized as a continuum involving, in sequential steps, the ratification of human rights treaties, the fulfillment of reporting requests by supervisory bodies, the implementation of norms in domestic law and rule-consistent behavior on the domestic level (Kent 1999: 236; Risse and Sikking 1999). While there is a general consensus in the literature that the commitment to the international human rights system[1] has consistently increased, there is still much debate over how to explain gaps between rhetorical and actual compliance understood as rule-consistent behavior. Some human rights scholars have maintained that non-compliance and "decoupling" between norms and behavior is the rule (Hafner-Burton and Tsutsui 2005), while others contend that international institutions and transnational advocacy networks are effective in socializing states into rule-consistent behavior (Risse and Sikking 1999; Jetschke 2011). Recently, scholars have also emphasized that National Human Rights Institutions (NHRI) may play an important role in increasing state compliance (Cole and Ramirez 2013). They are meant to serve as a bridge between international human rights law and domestic human rights practice, and to help localize human rights. This chapter demonstrates that this optimistic view is misplaced and political conflicts about human rights are still fought – not in the international arena between the West and Asian societies, but between local civil societies, domestic human rights institutions, and the various authoritarian regimes in Southeast Asia.

The chapter proceeds as follows. First, it provides an overview of compliance, which is understood as the ratification of major human rights instruments. It is shown that increasingly more states in Southeast Asia have signed the most important treaties of the international human rights regime. Second, the analysis shifts to the origin, mandate, and impact of National Human Rights Institutions (NHRI) that have been established in the last two decades. I discuss how they translate international human rights law into a domestic human rights landscape. Finally, human rights practices are analyzed using data from Freedom House (FH) and the Political Terror Scale (PTS). Moreover, this chapter also looks at the reports of the Universal Periodic Review in order to illustrate the major human rights concerns of Southeast Asian states.

## Southeast Asia's human rights commitment

### *Ratification of major human rights treaties*

When we look at the ratification of human rights treaties over time, we see a growing commitment of Southeast Asian states to these global instruments (see Figure 8.1; Mohamad 2002; Davies 2012). Although ratification has been fairly steady, we can also identify some significant periods of non-activity and non-ratification. These were longer in earlier periods (1975–1980; 1987–1989), when the consequences of human rights treaty ratification were less well known. The most recent period of inactivity, from 1998 to 2003, may be explained by the Asian economic crisis and its aftermath, when countries were still struggling to cope with the social and political effects of the crisis. There have also been times of unusually high activity, such as in 1992, when Cambodia signed nearly all human rights treaties due to the mandate of the 1991 Paris Peace Agreements, which pushed the country to follow basic human rights standards. Another input stems from Indonesia's democratization after 1999. Altogether, the bulk of ratifications have been signed in the past 15 years (23 of 58). This clearly shows a growing commitment toward human rights in the region. By the end of 2013, Southeast Asian states had ratified two-thirds (67 percent) of all human rights documents.

Although we have to acknowledge this overall positive trend, it should also be put into perspective, since the support for the different treaties varies

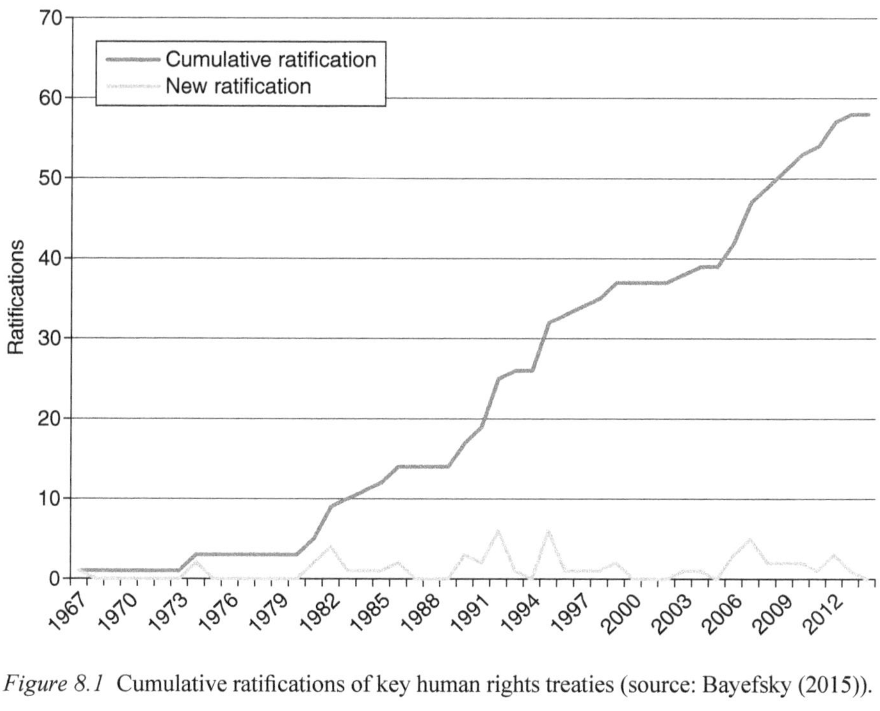


*Figure 8.1* Cumulative ratifications of key human rights treaties (source: Bayefsky (2015)).

tremendously (see Table 8.2). The CEDAW, the CRPD, and the CRC are the only treaties that have been signed by all Southeast Asian countries; the ratification of these treaties was also carried out quite quickly. All Southeast Asian states ratified the CRC within six years. Davies points to the historical significance of women's issues for the Southeast Asian states which hosted the ASEAN Women Leaders Conference in 1975 and formed the ASEAN Sub-Committee on Women in 1976. Interpreted in a more negative light, both of these issues may be regarded "qualitatively differently from human rights generally" (Davies 2012: 418f.) and, tellingly, other more contested and political human rights treaties – such as the CERD, the CESR, and the CCPR – have been signed by only six countries. From the "older" treaties the CAT enjoys the least support, and only half of Southeast Asian states have signed and ratified it.

While these general developments help discern important trends in the compliance of human rights instruments in Southeast Asia, they do not tell us much about the commitment of individual states to human rights. The support for human rights broadly correlates with regime type, since the region's democracies have signed significantly more treaties (Sorpong 2014). As is to be expected, Indonesia, the sole unqualified democracy in the region, has signed all treaties since its democratization in 1999. Apart from Indonesia, only Cambodia has signed all human rights treaties, since the 1991 Paris Accords mandated that the country follow global human rights standards. The Philippines and Thailand, which during the 1990s also experimented with more democratic forms of governance (before the coups of 2006 and 2014 reversed this development), also join this leading group. Interestingly, following these more democratic states we already find authoritarian Laos and Vietnam, although the latter signed the majority of human rights treaties in the early 1980s. The main proponents of the Asian values position, Singapore and Malaysia, have signed only three treaties – together with Myanmar (see Table 8.1).

## Weak compliance: reservations, reporting, and optional protocols

Despite these commitments, however, Southeast Asian states have put forward a number of reservations and declarations to the treaties they have signed, which cast their real commitment into question. Davies has examined these reservations and demonstrated that Southeast Asian states specifically hesitate to comply in three areas. First, they do not comply when their political and/or territorial sovereignty is involved. For instance, in a declaration to the CCPR, both Indonesia and Laos emphasized that the issue of self-determination and territorial integrity should be interpreted in accordance with international law governing friendly relations. Second, some states (Brunei, Indonesia, and Thailand) have objected to any form of mandatory arbitration of state disputes. A third area of reservation involves ensuring the primacy of national law, culture, and religion in any interpretation of the treaty. A number of states (Indonesia, Brunei, and Laos) have rejected several aspects of the treaties because they were not in line with their constitutions or their national cultures (Davies 2014: 420). These

*Table 8.1* Date of ratification of major human rights treaties

| *States* | *CERD 1965* | *CESCR 1966* | *CCPR 1966* | *CEDAW 1979* | *CAT 1984* | *CRC 1989* | *CPMW 1990* | *CRPD 2006* | *ICCPED 2006* |
|---|---|---|---|---|---|---|---|---|---|
| Brunei | | | | 2006 | | 1995 | | 2007S | |
| Cambodia | 1983 | 1992 | 1992 | 1992 | 1992 | 1992 | 2004 | 2007 | 1993 |
| Indonesia | 1999 | 2006 | 2006 | 1984 | 1998 | 1990 | 2012 | 2011 | 2010 |
| Laos | 1974 | 2007 | 2009 | 1981 | 2012 | 1991 | | 2009 | 2008 |
| Malaysia | | | | 1995 | | 1995 | | 2010 | |
| Myanmar | | | | 1997 | | 1991 | | 2011 | |
| Philippines | 1967 | 1974 | 1986 | 1981 | 1986 | 1990 | 1995 | 2008 | |
| Singapore | | | | 1995 | | 1995 | | 2013 | |
| Thailand | 2003 | 1999 | 1996 | 1985 | 2007 | 1992 | | 2008 | 2012 |
| Vietnam | 1982 | 1982 | 1982 | 1982 | | 1990 | | 2007 | |

Source: Bayefsky.com.

reservations seem to be brought forward to subvert or avoid certain treaty obligations – a pattern Linton documented for the ratification of CEDAW (Linton 2008). Despite the global rhetorical commitment toward human rights treaties, a look at Southeast Asian states' reservations reveals that some aspect of this commitment may be tactical or strategic.

This interpretation is confirmed when we look into reporting requirements. Each of the treaties mentioned above has certain compliance mechanisms, the main one being the creation of a committee to examine periodic reports, submitted by parties to these treaties, on the level of compliance with their provisions (see Table 8.2). Southeast Asian states have submitted 123 of the 193 required reports (64 percent). Rich argues that the reason for this may be the lacking state capacity to draft these reports, which sometimes requires technical and bureaucratic expertise and therefore does not necessarily reflect a lack of commitment to the human rights framework (Rich 2012).

Serious doubts about the commitment of Southeast Asian states to the international human rights regime, however, arise when we look at the status of optional protocols. Four of the six treaties have mechanisms with far more intrusive means of dealing with a nation's lack of compliance, including expert investigation and citizen complaints. These optional protocols have not been supported by Southeast Asian states. The only protocol that has been signed is the extensions to the CRC that focus on children in armed conflict and children as victims of sexual abuse, both of which do not come with the right of individual petition. Only Cambodia, Indonesia, and the Philippines have signed these protocols. Six signatories of the CEDAW have declined to sign the associated optional protocol on individual petition. Only Cambodia, Indonesia, the Philippines, and Thailand have endorsed it – although it has not yet been ratified by the Philippines and Thailand. Six Southeast Asian countries have not signed any optional protocol so far (Brunei, Laos, Malaysia, Myanmar, Singapore, and Vietnam). This hesitation to sign binding protocols with mandatory mechanisms shows a clear reluctance to international monitoring and the enforcement of rights.

*Table 8.2* Compliance with reporting: submission of HR treaty reports by ASEAN countries

| *Country* | *Reports submitted* | *Reports late or outstanding* |
|---|---|---|
| Brunei Darussalam | 1 | 3 |
| Cambodia | 13 | 18 |
| Indonesia | 9 | 8 |
| Laos | 21 | 6 |
| Malaysia | 3 | 2 |
| Myanmar | 5 | 1 |
| Philippines | 31 | 16 |
| Singapore | 4 | 2 |
| Thailand | 9 | 7 |
| Vietnam | 27 | 7 |

Source: UN (2012a, 2012b).

## Transmission belts: national human rights institutions

A different form of compliance is the establishment of National Human Rights Institutions (NHRIs), which are often described as a bridge between international norms and local implementation. NHRIs can become domestic actors in their own right and influence state compliance by challenging the state and mobilizing society (Cardenas 2011). To do this, NHRIs have to fulfill the two key functions of the protection and promotion of human rights. The former refers to the capacity to protect human rights through multiple means, such as processing (individual) complaints, investigating instances of abuse, and holding violators accountable; the latter relates to awareness-building and education in human rights (Cardenas 2011). In order to perform these functions effectively, NHRIs should have a broad mandate, enjoy a certain degree of independence from the executive branch of government, and have sufficient resources and close relations with civil society. This set of minimum standards was endorsed by the UN General Assembly in 1993, and since then has been widely accepted by the international community (Cardenas 2002; Stokke 2007). Five Southeast Asian states have established National Human Rights Commissions: Indonesia, Malaysia, Myanmar, the Philippines, and Thailand. Yet these differ immensely in terms of age, legal background, mandate, composition, and effectiveness.

## Origins and motivations

The establishment of all Commissions was the result of a combination of external and domestic factors. Driven by international norms of human rights, several reform movements within Southeast Asian societies have pushed for these institutions or, alternatively, authoritarian state leaders have intended to signal greater human rights compliance to appease international and domestic critics (Cardenas 2002). International pressure and domestic dynamics have also led to reform of these institutions. The oldest Commission in Southeast Asia is the Filipino Commission on Human Rights (CHR), which was established in the midst of a wave of political liberalization after the fall of President Marcos, in 1986. Driven by international norms and the wish to strengthen human rights, transparency, democracy, and the rule of law, President Aquino made human rights part of her campaign platform. The Commission's mandate was delineated in Article XII (Sections 17–19) of the 1987 constitution, which made it the first constitutionally mandated Human Rights Commission worldwide (Cardenas 2002: 32). In 1998, the mandate of the Commission was broadened, due to international pressure to give it more "teeth" to address ongoing human rights violations in the country (Cardenas 2002: 36).

Indonesia's Human Rights Commission (Komnas HAM) was established in 1993 by the Suharto regime, to deflect criticism of their poor human rights record in the aftermath of the Dili massacre in November 1991. Initiated by presidential decree, it was not only a hopeful symbol of the period of political openness (*keterbukaan*) in the early 1990s but also became a critical voice after this liberalization ended in 1996 (Cardenas 2002; Jetschke 2011: 155; Mohamad 2002: 238; Setiawan 2013). Renewed international pressure following another human rights crisis in East Timor and the country's democratization in 1999 forced the regime to establish a reformed Human Rights Commission. A new law on human rights replaced the 1993 presidential decree, and granted Komnas HAM far greater powers of investigation, research, and the important power of summons. It also brought Komnas HAM's legal status into conformity with the Paris Principles (Setiawan 2013: 47).

Thailand followed Indonesia with the establishment of the Thai National Human Rights Commission in 1999. A broader movement for political reform and good governance led to the promulgation of the liberal 1997 "people's constitution," which included a human rights catalog and called for a National Human Rights Commission (NHRCT) to protect and promote these rights. Following serious discussions about the role of the Commission and its independence from traditional politics, the New Rights Commission Act was enacted in 1999 and the NHRCT was established in July 2001 (Klein 2001; Harding 2006). However, in the wake of the coup against Thaksin, the liberal 1997 constitution was abolished. The new 2007 constitution retained the NHRCT, but "simplified" the selection procedure (see below).

Malaysia's Human Rights Commission (SUHAKAM) was established in 1999. Similar to the Indonesian case, its establishment was intended to deflect Malaysia's poor human rights record following the imprisonment of opposition leader Anwar Ibrahim in 1998. It benefited from the personal commitment of a high-ranking politician Musa Hitam, former deputy prime minister and former chairperson of the United Nations Commission on Human Rights, who later became the first chairman of SUHAKAM. He convinced Prime Minister Mahathir to experiment with a Human Rights Commission (Mohamad 2002: 238; Renshaw *et al.* 2011). Moreover, the foreign minister made certain that SUHAKAM was firmly based on the Paris Principles (Whiting 2003: 75). Finally, the youngest human rights institution is the Myanmar National Human Rights Commission. As part of the guided liberalization initiated by the Thein Sein government, the establishment of a human rights body in September 2011 aimed to send an important message to the international community that the government was willing to reform (Bünte and Portela 2012). However, the National Human Rights Commission was denied funding from the state budget and received financial contributions from the government instead – consequently its independence is more than dubious. The new legal framework for this body was only announced by the government in 2014 and met with strong criticism from civil society, due to the secrecy with which it was written (ANNI 2014).

## Composition, selection method, and mandate

The composition, selection method, and mandate of Southeast Asian National Human Rights Commissions also vary considerably. The Philippines and Thailand established relatively small NHRIs, whereas all the other Commissions comprise more than ten members. The Philippine Human Rights Commission has five members, who are appointed by the president for a period of seven years (Philippines Executive Order No. 163/1987). This allows political considerations to play a role in the selection, although the long tenure and the commissioners' full-time commitment to the position in practice guarantees the independence of their work (Stokke 2007: 8). The members of the Indonesian Human Rights Commission were initially selected by the president from a pool of "prominent national figures." Consequently, the first human rights commissioners were closely connected to members of the Suharto regime; however, the Commission managed to create some space for their work and, as a consequence, became a thorn in the regime's side (Stokke 1997: 17; Setiawan 2013: 42). In 1999, the selection process was modified. No more than 35 members are selected by the House of Representatives, on the recommendation of the plenary of the Commission (Indonesia Law 39/1999). This grants them somewhat more autonomy, although outsiders may find it difficult to gain entry (Stokke 1997: 17). Commissioners are elected for a period of five years and work part time; a reappointment for five years is possible. The Commission also has a nationwide network of branch offices and local commissions. In Malaysia, the Human Rights Commission is appointed by the Yang-Pertuan Agong (the titular head of state), on the recommendation of the prime minister. Until 2009, the tenure of the Commission was two years, with the possibility of reappointment. Candidates should come from a variety of "religious and racial backgrounds" (HRCMA 1999). The selection process gives the prime minister considerable influence. This, along with the short tenure of the commissioners, has raised doubts about the independence of the Commission, and civil society organizations pushed the UN Sub-Committee to downgrade the Malaysian Commission to "B"-level status, due to failed compliance with the Paris Principles.[2] The Malaysian government responded to this in May 2009 and reformed the institution in a bid to ensure SUHAKAM's compliance: SUHAKAM now has up to 20 commissioners, each of whom serves for three years (Renshaw *et al.* 2011: 196). In Thailand, the 11 members of the 1997 National Human Rights Commission (NHRC) were chosen by a Selection Committee consisting of the Supreme Court, the president of the Supreme Administrative Court judge, the president of the Supreme Administrative Court, the prosecutor general, the chairman of the Law Council, rectors or representatives of higher education institutions (five), human rights advocates (ten), politicians (five), and representatives of the public media (three) (Thailand National Human Rights Commission Act 1999). The new constitution of 2007 changed the selection process: The seven members of the NHRCT are selected by the king, with the advice of the Senate from persons with knowledge in the protection of rights. The proximity to the royalist elite and the selection process are signs of a lack of independence, which will not help in easing Thailand's polarization and evolving "human rights crisis" (ANNI 2015).

Myanmar's Human Rights Commission, which does not adhere to the Paris Principles, was chosen in secrecy and without any public consultation, in September 2011. The 15-member Commission, appointed by the president, consists of former ambassadors (three), civil servants (two), professors (three), and former government functionaries. It reflects the ethnic heterogeneity of the country, since the commissioners include Karen, Kachin, Shan, Chin, and Mon members (IBAHRI 2012). The next round of commissioners will be appointed after the 2015 elections. The new law stipulates that candidates be selected by the president on the recommendation of a board, whose members consist primarily of government representatives and two members of registered civil society organizations (ANNI 2014: 15). All in all, states have built up NHRIs, although they face serious difficulties in meeting the transparency and independence standards of the Paris Principles. In particular, the cases of Thailand, Malaysia, and Myanmar highlight the governmental assertion of influence in the selection of commissioners.

There is also a certain degree of variation with regard to the mandate of the individual Commissions. Nearly all mandates of NHRIs are framed with regard to the Paris Principles: to protect and promote human rights. Whereas the Indonesian, Thai, and Philippine Commissions have broader powers to investigate and take up complaints from individuals and groups, the mandates of the Malaysian and especially the Myanmar Commission are more limited. Although SUHAKAM's mandate covers "studies," the task of the Commission is purely to investigate and deliver conclusions to the relevant authorities. It has neither the power to act in court[3] nor powers of enforcement. When it finds that an infringement of human rights has occurred, it may refer the matter and its findings to the relevant authorities. The principal way of doing this consequently is to submit reports to Parliament (Whiting 2003: 77). The Indonesian, Thai, and Philippine NHRIs also possess certain quasi-judicial functions and can investigate past human rights violations. The Myanmar National Human Rights Commission stands out. It currently does not follow the Paris Principles and its mandate is rather narrowly focused on reporting abuses and giving advice to the government on human rights questions.

## Evaluating the impact of Human Rights Commissions

More than a decade ago, Sonia Cardenas concluded that:

> states have permitted these commissions to perform seemingly innocuous tasks, which have resulted in a high level of human rights demands and a growing awareness of human rights norms.... The longer term impact of these institutions is unclear, but it may depend on the extent to which the state is willing and able to meet these demands.
>
> (Cardenas 2002: 48)

Measuring the long-term impact is difficult, given the different regime trajectories in Southeast Asian states and the challenges they present for human rights.[4] When we look at the different human rights institutions from a perspective of socialization, agenda-setting, rule creation, accountability, and networking with civil society, we see that they certainly have different impacts at different times. The functions of these institutions change once countries experience an authoritarian regression (Thailand) or democratic opening (Indonesia).

Although the Philippine National Human Rights Commission looks promising on paper – constitutional foundation, independent selection of commissioners, and a broad mandate – its effectiveness and impact have been described as weak. The Asia-Pacific Human Rights Network concluded, in 2002, that its execution was poor and that civil society had little faith in it, perceiving it as comprising government lackeys (ANNI 2002: 109–118). A decade later the organization came to a similar conclusion: weak leadership, outreach to civil society only through personal (and not systematic) contacts, and little impact (ANNI 2013).

Following its inception by President Suharto in 1993, the Indonesian Human Rights Commission (Komnas HAM) made a significant contribution to the socialization of human rights. The Commission was particularly effective in educational activities, since it provided human rights training for members of the army and the police, for NGOs, and for the press. Given the repressive nature of the Suharto regime, this was novel.[5] Moreover, the most significant achievement in the early years was to highlight the human rights abuses of the military – for instance, in the cases of the murder of the labor activist Marsinah in 1993 and the death of pro-independence activists in East Timor (Liquisa) and West Papua (Timika) in 1995.[6] The reports on these incidents were extraordinary, since the military had never been subjected to criticism from state bodies before, let alone faced an inquiry. Although the security forces involved were not brought to justice and the overall human rights situation did not improve (see below), the detailed accounts of the events and the publicity they generated gave the Commission a high level of public legitimacy, especially in the eyes of civil society representatives (Setiawan 2013: 41f.).

After 1999 the role of Komnas HAM changed as the societal demand for investigating past human rights violations increased. The broader mandate of Komnas HAM and the growing public expectation of bringing human rights cases to court, however, also led to increasing internal divisions and factionalism within the Commission. Members became more aware of the consequences of their work and commissioners began to protect the interests of their organizations of origin. This not only strained the relationship with some NGOs but also had an impact on the effectiveness of the institution (Setiawan 2013: 52).

The Malaysian Human Rights Commission had to operate in a difficult environment, given its limited mandate and the semi-authoritarian character of the regime. In terms of socialization, SUHAKAM could improve the human rights culture, which is still in its infancy in Malaysia. In the words of Thio (2009: 1338):

> As a focal point and venue for human-rights concerns, the existence and operation of Suhakam has affirmed the legitimacy of human-rights concerns as an integral aspect of political discourse. The importance of this cannot be discounted in states where the idea of human rights has been delegitimized by projecting it as an alien, imperialistic discourse.

Public awareness of human rights has been raised in countless workshops; the Commission has also advised the government to sign certain human rights treaties such as ICCP, ICESR, CAT, and two optional protocols to the CRC (Thio 2009: 1300). SUHAKAM managed to broaden its mandate by focusing on socio-economic rights, which is consistent with the economic imperatives of a developing country (Whiting 2003: 82). With regard to accountability and political influence, SUHAKAM's record is mixed. On the one hand, SUHAKAM managed to irritate the government by criticizing some of its actions and pointing to ongoing human rights concerns; for instance, it repeatedly called on the authorities to remedy human rights abuses in relation to land disputes, indigenous peoples, and migrants, and urged respect for the human rights of internal security detainees. Several annual reports also demonstrate an ongoing attempt to push for the abolishment of the Sedition Act (Suhakam 2010, 2013, 2015).[7] Moreover, it held public inquiries over custodial deaths and alleged breaches of associational rights, and has requested to visit detention centers, although it has on occasion been denied access to detainees (Thio 2009: 1303). In addition, and to the surprise of many, it has directly challenged the government on several major human rights issues. For instance, it criticized the police for their brutality in handling certain public demonstrations, such as the Kesas Highway incident in November 2000 or the Bersih demonstrations in 2011. On the other hand, it shied away from very controversial topics and concentrated on "soft issues" only. Sensitive religious or racial questions, such as religious conversion or minority rights, were not addressed, despite the Commission being explicitly asked to do so. Although the Commission has issued recommendations against the demolition of places of worship, these statements have not become starting points from which to develop other relevant activities. Moreover, SUHAKAM has been unwilling to open investigations into individual complaints. Human rights NGOs and individual complainants have criticized the Commission's approach of turning a blind eye to the issue of freedom of religion (Thio 2009: 1321; Renshaw *et al.* 2010: 180; Whiting 2003; Setiawan 2013: 148). Its overall political impact is also limited, since none of SUHAKAM's reports of the past 14 years has been discussed in Parliament. Until 2009, the Malaysian government had never even issued a formal response to the annual reports. Consequently, the Malaysian state has not adequately met the human rights demands of its citizens. In light of this neglect by the government, SUHAKAM has turned to civil society. SUHAKAM has consulted broadly with members of civil society and could increase its legitimacy. Although civil society was initially skeptical and suspicious of the Malaysian government's motives in establishing SUHAKAM and regarded it as mere window-dressing to restore the credibility of the government in the light of serious human rights abuses (Renshaw *et al.* 2011: 185), public pressure from civil society pushed SUHAKAM to be more assertive.

The establishment of the Thai Human Rights Commission "marked a significant shift in the 'indigenisation' of rights and, and therefore the accommodation of rights to national culture" (Connors 2011: 107). As an offspring of the liberal reform period of the 1990s, the NHRC has not only been challenged by Thaksin's "electoral authoritarianism" from 2001 to 2006 but it has also suffered from the increasing polarization in Thai society since 2006. It has been further imperiled by the coups in 2006 and 2014. First, following the 2006 coup, the seven-member Commission was marred by infighting between royalists and opponents of the coup (see Connors 2011: 107f.). Second, in 2015, the military junta appointed new commissioners for the period 2016 to 2022 in secrecy and without any consultation with civil society. Allegedly, the majority of the members of the selection committee were from the military; consequently, it is no wonder that they chose candidates with rather questionable backgrounds, such as the leader of an ultra-royalist group – although he resigned after civil society groups strongly objected to his appointment (Prachathai 2015). Third, the Constitution-Drafting Committee proposed to merge the Human Rights Commission with the Ombudsman – a move that met with strong criticism from the regional UN High Commissioner for Human Rights (OHCHR 2015) and members of international civil society organizations, such as Human Rights Watch and the ICJ (Human Rights Watch 2015; ICJ 2015). Reacting to these developments, in October 2014 the ICC recommended that the NHRCT be downgraded from "A" status to a "B" due to its persistent deficiencies in the selection process. The Thai government has been granted a period of one year, until October 2015, to provide evidence of improvement.

The Myanmar Human Rights Commission (MNHRC) is the youngest and arguably the most controlled and least effective of the Commissions. It is still in the formative stage, since members of the Commission have to fully grasp their own role, the international environment, and the concept of human rights. Since Myanmar has been sealed off from the Western world due to self-isolation and Western sanctions from 1962 up until 2011, the concept of human rights is still new. Even the commissioners – most of them ambassadors and state officials – have little experience in the field of human rights (Interview, Commissioner, December 10, 2014). Notwithstanding, the MNHRC publicly recommended the government's ratification of ICCPR and ICESCR. Given the dismal state of human rights in the country, it will take time until the Commission can effectively socialize human rights ideas – even if they continue to conduct regular training sessions and workshops.

Following its inception in September 2011, the MNHRC quickly took steps to establish its credibility. In October 2011, it wrote an open letter to President Thein Sein requesting the release of political prisoners. The very next day, the president granted amnesty to more than 6,359 people, including a considerable number of political prisoners. Despite this initial albeit questionable success of the Commission, the MNHRC's role must be viewed critically. Although the MNHRC has begun to look into key human rights concerns, it has generally shied away from criticizing the government or the military. For instance, following a fact-finding investigation in Kachin State, it issued a general statement calling on all sides to avoid human rights violations, to promote landmine awareness, and to work together to establish peace. While this general call for peace is not problematic, the general impunity of the armed forces has been frequently criticized (ANNI 2015). Both the UN Rapporteur and civil society organizations have indicated the involvement of the military in various human rights violations. Unfortunately, the chair of the MNHRC has stated that the Commission will not investigate human rights abuses in conflict areas, demonstrating significant refusal to investigate the causes of human rights problems. The lacking "teeth" of the Human Rights Commission may be attributed to the early stage of Myanmar's protracted transition; the missing connections to "civil society" remain a concern. Thus far, the MNHRC has not reached out to civil society to fulfill its mandate but stays within the ambit of the state dominated by the military (Bünte forthcoming).

All in all, we may conclude that NHRIs have been established to appease powerful domestic and international critics, have contributed to the legitimacy of human rights in all five Southeast Asian states, and have lent fundamental support to the development of a domestic human rights movement in repressive countries. Most of the countries attempted to follow the Paris Principles in order to demonstrate human rights compliance. Some Human Rights Commissions, however, show fundamental weaknesses, such as lacking independence and a weak mandate.

## Southeast Asia's human rights record in practice

As Hathaway argues in her empirical study, the ratification of treaties does not necessarily guarantee the improvement of human rights practice (Hathaway 2002). Rather, it is a strategic act to show commitment. Do human rights treaties then make a difference in Southeast Asia? Does the introduction of National Human Rights Commissions go hand in hand with an improvement of human rights? Quantitative data from Freedom House and the Political Terror Scale (PTS) provide us with an overview of the human rights record over time, whereas the reports from the UN Human Rights Council's Universal Periodic Review (UPR) help us discern important human rights concerns.

## Quantitative overview of Southeast Asia's human rights record

In order to look at the rights actually enjoyed and exercised by groups and individuals, I examine the Freedom House data and the Political Terror Scale. Both indicators are widely used in comparative analyses of human rights practices and allow us to compare human rights violations over time.[8] The Freedom House dataset measures civil and political liberties on a 7-point scale, ranking states from most free (1) to least free (7). States ranking from 1.0 to 2.5 are considered free, those with values from 3.0 to 5.0 are seen as partly free, and from 5.5 to 7.0 as unfree. The Political Terror Scale is issued annually and uses Amnesty International and State Department data to indicate the use of terror by state agencies; it measures violations of physical and integrity rights (extrajudicial killings torture, disappearance, and imprisonment) on a 5-point fixed scale and is one of the most widely used indicators in comparative analyses of human rights practices. Level one on the scale indicates that states are under a secure rule of law, people are not imprisoned for their views, and torture is rare. Level three is characterized by extensive political imprisonment, execution, or other political murders and brutality. Unlimited detention (without or with trial) is accepted. The highest level is five, when terror has expanded to the whole population. The executives of these societies do not place any limits on their behavior in the pursuit of their goals (Gibney *et al.* 2015).

The Freedom House data do not paint a particularly encouraging picture for Southeast Asia (see Figure 8.2). On average, Southeast Asia's status of civil liberties and political rights has hardly improved over the last 40 years. On average, it remained in the unfree category (above 5) until 2002. From 2002 to 2005, values remain in the low "partly free category" (4.9–4.8) and fall back into the "unfree category" again in 2005 – developments that may be attributed to the crisis of the Thai state, the military coup in 2006, and democratic deficits in the Philippines (Croissant and Bünte 2011). Since 2008, however, we see a slow and gradual improvement. When we look at the individual country data, our diagnosis is confirmed. Brunei, Burma, Cambodia, Laos, and Vietnam are categorized as authoritarian for the past 40 years and we see barely any change in civil and political rights.[9] At the same time, Malaysia and Singapore remained "partly

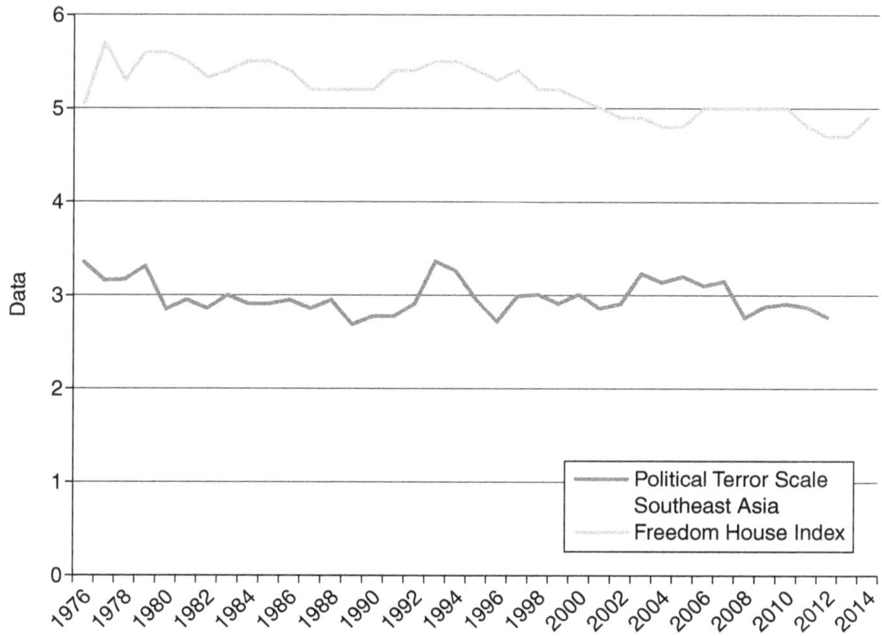


*Figure 8.2* Freedom House data and political terror scale data for Southeast Asian countries (source: own compilation based on Freedom House and PTS data).

free" over the past 40 years. The situation has been far more volatile in the more "democratic" states in the region. The Philippines has seen some improvements since democratization in 1986; Indonesia has made some progress in civil and political rights following democratization in 1998 and reforms in 2005 (see also Bünte and Ufen 2008). In both countries, however, progress is fragile and countries have experienced setbacks. The most volatile situation is found in Thailand, which saw a gradual opening and free phase from the mid-1990s until 2005. The 2006 and 2014 coups, however, have challenged these developments (Croissant and Bünte 2012).

Looking at the PTS data for Southeast Asia confirms the general picture. The level of state-induced violence has reduced only slightly over the past three decades, yet this regional average obscures important state differences. Brunei, Singapore, and Laos maintain a score of 1 to 2 throughout recent decades; while Singapore has a firm "rule of law," the small countries of Laos and Brunei fall under the radar of civil society organizations and consequently do not attract that much negative attention. With small populations and heavy state control, civil society is too weak to report human rights abuses. Moreover, neither state finds itself firmly on the US agenda. The scores for Malaysia and Vietnam shift between 2 and 3, and Indonesia between 3 and 4. The worst score, with the highest levels since 1988, is held by Myanmar.

Whereas the FH and PTS data help generalize trends over time, a look at the protocols of the UN's Universal Periodic Review (UPR) can discern important human rights concerns for individual countries. The UPR reviews the human rights record of every state in a five-year cycle. The review brings together state representatives, reports from all relevant UN treaty bodies, and submissions from civil society.

## Findings from the Universal Periodic Review (UPR)

As previously mentioned, the six ratifying ASEAN member states of the ICCPR are Cambodia, Indonesia, Laos, the Philippines, Thailand, and Vietnam. Indonesia, the Philippines, and Thailand have also established National Human Rights Commissions to socialize international human rights into domestic practice. The gap between human rights norms and practice is especially wide in Cambodia and Laos. In the case of Cambodia, for example, the High Commissioner pointed to the "increasing limitations on freedom of expression that have created a significant challenge for civil society, human rights defenders, the United Nations and ordinary Cambodians engaged in human rights" (UN 2013a: §45). The Special Rapporteur on Cambodia reported that many representatives from civil society organizations and journalists continued to encounter harassment, intimidation, and threats of defamation or incitement lawsuits. Moreover, violence is widespread and torture is a problem. Consequently, Cambodia was urged to prevent acts of torture and ill-treatment, including sexual violence in detention, and to put an end to any form of arbitrary and unlawful detention (UN 2013a: §19 and §20). ILO documentation also demonstrated serious violence against trade union leaders and members (UN 2013a: §52). Laos has similar problems, and the UPR documents reported allegations of torture and ongoing problems with enforced disappearances of human rights activists working on land grabbing. Since the last review in 2011, which entailed similar accusations, Laos has accessed CAT and enacted legal provisions to cope with the problem. Still, the disappearance of Sombath Somphone and other prominent human rights activists emphasizes the gravity of the problem (UN 2014: §22). The report on Vietnam, though acknowledging the revision of the constitution and the debate on human rights instruments (see Bui, Chapter 10, this volume), contained some problematic issues as well: freedom of information was "severely curtailed" and the blogosphere increasingly controlled (UN 2013b: §54 and §57). Other problems include: corruption in the judicial sector (UN 2013b: §48); limitations on organizing public protest – despite being legal according to the 1992 constitution – and difficulties in establishing social organizations outside the state's orbit of mass organizations (UN 2013b: §59). The Human Right Council's Periodic Review advised all three countries to strengthen existing human rights instruments and pushed for the creation of National Human Rights Institutions that follow the Paris Principles.

Despite its transition to democracy in 1998 and subsequent reforms, the UPR document on Indonesia reveals worrying messages: deep concerns about the numerous, credible, and consistent allegations of "widespread torture," especially in West Papua (UN 2012: §16 and §17) and the "climate of impunity for perpetrators of torture, including military, police and other state officials" (UN 2012: §31). Moreover, the report documents violence against certain minorities, in particular the Ahmadiyyah (UN 2012: §40; see also Ufen, Chapter 9, this volume). It also discloses a limited freedom of expression in conflict areas, such as West Papua and the Moluccas (UN 2012: §43). Here, we see allegations of a high incidence of rape perpetrated by military personnel (UN 2012: §22). The report raises the criticism that human rights organizations could not enter these areas (UN 2012: §44). Another concern is the introduction of Sharia laws in Aceh, which "legalized marital rape" (§23) and "provided for the punishments such as stoning and caning, and was in clear contravention of the prohibition of torture and cruel, inhuman or degrading punishment and the obligation to prevent and prohibit corporal punishment"; furthermore, women were disproportionally affected by these measures (UN 2012: §20, §21). Although the UPR praises the existence of several mechanisms to monitor the work of the police, the document also lists serious concerns regarding human rights mechanisms. For instance, the UPR criticized the attorney general for not taking up cases investigated by Komnas HAM, such as enforced disappearances during the student demonstrations in 1998 (Trisakti incident in May 1998, Semangi I and II in November 1998). Similarly, the report criticized the government for reducing the Komnas HAM's authority by stating that military officials should ignore the summons from Komnas HAM in connection with its investigations of gross violations of human rights (UN 2012: §4). Moreover, human rights courts were unable to secure the conviction of any of the alleged perpetrators of gross human rights violations in relation to the Tanjuk Priok (1984), East Timor (1999), and Abepura cases (2000), and alleged perpetrators of war crimes wanted by INTERPOL are serving in the Indonesian military forces (§32).

In the case of Thailand, the UPR expressed concerns about the dire human rights situation in the south, and persistent allegations of serious human rights violations, including widespread instances of extrajudicial killings and ill-treatment by the police and members of the armed forces, illustrated by incidents such as the Tak Bai and the Krue Se mosque incidents and the extraordinarily high number of killings during the war on drugs (UN 2011: §20; for the war on drugs see also Connors 2011: 108–119; Haberkorn 2013). Thailand's UPR session in May 2016 has highlighted the deteriorating human rights situation since the coup in May 2014. In particular, concerns were raised about the lack of freedom of information and expression and freedom of assembly and association (UN 2016).

Only the Philippines, a front runner in regional democratization and human rights in the region, received a somewhat positive review. The report acknowledged a "vibrant civil society environment" and "up-to-now relatively free media landscape" (UN 2012b: §33 and §34), although a number of concerns were also raised about "serious human rights violations, including torture, ill-treatment and extrajudicial killings, enforced disappearances, and harassment" (UN 2012: §15). Moreover, the UN also pushed for a reform of the National Human Rights Commission, since it "remained an institutionally weak body facing numerous challenges. It had no power to prosecute cases and a severely limited operational budget; its lack of credibility threatened its continued relevance in the country" (UN 2012b: §6).

## Conclusion

Measuring the state of human rights compliance is itself a contested issue. This chapter has concentrated on the ratification of human rights treaties and reservations thereof, and on the establishment of National Human Rights Institutions. For the region of Southeast Asia this exercise revealed a deep gulf between human rights rhetoric and human rights practice. Although more than two-thirds (67 percent) of the global human rights legal framework has been signed by the states of the region, Southeast Asian states' true commitment to human rights comes into question. The most important treaties, such as the ICPR and the CAT, have not been supported by the majority of states. Moreover, only the more democratic states have fully endorsed the international human rights treaty system (Indonesia, Philippines). In addition, the number of objections and reservations has also demonstrated an ongoing reluctance to come forward with binding mechanisms of arbitration and citizen complaints. The more democratic states in Southeast Asia have also established human rights institutions that act as a bridge between international and local institutions. Again, regime type matters for the impact of these institutions. The Indonesian and Philippine National Human Rights Institutions and their Thai counterpart (up until 2006) enjoyed broad support and had an important impact on the immediate post-authoritarian order. They helped put human rights on the political agenda and socialize human rights among members of the former military regimes. In the democratic era, these institutions also suffer from clientelism, infighting, weak leadership, and a lack of funding, all of which lead to legitimacy deficits of these institutions. In the more authoritarian states, such as Malaysia, Thailand (after 2006), and Myanmar, NHRIs are an important voice, challenge state power, and raise human rights consciousness.

The quantitative and qualitative views on human rights have shown that considerable obstacles to the enjoyment of rights in the region remain. Progress toward an implementation of political and civil rights is still slow and all states have significant human rights problems. Still, the ASEAN states seem to follow a particular approach to human rights, which Hiro Katsumata called "mimetic adoption" (Katsumata 2009). Katsumata sees this process as enhancing the legitimacy of Southeast Asian states without agreeing on these human rights principles as moral ends in their own right. The adoption is rooted in strategic motives and the reforms of the ASEAN Charter, the AICHR, and, most recently, the AHRD have occurred against a backdrop of no qualitative change within ASEAN member states' positions relative to global human rights standards. The findings of this chapter support this interpretation. However, it has also shown that there is still contestation over human rights at the domestic level. Here the role of domestic civil societies and established NHRIs in raising awareness about human rights comes into play. Changes in human rights practice simply need longer time horizons.

## Notes

1 The following treaties may be regarded as the main legal framework of the international human rights system: the International Convention on the Elimination of All Forms of Racial Discrimination (CERD, 1965); the International Covenant on Economic, Social, and Cultural Rights (CESCR, 1966); the Convention of the Elimination of All Discrimination against Women (CEDAW, 1979); the Convention against Torture and Other Cruel, Inhuman or Degrading Treatment or Punishment (CAT, 1984); the Convention on the Rights of Persons with Disabilities (CRPD, 2006); and the International Convention for the Protection of all Persons from Enforced Disappearance (ICCPED, 2006).

2 The Sub-Committee of National Institutions for the Promotion and Protection of Human Rights (ICC) determines the status of Human Rights Institutions. Retaining an "A" status is significant because otherwise the Commission loses its speaking rights within the UN Human Rights Council.

3 If a matter being investigated by SUHAKAM subsequently becomes the subject matter of any court proceeding, SUHAKAM must cease its own investigation.

4 For instance, in Thailand the Human Rights Commission was challenged by authoritarian tendencies under Thaksin, from 2001 to 2006, and the subsequent coup, which brought increased polarization between Thaksin loyalists and royalists, and between the rural poor and the urban aristocracy and middle class. This polarization was accompanied by increased street protests, violence, and human rights violations.

5 In these activities, Komnas HAM stressed the need for a dialogue between the opposed groups. This likely contributed to a positive perception.

6 Komnas HAM identified the military as being involved in all of these human rights violations.
7 The Sedition Act, originally enacted by the colonial authorities of British Malaya, criminalizes speech with "seditious tendency," including that which would bring hatred against the government or create hostilities between different races.
8 For measurement validity see Landmann (2004).
9 There is only one exception: Cambodia moved into the "partly free" category in 1993 and 1994, due to UN involvement. This trend reversed after 1994.

## Bibliography

ANNI (2012). "Philippines: Divided Leadership and Lacklustre Performance." In *ANNI Report on the Performance and Establishment of National Human Rights Institutions*, ed. Forum Asia. Bangkok, ANNI, pp. 58–75.

ANNI (2014). "All the President's Men." In *ANNI Report on the Performance and Establishment of National Human Rights Institutions in Asia*, ed. Forum Asia. Bangkok, ANNI, pp. 12–25.

ANNI (2015). "Thailand: Human Rights Crisis." In *ANNI Report on the Performance and Establishment of National Human Rights Institutions in Asia*, ed. Forum Asia. Bangkok, ANNI.

Bayefsky, A.F. (2015). "The UN Human Rights Treaty Systems" (bayefsky.com).

Bünte, M. (forthcoming). "Myanmar's Protracted Transition: Arenas, Actors, Outcomes." *Asian Survey*.

Bünte, M. and Portela, C. (2012). "Political Reforms and the End of Sanctions." Hamburg, German Institute of Global and Area Studies, *GIGA Focus International*, 3/2012, available at: www.giga-hamburg.de/dl/download.php?d=/content/publikationen/pdf/gf_international_12 03.pdf (accessed January 10, 2013).

Bünte, M. and Ufen, A. (2008): *Democratization in Post-Suharto Indonesia*. London, Routledge.

Cardenas, S. (2002). "National Human Rights Commissions in Asia." *Human Rights Review*, 4(1): 30–51.

Cardenas, S. (2011). "State Compliance and National Human Rights Institutions." In *Multidisciplinary Perspectives on National Human Rights Institutions, State Compliance, and Social Changed*, eds R. Goodman and T. Pegram. Cambridge, Cambridge University Press, pp. 29–51.

Christie, K. (1995). "Human Rights in Southeast Asia." *Political Studies*, XLIII, 204–218.

Ciorciari, J. (2012). "Institutionalizing Human Rights in Southeast Asia." *Human Rights Quarterly*, 34(3): 695–725.

Cole, W. and Ramirez, F. (2013). "Conditional Decoupling: Assessing the Impact of National Human Rights Institutions, 1981–2004." *American Sociological Review*, 78(4): 702–725.

Connors, M. (2011). "Ambivalent about Human Rights: Thai Democracy." In *Human Rights in Asia*, eds T. Davis and B. Galligan. Cheltenham, Edward Elgar, pp. 103–122.

Croissant, A. and Bünte, M. (2011). *The Crisis of Democratic Governance in Southeast Asia*. Basingstoke, Palgrave.

Davies, M. (2014). "States of Compliance? Global Human Rights Treaties and ASEAN Member States." *Journal of Human Rights*, 13(4): 414–433.

Davis, T. (2008). *Human Rights in Asia*. Cheltenham, Edward Elgar.

Eldridge, P. (2002). *The Politics of Human Rights in Southeast Asia*. London, Routledge.
Ford, M. (2008). "International Networks and Human Rights in Indonesia." In *Human Rights in Asia*, eds T. Davis and B. Galligan. Cheltenham, Edward Elgar, pp. 38–55.
Gibney, M., Cornett, L., Wood, R., Haschke, P., and Arnon, D. (2015). *The Political Terror Scale 1976–2015*. Data retrieved from the Political Terror Scale website: www.politicalterrorscale.org.
Gomez, J. and Ramcharan, R. (2012). "The Protection of Human Rights in Southeast Asia, Improving the Effectiveness of Civil Society." *Asia-Pacific Journal on Human Rights and the Law*, 2: 27–43.
Haberkorn, T. (2013). "Tracing an Uneven History: Notes on Sources and Trajectories of Thai State Violence." *Asian Journal of Peacebuilding*, 1(1): 109–116.
Hafner-Burton, E. and Tsutsui, K. (2005). "Human Rights in a Globalizing World: The Paradox of Empty Promises." *AJS*, 110(5): 1373–1411.
Harding, A. (2006). "Thailand's Reforms: Human Rights and the National Human Rights Commission." *Journal of Comparative Law*, 1: 88–100.
Hathaway, O.A. (2002). "Do Human Rights Treaties Make a Difference?" *The Yale Law Journal*, 111(8): 1932–2042.
Jetschke, A. (2011). *Human Rights and State Security. Indonesia and the Philippines*. Philadelphia, University of Pennsylvania Press.
Katsumata, H. (2009). "ASEAN and Human Rights: Resisting Western Pressure or Emulating the West?" *Pacific Review*, 22(5): 619–637.
Kent, A. (1999). *China, the United Nations and Human Rights*. Philadelphia, University of Pennsylvania Press.
Klein, J. (2001). "The Evolution of Thailand's National Human Rights Commission 1992–2001." In *Thailand's New Politics. KPI Yearbook 2001*, ed. M. Nelson. Bangkok, White Lotus, pp. 25–67.
Landmann, T. (2004). "Measuring Human Rights: Principle, Practice and Policy." *Human Rights Quarterly*, 26: 906–931.
Linton, S. (2008). "ASEAN States, their Reservations to Human Rights Treaties and the Proposed Commission on Women and Children." *Human Rights Quarterly*, 30(2): 436–493.
Mauzy, D.K. (1997). "The Human Rights and Asian Values Debate in Southeast Asia, Trying to Clarify the Key Issues." *Pacific Review*, 10(2): 210–236.
Mohamad, M. (2002). "Human Rights in Southeast Asia: Charting the Course of State Commitment." *Contemporary Southeast Asia*, 24(2): 230–251.
Peerenboom, R. (2003). "Beyond Universalism and Relativism: The Evolving Debates about Values in Asia." *Indiana International and Comparative Law Review*, 2003: 1–85.
Prachathai (2015). "Most of Committee Screening National Rights Commissioners are Military." Prachatai English Edition, July 30, available at: www.prachatai.com/english/node/5360 (accessed April 18, 2016).
Renshaw, C. (2013). "The ASEAN Human Rights Declaration 2012." *Human Rights Law Review*, 13(3): 557–579.
Renshaw, C., Byrnes, A., and Durbach, A. (2011). "Testing the Mettle of National Human Rights Institutions: A Case Study of the Human Rights Commission of Malaysia." *Asian Journal of International Law*, 1: 165–168.
Rich, R. (2012). "An Appreciation of the Human Rights Situation in Southeast Asia." In *The Crisis of Democratic Governance*, eds Marco Bünte and Aurel Croissant. Basingstoke, Palgrave, pp. 171–190.

Risse, T. and Sikking, K. (1999). "The Socialization of International Human Rights Norms into Domestic Practices: Introduction." In *The Power of Human Rights: International Norms and Domestic Change*, eds T. Risse, S. Ropp, and K. Sikking. Cambridge, Cambridge University Press.

Setiawan, K.M.P. (2013). *Promoting Human Rights: National Human Rights Commissions in Indonesia and Malaysia.* Dissertation, Leiden University, Leiden, Online Repository.

Sorpong, P. (2014). "The Limits and Potential of Liberal Democratization in Southeast Asia." *Journal of Current Southeast Asian Affairs*, 33(3): 19–47.

Stokke, H. (2007). "Taking the Paris Principles to Asia. A Study of Three Human Rights Commissions in Southeast Asia: Malaysia, Indonesia and the Philippines." *CMI Report*, No. 3. Bergen, Norway, available at: www.cmi.no/publications/publication/?2680=taking-the-paris-principles-to-asia.

Thio, L-A. (2009). "Panacea, Placebo, or Pawn: The Teething Problems of the Human Rights Commission of Malaysia (SUHAKAM)." *George Washington International Law Review*, 40: 1271–1342.

Thompson, M. (2001). "Whatever Happened to Asian Values?" *Journal of Democracy*, 12(4): 154–165.

Whiting, A. (2003). "Situating Suhakam: Human Rights Debates and Malaysia's National Human Rights Commission." *Stanford Journal of International Law*, 39: 59–81.

## Legal documents and reports

HRCMA (1999). Human Rights Commission of Malaysia Act, No. 597. Kuala Lumpur.

IBAHARI (2012). The Rule of Law in Myanmar. Challenges and Prospects. Report of the International Bar Association's Human Rights Institute (IBAHARI), London.

OHCHR (2015). Technical Note on the National Human Rights Commission of Thailand in the Draft 2015 Constitution, Office of the United Nations High Commissioner for Human Rights Regional Office for Southeast Asia (http://bangkok.ohchr.org/files/OHCHR%20on%20NHRI%20150327.pdf). Thailand National Human Rights Commission Act B.E. 2542 (1999), Bangkok.

Suhakam (2010–2015). Annual Reports. Human Rights Commission on Kuala Lumpur (online www.Suhakam.org.my).

UN (2011). Compilation prepared by the Office of the High Commissioner for Human Rights in accordance with paragraph 15 (b) of the Annex to Human Rights Council Resolution 5/1. Working Group on the UPR, twelfth session. Geneva, October 3–14 (http://lib.ohchr.org/HRBodies/UPR/Documents/session12/TH/A_HRC_WG.6_12_THA_2_Thailand_E.doc).

UN (2012a). Compilation prepared by the Office of the United Nations High Commissioner for Human Rights in Accordance with Paragraph 15 (b) of the Annex to Human Rights Council Resolution 5/1 and Paragraph 5 of the Annex to Council Resolution 16/21. Indonesia, March 12 (http://daccess-dds-ny.un.org/doc/UNDOC/GEN/G12/119/37/PDF/G1211937.pdf?OpenElement).

UN (2012b). Compilation Prepared by the Office of the United Nations High Commissioner for Human Rights in Accordance with Paragraph 15 (b) of the Annex to Human Rights Council 5/1 and Paragraph 5 of the Annex to Council 16/21. Philippines, March 30 (http://daccess-dds-ny.un.org/doc/UNDOC/GEN/G12/125/50/PDF/G1212550.pdf?OpenElement).

UN (2013a). Compilation Prepared by the Office of the United Nations High Commissioner for Human Rights in Accordance with Paragraph 15 (b) of the Annex to Human Rights Council Resolution 5/1 and Paragraph 5 of the Annex to Council Resolution 16/21, Cambodia (http://daccess-dds-ny.un.org/doc/UNDOC/GEN/G13/184/59/PDF/G1318459.pdf?OpenElement).

UN (2013b). Compilation Prepared by the Office of the United Nations High Commissioner for Human Rights in Accordance with Paragraph 15 (b) of the Annex to Human Rights Council Resolution 5/1 and Paragraph 5 of the Annex to Council Resolution 16/21, Viet Nam, November 7 (http://daccess-dds-ny.un.org/doc/UNDOC/GEN/G13/184/45/PDF/G1318445.pdf?OpenElement).

UN (2014). Compilation Prepared by the Office of the United Nations High Commissioner for Human Rights in Accordance with Paragraph 15 (b) of the Annex to Human Rights Council Resolution 15/1 (b) of the Annex to Human Rights Council Resolution 5/1 and Paragraph 5 of the Annex to Council Resolution 16/21. Lao People's Democratic Republic, November 12 (http://daccess-dds-ny.un.org/doc/UNDOC/GEN/G14/209/08/PDF/G1420908.pdf?OpenElement).

# 9 Undermining religious minority rights in Indonesia and Malaysia

## Fragile coalitions, wavering executive chiefs, and rogue groups as proxies[1]

*Andreas Ufen*

### Introduction

In Malaysia and Indonesia, both executive chiefs started their tenures with promises to uphold religious minorities' rights. Prime Minister Najib Razak themed his premiership "1Malaysia," thereby indicating his intention to bring the different ethnic and religious groups closer together. He also used the propagation of this inclusive approach to improve his international standing and called for a "global movement of the moderates" from all faiths to fight extremists in front of the UN General Assembly. In 2010, the government formed the Committee to Promote Inter-Religious Understanding and Harmony. Likewise, Indonesian President Susilo Bambang Yudhoyono portrayed himself as a staunch defender of religious minority rights. Almost at the end of his second term, in 2013, he even received the World Statesman Award for religious freedom from the Appeal of Conscience Foundation in New York – much to the dismay of human rights activists. In reality, it has turned out that most of Najib's and Yudhoyono's promises to improve inter-religious relations were empty. Religious minorities are increasingly under pressure; this statement does not refer primarily to the number of casualties in religiously tinged wars, the extent of repression by paramilitaries, etc., but rather to the contest over the compromises that have formed the basis of inter-religious relations as enshrined in the written and unwritten constitutions of the two countries. Today, Shi'ites and Ahmadis in Indonesia and Malaysia are being subjected to a kind of "religious cleansing." Christians in Malaysia are no longer allowed to use the word Allah in certain publications, and building permits for temples and churches are becoming more difficult to achieve. In Indonesia, even official permits are ignored by authorities in some cases. The Indonesian "state philosophy" Pancasila is still mostly unquestioned, but a range of regulations and laws now challenge the equal status of the six religions that it officially acknowledges. All these developments are part of a profound constitutional contestation,

> the process by which incumbent elites compete, bargain and struggle with oppositional groups … about what state institutions and the broader political order should look like, what rights should be granted, how these should be forced and particularly by whom.
>
> (Dressel and Bünte 2013: 4)

The debate on the place of religious minorities within the nation-state had already begun prior to Indonesia's and Malaysia's national independence. In both countries, the resulting formulas were not fully laical and liberal, but so broadly worded that religious minorities did not feel overly marginalized. In both countries this has changed over time. In Indonesia, the attempt to introduce the Jakarta Charter ("with the obligation for adherents of Islam to follow syari'ah") in the constitution utterly failed in 2002, but since then Islamists have made minor encroachments on the rights of religious minorities with the passage of certain laws, (inter-ministerial) decrees and local regulations, and by creating an atmosphere of intolerance, hate, and anguish. They are obviously attempting to redefine the role of Islam and other religions. In Malaysia, this contestation has also been present from the beginning. Islam was declared the religion of the state, but in a circumscribed form. A subsequent Islamization process, not unlike that in Indonesia, gradually rendered religious and ethnic minorities more and more vulnerable, peaking in 2001 when Prime Minister Mahathir claimed that Malaysia was an Islamic state, at a time when the rivalry of the United Malays National Organization (UMNO) with the Islamist Parti Islam Se-Malaysia (Pan-Malaysian Islamic Party (PAS)) had reached its apex. The legal position of minorities has also been impaired incrementally, but the debate over the constitutional and legal place of Islam, the privileges of Malays (as *bumiputeras*),[2] the status of shari'a courts, etc. has intensified in recent years. This is demonstrated, for example, by the rise of new civil society organizations established by religious minorities and Malay Muslims, all of which are able to mobilize large numbers of discontented supporters. Another indicator is the marked increase in legal cases regarding custody rights, apostasy, blasphemy, etc. (Freedom House 2010).

This chapter aims to uncover some of the situational and configurational political factors behind this increasing pressure on religious (and ethnic) minorities.[3] It argues that the explanation for the deterioration of religious minority rights is fourfold. First, in both countries, one of the central political contests is focused on the question of religion and its legal and constitutional position. Second, in order to hold their fragile coalitions of parties together, the pragmatically (or opportunistically) oriented executive heads have tried to take centrist positions, but in reality they have often given in to radicals. Third, in Malaysia, political parties politicized religious issues less intensively than in the past because PAS has toned down its Islamist agenda due to its position as a partner in the multi-religious and multi-ethnic opposition coalition;[4] in Indonesia, Islamist parties have increasingly shifted toward centerist positions. And fourth, because the political parties are somewhat more restrained in politicizing religion, rogue groups in tandem with a strengthened religious bureaucracy are playing an important role in determining the political agenda, in threatening minorities, and in creating an illiberal atmosphere.

## Pluralist constitutional platforms and deteriorating religious minority rights

### *The constitutional rights of religious minorities in Malaysia and Indonesia*

According to conventional wisdom, Malaysia is home to a moderate form of Islam. A significant syncretist heritage, multiculturalism, multi-religiosity, and the institutionalized accommodation of the interests of the different ethnic and religious groups have been effective obstacles to a radicalization of Islam. Religious freedom is generally respected. According to Article 11 of the constitution, every person has the right to profess and practice his or her religion. Islam is the religion of the federation according to Article 3(1) of the constitution, but according to Sundra Karean (2006) this only applies in relation to official ceremonies and sociocultural observances, and "it was not meant to assert the Islamic religion as one which was superior to other religions nor was it meant to institutionalise the state as a theocracy" (Sundra Karean 2006: 50). The sultans in nine of the country's 13 states are "Heads of Islam" and oversee the shari'a courts; in the remaining four states and the federal territories the highest Islamic authority is the king. Contradictions have arisen within the legal system due to the different status of Muslims and non-Muslims because it is a dual system with both civil and shari'a courts.

Indonesia also acknowledges the major rights of religious minorities, and the country has a history of tolerance and pluralism. Indonesians have the constitutionally guaranteed right "to worship according to their own religion or belief." Religious freedom is generally protected, but the belief in one supreme God (neutrally termed Tuhan, not Allah) is enshrined in the constitution. Besides Islam, the Pancasila recognizes Protestantism, Catholicism, Buddhism, Hinduism, and Confucianism (the latter since 2007). The Pancasila formula was once a means to safeguard the interests of religious minorities who feared domination by orthodox Muslims. Since independence in 1945, Islamists have fought for the inclusion of a passage in the constitution requiring the implementation of shari'a law for Muslims (the so-called Jakarta Charter). Because the great majority of MPs did not support the proposal when it was brought forward by smaller Islamist parties in 2002, the Pancasila has remained the core of a compromise between the Muslim majority and other religious groups (Hosen 2005; Salim 2008: 79ff.; Platzdasch 2009: 174ff.).

## The reality on the ground

Politics in Malaysia often centers around religion and ethnicity. The country is marked by a deeply engrained racism that is directly connected to Islam because religion itself is racialized, though the connection between a cultural and a genetic/biological notion of race in the official discourse is vague. A Malay who converts to another religion threatens the ideological foundation of Malayness. Thus, conversion is highly unlikely. In order to convert, a Muslim must obtain approval from a shari'a court, something which is very seldom granted. In some states, conversion is even punished with imprisonment or caning. Muslims who deviate from mainstream Islam may be subject to mandatory rehabilitation. A strong faction of the *bumiputeras*, especially the Malays, vehemently opposes any move that blurs the lines.

Religious minorities are in most cases free to practice their beliefs, but they nevertheless feel discriminated against. The most controversial issue in recent years has been the ban on the use of the word Allah by non-Muslims in Malay-language Bibles and other Christian publications such as the *Catholic Herald* (Neo 2014). The ban was issued in 2008 by the Internal Security Ministry (later part of the Home Ministry). The Roman Catholic Church argued that Christians in Malaya and Malaysia have used the word Allah for more than 400 years and filed a lawsuit against the ban. In January 2015, the Federal Court dismissed the latest appeal by the Catholic Church.

Besides, religious minorities frequently complain about temple demolitions, the limited funding for their places of worship, and difficulties in obtaining permits for the construction of these places and of cemeteries. Moreover, teachings of Islam that differ from those of Sunni Islam – for instance, Shia Islam and 56 Islamic sects deemed deviant – are banned; non-Muslim proselytizing of Muslims is also prohibited.

The shari'a courts only deal with Muslims, but time and again the different law systems collide. This has been compounded by Article 121 (1A), a 1988 constitutional amendment which stipulates that civil courts shall have no jurisdiction in respect of any matter within the jurisdiction of shari'a courts. The legal collisions are particularly tangible in cases of inter-religious marriage, decisions on custody rights, etc. (Liow 2009: 68ff.). In some states, elements of shari'a law have been incorporated into secular law. An example is *khalwat* (close physical proximity to an unrelated member of the opposite sex), which can be punished with imprisonment or caning.

In recent years, some prominent cases – such as those of Lina Joy, Revathi Masoosai, and Maniam Moorthy – have been in the public eye (Sundra Karean 2006: 54; Lopez 2015). Lina Joy, born Azlina Jailani, a Malay, sought to legalize her 1990 conversion from Islam to Christianity, but the Federal Court rejected her application to have "Muslim" taken off her identity card and ruled that the case fell under the jurisdiction of a shari'a court. A 2004 High Court judgment in *Lina Joy* v. *Majlis Agama Islam Wilayah* had previously "held that Malay ethnicity and Islam were simply inseparable" (Neo 2014: 759) and that as a Malay she must remain in the Islamic faith. Muslim-born Revathi Masoosai was detained because of apostasy and counseled daily in a rehabilitation center in Selangor for six months in 2007. Maniam Moorthy's dead body was "snatched" by the authorities and buried according to Muslim rites, although his relatives claimed he had never converted to Islam. Especially controversial are those cases regarding custody and religious conversion that involve both Muslims and non-Muslims. In some states, for example, the conversion of children to Islam with the permission of only one parent is allowed.

The above-mentioned cases have, arguably, mobilized and politicized religious minorities, who have felt increasingly vulnerable (Kaur 2014; Chong 2014; Puyok 2015). The establishment of Hindraf, the Hindu Rights Action Force, which protested in 2007 in an unprecedented, huge demonstration against the perceived discrimination and marginalization of the Indian Hindu minority, was a direct reaction not only to the Moorthy case but also to temple demolitions (Kaur 2014: 341; Govindasamy 2015).

The enforcement of public morality lies in the hands of the Islamic bureaucracy, which directly intervenes in the lives of minorities – with increasing intensity. The power of the religious bureaucracy has been strengthened over the years (Liow 2009: 43ff.; Maznah Mohamad 2013). Officials control religious activities and state governments administer mosques, appoint imams, and influence the content of sermons. The most important agency is the Department of Islamic Development Malaysia (JAKIM), which defines deviant beliefs. JAKIM is located within the prime minister's office, which was fundamentally strengthened during Mahathir's premiership. JAKIM officials are authorized to accompany police on raids and to enforce shari'a regulations on indecent dress, alcohol consumption, or *khalwat*.

The United States Commission on International Religious Freedom (USCIRF) placed Malaysia on tier 2 in 2014 among countries "where the violations perpetrated or tolerated by the government are serious and characterized by at least one of the elements of the 'systematic, ongoing, and egregious' standard" (USCIRF 2014: 5). Likewise, Malaysia's ranking on the Government Restrictions Index and the Social Hostilities Index by the Pew Research Center increased from 6.4 and 1.0 to 7.6 and 3.9 between 2007 (the baseline year of its research) and 2012 (Pew Research Center 2014: 63). Malaysia belongs to those countries in the survey with very strong government restrictions on religion (score above 6.6) and markedly increasing social hostilities involving religion. Religion has been politicized constantly over a long period of time, and the deterioration of minority rights has accompanied this process.

The deterioration of religious minority rights is also observable in Indonesia, where only specific forms of Islam are tolerated and deviance is being prosecuted with increasing intensity. Whereas in the past religious groups such as Ahmadiyah were tolerated, if only reluctantly, today they are subject to intimidation from vigilante groups countenanced by large parts of society and state. The United States Commission on International Religious Freedom thus placed the country, like Malaysia, on tier 2 in 2014 (USCIRF 2014). Indonesia has been on this tier, formerly the USCIRF's Watch List, since only 2009. According to USCIRF, the tradition of tolerance and pluralism is threatened. This is also reflected in the country's scores from the Pew Research Center for the Government Restrictions Index and the Social Hostilities Index; these increased from 6.2 and 8.3 to 8.3 and 8.5 between 2007 and 2012 (Pew Research Center 2014: 62). The already high scores for social hostilities are now at the same level as those for the highly restrictive legal and administrative framework.

Indonesia was never a country where religious communities lived side by side in perfect harmony, but in spite of (or because of) the harsh authoritarianism under Suharto, attacks on religious minorities were far less frequent and obvious than they are today. In glaring contrast to the low profile of Islamists in party politics, there is a widespread perception that Indonesian society should be cleansed of deviant beliefs, and violent incidents are on the rise (International Crisis Group 2008; Human Rights Watch 2013; CSW 2014).[5] Minority groups suffer from different forms of discrimination and are sometimes pressed to convert to Sunni Islam by local authorities.

A growing and organized vigilantism has been accompanied, and sometimes even initiated, by political reforms decided upon in Jakarta. An example is the blasphemy law, which has existed for a long time but has only recently been used excessively (Freedom House 2010). The 1965 Presidential Decree on the Prevention of Religious Abuse and/or Defamation was signed by Sukarno and directed against mystical indigenous beliefs (*aliran kepercayaan*). It was the basis for Law No. 5/1969, the blasphemy law, which was passed under Suharto. According to data provided by Amnesty International, at least 106 individuals have been convicted under the law since 2005 – in comparison to only ten during the New Order.[6] Another striking example of the rise of a conservative Islam is the highly contentious 2008 pornography law, which bans pornographic acts and images. The law defines pornography as “man-made sexual materials in the form of drawings, sketches, illustrations, photographs, text, voice, sound, moving pictures, animation, cartoons, poetry, conversations, and gestures.” The loose definition and the power it gives to authorities was seen by critics as a direct assault on basic civil liberties (Sherlock 2008).

The most controversial reforms with respect to religious minorities, however, were the 2006 Joint Decree on Religious Harmony, Empowering Religious Harmony Forums, and Constructing Houses of Worship and the 2008 Joint Decree on Admonition and Instruction to the Disciples, Members and/or Members of the Organising Board of the Jemaat Ahmadiyah Indonesia (JAI), and the Members of the Public, both of which legitimated attacks by Islamists. The 2006 decree resulted in the formation of Religious Harmony Forums (Forum Kerukunan Umat Beragama, FKUB) as advisory bodies to governors, mayors, and regents. The bulk of FKUB members belong to the majority religion in the respective area. Permits to build houses of worship require support by the congregation, people living in the area, the village head, recommendations by the FKUB itself, and the ministry of religion. The 2008 Anti-Ahmadiyah decree entailed further such regulations at lower administrative levels, even though local and provincial governments did not have the authority to deal with such matters (Human Rights Watch 2013; CSW 2014).

The Ahmadiyah community has existed in Indonesia since 1925 and now has approximately 400,000 to 500,000 members, with a stronghold in West Java.[7] Until the Indonesian Ulama Council (MUI) issued a *fatwa* in 2005, the community lived largely peacefully with the Sunni Islam majority in Indonesia, even though the MUI had issued a similar *fatwa* in 1980 that had declared the

Ahmadis to deviate from mainstream Islam. It is only since 2005 that a more or less systematically organized campaign against the group – which began with an assault on the Ahmadiyah headquarters in Parung, West Java in July of that year – has been carried out. Likewise, Shi'ites have been subject to prosecution only since approximately the same time. All these incidents are testimony to the growing clout of Islamist networks, which are able to connect with the police and other authorities at subnational levels. Another result of activities by these networks has been the issuance of shari'a or shari'a-inspired regulations by local governments. Michael Buehler (2013: 67) counted 169 such regulations issued in at least seven provinces and 51 districts and municipalities from 1999 to 2009.[8] Interestingly, they have been formulated mostly by parties classified as rather secular. This shows that the efforts to undermine religious minority rights emanate not only from Islamists but also from the (supposedly) moderate mainstream, and that the constellation of actors and interests may be most important.[9] An extraordinary case is Aceh, a region that received special autonomy rights after a long civil war (Salim 2008: 143ff.). Because of a 2003 presidential decree, Aceh's provincial government is allowed to implement shari'a law, including its penal code. A local special security patrol (*Wilayatul Hisbah*) enforces dress codes and regulations on alcohol consumption, gambling, etc. A range of religious communities (Sufis, Ahmadis, Shi'ites) are banned. To many Islamists, Aceh is at the forefront of a systematic Islamization.

To summarize, in both countries, political and constitutional contests are often focused on the role of Islam and religious minorities. For a long time this was directly reflected in party politics, but because of the specific coalition-building dynamics it has decreased in recent years. In Indonesia, this is predominantly indicated by the tendency to build huge, all-encompassing "rainbow coalitions." In Malaysia, the new coalition of opposition parties has resulted in PAS's softening of its stance on central issues, at least until mid-2015 (see note 4).

## Party system change, the weakening of executive heads, and the complicity with vigilantism

### *The moderation of political Islam within party systems in Malaysia and Indonesia*

The Malaysian political system is characterized by the marked restriction of basic human rights. However, this circumvention of groups critical of the regime is accompanied by pluralistic elections that produce an electoral authoritarian regime ranked by Freedom House in the middle of the spectrum from 1 to 7, with a 4 for political rights and a 4 for civil liberties. The ruling National Front (Barisan Nasional (BN)) and its predecessor, the Alliance, have always won the elections at the national level, in most cases with a two-thirds majority. The BN is led by UMNO and currently includes 13 parties. Many of them represent ethnic groups – that is, in the first instance, the Malay majority or the Chinese and Indian minorities. The distinction between these and other ethnic groups has had a deep impact on most Malaysians, who more often than not are unable to question the arbitrariness of a classification introduced by the British colonialists. Aside from UMNO, the best-known BN parties are the Malaysian Chinese Association (MCA), the Malaysian Indian Congress (MIC), and Gerakan (Parti Gerakan Rakyat Malaysia, Party Gerakan).

Malays are defined by Article 160 of the constitution as Muslims. It follows that ethnicity is tightly connected to religion, and ethnic and religious cleavages reinforce each other and shape the whole party system. Prime Minister Mahathir initiated a comprehensive, systematic Islamization process in the early 1980s (Liow 2009: 46ff.). Around the same time, Islamists, the so-called "Young Turks," took over leading positions within PAS and started to demand far-reaching reforms. This sparked a contest between UMNO and PAS for the "better" Islam. The government promoted a conservative version of Islam compatible with economic policies that aimed to enable integration into the world economy and attract investments from Western countries. Islam was, thus, an instrument not only to achieve modernity, but also to restrain liberal social and political forces. State Islam was moderate insofar as the establishment of an Islamic state and Islamic penal code was not the goal of Mahathir, who assessed the self-righteousness of many *ulama* with reservations. In order to keep civil society in check, the government marginalized and even criminalized sects such as Darul Arqam and used co-optation and repression to stimulate a conservative Islamization. Ironically, the most influential opposition politician, Anwar Ibrahim, was in the 1980s and 1990s the most important member of UMNO to propagate the Mahathirist version of political Islam.

Politics in Malaysia has changed since the late 1990s, when a new opposition movement arose after Anwar Ibrahim, the deputy prime minister at that time, was kicked out of UMNO and later imprisoned on charges of sodomy and corruption. Since then, the polarization between the regime and opposition parties has increased significantly, with the elections in 1999, 2008, and 2013 demonstrating the rising vulnerability of the once seemingly invincible BN. In the 2008 and 2013 elections, the opposition parties PAS, Democratic Action Party (DAP), and Parti Keadilan Rakyat (People's Justice Party (PKR)) achieved majorities in a few states, among them the two most successful economically, namely Penang and Selangor. Together they formed the Pakatan Rakyat (Peoples' Alliance). The 2013 elections in particular exhibited the weakness or even dispensability of UMNO's junior partners MCA, MIC, and Gerakan (Ufen 2013a). As these changes in the balance of power among the parties have been occurring, anti-establishment NGOs have taken to the streets. The best examples have been the huge demonstrations by Bersih, the Coalition for Clean and Fair Elections (Gabungan Pilihanraya Bersih dan Adil), and by Hindraf. This show of force has been without precedent in Malaysian history (Kaur 2014, Govindasamy 2015), and the blossoming of such NGOs has complicated the dynamics of the relationship between state, political society, and civil society.

The increased strength of the opposition was linked to the replacement of Prime Minister Mahathir with Abdullah Badawi. From the beginning, Badawi was perceived as much weaker than his predecessor, but the 2004 elections, which resulted in a huge victory for the BN, seemed to stabilize his position. He introduced the vague but essentially inclusive concept of Islam Hadhari or Civilizational Islam when he took office (Kessler 2013: 89ff.) and initiated a number of reforms, but he shied away from seriously fighting corruption or from substantially improving inter-ethnic and inter-religious relations. Badawi was stuck between the necessity to reform the polity and to approach the other parties within his coalition and the pressure from radical Malays who saw any kind of reform as a direct threat to their privileges.[10] In the 2008 elections, often described as a "political tsunami," the Barisan Nasional won with only a thin margin nationwide and, moreover, lost in five states.

The position of UMNO and the BN is now extremely fragile in comparison to their almost unchallenged predominance from independence in 1957 until the mid-1990s, when an opposition victory in the national elections was simply inconceivable. The elections, especially those in 2008 and 2013, have evinced the profound reconfiguration of ethnic and religious groups and a new logic of party politics from primordial issues (ethnicity and religion) toward a polarization between BN and Pakatan Rakyat with primordialism tending to become of secondary importance. The non-Malay ethnic and religious minorities were less scared of PAS because the so-called Erdogan faction, which was reform-oriented, was open to a pro-democratic coalition with DAP and PKR.[11]

In contrast to Malaysia, Indonesia has been slowly democratized since 1998 – that is, since the fall of Suharto. One might argue that the country is today the most democratic in Southeast Asia, though Freedom House recently downgraded it from "free" to "partly free" because of a controversial new law on mass organizations. In spite of this, Indonesia is an electoral democracy that has successfully held substantially free and fair elections. The public discourse is usually free from the restrictions faced by journalists in Malaysia. Paradoxically, increased openness and new actors often destabilize political systems. The first years after the end of the New Order were one of the most violent eras of Indonesian politics, with secessionist movements, religious strife, ethnic wars, etc. Democratization often means that long-suppressed and simmering conflicts are ignited, and this is also true of ethnic and religious mobilization. However, as of approximately 2002 these conflicts started to subside.

The 1999 elections established a fragmented party system in which parties with a rather secularist bent have repeatedly achieved majorities. They include the nationalist Partai Demokrasi Indonesia – Perjuangan (Indonesian Democratic Party – Struggle (PDI-P)) under the leadership of Megawati Sukarnoputri, the daughter of the first president, Sukarno; Partai Golongan Karya (Party of Functional Groups, Golkar); the New Order regime party; and, since 2004, Yudhoyono's Partai Demokrat (PD). Since 2009 personalist split-offs of Golkar have added to the fragmentation among the non-Islamic forces of the party system. These parties include Partai Gerakan Indonesia Raya (Greater Indonesian Movement Party, Gerindra), which is led by ex-general and former son-in-law of Suharto, Prabowo Subianto; Partai Hati Nurani Rakyat (People's Conscience

Party, Hanura), led by former general Wiranto; and Partai Nasdem (National Democratic Party) under media tycoon Surya Paloh (Ufen 2013b).

But even the Islamic parties such as Partai Amanat Nasional (National Mandate Party (PAN)) and Partai Kebangkitan Bangsa (National Awakening Party (PKB)), which are loosely linked to huge mass organizations (Muhammadiyah and Nahdatul Ulama, respectively), have generally opted for a moderate stance on religious issues. The largest Islamist parties, which tend to demand a much stronger role for shari'a within the legal system, have received a combined vote of less than 20 percent in all four elections since 1999. In 2014, the once quickly rising Islamist Partai Keadilan Sejahtera (Justice and Prosperity Party (PKS)), which is inspired by the Egyptian Muslim Brotherhood and shares many of its radical views, gained only 6.8 percent of votes because of its involvement in a spectacular corruption case. During the 2014 presidential campaign, PAN, Partai Persatuan Pembangunan (United Development Party (PPP)), and PKS (but not the PKB) combined forces to prevent a moderate Muslim, Jokowi, from winning the presidency. How far they are willing to compromise on liberal rights and democracy was evident with their support for Prabowo, one of the most dreaded New Order generals with a highly questionable human rights record, who openly ranted on abolishing direct elections during the campaign. In general, party politics in Indonesia takes place in a multiparty system with moderate polarization. The largest parties in Indonesia "have been wary of offending any large voting bloc, and this effectively means tolerating the most intolerant segments of the society.... Minority rights have thus become a major issue in democratic Indonesia" (Horowitz 2013: 256). The divide within the party system separates more secularist and Islamic/Islamist parties, but because of grand coalitions (or rainbow coalitions) at all levels and a tendency to seek consensus, religious and ethnic conflicts seldom flare up within party politics. In spite of enormous economic divisions and the religious and ethnic heterogeneity of the country, the politicization of religion (and the religionization of politics) within the party system has been moderate in terms of the impact of Islamists on policy-making, the platforms of the biggest parties, and the issues raised during election campaigns. In the enormously polarized 2014 presidential election, religion was politicized as part of a smear campaign against Jokowi, though the campaign in general dealt only marginally with the constitutional and political position of Islam (Ufen 2014).

To summarize, during the past decade, political parties in both countries have adopted more centerist positions with regard to religious issues. This is clearly observable in Indonesia, where even the PKS has stressed its pluralist credentials. This mechanism is rather more intricate in Malaysia, where PAS is more restrained than in the past but still frequently backslides toward its Islamism and where UMNO also often flip-flops when dealing with tricky questions pertaining to minorities.

## Weak executive heads and ungovernable civil societies[12]

In 2009, Malaysia's new prime minister, Najib Razak, started to reform the country's pro-*bumiputera* policies and propagated a new approach toward national unity among ethnic and religious groups by way of his "1Malaysia" campaign. He initiated the Government Transformation Program (GTP) and announced a New Economic Model (NEM) that aimed to implement transparent affirmative action programs with a focus on the bottom 40 percent of households to diminish disparities between the rich and the poor, the urban and the rural, and the *bumiputeras* and non-*bumiputeras*. In an effort to attract foreign investors, the prime minister allowed for majority-share ownership of companies in 27 service subsectors without requiring participation by *bumiputera* equity shareholders. These measures elicited stiff resistance from those *bumiputeras* who feared an end to their privileges. In 2013, therefore, Najib called for government departments and government-linked companies (GLCs) to rescue the newspaper close to UMNO, *Utusan Malaysia*, and he announced a RM31 billion Bumiputera Economic Empowerment Plan (BEEP), thus contradicting his original policies. Najib's zigzag course was also typical of his approach to liberalizing the political system (Ufen 2013a). He abolished, for example, the dreaded Internal Security Act (ISA), but replaced it with the potentially equally draconian Security Offenses (Special Measures) Act 2012 (SOSMA 2012). He also announced that the 1948 Sedition Act would be replaced by a new National Harmony Act and promised greater freedom of expression. However, this latter reform failed due to resistance from within his own party.

The reforms designed to enervate primordialism have effected its defiant resurrection in even more primitive forms. There has been a resurgence of Malay supremacists who aim to conserve pro-*bumiputera* rights and Muslim hegemony. In the 2013 elections, a major reason for the disastrous result for BN was the impact of these chauvinist groups, including Perkasa (Pertubuhan Pribumi Perkasa, Indigenous Empowerment Organization), which motivated non-Malays to vote for opposition parties (Noor 2013). The emergence of these "uncivil" groups has caused a growing split within the political elite between ultras and moderates, as well as a shift in the discourse and belligerence from within the party system toward certain sections of civil society. NGOs now fill a void left by UMNO because this party has to cooperate with BN member parties that represent ethnic and religious minorities. The Malay NGOs are, thus, more or less controlled proxies for Islamists and ultras within or close to UMNO. According to the supremacists, achieving national unity requires that *bumiputeras* be recognized as the country's core group (*bangsa teras*). In the so-called National Unity Memorandum, signed by 314 Malay NGOs at the Islamic Center in Kuala Lumpur in November 2014 and shortly before the UMNO Congress, these Malay groups reaffirmed their status as "original" settlers of the archipelago.[13] Moreover, they rejected the National Unity Consultative Council (NUCC), stating that it was "dominated by Malaysians who are said to be liberal."[14] The committee that drafted the Memorandum was headed by the chief of Perkasa,

Ibrahim Ali, a fiery racist and former UMNO MP famous among his supporters for his outspokenness.[15]

The UMNO cooperates with chauvinist groups such as Perkasa, which was founded in September 2008 following that year's elections (Govindasamy 2015).[16] Its patron is Mahathir, who began his political career as a Malay ultra. The extreme right-wing group is notorious for intimidating protesters. It claims a membership of more than 400,000, the majority of whom are believed to be members of UMNO. Moreover, there are strong indications that the organization is partially funded by the federal government.[17] Although the Kuala Lumpur government recently often used the Sedition Act to oppress the opposition, it shied away from applying the act to Ibrahim Ali, who had called for Bibles to be burnt if they contained the word Allah and other Arabic religious terms. Other organizations close to UMNO that are fighting for a stronger role for Islam include Pertubuhan-pertubuhan Pembela Islam (Organization for the Defense of Islam, Pembela) (Liow 2009: 117ff.), Pertubuhan Kebajikan dan Dakwah Islamiah Malaysia (Islamic Missionary and Welfare Association, Pekida), and Ikatan Muslimin Malaysia (Malaysian Muslim Network, Isma). These ethno-nationalist NGOs particularly blossomed under Prime Minister Badawi, and they are still thriving under Najib. Pekida, for example, consists of a range of NGOs and is a network created by gangs. In December 2011, Prime Minister Najib attended the Pekida annual meeting and promised aid in exchange for political support (Lemière 2014: 92).[18] The highly controversial takeover of Perak's chief minister post by an UMNO stalwart after three opposition members had left their party was accompanied by violent protests that were obviously stage-managed by Pekida members (Lemière 2014: 96). Pekida is not simply an ethno-nationalist and/or Islamist group, but also extends into the underworld. A part of it is an officially registered NGO; the other part is a network of gangsters (Lemière 2014: 100). Perkasa and Pekida are only the most well known among the infamous organizations, but there are hundreds of other groups that together form a Malay Muslim public that has a huge impact on the community at large. The latest example is the role of the National Silat Federation Pesaka under its president Ali Rustam that helped organize a controversial September 16 rally by so-called red shirts in Kuala Lumpur in reaction to the much bigger Bersih 4 rally a few weeks before.[19] These groups are connected to the blogosphere, which is also sponsored and to a large extent steered by UMNO and the bureaucratic machinery.[20] All these NGOs have significantly changed the public discourse on religion and ethnicity, and are able to intimidate members of the liberal opposition. Their rise occurred precisely at a time when Muslim *bumiputeras* felt increasingly threatened by a pro-democratic, multi-ethnic, and multi-religious opposition willing to do away with special privileges for *bumiputeras*, especially Malays. The current prime minister, who has been weakened by his party's poor showing in the 2013 elections, has to react to their demands and to defend the concept of Malay supremacy (*Ketuanan Melayu*) from time to time, especially at UMNO Congresses.

Like Najib, Yudhoyono was a frail leader. The contested position of presidents in Indonesia after 1998 is not new. Abdurrahman Wahid was toppled in

2001 not only because of his erratic leadership style, but also because he was deemed too liberal in his approach to religious issues. He took a clear stance against any form of Islamism and did not tolerate the undermining of religious minority rights. Ahead of his tenure, the Islamists had hoped to win the elections in June 1999, but they failed miserably; their subsequent attempts to reintroduce the Jakarta Charter into the Indonesian Constitution were met with resistance from an overwhelming majority in the People's Congress (MPR). Nevertheless, Wahid was not capable of preventing religiously motivated large-scale violence, such as that in the Moluccas, from occurring. Megawati Sukarnoputri, a rather conservative figure, had a stronger secular coalition behind her, especially with her own PDI-P, but she did accommodate Islamists. For instance, Hamzah Haz (PPP) was vice president in her broad coalition. All in all, these presidencies were too short to allow clear conclusions regarding their impact on the evolution of minority rights. However, during Megawati's tenure the government fought decisively against Muslim terrorists in the aftermath of the 2002 Bali bombing and was instrumental in achieving stable peace accords in Poso and the Moluccas that same year. The new strategy for handling radical Islamism led to the dissolution of the militant organization Laskar Jihad, the splintering of Jemaah Islamiyah (a network responsible for many of the bombings), and Front Pembela Islam's (Islamic Defenders Front (FPI)) adoption of a low-profile stance that saw it change its targets and strategies.

FPI, today the best known and most influential of the radical organizations (International Crisis Group 2008, 2012; Setara Institute 2010; Wilson 2014b), is most likely the outgrowth of militant groups that were initially mobilized by then defense minister and commander of the armed forces Wiranto in order to "secure" a special session of the People's Congress (MPR) against protesting students in November 1998.[21] From the beginning, FPI has been notorious for raids on "places of sin" such as bars and discotheques during the fasting month of Ramadan. A few days after the Bali bombing in 2002, FPI leader Habib Rizieq was arrested. FPI suspended many of its activities and dissolved its military arm, the Laskar Pembela Islam. In the following years, FPI seldom performed so-called sweepings of hotels, restaurants, etc. In connection with the MUI and Bakor Pakem *fatwas* and statements on the Ahmadiyah, FPI amplified its efforts to trigger the disbandment of the congregation. Thus, it was in 2005 that the organization started to shift its focus toward liberal Muslims and Ahmadis. In August of that year, FPI members almost attacked a gathering of liberal Muslims in Utan Kayu (Jakarta), but they were hindered by police forces. In June 2008 they carried out an attack on a demonstration by the National Alliance for the Freedom of Faith and Religion (AAKBB) in Central Jakarta and caused dozens of casualties. Habib Rizieq Shihab and Munarman, the commander of Komando Laskar Islam, were sentenced to prison in October 2008. However, due to complicity by state authorities and politicians, FPI as an organization did not have to lie low and has since even intensified its campaigns against liberals, Ahmadis, and Shi'ites.

One may argue that today the most successful strategy of moderate Islamists is to cooperate at different levels in a more or less informal coalition of conservatives from parties, bureaucracies, and civil society. This brings about piecemeal reforms in lawmaking together with a slow "cleansing" of religious minorities at the local level and the curtailing of individual freedoms in general. Most of the militants are Sunni Muslims. Other notorious groups besides the FPI are the Forum Komunikasi Muslim Indonesia (Indonesian Muslim Communication Forum (Forkami)), Hizbut-Tahrir Indonesia (HTI), and the Forum Umat Islam (Islamic People's Forum (FUI)). FUI was established in 2005, shortly after the MUI *fatwa* on liberal Islam and secularism was issued,[22] as a coalition of organizations such as FPI, HTI, and many others at the local level (Human Rights Watch 2013; Setara Institute 2010: 123ff.). Yudhoyono was eager to be perceived in Western countries as a devout but moderate Islamic leader, but, strangely he generally failed to clearly distance himself from rogue groups such as FPI. He frequently made controversial statements regarding religious minority rights. In 2005, for example, he expressed his openness towards *fatwas* from the MUI. Shortly afterwards, the MUI called Ahmadis apostates in another *fatwa* and, therefore, semi-officially legitimized the subsequent persecution of the sect by Islamist vigilantes. In 2007, the president told the MUI that everybody had to "take strict measures against deviant beliefs" and that the state could act after a *fatwa* had been issued (Crouch 2012).

The religious bureaucracy is part of the network responsible for the recent deterioration in religious minority rights (Hicks 2014). It consists of, among other organizations, the Ministry for Religious Affairs, the Coordinating Board for Monitoring Mystical Beliefs in Society (Bakor Pakem), and the MUI. Bakor Pakem, established in 1984 under Suharto and revived in recent years, reports to Indonesia's Attorney General's Office and has branches in every province and regency. Its task is to check on "religious beliefs that could endanger society and the state." Bakor Pakem cooperates with other government agencies and recommended the banning of the Ahmadiyah faith in April 2008. It has also led or initiated prosecution in some blasphemy cases.[23]

Yudhoyono's complicity is further indicated by his appointment of controversial figures to top positions within the administration. Ma'ruf Amin, chairman of the MUI, became a member of the Presidential Advisory Council, and former general Sudi Silalahi was inaugurated as cabinet secretary in 2004 and state secretary in 2009. Gamawan Fauzi was appointed minister of home affairs; he called the FPI a "national asset" and asked local governments to cooperate with the group. Most controversial, though, was Suryadharma Ali's (PPP) appointment as minister of religious affairs. He called for the banning of Ahmadiyah and the conversion of Shi'as to Sunni Islam. This kind of stance has been widespread within Islamic/Islamist parties. In 2009, the secretary general of the PPP visited Habib Rizieq in prison and said that Rizieq would be on his party's candidate list. A parliamentary initiative in 2010 to ban FPI was blocked by PKS, PPP, and PAN. Among the Muslim parties, only PKB supported the ban. In return, FPI announced its support for Prabowo and his coalition ahead of the 2014 presidential election (Wilson 2014b). Although the FPI was not wholeheartedly welcome, nobody rejected the alliance. Such cooperation appears to be paradigmatic. A member of the provincial Parliament in Jakarta unreservedly conceded that FPI actions are usually agreed upon by his party (Gerindra) and the leadership of FPI. He was surprised that "provocateurs" had been implicated in the recent violence surrounding protests against the then Jakarta governor designate Basuki Tjahaja Purnama (Ahok), who is Christian and a member of the ethnic Chinese community.[24]

The complicity of the state apparatus with Islamists has also been demonstrated through the former's inactivity in cases of minority suppression. The closures of the GKI Yasmin Church in Bogor and of the HKBP Filadelfia Church in Bekasi, West Java were declared illegal by the courts. But even after the local governments refused to allow the churches to reopen, the central government did not actively intervene.

It is not that Yudhoyono actively prepared the ground for radical Islamists; he was partially forced to heed the demands of Islamists within his coalition and at the subnational level, and to fill government posts with conservatives. At the least, he was unwilling to seek open confrontation with radicals.[25] Since Yudhoyono never talked about his stance on FPI, one can only assume that he more or less grudgingly tolerated infringements of religious minority rights and the initiatives of some of his Islamist coalition partners and top politicians. Only in February 2011 did Yudhoyono call for the disbanding of violent mass organizations following the attack on an Ahmadiyah gathering in Banten. FPI militia commander Munarman then threatened to overthrow Yudhoyono. During Ramadan in July 2013, a raid on establishments serving alcohol in Kendal, Central Java turned violent when the FPI were confronted by local residents and had to flee. The turmoil led to the killing of a woman. When the president criticized the FPI, Habib Rizieq Syihab called him a "loser" who was protecting the Ahmadiyah while whitewashing corruption in his own administration.[26]

## Concluding remarks

In Indonesia and Malaysia, central executive heads have been weak because they have been forced to balance different groups within their grand coalitions. In Malaysia, Najib has to heed the interests of ethnic and religious minorities within the Barisan Nasional and to accommodate the ultra faction of UMNO. Yudhoyono was always caught between the more secularist and the more Islamic/Islamist forces within the government and the general public. In both cases the result was a rather elusive, sometimes erratic policy in relation to religious minority rights and a strange mismatch between each leader's reputation as a reformer and the real policies on the ground. Najib and Yudhoyono both shied away from criticizing radicals and from taking clear decisions, instead only reacting and opportunistically seeking to play certain groups off against each other.

These leaders' approaches have to be analyzed against the background of party systems in which political Islam has evinced a low profile, in contrast to the politicization of religion in general. In Malaysia, the strong opposition coalition is built on a moderate stance on secularism and political Islam. This has diluted the competition within party politics between UMNO and PAS (although it does increase from time to time). UMNO is dependent on non-Muslim coalition partners, has to tone down its Islamic conservatism, and can hardly play the Islamic card openly. In Indonesia, the competition within party politics has always been restrained because in many instances parties form a kind of cartel in order to share the spoils of office. Only from time to time has competition between secularists and Islamists flared up; most politicians, even those from Islamist parties, avoid the outright politicization of religion. In both countries, parts of the religious bureaucracy and civil society, especially rogue groups, have taken the initiative in promoting conservative Islam and attempting to obtain dominance over religious minorities. Rogue networks such as Pekida and Perkasa in Malaysia and FPI in Indonesia are tolerated, and are sometimes even instrumentalized by administrative and political party elites in order to put specific issues on the political agenda.

In Malaysia, rogue groups mushroomed under Badawi and are increasingly influential under Najib. The prime minister's "volitional ambiguity" toward vigilantism has furthered the clout of these proxies. In Indonesia, these groups emerged earlier, but after the weakening of terrorist groups, the subsiding of civil wars in the Moluccas and Poso, and the increasing moderation of Islamist political parties, they predominantly set the agenda with respect to the role of a politicized Islam. Their rhetoric is as fiery as that of the Malaysian groups, but they are less controlled and instrumentalized, and their sheer existence is more contested and challenged. Although Indonesia is in many respects more democratic than Malaysia, the retrenchment of religious minority rights there is processing with much more violence and in a much more threatening way. Because the architecture of the presidential democracy is mostly established, and the constitution and the Pancasila (without the Jakarta Charter) are almost sacrosanct, Indonesian Islamists are attempting to change the written and unwritten constitution from the margins – in both a geographical and an institutional sense. It is not predominantly the Parliament or the constitutional court but rather the semi-official MUI, mayors, more or less legalized rogue groups, and the local police, etc. that are challenging the decades-old foundation of the nation-state with respect to minority rights. It follows that the deterioration of religious minority rights is not inevitable.[27] It is not the result of ideological contrasts inherent to different monotheistic worldviews, but rather of shifting power constellations. The targets and the strategies of Islamists change depending on political opportunity structures. Some religious minorities may live unchallenged in a country for decades before the mainstream suddenly "discovers" a disturbing "otherness" about them. Obviously, minorities serve as scapegoats and as symbols for deeper social tensions. The groups that fight these minorities, again, are often proxies of elite fractions that are in a battle with other elite fractions, usually over quite secular things. Whereas in Indonesia this contestation may lead in the long run to ever-fiercer competition between advocates of two contrasting state models and to fundamental constitutional reforms, in Malaysia the potential sequence is different. Here, two constitutional contestations are taking place at the same time: that centered on the question of autocracy versus democracy, as represented by the current ruling coalition and the Pakatan Rakyat opposition, respectively; and that centered on the place of Islam, *bumiputeras*, and religious and ethnic minorities within the nation-state.

## Notes

1 I am grateful to Marco Bünte, Björn Dressel, Tobias Hoheneder, and Kathrin Rupprecht for their valuable input.

2 Article 153 of the constitution guarantees special privileges for the *bumiputeras* (sons of the soil), who are mostly Malays. A Malay is legally defined as a person who professes the religion of Islam, habitually speaks the Malay language, and conforms to Malay custom. Other *bumiputeras* are East Malaysian ethnic groups such as the Dayak, Melanau, Bajau, Kadazandusun, Murut, etc.

3 This chapter does not focus on macro-sociological causes of the politicization of religion such as global tendencies to strengthen religious identities or shifting class structures in the wake of capitalist development (Hadiz 2011). For an approach explicitly including micro- and meso-sociological factors, see Sidel (2006). Likewise, Formichi (2014: 1f.) looks at "wider contexts of international politics, changing national political dynamics, legal provisions regulating religious minorities, and the local environment in which the attacks have occurred" and traces "the trajectory of the violent turn, bringing national politics and local dynamics into conversation with legal opinions in both the civil and religious realms." Hicks (2014: 323) "offers an interpretive framework that tries to avoid underplaying political power (as religious essentialism) or religion (as political instrumentalism)" and analyzes "wider processes of maintaining or securing both political and religious authority."

4 The chapter refers to developments until mid-2015. Since that time the PAS has split and a new, moderate National Trust Party (Parti Amanah Negara) has been established. The remaining PAS seems to be more assertive in terms of its original Islamist agenda.

5 See also reports by Setara and the Wahid Institute and their yearly counts of violent acts directed against religious minorities.

6 See Amnesty International, "Prosecuting Beliefs: Indonesia's Blasphemy Laws" (AI Index: ASA 21/018/2014), November 2014.

7 On Ahmadiyah see Crouch (2012), Platzdasch (2013), Hicks (2014).

8 The National Commission on Violence Against Women (Komnas Perempuan) (n.d.) counted 282 discriminatory policies against women inspired by Islamic law at the end of 2012 in contrast to only 154 such policies in 2009.

9 The passage of the pornography law was also promoted by a politician from the Partai Demokrat, Balkan Kaplele, who was chairman of a special committee responsible for drafting the bill.

10 Mahathir was able, with "his firm hand, his iron will and the force of his formidable character," to hold these tensions in check. In contrast, Badawi "was certainly not strong enough to control these poisonous growths once, after Dr Mahathir's time, they had matured in strength and tenacity, even virulence" (Kessler 2013: 93).

11 Yet, the intra-party fight between the Erdogans and the *ulama* or traditionalists resulted in the establishment of PAN (see note 4). Moreover, PAS went ahead with the plan to implement *hudud* laws in Kelantan.

12 The executive heads in Indonesia and Malaysia have much in common, even though the systems of government are markedly different. In both cases the leader's

accountability to the governing party coalition is relatively weak because of the presidential prerogatives in Indonesia and the presidential leadership style of Malaysian prime ministers, with their extraordinarily powerful prime minister's office. Nevertheless, both are generally dependent on multiparty coalitions.

13 While ignoring the status of *orang asli* (original people) who would have the right to depict themselves as the first inhabitants of the country.

14 *The Malaysian Insider*, November 23, 2014, "Recognise Bumiputeras as 'Core Group' for National Unity, say Malay Groups."

15 In 2013 he stood as an independent candidate but was ultimately supported by UMNO. The vice president of Perkasa, Zulkifli Noordin, was an UMNO candidate in Shah Alam. Neither was able to gain a plurality.

16 Following the split of PAS, the party surprisingly announced that they have started to cooperate with Perkasa on issues related to Islamic and Malay interests (see *The Malaysian Insider*, October 17, 2015, "PAS–Perkasa Cooperation on Issues Nothing Strange Says Youth Wing." Perkasa's new stance was probably linked to the widening rift between Mahathir and Najib.

17 See *Free Malaysia Today*, November 11, 2014, "Are Isma, Perkasa Funded by Govt Grants?" (www.freemalaysiatoday.com/category/nation/2014/11/11/are-isma-perkasa-funded-by-govt-grants/).

18 Sophie Lemière (2014) interprets this as "connivance militancy" and distinguishes between different types with respect to the degree of militancy.

19 *The Malaysian Insider*, October 25, 2015, "We're Ready to Go to War if Need Be, Says Silat Leader."

20 UMNO used so-called cyber-troopers during the 2013 election campaign. See also Najib's concession that the party hires bloggers to write for it in *The Malaysian Insider*, November 30, 2014, "Najibs Mocking of Pro-UMNO Bloggers Will Backfire Says ex-NST Editor." Moreover, the regime holds sway over state TV and radio stations and newspapers such as the fiery UMNO mouthpiece *Utusan Malaysia*.

21 In 2000, FPI backed Wiranto when he was investigated by the National Commission for Human Rights (Komnas HAM) because of human rights violations in East Timor and besieged the Komnas HAM office. In 2004, FPI endorsed Wiranto as presidential candidate.

22 The MUI issued this controversial *fatwa* in 2005 against secularism, pluralism, and liberalism (known in Indonesia under the acronym SIPILIS).

23 See Human Rights Watch, July 12, 2012, "Indonesia: Shia Cleric Convicted of Blasphemy. Amend Blasphemy Law, Abolish Islamist Legal Board."

24 *Kompas*, October 4, 2014, "Adik Uje Sebut Aksi Unjuk Rasa Selalu Koordinasi dengan Gerindra."

25 Only at the end of his tenure did Yudhoyono appoint a potential reformer, Lukman Hakim Saifuddin, as minister for religious affairs, after Suryadharma Ali was forced to resign because of a corruption scandal.

26 *Kompas*, July 22, 2013, "Pesan Presiden SBY untuk FPI."

27 Since the transfer of power from Yudhoyono to Jokowi, for example, policies with regard to religious minorities seem to be changing: a progressive draft law on religious harmony (RUU Kerukunan Beragama) has been prepared.

## Bibliography

Buehler, M. (2013). "Subnational Islamization through Secular Parties: Comparing Shari'a Politics in Two Indonesian Provinces." *Comparative Politics*, 46(1): 63–82.

Chin, J. (2014). "Najib's Pyrrhic Victory and the Demise of 1Malaysia." *Southeast Asian Affairs*, 2014: 175–189.

Chong Eu Choong (2014). "The Christian Response to State-led Islamization in Malaysia." In *Religious Diversity in Muslim-majority States in Southeast Asia: Areas of Toleration and Conflict*, eds B. Platzdasch and J. Saravanamuttu. Singapore, ISEAS, pp. 290–320.
Christian Solidarity Worldwide (CSW) (2014). *Indonesia Report: Pluralism in Peril*, February 14, available at: www.csw.org.uk/2014-indonesia-report.
Crouch, M. (2012). "Judicial Review and Religious Freedom: The Case of Indonesian Ahmadis." *Sydney Law Review*, 34 (3), 545–572.
Dressel, B. and Bünte, M. (2014). "Constitutional Politics in Southeast Asia: From Contestation to Constitutionalism?" *Contemporary Southeast Asia*, 36(1): 1–22.
Formichi, C. (2014). "Violence, Sectarianism, and the Politics of Religion: Articulations of Anti-*Shi'a* Discourses in Indonesia." *Indonesia*, 98(October): 1–27.
Freedom House (2010). "Policing Belief: The Impact of Blasphemy Laws on Human Rights," available at: https://freedomhouse.org/report/special-reports/policing-belief-impact-blasphemy-laws-human-rights#.VMnme2c5Bjr.
Govindasamy, A.R. (2015). "Social Movements in Contemporary Malaysia: The Cases of BERSIH, HINDRAF and Perkasa." In *Routledge Handbook of Contemporary Malaysia*, ed. M.L. Weiss. London and New York, Routledge, pp. 116–126.
Hadiz, V.R. (2011). "Indonesian Political Islam: Capitalist Development and the Legacies of the Cold War." *Journal of Current Southeast Asian Affairs*, 30(1): 3–38.
Hicks, J. (2014). "Heresy and Authority: Understanding the Turn against Ahmadiyah in Indonesia." *Southeast Asia Research*, 22(3): 321–339.
Horowitz, D.L. (2013). *Constitutional Change and Democracy in Indonesia*. Cambridge, Cambridge University Press.
Hosen, N. (2005). "Religion and the Indonesian Constitution: A Recent Debate." *Journal of Southeast Asian Studies*, 36(3): 419–440.
Human Rights Watch (2013). *In Religion's Name: Abuses against Religious Minorities in Indonesia*. New York, www.hrw.org/reports/2013/02/28/religion-s-name-0.
International Crisis Group (2008). *Indonesia: Implications of the Ahmadiyah Decree*. Asia Briefing No. 78, Jakarta/Brussels, July 7.
International Crisis Group (2012). *How Indonesian Extremists Regroup*. Crisis Group Asia Report No. 228, Jakarta/Brussels, July 16.
Kaur, A. (2014). "Hindraf as a Response to Islamization in Malaysia." In *Religious Diversity in Muslim-majority States in Southeast Asia: Areas of Toleration and Conflict*, eds B. Platzdasch and J. Saravanamuttu. Singapore, ISEAS, pp. 341–358.
Kessler, C. (2013). "The Abdullah Badawi Premiership: Interlude or End-Game?" In *Awakening: The Abdullah Badawi Years in Malaysia*, eds B. Welsh and J. Chin. Petaling Jaya, SIRD, pp. 66–96.
Lemière, S. (2014). "Gangsta and Politics in Malaysia." In *Misplaced Democracy. Malaysian Politics and People*, ed. S. Lemière. Petaling Jaya, SIRD, pp. 91–108.
Liow, J.C. (2009). *Piety and Politics. Islamism in Contemporary Malaysia*. New York, Oxford University Press.
Lopez, C. (2015). "Interfaith Relations in Malaysia." In *Routledge Handbook of Contemporary Malaysia*, ed. M. Weiss. London and New York, Routledge, pp. 324–336.
Maznah Mohamad (2013). "Bureaucratic Islam in Malaysia: Homogenizing and Ring-fencing the Muslim Subject." In *Encountering Islam: The Politics of Religious Identities in Southeast Asia*, ed. Y. Foong. Singapore, ISEAS, pp. 103–132.
National Commission On Violence Against Women – Komnas Perempuan (n.d.). *National Human Rights Institution Independent Report on the Review of Indonesian*

*Report on the Implementation of the International Covenant on Civil and Political Rights in Indonesia, 2005–2012*, submitted to UN Human Rights Committee, available at: http://tbinternet.ohchr.org/Treaties/CCPR/SharedDocuments/IDN/INT_CCPR_NGO_IDN_14711_E.doc.

Neo, J.L. (2014). "What's in a Name? Malaysia's 'Allah' Controversy and the Judicial Intertwining of Islam with Ethnic Identity." *International Journal of Constitutional Law*, 12(3): 751–768.

Njoto-Feillard, G. (2015). *Religious Pluralism and Tolerance in Jokowi's Indonesia.* ISEAS Perspectives 10/2015.

Noor, F.A. (2013). "The Malaysian General Elections of 2013: The Last Attempt at Secular-inclusive Nation-building?" *Journal of Current Southeast Asian Affairs*, 32(2): 89–104.

Pew Research Center (2014). *Religious Hostilities Reach Six-year High*, available at: www.pewforum.org/2014/01/14/religious-hostilities-reach-six-year-high/.

Platzdasch, B. (2009). *Islamism in Indonesia: Politics in the Emerging Democracy*. Singapore, ISEAS.

Platzdasch, B. (2013). "Religious Freedom in Contemporary Indonesia: The Case of the Ahmadiyah." In *Encountering Islam: The Politics of Religious Identities in Southeast Asia*, ed. Hew Yew Foong. Singapore, ISEAS, pp. 218–246.

Puyok, A. (2015). "Rise of Christian Political Consciousness and Mobilization. In *Routledge Handbook of Contemporary Malaysia*, ed. M. Weiss. London and New York, Routledge, pp. 60–71.

Salim, A. (2007). "Muslim Politics in Indonesia's Democratisation: The Religious Majority and the Rights of Minorities in the Post-New Order Era." In *Indonesia. Democracy and the Promise of Good Governance*, eds R. McLeod and A. MacIntyre. Singapore, ISEAS, pp. 115–137.

Salim, A. (2008). *Challenging the Secular State: The Islamization of Law in Modern Indonesia*. Honolulu, University of Hawai'i Press.

Setara Institute (2010). *The Faces of Islam "Defenders": Religion, Radicalism and Its Implications on Assurance of Religious/Belief Freedom in Jabodetabek and West Java.* Jakarta.

Setara Institute (2013). *Leadership Without Initiative: The Condition of Freedom of Religious/Belief in Indonesia 2012*. Jakarta.

Sherlock, S. (2008). "Parties and Decision-making in the Indonesian Parliament: A Case Study of RUU APP, the Anti-pornography Bill." *Australian Journal of Asian Law*, 10(2): 159–183.

Sidel, J.T. (2006). *Riots, Pogroms, Jihad: Religious Violence in Indonesia*. Ithaca, NY, Cornell University Press.

Sundra Karean, V. (2006). "The Malaysian Constitution and its Identity Crisis: Secular or Theocratic?" *LAWASIA Journal*, 1: 47–61.

Ufen, A. (2013a). "Introduction: The 2013 Malaysian Elections: Business as Usual or Part of a Protracted Transition?" *Journal of Current Southeast Asian Affairs*, 2: 3–17.

Ufen, A. (2013b). "Lipset and Rokkan in Southeast Asia: Indonesia in Comparative Perspective." In *Political Parties in Southeast Asia. Clientelism and Electoral Competition in Indonesia, Thailand and the Philippines*, eds D. Tomsa and A. Ufen. Abingdon, Routledge, pp. 40–61.

Ufen, A. (2014). "Jokowi's Victory. The End of the New Order in Indonesia?" *Asia Policy Brief*, Bertelsmann Stiftung, 05/14, 1–7, available at: www.bertelsmann-stiftung.de/de/publikationen/publikation/did/jokowis-victory-the-end-of-the-new-order-in-indonesia/.

USCIRF (United States Commission on International Religious Freedom) (2014). *Annual Report*, available at: www.uscirf.gov/sites/default/files/USCIRF%202014%20Annual%20Report%20PDF.pdf.

Wahid Institute (2010). *Islam, The Constitution, and Human Rights: The Problematics of Religious Freedom in Indonesia*. Jakarta.

Wahid Institute (2014). *Laporan Tahunan: Kebebasan Beragama/Berkeyakinan dan Intoleransi 2013*, Jakarta, available at: www.wahidinstitute.org/wi-id/images/upload/dokumen/laporan_kbb_2013_wi.pdf.

Wilson, I. (2014a). "Morality Racketeering: Vigilantism and Populist Islamic Militancy in Indonesia." In *Between Dissent and Power: The Transformations of Islamic Politics in the Middle East and Asia*, eds B.T. Khoo, V. Hadiz and Y. Nakanishi. Basingstoke, Palgrave Macmillan, pp. 248–274.

Wilson, I. (2014b). *Resisting Democracy: Front Pembela Islam and Indonesia's 2014 Elections*. ISEAS perspective 10/2014, available at: www.iseas.edu.sg/documents/publication/ISEAS_Perspective_2014_10-Resisting_Democracy.pdf.

# 10 Vietnam's constitutional politics in focus

## Investigating the arenas of the rule of law and human rights

*Bui Hai Thiem*

### Introduction

Between 2011 and 2013, Vietnam's party-state initiated a constitutional reform process that invited different social actors into the political space. While ultimately no far-reaching reform was incorporated into the 2013 revision of the constitution, the strenuous public debates over constitutional amendments demonstrated potential for change in the two most contested arenas: the rule of law and human rights. Since the collapse of the Soviet Union and the socialist bloc in the early 1990s, as a one-party-state Vietnam has made a concerted effort to adapt its socialist theoretical foundations to a market economy and substantially transform key legacies. Since then, the "socialist-oriented" market economy and the socialist law-based state concepts have been hailed as the most important theoretical achievements of the Communist Party of Vietnam (CPV). CPV theorists have claimed the doctrine that Vietnam is a socialist law-based state as a distilled version of the rule of law toward which Vietnam is moving (see e.g., Hoang Chi Bao 2002; Tran Ngoc Hien 2008; Tran Ngoc Duong 2011). Building on the legacy of "socialist legality," the doctrine has been given multiple meanings and dimensions. It is developing concurrently as a fundamental value, a basic principle of the constitution, and a set of institutions to support its realization. However, the human rights regime based on the concept is insufficient and inconsistent, exposing disconnects with international human rights laws that Vietnam recognizes. Rather than evolving independently, the current dynamic discourse on human rights has emerged in Vietnam within this broader context.

The literature on the concept of socialist law-based state and human rights in Vietnam tends not to be directly on point. Little attention has been paid to the subtle shifts in the human rights discourse taking place within the general context of the socialist law-based state or to the implications of these shifts. This chapter argues that the changing discourse on human rights in Vietnam is likely to transcend the socialist law-based state concept to create a new human rights identity, and the identity-shaping process will have major implications for the evolution of human rights there as both an ideal and a regime. The process is characterized by contestations and challenges of ideas and values by both party-state and non-state actors that are unprecedented in Vietnamese political and legal discourse.

The chapter therefore first investigates how the "socialist" rule of law evolved from simply socialist legality to a socialist law-based state. It then links this development to the human rights regime and the changes in the discourse on human rights that have taken place during the constitutional reform process. In setting out the context and content of constitutional reform, the chapter seeks to deconstruct the socialist rule of law and interpret the discourse of human rights accordingly. It identifies subtle changes in that discourse as the party-state engages more deeply and substantively with international human rights law. To make sense of these changes, it is important to understand the mechanism of the socialization of human rights within Vietnam's politically closed authoritarianism. The chapter also attempts to illuminate the implications of this change for the progression of Vietnam's human rights regime and ideals.

## Gradual moves to a rule of law discourse

In Vietnam, the discussion of human rights comes within the broad framework of *Nhà nước pháp quyền xã hội chủ nghĩa* (the socialist law-based state). The discourse on human rights does not have independent standing separate from the state doctrine because it is rooted in the traditional dominance of the socialist legality concept (*pháp chế xã hội chủ nghĩa*) and the doctrine of a socialist law-based state – a doctrine that has emerged as an indigenous variant of the rule of law since the early 1990s. That is why the point of departure for any research on human rights discourse in Vietnam must be socialist legality and the law-based state.

## Socialist legality

The core idea on which the concept of socialist legality is based is that in governing the state attaches increasing importance to the role and rule of law. However, there is vigorous domestic debate about its significance. As John Gillespie argues, "For most of Vietnam's history, laws were marginalized and play a relatively minor role compared with regulation through moral virtue, administrative measures, and self-regulation by village officials or families" (2010: 78). Mark Sidel (2008) details how, early on during its period in power, the CPV marginalized laws and describes the efforts of intellectuals like Nguyen Huu Dang, Nguyen Manh Tuong, and Vu Dinh Hoe to convince the CPV to recognize the role of laws in governance. They made little headway. In 1959 the CPV (mirroring the Soviet state apparatus) even abolished the Ministry of Justice, which was not re-established until 1980. Generation by generation, CPV leaders have emphasized leadership by revolutionary moral principles and rule by virtue – both of which are core neo-Confucian governance values. Writings by Ho Chi Minh such as *Revolutionary Morality* (1958) and *Improving Revolutionary Morality, Sweeping Clean Individualism* (1969) have become classic texts for educating CPV members (Ho Chi Minh 2000). They have left a profound imprint on every Party Congress Resolution, many Central Committee

Plenum Resolutions, and discussions by such CPV theorists and scholars as Dang Xuan Ky (1994), Nguyen Duc Binh (2006), and Le Huu Nghia (2007). In recent years, campaigns for "studying and following Ho Chi Minh's moral example" and "criticism and self-criticism" have clearly emphasized moral virtue as the most critical value in governance.[1]

The realities of CPV governance, however, have demonstrated that leadership by moral virtue is insufficient and that laws are needed to regulate state–society relations. In particular, excesses in the execution of Chinese-style land reforms between 1953 and 1956 ultimately required public apologies from Ho Chi Minh and Vo Nguyen Giap – top CPV leaders regarded as highly virtuous – and the demotion of Party Secretary Truong Chinh. Recognizing the problem, late in 1952 the CPV imported the Soviet idea of socialist legality as a legal-rational supplement in governance that sees law as politically expedient. At its Third National Congress in 1960, for the first time the CPV officially endorsed the socialist legality doctrine (CPV 1960).

All Party Congresses through to the most recent in 2011 have reaffirmed this doctrine as making state management more effective. As Gillespie (2010) pointed out, four fundamental principles underlie the socialist legality doctrine: rule by the party leadership; the class-based nature of law (law as expressing the will of the ruling class); the ready substitution of policy for law; and the predominance of the collective interest over individual rights. These core principles are theoretical anchors for the CPV, and prevail throughout official political and legal discourse. However, since the country embarked upon *Doi Moi* (market-based reforms) in 1986 they have been periodically subject to challenge and to some extent have been eroded.

However, the principle that party leadership of the state and society is paramount – affirmed in Article 4 of both the 1980 and 1992 constitutions – is ambiguous and is practiced inconsistently. Despite continued calls to reinforce party leadership in every aspect of governance, Party Congresses regularly criticize the state's ineffectiveness. As a consequence, not only has socialist legality not been well observed, it has even been undermined. The Political Report presented to the sixth Party Congress in 1986 acknowledged that "it is increasingly common that the laws and discipline of the state are violated" (CPV 1986). The CPV has recognized that overlaps in the functions, tasks, and organization of the party and the state are a root cause of this problem, but it has struggled with "renovating the way of party leadership" (CPV 1986).

Gainsborough (2012) has observed that a question central to any attempt at political reform in Vietnam is how to redefine the relationship between the party and the state. This question, which is closely linked to the other three core principles of socialist legality doctrine, goes to the heart of the inherent tension between party supremacy and effective governance. The CPV itself has been fully aware of this issue since the early 1990s:

> Realities over the past few years have indicated that for the renovation and improvement of the political system, the building and practice of socialist

> democracy, *the pivotal issue is to clearly delineate functions and well handle the relationship between the Party, the State and mass organizations*; resolutely combat bureaucratic bad practices and acts infringing on people's mastership, and at the same time criticize and overcome distortions.
>
> (CPV 1991b; emphasis added)

Socialist Vietnam's emphasis on the class-based nature of law is being called into question now that the country has opted for a market economy integrated with the rest of the world. Further, if law is considered to represent the will of the ruling class, it may be interpreted that the CPV has failed to execute that will or fulfill its leadership mission. The Political Report to the seventh Party Congress in 1991 admitted that "Many laws and ordinances that have been promulgated have not [been] strictly and consistently implemented. Many cases of breaching laws have never been brought to court; there have been delays in court hearings or the judgments are not strict" (CPV 1991a). Law understood as the will of the ruling class depends to a great degree on discretionary control by the CPV. In a market economy, this poses difficulties for businesses. There have been numerous complaints about "opaque and constantly changing regulations, intrusive government inspection and official corruption" (CPV 1991a). The introduction and practice of a market economy and international economic integration require that national law be characterized by stability, transparency, accessibility, consistency, and limits on discretionary application and alignment with widely accepted standards. In short, law whose enforcement depends on what the party-state considers expedient is incompatible with the smooth operation of a market economy.

Furthermore, the party-state has found it difficult to restate policies and guidelines as laws for regulating economic and social activities. In 1991 the CPV acknowledged that it needed to turn policies and guidelines into laws because "there has been a lack of many necessary laws in the economic field and in the field of internal affairs and administration" (CPV 1991a). The frequent conflation of policy and guidelines with laws and the lack of a clear delineation between them have resulted in ineffective governance and inconsistency, overlaps, and a lack of both the viability and enforceability of laws. The crux of the problem is the long tradition that party policies and guidelines have regulatory power over not only party members but also the whole of society. That notion has proven hard to sustain in a market economy where only laws can support such power. Increased CPV legalization efforts are thus essential to infuse legal-rational authority into the party's legitimacy to rule (Thayer 2009).

When individual rights are arbitrarily subordinated to collective interests – themselves often vague, loosely defined, and thus easily manipulated by powerful interest groups – there is a significant risk that the legitimate interests of the people will be damaged and their rights blatantly violated. Such problems have been particularly evident and have increasingly created pressures related to policies and laws regarding land rights since the first land law in the *Doi Moi* era was enacted in 1987. Many voices have been calling for greater respect for individual rights to ensure justice for the people. They often express themselves in the form of petitions initiated by well-known intellectuals and former high-ranking officials, such as the Group of 72, which advanced a radical seven-point petition on constitutional amendments in January 2013, or those speaking out in the bauxite mining controversy in 2009. These issues have captured the attention of the party-state, which has recognized the need for a new theoretical foundation.

## The socialist law-based state and human rights

Although after *Doi Moi* socialist legality could not keep up with the demands of governance, party theorists and legal scholars nevertheless sought to defend its relevance and the core principles. They argued that the doctrine simply needed to be updated. Inspired by the Soviet doctrine of *pravovoe gosudarstvo*, the law-based state (Gillespie 2004), and the idea of the rule of law as a critical governance value in Western liberal discourse, the CPV formulated the doctrine of the socialist law-based state. Matthieu Salomon and Vu Doan Ket (2010: 136) refer to this doctrine as "dualist thinking, mixing 'rule of law' and 'rule of the Party'." While it captures a prominent feature of the doctrine, their view may be reductionist. In fact, "rule of the party" is only one, though possibly the most important, principle of socialist legality. For a more nuanced approach, I argue that the socialist rule of law version that CPV theorists advocate as the most significant theoretical post-*Doi Moi* achievement represents a syncretism of "socialist legality" and "the law-based state" which has a broader embrace.

Once exposed to international standards and values in governance as a consequence of its decision to adopt an open-door policy, the CPV was attracted by the rhetorical power of the rule of law. However, the road to a socialist law-based state has not been smooth (Do Muoi 1992). Basically, it has reflected dualist CPV thinking on how to organize state powers. On the one hand, the CPV clings to the doctrine of "unity of powers" and repudiates the concept of the separation of powers or a checks-and-balances system. This leaves little space left for the concept of judicial independence and, as noted by Ginsburg (2010), "the scope of judicial power in the regulatory arena is subject to ultimate control by strong political powers." Not only can the CPV control judicial power but the legislative and the executive can also influence it.

However, faced with widespread bureaucratic corruption and abuse of powers, the CPV is seeking to establish a formal normative structure to check bureaucratic powers. Here, "normative structure" means a collection of norms and institutions that can regulate and prescribe behavior, constitute identity (understood as the distinctive purpose ascribed to an actor, including self-understanding), and shape the interests of social and political actors. Traditionally, to monitor and punish bureaucratic errors and malfeasance, the CPV has relied on its own apparatus, especially the control committee system at every level of party organization, and on the practice of criticism and self-criticism.

However, the party has also come to realize that these alone have not been sufficient to curb rampant corruption and the proliferation of complaints from the public. Yet, though the need for legal-rational processes to control state powers has become obvious, the CPV hesitates to grant more substantive powers to the branches of government for fear they would become more independent of party leadership. The CPV has been struggling to find a way to accept constitutional and legal constraints on its power while retaining the capability to deal with governance problems even as they are mounting.

While every Party Congress still reaffirms "strengthening socialist legality," the term itself has fallen out of use since the doctrine of the socialist law-based state was formally endorsed by the Seventh National Congress Resolution of the CPV in 1991 and incorporated into the 1992 constitution by a 2001 resolution of the National Assembly on constitutional amendments in 2001.[2] The doctrine has since been popularized by party-state documents and writings by party theorists and scholars. Still, the core principles of socialist legality are not only unchanged but also incrementally updated by the CPV to flesh out the notion of the socialist law-based state. As noted by Gillespie, in Vietnam, "writers use *nhà nước pháp quyền* as a convenient rubric to smuggle socialist legality and liberal democratic ideas into the 'rule of law' discourse" (Gillespie 2004). When it comes to more concrete details and questions about the socialist law-based state, however, analysis and discussion are usually missing or there is simply recourse to the official line set out in party documents. Due to the lack of substantive discussion, consensus has been slow to emerge on how to resolve the tensions between social legality and the liberal democratic concept of rule of law. The doctrine of the socialist law-based state is in fact designed to embrace the rhetorical power of the rule of law and at the same time reconcile inherent tensions.

The first major tension to note is between the powers of party leadership and the powers of the state, or between the traditional notion of unity of powers and separation of powers. The CPV has tried to manage this tension by highlighting the requirements for clearer coordination, allocation, and control of powers among the legislative, executive, and judicial branches. The insertion of the term "control of power" into the eleventhth Congress Resolution in 2011 was the result of a consensus that emerged from long-standing and heated internal debates to define a key characteristic of the socialist law-based state. In making the insertion, the CPV has come to accept that powers should be checked. In fact, in 2007 it dissolved some powerful specialized commissions, transferring their functions to state institutions.[3]

Greater recognition of the role of the power of the courts – and efforts to reform the court system in order to clarify bureaucratic and judicial powers so that courts can deal more effectively with cases – are major steps toward building the law-based state. Both the legislative and executive branches have been granted more discretion. The National Assembly has shown growing confidence in holding the executive accountable – though with limited effect – and has actively embraced broader powers of oversight and legislating. The executive has become more dynamic and more autonomous in decision-making and administration.

Concern has been expressed that without there being a formal normative structure, the CPV can at its own discretion withdraw these powers at any time. This is in fact what happened in mid-2012, when the Anti-Corruption Central Steering Committee was returned from the administration to the CPV, with the General Secretary as its head, and the CPV Commissions on Internal Affairs and Economic Affairs were reconstituted.[4] This has led to difficulties in applying the anti-corruption law; the party decisions sent a mixed message about whether the party-state genuinely intended to build up the rule of law.

The second tension is the role of the constitution in relation to party policies and its power to regulate party organizations and members. On the one hand, party lines and party resolutions still prevail. CPV General Secretary Nguyen Phu Trong asserts that the significance of the constitution is second to that of the CPV political platform (VnExpress 2013). On the other hand, the CPV has been placing more emphasis on the importance of the constitution and laws, and on the expression of policies in the form of laws. It stresses that "the state manages society by law," basically meaning that rule by law will replace rule by decree. Although it continues to hold an instrumentalist view of law, the CPV has signaled that it will refrain from issuing policies, guidelines, instructions, and directives in order to manage governance. The formal supremacy of the constitution is widely accepted, the need for a more effective mechanism of enforcing constitutional protection is recognized, and there have been efforts to make the constitution itself less a party policy document and more a legally enforceable text. Pressures have been building for more conspicuous and concrete constitutional and legal constraints on operations of the party and its members.[5] The intent of these efforts was to ensure that party members and non-members are equal before the law[6] and that the CPV and its members are accountable to the law.

The final tension to be reconciled concerns human rights and what they mean within the party-state structure. Before the 1990s, human rights were downplayed in mainstream political and legal discourse in Vietnam. They also had little influence on the behavior of the party-state. Human rights basically mean individual rights, but the party-state's dominant notion has been to promote state and collective interests. However, as Vietnam has become integrated into regional and global economies, the party-state has become conscious of the need to give more effective respect and protection to human rights. In principle, it has accepted that because a human rights regime is an integral part of the rule of law, the state is obliged to acknowledge, respect, and protect it. The question is now how can the party-state embrace internationally recognized governance values within the doctrine of the socialist law-based state? Today this is the critical arena for discourse on human rights in Vietnam.

The official view of human rights is rooted in the legal positivist tradition of socialist thought that sovereign rights prevail over human rights; it reflects "deeply entrenched communitarian views that human rights should be assessed according to broad social outcomes rather than individual needs" (Gillespie 2006). Therefore, the party-state enacts laws to guarantee human rights to the extent that they do not encroach upon sovereign rights. Further, human rights can only emanate from the laws promulgated by the state.

As noted by Gillespie, socialist legality may be seen as "an extreme manifestation of legal positivism" (2004) where there is no space for natural rights. Thus, official discourse in Vietnam has only addressed state interests as represented by the CPV. Human rights are so politically sensitive that they are virtually taboo in state-regulated media and public discussions. Nevertheless, the term "human rights" has appeared sporadically in the discourse of top leaders. In a speech to the fifth CPV Congress in 1982, General Secretary Le Duan stressed that the establishment of the people's administration, national independence, reunification, and economic, cultural, and social achievements in themselves "guarantee authentic human rights" (CPV 1982). In other words, the official view was that because socialist legality ensured human rights, discussion of human rights would be either unnecessary or irrelevant; the focus should be on socialist legality.

## Human rights ideals in post-*Doi Moi* Vietnam

The notion and practice of human rights began to change markedly in the late 1980s when the country adopted market-based reforms and opened its economy to the world. The development of the socialist law-based state from 1992 onward has brought human rights language into official discourse. Since – like the concept of rule of law itself – it is too rhetorically powerful to be ignored, human rights has gained political and legal currency in Vietnam. This new development under the doctrine of socialist rule of law has been attributed mainly to the move toward a market economy and the increasingly deeper integration of Vietnam into the international community, both economically and politically.

Traditionally, the Vietnamese party-state has adopted a communitarian view of human rights, prioritizing economic, social, and cultural rights over individualistic political and civil rights. The country's economic success since *Doi Moi* – which has brought reductions in poverty and progress toward achieving the UN Millennium Development Goals – has helped support the CPV's claim that it has protected and advanced human rights in Vietnam. However, the introduction of market reforms and the requirement for increased legalization to accommodate development needs has promoted a turn in human rights discourse toward more recognition and protection of individualistic political and civil rights.

Incorporation of human rights discourse into the legal sphere was first evidenced by the recognition in the Criminal Code of 1985 and the Criminal Procedures Code of 1988 of the presumption of innocence for defendants and of a victim's right to compensation.[7] In 1992, the Party Secretariat issued Directive No. 12 on "Human Rights and the Viewpoint, Policy of the Party," stating that the state should "be prepared to express willingness to cooperate in international relations for human rights, and at the same time, fight against plots to take advantage of the issue against us" (Pham Binh Minh 2010). However, the party-state leaders and theorists needed fresh ideas to reconcile the inherent tension between socialist legality and human rights. In the early 1990s, coincidentally an opportunity arose when debate about "Asian values" began in the Asia-Pacific region. Vietnamese leaders and officials could find useful elements in the argument of cultural relativism and the "developmental state" model to refine their approach to reconciling human rights with the doctrine of the socialist law-based state. It incorporated exactly the performance-based legitimacy that Vietnam's party-state had been seeking since *Doi Moi* (Thayer 2011).

The arguments in favor of Asian values have in fact provided fundamental building blocks for the Vietnamese doctrine of the law-based state and a sharper theoretical weapon to respond to international criticism of the country's human rights record. This explains why, as some commentators have put it, "laws are not promulgated to furnish people and groups with new and equal rights, but primarily to enable the central state agencies to rule the country and the new market economy in a more effective and legitimate way" (Gammeltoft and Hernø 2000: 170). In Vietnam's model of the socialist law-based state, individual rights are still secondary to the interests of the state and every citizen is obliged to contribute to the collective good.

The prevailing mindset in Vietnam asserts that there is an exclusive association between development and state-led industrialization (Gammeltoft and Hernø 2000). This trend has been reinforced by the country's impressive economic development and political stability after *Doi Moi*. Thanks to economic growth, the middle class in Vietnam is not only much larger; it has grown increasingly vocal in demanding rights and democratic freedoms. At the same time, Vietnam's party-state has become more confident about opening up the discourse on human rights to the international community. In 2013 Vietnam successfully bid for a seat on the UN Human Rights Council. It has also engaged in dialogue on human rights with such Western countries as the United States, Australia, Switzerland, the European Union (EU), and Norway. In this discourse, Vietnam's party-state has revived various elements of the Asian values argument to justify its practices. It is not alone in this respect: the legacy of the Asian values debate is still embedded in the discourse of China, Cambodia, Laos, and many other Asian countries.

Until a more effective theoretical response emerges to justify their approach to human rights, Asian states with authoritarian regimes still have to rely on the Asian values line of defense to respond to criticisms by the international community. More significantly, an implicit reason is that, as a German critical theorist put it, the audience that the Asian values thesis addresses is "not the West, and Western values, but emancipated, well-educated Asians, especially those in the new middle class" (Senghaas 2002: 85). Because this middle class is a growing audience in Vietnam, it is not surprising that the party-state's model of a socialist law-based state continues to rely on the core Asian values argument, as Vietnamese Foreign Minister Pham Binh Minh has made explicit (2010: 19):

> During dialogues, Vietnam has always emphasized the necessity to implement harmoniously civil, political rights and economic, social, cultural

> rights. Moreover, we highlight the difference in the historical, political, economic, cultural, and social context of Vietnam from other countries, particularly the United States and other Western countries, thus affirming the difference in our approach to human rights from that of other countries. At the same time, we stress the principle of national independence and sovereignty, of not using human rights to impose any viewpoint and interfere in each other's internal affairs.

Although it remains firm on many traditional understandings of human rights embedded in the Asian values argument, this formulation demonstrates two important changes: (1) There is clearly a departure from the orthodox socialist notion of the hierarchy of rights in which economic, social, and cultural rights always prevail over civil and political rights. The emphasis on a harmonized approach to all these rights indicates that no particular rights will either be prioritized or prejudiced over others. (2) Promoting human rights is no doubt the obligation of the state. This differs from the traditional party-state message that it is everyone's obligation to promote human rights. The support of the people for the party-state and their political participation is conditional on effective implementation by the state of its obligations – ending the age-old perception that the state grants rights and well-being to the people for which the latter should simply be thankful.

This change in the approach to human rights is modeled on the legalization efforts of the party-state to build the socialist law-based state. It represents a trend of juridification which Ran Hirschl (2006) terms rationalized processes. The obvious change during these processes is the gradual spread of human rights discourse into political, social, and legal spheres from which it was previously excluded or in which it played only a minimal role. A key element of the rule of law which has also been incorporated into the law-based state doctrine is that the laws and practices of the state are consistent with international human rights norms and standards.

The mixed-market economy and the law-based state model resulted in pressure for increasing legalization and for the localization of international norms and standards on human rights. Vietnam's closer relations with the United States, EU, World Bank, International Monetary Fund, and World Trade Organization and its membership in the Association of Southeast Asian Nations (ASEAN) have all contributed to the new governance thinking and values. The ASEAN Charter, of which Vietnam is a signatory and which serves as the organization's constitution, has codified adherence to the rule of law and protection of human rights as interlinked and mutually reinforcing principles of governance. Meanwhile, engagement by Vietnam's government with the Universal Periodic Review (UPR) mechanism of the UN Human Rights Council has given more vibrancy to human rights discourse and has facilitated the participation of different social actors, such as NGOs and hybrid actors.[8]

But the task has only just begun. Despite tremendous efforts by the Vietnamese party-state to build up the legal and the judicial systems in recent decades, there are still many loopholes in the formal guarantees of human rights, not to mention considerable discrepancy between legal requirements and their enforcement. Notably, limited access to justice and the relative weakness of the judicial system are significant obstacles to the protection of human rights.

The party-state is well aware of many issues arising from the intersection of Vietnam's criminal code with international human rights standards. A Ministry of Justice report (2012) on a review of the compatibility of criminal law and criminal procedures with international human rights treaties, to which Vietnam is a party, identified these shortcomings:

> There remain some incompatible problems between Vietnam's criminal law, criminal procedures law and international standards, including legal rules on protection against arbitrary and illegal detention and imprisonment, the right to fair trial, some groups of rights of children and women.... *Some specific crimes stipulated in the Criminal Code shall be amended in accordance with requirements of international legal instruments* [emphasis added].

While these issues are now on the political agenda of the party-state, putting through an amendment to the Criminal and Criminal Procedure Codes in that direction is likely to be problematic.

Within Vietnam, these issues continue to provoke many critical voices and generate pressure from intellectuals and scholars. Heated debates are taking place in cyberspace and in the blogosphere where the party-state has limited control. The Internet and social media have provided an effective vehicle for circulation and deliberation of different ideas given that more than 32 million Vietnamese – over one-third of the population – use the Internet regularly (Vietnam Internet Center 2013). Generally, the new middle class use these media to demand greater democratic freedoms.

## Human rights and the constitutional reform process

Public debates on constitutional issues in post-*Doi Moi* Vietnam date back to 1991/1992 and the framing of the 1992 constitution. Those debates focused on the constitution's incompatibility with new economic priorities, the need for more individual freedoms, separation of powers, the rule of law, and government efficiency (Heng 1992). Discussions were mostly limited to party-state-sponsored channels for deputies of the National Assembly, government officials, and scholars in state-owned institutions. In 2001 there were also heated debates about central constitutional issues before some minor amendments were made to the 1992 constitution, though those were silent on human rights. However, discussions of human rights issues as a core theme have since gained momentum that reached an unprecedented level between 2011 and 2013 during the constitutional reform process.

Over the past two decades, discourse on human rights in Vietnam has thus undergone a subtle shift from unalloyed legal positivism to a more open and substantive debate. This change is most evident in the recent discussion of constitutional reform in Vietnam with human rights as a central theme – a consequence of efforts by progressive and radical intellectuals and scholars to identify a more effective legal-rational model to promote and protect human rights in Vietnam. Anthony Langlois considers this alternative model to have "its roots in natural law and right, ascertained by the proper use of right reason and enshrined in positive law" and "underlies most contemporary thought on human rights theory" (Langlois 2001: 9). Thus, discussion related to the constitutional amendment process has challenged the conventional assumption that "discourses that shape official attitudes to human rights primarily take place within party and state circles" (Gillespie 2006).

Throughout, support for liberal universalism, particularly the theory of natural rights, has been growing. It has gained legitimacy by invoking the values of the first Constitution of Vietnam in 1946 which – promulgated at the outset of the revolution against the French colonial regime – was liberal and democratic. The tide of support for liberal universalist concepts is based on a consensus among scholars and intellectuals in Vietnam about the relevance of many great legacies of constitutional ideas and culture to building a law-based state and recognizing and protecting human rights (Nguyen Si Dung 2011). It is important to keep in mind that the liberal universalist discourse in Vietnam has largely focused on the conception of human rights in terms of negative freedoms: "the absence of external restrictions or constraints on the individual, allowing freedom of choice" (Heywood 2007: 31). Previous proposals to draft laws on freedom of association, the right to demonstrate, and access to information, and efforts to institutionalize Article 69 of the 1992 constitution, have been revived.[9] Although to date these proposals have all been shelved, the current challenges to the dominant socialist ideology and the firm control of the party-state over this political and constitutional discourse are considerable.

Human rights are recognized, provided for, and guaranteed by the state in the constitution and a number of other laws. As noted by Randall Peerenboom, the government's desire for legitimacy both domestically and internationally is an important force pushing for rule of law and new rules and human rights norms (Peerenboom 2004: 15). Although the 1992 constitution devotes a chapter to rights and obligations, it frames human rights rigidly within the context of citizens' rights (Art. 50, ch. V). For years, however, this has been called into question on the grounds that it has actually reduced human rights to the will of the state (Langlois 2012: 444).

In the constitutional amendment debate, advocates of liberal universalism have been allowed to voice their criticisms of this reductionist approach, maintaining that human rights are natural rights with universal moral standards that are not grants from the state. The major issues are succinctly presented by a leading Vietnamese academic:

> It is wrong to conflate human rights with citizens' rights as in Article 50 of the current Constitution and causes misunderstanding that in Vietnam, only

> Vietnamese citizens have human rights but foreigners have not.... Another problem in the Constitution of Vietnam is that human rights are stipulated as granted by the State. It is easily misunderstood that human rights are something the State bestows on the people. The rules are evident in the Chapter on the rights and obligations of citizens in constitutions of Vietnam like Article 53, 54, 56, 57, 58 ... of the 1992 Constitution which all provide that the State recognizes and gives citizens the rights in a wishful thinking and at its own discretion, not in the way that citizens are naturally entitled to these rights.
>
> (Nguyen Dang Dung 2011)

The rigid formula fixed by the "socialist legality" mentality that the state grants human rights is evident throughout the 1992 constitution; it appears more than 20 times (Bui Ngoc Son 2011). Scholars in the new generation educated in the West and inspired by the liberal universality of human rights – such as Vu Cong Giao, Bui Ngoc Son, and Vo Tri Hao – have been deeply critical of the entrenchment of the Soviet mentality in Chapter V of the constitution. They argue that this orientation contravenes the supreme object and purpose of the constitution: to protect human rights. Thus, there has emerged a consensus among scholars that human rights should be treated as distinct from citizens' rights in new constitutional amendments.

Vo Tri Hao (2012) points out the detrimental effects of stipulating that human rights are equated with the constitutional rights of citizens, which are in turn equated with rules embodied in every legal normative document. This criticism states that the dominance of the Soviet mentality in the constitution deprived the constitutional rights of citizens of their substantive meaning, directly affecting how courts apply the document and the protection they provide to citizens. The term "in accordance with laws" is often criticized for its ambiguity and the potential it offers for abuse of power by the authorities (Vo Tri Hao 2012). In a detailed analysis of many articles in the second draft of the 1992 Constitutional Amendments released for public consultation in January 2013, Hoang Xuan Phu made a number of critical comments on how the new draft would reduce some human rights: "The regressive changes in the draft Constitutional Amendments have been made with intention and careful deliberation. They even make use of sophisticated legal tactics to implement and conceal their purposes" (2013).

The party-state has come to acknowledge some problems with its approach to rules and norms related to human rights. The concern is partly reflected in the Ministry of Justice's report that identifies the possible scope of constitutional amendments related to human rights (Ministry of Justice 2012). The report emphasizes clear delineation between human rights and citizens rights, concretization of substance, and procedures for implementaing some direct democratic rights of citizens (participation in referenda, governance over the state and society, access to information, peaceful assembly and association), and the addition of some important rights incorporated into international human rights treaties (prohibition of the death penalty, torture, double jeopardy for the same crime, the right to enjoy development, a healthy and peaceful environment, and social security). The Ministry of Justice argues that human rights and freedoms and citizens' rights can only be limited by laws enacted by the National Assembly and the laws should make explicit their scope, time frame, conditions, and procedures. The Ministry further stresses the obligation of state institutions to respect, guarantee, and promote both human and citizens' rights and to harmonize human rights, citizens' rights, and popular sovereignty in a socialist law-based state.

Faced with sustained criticisms and contestation during the constitutional debates – particularly from prominent members of the Group of 72, full-time deputies of the National Assembly, and scholars in online forums and the mass media – the third draft of the amendments to the 1992 constitution and the final version approved by the National Assembly in November 2013 seemed to make some concessions: "In the Socialist Republic of Vietnam, human rights and citizens' rights in the political, civil, economic, cultural, and social sphere are recognized, respected, and protected in accordance with the Constitution and law." However, the response of the Vietnamese party-state has been extremely cautious. It has justified ideas about limitation of rights, abuse of rights, duties inseparable from rights, and individual rights to land ownership by invoking state socialism, popular sovereignty, and elements of Asian values that argue for cultural relativism. The Constitution Amending Committee resolutely defended their position on these issues as the stronghold of a socialist law-based state. The final draft of the amended constitution approved in 2013 retains that view.

Most remarkably, the argument that the constitution should restrict the discretion of individual officials and state agencies in protections for human rights gained ground. Article 14 (2) of the 2013 revision was the most progressive advance over previous constitutions: "Human rights and citizen's rights shall only be restricted in imperative circumstances for reasons of national defense, national security, social order and security, social morality, and the health of the community." That this idea is enshrined for the first time in the revised constitution is indicative of deepening constitutional discourse in a Western liberal sense. While there may be a large gap between written rules and actual implementation due to the apparent lack of a basis for respect for the rule of law, the very recognition of this idea in the revised constitution provides a firmer foundation for translating the discourse into constitutional practice.

The discussions on human rights in the process of amending the constitution of Vietnam have been neither as static nor as fixed as the orthodox "socialist legality" doctrine might suggest. Even when the amended constitution was ratified in November 2013, it was not certain which particular strand of thought dominated the articles on human rights. Although there were liberal influences, no consistent body of ideas had inspired a comprehensive and definitive set of amendments. Rather, because the final outcome depended on the decision of political authority – not the rhetorical power or appeal of any ideologies – the result has once again been a syncretic combination of many different ideas. However, one thing which is certain from the discourse is that the doctrine of socialist legality is being further undermined.

Finally, there has been a significant change in the emergent discourse on human rights. Until quite recently the emphasis on the class-based nature of law and the binary dichotomy between the socialist and capitalist character on the legal rights of individuals were still dominant in Vietnamese legal discourse. However, in the debates over amendments to the constitution, interest in the class-based nature of laws plunged and there is no longer any class-based typology of human rights in the discourse. This notable change paves the way for more dynamic interpretations of human rights and opens a path for recourse to international human rights law as a higher ground for reasoning.

## Conclusion

The introduction of a market economy in Vietnam, formulation of a socialist law-based state doctrine, and exposure of long-held socialist norms of human rights to liberal universalism have paved the way for expanded discourse on human rights. As may be seen from the debate on the 2011 to 2013 Constitutional Amendments, human rights discourse is dynamic and changing. Throughout the amendment process there were serious contestations and challenges where, despite resistance by CPV ideologists, many participants argued forcefully for moving the discourse on human rights from the periphery to the core of the evolving doctrine of socialist law-based state and the rule of law. The new chapter on human rights and citizens' rights in the constitution as amended in 2013 makes it clear that new human rights ideals influenced by liberal thought are gaining ground against orthodox socialist ideals. However, the difficult and slow process of drafting laws on citizens' rights demonstrates the CPV's lack of consistency and clear thinking on how to move forward to address the social demand for more political space.

It should be noted that so far in Vietnam, efforts to institutionalize a more effective and consistent legal-rational model of human rights have failed. Although the constitution was amended to refer specifically to human rights, prospects of a coherent and consistent human rights regime are uncertain. As may be seen in the debates and the final constitutional amendments, the new thinking on the rule of law and human rights as transplanted from the Western liberal tradition is underdeveloped. Although they may be appealing to many due to the rhetoric of universality, freedom, and egalitarianism, these theoretical proposals need to be subjected to more critical scrutiny and deliberation. Contestation during the constitutional amendment process may well have been a good beginning for a long march toward building a desirable human rights regime based on the rule of law. Now that the new thinking has been set in motion, it is likely to go beyond revealing fissures in the party-state's discourse to produce constitutive effects for the behavior and identity of the party-state on human rights.

Proponents of the new thinking have in effect attempted to substitute another set of universal normative principles, implying their ideological hegemony over other perspectives. In fact, the proponents have not done justice to "the plurality of traditions of reason – among which liberalism is only one – and to the plurality of values exhibited around the world" (Langlois 2001: 7). In this respect, they have followed the same path and fallen into the same trap as the proponents of orthodox socialist ideas. The more effective and consistent legal-rational model that most scholars seek does not work or is simply utopian; only a political model of human rights can serve Vietnam's current circumstances.

This analysis has shed light on the continuing constitutional amendment process and how Vietnam's party-state has responded. While at a high level of abstraction the party-state has accepted the universality of human rights, it diverges from Western countries and international institutions in terms of the content, justification, interpretation, and application of these rights. The interim solution to the impasse is necessarily a syncretism that enables "new and contradictory substantive ideas to enter and enlarge the range of values applied to new situations" (Gillespie 2004: 172). While the socialist legality doctrine is in decline and a law-based state is still at an embryonic stage, such a syncretism can only survive with a more dynamic and tolerant political model of human rights sanctioned by the Vietnamese party-state.

## Notes

1 In December 2011, the fourth Plenum of the eleventh Tenure Central Committee of the CPV issued the resolution on "Some urgent issues on party-building now" and relaunched the campaign for "criticism and self-criticism" at every party organization level.
2 See Resolution No. 51/2001/QH10 dated December 25, 2001 issued by the National Assembly of Vietnam, and Article 2 of the 1992 Constitution amended in 2001.
3 Five Commissions were either abolished or merged into other party commissions in 2007: the Commission on Internal Affairs, the Commission on Economic Affairs, the Commission on Science and Education, the Commission on Internal Political Security, and the Commission on Finance and Administration.
4 These decisions were made at the fifth and sixth Plenums of the CPV Central Committee in May and October 2012, respectively.
5 Nguyen Van An, former chairman of the National Assembly of Vietnam; Nguyen Dinh Loc, former minister of justice, and the Central Committee of the Vietnam Fatherland Front have all publicly voiced their opinions about the need for a law on the CPV.
6 A constitutional rule under Article 52 of the 1992 Constitution.
7 See texts of the revised Criminal Code of 1985 and the Criminal Procedures Code of 1988, available at: http://thuvienphapluat.vn/archive/Bo-luat-Hinh-su-1985–17-LCT-HDNN7-vb37003.aspx.
8 For example, in June 2013 60 local NGOs prepared and submitted a shadow report under the United Nations Human Rights Council's Universal Periodic Review to make an assessment of and recommendations on Vietnam's implementation of its obligations on human rights. Hybrid actors are those which "can resemble state agencies but pursue private (non-state objectives) or look like non-state agencies but aim to realize state policies (Gillespie 2010: 28).
9 Article 69 of the 1992 constitution states: "citizens have the right to freedom of speech, freedom of press, access to information, the right to assembly, association and demonstration in accordance with legal rules."

## Bibliography


Bui Ngoc Son (2011). "Phân tích thực nghiệm về mức độ chi tiết hóa Hiến pháp và một số gợi mở cho sửa đổi Hiếnpháp 1992" [An Empirical Analysis of the Detailed Rules of the Constitution and Some Suggestions for the Amendments of Constitution 1992]. *Tạp chí Nghiên cứu lập pháp* [*Journal of Legislative Studies*], available at: www.nclp.org.vn/nha_nuoc_va_phap_luat/phan-tich-thuc-nghiem-ve-muc-111o-chi-tiet-hoa-hien-phap-va-mot-so-goi-mo-cho-sua-111oi-hien-phap-1.

CPV (1960). National Congress Resolution, available at: http://123.30.190.43:8080/tiengviet/tulieuvankien/vankiendang/details.asp?topic=191&subtopic=8&leader_topic=220&id=BT990537556.

CPV (1982). CC Political Report at the Fifth National Congress, available at: http://123.30.190.43:8080/tiengviet/tulieuvankien/vankiendang/details.asp?topic=191&subtopic=8&leader_topic=222&id=BT590634673.

CPV (1986). CC Political Report at the Sixth National Congress, available at: http://123.30.190.43:8080/tiengviet/tulieuvankien/vankiendang/details.asp?topic=191&subtopic=8&leader_topic=223&id=BT1260354904.

CPV (1991a). Central Committee Political Report at the Seventh National Congress in 1991, available at: http://123.30.190.43:8080/tiengviet/tulieuvankien/vankiendang/details.asp?topic=191&subtopic=8&leader_topic=224&id=BT1260354741.

CPV (1991b). Seventh CPV National Congress Resolution, available at: http://123.30.190.43:8080/tiengviet/tulieuvankien/vankiendang/details.asp?topic=191&subtopic=8&leader_topic=224&id=BT2440658679.

Dang Xuan Ky (1994). "Tư tưởng đạo đức Hồ Chí Minh" [Ho Chi Minh's Thought on Ethics]. *Tạp chí Cộng sản* [*Communist Review*], 5 (May).

Do Muoi (1992). *Sửa đổi Hiến pháp, xây dựng nhà nước pháp quyền Việt Nam, đẩy mạnh sự nghiệp Đổi Mới* [*Amending the Constitution, Establishing a Law-based State, and Promoting Doi Moi Cause*]. Hà Nội, Nhà xuất bản Sự thật.

Gainsborough, M. (2012). "Elites v. Reform in Laos, Cambodia, and Vietnam." *Journal of Democracy*, 23(2): 34–46.

Gammeltoft, T. and Hernø, R. (2000). "Human Rights in Vietnam: Exploring Tensions and Ambiguities." In *Human Rights and Asian Values: Contesting National Identities and Cultural Representations in Asia*, eds M. Jacobsen and O. Bruun. Richmond, UK, Curzon Press, pp. 159–177.

Gillespie, J. (2004). "The Conceptions of Rule of Law in Vietnam." In *Asian Discourses of Rule of Law*, ed. R. Peerenboom. London, RoutledgeCurzon, pp. 146–182.

Gillespie, J. (2006). "Evolving Concepts of Human Rights in Vietnam." In *Human Rights in Asia: A Comparative Legal Study of Twelve Asian Jurisdictions, France and the USA*, eds R. Peerenboom, C.J. Petersen, and A.H.Y. Chen. New York, Routledge, pp. 452–486.

Gillespie, J. (2010). "The Jurification of State Regulation in Vietnam." In *Legal Reforms in China and Vietnam: A Comparison of Asian Communist Regimes*, eds J. Gillespie and A.H.Y. Chen. London, Routledge, pp. 78–102.

Ginsburg, T. (2009). "The Judicialization of Administrative Governance: Causes, Consequences and Limits." In *Administrative Law and Governance in Asia*, eds T. Ginsburg and A.H.Y. Chen. London, Routledge, pp. 1–20.

Heng, H.K.R. (1992). "The 1992 Revised Constitution of Vietnam: Background and Scope of Changes." *Contemporary Southeast Asia*, 14(3): 221–230.

Heywood, A. (2007). *Political Ideologies.* New York, Palgrave Macmillan.

Hirschl, R. (2006). "The New Constitutionalism and the Judicialization of Pure Politics Worldwide." *Fordham Law Review*, 75(2): 721–754.

*Ho Chi Minh toan tap* [*Ho Chi Minh's Collected Works*], Vol. 9 (1958–1959) (Ha Noi: Nha xuat ban chinh tri quoc gia, 2000), pp. 288–301 and the CPV official website, available at: http://dangcongsan.vn/cpv/Modules/News/NewsDetail.aspx?co_id=30178&cn_id=152053.

Hoang Chi Bao (2002). "Từ những đặc điểm của thời kỳ quá độ lên chủ nghĩa xã hội đến việc xây dựng Nhà nước pháp quyền xã hội chủ nghĩa ở Việt Nam hiện nay" [From Characteristics of a Transitional Period to Socialism to the Construction of a Socialist Law-based State in Vietnam Nowadays]. *Tạp chí Triết học [Journal of Philosophy]*, 1: 28–33.

Hoang Xuan Phu (2013). "*Teo dần quyền con người trong Hiến pháp 1992*" [*Shrinking Human Rights in Constitution 1992*]. Hoang Xuan Phu Blog, January 15, available at: http://hpsc.iwr.uni-heidelberg.de/hxphu/index.php?page=readwriting&w=TeoDanQuyenConNguoiTrongHienPhap-20130115.

Langlois, A. (2001). *The Politics of Justice and Human Rights: Southeast Asia and Universalist Theory*. New York, Cambridge University Press.

Langlois, A. (2012). "Human Rights." In *Introduction to International Relations*, eds R. Devetak, A. Burke, and J. George. Port Melbourne, Australia, Cambridge University Press, pp. 441–449.

Le Huu Nghia (2007) "Năm mươi năm phấn đấu thực hiện lời dạy của Chủ tịch Hồ Chí Minh về học tập, nghiên cứu lý luận và đào tạo, bồi dưỡng cán bộ" [Fifty Years of Striving for Implementing the Teachings of President Ho Chi Minh on Studying Theories and Training Cadres]. *Tạp chí lịch sử Đảng [Journal of Party History]*, available at: www.hcma.vn/B%C3%80IVI%E1%BA%BETCHUY%C3%8AN%C4%90%E1%BB%80/tabid/94/ctl/Details/mid/439/ItemID/597/Default.aspx.

Ministry of Justice of Vietnam (2012). "Report on the Review of Compatibility of Criminal Law and Criminal Procedures Law with International Human Rights Treaties to which Vietnam is a Party," prepared for *The First Legal Policy Dialogue in 2012* on Improvement of Laws on Human Rights organized by the Ministry of Justice of Vietnam and the United Nations Development Program in Vietnam, Ha Noi, May 23, 2012, available at: www.moj.gov.vn/htpl/datctcclvbvq/Lists/CacTaiLieuThamKhao/View_Detail.aspx?ItemID=30.

Nguyen Dang Dung (2011). "Cách tiếp cận hay là cách thức quy định nhân quyền trong Hiến pháp" [An Approach to or a Way of Stipulating Human Rights in the Constitution]. *Tạp chí Nghiên cứu lập pháp* [*Journal of Legislative Studies*], available at: www.nclp.org.vn/nha_nuoc_va_phap_luat/cach-tiep-can-hay-la-cach-thuc-quy-111inh-nhan-quyen-trong-hien-phap.

Nguyen Duc Binh (2006). "Xây dựng Đảng ta thật vững mạnh" [Building and Strengthening our Party]. *Nhân Dân*, February 23.

Nguyen Si Dung (2011). "Hoc o Hien phap 1946" [Learn from Constitution 1946]. *Tia Sang*, September 16, available at: http://tiasang.com.vn/Default.aspx?tabid=116&CategoryID=42&News=4377.

Pham Binh Minh (2010). "Đối thoại của Việt Nam với các nước về Dân chủ, Nhân quyền" [Vietnam's Dialogues with Other Countries on Democracy and Human Rights]. *Tạp chí lý luận chính trị* [*Journal of Political Theory*], 7: 16–21.

Salomon, M. and Vu Doan Ket (2010). "Achievements and Challenges in Developing a Law-based State in Contemporary Vietnam: How to Shoe a Turtle?" In *Legal Reforms in China and Vietnam: A Comparison of Asian Communist Regimes*, eds J. Gillespie and A.H.Y. Chen. London, Routledge, pp. 134–154.

Senghaas, D. (2002). *Clashes within Civilizations: Coming to Terms with Cultural Conflicts*. London, Routledge.

Sidel, M. (2008). *Law and Society in Vietnam*. New York, Cambridge University Press.

Thayer, C. (2009). "Political Legitimacy of Vietnam's One Party-State: Challenges and Responses." *Journal of Current Southeast Asian Affairs*, 28(4): 47–70.

Thayer, C. (2011). "Political Legitimacy in Vietnam under Challenge.", In *Political Legitimacy in Asia*, eds J. Kane, H.-C. Loy, and H. Patapan. New York, Palgrave Macmillan, pp. 39–59.

Tran Ngoc Duong (2011). "Kiểm soát quyền lực nhà nước trong xây dựng nhà nước pháp quyền xã hội chủ nghĩaViệt Nam" [Checking the State Power in the Construction of a Socialist Law-based State in Vietnam]. *Tạp chí Nghiên cứu lập pháp* [*Journal of Legislative Studies*], 16: 5–9.

Tran Ngoc Hien (2008). "Kinh tế thị trường định hướng xã hội chủ nghĩa với nhà nước pháp quyền và xã hội dân sự nước ta" [Socialist-oriented Market Economy, the Law-based State, and Civil Society in our Country]. *Tạp chí Cộng sản* [*Communist Review*], 787(May): 50–55.

Vietnam Internet Center, Ministry of Information and Communication (2013). Available at: www.thongkeinternet.vn/jsp/thuebao/table_dt.jsp.

VnExpress (2013). "Tổng Bí thư: Đề phòng thế lực muốn xóa bỏ Điều 4 Hiến pháp" [General Secretary: Take Caution of Hostile Forces' Attempt to Remove Article 4 of the Constitution]. *VnExpress.net*, September 28, available at: http://vnexpress.net/tin-tuc/thoi-su/tong-bi-thu-de-phong-the-luc-muon-xoa-bo-dieu-4-hien-phap-2886937.html.

Vo Tri Hao (2012). "Hoàn thiện kỹ thuật lập hiến đối với Chương V Hiến pháp" [Improving Constitutional Techniques for Chapter V of Constitution 1992]. *Tia Sang*, July 2, available at: www.tiasang.com.vn/Default.aspx?tabid=116&CategoryID=42&News=5338.

# 11 Racial politics and imperatives and the constitutional special position of the indigenous Malays in a new society

## Asserting interests and the non-contestation of rights in Singapore's communitarian constitutionalism

*Eugene K.B. Tan*

## Introduction

Upon securing independence from Malaysia on August 9, 1965, the imperative was for Singapore to build a Singaporean Singapore society. This was notwithstanding the relatively large ethnic Chinese majority on the city-state of about two million people. Nurturing such a new society was a geopolitical necessity given its location in Southeast Asia. With its survival as an accidental nation-state under grave threat, the choice for Singapore's leadership was clear. To subject ethnic minorities to a subordinate status would not only be a betrayal of the founding ideal of the fledgling nation-state and risk internal strife; it would also invite interference in Singapore's domestic politics from neighboring countries ostensibly seeking to protect their co-ethnics in Singapore.

When Thomas Stamford Raffles set up a trading post in Singapore on behalf of the British East India Company in 1819, conventional wisdom has it that it was a backwater settlement of 150 Malays along the banks of the Singapore River and some 30 Chinese engaged in pepper and gambier planting. Subsequently, the development of Singapore as an entrepôt and a regional emporium attracted traders, requiring migration of people from other parts of Asia to attend to the increased economic activity. By 1824, with the conclusion of the Anglo-Dutch Treaty and the Treaty of Cession resulting in the British acquiring unchallenged sovereignty over Singapore, the local population had reached 10,683 (comprising Malays 60 percent, Chinese 31 percent, Indians 7 percent, and others 2 percent).[1]

Further and rapid migration led very quickly to the indigenous Malays becoming a minority within 50 years of the commencement of the colonial period. By 1867, the Chinese community had become the majority, making up 65 percent of the population of 55,000. By 1959 when the British granted Singapore self-government, the racial composition had already long stabilized with the ethnic Chinese making up about three-quarters of the population, the Malays no larger than one-sixth of the total population, and the Indians one-twelfth. The Malays were, however, the majority once again during Singapore's short-lived and tumultuous merger with Malaysia between September 1963 and August 1965. Since independence, with the government's strategic intervention on the demographic front, these racial ratios – seen as a foundational prerequisite for Singapore's success – have been maintained.

This brief historical and demographic overview suggests that the majority–minority status within a society can be fluid and may easily mutate into a citizen–subject type of relationship.[2] In any multi-ethnic society it is inevitable that there will be majority and minority communities and the concomitant contestation for finite resources of the state. Majoritarianism is problematic if it results in exclusivity, privilege, and preference for the majority, and discrimination and marginalization of the minorities. Path dependence also means that the aspiration of multiracialism and equal citizenship, however inchoately expressed, would have to contend with extant colonial practices in an earlier and extended period.

In Singapore, the notion of relegating the ethnic minorities to a subordinate status was a non-starter. In the negotiations for internal self-government in 1957 to 1958, all key stakeholders in London and in Singapore embraced the ideal of civic citizenship for all, but with a "special position" for the Malays. This was a tacit recognition that colonial rule had disadvantaged the Malays and that their interests must be safeguarded in the headlong rush to self-government and, eventually, to *merdeka* (independence). There was the cautious belief that racial contestation could be avoided through a deliberate process of constitutional recognition and political commitment to the Malays' special position, even if there were competing conceptions of what it meant and entailed.

This chapter comprises three sections. In the first section, I examine how Article 152 of the Singapore Constitution recognizes the Malays as Singapore's indigenous people. This constitutional recognition, however, did not and has not resulted in the provision of special rights to the Malay-Singaporeans by virtue of their race, language, and religion. There is no affirmative action policy in favor of the Malays or any minorities. Concessions or benefits to any racial group, when provided, are carefully couched to avoid any sense of entitlement or legal rights. This is elaborated in the second section, which explores two significant policies, namely the Group Representation Constituency and the free tertiary education benefit, that give effect to protecting the interests of the Malays. In the third section, I examine the institution of National Service in Singapore as a contested expression of equal citizenship vis-à-vis the Malay community, and where the interests of the state predominate over the rights of the individual and the concerns of the community.

Focusing on the significant Malay-Singaporean minority, I argue that the conscious avoidance of a rights-based legal regime in the management of ethnic issues in Singapore has removed a significant element of contestation and depoliticized, to a large extent, the postcolonial nation-building project. Central to this is the constitutional and political approach toward the special position of the Malays. The constitution, laws, and policies have structured and moderated the expectations of the majority and minority communities with regard to their rights, interests, and power. Further, interests, duties, and responsibility – rather than rights and entitlement – are the de facto collective language of citizenship, wherein the larger good of the state and society takes ultimate precedence. These two significant constitutional practices ensured that Singapore's constitutional and political model as a sovereign state diverged from the liberal Western model from the outset.

In responding to the state's management of ethnic relations, Singapore's ethnic minorities and the ethnic Chinese majority have embraced civic citizenship based on civic nationalism as the most democratic form of non-majoritarian, non-plebiscitarian accommodation. Second, the ethnic minorities have not forfeited their individual group's collective claim to a distinctive identity. Third, they have not demanded special concessions or sought privileges from the state in order to maintain their own culture, values, and way of life. Fourth, notwithstanding the occasional bumps in the nation-building quest, the ethnic minorities have not sought a competing nationalist ideology and separatist cause. What undergirds the multiracial ethos is the tacit recognition of a particularistic ideal of constitutionalism where interests and accommodation are valorized in the construction of an overarching Singaporean identity that is distinct from the component sectarian and subnational identities.

## The Singapore Constitution and the entrenching of multiracialism

In the official narrative, Singapore's steadfast commitment to the multiracial ethos contributed to its failed political merger with the Federation of Malaysia between September 1963 and August 1965. Singapore's rigorous objections to the federal government's goal of an ethnic-based Malay-Malaysia translated into a tumultuous merger marked by mutual suspicion, political maneuvering, and confrontation culminating in Singapore's sudden, but negotiated, independence in 1965. In the fledgling nation-building efforts in the aftermath of Separation, the government consciously sought to develop a "Singaporean Singapore" identity, while symbolically recognizing the special position of the indigenous Malays (Lee 1998: 540–663; Lau 1998). According to the founding Prime Minister Lee Kuan Yew, this was necessary "[b]ecause we, the Chinese majority in Singapore, suffered communal bullying and discrimination during the two years we were a part of Malaysia, the first-generation leaders vowed that we would never bully or discriminate our bullies" (Lee 2004).[3]

The centerpiece of the Singapore state's attempt at inclusive citizenship for the minorities, especially the Malays, is found in Article 152 of the Singapore Constitution. This provision pre-dates independent Singapore's Constitution. Article 152(1) states that: "It shall be the responsibility of the Government constantly to care for the interests of the racial and religious minorities in Singapore." In particular, Article 152 recognizes the "special position of the Malays" by virtue of their being the indigenous people of Singapore.[4] Article 152(2) states that:

> The Government shall exercise its functions in such manner as to recognise the special position of the Malays, who are the indigenous people of Singapore, and accordingly it shall be the responsibility of the Government to protect, safeguard, support, foster and promote their political, educational, religious, economic, social and cultural interests and the Malay language.

Clearly, Article 152 of the Singapore Constitution legitimizes and constitutionally protects minority claims to cultural diversity and autonomy in Singapore. In practice, this is in sync with the Singapore government's approach to the management of ethnic relations. The political commitment to equality was manifested in the constitutional principle and requirement of the government of the day having a responsibility to care for the interests of racial and religious minorities. This commitment was agreed to between the colonial government in London and the All-Party delegation from Singapore, and was incorporated into the preamble of the 1959 constitution of the Colony of Singapore that granted internal self-government to Singapore. The relevant portion of the preamble read:

> And ... it is hereby expressly affirmed, that it shall be the responsibility of the Government of Singapore constantly to care for the interests of racial and religious minorities in Singapore, and in particular that it shall be the deliberate and conscious policy of the Government of Singapore at all times to recognise the special position of Malays, who are the indigenous people of the Island and are in most need of assistance, and accordingly, that it shall be the responsibility of the Government of Singapore to protect, safeguard, support, foster and promote their political, educational, religious, economic, social and cultural interests and the Malay language.[5]

The substance of this preamble, albeit trimmed and less effusive, is now found in Article 152 of the Constitution of the Republic of Singapore. Hence, right from its sovereign founding moment, equality in a polyglot Singapore was nuanced and certainly not fixated on formal equality. While formal equality is a constitutional prescription and studiously observed, there is also the tacit and sophisticated understanding that formal equality must also allow for unequal treatment to the extent necessary to achieve substantive equality. This is the substance of the constitutional treatment of minorities in Singapore. In rebutting the notion of a formalistic and legalistic understanding and approach to racial equality (and, in turn, recognizing the centrality of substantive racial equality), Lee (2009) stated robustly his conception of racial equality in the Singapore Constitution in his final parliamentary speech in 2009:

> We explicitly state in our Constitution a duty on behalf of the Government not to treat everybody as equal. It [racial equality] is not reality, it is not practical, it will lead to grave and irreparable damage if we work on that principle. So this was an aspiration.... You suggest to the Malays that we should abolish these provisions in the Constitution and you will have grave

> disquiet.... The American Constitution does not say that it will treat blacks differently but our Constitution spells out the duty of the Government to treat Malays and other minorities with extra care.... And I thought to myself, perhaps I should bring this House back to earth and remind everybody what is our starting point, what is our base, and if we do not recognise where we started from, and that these are our foundations, we will fail.... Today, 44 years later, we have a Malay community, I believe, at peace, convinced that we are not discriminating against them, convinced that we are including them in our society.

Scholars and politicians alike have generally interpreted Article 152 as being directory and non-justiciable, rather than being mandatory and rights bearing (Tan K.Y.L., 2004: 102–104). Article 152 has been described as being "paradigmatic" for its deliberate approach of precluding rights-based protection. In turn, this entails a "judicious balancing approach" and non-adversarial methods of engagement to resolve differences and diffuse hostilities between the different ethnic groups (Neo 2008). Although it has yet to be judicially interpreted, then Chief Justice Chan Sek Keong (2007) likens Article 152 to the Indian Constitution's Directive Principles of State Policy.[6] The legal effect of such a provision is that it elevates the principle of minority protection into one of salutary constitutional importance but not amounting to a prescriptive constitutional guarantee that could lend itself to significant political and juridical intervention and contestation. As such, Article 152 is more of a symbolic but powerful shield rather than a sword, one which the minorities can assert collectively against the government of the day if it fails to care adequately for them.

Not surprisingly, perceptions toward Article 152(2) differ, reflecting the somewhat multifarious nature of the emblematic constitutional provision. Some Malays believe that the provision confers a special status upon them, which in turn requires the government to provide special rights, privileges, and affirmative action policies such as quotas. This stance is not shared by others (Malays and non-Malays alike) who argue that a privileged position for the Malays has no place in Singapore's multiracialism, and would also undermine the meritocracy ideal and foment a potentially debilitating crutch mentality within the Malay community.[7]

The Singapore state strives to scrupulously adhere to a non-Chinese orientation in governance. For example, the national symbols of the Singapore state are more Malay-centric than Chinese. In a symbolic recognition of the indigenous Malay heritage of Singapore, Malay language is the sole national language, despite it being used almost exclusively by the Malays.[8] Article 153A prescribes the official languages and national language, with Malay having the distinction of being both the national and an official language. Thus, Singapore's national anthem, *Majulah Singapura* ("Onward Singapore") , is sung in Malay by schoolchildren every morning in national schools. In a similar fashion, Singapore's motto, also *Majulah Singapura*, was incorporated into Singapore's coat of arms. Further, the long-standing pre-independence practice of military parade commands being executed in Malay was retained.[9]

These explicit manifestations of recognition and accommodation, and an implicit disavowal of contestation, are integral elements of the multiracialism ethos that has been identified with the People's Action Party (PAP) government, which has governed Singapore continuously since 1959. The various groups' ethnic identities, cultures, and religions are neither explicitly encouraged nor are they suppressed by the state. As David Brown observes, "the Malay minority [in Singapore] has been depicted as the symbolic ethnic core of the nation, but Malay culture continues to be marginal in the emergent Singaporean national culture" (Brown 2009: 145). Neither has Singapore opted to constitutionalize the ethos of accommodation of diversity, a hallmark of its multiracialism, mindful of calibrating the appropriate constitutional and political expectations toward the special position of the Malays.[10]

Hence, Singapore eschews a rights-based approach when it comes to matters pertaining to ethnicity (such as race, language, and religion). Like most liberal democratic constitutions, the fundamental liberties provided for under the Singapore Constitution proceed on the premise that the individual, rather than a community, is the bearer of such rights.[11] Nonetheless, the law is greatly relied upon to maintain a strict regime in matters of race and religion. There are many legal instruments in the statute books allowing the government to act determinedly, swiftly, and even pre-emptively, against real and apparent threats to ethnic stability (Tan, E.K.B, 2004, 2005; Tan, K.Y.L., 2004).

While Singapore adopts a civic conception of citizenship, it also urges a conscious formation and sustenance of distinctive ethnic identities of the majority and minority communities. This is amplified in Article 12(3)(a) of the constitution, which states that the equal protection provision (Article 12) does not invalidate or prohibit any provision regulating personal law.[12] There are a number of primary and subsidiary legislative provisions relating to personal law. While most of these relate to the application of Islamic law to Muslims, there is also recognition of the religious sensitivities and requirements of other minority communities.[13]

The constitutional reality is that no Singaporean government of the day can govern or legislate against the interests of the racial and religious minorities without being subjected to scrutiny under either Article 12 or Part VII of the constitution. More importantly, it would also be politically untenable to do so. Put simply, multiracialism is a constitutionally entrenched obligation and a political imperative. Further, Article 153 also reinforces the special position status of the Malays by providing that the legislature "shall by law make provision for regulating Muslim religious affairs and for constituting a Council to advise the President in matters relating to the Muslim religion."[14] Consequently, the Administration of Muslim Law Act (AMLA) was enacted in 1966 to regulate Muslim religious affairs and to constitute a council to advise the government on matters relating to the Muslim religion in Singapore, and provides for the establishment of the Syariah Court.[15] The AMLA provides for a limited degree of legal pluralism for the Muslim community, who are governed by Islamic law in matters of personal law such as marriage, divorce, and succession. There is no similar constitutional provision for the other religions.

There is also a semblance of preferential treatment extended to the Malay-Muslim community, although these tend not to have any distorting effect on national policy. Although the linkage with Article 152 of the Singapore Constitution was never relied upon by the government, the Malay-Muslim community enjoys several privileges not accorded to the other races, such as free tertiary education (albeit qualified in 1989), state support for the mosque-building program, and the appointment of a minister in-charge of Muslim affairs to assist in the governance of a significant and important minority.[16] The Presidential Council of Minority Rights (PCMR), a constitutional organ, was also established as a commitment to the multiracial ethos.[17]

Of significance, Singapore's civic conception of citizenship also urges a conscious formation and sustenance of distinctive ethnic identities of the majority and minority communities. But the convergent civic and apparent divergent ethnic identities naturally at times compete, contest, and conflict. This gives rise to a variegated discourse on belonging, identity, and citizenship denominated in terms of societal interests over sectarian ones. Similarly, the heterogeneity of Singapore requires that careful attention be given to the design of institutions if multiracialism is to be sustained. As John Ikenberry (2003: 356) observes, "Ethnic divisions put at risk the nation-state, but they also provide a powerful incentive for the designing and building of state institutions."

The virtue of Article 152 and related provisions in the Singapore Constitution is that they constitutionally recognize the ethnic minorities in Singapore. Such recognition extends to their having distinct cultures, religions, and languages with the state's tacit support. Purposeful recognition reduces contestation. As the philosopher Charles Taylor (1994: 26) aptly puts it, "Due recognition is not just a courtesy we owe people. It is a vital human need."

More importantly, recognition has vitally important signaling effects – not just to the minority communities but to the ethnic Chinese community as well. This recognition of minorities as equal citizens helps ensure that the right of membership in a nation-state is substantively endowed, expressed purposefully, and honored meaningfully through being recognized by others as an equal, treated by the same standards and values, and accorded the same level of respect and dignity as all other members of that community. Thus, benefits, policy exceptions, preferences, and the like, when provided, are carefully structured to avoid any sense of entitlement or legal rights. I next examine how, despite the constitutional safeguards for the ethnic minorities, expectations have been structured toward one of emphasizing interests rather than rights.

## Language of accommodation for ethnic minorities: interests rather than rights

The arguable, potentially contentious, point of Article 152 has revolved around whether the provision specifically confers group rights upon the Malays, which would also entail special rights for them. Like most postcolonial constitutions, the Singapore Constitution is framed on the premise of individual rights. The fundamental liberties in Part IV of the constitution posit the individual as the rights-bearer. This interpretation is buttressed by the 1966 Constitutional Commission's report that the

> best way and most appropriate way of safeguarding the rights of the racial, linguistic and religious minorities in the Republic would be specially to entrench in the Constitution the fundamental rights of both the individual and the citizen (which would include prohibition against discriminatory treatment on the ground only of race, descent, place of origin or religion).[18]

In referring to the minorities in Singapore, the constitution – specifically Article 152 – does not use "right" or "rights." Instead, "interest(s)" is consciously adopted. As such, the safeguards in the constitution ought to be construed as being political in intent and effect, rather than legal, in substance. The special position of the Malays does not amount to special rights for them, as is the case in Malaysia. Likewise, the constitutional exhortation to the government to care for racial and religious minorities does not include the policy and language of affirmative action. Notably, Article 152 has not been a source of significant contestation or disaffection. In part, this reflects the even-handed approach toward the management of ethnic relations in Singapore. It also suggests that the government's consistent approach toward Article 152 since the throes of independence has not only managed expectations of the various communities but also set the tone for ethnic relations in Singapore.

Furthermore, given the centrality of "interests" in Article 152, the management of ethnic relations in Singapore has cohered resolutely around the careful policy of balancing interests without resorting to a language of rights or entitlement. The interests of the minorities have to be balanced against the interests of the majority ethnic Chinese community, and vice versa. In turn, this entails responsibility on the part of all key stakeholders in not pushing excessively for their community's interests, and for the government to always remain impartial. We now examine two policy initiatives, namely the introduction of the Group Representation Constituency (GRC) scheme into the electoral regime, and the tweaking of the policy of free education for the Malay community. Both impacted significantly on the Malay community and where the intent of Article 152, even if not specifically referred to, is given cognizance.[19]

## Ensuring political representation of racial minorities

First implemented in the 1988 general election, the Group Representation Constituency (GRC) electoral system is celebrated as Singapore's *sui generis* attempt at sustaining multiracialism through electoral integration by ensuring the adequate representation in Parliament of Members of Parliament (MPs) from the Malay, and Indian and other minority communities. The PAP government maintains that the GRC system has ensured that the minority races' needs, concerns, and views are not ignored or neglected in an ethnically Chinese-dominant

Singapore. Further, it had claimed that the electorate, especially the young voters, preferred "candidates who were best suited to their own needs without being sufficiently aware of the need to return a racially balanced slate of candidates," resulting in voting along racial lines.[20]

Under the GRC scheme, voters elect in an enlarged electoral district, on a "one person, one vote" basis, a team of MPs rather than an individual MP. A political party contesting in a GRC has to field a multi-member team of which at least one member must be from a designated minority race. To ensure adequate Malay parliamentary representation, three-fifths of the total number of GRCs must be designated constituencies where at least one of the candidates in every group shall be a person belonging to the Malay community.[21]

In ostensibly seeking to protect the interests of the racial minorities through adequate parliamentary representation, the GRC scheme should be construed as a policy and constitutional expression of Article 152, even if the government has never explicitly linked the scheme to it. The supposed racial bias in the electoral behavior would particularly threaten the political representation of the ethnic Malay community, the most significant minority race community. Then First Deputy Prime Minister Goh Chok Tong (*Singapore Parliament Reports* 1988a) explained:

> It is make-belief to pretend that race and language do not affect voter preferences.... Paradoxical as it may seem, to ensure that multi-racialism succeeds in Singapore, we have to openly recognise that race does play a part in politics.... Loyalty to one's own community, to race, to one's religion and language is stronger than loyalty to the nation, particularly if that nation is a new one and has many races.... For Singapore to remain a beautiful, peaceful country for many more generations, it is wise of us to strengthen the political framework before it is weakened by disillusionment, despondency and despair when one community finds itself thrown out of Parliament by the electoral system.

Initially, the Malay parliamentarians from the ruling People's Action Party (PAP) did not support the GRC proposal. Their concern was that a minority race candidate would be perceived to have "leaned on" a Chinese candidate in order to get elected. However, after the ruling party suffered electoral setbacks in the 1984 general election, the minority PAP MPs agreed to the GRC proposal to ensure that minority race candidates, especially first-time Malay candidates, would be elected in future elections in fair numbers. The PAP government argued that it had to take the lead in entrenching multiracialism. At the third reading of the Bill, First Deputy Prime Minister Goh (*Singapore Parliament Reports* 1988b) remarked:

> [Our GRC/Team MPs concept] is benevolent. The constitutional change is initiated by the majority to directly benefit the minority communities without any direct benefit to itself. It is our way of sharing our future

> together, of giving Singaporeans, whether Malays, Indians, Chinese, Eurasians or Others, that feeling of belonging to a single nation.... On its own, it [the GRC] will not ensure success in building up or strengthening our multiracial society. It is a formal institutional arrangement. For us to succeed, we must have the same spirit as the Swiss to search for consensus, to work through informal as much as formal arrangements, to make every citizen, whichever community, he belongs to, feel that he is a Singaporean.

Given this bias in favor of the minorities, Parliament was careful to explicitly provide for Article 39A(3) of the constitution which states that no laws relating to the GRC scheme are invalid for being inconsistent with the equal protection clause under Article 12 or be considered a "differentiating measure" under Article 68. The GRC scheme is potentially inconsistent with Article 12 on two counts: (1) That the GRC "prefers" the minority races by giving them a designated number of elected parliamentary seats. (2) That a voter in a multi-member GRC electoral ward has more voting power than his counterpart in a single-member constituency (SMC), as the former's single vote would place up to six MPs while the latter's vote elects only one MP.

Unsurprisingly, critics regard the GRC scheme as an unabashed attempt to stem the PAP's electoral decline, and help extend its electoral dominance (Tan, E.K.B. 2005). GRCs are now the dominant electoral division. Today, there are 16 GRCs and 13 single-member constituencies in Singapore's thirteenth Parliament, which has 89 elected seats, with 76 seats for the GRCs. But the language of interests was and remains dominant in justifying the creation of the GRC electoral innovation: that of the larger interest of entrenching multiracialism in Singapore, and protecting the interest of the minorities by their having adequate legislative representation.[22]

## Modifying the principle of free education for Malays: tweaking or compromising?

The policy of free education for the Malays up to the tertiary level had long been accepted as an explicit manifestation of the special position of the Malays. Introduced in 1960, this policy was also seen as integral to the effort to uplift the Malay community's relatively low educational standards. In 1989, the government proposed to modify the policy by having Malay students whose families could afford the tuition fees meet all or part of the cost of their tertiary-level education at the local polytechnics or universities, as well as at independent secondary schools. The government assured the Malay community that the scheme would not result in a change in the actual expenditures on free education for the Malays. Instead, the use of means testing would help ensure that more funds would be available for educational purposes administered by the Malay self-help group, Mendaki.

Again, the language of community interests was flagged. The modification to the free education policy was rationalized as benefitting the entire Malay community. This significant change to a long-standing policy initiative, assumed by many in the Malay community as an Article 152 entitlement and right, was explained in the logic of rationality, equity, and interest of the community (as opposed to the interest of a Malay individual or family). As a prominent Malay community leader had put it, "The whole objective of the scheme was really to support needy students and the savings under such a scheme would then enable Mendaki to extend financial assistance to more Malay students or finance other education-related projects" (Ridzwan Dzafir 2009: 196). In a rare parliamentary intervention (in what was to be his last term as a cabinet minister) in 2009, Minister Mentor Lee Kuan Yew stressed race equality in Singapore as an ideal, an aspiration to strive toward:

> As Malays have progressed and a number have joined the middle class with university degrees and professional qualifications, we have asked Mendaki to agree not to have their special rights of free education at university but to take what they were entitled to; put those fees to help more disadvantaged Malays. So, we are trying to reach a position where there is a level playing field for everybody which is going to take decades, if not centuries, and we may never get there.

It is worth noting that the expectation of free education for Malays from primary to tertiary level as a right is arguably not misplaced. When Singapore was making the necessary constitutional changes prior to merging with Malaya to form the Federation of Malaysia in 1963, Singapore explicitly maintained the policy of free education for the Malays in Singapore even though the Federal Constitution then had prohibited the federal government in Kuala Lumpur from discriminating in education among the races. On the other hand, the Malaysian Federal Constitution of 1963 had provided for reservations of public service positions for the Malays, as well as the reservation of a proportion of permits or licenses for selected trade and business in Malaysia. Singapore's state constitution, however, did not provide for these reservations. It would appear that free education for the Malays plays a unique role within Singapore's Article 152 framework.

The GRC scheme and the modified free education scheme for Malays suggest a certain degree of reflexive responsiveness on the part of the government in adjusting to changing circumstances and to keep Article 152 relevant. In both initiatives, the minorities, especially the Malays, are not accorded roles and identities as subjects. Instead, the identity as citizens is evident. Nonetheless, the biggest challenge to claims of inclusive citizenship does not revolve around Article 152. In the third section, I examine the role of the Malays in the Singapore military. Ironically, the very areas (i.e., Malay race and Muslim religion), which are accorded explicit recognition under Articles 152 and 153, are key concerns in the full integration of Malays in Singapore's citizen armed forces.

## Differentiated and contested belonging and recognition? Of Trojan horses, loyalty, and citizenship ambiguity

Since the days of the republican city-states of ancient Greece, the metaphor of military service and citizenship as integral to nation-building has been a powerful one. Military service is idealized as being capable of expanding the citizenship rights of minorities (be it racial, religious, linguistic, or gender). Military service, especially during times of conflict against an external aggressor, embodies the ultimate sacrifice that a citizen is prepared to make in defense of the state's sovereignty and territorial integrity. Beyond the confines of the barracks, military recruitment and placement policies have tremendous potential to shape society. National Service in defense of one's country nurtures national and civic consciousness. In particular, the politics of identity and citizenship are intimately and fundamentally influenced, shaped, and determined. In this regard, the role of citizens, especially the minorities, in the military shapes the discourse of citizenship in more ways than one.

Security concerns are dominant themes in independent Singapore's governance and historiography. This strategic anxiety of a miniscule population is shaped by its assessment of Southeast Asia as a volatile neighborhood, a history of uneasy relationships with its closest neighbors, and an abiding concern with the primordial pulls of race, language, and religion.[23] In turn, these geographical, historical, and cultural angsts and ambivalences have created a citizenship ambiguity for the Malay-Muslims in the discourse on multiracialism and citizenship.

The Singapore Armed Forces (SAF) is a largely conscript defense force and is steadfastly portrayed as one of the pillars of Singapore's multiracial ethos. Born of and sustained out of "a chronic sense of its [Singapore's] own vulnerability,"[24] the SAF is promoted and celebrated by the government as an institution that is non-racial and one that bonds the servicemen regardless of their class, race, language, or religion, in the defense of Singapore's sovereignty.[25] In *Defending Singapore in the 21st Century*, the Ministry of Defence declares that "National Service remains the only viable option for building up a defence force capable and formidable enough to deter an external attack" (Ministry of Defence 2000: 41). Introduced in March 1967, all medically fit males aged 18 are enlisted to serve National Service for up to two years (previously, two and a half years). This is followed by reserve service until 40 years of age for non-commissioned officers and 50 years of age for commissioned officers.[26]

Military service is seen as being central to full Singaporean citizenship. In the official discourse, National Service is portrayed as being integral to full, as opposed to formal, citizenship for Singaporean males. National service is an important rite of citizenship for a "nation-in-arms … a garrison state with a garrison mentality to match" (Tan, T.Y., 2001: 277). Mandatory military service can therefore provide a shared experience of Singaporean society. It has also become a traditional training ground for Singapore's future leaders, especially in politics.[27] For a society where the concerns of survivalism and vulnerability are ever present, compulsory National Service is a key institution in the defense of

Singapore and in the nation-building process. National service is undoubtedly a sociopolitical process in societal homogenization in the civic sense.

Although the military is also seen as an institution of nation-building through its efforts in racial integration,[28] the government has always insisted that SAF's operational requirements take clear precedence over the nation-building function. From a largely ethnic Malay police force and armed forces, the government, upon gaining independence, sought to recruit more Chinese and Indians into the police and armed forces. When National Service was introduced, politicians and citizens alike shared the explicit understanding that the new National Service laws require every young Singaporean male citizen be conscripted, irrespective of racial background (Peled 1998: 99). As it turned out, this was not the case. Between 1969 and 1973, universal conscription of Malays was not practiced so as to "racially balance" Singapore's defense force from a predominantly Malay fighting force to a mixed-race force. Such a policy is perhaps not all that surprising.

The Singapore government was motivated by a deep concern and abiding fear that in a crisis the soldiers could not be trusted to be impartial. It took a leaf from the racial disturbances in Singapore in 1964, and the May 13, 1969 riots in Malaysia where the Malaysian military and police personnel (who were overwhelmingly Malay in both situations) were partial in the conflict, resulting in significant Chinese casualties (Peled 1998: 111–112).[29] As Stanley Bedlington (1981: 260) remarked more than two decades ago, "The government cannot be expected to tolerate the domination of its military and police by an ethnic group which forms only 15 percent of the population as a whole and whose loyalties can be reasonably questioned." Former Prime Minister Lee Kuan Yew wrote in his memoirs, "Independent Singapore could not continue the old British practice of having a city of three-quarters Chinese policed and guarded by Malay policemen and soldiers" (Lee 2000: 31).

The government's quest for a more "mixed-race" SAF consequently led to the dual effort in ramping up the recruitment of more non-Malays and concomitantly reducing the Malay proportion in the SAF. Between 1969 and 1973, few Malays were enlisted. In addition, regular Malay soldiers' careers apparently suffered significant detriment to their career prospects through the conscious policy of "racially balancing" the rank and file of the military to make it more indicative of Singapore's racial composition.[30] Since 1985, however, all eligible Malays have been enlisted for National Service. By 2000, there was predominance and over-representation of ethnic Chinese in the officer ranks in contrast to the 1980s when there were more non-Chinese officers, and in the 1960s when the Malays constituted the backbone of the SAF's predecessor.[31] A racially balanced personnel, with an over-representation of ethnic Chinese military personnel in all ranks, will persist as a desired state of affairs even as there are now more Malay commissioned officers and with more holding senior positions. Yet, closer integration in society and the SAF does not remove the security concerns that are the major hindrance to the ethnic Malays playing a fuller role, not just in the SAF but also in the larger security apparatus, including the intelligence services.

The state's and government's sense of vulnerability is overriding and is attributed to the acrimonious political union of Singapore in Malaysia where racial concerns were central in the July and August 1964 riots culminated dramatically in the failed merger with Malaysia and Singapore's subsequent independence.[32] Furthermore, the security perspective of Singapore as a small, predominantly ethnically Chinese state in a Malay-Muslim world sustains and heightens the country's entrenched sense of vulnerability. It was in this context that the SAF came into being, and whose influence on society and half of Singapore's population is substantive. This state of perpetual vulnerability breathes life into Singapore's defense posture and policies.

The key hindrance to closer Malay integration in the defense force stems from the Singaporean political elites' belief that primordial loyalties of ethnicity and religion will trump the civic and secular loyalties of the Singaporean nation. The tacit institutional ambiguity of their National Service role and their place within the larger national security apparatus are major issues that continue to gnaw at the Malay-Muslims, resulting in some degree of angst, distrust, and misunderstanding between the Malay-Muslims and the government. More than three decades ago, this alleged loyalty dilemma was the "focal point of Malay dissatisfaction with if not alienation from the Singapore political system" (Bedlington 1981: 259).[33]

Meritocracy is explained as the reason for the low or non-deployment of Malay-Muslims in sensitive units and in high staff and command positions. Yet, this belies the true issue at heart: that the origins of the role of the Malay-Muslims in the SAF may be traced to the government's early doubts as to whether the Malay-Muslim soldier can rise above his racial and religious loyalties in the defense of Singapore. In the government's view, race and religion may conflict with, if not trump over, patriotic pulls for a Malay-Muslim soldier. This position was never publicly enunciated until 1987, 20 years after the introduction of NS, when BG (NS) Lee Hsien Loong, then junior defense minister, stated first in a constituency tour and, later in Parliament the government's longstanding concern with the purported dual-loyalty conflict faced by the ethnic Malays resulting in the need for an exclusionary ethnic manpower policy in the national security apparatus (*Singapore Parliament Reports* 1987):

> If there is a conflict, we don't want to put any of our soldiers in a difficult position where his emotions for the nation may be in conflict with his emotions for his religion.... We don't want to put anybody in that position where he feels he is not fighting a just cause, and perhaps worse, maybe his side is not the right side.... The SAF is not only an institution for nation building; it also has an operational role. Its operational role is to defend Singapore against armed attack in case of war. We cannot post a soldier, a national serviceman, to the SAF, or for that matter post him to any particular post in the SAF, simply for purposes of nation building alone. He is there not just for his education but to fulfill a role, an operational role. We have to take this into account. We still have to remember that in a multi-racial

> society, as was pointed out by Dr Goh [Keng Swee] 10 years ago but it is still true, "the ethnic distribution of soldiers is obviously an important yet delicate subject".

Earlier on, in November 1986, Israel's President Chiam Herzog's state visit to Singapore incurred the displeasure of Malaysia. In the ensuing bilateral spat, the government questioned the loyalty of Singaporean Muslim organizations when it perceived that they reacted to the visit in the same manner as the Malaysians. Then Prime Minister Lee Kuan Yew remarked that "It is a reminder that in certain circumstances the Malay Singaporean reacts with the emphasis on Malay/Muslim rather than Singaporean" (Leifer 1988: 349). More than a decade later, Lee (2001) reaffirmed the government's concern:

> We must never put the person in a situation where he may face a conflict of loyalties. I said in answer to a question some nearly two years ago that it is a difficult matter to put a Malay Muslim of deeply religious family background in charge of a machine-gun. We should never have to ask this of anyone. Some of you were disturbed by my frankness. But when I faced crises in the 1960s I could not afford to be wrong. Was this discrimination or was it common sense – a policy of prudence?... We uphold meritocracy, which means the most qualified and suitable person for the job. For nearly every job, a person's race and religion are irrelevant. But in the security services, because of our context, we cannot ignore race and religion in deciding suitability.... Our concerns about conflicting loyalties are real. We know of at least one case where foreign intelligence agencies approached one of our senior officers because he was Malay. Fortunately, he reported the approach to his superiors. We had judged his loyalty correctly. So we are not just dealing with hypothetical situations. Potential adversaries see this as a fault line in our society, and they will exploit it whenever they can.[34]

This is the tightrope situation for the Malay-Muslims and the government to tread. The rites and rituals of citizenship require that they perform compulsory National Service, yet their loyalty remains in some doubt. The concern, although weakening, remains over whether the Malay community are differentiating and distancing themselves from the larger Singaporean society.[35] This reiterates the government's long-standing position, first elaborated in Parliament in March 1987, that the deeper integration of the Malays in Singapore society is the prerequisite for greater Malay participation in the SAF. Yet, so long as there is distrust, the common space and nation-building mechanism *par excellence* that National Service is promoted as becomes a contested symbol of the loyalty of the Malay-Muslims and prevents their meaningful participation as full-fledged citizens.[36]

At the same time, the government is alive to the need for the ethnic composition of the SAF to be balanced. An ethnically skewed military, more likely than not, will heighten ethnic consciousness and exaggerate ethnic insecurities of ethnic groups not adequately represented in the military. As a key coercive arm of the state, the military demographics may either result in the military as a cause of violence or a restraint (Petersen and Staniland 2008). This caution was reasonable at independence given that race relations were relatively polarized. However, going forward, if the multiracial and inclusive citizenship ideology is not to be discredited, closer integration in the armed forces would require doing away with the operational worldview of the Malay-Muslim servicemen's susceptibility to potential disloyalty.

For the government, its stance is that the full integration of Malay servicemen cannot be forced. The government's policy approach to integration of Malays in the SAF is an incremental one, buttressed by its stand that the role of Malays in the SAF is not static.[37] Although there is universal conscription of all fit Malay-Muslim males today, they tend to be concentrated in the non-sensitive military units and in non-military sectors such as the civil defense and police forces (Huxley 2000: 102–104). But there has been significant progress since the 1970s, and progress continues to be made.[38] Gone are the days of well-publicized exceptions of Malay deployment in the SAF in the mass media to highlight the growing integration of the Malays in the defense structure. Notwithstanding these developments, the security paradigm is oriented on race as being powerfully salient and critical in the security affairs of a society still self-assessed to be not fully integrated.

To be sure, the concerns of the government are real rather than imagined. The heightened fears of religious loyalties and their destructive effect on a military fighting machine have conspired to limit the role of Malay-Muslim servicemen in Singapore's defense apparatus. Where the Malay-Muslim servicemen are concerned, National Service as an institution of multiracialism, if not carefully managed, could accentuate perceptions of a less than inclusive multiracialism. In turn, the special position of the Malays is unwittingly undermined.

## Conclusion

In 1959, Singapore secured internal self-government with the promise to care for the interests of racial and religious minorities in Singapore. The path dependence of this promise remains, sustains, and nourishes the nation-building endeavor, and is a core component of the PAP government's performance legitimacy. Notwithstanding the civic concept of citizenship in Singapore, this process is greatly aided by Article 152 of the Singapore Constitution, which urges a conscious formation and sustenance of distinctive ethnic identities of the majority and minority communities. It encapsulates the state's and the government's political promise to always care for the interests of the racial and religious minorities in Singapore and to recognize the special position of the Malays.

The Singapore approach to ethnic relations, in particular to the management of the ethnic minorities, seeks to reconcile the political elites' and society's antipathy against affirmative action on the one hand, and the strategic importance of uplifting the minorities, especially the Malays, on the other. It is also about the commitment toward and the imperative of formal and substantive racial equality wherein the national effort toward equal opportunity, rather than equal outcomes, is part of the Singaporean multiracial ethos. To be sure, it remains a work-in-progress, as the integration of the Malays into Singapore's military vividly demonstrates.

There has been the abiding and conscious avoidance of a (group) rights-based legal regime in the management of ethnic issues as part of the postcolonial nation-building project. Interests, duties, and responsibility – rather than rights and entitlement – constitute the de facto language of citizenship. In examining the public discourse on race, the uncontested description of or reference to the Malays as the "indigenous people" is barely used. Neither is the political relationship between the Malays and the state overtly defined by indigenity. In comparison with Malaysia, Australia, Canada, or the United States, there is little traction for the indigenity discourse as part of the larger constitutional narrative in Singapore. The Singapore constitutional experience vis-à-vis pluralism in a multi-ethnic polity highlights that differentiated role of rights and interests. The political role and importance they play are very much a product of socio-legal and political recognition. Article 152 of the Singapore Constitution may be likened to a constitutional shield (used reactively), as opposed to a political sword (used proactively).

Consequently, the constitutional posture and attitude toward the special position of the Malays establishes and facilitates the conscious avoidance of a rights-based legal regime in the management of ethnic issues since the establishment of self-governing Singapore. In that regard, Article 152 has depoliticized, to some extent, the postcolonial nation-building project in Singapore. Further, Article 152 creates the foundational substratum for interests, duties, and responsibility – rather than rights and entitlement – as the de facto language of citizenship, wherein the larger good of the state and society takes ultimate precedence. Rights are regarded as an inappropriate means to undergird multiracialism and securing purposeful citizenship for all Singaporeans. It is seen as promoting contestation and confrontation, and hence is inherently problematic for nation-building.

The non-framing of ethnic minority positions in terms of rights does not remove the central importance of addressing the interests, needs, and concerns of the indigenous Malays in managing issues of race, language, religion, and belonging in the Singapore political milieu. In fact, given the dominant discourse of the larger good of the state and society taking precedence over sectarian concerns, the constitutional framework urges the emphasis on and recognition of competing interests and balancing them as securing the state's even-handed approach to competing and conflicting concerns in a multiracial society. This is not to suggest that rights are inconsequential. They matter immensely but their relevance is primarily at the individual level. At the societal level, interests are defining, with the imperative of ensuring that rights are not regarded as "trumps." Notwithstanding the focus on interests, the convergent civic and divergent ethnic identities will compete, giving rise to a variegated and, at times, contested

discourse on belonging, identity, and citizenship. The discourse has shifted toward the quality of citizenship belonging, as the Malays' role in the Singapore military establishment poignantly demonstrates. The interactions on this pivotal issue of inclusiveness and belonging will have a long-lasting impact on the nation-building process.

The Singapore experience suggests that the deliberate avoidance of framing ethnic minority positions in terms of rights has been critical in reducing contestation. But this approach has been accompanied by a focus on, if not the valorizing of, interests of the state. Furthermore, and just as critical, is the recognition and accommodation of the minority communities within the complementary framework of an overarching Singaporean civic identity and loyalty. This approach may not be entirely relevant in other countries grappling with the challenges of pluralism, but it does offer a viable, alternative approach to the liberal democratic emphasis on rights for how we could think about constitutional practice in Southeast Asia – one that seeks to adopt an even-handed approach toward the balancing of rights and interests at the individual, community, and statist levels.

## Notes

1 Anthony Reid (2010) notes that Singapore has had a high foreign-born population content throughout its history. Lily Rahim (2009) describes Singapore as a "colonial settler society" but her analysis is built on the somewhat questionable binary of the ethnic Chinese immigrants as "colonizing outsiders" and the Malays as the "natives."

2 See Gladney (1998) for a further discussion.

3 As Prime Minister Lee Hsien Loong (2015) put it recently:

> One of our most remarkable achievements over these last 50 years, has been our racial and religious harmony. It stems from a strong belief in the ideal of a multiracial society where everybody is equal, regardless of race, language or religion, and it was the most fundamental reason why we left Malaysia and went our own way on 9 August 1965. Since then, we have held firmly to the belief that before race, language and religion, first and foremost, we should all be Singaporeans together and so, we have built a fair and just society, based on meritocracy, where ability and not your background or the colour of your skin, determines how well you do, determines what contributions you make, and what rewards you get.
> (Transcript available online: sg/mediacentre/transcript-speech-prime-minister-lee-hsien-loong-onepeoplesgs-community-leaders (accessed October 26, 2015))

4 The Singapore Constitution does not define who a Malay is. In contrast, Article 160(2) of the Malaysian Constitution defines a "Malay" as "a person who professes the religion of Islam, habitually speaks the Malay language, conforms to Malay custom." On the Malays and "Malayness," see generally Milner (2008). See also Syed Muhd Khairudin Aljunied (2009). On Malay ethnicity and its shifting boundaries as a response to trade, see Andaya (2008).

5 Singapore (Constitution) Order in Council, 1958 (SI No. 1956 of 1958).

6 Although the Directive Principles of State Policy are not enforceable by any Indian court, the Indian state is duty-bound to apply the principles in making laws: see Article 37, and Part IV generally of the Indian Constitution.

7 See also Huang-Thio (1964).

8 Besides English, the assigned mother-tongue languages of the three main ethnic groups, namely Mandarin, Malay, and Tamil, were adopted as official languages. However, few non-Malay Singaporeans can speak the Malay language. Malay is, of course, the *lingua franca* of Singapore's immediate neighbors. D.J. Enright (1969: 120–121) described Malay in Singapore as the "nominal" national language used as a "linguistic red herring to distract attention from the real problem, or the real problem as reflected in the rivalry between the English and Chinese languages."

9 Independent Singapore's first head of state was Malay. The second was Eurasian while the third was Indian.

10 Canada has constitutionalized its commitment to multiculturalism. Article 27 of The Constitutional Act, 1982 reads: "This Charter shall be interpreted in a manner consistent with the preservation and enhancement of the multicultural heritage of Canadians." On the Canadian experience in accommodating diversity, see Kymlicka (2003).

11 See the discussion on Singapore in Castellino and Redondo (2006: 193–236).

12 Article 12 of the Singapore Constitution reads as follows:

> (1) All persons are equal before the law and entitled to the equal protection of the law.
>
> (2) Except as expressly authorised by this Constitution, there shall be no discrimination against citizens of Singapore on the ground only of religion, race, descent or place of birth in any law or in the appointment to any office or employment under a public authority or in the administration of any law relating to the acquisition, holding or disposition of property or the establishing or carrying on of any trade, business, profession, vocation or employment.
>
> (3) This Article does not invalidate or prohibit –
>
> (a) any provision regulating personal law; or
>
> (b) any provision or practice restricting office or employment connected with the affairs of any religion, or of an institution managed by a group professing any religion, to persons professing that religion.

13 For instance, the Prisons Regulations (Cap 247, Rg 2, 2002 Rev Ed) reg 103(2)) provides that Jewish prisoners may not be compelled to work on Saturdays if they claim exemption and they may also keep such festival days as may be allowed by the government. Similarly, reg 103(3) of the Prisons Regulations allows Muslim prisoners to observe the fast of *Ramadan* and to labor at reduced tasks during the fast.

14 Some 99.6 percent of Malays are Muslims.

15 Cap. 3, 1999 Revised Edition.

16 On the mosque-building program, see Green (2007).

17 The PCMR has the general function of considering and reporting on "matters affecting persons of any racial or religious community in Singapore" as may be referred to the Council by Parliament or the government. Its particular function is to draw attention to any Bill or to any subsidiary legislation if the Council deems them to be a differentiating measure: see, generally, Part VII of the Singapore Constitution. A differentiating measure is:

> any measure which is, or is likely in its practical application to be, disadvantageous to persons of any racial or religious community and not equally disadvantageous to persons of other such communities, either directly by prejudicing persons of that community or indirectly by giving advantage to persons of another community.
>
> (Article 68, Singapore Constitution)

To date, there has been no negative report by the PCMR.

18 Constitutional Commission (1966: para 11). See also para 24 of the Commission's report, as well as Articles 12 and 16 of the constitution.

19 Another significant expression of the government's protecting the interests of the minorities is the formation and continued support for the ethnic self-help groups. The Malays have two such groups (Mendaki and the Association of Muslim Professionals) and the Indians have the Singapore Indian Development Association (SINDA). The Chinese self-help group, the Chinese Development Assistance Council (CDAC), was established after the Malay and Indian self-help groups were established. Due to space constraints, an examination of the ethnic self-help groups is not attempted in this chapter.

20 *Singapore Parliament Reports* (1988a). Since voting is secret and exit polls on polling day prohibited, it is unclear (save for anecdotal evidence) how the PAP government arrived at its conclusions on Singaporeans' voting behavior.

21 See section 8A(3) and section 8(1)(b)(i) of the Parliamentary Elections Act. Section 8A(2) of the same Act provides that for each general election, the number of MPs returned by all GRCs shall not be less than one-quarter of the total number of elected MPs.

22 While the intent and design of the GRC scheme is ostensibly to further protect the interests of the minorities, the scheme has also been helpful to the electoral fortunes of the PAP. See further Tan, E.K.B. (2013).

23 A thoughtful discussion of the "structural tension" in Singapore's bilateral relations with Malaysia is found in Leifer (2000). See also Shirashi (2009).

24 Tan (2001: 276).

25 Under the law, both men and women may be conscripted, although only men have been enlisted since 1967.

26 See Enlistment Act (Cap. 93, 2001 Revised Edition).

27 In the newest Cabinet formed in September 2015, seven of the 20 Cabinet Ministers, including the Prime Minister and one Deputy Prime Minister, were former professional military officers. This included the immediate past Chief of Defence Force who entered politics in the September 2015 general election.

28 See National Library Board and National Archives of Singapore (2007: 79–81).

29 That the SAF played a key role in maintaining law and order in Singapore in the spillover of racial disturbance from Malaysia's May 1969 riots is described in Ministry of Defence Singapore (2007: 32–34).

30 See, further, Bedlington (1981), Peled (1998: 106–118), Huxley (2000: 9–10, 102).

31 Huxley (2000: 114–115). No precise figures were given by Huxley; nor are the figures available in the public domain.

32 On the failed merger, see Lau (1998). On the seeds of failure in the formation of the Federation of Malaysia in 1963, see Tan, T.Y. (2008).

33 Ismail Kassim (2008: 59) notes:

> As part of the separation agreement, the Tunku [Abdul Rahman, Malaysia's Prime Minister between 1957 and 1970] offered Singapore Malays land in Johore and the option of becoming Malaysian. Only a handful accepted; the vast majority preferred to take their chances with Lee [Kuan Yew] and the PAP.

34 For a summary of the main points of the position paper prepared by Majlis Pusat and the AMP for the dialogue, see Ismail Kassim (2008: 200–202).

35 "Integrate or Separate: Malays' Pick." *The Straits Times*, March 4, 2001.

36 On the Malay alienation as a consequence of the exclusionary manpower policy, see Peled (1998: 118–125). Lily Rahim (1998: 107) argues that the government has "mistaken Malay political alienation and dissent for disloyalty."

37 "Role of Malays in SAF has Evolved." *The Straits Times*, March 4, 2001.

38 See replies by the Defense Minister to parliamentary questions on the deployment of Malay-Muslim personnel within the SAF: *Singapore Parliament Reports* (2014a, 2014b). Depending on one's perspective, the integration of Malays in the SAF is either seen as the glass being half empty or half full.

## Bibliography

Andaya, L.Y. (2008). *Leaves of the Same Tree: Trade and Ethnicity in the Straits of Melaka*. Honolulu, University of Hawaii Press.

Bedlington, S.S. (1981). "Ethnicity and the Armed Forces in Singapore." In *Ethnicity and the Military in Asia*, eds C. DeWitt, C. Ellinwood, and C.H. Enloe. New Brunswick, NJ, Transaction Books, pp. 242–266.

Brown, D. (2009). "Ethnic and Nationalist Politics in Southeast Asia." In *Contemporary Southeast Asia*, ed. M. Beeson. Basingstoke, Palgrave Macmillan, pp. 143–156.

Castellino, J. and Redondo, E.D. (2006). *Minority Rights in Asia: A Comparative Legal Analysis*. Oxford, Oxford University Press.

Chan, S.K. (2007). "Culture and Legal Practice." Keynote speech by the Chief Justice of Singapore at the International Bar Association Conference, Singapore, October 15.

Constitutional Commission (Wee Chong Jin, Chairman) (1966). *Report of the Constitutional Commission, 1966*. Singapore, Government Printer.

Enright, D.J. (1969). *Memoirs of a Mendicant Professor*. London, Chatto & Windus.

Gladney, D.C., ed. (1998). *Making Majorities: Constituting the Nation in Japan, Korea, China, Malaysia, Fiji, Turkey, and the United States*. Stanford, CA, Stanford University Press.

Green, A. (2007). *Continuing the Legacy: 30 Years of the Mosque Building Fund in Singapore*. Singapore, Majlis Ugama Islam Singapura.

Huang-Thio, S.M. (1964). "Constitutional Discrimination under the Malaysian Constitution." *Malayan Law Review*, 6(1): 1–16.

Huxley, T. (2000). *Defending the Lion City: The Armed Forces of Singapore*. St. Leonards, NSW, Allen & Unwin.

Ikenberry, G.J. (2003). "What States Can Do Now." In *The Nation-State in Question*, eds T.V. Paul, G.J. Ikenberry, and J.A. Hall. Princeton, NJ, Princeton University Press, pp. 350–371.

Ismail Kassim (2008). *A Reporter's Memoir: No Hard Feelings*. Singapore, Ismail Kassim.

Kymlicka, W. (2003). "Being Canadian." *Government and Opposition*, 38(3): 357–385.

Lau, A. (1998). *A Moment of Anguish: Singapore in Malaysia and the Politics of Disengagement*. Singapore, Times Academic Press.

Lee, H.L. (2015). Transcript of speech by Prime Minister Lee Hsien Loong at the OnePeople.Sg's Community Leaders' Conference at The Grassroots Club, Singapore, October 4.

Lee, K.Y. (1998). *The Singapore Story: The Memoirs of Lee Kuan Yew*. Singapore, Times Editions and The Straits Times Press.

Lee, K.Y. (2000). *From Third World to First – The Singapore Story: 1965–2000, Memoirs of Lee Kuan Yew*. Singapore, Singapore Press Holdings and Times Editions.

Lee, K.Y. (2001). "Loyalty and the SAF." Speech at the dialogue session with the Association of Muslim Professionals and the *Majlis Pusat*, March 2.

Lee, K.Y. (2004). Speech at the People's Action Party fiftieth anniversary celebrations, November 21.

Lee, K.Y. (2009). Parliamentary speech at the debate on the "Nation Building Tenets" motion, Singapore Parliament Reports, vol. 86 (August 19, 2009), available at: https://sprs.parl.gov.sg/search/topic.jsp?currentTopicID=00073711-ZZ&currentPubID=00075281-ZZ&topicKey=00075281-ZZ.00073711-ZZ_1%2B%2B.

Leifer, M. (1988). "Israel's President in Singapore: Political Catalysis and Transnational Politics." *The Pacific Review*, 1(4): 341–352.

Leifer, M. (2000). *Singapore's Foreign Policy: Coping with Vulnerability*. London, Routledge.

Lily Zubaidah Rahim (2009). *Singapore in the Malay World: Building and Breaching Regional Bridges*. London and New York, Routledge.

Milner, A. (2008). *The Malays*. Malden, MA, Wiley-Blackwell.

Ministry of Defense (2000). *Defending Singapore in the 21st Century*. Singapore, Ministry of Defense.

Ministry of Defense Singapore (2007). *40/40: 40 Years and 40 Stories of National Service*. Singapore, Landmark Books for Ministry of Defense.

National Library Board and National Archives of Singapore (2007). *Singapore: The First Ten Years of Independence*. Singapore, National Library Board and National Archives of Singapore.

Neo, J.L.-C. (2008). "The Protection of Minorities and the Constitution: A Judicious Balance?" In *Evolution of a Revolution: Forty Years of the Singapore Constitution*, ed. L.-A. Thio and K.Y.L. Tan. London and New York, Routledge, pp. 234–259.

Peled, A. (1998). *A Question of Loyalty: Military Manpower Policy in Multiethnic States*. Ithaca, NY, Cornell University Press.

Petersen, R. and Staniland, P. (2008). "Resentment, Fear, and the Structure of the Military in Multiethnic States." In *Intra-State Conflict, Governments and Security: Dilemmas of Deterrence and Assurance*, ed. S.M. Saideman and M.-J. Zahar. London and New York, Routledge, pp. 96–119.

Reid, A. (2010). "Malaysia/Singapore as Immigrant Societies." National University of Singapore – Asia Research Institute, Working Paper Series No. 141 (July).

Ridzwan Dzafir (2009). *Ridzwan Dzafir: From Pondok Boy to Singapore's "Mr ASEAN" – An Autobiography*. Singapore, Editions Didier Millet.

Shirashi, T. (ed.) (2009). *Across the Causeway: A Multi-dimensional Study of Malaysia–Singapore Relations*. Singapore, Institute of Southeast Asian Studies.

*Singapore Parliament Reports* (1987). Vol. 49, col. 375 (March 17).

*Singapore Parliament Reports* (1988a). Vol. 50, no. 3, cols 181–192 (January 11).

*Singapore Parliament Reports* (1988b). Vol. 51, no. 1, cols 27–53 (January 11).

*Singapore Parliament Reports* (2009). Vol. 86 (August 19).

*Singapore Parliament Reports* (2014a). Vol. 92 (May 29).

*Singapore Parliament Reports* (2014b). Vol. 92 (July 7).

*Straits Times, The* (2001a). "Integrate or Separate: Malays' Pick." March 4.

*Straits Times, The* (2001b). "Role of Malays in SAF Has Evolved." March 4.

Syed Muhd Khairudin Aljunied (2009). "British Discourses and Malay Identity in Colonial Singapore." *Indonesia and the Malay World*, 37(107): 1–21.

Tan, E.K.B. (2004). " 'We, the Citizens of Singapore': Multiethnicity, its Evolution and its Aberrations." In *Beyond Rituals and Riots: Ethnic Relations and Social Cohesion in Singapore*, ed. L.A. Eng. Singapore, Eastern Universities Press, pp. 65–97.

Tan, E.K.B. (2005). "Multiracialism Engineered: The Limits of Electoral and Spatial Integration in Singapore." *Ethnopolitics*, 4(4): 413–428.

Tan, E.K.B. (2013). "Autochthonous Constitutional Design in Post-colonial Singapore: Intimations of Confucianism and the Leviathan in Entrenching Dominant Government." *Yonsei Law Journal*, 4(2): 273–308.

Tan, E.K.B. (2015). "Singapore." In *Keeping the Faith: A Study of Freedom of Thought, Conscience, and Religion in ASEAN*. Jakarta, Human Rights Resource Center, pp. 416–480.

Tan, K.Y.L. (2004). "The Legal and Institutional Framework and Issues of Multiculturalism in Singapore." In *Beyond Rituals and Riots: Ethnic Pluralism and Social Cohesion in Singapore*, ed. L.A. Eng. Singapore, Institute of Policy Studies and Eastern Universities Press, pp. 98–113.
Tan, T.Y. (2001). "Singapore: Civil–Military Fusion." In *Coercion and Governance: The Declining Political Role of the Military in Asia*, ed. M. Alagappa. Stanford, CA, Stanford University Press, pp. 276–293.
Tan, T.Y. (2008). *Creating "Greater Malaysia": Decolonization and the Politics of Merger*. Singapore, Institute of Southeast Asian Studies.
Taylor, Charles (1994). "The Politics of Recognition." In *Multiculturalism: Examining the Politics of Recognition*, ed. A. Gutmann. Princeton, NJ, Princeton University Press, pp. 25–73.

# Part IV

# Constitutional politics and the rule of law

# 12 Courts and constitutional politics in Southeast Asia

*Björn Dressel*

## Introduction

Over the past 25 years, the role of courts in asserting the supremacy of constitutions while providing equitable justice as part of the expansion of the rule of law has become a central topic of debate in Southeast Asia. Consider the role of courts in Thailand's continuing political turmoil, the high-profile religious and political cases in Malaysia, or the continuing struggles of courts in Burma and Cambodia to assert their independence from politics. These are struggles not only about notions of the rule of law but also about the extent to which the law has acquired primacy over politics – a critical aspect of current constitutional trajectories in Southeast Asia.

Courts, particularly those charged with judicial review of constitutional issues, are critical to this process. With political governance playing an increasingly important role as part of the "judicialization of politics," which Hirschl describes as "the ever-accelerating reliance on courts and judicial means for addressing core moral predicaments, public policy questions, and political controversies" (2006: 721), the region's courts have been at the center of contestation in disputes ranging from human rights protection to religious matters and broad public policy questions. They have therefore become critical to the extent to which the rule of law is conceptualized and applied fairly in Southeast Asia.

Yet, like the institution of the judiciary itself, the trend of judicializing the constitutional and political arena and its consequences are not well understood. In fact, though well documented for the United States, Europe, and Latin America (see Tate and Vallinder 1995; Epp 1998; Feeley and Rubin 1998; Stone Sweet 2000; Shapiro and Stone Sweet 2002; Sieder *et al.* 2005b), the judicialization of politics in Asia, particularly Southeast Asia, has rarely been explored (though see, for tentative exploration, Ginsburg and Chen 2009; Harding and Nicholson 2010; Dressel 2012). This is perhaps not surprising. The region still battles legacies of executive dominance and an unusual degree of regime diversity that all have higher visibility than what happens within courts. In fact, almost 20 years ago, because so many regimes were neither democratic nor constitutional, a leading scholar claimed that "a majority of Southeast Asian countries are unlikely candidates for the judicialization of politics" (Tate 1994: 188).

Much has changed. As political and economic liberalization has advanced (though certainly not in a straight line), many countries have become concerned about not only the rule of law but also about accountability and rights issues. As countries emerging from authoritarian rule consolidate recent democratic gains, promoting the rule of law has gained traction. Many less than liberal regimes have also chosen to reform constitutions and courts to tighten social control, enhance legitimacy, and ensure credible policy outcomes (see Ginsburg and Moustafa 2008). As a result, in many countries the courts have become central to political life to an unprecedented degree.

Underlying many of these changes is the orthodoxy that empowered courts are a force for liberal constitutionalism (if not good governance at large). They are seen as critical to upholding the rule of law by protecting basic rights and freedoms and ensuring that the commitments of state actors in areas like property rights are credible. Courts, it is also assumed, give citizens stability and security when their interpretations of laws mitigate societal conflict. Courts are thought to hold government actors accountable and to provide political checks and balances, thus limiting government and making it more responsive. In short, the common view is that by promoting the rule of law, constraining governments, and gradually judicializing governance, courts are critical to constitutional governance (Shapiro 1981; Feeley and Rubin 1998; Kapiszewski *et al.* 2013).

But are these common assumptions correct? A close look at what is happening across Southeast Asia raises numerous questions. For starters, the tremendous variation in patterns of judicial behavior in constitutional matters calls for more attention to the nuances of judicialization as it unfolds. And judicial activism – ostensibly to promote the rule of law and make governments more accountable, responsive, and stable – has had at best ambiguous effects. Some courts have actively intervened to promote constitutional practice by checking executive abuse, upholding the supremacy of law, and protecting the rights of citizens (e.g., the Philippines, Indonesia). Others have subverted the rule of law and undermined mechanisms of accountability on behalf of narrow interests (e.g., Thailand). Still others have avoided any engagement with core issues of political and constitutional governance, raising questions about their independence (e.g., Malaysia, Singapore).

Here we confront serious questions, both empirical and theoretical, that emerge from the dramatic variations in judicial performance and behavior in Southeast Asia. How do the variations inform scholarly debate about courts and constitutional politics? More specifically, how does the judicialization trend affect the rule of law and constitutionalism? Under what conditions does judicial engagement reinforce or support a move to liberal constitutional governance? And when does it lead to other patterns of constitutional politics?

The basic argument advanced here is that it is necessary to differentiate patterns of constitutional politics to understand the extent to which judicialization supports different patterns. I apply a strategic interaction argument that considers how citizens and elites interact to achieve equilibrium (Ferejohn 2006; Przeworski 2006) and argue that a country's pattern of constitutional politics reflects the degree of equilibrium (or otherwise) based on supply-side dynamics (the elite's institutional empowerment of courts) and demand-side aspects (support, on and off the bench, for more or less extensive notions of the rule of law). From this perspective, courts are critical: sometimes they embody patterns and sometimes they are sources of change as they respond to shifts in demand and supply. In fact, except for the liberal constitutional equilibrium where actors agree to settle contentious issues mainly through institutions such as the courts, other patterns of constitutional politics seem less stable and thus ultimately more likely to change over time. It is these patterns that tend to exacerbate contestation within as well as outside the courts.

To elaborate this argument, the chapter is organized as follows. First, it engages with the literature to extract a basic typology of judicial patterns. The purpose is to move the debate away from causes of judicialization to its effects: how greater judicial engagement may, or may not, support the rule of law and thus ultimately constitutionalism. Then come empirical illustrations of patterns identified and their drivers. The chapter closes with reflections on what developments in Southeast Asia can contribute to the study of constitutionalism and judicial politics.

## Conceptualizing judicialization in Southeast Asia

Over the past 25 years states in Southeast Asia have begun to create or modify courts to embrace forms of judicial, and more narrowly constitutional, review (Table 14.1). As existing courts are given more power and specialized constitutional courts are introduced with power to strike down incompatible legislation and administrative actions, the judicialization trend has become critical in shaping constitutional practice and the rule of law. Indeed, courts have become involved not only in such common rights areas as criminal due process and classic civil liberties, but increasingly in core political matters, such as executive powers, electoral disputes, and collective identity and nation-building processes.

Yet the effects in the region of what is generally summarized as the judicialization of politics (Hirschl 2006, 2008) on the rule of law and constitutional practice are not well understood. This is due partly to conceptual ambiguities arising from the judicialization phenomenon itself, partly to the fact that research thus far has mainly focused on what is driving it rather than its effects (Dressel 2012). This is of concern given the considerable diversity in judicial patterns and the varied impact on constitutional trajectories in the region.

The region actually demonstrates distinct clusters of high court behavior, with considerable nuances. For instance, courts in Indonesia, the Philippines, and Thailand are all considered highly activist, yet they have often gone in quite different directions. In Indonesia and the Philippines courts have regularly intervened to expand the scope for constitutional rights and politics, while the Thai Constitutional Court – often in concert with other Thai courts – has increasingly closed down the space for rule-bound governance in favor of elite interests. Meanwhile, the behavior of traditionally restrained courts, such as the High

Court of Malaysia, has been highly uneven in terms of the rule of law, while courts in the socialist republics of Vietnam and Laos and in places as diverse as Burma, Singapore, and Cambodia have yet to engage much in constitutional matters at all.

The question that then emerges is: Given this diversity in the behavior of courts, under what conditions do courts engage in building up the rule of law and expanding constitutional practice to check executive abuse, uphold the supremacy of law, and protect citizen rights?

Thus far the literature has been relatively mute on these points. Instead, there is debate about how the concept itself has been stretched to cover different, though sometimes related, processes (see Hirschl 2006). For instance, the capture of social relations and popular culture by law as modern societies grow ever more complex – often described as "juridification" (see, for a good overview, Blichner and Molander 2008) – deserves thoughtful separation from the much-analyzed intervention of the courts in public policy as part of "ordinary" constitutional rights jurisprudence. Another relevant area is the even narrower reliance on courts and judges to deal with "megapolitics" – core political controversies and deep moral dilemmas related to such areas as executive branch prerogatives, electoral politics, and regime change (Hirschl 2008: 99–100).

In essence, two notions may be identified. Narrowly, the term refers to how, in exercising their review powers, judges influence public policy, especially as constitutional or supreme courts come to dominate policy-making, previously the prerogative of legislatures and executives (Sieder *et al.* 2005a: 3). More broadly, judicialization encompasses not only the expansion of the scope of "judge-made law" but also the increased intervention of judicial processes and court rulings in political and social life; for instance, when social actors use courts to advance their own interests, political actors become more responsive to court actions, and state legitimacy is increasingly constructed in terms of the rule of law (Domingo 2004: 108–110).

Likewise, what is driving the trend is debated. Some authors have anchored constitutional transformation and judicialization in macro-processes of democratization and modernization (Shapiro 1999; Sunstein 2001). Others highlight the spread of rights consciousness and legal structures supporting mobilization by civil society as part of judicialization from "below" or even "abroad" (Epp 1998; Slaughter 2000). Other scholars have drawn attention to structural dynamics and the actors as part of judicialization from "above." These micro-level theories argue that self-interested strategic actors may have political reasons for empowering judges, such as the "insurance model" which views judicial empowerment as a form of strategic insurance in times of growing electoral competition (Ramseyer 1994; Ginsburg 2003); and the "hegemonic preservation model" which sees growing judicial empowerment and thus control of the law as a way for elites to preserve power even as they become vulnerable to majoritarian politics (Hirschl 2008: 741).

Unfortunately, no current model has managed to explain under what conditions courts become willing to expand the rule of law and constitutional practice. In fact, contributions in this collection and beyond suggest that judicial behavior results from a complex interplay between institutional, ideational, and broader structural factors that enable or even compel judges to breach traditional constraints. Among them (see Kapiszewski *et al.* 2013) are enduring national, institutional, and political structures (e.g., the powers, scope, and size of judicial institutions); contemporary political dynamics that press courts to take more responsibility for governance and public policy (e.g., elite support for courts, public opinion, and active social movements); and the incentives, capacities, and motives of individual judges and intra-court relations (e.g., court leadership and the values and preferences of judicial majorities).

In short, contextual political conditions, forces, and factors are propelling courts to expand the rule of law and engage more deeply in constitutional politics, but it is not clear when certain factors become relevant and how they are interwoven. To evaluate these ambiguities we propose a simple typology of the patterns of constitutional politics along two conceptual dimensions:

- *The supply of judicialization:* court empowerment as highlighted by the frequency of judicial interventions in high-profile political cases – what Hirschl and others call "megapolitical" cases (Hirschl 2008).
- *Demand for the rule of law:* demand on and off the bench for the rule of law, whether through "thin" readings, as those that are mainly procedural, or "thick," as dealing with the substance of the rule of law (Peerenboom 2004).

Together, these dimensions allow us to conceptually capture diversity in constitutional politics patterns through four ideal types and to trace the dynamic change that occurs when judiciaries engage in countries over time (see Figure 12.1).

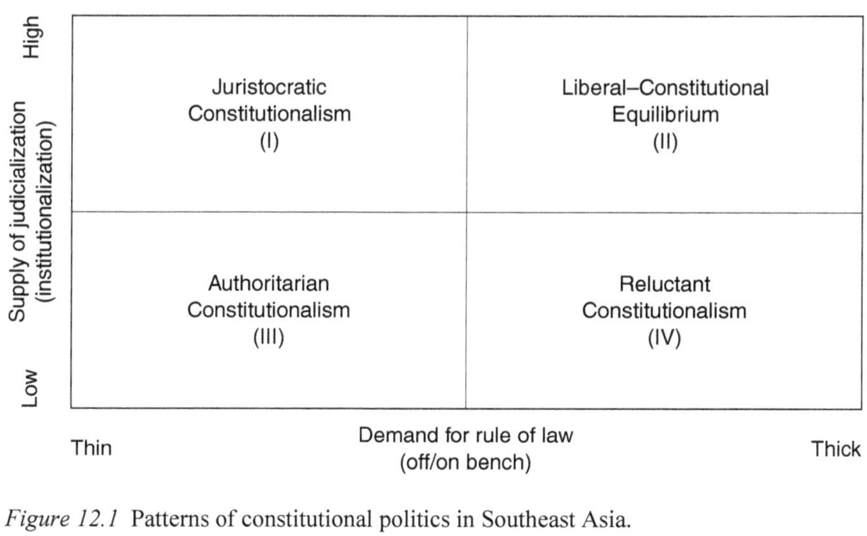


*Figure 12.1* Patterns of constitutional politics in Southeast Asia.

Implicit in this typology are two arguments:

1 It is necessary to differentiate the types of constitutionalism beyond the simple liberal dichotomy that some theorists have suggested in order to better understand how judicialization supports what actually happens as courts do or do not evolve as independent branches of government.
2 The pattern of a country's constitutional politics is best understood in terms of an equilibrium – a stable set of institutions or behavior) – that is the outcome of the supply dynamics created by elite-driven empowerment of the courts and the demand aspects created by the degree to which the people demand more or less extensive notions of the rule of law.

Using this strategic interaction framework, equilibria are stabilized in circumstances where empowerment of the courts is supported by popular demand for deeper notions of the rule of law (a liberal constitutional equilibrium). The situation is self-reinforcing insofar as actors seek to address contentious issues through constitutional means – within the parameters of the rule of law and principally through institutions like the courts. However, pressure for movement to a different equilibrium point is likely where demand outstrips institutional supply (reluctant constitutionalism), or where given the demand structure in place the polity has "oversupplied" courts with powers (juristocratic constitutionalism). In fact, even where there is little interest in a deeper notion of the rule of law and little institutionalization of judicial powers (authoritarian constitutionalism), pressure for change is likely to build as contentious issues are either completely suppressed or resolved by extra-constitutional means in ways that, over time, become too costly in terms of the accompanying repression and unpredictability. In short, disequilibrium generates greater contestation, which in turn animates changes over time.

The next section will briefly illustrate actual patterns and trajectories of court involvement in matters of rule of law and constitutional politics in order to illuminate factors that explain variances and to seek commonalities. But first a word of caution. For illustrative purposes some clusters and trajectories described are somewhat overdrawn. Constitutional patterns vary greatly not only from country to country but also over time within a country; court behavior may be merely temporary, whether because judges are propelled into the political fray in reaction to exceptional events (political crisis, deadlock), or the political response to judicial activism is institutional change that curbs judicial powers. However, as we shall see, once institutional practices are engrained, the resultant stable patterns of judicial governance allow us to characterize the behavior of a country's courts more consistently.

## Trajectories of constitutional politics in Southeast Asia

In exploring the role of courts in constitutional politics, we look most closely at Supreme and Constitutional Courts because they are the ones most likely to shape constitutional politics.

### *A self-reinforcing liberal constitutional equilibrium: the Philippines and Indonesia*

The Indonesian Constitutional Court and the Philippines Supreme Court have both emerged as central actors within what has become a stable constitutional polity. Both are closely tied to popularly supported democratic transitions and have also triggered far-reaching reforms of courts. The Indonesian Constitutional Court was established in 2003 as part of sweeping post-Suharto amendments after the 1998 popular *Reformasi* movement; the much older Philippines Supreme Court saw its powers reinforced by the 1987 constitution that was the direct outcome of the 1986 People's Power revolution. Both have since become respected as the principal arena for resolving contested political issues (Mietzner 2010; Cienca 2012).

The evolution of the Indonesian court is particularly telling (see, for a good overview, Butt 2012, 2015). In less than a decade the court has taken on several highly contested cases critical to the constitutional and democratic trajectory of the polity. It has invalidated national legislation as unconstitutional[1] and imposed obligations on the state based on principles implied in the constitution, such as the protection of citizens from corruption and the right to a fair trial, access to justice, and legal aid.[2] It has also become involved in economic questions (privatization[3]); public policy (allocation of the national education budget[4]); and contentious religious matters (polygamy and blasphemy) – in the process defining the place of Islam in Indonesia.[5] Perhaps most notable has been its consistent support for open democratic elections, whether by controversially allowing former members of the Communist Party to stand for the legislature on the grounds that the constitution protects citizens from discrimination,[6] or by ensuring that every eligible Indonesian with a valid identity card may vote[7] and finding that the party system should not be tilted in favor of larger parties.[8]

The pattern for the Philippine Supreme Court is similar. Despite its long history at the apex of the ordinary court hierarchy, it too has used the expanded scope of judicial review under the 1987 constitution to consistently uphold constitutional principles and protect civil liberties and human rights, while clearly delineating executive powers and prerogatives. For instance, it has invalidated presidential appointments,[9] during the Aquino presidency (1987–1992) restricted the sale of state property,[10] and under Ramos rejected efforts to amend the constitution via the Initiative Referendum Act (1992–1998).[11] It later cleared the deadlock emerging from the 2001 impeachment of President Estrada by swearing in Vice President Macapagal Arroyo (and later justifying it in a questionable decision[12]) before invalidating multi-billion-dollar contracts;[13] it has extensively reviewed political and civil liberties cases[14] and rejected initiatives for constitutional change[15] under the Macapagal Arroyo presidency. A similar pattern has emerged under President Aquino III (2010–2016), where the court has intervened to end executive pork-barrel practices and to limit executive discretion in budgetary allocations.[16]

In short, both courts have become critical to advancing the rule of law and strengthening constitutional practice, and have thus gradually transformed political contestation toward the constitutional space and strengthened the primacy of law by insisting on rule-bound governance. Their growing empowerment and institutionalization has been highlighted by their activist interventions in the political realm and by consistent support from citizens not only for the institution of the judiciary but also for a deeper understanding of the rule of law, which has allowed the courts to gradually expand leadership into the political realm.

Not that the trajectory has always been smooth in either case. There have been allegations that the courts have become politicized, impeachment proceedings against chief justices, and evidence of corruption and declining professionalism in the judiciary at large. And yet, with heavier caseloads and public approval ratings well above those for other institutions, the two courts have become the principal avenue for resolving political controversies for citizens and elites alike. Hence, with the support of elites, there has been a mutually reinforcing equilibrium in which the courts can push for both the institutionalization of their role and a deepening of the rule of law, and thus support constitutional practice which is more akin to that of liberal Western democracies.

### *Authoritarian constitutionalism: Singapore and Malaysia*

The trajectories of the Singaporean and Malaysian Federal Courts highlight a pattern common to many states in Southeast Asia, from the socialist states of Vietnam and Laos to the soft authoritarian states of Burma and Cambodia (see Tan 2014; Tushnet 2015). Despite considerable diversity, they illuminate the limits of judicial autonomy in constitutional matters and the circumscribed space for constitutional contestation where the executive is dominant and statist/communitarian ideologies limit the range of judicial activism.

The Singaporean court is particularly interesting because its duality has made it the model for many states in the region. Singapore's legal system is regularly ranked among the best in the world in terms of professionalism and efficiency, yet within the soft authoritarian rule of the People's Action Party (PAP) serious questions have been raised about judicial impartiality, particularly in politically sensitive cases (Littlemore 1998; Worthington 2001; International Bar Association 2008; Sim 2011). In fact, although the government has gone to great lengths to stress the role of an independent judiciary in ensuring good governance,[17] some have argued that given PAP dominance, in terms of separation of powers "the legislature and the judiciary are disenfranchised by the executive, and the legal profession has no capacity to challenge or even advise the executive" (Worthington 2003: 133).

Since it was founded in 1957 the court has exercised its judicial review powers very cautiously – of 79 cases, the applicant won in 22, or 27.8 percent – and virtually none of its cases addresses substantive constitutional or political issues. While this partly reflects a lack of open contestation in a tightly controlled political system, it also illustrates government efforts to exert subtle control, particularly over the Supreme Court, through such means as removal of external review of Singapore's courts (appeals to the Privy Council ceased in 1994); legislation to curtail court sentencing prerogatives; direct influence over the terms of appointment through the exercise of executive discretion in appointing Supreme Court judges (many of whom are linked to the PAP inner circle); rotation of judges through legal service positions; lack of tenure for many judges; and extension of contracts at the Supreme Court beyond legal retirement age at the will of the prime minister. These are in addition to tight regulation of judges through corporatist control of such gateways to the bench as the Singapore Law Society and institutions of higher legal education, which have often reinforced judicial communitarian/statist ideology (Seow 2006; Li-ann 2014).

However, whether the pattern is sustainable remains to be seen. Demands for more judicial independence and a more substantial notion of the rule of law have occasionally emerged even in a tightly controlled system like Singapore's – demands that are likely to increase with the recent death of founding father and "minister mentor" Lee Kuan Yew, and subsequent disquiet among Singaporeans over the challenges the country faces (Welsh 2015).

The trajectory of Malaysia illustrates a more volatile pattern of judicial engagement in matters of constitutional politics. It is the result of more complex sociopolitical structures that sometimes give the executive less control over judicial institutions given strong citizen demand for the rule of law supported by a vibrant legal class. The multi-ethnic UMNO coalition in power since independence in 1957 has repeatedly attempted to follow the Singapore trajectory by containing the constitutional space, particularly when confronted by growing political contestation, as it has in recent years.

Here, too, the sustainability of the pattern may be questionable, as the volatile engagement of the Malaysian Federal (formerly Supreme) Court in constitutional and political matters vividly illustrates. For instance, after the 1957 constitution the Supreme Court promptly imposed upon itself strict literalism and restraint in political matters (Lee 1995: 2). In the first 32 years of independence, the court found unconstitutional only seven statutory provisions (three were reinstated on appeal, one was struck down by the Privy Council, and three were upheld), and in cases involving fundamental rights the court insisted on a narrow reading of the constitution (Harding 2012: 213–219).

However, during the Mahathir premiership (1982–2003) this pattern was challenged by growing executive assertiveness and intra-elite tensions, which drew the courts into political and constitutional conflicts related to the powers and immunity of Malaysian royalty (1983, 1992) and to the political leadership itself (1988). But judicial efforts to chart a more assertive, if not actually activist, path during these constitutional crises were short-lived, as highlighted by the gradual subjugation of the judiciary after Lord President of the Court Tun Salleh and five colleagues were removed at the height of the 1988 crisis and constitutional amendments then further limited court powers (Khoo Boo Teik 1999). Attacks on judicial independence grew, as did attempts to instrumentalize the courts in political cases, such as the 1998 sodomy trial against opposition leader Anwar Ibrahim (Wu Min Aun 2007).

Gradual efforts under the Badawi premiership (2003–2009) to rebalance executive–judicial relations, such as reforms to depoliticize appointments and tackle corruption within the judiciary, have done little to change the pattern. In fact, despite being forced to deal with a host of high-profile political and constitutional questions, the court has usually avoided adopting a clear position on highly contested religious cases[18] – to the point that questions of jurisdictional boundaries between Syariah and civil courts have not been resolved. The court has also ruled that the separation of power doctrine is merely political and therefore not sufficient to support a finding of unconstitutionality[19] – a position widely seen as being at odds with global practice (Foo 2010; Harding 2012: 203–204). Meanwhile, the questionable conviction of Anwar Ibrahim in his second sodomy trial in 2015, despite his acquittal in 2012, and the recent decisions of the highest court in the "Allah"[20] and "Borders"[21] cases suggest that the court has begun to either directly follow executive interests in political cases or at the minimum restrain itself from addressing major issues that are at the heart of an increasingly contested polity (Lee 2014; Neo 2014).

What has emerged in Malaysia is thus a trend of growing judicialization in core political matters, even though courts have evaded it whenever possible, particularly when cases are seen to be at odds with executive interests. And, as in Singapore, courts have increasingly become tools for the regime to silence critics via defamation suits and politically motivated criminal proceedings.[22] However, the sustainability of that approach is questionable, given that the behavior of the courts increasingly conflicts with demands for constitutional adjudication, highlighted by heightened political protest and declining public confidence in the judiciary itself (Lee 2014).

In short, Singapore, and to a lesser degree Malaysia, illustrate a kind of "authoritarian constitutionalism." Both governments seek to contain adjudication of political and constitutional matters by controlling the court system, referencing communitarian ideology, and using the courts against individuals or groups challenging the regime. Meanwhile, efforts have been made to ensure that courts are professional and independent in commercial matters. That dual system of justice has become an appealing proposition to other states in the region seeking to balance growing demands, both internal and external, for the rule of law with attempts to retain the political status quo.

Yet the Malaysian case demonstrates that the constitutional politics pattern is difficult to sustain over the long run. Executive interference in high-profile political cases has eroded public confidence in the courts; and the apparent reluctance of the courts to defend core constitutional matters has only exacerbated political conflict. Even in Singapore, where the political space has been tightly contained, it may be that the polity is in for a major overhaul, since the recent death of Lee Kuan Yew has left the leadership to deal with growing public concerns about an uncertain future. Given these challenges, there is no doubt that the own trajectory of the judiciary will have an important role to play in the institutional and constitutional transformation ahead.

### *Juristocratic constitutionalism: Thailand*

Thailand's pattern of constitutional politics since the turn of the millennium may probably be best described as "juristocratic constitutionalism" in that the courts have come to dominate the political and constitutional space at the expense of majoritarian democratic institutions. The pattern is the unexpected outcome of liberal constitutional reforms in the mid-1990s that sought to promote both a gradual deepening of the rule of law and empowerment of the judiciary. However, the process was gradually reversed as traditional elites, faced with political challenges from forces aligned with ousted former PM Thaksin Shinawatra (2001–2006), began to instrumentalize the judiciary.

Established in 1998 by Thailand's 1997 "People's Constitution," the court was envisioned as the guardian of the new liberal architecture and hub of a network of oversight agencies to strengthen rule-based governance (Leyland 2008; Harding 2010). The court enjoyed comparatively broad jurisdiction and (at least formally) solid safeguards for its independence. Briefly dissolved by the 2006 military coup,[23] it was then reconstituted by the 2007 constitution that significantly enlarged the political role of the court by involving it in the selection of senators and candidates for independent agencies; allowing it to propose laws directly to the House of Representatives; and, most controversially, giving it the power to dissolve a political party if one of its leaders is found guilty of election fraud (Dressel 2009: 311–312). The 2015 constitution enhances these powers, particularly with regard to the interpretation of the vague constitutional basic order (DRKS: the "Democratic Regime with the King as Head of State"), thus maintaining the critical role of the Constitutional Court (and judiciary at large) in Thailand's current governance structure (Glaser 2015).[24]

Few observers would have predicted that the Thai Constitutional Court would use its new powers to radically transform the political and constitutional space, especially since it was criticized early on for its conservatism during the Thaksin administration (Klein 2003). But the growing judicial assertiveness gradually became more visible, particularly as political tensions built over the populist Thaksin government and its 2006 post-coup reconstituted successors. For instance, in cooperation with other parts of the judiciary and oversight agencies, the Constitutional Court annulled the April 2006 general elections;[25] dissolved the major Thai Rak Thai (TRT) party in 2007; and barred 111 of its members from public office for five years[26] (a decision by the interim Constitutional Tribunal), before finding Prime Minister Samak Sundaravej guilty of a conflict of interest for hosting a popular cooking show on TV;[27] it then dissolved the People's Power Party (PPP), the political successor to the TRT, in 2008, deposing Prime Minister Somchai Wongsawat in the process.[28] It also blocked efforts by the Yingluck Shinawatra government (2011–2014) in 2013 to change the 2007 constitution under a questionable interpretation of Article 68 of that constitution, which prevents action aimed at "overthrowing the democratic regime with the king as head of state" (Glaser 2012). It then moved to annul the 2014 general election results[29] before removing Thaksin's sister as prime minister, with seven members of her cabinet, in 2014 for the unconstitutional transfer of a security officer.[30]

Such unprecedented judicial involvement has profoundly altered the political landscape in Thailand: the judges, often hand in hand with other oversight agencies, have effectively destroyed Thailand's largest and most successful political party, forced the resignation of three prime ministers, and kept pressure on the popular Thaksin to remain in exile. Meanwhile the interventions of the constitutional court have also raised concerns about the trajectory of constitutionalism in Thailand, given that so far its decisions have almost exclusively benefitted only one side of the political divide (Glaser 2012). In fact, with many observers linking the unprecedented judicial interventions to a 2006 speech by King Rama IX which urged the courts to solve the political stand-off (see Mérieux, Chapter 7, this volume, for the ramifications of the speech), it is hard to see the court as a neutral arbiter of political conflict and an impartial guardian of the constitution and the rule of law (Chaturon Chaiseng 2009; Dressel 2010; McCargo 2015).

However, whether such intensive judicial involvement – now enshrined in the 2015 constitution – is sustainable in the long run is questionable. Not only do the courts all now stand accused of double standards in the application of the rule of law, but the high court's constitutional interpretations seem increasingly at odds with popular demand, as highlighted by continuing public protest. Meanwhile, the open involvement of the military since the 2006 coup and its support for a narrow reading of the rule of law has demonstrated a gradual move in Thailand to an authoritarian constitutional space in which court decisions are strategically employed against majoritarian demands. Yet, with a royal succession looming on the horizon and political polarization as deep as ever, demands for constitutional adjudication and equitable judicial application of the rule of law are likely to increase

### *Reluctant constitutionalism: pre-1987 Philippines compared to post-1945 Japan*

The category of reluctant constitutionalism is perhaps the hardest to conceptualize. It captures a rare situation in which demands for a substantive rule of law are matched by low levels of judicialization. This is best understood as the result of self-imposed doctrinal or cultural constraints within courts rather than of institutional rules or executive interventions limiting their actions. However, the sustainability of this constitutional pattern is questionable, as illustrated here by the trajectory of the Philippines Supreme Court prior to 1987, although the post-1945 experience of the Japan Supreme Court presaged that such change might occur very slowly unless there is a transformation in the political environment.

The early history of the Philippines Supreme Court, which emerged from US colonial efforts in 1901 and was then gradually indigenized and institutionally consolidated under the 1935, 1973, and 1987 constitutions, provides a good illustration of the reluctant constitutional pattern. In fact it emerging quickly as "a respected, independent and powerful legal force in Philippines politics and government" (Tate 1994) that provided one of the "most important legitimizing institutions in the Philippines" (Tate and Haynie 1993) in the twentieth century. Nevertheless, the court was steadfast in avoiding being drawn into political conflict as part of its strict adherence to the "political question" doctrine developed by its US counterpart (Rillo 2003).

In hindsight, its reluctance was somewhat surprising. Both the 1935 and 1973 constitutions afforded the court considerable judicial powers which gave it discretion to adjudicate high-level political cases. Yet, as is clear from a series of critical decisions pre- and post-independence,[31] the judges held to a restrained doctrinal view, even though frictions within the bench became gradually more obvious in response to a growing number of habeas corpus[32] and constitutional amendment cases[33] as part of the authoritarian turn in the Marcos presidency (1965–1981). In fact, in what would became a landmark case in the Marcos period, *Javellana* v. *Executive Secretary*,[34] the court decided by a slim majority to allow the fraudulent ratification of the 1973 constitution based on the political question doctrine. The decision considerably damaged its public standing (Gatmaytan-Magno 2007).

And yet what some saw as the consequence of an increasingly stacked court under Marcos (Celoza 1997: 83–84; Dezalay and Bryant 2010: 134) is perhaps best understood as an outcome of the dominant internal judicial culture, the more so as there is little actual evidence of direct executive influence on the justices. The reactions to *Javellana*, however, also illustrate that the judicial restraint was increasingly out of sync with growing demands for constitutional adjudication. In fact, in direct reaction to *Javellana*, constitutional drafters in 1987 specified that judicial powers included the duty to "settle actual controversies involving rights … and to determine whether there has been a grave abuse of discretion amounting to excess of jurisdiction" by any branch of government (Article VIII, Section 1). This softened the political question doctrine by mandating judicial involvement in these matters. Combined with broader changes to court powers, this in fact initiated a gradual transformation of the Philippines Supreme Court in line with demands for liberal constitutional politics.

However, a quick flashback to post-war Japan is a vivid reminder that such transformations can take time. Like the pre-1987 Philippines Supreme Court, the Supreme Court of Japan, despite considerable nominal independence, has to this day chosen not to engage at all with mega-political cases. Since its founding in 1947 the court has struck down only eight statutes as unconstitutional grounds (the German Constitutional Court has struck down 600), and even those constitutionality rulings have been less than momentous. In cases of significant political impact it has simply avoided ruling on the constitutional merits at all.

To explain this unusual pattern, observers of the Japanese courts have pointed out that activism has been kept at bay less by direct interventions against liberal-activist judges[35] than by the internal organizational structure and the related legal culture within the Supreme Court (O'Brian and Ohkoshi 2001). It has similarly been suggested that Supreme Court judges view the constitution as more an articulation of political principles than a source of law (Matsui 2011), or as part of a legacy of German "organ theory" in Japanese law that limits constraints on public authority through judicial review by ensuring the autonomy of each state organ (Ginsburg and Matsudaira 2012).

To be sure, reforms in the 1990s to expand the rule of law in Japan, and by extension the role of courts, have yet to make much impact. While the courts are independent and even activist on rights issues, they are averse to any ruling that might involve them in political issues, as illustrated in recent cases dealing with whether visits of high-ranking politicians to the Yasukuni Shrine may have violated the separation of state and church;[36] whether involvement of Japan's self-defense forces in Iraq violated Article Nine;[37] and whether former "comfort women" and forced laborers from other Asian countries could claim compensation.[38] However, criminal prosecutions of corrupt politicians, often as a direct result of citizen engagement, court interventions in electoral matters, and growing encouragement from former justices for the court to take a more active role in constitutional matters, suggest that a gradual move of the courts toward a more liberal constitutional equilibrium may not be unimaginable (Matsudaira 2011).

The trajectories of the Philippines Supreme Court in the early twentieth century and of the Japanese court later are vivid reminders of how cultural traits might produce a reluctant pattern of constitutional politics, marked by low levels of judicialization despite considerable independence of courts and demands for a deeper rule of law. Yet when court behavior is more and more at odds with growing demands, as it was in the Philippines, change is likely – though Japan reminds us that without major political change the process may drag on. The fact that so few countries in the region exhibit this particular pattern also makes it clear that it can only emerge in a unique context where there is an uninterrupted, engrained judicial culture – fairly rare in a region marked by authoritarian legacies and recent political changes.

## Conclusion

Evaluating the effects of judicialization on constitutional politics in the region is not easy. While courts are clearly becoming more important, if not consequential, to constitutional practice and governance in Southeast Asia, it is equally clear that their involvement has been varied and complex. Because courts are deeply embedded in the sociopolitical context in which they operate, they can act as supporters of illiberal and authoritarian political patterns as well as drivers or consolidators of a deeper application of the rule of law and liberal constitutionalism.

It is tempting from a quick glance at the region to view judicial engagement in support of liberal constitutionalism largely as the outcome of the political regime in place: the more vibrant and established democracies in the region (the Philippines, Indonesia) also host some the most activist and liberal courts in the region. This is not surprising. Political liberalization and democratization have meant a considerable repositioning of the judiciary in terms of their constitutional powers and mandates in the Philippines, and in Indonesia and Thailand have even established specialized new constitutional courts with far-reaching powers. Yet, the roller-coaster that the Thai Constitutional Court has ridden since its creation in 1997 is also a reminder that the link between expanded judicial review powers and liberal constitutional practice is hardly clear-cut; similarly, a look at the neighboring Japanese Supreme Court highlights how even in established democracies, courts may limit their involvement in constitutional matters despite judicial reforms intended to broaden their role in governance. It appears that institutional empowerment, while important, is not sufficient in its own right to explain the behavior of courts.

In fact, the theme that emerges from the diverse trajectories in the region is that for understanding where courts are it is necessary to scrutinize the interplay between supply and demand dynamics. Clearly, more competitive elite structures, emerging from the fragmentation of political power, provide the courts with the institutional space to engage in constitutional matters, while on the demand side – the support judges receive for applying the rule of law and protecting constitutional rights from the public and legal complex – is often crucial in animating judges to test the boundaries given to them. Both supply and demand also influence the expression of judicial philosophy by determining the views that may be expressed on the bench, whether exerted through the appointment process or by sanctioning internally the behavior of judges. The permutations of the Thai Constitutional Court over the past decade, the result of a politicized appointment process and close affiliation with an anti-liberal ideology of the traditional trinity of nation, religion, king, is a case in point.

Judicial reforms and rule of law discourses notwithstanding, elites in the region have increasingly appropriated the judicialization trend for their own purposes, whether by leaving the door open to "regimes of exception" in the name of security and public order, or more subtly by establishing a dual legal order, where the rule of law is applied differently in commercial and political matters (Jayasuriya 2001). In either case, political actors not only maintain reserve powers but judges act so as to consolidate hegemonic interests. Singapore's pattern of a highly professional judiciary that does not speak to political matters has much appeal for neighboring regimes, though it seems to be more difficult to achieve for more diverse and contested states (e.g., Malaysia), or when new social forces seek accommodation within rapidly transforming societies (e.g., Vietnam, Myanmar).

Meanwhile, liberal constitutional states are not only an exception in the region but within them judges also face challenges. In fact, as highlighted by the impeachment of chief justices in the Philippines (2014) and Indonesia (2015), these courts regularly struggle not only with issues of internal capacity and professionalism but also with executive encroachment and interference from political actors. However, public support for these institutions, including public outcry over political interference, supports an equilibrium that makes it hard for political actors to exert control over the courts. This is particularly true where courts have great public legitimacy and judges have carefully nurtured public support for their own benefit (see Deinla, Chapter 14, this volume) – though the executive assault on the Malaysian Federal Court in 1988 is a painful reminder of the ever-present dangers for even established courts.

What might come next? The spread of a liberal constitutional equilibrium in Southeast Asia is likely to take time – institutional reforms and judicial empowerment notwithstanding. In fact, given a highly diverse region and the complex interplay among structural, political, and cultural patterns in animating judicial behavior, considerable diversity in patterns of constitutional politics is likely to be evident for years to come.

What is happening in Southeast Asia offers new theoretical and empirical insights for the scholarly debate. It urges us to adopt a more pluralized understanding of constitutionalism; raises critical questions about the often-postulated link between judicial empowerment and liberal constitutional practice, and offers insights into factors that shape the behavior of the judiciary as they attempt to navigate this rapidly changing environment. No doubt, as highlighted throughout this volume, how courts in Southeast Asia manage constitutional contestation in the rule of law space will be critical to the trajectory of constitutionalism in Southeast Asia.

## Notes

1 See, MK Decisions: 6/PUU-V/2007 and 012–022/PUU-IV/2006; 013/2003; 9/PUU-VII/2009 and 98/PUU-VII/2009; 011–017/2003.
2 MK Decision 006/PUU-I/2003; 006/PUU-II/2004.
3 MK Decision 001–021–022/PUU-I/2003.
4 MK Decision 011/PUU-III/2005; MK Decision 026/PUU-III/2005.
5 MK Decision 12/PUU-V/2007.
6 MK Decisions 14–17/PUU-V/2007 and 15/PUU-VI/2008.
7 MK Decision 102/PUU-VII/2009.
8 MK Decision 110–111–112–113/PUU-VII/2009.
9 *Brillantes* v. *Yorac* (1990).
10 *Garcia* v. *Board of Investments* (1989).
11 *Santiago* v. *Comelec* (1997).
12 *Estrada* v. *Arroyo* (2001).
13 *Chavez* v. *Public Estates Authority – Amari* (2002); *La Bugal-B'laan Tribal Association, Inc.* v. *Ramos* (2004 January); *Information Technology Foundation of the Philippines* v. *Comelec* (2004); and *Agan Jr.* v. *Philippine International Air Terminals Co., Inc.* (2004).
14 *BAYAN* v. *Ermita* (2006); *Senate* v. *Ermita* (2006); *David* v. *Arroyo* (2006).
15 *Lambino* v. *Comelec* (2006).
16 See DAP (http://sc.judiciary.gov.ph/pdf/web/viewer.html?file=/jurisprudence/2014/april2014/204819.pdf) and PDAF (http://sc.judiciary.gov.ph/jurisprudence/2013/toc/november.php) decisions by the SC.
17 See Lee Kuan Yew's speech to the International Bar Association in 2007, "Good Governance, Sound Judiciary Contribute to Singapore's Stability: MM Lee." Channel News Asia, available at: www.channelnewsasia.com/stories/singaporelocalnews/view/305629/1/.html.
18 *Subashini Rajasingham* v. *Saravanan Thangathoray & other appeal* [2008] 2 MLJ 147; see also *Shamala Satiyaseelan* v. *Dr. Jeyaganesh C Mogarajah and Anor* [2004] MLJ 648.
19 *Public Prosecutor* v. *Kok Wah Kuan* [2008] 1 MLJ1.
20 *Titular Roman Catholic Archbishop of Kuala Lumpur* v. *Menteri Dalam Negeri and Anor* [2010] 2 MLJ 78.

21 NO: 25–137–06/2012.
22 See defamation law suit against online newspaper Malaysiakini by P.M. Najib in 2015 for blogposts by readers – a case incidentally assigned to a judge in a temporary position – or the conviction of opposition leader Anwar Ibrahim in 2015.
23 Article 35 of the 2006 interim constitution established a constitutional judicial committee comprising the president of the Supreme Court (as chair), president of the administrative court (as deputy chair), five supreme court judges, and two administrative court judges. This committee performed the functions of the constitutional court. Once the 2007 constitutional was in force, Article 300 provided that the aforementioned committee was to act as caretaker until the new constitutional court judges were appointed, which was the case in 2010.
24 See, Article 7, stating: "Whenever no provision under this Constitution is applicable to any case, it shall be decided in accordance with the constitutional convention in the democratic regime of government with the King as Head of State," as well as Book III, Section 1–3. Source: Draft Constitution 2015 (English translation; ©2015 Pakorn Nilprapunt, Chintapun Dungsubutra, Vareerat Ratanaviboonsom and Natthanicha Aneksomboonphol, Office of the Council of State of Thailand).
25 Constitutional Court Decision No. 9/2549 (2006).
26 Constitutional Tribunal Decision No. 3–5/2550 (2007).
27 Constitutional Court Decision No. 12–13/2551 (2008).
28 Constitutional Court Decision No. 20/2551(2008).
29 Decision, March 21 2014 (based on the fact that elections were not held on the same day), available at: www.bangkokpost.com/learning/learning-from-news/401033/consitution-court-voids-feb-2-election.
30 Decision, May 2014, available at: http://theconversation.com/thai-judiciary-wins-another-round-against-elected-government-26403.
31 See, e.g., *Barcelon* v. *Baker* (5 Phil. 87 1905); *Abueva* v. *Wood* (45 Phil. 612 1924); *Alejandro* v. *Quezon* (46 Phil. 83 1924); *Vera* v. *Avelino* (77 Phil. 192 1946); *Avelino* v. *Cuenco* (83 Phil. 17 1949) *Osmena, Jr.* v. *Pendatun* (109 Phil. 863 1960).
32 *Lansang* v. *Garcia* (42 SCRA 448 1971); *Aquino, Jr.* v. *Enrile* (59 Phil. 183 1973); *Padilla-Garcia* v. *Enrile* (206 Phil. 392 1983).
33 *Gonzales* v. *COMELEC* (21 SCRA 774 1967); *Tolentino* v. *COMELEC* (41 SCRA 702 1971); *Sanidad* v. *COMELEC* (L-44640 1976).
34 50 SCRA 30 (1973).
35 Widely debated exceptions were the cases against Judge Fukushima, a member of the leftist Young Jurist League (YJL) in the 1960s and the non-renewal of Judge Miyamoto Yasuaki in 1971.
36 Yasukuni Shrine, 1940 Hanji 122 (Sup. Ct. 2nd Bench decision, June 23, 2006).
37 Nagoya High Court, April 17, 2008 (unpublished decision).
38 See Nagoya High Court ruling May 31, 2007, 54 Shomu Geppo 287. The Supreme Court refused to hear the appeal (Sup. Ct. decision, November 11, 2008).

## Bibliography

Blichner, L.C. and Molander, A. (2008). "Mapping Juridification." *European Law Journal*, 14(1): 36–54.

Butt, S. (2012). "Indonesia's Constitutional Court: Conservative Activist or Strategic Operator?" In *The Judicialization of Politics in Asia* ed. B. Dressel. Abingdon and New York, RoutledgeCurzon, pp. 98–117.

Butt, S. (2015). *The Constitutional Court and Democracy in Indonesia*, Brill, Nijhoff.

Celoza, A. (1997). *Ferdinand Marcos and the Philippines: The Political Economy of Authoritarianism*. Westport, CT, Praeger.

Chaturon Chaiseng (2009). *Thai Democracy in Crisis: 27 Truth*. Bangkok, A.R. Information.

Cienca Jr., A.N. (2012). "From Judicialization to Politicization of the Judiciary: The Philippine Case." In *The Judicialization of Politics in Asia*, ed. B. Dressel. Abingdon and New York, Routledge, pp. 117–139.

Dezalay, Y. and Bryant, G. (2010). *Asian Legal Revivals: Lawyers in the Shadow of Empire*. Chicago, IL, University of Chicago Press.

Domingo, P. (2004). "Judicialization of Politics or Politicization of the Judiciary? Recent Trends in Latin America." *Democratization*, 11(1): 104–126.

Dressel, B. (2009). "Thailand's Elusive Quest for a Constitutional Equilibrium, 1997–2007." *Contemporary Southeast Asia*, 31(2): 296–325.

Dressel, B. (2010). "Judicialization of Politics or Politicization of the Judiciary? Considerations from Recent Events in Thailand." *The Pacific Review*, 23(5): 671–691.

Dressel, B. (ed.) (2012). *The Judicialization of Politics in Asia*. Abingdon and New York, Routledge.

Dressel, B. (2012). "The Judicialization of Politics in Asia: Towards a Framework of Analysis." In *The Judicialization of Politics in Asia*, ed. B. Dressel. Abingdon and New York, Routledge, pp. 1–14.

Epp, C.R. (1998). *The Rights Revolution: Lawyers, Activists and Supreme Courts in Comparative Perspective*. Chicago, IL, University of Chicago Press.

Feeley, M. and Rubin, E. (1998). *Judicial Policy Making and the Modern State: How the Courts Reformed America's Prisons*. Cambridge, Cambridge University Press.

Ferejohn, J. (2006). *Self-enforcing Democracy*. Palo Alto, CA, Stanford University.

Foo, R.S.K. (2010). "Malaysia: Death of a Separate Constitutional Judicial Power." *Singapore Journal of Legal Studies*: 227–255.

Gatmaytan-Magno, D. (2007). "Changing Constitutions: Judicial Review and Redemption in the Philippines." *UCLA Pacific Basin Law Journal*, 25(1): 1–24.

Ginsburg, T. (2003). *Judicial Review in New Democracies. Constitutional Courts in Asian Cases*. Cambridge, Cambridge University Press.

Ginsburg, T. and Chen, A.H.Y., eds (2009). *Administrative Law and Governance in Asia. Comparative Perspectives*. New York, Routledge.

Ginsburg, T. and Matsudaira, T. (2012). "The Judicialization of Japanese Politics?" In *The Judicialization of Politics in Asia*, ed. B. Dressel. Abingdon and New York, Routledge, pp. 17–37.

Ginsburg, T. and Moustafa, T. (2008). *Rule by Law: The Politics of Courts in Authoritarian Regimes*. Cambridge and New York, Cambridge University Press.

Glaser, H. (2012). "Thai Constitutional Courts and the Political Order." *Seoul Law Journal*, 53 (2): 65–163.

Glaser, H. (2015). "Constitutional Conflict and Restatement: The Challenge and Transformation of the Hegemonic Basic Consent in Thailand." In *Norms, Interests, and Values. Conflict and Consent in the Constitutional Basic Order*, ed. H. Glaser. Baden Baden, Nomos, pp. 291–344.

Harding, A. (2010). "The Constitutional Court of Thailand 1998–2006. A Turbulent Innovation." In *New Courts in Asia*, eds A. Harding and P. Nicholson. Abingdon and New York, Routledge.

Harding, A. (2012). *The Constitution of Malaysia: A Contextual Analysis*. New York, Hart Publishing.

Harding, A. and Nicholson, P. (2010). *New Courts in Asia*. Abingdon and New York, Routledge, pp. 122–140.

Hirschl, R. (2006). "The New Constitutionalism and the Judicialization of Pure Politics Worldwide." *Fordham Law Review*, 75: 721–754.

Hirschl, R. (2008). "The Judicialization of Mega-politics and the Rise of Political Courts." *Annual Review of Political Science*, 11: 93–118.

International Bar Association (2008). *Prosperity versus Individual Rights? Human Rights, Democracy and Rule of Law in Singapore.* London.

Jayasuriya, K. (2001). "The Exception Becomes the Norm: Law and Regimes of Exception in East Asia." *Asian-Pacific Law and Policy Journal*, 2(1): 108–124.

Kapiszewski, D., Silverstein, G., and Kagan, R.A., eds (2013). *Consequential Courts. Judicial Roles in Global Perspective.* Cambridge, Cambridge University Press.

Khoo Boo Teik (1999). "Between Law and Politics: The Malaysian Judiciary since Independence." In *Law, Capitalism and Power in Asia*, ed. K. Jayasuriya. London and New York, Routledge, pp. 205–232.

Lee, H.P. (1995). *Constitutional Conflicts in Contemporary Malaysia.* Kuala Lumpur and New York, Oxford University Press.

Lee, H.P. (2014). "Constitutional Developments in Malaysia in the First Decade of the Twenty-first Century: A Nation at the Crossroads." In *Constitutionalism in Asia in the Early Twenty-first Century*, ed. A.H.Y. Chen. Cambridge, Cambridge University Press, pp. 244–269.

Leyland, P. (2008). "Thailand's Constitutional Watchdogs: Dobermans, Bloodhounds or Lapdogs?" *Journal of Comparative Law*, 2: 151–177.

Li-ann, T. (2014). "We are Feeling Our Way Forward Step by Step: The Continuing Singapore Experiment in the Construction of Communitarian Constitutionalism in the Twenty-First Decade." In *Constitutionalism in Asia in the Early Twenty-First Century*, ed. A.H.Y. Chen. Cambridge, Cambridge University Press, pp. 270–295.

Littlemore, S. (1998). Report to the International Commission of Jurists Geneva, Switzerland, on a Defamation Trial in the High Court of Singapore, *Goh Chok Tong* v. *J. B. Jeyaratnam*. August 18–22.

Matsudaira, T. (2011). "Judicialization of Politics and the Japanese Supreme Court." *Washington University Law Review*, 88: 1559.

Matsui, S. (2011). "Why is the Japanese Supreme Court So Conservative?" *Washington University Law Review*, 88: 1375–1423.

McCargo, D. (2015). "Thailand in 2014: The Trouble with Magic Swords." In *Southeast Asian Affairs 2015*, eds D. Singh and V. Nair. Singapore, ISEAS, pp. 335–358.

Mietzner, M. (2010). "Political Conflict and Democratic Consolidation in Indonesia: The Role of the Constitutional Court." *Journal of East Asian Studies*. 10(3): 397–424.

Neo, J.N. (2014). "What's in a Name? Malaysia's 'Allah' Controversy and the Judicial Intertwining of Islam with Ethnic Identity." *I•CON*, 12(3): 751–768.

O'Brian, D.M. and Ohkoshi, Y. (2001). "Stifling Judicial Independence from Within: The Japanese Judiciary." In *Judicial Independence in the Age of Democracy: Critical Perspectives from Around the World*, eds P.H. Russel and D.M. O'Brian. Charlottesville and London, University of Virginia Press, pp. 37–61.

Peerenboom, R. (2004). "Varieties of Rule of Law: An Introduction and Provisional Conclusion." In *Asian Discourses of Rule of Law*, ed. R. Peerenboom. London and New York, Routledge, pp. 1–55.

Przeworski, A. (2006). "Self-enforcing Democracy." In *The Oxford Handbook of Political Economy*, eds B. Weingast and D. Wittman. New York, Oxford University Press, pp. 312–328.

Ramseyer, M.J. (1994). "The Puzzling (In)Dependence of Courts: A Comparative Approach." *Journal of Legal Studies*, 23: 721–747.

Rillo, M.C. (2003). *To Meddle or not to Meddle: The Political Question Doctrine in Light of the Expanded Power of the Supreme Court*. Dissertation, Ateneo de Manila University.

Seow, F.T. (2006). *Beyond Suspicion? The Singapore Judiciary*. New Haven, CT, Yale University Press.

Shapiro, M. (1981). *Courts: A Comparative and Political Analysis*. Chicago, IL, Chicago University Press.

Shapiro, M. (1999). "The Success of Judicial Review." In *Constitutional Dialogues in Comparative Perspective*, eds S.J. Kenney, W.M. Reisinger, and J.C. Reitz. New York, Palgrave Macmillan, pp. 193–219.

Shapiro, M. and Stone Sweet, A. (2002). *On Law, Politics, and Judicialization*. New York, Oxford University Press.

Sieder, R., Schjolden, L., and Angell, A. (2005a). Introduction. In *The Judicialization of Politics in Latin America*, eds R. Sieder, L. Schjolden, and A. Angell. New York and Basingstoke, Palgrave Macmillan, pp. 1–21.

Sieder, R., Schjolden, L. and Angell, A., eds (2005b). *The Judicialization of Politics in Latin America*. New York and Basingstoke, Palgrave Macmillan.

Sim, C. (2011). "The Singapore Chill: Political Defamation and the Normalization of a Statist Rule of Law." *Pacific Rim Law and Policy Journal*, 20(2): 331–345.

Slaughter, A.M. (2000). "Judicial Globalization." *Virginia Journal of International Law*, 40: 1103–1124.

Stone Sweet, A. (2000). *Governing with Judges: Constitutional Politics in Europe*. Oxford, Oxford University Press.

Sunstein, C.R. (2001). *Designing Democracy. What Constitutions Do*. Oxford, Oxford University Press.

Tan, K.Y. (2014). "Constitutionalism in Burma, Cambodia and Thailand: Developments in the First Decade of the Twenty First Century." *Constitutionalism in Asia in the Early Twenty-First Century*, ed. A.H.Y. Chen. Cambridge, Cambridge University Press, pp. 219–243.

Tate, N.C. (1994). "The Judicialization of Politics in the Philippines and Southeast Asia." *International Political Science Review*, 15(2): 187–197.

Tate, N.C. and Haynie, S.L. (1993). "Authoritarianism and the Functions of Courts: A Time Series Analysis of the Philippine Supreme Court, 1961–1987." *Law and Society Review*, 27(4): 707–740.

Tate, N.C. and Vallinder, T., eds (1995). *The Global Expansion of Judicial Power*. New York, New York University Press.

Tushnet, M. (2015). "Authoritarian Constitutionalism." *Cornell Law Review*, 100(2): 391–461.

Welsh, B. (2015). "Lee Kuan Yew's Political Legacy – A Matter of Trust." *New Mandela*, March 24, available at: http://asiapacific.anu.edu.au/newmandala/2015/03/24/lee-kuan-yews-political-legacy-a-matter-of-trust/.

Worthington, R. (2001). "Between Hermes and Themis: An Empirical Study of the Contemporary Judiciary in Singapore." *Journal of Law and Society*, 28(4): 490–519.

Worthington, R. (2003). *Governance in Singapore*. London and New York, Routledge-Curzon.

Wu Min Aun, J. (2007). "The Saga of Anwar Ibrahim." In *Constitutional Landmarks in Malaysia*, eds A. Harding and H.P. Lee. Singapore, LexisNexis, pp. 273–291.

# 13 Contesting constitutionalism in Vietnam

## The justifications and proposed models of judicial review in the 2013 constitutional amendment process

*Huong Thi Nguyen*

### Introduction

Vietnam remains a one-party authoritarian regime; yet despite the restrictive political environment there has been a strong demand for judicial review in Vietnam in order to protect rights and promote the rule of law. This chapter examines the 2013 constitutional amendment debate on the establishment of a judicial review mechanism and sheds light on the contestation of major social forces in Vietnam. The seemingly technical discourses on constitutional amendments and constitutional review reveal actual competition of political ideas and intellectual creativity on what the rule of law and constitutionalism mean in the Vietnamese political context. Yet the contestation of constitutional ideas within the one-party regime contains its own ambiguity regarding the position of the Communist Party within the constitutional structure, and, in particular, regarding the power of a constitutional review mechanism. Despite the creativity and significant diversity of constitutional discourses, public intellectuals[1] in Vietnam seem to take the leadership of the Communist Party for granted and try to reconcile liberal concepts of constitutionalism with the constraints of the political regime instead of defying it.

The topics I examine in this chapter, the justifications of constitutional review and proposals of judicial models, each illustrate the contestation and ambiguity of constitutional ideas in contemporary Vietnam. I argue that while the progressing constitutionalism inspires the public intellectuals' demands for a strong and independent judicial review mechanism, the political constraints of the one-party regime continue to be a hindrance to the establishment of such a mechanism, as the reality of the supremacy of the Party unsurprisingly prevails over the ideational supremacy of the constitution. I suggest that, in the end, proponents of judicial review in Vietnam cannot avoid tackling the question of political reforms and the reform of legal education as necessary conditions for establishing a serious judicial review mechanism. I will start by laying out the background of the ideational transformation in Vietnam over the past two decades and during the 2013 constitutional amendment process. Next I will examine the contestation and ambiguity of constitutional ideas regarding the justifications of constitutional review and proposed models of judicial review. I will end with a forward-looking conclusion on the implications of the contestation of ideas for constitutional reform in Vietnam.

## The rising constitutional contestation in Vietnam: a background

The Socialist Republic of Vietnam is a one-party communist regime where basic political freedoms are restricted and the entire state and judiciary apparatus is controlled by the Communist Party of Vietnam. The country has been undergoing major transformations over the past two decades. In 1986, the economic "Renovation" abolished the centrally planned economy and moved toward a "socialist market economy under state guidance" combined with a "civilized and equitable society" (Beresford 2008: 221). This reform has not only transformed the Vietnamese economy but has also been a catalyst for the importation of new ideas. Opening the country to the external world especially through foreign trade and accession to global institutions required the adoption of international practices, rules, and legal standards that are at odds with the Soviet legal and political system (Koh 2010: 224). The new economic system and social changes resulted in diverging social interests (Vuving 2010) and transformed the conceptions of law in Vietnam (Gillespie 2005, 2010). The contestation of constitutional ideas occurs within this transformational context.

In 1992, Vietnam adopted the first post-Renovation constitution to reflect the policy changes adopted in the late 1980s (Hiang Khng 1992). The 1992 Constitution replaced the 1980 Constitution to keep pace with societal changes and economic liberalization (Sidel 2009: 83). In 2001, the 1992 Constitution was amended, to include, among others, two important but ambiguous concepts: the "state governed by law" (*nha nuoc phap quyen*) and "distribution and coordination among state bodies" (Sidel 2009: 120). The interpretation of the concept "state governed by law" has remained ambiguous and has opened discursive spaces for competing political ideas to operate (Gillespie 2004). Over the past few years, domestic intellectuals have pushed for further constitutional reforms to give substance to the concept of "state governed by law" in the constitution, focusing especially on the limitation of state powers. In addition, these intellectuals have dedicated special attention to building up a "constitutional protection" (*bảo hiến*) mechanism in the form of judicial review. The party itself seemed to feel compelled to include a "constitutional protection" mechanism as part of future judicial and constitutional reforms, and it has endorsed and funded studies on different models of judicial review (Communist Party of Vietnam Political Bureau 2005). Opposition groups invoking constitutional rights and international human rights as their legitimizing basis have also called for a mechanism to enforce constitutional rights against abuses of power by the party-state. In online blogs, forums, and social networks, law students and scholars have been discussing the need for constitutional mechanisms to protect citizens' rights as well as debating different constitutional court models that are appropriate for Vietnam.

In August 2011, the Vietnamese state launched an official constitutional amendment process. Although the need to amend the 1992 Constitution was first discussed at the National Assembly in 2010 to respond to the potential unconstitutionality of a plan to abolish the District People's Councils, public intellectuals quickly seized the opportunity to raise other fundamental constitutional issues that needed to be reformed (Nguyen 2012). In particular, establishing a constitutional court figured among the priorities of the amendment plan in 2011. The first draft of the amendments was released for public comment on January 2, 2013. Initially, the public had until March 2013 to contribute its opinions, but an unprecedentedly vibrant public debate on the amendments occurred: official sources estimated that 20 million "opinions" were received in the first three months of 2013 (Linh Thu 2013). In May 2013, the National Assembly voted to extend the time to receive public comments until September 2013. The final draft was adopted on November 28, 2013, with a near-unanimous vote of 486 out of 488 members of the National Assembly voting in favor (Hoang *et al.* 2013). Not all of the civil society's inputs made it to the final draft, however, including the demand for a constitutional review mechanism. Although a Constitutional Council figured in the amendment drafts, it was withdrawn from the last draft in November 2013.

Several issues were central to the 2013 constitutional amendment agenda and public debates: the role of the Communist Party of Vietnam in the political system (as stated in Article 4 of the 1992 Constitution), separation of powers, human rights and citizens' rights, land ownership, constitutional protection (judicial review), and organizing a referendum for the people to approve the amendments. There was a clear discrepancy between the party-state's position and public opinion on those issues at large. Regarding the party-state leadership, there were non-negotiable items that the party insisted on maintaining: the party's monopoly of power, control over the national army, the public ownership of land, the limitation of rights (especially civil and political rights), and the refusal to organize a referendum for the people to have the last word in the amendment process. The party-state leadership's position was reflected in various amendment drafts from January 2013 onward, as well as in the final draft of November 2013. Moreover, although a Constitutional Council figured in the early drafts, the final amendments excluded such an amendment altogether. However, reading newspapers and independent blogs, one may be surprised at the liberal tone of the broader constitutional discourse by public intellectuals and lawyers.

While it is difficult to measure "public opinion," a few surveys and petitions that were independently undertaken by well-known public intellectuals convey to some extent what was going on in the public discourse. I refer in particular to the survey on the website hienphap.net and Petition 72. The website hienphap.net was initiated by three well-known Vietnamese public intellectuals – Mathematics Professor Ngo Bao Chau at the University of Chicago, renowned for receiving the Fields Medal in 2010; Physics Professor Dam Thanh Son, also at the University of Chicago;[2] and Nguyen Anh Tuan, former editor-in-chief of

VietnamNet, one of the most liberal online state-owned newspapers. With the website, they intended to "create an additional dialogic space for all those who care about the constitutional amendment, so that they can discuss about this matter in a serious and democratic way" (Cùng Viết Hiến Pháp 2013). Founders of the website also share their definition of a constitution with a liberal tone:

> A Constitution is the fundamental law of a nation. It has to contain basic principles that set out the foundations to establish the political regime and the organization and functions of the State, and to protect fundamental rights of citizens.
>
> (Cùng Viết Hiến Pháp 2013)

The website carried out an online Survey on Opinions about the 2013 constitutional amendments draft between January and March 2013. The website reported that 4,800 people participated and 3,122 complete answers were received (Kết Quả Khảo Sát 2013). Although there was no report on the background of the participants, given that this was an online survey it may be reasonably assumed that most participants belonged to the educated middle class (as they had access to the Internet).

For the question "Should there be a limitation clause on human rights in the Constitution?," 80.6 percent of participants responded No; only 9.8 percent responded Yes. Most participants who responded No gave a general reason that such provision could easily be abused to violate human rights (Tổng Hợp Ý Kiến Khảo Sát 2013).[3] Some 86.8 percent of participants responded that a provision on the leadership of the Communist Party of Vietnam should not have a place in the constitution. Some 91.6 percent responded No to a provision requiring the army to be loyal to and to defend the Communist Party (Tổng Hợp Ý Kiến Khảo Sát 2013).[4] Some 92.5 percent of respondents responded Yes to the separation of state powers into legislative, executive, and judiciary power; the general reason given being "separation of powers has been applied widely in the world and is seen as the main principle of a rule of law state" (Tổng Hợp Ý Kiến Khảo Sát 2013).[5] Some 95.5 percent of respondents agreed that there should be a provision on the independence of the judiciary, and 88.2 percent of respondents responded Yes to establishing an organ to protect the constitution (judicial review) (Tổng Hợp Ý Kiến Khảo Sát 2013).[6]

Another appeal to public opinion by public intellectuals inside the country could also help convey a broader understanding of public opinion about constitutional demands in Vietnam. On January 19, 2013, 72 public intellectuals inside the country released the Petition on the 1992 Constitution's Amendment (publicly known as Petition 72) (Kiến Nghị 2013; Kiến Nghị Hiến Pháp Bỏ Điều 4 2013). By November 2013, the Petition had reportedly received 15,000 signatures (Lời Kêu Gọi 2013). On February 4, 16 representatives of the Petition 72 group, led by Nguyen Dinh Loc, former Minister of Justice and member of the 1992 Constitution Drafting Committee, met with the Vice-Head of the Constitutional Amendment Drafting Committee in order to directly hand them the

Petition (Trao Kiến Nghị 2013; Trao Bản Kiến Nghị 2013). The event was also reported in state-owned media, although the content of the petition was neither published nor discussed there (Nhân Sỹ Trí Thức Gửi Bản Kiến Nghị 2013).

The petition stressed seven demands, among them: to respect the sovereignty of the people, which means removing the provision on the leadership of the Communist Party; to revise rights provisions "according to the spirit of the 1948 Universal Declaration of Human Rights and international covenants to which Vietnam is a signatory" (Kiến Nghị 2013); private land ownership; separation of powers with an independent judiciary and a constitutional court; the army's loyalty to the people instead of to the Communist Party; and organization of a referendum for the people to have the final word in the amendment process. The Petition also proposed an alternative constitution draft that is liberal in essence – proposing multiparty democracy and individual rights, among others (Kiến Nghị 2013).

The Survey and Petition are relevant here because they were two important moments that were initiated by the civil society in the constitutional amendment process in 2013. They also attracted the attention of the public because they were launched by well-known public intellectuals who maintain good relations with the current political regime, yet the Survey and Petition are liberal in their approach and content. The Survey and Petition may reflect the points of view of the urban middle class on the Internet, but they were widely circulated on dissident blogs and new media as well, and thus received the endorsement of a wider audience than merely the elite middle class. One may say that the Survey and Petition do not reflect the views of other marginalized groups. Yet a widespread consultation process organized by 17 Vietnamese civil society organizations with seven vulnerable groups in Vietnam (ethnic minorities, people with disability, migrant workers, people with HIV, LGBT people, women, and youth) in various locations in the country (iSEE 2013a)[7] yielded similar liberal demands, although they only focused on human rights issues (and not "sensitive" matters such as questions on the political regime). The consultation resulted in a series of recommendations, ranging from the general aspiration on the nature of the constitution (iSEE 2013b: 3)[8] to specific changes to the amendment draft, including many recommendations on equality, human rights and the state's obligation in ensuring those rights, and establishing an independent Constitutional Court (with adjudicatory power) and an independent National Human Rights Commission (iSEE 2013b).

The above overview of the Vietnamese context and the 2013 constitutional amendment process reveals an emerging constitutional contestation in Vietnam – the genuine societal interests in constitutional changes and the efforts to influence the constitutional agenda through public surveys, consultations, and petitions, as well as competitions of divergent ideas, notably between the state-party officials and public intellectuals. Although the final amendments reflect the position of the political leadership, understanding such competition of ideas will help one understand the development of constitutionalism in Vietnam for the years to come. In the following sections, I will examine in more detail the debate on establishing a judicial review mechanism: the competing justifications of constitutional review and the proposed models of constitutional review.

## Justifications of judicial review: the particularity of the concepts of constitutional review, democracy, and rule of law in the one-party regime

There are three main competing justifications of constitutional review: one is vague and concerned mostly with preserving the supremacy of the National Assembly; the other two are about fundamental values and tradition on the one hand, and the rule of law more generally on the other. One particularity of the Vietnamese discourse on constitutional review is the preoccupation with justifying constitutional review, especially independent constitutional review, within the one-party political context.

### The official discourse: a vague justification for "supervision of constitutionality"

The official justification of building a constitutional review mechanism came from the Communist Party's tenthth and eleventh National Congresses' Resolutions, in which the ruling party acknowledged the need to "build a mechanism to *adjudicate* on constitutional violations in the legislative, executive, and judiciary activities" (Nguyen Van Thuan 2013). However, there are no additional details. The need to "supervise the constitutionality" is the vague wording of a justification that aims, perhaps, to avoid tackling the root of the unconstitutionality of acts. Members of the National Assembly who refer to this function often direct their efforts to fit the Constitutional Council within the current power structure instead of making it a counter-force (Bao Cam 2013). Their goal seems simply to create a body to "check the constitutionality of legal documents" without inquiring more deeply why the unconstitutionality of legal documents would be a problem (such as the implications of unconstitutionality to citizens' lives – rights violations, abuse of power, corruption, and so on). In touching only the surface of the matter, they seek to maintain the status quo power structure – the supremacy of the National Assembly, and, arguably, the supreme control of the Communist Party. State officials who contributed their opinion on constitutional review relied heavily on the Communist Party's resolutions as the political justification for constitutional review. State officials such as Pham Hong Quang, Head of the Department of Criminal and Administrative Law of the Ministry of Justice, even refers to the leadership role of the Communist Party as the justification for constitutional review:

> The consideration to establish a constitutional protection mechanism is an objective need. [We] should avoid thinking that a constitutional protection mechanism only suits the bourgeois rule of law state. Constitutional protection is the need, the demand that emanates from the organization of the

> socialist rule of law state apparatus. First of all, the acknowledgment of the leadership role of the Party in Article 4 of the 1992 Constitution has undeniably expressed the absolute consent and support by the people for the legitimate party that has led the State, society, and all the people to great achievements throughout history. In the reality of the state management activities under the leadership of the Party, state organs that are assigned with legislative, executive, and judicial functions, for many objective and subjective reasons, may unavoidably, intentionally or unintentionally, enact acts or take the actions that violate the Constitution and the law, infringing upon the legitimate rights and interests of the citizens, although the Constitution and the law have prescribed otherwise. Thus, more than ever, the existence of a constitutional protection mechanism aims precisely to protect the policies and directives of the Party, to ensure their implementation in the right direction. In other words: *Protecting the Constitution, or building a constitutional protection mechanism, is protecting the Party.*
>
> (Pham Hong Quang 2013)[9]

The consequence of such a justification is the proposal of models of weak constitutional review: a Constitutional Council that is subordinate to the National Assembly (Bao Cam 2013), or a proposal to entrust the constitutional review power to the existing Supreme People's Court (Pham Hong Quang 2013), and, in the final draft, the absence of constitutional review altogether. I will elaborate more on those proposals of judicial review later in the chapter.

## Justifications of judicial review by public intellectuals and lawyers

For proponents of judicial review, justifying judicial review in the Vietnamese context equals refuting the argument that judicial review comes out of and only suits liberal democracies. Some particularities of the justification of constitutional review in Vietnam concern the role of the Communist Party and the one-party regime. Here lies the creativity of the Vietnamese constitutional discourses. As a general matter, the mainstream elite refers to the Communist Party's National Congresses' Resolutions as the justification for their demands of constitutional review – since constitutional protection is a need stated by the leadership, establishing a constitutional review mechanism is undisputable. However, there is much distance to travel from justifying *a* constitutional review mechanism to justifying *a strong and independent* constitutional review mechanism. The most frequent justification of judicial review by public intellectuals in Vietnam involves democracy and rule of law. However, what they mean by democracy and rule of law is not the same as in the context of liberal democracies because, within the one-party regime, there are constraints about what they are allowed to discuss.

***Socialist democracy and rule of law***

The democracy justification of constitutional review in Vietnam draws from the sovereignty of the people. The constitution is supreme because it emanates from the sovereign power of the people; thus, in order for the sovereign power of the people to be respected, there has to be an effective mechanism to protect the constitution. The newly introduced concept "socialist rule of law state" in Article 3 of the 1992 Constitution as amended in 2001 (that some authors refer to as "law-based state") contributes to reinforcing the idea of the supremacy of the constitution, and especially of the function of the constitution in limiting the government's power. However, while drawing on those concepts to justify judicial review, proponents of strong and independent judicial review also take care to clarify that appealing to democracy and rule of law have nothing to do with multiparty democracy, and it is thus not a challenge to the Communist Party. For proponents of independent judicial review such as Tran Ngoc Duong, a former member of the Committee on Laws of the National Assembly,

> the establishment of an independent constitution protection mechanism aims to continue to improve and deepen the nature of our state – the socialist rule of law and the socialist democracy nature. It is unimaginable that a democratic, rule of law state does not have an independent constitutional protection institution.
>
> (Tran Ngoc Duong 2013)

Tran Ngoc Duong justifies constitutional review ("constitution protection") by stating that the nature of the constitution is as the supreme law of the country, which emanates from the sovereign power of the people and thus "is above the legislative, executive, and judicial powers and contains particular values of a state" (Tran Ngoc Duong 2013). The constitution specifies the organization of state powers and is the instrument through which the sovereign people limit the power of the government. To protect the constitution is thus to protect the democratic regime and the sovereign power of the people. For him, a constitutional protection mechanism thus "has nothing to do with a multiparty regime," but rather with theories of the sovereignty of the people, rule of law, and respect for democracy.

For Truong Dac Linh, law lecturer at Ho Chi Minh City University of Law, there is a close relationship between democracy, the rule of law, and the constitution:

> The rule of law is the primary principle and the utmost requirement of democracy. In turn, the Constitution, as the fundamental law of the state with the highest authority over all power institutions in the society, is the legal basis and the indispensable principle of the rule of law state.... But the existence of the Constitution is only a necessary condition, not a sufficient condition, of a democratic regime, of a rule of law state.... [I]n order for the

> constitutional regime to be respected and guaranteed in real life, there needs to be an effective mechanism to protect and restore the constitutional order.
> (Truong Dac Linh 2013)

Nguyen Nhu Phat, a public intellectual, professor, and high-ranking member of the Institute of State and Law in Vietnam, wrote an insightful article entitled "[The Need to] Protect the Constitution Emanates from the Need to Erect and Develop a Rule of Law State" which was published on the website of the National Assembly's delegates ("The People's Delegates"). Using the rule of law as the main justification for judicial review, he argues for a strong judicial review power that is not subordinate to the National Assembly and whose decisions are final. For him, given the nature of the constitution as "a special legal document, with profound political-legal and declaratory characters," the protection of the constitution must start from the particularity of such a document (Nguyen Nhu Phat 2013a). His concern here is about an impartial implementation of the constitution that would not put the state's interests before citizens' interests. He talks about the unavoidable conflicts of interest and the conflict of powers between citizens and the state, especially on matters of citizens' rights. Thus,

> one cannot rely on the legal system of the National Assembly and of the Government to resolve fundamental problems of the Constitution, but can rely on the Constitution itself, through proper constitutional interpretation [by an independent judicial review mechanism] to work out the criteria of constitutionality [upon which conflicts will be resolved].

If constitutional protection necessarily involves competing interpretations of constitutional provisions, principles, and values, entrusting constitutional review to a state organ would result in failure to protect the constitution concerning people's constitutional rights. For Nguyen Nhu Phat, the number of political parties in the political regimes has no impact for constitutional adjudication, the need for which is justified by the necessity of maintaining the integrity of constitutional order regardless of the political machine which operates within that order. What matters is that "political parties, or, the political party, in a rule of law State, are only allowed to exist and operate under the swagger-cane of the Constitution" (Nguyen Nhu Phat 2013a).

Thus, Vietnamese public intellectuals bring within the rule of law concept various justifications of constitutional review, including rights protection and the limitation of state powers. The reference to those justifications does not point to the same thing. For instance, the nuances of different theories of democracy in liberal democracies, which emphasize political competition and different levels of procedural and substantive guarantees to citizens' participation in the democratic process, do not exist in the Vietnamese mainstream elites' justifications of judicial review. Thus, democracy, as a justification of judicial review, is conditioned by existing political ideologies such as the socialist ideologies of the state.

Judicial review in a "socialist democracy" and in a "socialist rule of law" state will likely be a weak institution that is subordinate to the ruling party, at least when it is first established.

### *Fundamental values and tradition*

Bui Ngoc Son, law lecturer at Hanoi National University Faculty of Law, justifies his proposal of a Constitutional Council model through interpreting and reminding people of the "spirit of constitutional protection" as one of the traditions in Vietnamese history. For him,

> Vietnam has a tradition of checking the conformity of the monarch's acts to the fundamental moral-political norms, performed by scholars and mandarins through institutionalized activities of advising, educating, and recording history. The establishment of an independent constitutional protection organ is coherent with this tradition.
>
> (Bui Ngoc Son 2013)

Bui Ngoc Son refers to the advisory bodies established by the Nguyen dynasty in the thirteenth century to provide advice to monarchs on fundamental moral and political norms, historical experiences in governing the country by the monarch's predecessors, supervising the monarch's deeds and speech, and ensuring their conformity with tradition. Such counsel and supervision had merely advisory effects, but, in Bui Ngoc Son's words, "the power of tradition ensures the effectiveness of such advisory institutions" (Bui Ngoc Son 2013). However, it is not clear from Bui Ngoc Son's historical example how talking about the "spirit of constitutional protection" in historical dynasties would help in explaining why this historical precedent is relevant in the context of a modern constitutional protection mechanism. The king had the final word on all affairs, but in modern constitutionalism the question of whether the government or the courts should have the final word in cases of disagreement is still a matter for debate. In addition, if history is relevant, then does it mean that the structure of judicial review should only be the equivalent of what existed in the past; that is, an advisory function only? It does not seem to be the case in Bui Ngoc Son's proposal, because he ended up proposing a mechanism based on the French Constitutional Council model. Referencing Vietnamese history seems to serve the political justification purpose: that those who advocate for an independent constitutional protection mechanism do not aim to import a Western model that would potentially subvert the Communist Party's power, and that there is nothing abnormal about advocating for such a mechanism given that there is a historical precedent.

Most of what public intellectuals, such as Nguyen Nhu Phat and Bui Ngoc Son, argue aims at the justification of strong judicial review (the German model in Nguyen Nhu Phat's proposal and the French model in Bui Ngoc Son's) in a one-party political context. Bui Ngoc Son refers to history and tradition while

Nguyen Nhu Phat and others find ways to assure their audience that a strong constitutional review mechanism is required by the rule of law and socialist democracy, and that it is compatible with (and thus not threatening to) the existing power structure. The logic of these justifications is similar to the context of countries with parliamentary regimes: there needs to be a way to ensure that judicial review does not challenge the fundamental principle of the supremacy of the legislative power. In the Vietnamese situation, the political conventional rule to contend with is not quite the supremacy of the legislative power, but the dominating power of the Communist Party. The competing justifications of constitutional review result in different proposed models. Not surprisingly, the party-state opted for a weak model of judicial review, and ultimately decided to discard the adoption of a constitutional review mechanism altogether. Proponents of the supremacy of the constitution tried to push for a strong and independent mechanism of review, without success in the end.

## Competing proposals of constitutional review models

Regarding proposals of models of constitutional review for Vietnam in the 2013 constitutional amendment debate, there are again competing visions and a divergence between the official view and the demands from public intellectuals. The official draft merely proposed a weak model at first, then the leadership decided to discard the amendment on constitutional review altogether. State officials also suggested entrusting the constitutional review power to the existing Supreme People's Court. Public officials leaned toward an independent and strong judicial review mechanism, although there was divergence within the models they proposed.

## Proposals of weak constitutional review

### *A weak and subordinate Constitutional Council model suggested in the official amendment drafts*

In the second amendments draft as of July 2013, the party-state adopted a weak Constitutional Council model which would report to and be subordinate to the National Assembly and which would not have any adjudicative power. The new constitutional draft contains only one article regarding the Constitutional Council. According to this new Article 120, "the Constitutional Council is an organ *established by the National Assembly*."[10] That Constitutional Council would examine the constitutionality of legal norms promulgated by the National Assembly, the President of the Republic, the government, the Prime Minister, the People's Supreme Court, and the People's Procuracy. But, after detecting constitutional violations, it would only have the very limited power to "petition" the National Assembly to amend a law, or to request other relevant state organs to amend their own acts. There were no details in the draft constitution about the organization, its concrete powers, or the appointment and tenure of members of the Constitutional Council. Clause 3 of Article 120 leaves those issues to ordinary law to determine. In brief, the model of the Constitutional Council that the constitutional amendment draft set out would look more like a committee of the National Assembly. The official discourse made it unequivocal that "the low-level constitutional protection mechanism" was adopted to respond to "two basic particularities of Vietnam": the "one-party regime"; and the "National Assembly [being] *asserted by the Party* as the supreme state organ" (Nghia Nhan 2013).[11]

In the third draft as of October 2013, the Constitutional Council was the dominant model. The amendment drafts suggest the Constitutional Council model with limited power. There are two drafting proposals for the Constitutional Council. Both provide that the Constitutional Council "is an organ established by the National Assembly" with three powers. First, the Constitutional Council would:

> examine the constitutionality of the law and resolutions enacted by the National Assembly. Provisions or documents that are determined unconstitutional by the Constitutional Council would be suspended until the National Assembly reexamines them at the next working session. If two-thirds of the National Assembly votes to maintain the provision or document, then the later continues to remain in force.

The second proposal does not mention the two-thirds veto provision. Second, the Constitutional Council would "examine the constitutionality of documents issued by the President, the Standing Committee of the National Assembly, Government, the Prime Minister, Ministers, Head of ministry-level organs, the People's Supreme Court and the Supreme People's Procuracy." If the Constitutional Council decides that some provisions or documents are unconstitutional,

> their implementation is suspended until the organ which issued the document amends or repeals the unconstitutional provisions or documents. If the issuing organ fails to amend or repeal the document, the Constitutional Council petitions competent organs to examine and decide.
>
> (Nguyen Van Thuan 2013)

There is a nuanced difference between the two proposals: in the second, the Constitutional Council would be slightly more interfering – it would order the issuing organ to repeal or amend the provisions or documents it deems unconstitutional. In the first, the Constitutional Council's authority would stop short at its decision on the constitutionality of a document, and it would not have the authority to issue orders to the issuing organ to take remedying measures (Dang Minh Tuan 2013). Third, the Constitutional Council would "examine the constitutionality of international treaties that were signed on behalf of the State before they were submitted to ratification by the National Assembly and the President." Besides the clause on the three general powers of the Constitutional Council, the draft amendments do not specify further details. Draft Article 117 provides only that "[t]he organization, mission, concrete jurisdiction, procedure before the Constitutional Council, as well as the number of members of the Council and their tenure will be specified by law" (Nguyen Van Thuan 2013).

It is clear from the draft, however, that the Constitutional Council is meant to be subordinate to the National Assembly. Draft Article 117 clause 2 states first hand that "the Constitutional Council is responsible before and has to report its activities to the National Assembly." According to draft Article 70 clause 7, the National Assembly would select, revoke, and dismiss the president of the Constitutional Council, and approve the list of members of the Constitutional Council. There are no more details on who has the power to nominate candidates or suggest them to the National Assembly, or who may dismiss or revoke the president of the Constitutional Council (Dang Minh Tuan 2013).

### *Proposal to give constitutional review power to the Supreme People's Court*

State officials such as Pham Hong Quang, head of the Department of Criminal and Administrative Law of the Ministry of Justice, suggest giving to the existing Supreme People's Court the exclusive constitutional review power. The Supreme People's Court would have the power to: (1) adjudicate the constitutionality of all norms enacted by state organs and international treaties before ratification; (2) interpret the constitution; (3) examine the constitutionality of the legal basis of decisions and judgments by lower level courts; (4) examine and decide the constitutionality of state organs and state officials' acts in order to protect constitutional rights and legitimate interests of citizens; and (5) dissolve associations whose activities violate the constitution (Pham Hong Quang 2013). The constitutional review power of the Supreme People's Court would apply only to legal norms that have entered into force; that is, the proposed model is an a posteriori review model.

Pham Hong Quang, however, does not concern himself with ensuring the structural independence of the Supreme People's Court that would allow it to execute its tasks in a more effective way. He still suggests that the Chief Judge of the Supreme People's Court and the Chief Judge of the Constitutional Chamber of the Supreme People's Court be elected by the National Assembly from among members of the National Assembly. The term lengths of judges of the Constitutional Chamber and of the Supreme People's Court correspond with the term length of the National Assembly – a new National Assembly would elect new judges. Other organizational matters of the Constitutional Chamber, including appointment and dismissal rules, term length, and so on may be determined by an ordinary law. Thus, it seems that although Pham Hong Quang advocates for the need of a constitutional review power of the Supreme People's Court, he still sees the Supreme People's Court as subordinate to the National Assembly. It is unclear how this model will be more effective than the subordinate Constitutional Council model that is suggested in the constitutional amendment drafts.

## Proposals of a strong and independent constitutional review model by public intellectuals

Liberal scholars who have referred to the rule of law, rights protections, and the separation of powers are unequivocal in advocating for a strong adjudicatory constitutional review model, regardless of the actual structure of the review mechanism. There are two different suggested models: the model of a centralized Constitutional Court and a strengthened Constitutional Council model.

### *Centralized Constitutional Court model*

Nguyen Nhu Phat suggests a complete separation between the constitutional court and the ordinary court system (Nguyen Nhu Phat 2013a, 2013b). He does not specify a particular structure of constitutional review, but suggests that the procedure which leads to the constitutional review institution be separated from the ordinary court system, meaning that there would be no certification mechanism. All levels of ordinary courts must be exhausted before a case may be brought before the constitutional review institution. The latter has adjudicatory, court-like powers. It seems that the model Nguyen Nhu Phat has in mind is a posteriori review. The decisions of the court would not have binding force upon ordinary judges; however, though Nguyen Nhu Phat does not state this clearly, it is reasonable to suggest that, as a matter of fact, ordinary judges would have the incentives to look at constitutional precedents in deciding their own cases. In case there are no precedents, there is still a chance for the gradual building up of constitutional analysis that can eventually be resolved in the final instance by a Constitutional Court. This proposal suggests a combination between bottom-up constitutional jurisprudence-building and a centralized constitutional review organ that would have the last word in deciding the constitutionality of cases.

### *The strong Constitutional Council model*

Vietnamese mainstream elites seem to share the view that a Constitutional Council may be appropriate for Vietnam in the current political context, but it should only be considered as a transitional model. During the constitutional amendment process in 2013, the Drafting Committee of the 1992 Constitutional Amendments published a book entitled *Organizational Models and Operation of Constitutional Councils in Some Countries in the World*, co-authored by various public intellectuals and jurists. The book reviews the models and experiences of Constitutional Councils in the world, and recommends that "in the long term, the Constitutional Court model seems to be more appropriate than the Constitutional Council model," and that

> if the Constitutional Council model is adopted, it should only be seen as a transitional step, and the Constitutional Council should have functions and authority that reflect the trend of reforms of constitutional councils that are

> happening in the world, and that suit the direction and the requirement of the establishment and perfection of a rule of law state in Vietnam.
>
> (Ban Bien Tap Du Thao 2013: 126)

For the authors of the book, the Constitutional Council modeled in the constitutional amendment draft "is not an independent constitutional adjudication organ, but seems to be an institution of political nature." Yet "Constitutional Councils with many political characteristics will have [a] limited role in protecting the Constitution" (Ban Bien Tap Du Thao 2013: 127). Thus, they proposed that if a Constitutional Council model is adopted, the constitutional amendments should "enhance its independence, expand its power and facilitate citizens' access to this organ" (Ban Bien Tap Du Thao 2013: 127).

Concretely, in terms of organization, the Constitutional Council should be constituted from the legislative, executive, and judicial branches (instead of merely the legislative branch). Its members should be specialized (that is, have diplomas and experience) in politics, administration, and law. The Constitutional Council should not only have a priori review power, but should also have the power to adjudicate the constitutionality of statutes that have entered into force (that is, a posteriori review), other legal norms, and administrative acts by executive organs. The Constitutional Council should also have the power to supervise elections, referendums, and the signing and ratification of international treaties. The constitution should also give the people the ability to bring claims to the Constitutional Council, either indirectly through ordinary courts and through members of the National Assembly, or directly when other existing legal actions have been exhausted without having their constitutional rights protected (Ban Bien Tap Du Thao 2013: 127). Thus, even when public intellectuals go along with the Constitutional Council model proposal, what they have in mind is not a subordinate organ but an independent and strong constitutional review mechanism with significant public access. Ultimately, even such a strong Constitutional Council model should only be seen as transitional, with a Constitutional Court model as the ultimate goal.

## Conclusion: prospects for constitutional review in Vietnam

I have examined the debate surrounding the establishment of a constitutional review mechanism for Vietnam, focusing in particular on competing justifications of judicial review and proposals for constitutional review models in the 2013 constitutional debate. The failure of proponents of judicial review to get a constitutional review model adopted in 2013 was proof that the reality of the supremacy the party prevailed over the ideational supremacy of the constitution. The failure to adopt a constitutional review mechanism, even a weak and subordinate one, was perhaps an indication that the party-state was suspicious of its capacity to keep such a mechanism under control if it was established. However, given the strong demands for judicial review, the momentum of the progressing constitutionalism in Vietnam will probably continue, and the constitution is likely to face another amendment in the years to come.[12] If such an occasion occurs again within the current political regime, reformers may still need to compromise with the constraints of the political system. The compromise may involve adopting a Constitutional Court or a Constitutional Council with weak powers. But advocating for the public's direct access to the constitutional review mechanism and for the constitutional review body's unrestricted jurisdiction over rights-adjudication matters are crucial for the newly established institution to gradually assert its power in the long term. It is not realistic for constitutional review proponents to insist on their ideal model. Instead, they could assess what is possible, and find a strategic way to negotiate and establish a judicial review authority from that opening of possibility.

That said, serious proponents of constitutionalism and constitutional review cannot always avoid the fundamental question of the nature of the political regime. Although public officials in Vietnam have voiced their preference for a strong and independent Constitutional Court or Constitutional Council, it is not clear how a separate constitutional review institution would maintain its independence vis-à-vis the National Assembly and the Communist Party of Vietnam. Even if the constitution provides for separation of powers and judicial independence, within the current political structure most members of the new institution would have to be selected and/or approved by the Communist Party of Vietnam (through its control over the National Assembly, the government, the Supreme Court, and other sociopolitical mass organizations). It is true that the European model of the centralized Constitutional Court was designed to deal with the issue of a weak judiciary structure, but simply adding another institution on top of the current structure does not automatically guarantee its independence and superior competence. That is especially the case if there is no guarantee of genuine independence in the appointment process and in the operation of the court, as well as in the quality of judges and the quality of the legal education. In other words, reformers cannot simply talk about establishing a Constitutional Court in Vietnam while avoiding other structural reforms, such as the reforms of the political system and of legal education.

## Notes

1 By public intellectuals, I refer to the mainstream elite who have a position within the system, either academically or politically; for example, lawyers, law professors, civil society leaders, and party and state officials.

2 Both Professors Ngo Bao Chau and Dam Thanh Son grew up in Vietnam and built their professional career abroad.

3 Question 5.

4 Question 16.

5 Question 19.

6 Questions 20 and 21.

7 Forty-five consultations were organized with 980 individuals from the seven targeted vulnerable groups from 13 provinces and cities.

8 The Constitution … should take roots from diversity, aiming at establishing equality among individuals, groups and communities. The Constitution, instead of

narrowing the international human rights standards, should clearly recognize the international human rights Vietnam has committed to implement when it signed the International Covenants on Human Rights. It should also reinforce the widely recognized international norms that Vietnam has the obligation to observe.

9 Unless otherwise noted, all quotations are my own translation.
10 Emphasis added.
11 Deputy Minister of Justice Hoang The Lien's speech. Emphasis added.
12 For example, the experience of the 1992 and 2001 constitutional amendments – the demands that had been quelled at those times resurfaced to be the momentum for subsequent constitutional revisions (Hiang Khng 1992, Sidel 2002).

## References


Ban Bien Tap Du Thao Sua Doi Hien Phap Nam 1992 [The 1992 Constitution Amendments Editorial Board] (2013). *Mô Hình Tổ Chức Và Hoạt Động Của Hội Đồng Hiến Pháp Ở Một Số Nước Trên Thế Giới* [*Organizational Models and Operation of Constitutional Councils in Some Countries in the World*]. Hanoi, NXB Chinh Tri Quoc Gia.

Bao Csm (2013). Đề nghị có Hội đồng hiến pháp [Proposals to Adopt a Constitutional Council]. *Thanh Nien*, September 26, 2013, available at: www.thanhnien.com.vn/pages/20130926/de-nghi-co-hoi-dong-hien-phap.aspx (accessed March 15, 2015).

Beresford, M. (2008). "*Doi Moi* in Review: The Challenges of Building Market Socialism in Vietnam." *Journal of Contemporary Asia*, 38(2): 221–243.

Bui Ngoc Son (2013). Tinh thần bảo hiến trong truyền thống Việt Nam [The Constitutional Protection Spirit in the Vietnamese Tradition]. *Dai Bieu Nhan Dan*, September 23, available at: http://daibieunhandan.vn/default.aspx?tabid=76&NewsId=293106 (accessed March 15, 2015).

Communist Party of Vietnam Political Bureau (2005). Resolution 49-NQ/TW on Strategy to Judicial Reforms until 2020, June 2. Hanoi.

Cùng Viết Hiến Pháp [Write the Constitution Together] (2013). *Cung Viet Hien Phap*, available at: http://hienphap.net/cung-viet-hien-phap/ (accessed December 16, 2013).

Dang Minh Tuan (2013). Cơ cấu, tổ chức và chức năng, nhiệm vụ của Hội đồng Hiến pháp trong Dự thảo sửa đổi Hiến pháp năm 1992 [The Structure, Organization, and Functions, Mission of the Constitutional Council in the Draft Amendments to the 1992 Constitution]. *Dai Bieu Nhan Dan*, August 28, available at: http://daibieunhandan.vn/default.aspx?tabid=76&NewsId=290677 (accessed March 15, 2015).

Duong Phi Anh (2013). Trật Tự Pháp Luật: Vấn Đề Không Nhỏ Của Hiến Pháp [Legal Order: A Not-so-small Issue of the Constitution]. *Cung Viet Hien Phap*, March 10, available at: http://hienphap.net/2013/03/10/trat-tu-phap-luat-van-de-khong-nho-cua-hien-phap-duong-phi-anh/ (accessed December 16, 2013).

Gillespie, J. (2004). "Concept of Law in Vietnam: Transforming Statist Socialism." In *Asian Discourses of Rule of Law: Theories and Implementation of Rule of Law in Twelve Asian Countries, France and the U.S.*, ed. R. Peerenboom. London, Routledge, pp. 142–179.

Gillespie, J. (2005). "Changing Concepts of Socialist Law in Vietnam." In *Asian Socialism and Legal Change: The Dynamics of Vietnamese and Chinese Reform*, eds J. Gillespie and P. Nicholson. Canberra, ANU E Press, pp. 45–76.

Gillespie, J. (2006). "Evolving Concepts of Human Rights in Vietnam." In *Human Rights in Asia: A Comparative Legal Study of Twelve Asian Jurisdictions, France and the USA*, ed. R. Peerenboom. Abingdon, Routledge, pp. 452–486.

Gillespie, J. (2010). "The Juridification of State Regulation in Vietnam." In *Legal Reforms in China and Vietnam: A Comparison of Asian Communist Regimes*, eds J. Gillespie and A. Chen. London, Routledge, pp. 78–102.

Gillespie, J. (2011). "Exploring the Limits of the Judicialization of Urban Land Disputes in Vietnam." *Law and Society Review*, 45(2): 241–275.

Hiang Khng, R.H. (1992). "The 1992 Revised Constitution of Vietnam: Background and Scope of Changes." *Contemporary Southeast Asia*, 14(3): 221–230.

Hoang, C., M. Thang, D. Yen, and H. Duyen (2013). 97,59% Ấn Nút Thông Qua Hiến Pháp [97.59% Pressed Yes to Adopt the Constitution]. *Vietnamnet*, November 21, available at: http://vietnamnet.vn/vn/chinh-tri/151344/97-59-an-nut-thong-qua-hien-phap.html (accessed December 12, 2013).

iSEE – Viện Nghiên Cứu Xã hội, Kinh tế và Môi trường [The Institute for Studies of Society, Economics and Environment] (2013a). Kết Quả Tham Vấn Bảy Nhóm Xã Hội Cho Sửa Đổi Hiến Pháp 1992 [The Results of the Consultation with Seven Social Groups on the Amendments to the 1992 Constitution], March 11, available at: http://isee.org.vn/vi/Blog/Article/ket-qua-tham-van-bay-nhom-xa-hoi-cho-sua-doi-hien-phap-1992 (accessed December 16, 2013).

iSEE – Viện Nghiên Cứu Xã hội, Kinh tế và Môi trường [The Institute for Studies of Society, Economics and Environment] (2013b). Góp ý với Dự Thảo Sửa Đổi Hiến Pháp của 7 Nhóm Xã Hội, Nhóm Yếu Thế và Dễ Bị Tổn Thương [Comments on the Constitutional Amendments Draft from Seven Social and Vulnerable Groups], March, available at: http://hienphap.files.wordpress.com/2013/03/gop-y-sua-doi-hien-phap-1992-cua-7-nhom-xa-hoi.pdf (accessed December 16, 2013).

Kết Quả Khảo Sát [Survey Results] (2013). *Cung Viet Hien* Phap, March, available at: http://hienphap.net/ket-qua-khao-sat (accessed December 14, 2013).

Kiến Nghị Hiến pháp bỏ Điều 4 [Petition to Abolish Article 4 of the Constitution] (2013). *BBC Vietnamese,* January 23, available at: www.bbc.co.uk/vietnamese/vietnam/2013/01/130123_constitution_petition.shtml (accessed December 16, 2013).

Kiến Nghị về Sửa Đổi Hiến Pháp 1992 [Petition on the 1992 Constitution's Amendment (Petition 72)] (2013). *Boxitvn*, January 19, available at: http://boxitvn.blogspot.com/2013/01/kien-nghi-ve-sua-oi-hien-phap-1992.html (accessed December 12, 2013).

Koh, D. (2010). "Modern Law, Traditional Ethics, and Contemporary Political Legitimacy in Vietnam." In *Vietnam's New Order: International Perspectives on the State and Reforms in Vietnam*, eds S. Balmie and M. Sidel. New York, Palgrave Macmillan, pp. 217–236.

Linh Thu (2013). Từ 'Không Cấm Kỵ' Đến 'Phút Lịch Sử' [From "No Taboo" to the "Historical Moment"]. *Vietnamnet*, November 29, available at: http://vietnamnet.vn/vn/chinh-tri/151417/tu-khong-cam-ky-den-phut-lich-su-.html (accessed December 12, 2013).

Lời Kêu Gọi Dừng Việc Thông Qua Dự Thảo Hiến Pháp Nước Cộng Hòa Xã Hội Chủ Nghĩa Việt Nam Năm 1992 (Sửa Đổi 2013) [Appeal to Suspend the Adoption of the 2013 Amendments of the 1992 Constitution of the Socialist Republic of Vietnam] (2013). *Boxitvn*, November 16, available at: www.boxitvn.net/bai/21101 (accessed December 16, 2013).

Nghia Nhan (2013). Sửa đổi Hiến pháp: Tạo điều kiện cho người dân thực thi tự do [Amending the Constitution: Creating the Conditions for the People to Exercise Freedom]. *Du Thao Online*, February 23, available at: http://duthaoonline.quochoi.vn/

DuThao/Lists/TT_TINLAPPHAP/View_Detail.aspx?ItemID=965 (accessed March 15, 2015).

Nguyen Minh Tuan (2013). Quyền biểu tình: Nên quy định thế nào [The Right To Protest: How To Regulate]. *Tia Sang*, March 14, available at: http://tiasang.com.vn/Default.aspx?tabid=116&CategoryID=42&News=6195 (accessed December 16, 2013).

Nguyen Nhu Phat (2013a). Bảo vệ Hiến pháp xuất phát từ nhu cầu xây dựng và phát triển Nhà nước pháp quyền [Protecting the Constitution as a Need to Establish and Develop the Rule of Law State]. *Dai Bieu Nhan Dan*, September, 9, available at: http://daibieunhandan.vn/default.aspx?tabid=76&NewsId=291432 (accessed March 15, 2015).

Nguyen Nhu Phat (2013b). Nên mở rộng thẩm quyền của Hội đồng Hiến pháp [Should Expand the Power of the Constitutional Council]. *Dai Bieu Nhan Dan*, September 9, available at: http://daibieunhandan.vn/default.aspx?tabid=76&NewsId=291632 (accessed December 16, 2013).

Nguyen Van Thuan (2013). Về mô hình cơ quan bảo vệ Hiến pháp trong Dự thảo sửa đổi Hiến pháp năm 1992 [About the Constitutional Protection Organ Model in the 1992 Constitutional Amendments Draft]. *Dai Bieu Nhan Dan*, September 3, available at: http://daibieunhandan.vn/default.aspx?tabid=76&NewsId=291114 (accessed March 15, 2015).

Nguyen, T.H. (2012). "Pursuing Constitutional Dialogue within Socialist Vietnam: The 2010 Debate." *Australian Journal of Asian Law*, 13(1): 1–18.

Nhân Sỹ Trí Thức Gửi Bản Kiến Nghị Sửa Đổi Hiến Pháp 1992 [Personalities and Intellectuals Submitting the Petition on Constitutional Amendments] (2013). *Song Moi*, February 5, available from: www.baomoi.com/Nhan-sy-tri-thuc-gui-ban-kien-nghi-sua-doi-Hien-phap-1992/122/10343640.epi (accessed December 14, 2013).

Pham Hong Quang (2013). Bình luận về tính hợp lý và khả thi giao cho hệ thống tòa án nhân dân thực hiện nhiệm vụ bảo hiến [Comments on the Reasonableness and Feasibility in Conferring Upon the People's Courts System the the Constitutional Protection Mission]. *Cong Thong Tin Bo Tu Phap*, February 22, available at: http://moj.gov.vn/hienphap1992/News/Lists/giaidapthacmac/View_Detail.aspx?ItemID=5225 (accessed March 15, 2015).

Sidel, M. (2002). "Analytical Models For Understanding Constitutions And Constitutional Dialogue in Socialist Transitional States: Re-Interpreting Constitutional Dialogue In Vietnam." *Singapore Journal of International and Comparative Law*, 6(1): 42–89.

Sidel, M. (2008). *Law and Society in Vietnam: The Transition from Socialism in Comparative Perspective*. Cambridge, Cambridge University Press.

Sidel, M. (2009). *The Constitution of Vietnam: A Contextual Analysis*. Portland, OH, Hart Publishing.

Toàn Văn Dự Thảo [Amendments – All Drafts]. *Du Thao Online*, available at: http://duthaoonline.quochoi.vn/DuThao/Lists/DT_DUTHAO_NGHIQUYET/View_Detail.aspx?ItemID=32&TabIndex=1&LanID=53 (ccessed June 13, 2014).

Tổng Hợp Ý Kiến Khảo Sát Trên Trang Cùng Viết Hiến Pháp [Summary of Survey Opinions on Cung Viet Hien Phap Website] (2013). *Cung Viet Hien Phap*, March, available at: http://hienphap.files.wordpress.com/2013/03/te1bb95ng-he1bba3p-c3bd-kie1babfn.pdf (accessed December 13, 2013).

Tran Ngoc Duong (2013). Kiểm soát tính hợp hiến của các đạo luật và điều ước quốc tế mà QH đã phê chuẩn [Control the Constitutionality of Statutes and International Treaties that the National Assembly Has Ratified]. *Dai Bieu Nhan Dan*, May 30, available at: http://daibieunhandan.vn/default.aspx?tabid=76&NewsId=281910 (accessed March 15, 2015).

Trao Bản Kiến Nghị Sửa Đổi Hiến pháp [Submitting the Petition on Constitution Amendments] (2013). *BBC Vietnamese*, February 5, available at: www.bbc.co.uk/vietnamese/vietnam/2013/02/130205_constitution_intellectuals.shtml (accessed December 16, 2013).

Trao Kiến Nghị Dự Thảo Sửa Đổi Hiến Pháp [Submitting the Petition on Constitutional Amendments] (2013). *Anh Ba Sam*, February 4, available at: www.basam.info/hien-phap/1-trao-kien-nghi-du-thao-sua-doi-hien-phap/ (accessed December 14, 2013).

Truong Dac Linh (2013). Bàn về tài phán hiến pháp và thẩm quyền của cơ quan tài phán hiến pháp ở Việt Nam [Comment on Constitutional Adjudication and the Powers of a Constitutional Adjudication Organ in Vietnam]. *Cung Viet Hien Phap*, February 5, available at: http://hienphap.net/2013/02/05/ban-ve-tai-phan-hien-phap-va-tham-quyen-cua-co-quan-tai-phan-hien-phap-o-viet-nam-truong-dac-linh/ (accessed December 16, 2013).

Uy Ban Du Thao Sua Doi Hien Phap Nam 1992 [The 1992 Constitution Amendment Drafting Committee] (2013). Báo cáo: Thuyết minh về Dự thảo Sửa đổi Hiến pháp năm 1992 [Report: Description of the Draft Amendments to the 1992 Constitution]. January 5, available at: http://hagiang.gov.vn/province/Documents/B%C3%A1o%20c%C3%A1o%20thuy%E1%BA%BFt%20minh.pdf (accessed June 13, 2014).

Vietnam (1992). Constitution of the Socialist Republic of Vietnam as Amended in 2001, available at: www.vietnamlaws.com/freelaws/Constitution92(aa01).pdf (accessed March 15, 2015).

Vuving, A. (2010). "Vietnam: A Tale of Four Players." In *Southeast Asian Affairs 2010*, ed. D. Singh. Singapore, Institute of Southeast Asian Studies, pp. 367–391.

# 14 Constitutional politics and the Philippine Supreme Court

## The role of public support in mitigating politicization of the judiciary

*Imelda Deinla*

### Introduction

In this study, the central question being asked is: *Why would a politicized court actually rule against the policy preferences of the political actors?* This may appear to be an oxymoron, especially in the light of some views that constitutional politics may only do well in a democracy where courts are "independent." On the contrary, we make an assumption of a "political court," the Philippine Supreme Court, in view of its historical and institutional embeddedness in wider politics. This may also help us in re-examining our views about an "activist court" and under what conditions it assumes this behavior. But how does a court actually assert itself against the wishes or interests of political actors or render decisions that guard against affronts to constitutional norms and principles? Does the court make strategic calculations of the possible behavior of other political actors, the executive or the legislative, or does it rely on something else, including the wealth of prior jurisprudence?

This chapter proposes that the public also poses a significant constraint to court behavior, and which the court also depends on for its legitimacy. Public support and legitimacy – features that have received scant attention in the study of constitutional politics – are posited as key factors in determining the ability of the Court to render decisions contrary to policy preferences. Does the public provide an adequate anchor for the Court to pursue constitutional rule-making and thus advance the rule of law? Using the Philippine Supreme Court as a case study, this chapter seeks to illuminate these questions and to provide a framework to better understand and capture the multiplicity of drivers involved in constitutional politics and how the Court manages the interplay of various factors affecting constitutional rule-making in the context of a democratizing state like the Philippines.

## A framework of study: constitutional politics as political regulation

The core idea of constitutional politics has largely involved the centrality of the courts in resolving political disputes. This is of course for good reason, as courts' decisions have been thought to have increasingly impacted the policies and behavior of other non-judicial state actors, the executive and legislative (Sweet 2000). Thus, early studies of constitutional politics have been widely associated with "judicialization of politics" (Tate and Vallinder 1997), and courts' decisions have come to be known as "judicialized politics" (Tate 1994: 188–189; Shapiro 1994) or "judicialized legislation" or "judicialized governance" (Sweet 2000). In recent years, the courts' role in adjudicating mega-politics, or those issues that have tremendous political and constitutional significance, has increased dramatically (Hirschl 2008: 93–97).

The courts in Southeast Asia, in particular the emergence of Constitutional Courts and Supreme Courts with power of judicial review, have gained special attention due to their constitutional review authority as a consequence of democratization or the adoption of liberal market reforms starting in the 1980s (e.g., Peerenboom 2002; Ginsburg 2003; Dressel 2012). These studies have begun to locate courts and decision-making within the broader sociopolitical and historical contexts and the way courts interact with political actors. Current literature has however overlooked other factors that play a major role or influence in the courts, its formation, and its decision-making process. This involves looking at other actors driving democratization and constitution-making, namely the public.

To place the public in the discourse of constitutional politics one has to start scaling back the primacy of the courts in its role in resolving contentious politics. This chapter situates constitutional politics as only one among other forms of political regulation. In reality, regulation is carried out through different modes of non-legalistic and informal mechanisms whose normative basis may come from other social values or structures of authority (Braithwaite 2002). Major democratic milestones in the Philippines – and watersheds – have emerged from or are driven by extraordinary measures such as the direct exercise to change governments. Having a legal culture that is underpinned by elite domination (Hutchcroft 1998; Sidel 1999), political elites have an array of non-legal menus from which they can choose. Such were the people power events in 1986 and 2001 which, despite being triggered by critical events, were concluded by "backroom" agreements among critical players, factions of the elite that agreed to facilitate a regime or leadership change. The use of threats or violence against political opponents or mustering public support for mass protests, *coups d'etat*, negotiations, and mediation have been employed at various times in political dispute resolution (see Figure 14.1). The 1987 Constitution that provides extensive powers to the Philippine Supreme Court was in fact a product of these extraordinary non-legal exercises.

Conceiving constitutional politics within the broader spectrum of political regulation allows us to better describe the political environment where the court itself is being embedded, and its place in the societal framework of political

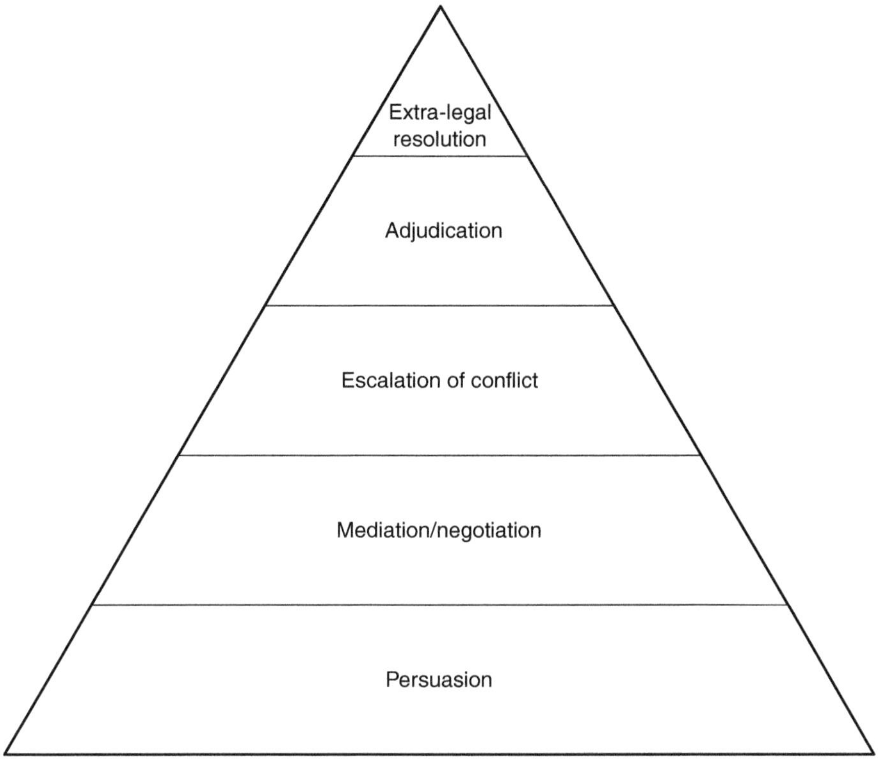


*Figure 14.1* Pyramid of political regulation in the Philippines.

regulation. This also enables us to see the courts as "political actors" on and off the bench (Hirschl 2008) that seek to enhance its legitimacy from the different political actors (Shapiro 1964; Tamanaha 2012). By recognizing the various mechanisms in political regulation, we can also imagine who the political actors are that court members interact with, including ideological considerations that it may take into account (see Kapiszewski 2011: 477–479), and the interlocking roles of the legal or "judicial elites" (Hirschl 2004) in the process of political dispute resolution.

In this chapter, the politicization of the court is not only seen as a function of the judicialization of politics, nor as a consequence of the courts' increasing decisions on political matters (Ferejohn 2002; Haynie 1998). The Philippine Supreme Court's politicization is inherent to the institution. This is by virtue of the Court's inherent vulnerability to the asymmetry of power relations in the wider social order manifested in the persistence of elite and personalistic politics and state institutions (Raquiza 2012; Haque 2007; Thompson 1995). The degree of being "politicized" however can vary across periods depending on the extent to which courts take "political considerations" rather than adherence to established legal norms and in their involvement in non-judicial modes of settling issues involving political elites – as well as their own ranks. A court may thus be judged as "politicized" through its actions within and outside of the bench (ex. *Macias* v. *Arula* 1982).

The Philippine Supreme Court was invested with its political character from the moment it was constituted as a colonial state institution in the American period and through current practices in the appointment of court members and personnel. Despite the appointment reform process in the 1987 Constitution which created the Judicial and Bar Council (JBC), Court members' appointment still rests with the executive by virtue of having the most numbers of executive-appointed members in the Council and the president having the ultimate decision to appoint. The recent case of *Jardeleza* v. *Sereno* (2014) meant that JBC's vetting function of candidates would be severely restricted by putting the onus of proof on the Council in their role of scrutinizing the nominees' qualifications rather than on applicants showing their fitness for the position.

The Court itself is part of or drawn from among the Philippine elites, the widely regarded "legal elites," who have actively taken part in key political (Figure 14.1) and business activities, even prior to their appointments to the bench. The Philippine legal profession enjoys considerable prestige as a profession. The members of the judiciary come from those ranks of lawyers and legal academics who at some point have acted as intermediaries among the elites, as activists, and as the repository of legal knowledge that maintains the legitimacy of the Philippine state as a whole (Desalay and Bryant 2010). Members of the legal profession have interlocking roles in political resolution as citizens, members of civil society, as lawyers or mediators employed by various political or business groups or interests, as politicians or government officials, as oppositionists or supporters of rebels or coup plotters. While the political elites are mostly coming from family dynasties or clans of the landed and business groups (Querubin 2010), lawyering has also become a pathway to political power itself and to important positions in state institutions (Desalay and Bryant 2010). The case of a questionable election of officers of the Integrated Bar of the Philippines (IBP) in 1989 highlights the highly political role of the legal profession and the underlying social connections at work behind it (Laserna 2009). The IBP is the nationwide association of lawyers in the Philippines whose representative sits as one of seven members on the JBC.

The political pressure being exerted on the Court thus comes from a variety of political actors, the executive, the ruling coalition, various elites out of power, and the public at large. Given the personality oriented, largely non-programmatic, and predatory nature of party politics in the Philippines, the fragmented nature of the elites (see Helmke and Rosenbluth 2009) does not provide sufficient insurance to respect court autonomy or that political guarantee from outgoing coalitions can be relied on (Ramseyer and Rasmusen 2003). With shifting allegiances and trends of alternating elites in power, collusion among the contending elites can happen to attack the court, as shown in the failed impeachment proceedings against Chief Justice Hilario Davide in 2001.

## The role of the public in constitutional politics

The role of the public in constitutional politics has been given scant attention (Barnum 1985: 662–664). Studies on the influence of the public – expressed through public opinion – in judicial decision-making are a recent exploration mostly in the United States (Barnum 1985), Latin America (Kapiszewski 2011), and much less so in authoritarian regimes (Moustafa 2003). In the Philippines where the public has played a major role in constitutional moments, few studies exist to analyse the influence of the public in judicial decision-making (Chan 2002; Molo 2002). This study recognizes the prominent role of the Philippine public as a potent political force in itself, organized or through spontaneous concerted actions, driving constitutional developments and functions as "judicial support structures" (Moustafa 2003: 897). The public was instrumental in the people's power revolt in 1986 that brought back formal democracy and also overwhelmingly ratified the 1987 Constitution. The Philippine civil society which has initiated mass movements and advocacies has a relatively broad base that primarily accounts for its power when exercised collectively. Civil society organizations cover various sectors – youth, women, academics, farmers, laborers, informal settlers, and professionals – who, either on their own or working with or pressuring other institutions such as the Church and media, can indeed exercise influence over any branch of government, including the judiciary. Issue-oriented political movements have come about assisted by factors that include a relatively free media, accessibility of new forms of communication technology, and a retained sense of a shared history of repressive rule.

The public as a "political pressure" is therefore an enabler and a constraint to court decision-making. *This study seeks to explain how the court gives more consideration to public opinion over other competing political pressures*. It is posited here that a court which is not or is less attentive to the public tends to be more vulnerable to political pressure and is most likely to suffer a political attack. A court which takes account of public opinion or expectations is more insulated from political attack. This kind of court also plays a greater veto role in national politics and is more likely to deliver judgments that are in accord with the democratic aspirations of the constitution.

Through its legal and extra-legal actions, individually or as a group, the judiciary may also influence the formation of public opinion and the kind of support it gets from the public. Legitimacy is understood here as not simply derived from the qualities vested by law or the constitution or what is termed "legal legitimacy"; it is also one that is attributed to the perception of effectiveness of outcomes or which corresponds to citizens' preferences (Scharpf 1997; Shapiro 1981). The Court's actions in and out of the courtroom shape public perception of its legitimacy and capacity that is being fed back to the judiciary and taken into account in its decision-making.

In showing the dynamics of public support and judicial decision-making, this study juxtaposes public opinion surveys of the three state institutions across the five presidential administrations since 1986 with how the Supreme Court has decided selected cases. Through this, it will demonstrate how the Court has steadily consolidated its power and maintained its legitimacy despite the persistence of political upheavals and its enmeshment in political controversies. Salient political developments in the five governments – Aquino 1 (Corazon Aquino, 1986–1992), Ramos (Fidel Ramos, 1992–1998), Estrada (Joseph Estrada, 1998–2001), Arroyo (Gloria Macapagal-Arroyo, 2001–2010), and Aquino 2 (Benigno Aquino III, 2010 to the present) – will be discussed to provide the context for public opinion and to show the quality of democratization across the various periods. An outcome of this exercise is to produce a typology of the Court in relation to broader political trends at least in the context of the Philippines.

There is, however, a constraint upon the methodology used in the research due to the paucity of available data. There are very few public opinion surveys on specific issues that were brought for adjudication – or at most three cases, where public opinion surveys were taken before the Court for decision. Thus, a much broader performance rating of the Court and its successive Chief Justices across the five administrations will instead be used to show the level of public support and legitimacy achieved by the Court and its leaders. The quarterly performance surveys by Social Weather Stations (SWS), an independent polling organization, are used in this chapter. These surveys have been conducted since 1988 and take on a multi-stage random sampling of at least 1,200 respondents nationally through face-to-face interviews.

## Democratization and the politics of judicial consolidation (1986–2015)

The transition to democracy provided the opportunity for renewal and capacity-building of a court long under the mantle of dictatorship. The Supreme Court, the apex of the Philippine judiciary, is regarded as one of the most powerful and highly respected courts in the world (Tate 1997; Tate and Haynie 1993). It suffered a major setback under the Martial Law regime from 1972 to 1986 when it was largely perceived as serving the interests of the ruling elites and legitimated the regime through decided cases (*Planas* v. *Commission on Elections*, 1973); *Javellana* v. *Executive Secretary*, 1973). Since the adoption of the 1987 Constitution which restored the separation of powers among the three major state institutions, the Supreme Court has steadily regained its power, influence, and prestige. In fact, the Court has been regarded as a "superjudiciary" by virtue of its expansive review powers under the charter (Agabin 2011).

The 1987 Constitution laid down the foundation for a post-authoritarian judiciary and marked the beginning of judicial consolidation. Constitutional innovation and institutional design were clearly fashioned against the resurgence of monopoly of state power. The power of judicial review, guarantees of individual freedoms and human rights, and strict stipulations on the exercise of emergency powers by endowing the Court to review the factual basis of an emergency proclamation, and broad powers to "determine grave abuse of discretion amounting to lack or excess of jurisdiction" on any part or instrumentality of the state (1987 Constitution Sec. 1 Article VIII) are meant to act as a check on "creeping" authoritarianism, or the progressive increase of government powers. This allowed the Court to override the doctrine of "political questions" that was often invoked by the Marcos Court to recuse itself from assuming jurisdiction over critical political cases.

Institutional designs that seek to insulate the Court from political influence or interference include the provision on fiscal autonomy, the power of appointment, and the discipline and administration of auxiliary and lower courts. The establishment of the Judicial and Bar Council, with the Chief Justice as *ex-officio* Chair, as a constitutional body ensures that Court appointments are not politicized and that the Court plays an indispensable role in the selection of judges. This was not so under the Marcos regime which exercised control of both the appointment and supervision of the lower courts.

The following sections discuss the process of democratization that has taken place side by side with the renewal and consolidation of the Philippine Supreme Court. What has been understudied in constitutional politics is that democratic transition is also a process of judicial consolidation and response. The judiciary consolidates itself as an institution through how it calculates and uses its power in response to wider political processes.

## Aquino 1: turbulence in the period of formal democracy and judicial legitimacy

Regaining the legitimacy of the Supreme Court was the legacy of the Aquino 1 government and the defining feature of the Court during this period. Amidst the uncertainty of democratic transition coupled with power struggles among competing elites, the Court legitimized the "revolutionary government" and thus defended the democratic process. As has been the case in other post-revolutionary regimes, the new government sought to legitimize its rule by reorganizing the Supreme Court. President Corazon Aquino asked the incumbent justices to resign and in their place appointed lawyers who opposed Marcos or law professors with no previous judicial experience. In a landmark ruling, the Supreme Court bestowed formal legitimacy on Aquino I (*Lawyers League* v. *Aquino*, 1986). This case recognized the "residual" power of the people to change government and that the legitimacy of the government is for the people to judge. During this period the Court played a stabilizing function by affirming the legitimacy of the government against both legal and extra-legal challenges, including at least seven coup attempts by military-elite factions who were either loyal to Marcos or who felt excluded in the transition to the new government (*Davide Fact Finding Report* 1990).

This period also heralded a more visible Court before the public. It was the newly appointed Chief Justice Claudio Teehankee, a hold-over from Marcos, who had shown steadfast independence from the regime, and who performed a widely televised oath-taking of the President on February 25, 1986. The case of

*Beltran and Soliven* v. *Makasiat* (1988), where the Court sustained a libel case brought by the President against a newspaper editor who wrote an article for allegedly "hiding under the bed" during a failed coup attempt in 1987, became a precedent in the use of live coverage of court proceedings. In this case, the accusation was taken seriously by the administration in light of destabilizing challenges to the government, and the President's testimony in Court was broadcast live on television. In many ways, this case showed how public trial could be used to generate public support. The political role of visual technology through the use of live coverage has since become a feature of impeachment trials in the Philippines. It marked the beginning when the Chief Justice and the entire judiciary were put in the spotlight and at the center of political conflict.

## Ramos: stability in democratic transition and judicial strengthening

As the first freely elected government after Marcos, the Ramos administration ushered in a period of relative stability and modest economic growth. By contrast to the turbulent years of Aquino I, a period of *rapprochement* among the elites was made possible through Ramos's politics of inclusive accommodation and political settlement with factional elites, and communist and Muslim insurgency groups (Rivera 2002). Ramos appointed an "experienced" Court that was drawn mostly from the judiciary and former government officials. While the appointment of justices who understood the dynamics of legislative and executive work strengthened the Court's capacity, this also became a pathway to play politics. The growing power of the Court in deciding cases of far-reaching importance provided a window of opportunity for both political and business elites to influence or put pressure on the justices. The structure of the Court contributed to this as cases are raffled to a division and then to a particular justice, the *ponente*, for drafting the decision. A practice developed where other justices deferred toward the findings of the *ponente* which sparked a growing perception that it facilitated judicial corruption (Haynie 2004).

Institutional consolidation of the Court was achieved under the Ramos presidency. This is an achievement that has remained unnoticed and less scrutinized, since most studies focus on the "power relationship" among state institutions. As discussed later, the Court began to present a more unified front than the political actors. During this period the Court handed down more unanimous decisions than a divided court. Despite the perception to the contrary, this trend has continued in subsequent administrations, with very few exceptions.

The Court under Ramos, which is generally regarded to have been satisfactory, was perceived to adopt a divergent stance between political and economic cases. It was during this period where the government was instituting economic liberalization policies that would break the monopoly of certain oligarchs. Having Court members that were recruited from the legislature and legal practitioners meant that they had ties other than the executive and economic progress offered opportunity for corruption. Both the government and the Court were in fact implicated in major corruption scandals (Coronel and Tordesillas 1998). The then vice president Estrada labeled judges "hoodlums in robes" given how they derailed the cases he was pursuing as chief of the Presidential Anti-Crime Commission ("Estrada and the Hoodlums in Robes" 2008). In the case of *PLDT* v. *NTC* (1995) a judge in the Supreme Court was suspected of having allowed a lawyer for a party to write the decision for the Court. In this case involving the issue of telecoms deregulation, the Court initially decided against the government measure. That decision was widely discussed in public as having been decided based on massive pay-offs to certain justices and resulted in the resignation of the justice who penned the decision.

The ruling coalition – backed by elites favoring economic liberalization and dismantling the oligarchs formed during the Marcos years – was also interested in extending the presidential term limits in order to continue the reform programs. The position of the Court toward political cases was, however, to resist attempts to change the constitutional balance of power. This coincided with strong public sentiment against constitutional amendment for fear of the recurrence of a dictatorship and perpetuating the terms of dynasties or clans. This was the period when, for the first time, the elites were trying to undo constitutional provisions on presidential term limits. The ruling coalition was collecting a million signatures to initiate a referendum to amend the constitution for that purpose. In a case which ensued called the PIRMA Case, the Supreme Court decided that the enabling law proposed by legislature to amend the constitution was inadequate in meeting the required standards for constitutional amendments (*Santiago* v. *COMELEC*, 1997).

## Estrada: democratic populism, elite fragmentation, and a strong judiciary

During the short-lived Estrada administration, the Supreme Court was seen as being independent in an environment of widespread corruption, cronyism, and administrative incompetence (Hedman 2001; Putzel 2001). A charismatic politician elected to the presidency by a wide margin, Estrada's time in office was marked by divisive elite contestation as the administration became beholden to rent-seeking politicians. It also came under criticism from supporters of the previous administration, including the Catholic Church hierarchy and civil society organizations who decried Estrada's populism. Estrada himself was perceived to be close to "Chinese" businessmen or businessmen involved in illegal activities. It was his close ties to "dubious" business associates that precipitated events leading to his impeachment as president and subsequently, his conviction for the crime of plunder (Rodis 2013; *People of the Philippines* v. *Estrada*, 2007).

During this period the Court gained more prominence by playing an important role in national politics – and where it behaved autonomously from the appointing power. First, Chief Justice Hilario Davide, an appointee of President Estrada, acted as the presiding officer in the trial of the sitting president, a first in the history of the country, in December 2000. Second, the Court legitimized the Arroyo government propelled to power by a second "people power revolt" which ousted Estrada on January 20, 2001. That event was triggered by legal and extra-legal delaying tactics employed by Estrada and his allies in the impeachment trial that was televised live on television and radio. Led by a coalition from organized civil society groups, church leaders, left-wing organizations, and the middle class, a series of mass demonstrations were held at the EDSA Shrine. With members of Estrada's cabinet resigning from their posts and military leadership withdrawing their support to the president, Chief Justice Davide swore the new President into office at noon on the fourth day of mass gatherings. It was the Court which broke the impasse in the negotiations between the Estrada and Arroyo camps, though this decision was viewed by some as patently "biased" in favor of the new Arroyo administration.

The Court justified the ouster of Estrada based on the maxim, *salus populi est suprema lex* (the voice of the people is the supreme law) (SC *En Banc* Resolution, January 20, 2001) which further affirmed direct democracy. Subsequently, the Court issued a ruling (*Estrada* v. *Arroyo*, 2001) justifying Arroyo's presidency which could be argued as being bereft of legal precedent but driven by public and elite pressure. In this case, the Court made a distinction between the first and second people power "revolts"; the former was an act of extra-constitutional powers to the people, while the latter was a legal question involving the exercise of the people's freedom of expression and assembly to petition redress of grievances and thus only involved the office of the presidency. A reading of the case would show, however, that the Court justified its findings on questions of facts based on certain "antecedent" evidence or events prior to Estrada's departure from the presidential palace (Putzel 2001). In this instance, the public were mostly the middle class and professional groups, as Estrada continued to enjoy the support from the Manila urban poor and "displaced" elites from the Marcos regime.

The Estrada administration marked a turning point for the Supreme Court, as it became the focal point for contending elites and civil society. This was a period characterized by "legal and extra-legal experimentation" by various political forces to test the efficacy of constitutional provisions on checks and balances and the accountability of state officials, in cases such as *Bayan* et al. v *Executive Secretary* (2000) and *Estrada* v. *Desierto* (2001). However, the Court's ever-increasing power was seen by the elites as both an opportunity and a threat, and thus motivated initiatives to either discredit or co-opt it. During this time, the opposing political camps appealed to the public for support while the Court remained silent. It was the institution of the Court that would remain united in the face of political upheaval. Thus, it is not surprising that an open confrontation between the Lower House, composed of locally elected politicians, and the judiciary would emerge during the Arroyo government, a condition that would subsequently re-emerge via the executive–judicial confrontation in the current Aquino 2 government.

## Arroyo: democratic deficit and leadership crisis

The Arroyo government was brought about by an extra-constitutional act of people power, known as *EDSA Dos*, which also marked a regression to disruptive elite contestation and collusion, and acts that are much more typical of authoritarian rule. It was during Arroyo's term that Freedom House downgraded the Philippines' democracy status from "free" to "partly free" (Freedom House 2015). The breakdown of the fragile "rainbow coalition" that supported Arroyo's takeover of power from Estrada led the administration to turn to the military and conservative elite factions for support. During her presidency, Arroyo had to face challenges to her power. These were the failed EDSA *Tres* protest in April 2001 carried out by Estrada's mainly mass supporters in Manila, and several instances of mass demonstrations and coup attempts calling on Arroyo to step down or forcibly removing her from power. In addition, the opposition in the Lower House filed impeachment complaints against her that were thwarted by the majority. Politically, the failures of these extra-constitutional movements could be ascribed both to elite fragmentation and civil society divisions. The Supreme Court however should be credited for averting a grave constitutional crisis that would have led the country into more political instability.

The two failed impeachment trials against Chief Justice Hilario Davide, the first-ever attempt at impeaching a Chief Justice, were emblematic of the politics during this period and also severely affected the Court's legitimacy for the first time since 1986. This Court was seen as "highly politicized" and was known as the Arroyo Court (Vitug 2013). These episodes witnessed the tacit collusion among the "competing" elites as they fought for political survival or to protect the economic interests of Marcos's cronies. The proponent of the first impeachment complaint was former President Estrada, but it was dismissed by the House Committee on October 22, 2003. The second impeachment complaint was shrouded in mystery because it was initiated by legislators from the Nationalist Peoples' Coalition (NPC), a political party headed by businessman Eduardo Cojuangco Cojuangco, a known Marcos crony and previous ally of Estrada who later aligned himself with Arroyo's "Sunrise Coalition."

Chief Justice Davide, who was highly regarded for his competence and integrity (Social Weather Stations 2001), was an obvious target of elite collusion. This was due to a number of decisions the Court handed down in the early years of the Arroyo government that threatened crony interests, certain factions of the oligarchs, and those who resisted public accountability. These cases included rulings that affirmed the legitimacy of the Arroyo government (*Estrada* v. *Arroyo*, 2001; *Estrada* v. *Desierto*, 2001), the reopening of the murder case against Senator Panfilo Lacson (*People of the Philippine* v. *Lacson*, 2003), the declaration of coco levy funds (claimed by Cojuangco) as "public funds" (*PCGG* v. *Ballares* et al., 2001), the return of \$683 million from Marcos's Swiss bank account to the government (*People of the Philippines* v. *Sandiganbayan, Marcos*, 2003), and affirming the conviction of Estrada for plunder (*Ejercito* v. *Sandiganbayan*, 2006). The Arroyo government also faced a string of corruption exposés, in particular the Jose Pidal account, a PHP500 million account allegedly belonging to Arroyo's husband, and Cojuangco's threat to leave the coalition and launch his own campaign for the presidency in 2004.

A looming constitutional crisis between the legislative and judiciary that arose as a result of the Supreme Court's ruling on the second impeachment case (*Francisco* v. *House of Representatives*, 2003) was averted when the Lower House deferred to the Court's decision. At that time, the Court had huge support from civil society and from former President Cory Aquino, which saw the impeachment move more as an assault against democracy and the rule of law. The failed Davide impeachments, however, led to a more compromised judiciary. The impeachment was not only a personal assault on the chief justice but on the institution itself and sent a warning signal to the justices. Subsequently, public support for the Supreme Court declined. The legislature's submission to the Court decision on the second impeachment seems to have been achieved through a compromise settlement worked out by former President Arroyo herself ("Arroyo Seeks Impeachment Solution" 2003). It was not clear what the details of this settlement were, but it was apparent that the Supreme Court became increasingly perceived as biased toward the executive, particularly after the retirement of Davide and the appointment of new justices. This may not be an entirely incorrect assessment, given that almost all corruption and impropriety cases against Arroyo or her allies were decided in her favor.

The Court however performed differently – and consistently – in key constitutional cases that would have affected constitutional boundaries of power and the exercise of rights. In these cases, the Court clearly ruled against the executive policy preferences that would have eroded constitutional democracy. These generated mass protests, short of people power, that reminded the Court of its constitutional duty. These cases include the invalidation of the state of emergency following a failed *coup d'état* (*David* v. *Arroyo*, 2006), the promulgation of the rules on the writ of *amparo* and writ of *habeas data* to combat the increase in extra-judicial killings and enforced disappearances (A.M. No. 07-9-12 2007), the illegality of popular initiatives that would amend the constitution to change the form of government (*Lambino* v. *COMELEC*, 2006), the striking down of the "calibrated pre-emptive response" (CPR) policy directed at pre-empting the holding of anti-government rallies (*Bayan* v. *Ermita*, 2006), and partly invalidating grants of executive privilege or exemption from congressional investigations (*Senate* v. *Ermita*, 2006).

The case of *North Cotabato* v. *RP Peace Panel* (2008) was significant, as the Court unanimously invalidated the Memorandum of Agreement on Ancestral Domain (MOA-AD) negotiated by the government with the Moro Islamic Liberation Front in 2008. There was a huge public outcry – which included local and national elites in Mindanao and Manila – against the establishment of the Bangsamoro Juridical Entity. In a Pulse Asia survey from October 14–27, 2008, disagreement by the public for the creation of a much larger independent territory for the Bangsamoro region was 46 percent, with only 16 percent of the public agreeing and the remaining 33 percent undecided.

## Aquino 2: policy of good governance and judicial re-consolidation

The current administration of President Benigno Aquino, son of Corazon Aquino, was elected on a platform to fight corruption and greater accountability for government officials. The policy of good governance is being pursued as a means to advance economic development. The "inherited" Court from Arroyo was seen as an obstruction to the pursuit of this policy. The then Chief Justice Renato Corona was viewed as a "midnight appointee" by Arroyo and the Court was "packed" with Arroyo appointees. The executive assault on the judiciary was borne out of the assessment that it would not be a "friendly" court. The actuations of the early Court in Aquino 2 show that ruling against policy preferences can be given, not only by an activist or autonomous court, but by one that is highly politicized.

A divided "politicized" judiciary may also give way to an autonomous court. The early decisions of the Court in Aquino may be argued to be "politicized" against the administration. These cases include such decisions as the unconstitutionality of the Truth Commission to conduct a fact-finding investigation of large -scale reports of corruption in the previous administration (*Biraogo* v. *The Philippine Truth Commission*, 2010), restraining the implementation of Executive Order No. 2 that would reverse the appointments made by Arroyo before the first day of the constitutional ban on appointments prior to the 2010 presidential elections, called the "midnight appointments" (*General* v. *Arroyo* et al., 2011), and suspension of impeachment proceedings against former Ombudsman Merceditas Gutierrez, an Arroyo appointee who was alleged to have wavered in investigating corruption cases involving Arroyo and her cohorts (*En Banc Status Quo Ante* Order, September 14, 2010). In 2011, the Supreme Court also issued restraining orders allowing Arroyo and her husband to travel out of the country while plunder charges against them were being heard. In response to unfavorable decisions, President Aquino remarked that these highly disadvantageous and biased cases were acts of *pang-aapi* (harassment) of the executive by the judiciary (Vitug 2012).

The impeachment of Chief Justice Corona on December 12, 2011 highlights the power of a strong and popular executive that is nonetheless contingent upon public support. Public support for the impeachment was overwhelming but did not extend to a complete loss of support for the entire institution of the judiciary, assisted by the fact that the rest of the judiciary remained "silent." The Court's – and that of Justice Corona's performance ratings – suffered, despite the efforts of the Office of Court Administrator to issue public statements supporting the embattled Chief Justice (Santos 2012). This was the first time that an administrative arm of the Court was used in a politically charged concern. The appointment of Justice Lourdes Sereno in 2012 as Chief Justice also served to break the hold of Arroyo justices.

The impeachment, though a low point for the Court, was a turning point to recuperate from this legitimacy crisis. After the impeachment the Aquino 2

Court did not hold back but seized the opportunity to shore up its institutional support. Four months after the impeachment proceedings, on April 24, 2012, the Supreme Court voted 8 to 6 to expropriate Hacienda Luisita, a 4,915-hectare estate owned by President Aquino's family (*Hacienda Luisita* v. *PARC*, 2012). Corona's removal from office actually assisted the Court in getting better performance ratings, as shown by the upward movement of its net satisfaction ratings from June 2012 (Figure 14.2). The subsequent decision of the Court in *Belgica* v. *Executive Secretary* (2013) indicates the Court's resolve to regain its legitimacy and credibility. In this case, the Court declared unconstitutional the pork barrel arrangement that was a perennial source of patronage and corruption among politicians. The Supreme Court's ruling in this case reversed three of its earlier rulings (*Philconsa* v. *Enriquez*, 1994, *Sarmiento* v. *Treasurer*, 2001, *LAMP* v. *Budget Secretary*, 2012), sustaining the validity of the pork barrel system. A public opinion survey taken by Pulse Asia in September 2013 showed that 45 percent of respondents supported the repeal of a key component of the system, the Priority Development Assistance Fund (Pulse Asia 2013). This coincided with the massive protests held in Manila and other parts of the country calling for the abolition of the pork barrel system ("Pork Barrel Protest Grips the Philippines" 2013).

The continued verbal attack against the Court by the President after this ruling – including pronouncements that he would run for a second term if only to counter the Court's "over-reach," has not affected the standing of the Court before the public, as shown by its consistent performance ratings. The fact that the President backed down from his overtures for a second term when public opinion was not supportive (Dizon 2014) indicates that he was unable to muster strong public opinion against the Court. The Court is in fact in a better position in this government, which recently lost a huge part of public trust because of the Mamasapano incident that also triggered calls for the President to resign (Pulse Asia Research 2015). In this incident, the President is accused of being responsible for the military operations in Mindanao which resulted in the death of 44 policemen (Rappler.com 2015).

The case of *Imbong* v. *Ochoa* (2014) involving the passage of the Reproductive Health Law, which was upheld in most part by the Supreme Court in April 2014, is another example of strong public opinion that coincides with the government's preference. National surveys (Social Weather Stations 2013, Pulse Asia 2013) revealed that more than 60 percent of respondents expressed approval for the law. Despite a strong lobby by the Catholic Church, a powerful sector of the public, and "pro-life" advocates against its passage, the Court sustained most parts of the legislation but was also careful to sustain the more punitive aspects of the law.

## Public opinion surveys and public support for the Court

Longitudinal public opinion surveys taken by the Philippine Social Weather Stations from November 1990 to December 2014 reveal a relatively stable confidence rating by the public for the Supreme Court since the democratic transition. In these surveys, respondents were asked a simple question on whether they were satisfied or not with the performance of each major state institution: the Supreme Court, the Cabinet (executive), the Senate (upper legislature), and Congress (lower legislature). The aggregate of the graph shown in Figure 14.2 shows that the Court enjoyed higher satisfaction ratings relative to the executive and became more pronounced when the Court decided cases that were highly supported by the public, such as the PIRMA case in Ramos, the EDSA Dos case in Arroyo, and the pork barrel case in Aquino 2. One exception was in 2011 during the successful impeachment of Chief Justice Corona.

By comparison to both houses of the legislature, the Court's ratings were generally lower than the Senate and only on par with Congress. The Senate is always perceived to be independent from the Executive, particularly during the Estrada and Arroyo governments (Figures 14.2 and 14.3). However, starting in September 2013 the Court edged out the Senate as the most appreciated institution with a rating of +41 as against the Senate's +36 rating, as the Court recovered from its lowest point during impeachment and appears to have maintained its position as the most appreciated state institution in the Philippines since then. It may be argued that the Court's decision in November 2013 to declare the pork barrel arrangement unconstitutional has been favorably received by the public. The Court enjoyed the highest public support at times when the Court ruled on major constitutional issues (Estrada ouster) or was about to

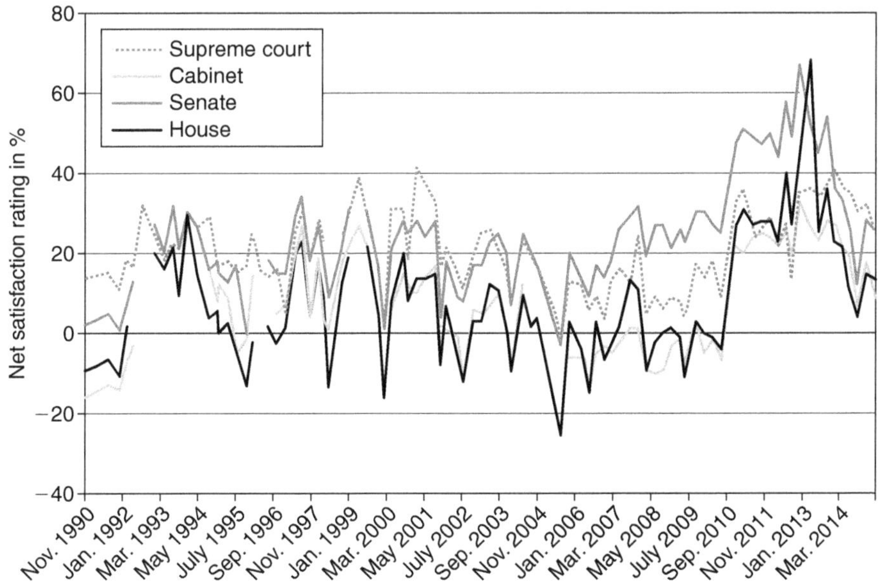


*Figure 14.2* Public satisfaction with key government institutions

Notes

Net ratings = % satisfied – % dissatisfied.

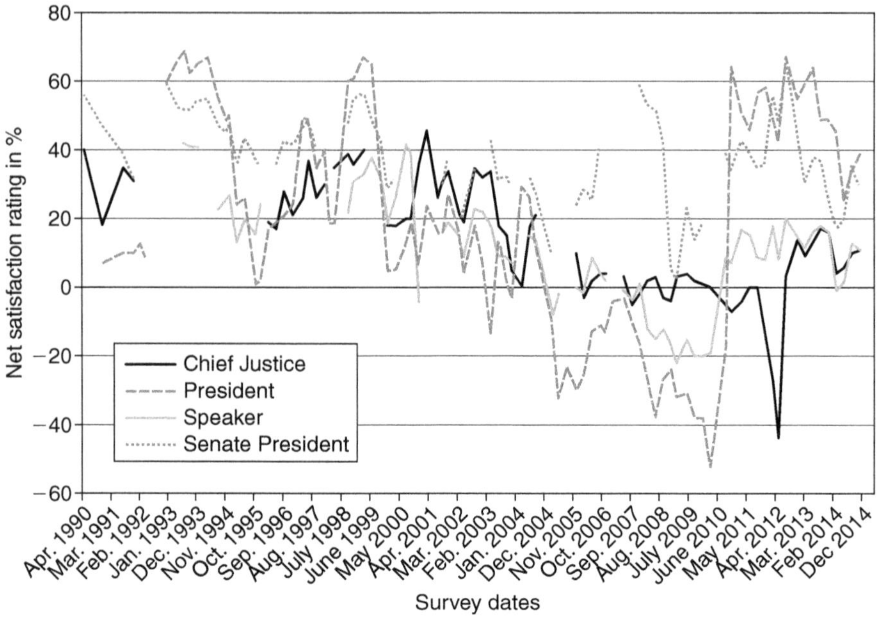


*Figure 14.3* Public satisfaction with key government officials.

Notes
Net ratings = % satisfied – % dissatisfied.

decide on a significant constitutional case (pork barrel case). The Court received its lowest performance rating when it was perceived to have close affinity with the Executive (the Arroyo Court; see Figures 14.2 and 14.3) or highly corrupt (Ramos in 1997). A negative rating, equivalent to poor net satisfaction, was received by the Court coinciding with the retirement from office of Chief Justice Hilario Davide in May 2005. However, Davide had always been perceived as independent and enjoyed a high credibility reputation. From March 2006 to March 2010, the Court received more single-digit net satisfaction ratings (equivalent to "neutral") than in any other administration, as the Court was perceived to be supportive of an increasingly legitimacy-challenged president, namely Gloria Macapagal Arroyo. On public perception of the leaders, the Chief Justice scored a lower rating than others, as media attention or coverage mostly affect the three top officials. An exception was during the early Davide period in Arroyo. However despite these lower ratings, the Chief Justice has fewer negative fluctuations except during the Corona impeachment, which means that they are more insulated from negative public support.

## A typology of judicial behavior of the Philippine Supreme Court

Based on the above discussion, we can establish a relationship between the type of court and the democratization trends in the five administrations and how court legitimacy has been established or affected during these periods. The findings suggest that a better quality of democracy and a more stable political environment generates strong capacity and legitimacy for the Supreme Court. An unstable democratic regime, but with the presence of a vibrant mass movement or active civil society, also generates a responsive judiciary. On the other hand, an unstable regime that veers toward authoritarianism tends to stifle judicial capacity and thus generates institutional instability in the Court and also weak support from the public. At least in the Philippine context, we may say that an "active public" has become a staple of democratization even during episodes of pressures on democratization, such as threats of military-led *coups d'état*, traditional elite-induced power grabs, or the government's use of excessive restraint, violence, and intimidation to stifle opposition against the government. Table 14.1 summarizes the trends in democratization and the corresponding perception of the Court's legitimacy.

To summarize, it is possible to draw a correlation between public support and trends in democratization and the consequent behavior of the Court. The typology shown in Table 14.1 presents a sketch of Court behavior when public support and the quality of democratic practice interact with each other. It also shows that the dynamics of constitutional practices are fashioned within and outside state institutions. This chapter shows how public support enables the Court to assert its judicial power and its role in sustaining or re-creating constitutional democracy. Through this study, we have shown that judicial activism by the Supreme Court is impelled by strong public support. At least in the Philippine context, judicial assertiveness has its foundation in the democratic constitution and in the people who empowered it.

Table 14.1 shows how strong public support trumps a high degree of political pressure. A strong public is engendered in an environment of a higher quality of democracy. By better democracy we mean, in the context of a democratizing polity like the Philippines, a more stable ruling coalition with generally high levels of tolerance for public expression or dissent, when public information may be freely accessed, and where political parties – despite their fragmented nature – are less predatory or clientelistic. While Philippines-style democracy may not be comparable in all respects to more stable Western democracies, that these

*Table 14.1* Typology of judicial behavior of the Philippine Supreme Court

| | | | |
|---|---|---|---|
| Public support | H | Activist Court | Autonomous Court |
| | L | Reactive Court | Assertive Court |
| | | L | H |
| | | Democratic quality | |

qualities exist – and that the Supreme Court could from time to time assert is authority and see its decisions respected by other political actors – show that democracy is not all a fiction in the Philippines (see Dressel 2011).

We may conclude that the Supreme Court under various governments shows more tendencies in one category over the other. However, the Court is generally activist or assertive – and, regardless of the quality of democratization, when the Court's own authority is threatened, when there is danger that state authorities will be exceeded, and when there are threats to the exercise of fundamental freedoms. It should be noted that these issues also receive higher awareness and support from the public. An autonomous Court is one that can use its judicial power effectively and with more confidence in important political issues. The Courts in Ramos and Aquino 2 – both periods of relative political stability and better economic performance – exhibit this behavior. Autonomy, however, does not mean a complete absence of political influence as when Court members, due to lack of strong accountability mechanisms, become vulnerable to corruption. This was exhibited in Ramos where there was high public support but the Court was not held accountable. Lower quality of democratization with a low level of public support may generate a reactive Court. With a low level of public oversight, the Court becomes more attuned to opportunistic activities. This is a Court that operates in a highly constrained political environment with little legitimacy; it generally favors government actions or policies but also takes some counter-majoritarian decisions in extremely critical issues, such as the maintenance of constitutional democracy. The Arroyo Court, a period of democracy deficit, displays this kind of behavior.

Higher quality democratization but a low level of public support generates a Court that tries to regain credibility by taking decisions that would bolster its support. This is the assertive Court emerging from the impeachment of the Chief Justice in Aquino 2 and has since regained higher levels of public support. However, internal conflicts in the Court such as the Jardeleza affair could open it to greater political intervention that could as a consequence erode this gain. A low quality of democratization but a high level of public support generates an activist Court, one that uses high public support to assert its power even in the face of intense political pressure or chaos. This is the Court in the Estrada period which underwent a democratic malaise. The Court, and even the public, was able to be assertive during these times due to the breakdown of political controls, which allowed it space for maneuver through the difficult political environment.

## Conclusion

That Philippines democracy withstands the uncertainties of transition is owed in large part to the role of the Philippine Supreme Court in policing constitutional boundaries in the exercise of state power and the protection of individual rights. The post-authoritarian period from 1986 saw the competing influence of political elites and the public that impacted the Court's capacity to safeguard constitutional democracy and steer the country toward observance of the rule of law. The Court is itself embedded in a fluid constellation of elite power and is a politicized Court, both on and off the bench. A strong public – and its continuing support for the Court as guardian of constitutional democracy – has enabled the Court to be attentive to its legal constraints and to assert its judicial review powers in the face of pressure and threats to its members and to the institution of the Court. The continuing trust that the public places in the Court – as a mechanism to resolve important political disputes – means that unconstitutional or extra-constitutional measures are losing their appeal among key political actors – and the greater public – in resolving contentious political issues. This is shown in the public's attitude toward the formation of a "transition council" to force the resignation of incumbent President Aquino and take the reins of state authority which was one of deep mistrust. The Court has certainly gained greater legitimacy with increased public support that it can in turn deploy to assert its authority as the ultimate and most authoritative arbiter of political disputes. Public opinion however is feeble and can be manipulated to suit certain political agenda. Just as it has to resist elite capture, the Court also needs to guard itself against unreasoned public opinion. To further enhance its legitimacy and capacity, the Court needs to be mindful of how it generates public support through its actions in and out of the courtroom.

## References


1987 Philippine Constitution at www.gov.ph/constitutions/the-1987-constitution-of-the-republic-of-the-philippines/ (accessed March 20, 2015).

Agabin, P. (2011). *Mestizo: The Story of the Philippine Legal System*. University of the Philippines College of Law, Quezon City.

*Andres Sarmiento* et al. v. *Treasurer of the Philippines* et al., G.R. No. 125680 and 126313 (2001), available at: www.chanrobles.com/scresolutions/resolutions/2001/september/125680.php (accessed October 11, 2014).

"Aquino: No More Second Term" (2014). *Philippine Daily Inquirer*, October 29, available at: http://newsinfo.inquirer.net/647467/aquino-no-more-2nd-term (accessed February 20, 2015).

Arjomand, S.A. (2003). "Law, Political Reconstruction and Constitutional Politics." *International Sociology*, 18(1): 7–32.

"Arroyo Seeks Impeachment Solution" (2003). CNN, October 27, 2003, available at: http://edition.cnn.com/2003/WORLD/asiapcf/southeast/10/27/judge.impeachment.reut/ (accessed March 20, 2015).

*Articles of Impeachment against Chief Justice Renato C. Corona* (2011). Available at: www.gov.ph/2011/12/12/articles-of-impeachment-against-chief-justice-renato-c-corona-december-12-2011/ (accessed February 20, 2015).

Barnum, D.G. (1985). "The Supreme Court and Public Opinion: Judicial Decision Making in the Post-New Deal Period." *Journal of Politics*, 47(2): 652–666.

*BAYAN* et al. v. *Eduardo Ermita* et al., G.R. Nos 169838, 169848, 169881 (2006). Available at: at www.lawphil.net/judjuris/juri2006/apr2006/gr_169838_2006.html (accessed November 4, 2014).

*BAYAN* et al. v. *Executive Secretary* et al., G.R. Nos 138570, 138572, 138587, 138680, 138698 (2000). Available at: www.lawphil.net/judjuris/juri2000/oct2000/gr_138570_2000.html (accessed November 4, 2014).

*Belgica* et al. v. *Executive Secretary* et al., G.R. No. 208566 (2013). Available at: http://sc.judiciary.gov.ph/pdf/web/viewer.html?file=/jurisprudence/2013/november2013/208566.pdf (accessed February 23, 2015).

*Biraogo* v. *The Philippine Truth Commission*, G.R. No. 192935 (2010). Available at: http://sc.judiciary.gov.ph/jurisprudence/2010/december2010/192935.htm (accessed November 4, 2014).

Braithwaite, J. (2002). *Restorative Justice and Responsive Regulation*. New York, Oxford University Press.

Braithwaite, J. and Ayres, I. (1992). *Responsive Regulation: Transcending the Deregulation Debate*. New York, Oxford University Press.

Chan, G.L. (2002). "Lobbying the Judiciary: Public Opinion and Judicial Independence." *Philippine Law Journal*, 77(1): 73–95.

*Chavez* v. *Public Estates Authority* et al., G.R. No. 133250 (2003). Available at: http://sc.judiciary.gov.ph/jurisprudence/2003/nov2003/133250.htm (accessed November 10, 2014).

"CJ Sereno Manipulated JBC to Keep Jardeleza Off List – Brion" (2014). GMA News, September 5, available at: www.gmanetwork.com/news/story/377902/news/nation/cj-sereno-manipulated-jbc-to-keep-jardeleza-off-list-brion (accessed February 10, 2015).

*Code of Judicial Conduct* (2004). A.M. No. 03-05-01-SC, April 27, available at: www.sc.judiciary.gov.ph.

Coronel, S. and Tordesillas, E. (1998). "The Grandmother of all Scams," March 18–20, available at: http://pcij.org/stories/1998/amari.html (accessed January 12, 2015).

*David* v. *Arroyo*, G.R. No. 171396 (2006). Available at: http://sc.judiciary.gov.ph/jurisprudence/2006/may2006/G.R.%20No.%20171396.htm (accessed November 20, 2014).

*Davide Fact-Finding Commission Report* (1990). Available at: www.gov.ph/1990/10/03/the-final-report-of-the-fact-finding-commission-october-1990/ (accessed January 10, 2015).

*De Castro* v. *Judicial Bar Council* G.R. No. 191002 (2010). Available at: http://sc.judiciary.gov.ph/jurisprudence/2010/march2010/191002.htm (accessed November 10, 2014).

Desalay, Y. and Bryant, G. (2010). *Asian Legal Revivals: Lawyers in the Shadow of Empire*. Chicago, IL, University of Chicago Press.

Dizon, M. (2014). "Aquino: No more second term." Inquirer.net, October 29, available at: http://newsinfo.inquirer.net/647467/aquino-no-more-2nd-term.

Dressel, B. (2011). "The Philippines: How Much Real Democracy?". *International Political Science Review*, 32(5): 529–545.

Dressel, B. (2012). *The Judicialization of Politics in Asia*. New York, Routledge.

*Ernesto Francisco* et al. v. *House of Representatives* et al., G.R. Nos 160261–63, G.R. Nos. 160277, 160292, etc. (2003). Available at: http://sc.judiciary.gov.ph/juris prudence/2003/nov2003/160261.htm (accessed January 12, 2015).

"Estrada and the Hoodlums in Robes" (2008). GMA News, September 11, available at: www.gmanetwork.com/news/story/119704/news/estrada-and-the-hoodlums-in-robes (accessed September 23, 2014).

*Estrada* v. *Sandiganbayan*, G.R. No. 148560 (2001). Available at: http://sc.judiciary.gov.ph/jurisprudence/2001/nov2001/148560.htm (accessed November 10, 2014).

*Estrada* v. *Sandiganbayan*, G.R. Nos 157294–157295 (2006). Available at: www.lawphil.net/judjuris/juri2006/nov2006/gr_157294_2006.html (accessed November 10, 2014).

*Estrada* v. *Arroyo*, G.R. No. 146738 (2001). Available at: http://sc.judiciary.gov.ph/jurisprudence/2001/mar2001/146710_15.htm (accessed March 15, 2015).

Ferejohn, J. (2002). "Judicializing Politics, Politicizing Law." *Law and Contemporary Problems*, 65(3): 41–68.

*Francis H. Jardeleza* v. *Chief Justice Maria Lourdes P.A. Sereno*, G.R. No. 213181 (2015). Available at: http://sc.judiciary.gov.ph/pdf/web/viewer.html?file=/jurisprudence/resolutions/2015/01/213181.pdf (accessed February 19, 2015).

*Francisco* v. *House of Representatives*, G.R. No. 160261 (2003). Available at: http://sc.judiciary.gov.ph/jurisprudence/2003/nov2003/160261.htm (accessed February 10, 2015).

Freedom House (2015). *Freedom in the World Report 2004*, available at: www.freedom-house.org/report/freedom-press/freedom-press-2004 (accessed March 15, 2015).

"Friend or Foe?" (2014). Asian Journal, August 23, available at: http://asianjournal.com/editorial/friend-or-foe/ (accessed January 15, 2015).

Ginsburg, T. (2003). *Judicial Review in New Democracies: Constitutional Courts in Asian Cases*. New York, Cambridge University Press.

*Hacienda Luisita* v. *Presidential Agrarian Reform Council*, G.R. No. 171101 (2012). Available at: http://sc.judiciary.gov.ph/jurisprudence/2012/april2012/171101.htm.

Haque, M.S. (2007). "Theory and Practice of Public Administration in Southeast Asia: Traditions, Directions and Impacts." *International Journal of Public Administration*, 30(12–14): 1297–1326.

Haynie, S. (1998). "Paradise Lost: Politicization of the Philippine Supreme Court in the Post-Marcos Era." *Asian Studies Review*, 22(4): 459–473.

Haynie, S. (2004). "Structure and Context of Judicial Institutions in Democratizing Countries: The Philippines and South Africa." *Arellano Law and Policy Review*, 5(2): 36–38.

Hedman, E. (2001). "The Spectre of Populism in Philippine Politics and Society: Artista, Masa, Eraption!" *South East Asia Research*, 9(1): 5–54.

Helmke, G. and Rosenbluth, F. (2009). "Regimes and the Rule of Law: Judicial Independence in Comparative Perspective." *Annual Review of Political Science*, 11: 345–366.

Hirschl, R. (2004). "The Political Origins of the New Constitutionalism." *Indiana Journal of Global Legal Studies*, 11(1): 71–108.

Hirschl, R. (2008). "The Judicialization of Mega-politics and the Rise of the Political Courts." *Annual Review of Political Science*, 11: 93–118.

Hutchcroft, P. (1998). *Booty Capitalism: The Politics of Banking in the Philippines*. New York, Cornell University Press.

*Imbong* et al. v. *Paquito Ochoa* et al., G.R. Nos 201489, 204934 (2014). Available at: http://sc.judiciary.gov.ph/pdf/web/viewer.html?file=/jurisprudence/2014/april2014/204819.pdf (accessed March 10, 2015).

*In the Matter of the Inquiry into the 1989 Elections of the Integrated Bar of the Philippines*, A.M. No. 491 (1989). Available at: www.lawphil.net/judjuris/juri1989/oct1989/am_491_1989.html (accessed February 20, 2015).

"Jardeleza's SC Entry and Sereno's Eroding Clout" (2014). August 20, available at: www.rappler.com/newsbreak/66794-jardeleza-sc-sereno-clout (accessed March 20, 2015).

*Javellana* v. *Executive Secretary*, G.R. No. L-13142 (1973). 50 SCRA 30.

*Joseph Estrada* v. *Gloria Macapagal-Arroyo, Joseph Estrada* v. *Aniano Desierto*, G.R. Nos 146738, 146710–146715 (2001). Available at: http://sc.judiciary.gov.ph/jurisprudence/2001/mar2001/146710_15.htm (accessed October 10, 2014).

Kapiszewski, D. (2011). "Tactical Balancing: High Court Decision Making on Politically Crucial Cases." *Law and Society Review*, 45(2): 471–506.

Laserna, M. (2009). *IBP Rotation Role*, May 8, available at: http://attylaserna.blogspot.com.au/2009/05/ibp-rotation-rule.html (accessed February 12, 2015).

*Lawyers against Monopoly and Poverty (LAMP)* v. *the Secretary of Budget and Management* et al., G.R. No. 164987 (2012). Available at: http://sc.judiciary.gov.ph/jurisprudence/2012/april2012/164987.htm (accessed March 10, 2015).

*Lawyers League for a Better Philippines* v. *Aquino*, G.R. Nos 73748–22 (1986). Available at: https://archive.is/n6RPR (accessed March 20, 2015).

*Luis Beltran* v. *Ramon Makasiar* et al., G.R. Nos. 82827, 83979, 82585 (1988). Available at: www.lawphil.net/judjuris/juri1988/nov1988/gr_82585_1988.html (accessed October 10, 2014).

Macairan, E. (2015). "SC Suspends Impeachment Hearing v. Ombudsman." Philstar.com, September 15, available at: www.philstar.com/headlines/611801/sc-suspends-impeachment-hearing-vs-ombudsman (accessed March 20, 2015).

*Macias* v. *Arula* (1982). 115 SCRA 135.

Mangahas, M. (2013). "The Value of Statistical Competition." Available at: www.nscb.gov.ph (accessed February 24, 2015).

Meruenas, M. (2014). "CJ Sereno Manipulated JBC to Keep Jardeleza off List." *Brion*, September 5.

Molo, A.B. (2002). "Navigating Through Shifting Sands: Reinforcing Judicial Independence in the Philippine Context." *Philippine Law Journal*, 77(1): 48–72.

Moustafa, T. (2003). "Law Versus the State: The Judicialization of Politics in Egypt." *Law and Social Inquiry*, 28: 883–930.

Panganiban, A. (2004). "Judicial Activism in the Philippines." *Philippine Law Journal*, 79: 2.

Peerenboom, R. (2002). *China's Long March toward Rule of Law*. New York, Cambridge University Press.

*People of the Philippines* v. *Joseph Estrada,* Crim Case No. 26558, Sandiganbayan, Special Division (2007). Available at: www.lawphil.net/courts/sandigan/sb_26558_2007.html (accessed March 3, 2015).

*People of the Philippines* v. *Panfilo Lacson*, G.R. No. 149453 (2003). Available at: http://sc.judiciary.gov.ph/jurisprudence/2003/oct2003/149453.htm (accessed November 20, 2014).

*Philconsa* v. *Enriquez*, G.R. No. 113105 (1994). Available at: www.lawphil.net/judjuris/juri1994/aug1994/gr_113105_1994.html (accessed November 10, 2014).

*Planas* v. *COMELEC*, G.R. No. L-35925 (1973). Available at: www.lawphil.net/judjuris/juri1973/jan1973/gr_35925_1973.html (accessed October 20, 2014).

*PLDT* v. *NTC*, G.R. No. 94374 (1995). Available at: www.lawphil.net/judjuris/juri1995/feb1995/gr_94374_1995.html (accessed November 10, 2014).

"Pork Barrel Protest Grips the Philippines" (2013). *Asia Sentinel*, August 26, available at: www.asiasentinel.com/politics/pork-barrel-protest-grips-the-philippines/ (accessed January 10, 2015).

*Province of North Cotabato,* et al. v. *The Government of the Republic of the Philippines Peace Panel on Ancestral Domain* (GRP) et al., G.R. Nos 183591, 183752, 183893, 183951, 183962 (2008). Available at: http://sc.judiciary.gov.ph/jurisprudence/2008/october2008/183591.htm (accessed October 20, 2014).

"Pulse Asia Nationwide Survey on the Pork Barrel" (2013). September 14–27, available at: www.cenpeg.org/2013/gov/oct/PULSE_ASIA_on_pork_barrel_Oct_2013.pdf.

Pulse Asia Research March (2015). Ulat ng Bayan First Quarter Survey, March, available at: www.pulseasia.ph.

Punay, E. (2011). "SC Won't Stop Impeach Proceedings v. Merci." Philstar, February 16, available at: www.philstar.com/headlines/657497/sc-wont-stop-impeach-proceedings-vs-merci (accessed March 10, 2015).

Putzel, J. (2001). "A Muddled Democracy – 'People Power' Philippine Style." LSE Working Paper Series no. 14, available at: www.lse.ac.uk/internationalDevelopment/pdf/WP/WP14.pdf (accessed March 10, 2015).

Ramseyer, J.M. and Rasmusen, E. (2003). *Measuring Judicial Independence: The Political Economy of Judging in Japan*. Chicago, IL, University of Chicago Press.

Rappler.com (2015). Senate draft report, "Aquino must bear responsibility," March 17, available at: www.rappler.com/nation/87112-senate-report-mamasapano-aquino-responsible.

Raquiza, A. (2012). *State Structure, Policy Foundation and Economic Development in Southeast Asia: The Political Economy of Thailand and the Philippines*. Routledge, New York

*Raul Lambino* v. *Commission on Elections, Mar-Len Abigail Binay* et al. v. *Commission on Elections,* G.R. Nos 174153, 174299 (2006). Available at: http://sc.judiciary.gov.ph/jurisprudence/2006/october2006/174153.htm (accessed November 10, 2014).

*Republic of the Philippines* v. *Ballares* et al., G.R. Nos 147062–147064 (2001). Available at: http://sc.judiciary.gov.ph/jurisprudence/2001/dec2001/147062_64.htm (accessed October 20, 2014).

*Republic of the Philippines* v. *Sandiganbayan, Ferdinand Marcos* et al., G.R. No. 152154 (2003). Available at: http://sc.judiciary.gov.ph/jurisprudence/2003/jul2003/152154.htm (accessed October 21, 2014).

Rivera, T.C. (2002). "Transition Pathways and Democratic Consolidation in Post-Marcos Philippines." *Contemporary Southeast Asia*, 24(3): 466–475.

Rodis, R. (2013). "Estrada's Plunder Conviction Remembered." Inquirer.net, August 28, available at: http://globalnation.inquirer.net/84269/estradas-plunder-conviction-remembered/ (accessed March 30, 2015).

*Santiago* v. *COMELEC*, G.R. No. 127325 (1997). Available at: www.lawphil.net/judjuris/juri1997/mar1997/gr_127325_1997.html (accessed October 24, 2014).

Santos, D. (2012). " 'You'll Never Walk Alone' Sung at Mass for Corona." Available at: www.rappler.com/nation/884-you-ll-never-walk-alone-sung-at-mass-for-corona (accessed March 12, 2015).

Scharpf, F. (1997). "Economic Integration, Democracy and the Welfare State." *Journal of European Public Policy*, 4(1): 18–36.

SCPIO (2015). Twitter post, March 20, available at: https://twitter.com/SCPh_PIO/status/578752529292365824.

*Senate of the Philippines,* et al. v. *Eduardo Ermita* et al., G.R. Nos 169777, 169659, 169660, 169667, 169834, 171246 (2006). Available at: www.lawphil.net/judjuris/juri2006/apr2006/gr_169777_2006.html (accessed October 20, 2014).

Shapiro, M. (1964). *Law and Politics in the Supreme Court: New Approaches to Political Jurisprudence.* New York, Free Press of Glencoe.

Shapiro, M. (1981). *Courts: A Comparative and Political Analysis*. Chicago, IL, University of Chicago Press.

Shapiro, M. (1994). "Juridicalization of Politics in the United States." *International Political Science Association*, 15(2): 101–112.

Sidel, J. (1999). *Capital, Coercion and Crime: Bossism in the Philippines*. Stanford, CA, Stanford University Press.

Social Weather Stations (2001). Performance ratings of the new administration, available at: www.sws.org.ph/pr032901.htm (accessed March 30, 2015).

Sweet, A.S. (2000). *Governing with Judges: Constitutional Politics in Europe*. Oxford, Oxford University Press.

Tamanaha, B. (2012). “The Several Meanings of Politics in Judicial Politics Studies.” *Emory Law Journal*, 61(4): 759–778.

Tate, C.N. (1994). “The Judicialization of Politics in the Philippines and Southeast Asia.” *International Political Science Review*, 15(2): 187–197.

Tate, C.N. (1997). “Courts and the Breakdown and the R-creation of Philippine Democracy: Evidence from the Supreme Court’s Agenda.” *International Social Science Journal*, 49(152): 279–291.

Tate, C.N. and Haynie, S. (1993). “Authoritarianism and the Functions of Courts: A Time Series Analysis of the Philippine Supreme Court, 1961–1987.” *Law and Society Review*, 27(4): 707–740.

Tate, C.N. and Vallinder, T. (1997). *The Global Expansion of Judicial Power*. New York, New York University Press.

*The Province of North Cotabato* v. *Republic of the Philippines*, G.R. Nos 183591, 183752, 183893, 183951 (2008). Available at: http://sc.judiciary.gov.ph/jurisprudence/2008/october2008/183591.htm (accessed October 11, 2014).

*The Rule on the Writ of Amparo*, A.M. No. 07—12-SC (2007). Available at: www.lawphil.net/judjuris/juri2007/sep2007/am_07-9-12-sc_2007.html (accessed October 10, 2014).

Thompson, M. (1995). *The Anti-Marcos Struggle: Personalistic Rule and Democratic Transition in the Philippines*. New Haven, CT, Yale University Press.

“TIMELINE: Mamasapano Clash” (2015). Rappler.com, February 7, available at: www.rappler.com/nation/82827-timeline-mamasapano-clash (accessed March 30, 2015).

Trochev, A. and Ellett, R. (2014). “Judges and their Allies, Rethinking Judicial Autonomy through the Prism of Off-bench Resistance.” *Journal of Law and Courts*, 2(1): 1–20.

Vitug, M. (2012). *Hour Before Dawn, The Fall and the Uncertain Rise of the Philippine Supreme Court.* Quezon City, Cleverheads Publishing.

Vitug, M. (2013). “God and the Supreme Court.” Rappler.com, March 26, available at: www.rappler.com/thought-leaders/24756-god-supreme-court-rh-law (accessed February 25, 2014).

# 15 The rule of law in illiberal contexts

## Cambodia and Singapore as exemplars

*Stephen McCarthy and Kheang Un*

### Introduction

The rule of law in Singapore has been criticized by liberal democrats for its illiberal nature; yet it remains an attractive model for certain newly developing countries, including Cambodia, that aspire to achieve economic development without more liberal forms of democracy. Unlike some other countries in Southeast Asia, there is less evidence of meaningful constitutional contestation taking place – bargains and struggles among elites, opposition forces, and civil society – over state institutions, the broader political order, and the granting and enforcement of rights. To be sure, civil and political struggles over representation, human rights issues, and fair compensation have been rife in recent years. However, in these single-party-dominated regimes a lack of constitutional contestation is particularly evident in the area encompassing the rule of law, courts, and justice. This is not to say that the rule of law and justice mechanisms as understood by the countries' elites are absent from these regimes. Rather, that understanding the rule of law as it is understood by the elites offers better insight into the trajectory of political development and the obstacles to Western ideals for legal reform.

This chapter traces the recent convergence of the rule of law in Singapore and Cambodia in the face of each country's political, historical, and social differences, and the obstacles confronting Cambodia's judicial and legal reform program. Over the past decade Cambodia has seen a series of legal reforms and an increase in the use of legal proceedings, including defamation and disinformation lawsuits against opposition politicians and members of civil society. We argue that this is a product of a strategic calculation by the Cambodian ruling elites to utilize a more subtle and legitimate strategy of social control. The legal reforms already introduced, those soon coming into effect, and the role of the judiciary in relation to each may be better understood through insight into the rule of law in Cambodia and by placing it in the context of other exemplars in the region – in particular Singapore. However, differences will remain, as the judiciary's role in society and public policy is intertwined with and impacted by each country's understanding of the rule of law that has evolved through a series of historical, political, institutional, cultural, and economic factors. Therefore, this chapter undertakes a comparative analysis of the two countries' legal traditions and political-historical trajectories in order to discern the development of the role of the courts and their power in judicial review.

This approach is consistent with recent calls for more comparative research on the rule of law in order to better understand the nature of democracy and authoritarianism in Asia (Fukuyama 2010, 2012). While electoral gains by opposition movements in Singapore (2011) and Cambodia (2013) illustrate that the meaning of democracy and the rule of law is contested locally, we argue that understanding the rule of law as it is understood by the countries' elites themselves offers more insight into the true nature of the regimes in question than comparing and classifying polities as examples of "competitive authoritarianism" or "electoral authoritarianism" on the basis of their democratic deficiencies (Levitsky and Way 2010; Schedler 2006). In addition, we analyze whether Singapore's lessons may be applied in large, poor, and underdeveloped authoritarian regimes; and whether the Singapore model can be sustained or replicated in the case of Cambodia (Silverstein 2007).

## Rule of law in illiberal democracies

Democratization theorists have long argued the importance of the rule of law for liberal democracies. Indeed, one of the distinguishing features of liberal democracy over competitive or electoral authoritarianism is the existence of a democratic or "true rule of law" which grants all citizens political and legal equality, and makes the state and its agents subject to the law (Diamond 1999: 11). Laws must be promulgated in advance and then fairly and consistently applied by relevant state institutions, including the judiciary, across equivalent cases (O'Donnell 2004: 33). Without an independent judiciary there will be an absence of checks and balances and no guarantee that state institutions, or the rich and powerful, or both in combination, will act within legal and institutional boundaries. Ideally, an independent judiciary holds everyone equal before the law, protects political and civil rights, and holds elected officials and their associates accountable for illegal actions (Huber 1999: 197). An independent judiciary can mediate conflicts among political actors and political institutions and societal organizations in a legitimate fashion, a process that can minimize political violence and confrontation that could jeopardize political order, civil and political rights, and hence democratic and economic advancement (Gunther *et al.* 1995: ch. 1).

Judicial independence can be compromised by institutional weakness, such as limited resources, low salaries, lack of trained personnel, and low intra-institutional cooperation. Low salaries make judges and court officials susceptible to compromise and corruption; the latter is defined as court officials' engagement in "procedural, substantive and/or administrative behavioral patterns for private benefits" (Buscaglia 2007: 68). A lack of intra-institutional cooperation is a weakness found in many newly emerging democracies like Cambodia. Since no single agency can enforce horizontal accountability, the judiciary cannot perform its role effectively unless it receives support from other government institutions – particularly the police who investigate crimes and execute court orders and rulings – but also the support of the army (Frankel 1993: 27). Judicial independence can also be compromised by patron-clientelism. When power, resources, and loyalty flow through patron-client networks, any meaningful reform would affect the interests of these networks and is thus self-defeating. Consequently, elites, through their patronage networks, tend to resist any effort to reform and strengthen political institutions – including the judiciary – aimed at making them more efficient, effective, and independent.

It is important to note that this democratic or true rule of law is of an ideal type – the proximity of a country's rule of law, including its judicial system to this type, indicates the level of its independence, and hence its effectiveness in the protection of civil and political rights, and in reviewing and vetoing legislative and executive decisions deemed to be undemocratic. Yet it fails to adequately explain the rule of law and judicial conditions that are intertwined with the wider social, political, and economic realities found in many countries in Southeast Asia. In single-party dominant regimes, elites could deny that economic growth requires democratization; rather, the rule of law should be narrow, proceduralist, and divorced from democracy promotion. Indeed, the minimum requirement for this thin or narrow version of the rule of law in a developmental context could be that it secures property rights and enforces contracts in order to promote economic development – usually driven by foreign investment. This scenario is popular with advocates of the "Beijing Consensus" as an alternative to the "Washington Consensus" that has been promoted in various forms by Western governments and international financial institutions since before the end of the Cold War. To be sure, the Beijing Consensus argument has gained further resonance in East Asia and elsewhere following the Global Financial Crisis (Beeson 2011; Silverstein 2003). While Singapore was an early exemplar of this approach, we argue that in Southeast Asia Cambodia's Hun Sen has followed Singapore's lead and become a new member of the Beijing Consensus club by pursuing an ordered society wherein human rights are subordinated to political stability and economic growth (Ledgerwood and Un 2003: 537–539).

Moreover, like Singapore, Cambodia lacks the democratic fullness required to approximate a Western liberal democracy and subsequently should more appropriately be labeled a semi-authoritarian, semi-democratic, or illiberal regime. These types of regime possess a "thin rule of law" as part of their institutional structure; and not just "rule by law" which is a procedural description of behavior that can also occur in liberal democracies – connoting the enforcement of the law by the executive, judiciary, or various arms of the state without regard for or at the expense of justice. As such, the thin rule of law constitutes a structural category in itself that may be used to identify semi-authoritarian or illiberal regimes. While staging elections may be manageable for authoritarian regimes, changing the rule of law means addressing the structure and distribution of power and as such is less desirable for elites in these countries. The kind of rule of law found in each country is therefore a far more important indicator of the quality of democracy, and differences in the rule of law are more reflective of the particular regime type. This can be illustrated by examining the evolution of the thin rule of law in Singapore and Cambodia despite their undergoing starkly different political, historical, and legal trajectories.

## The Singaporean rule of law

Singapore inherited English common law from Great Britain when it acquired sovereignty of the island in 1824. The courts set up by the British under the Second Charter of Justice in 1826 would later interpret this Charter to have imported the whole body of English law into its Straits Settlements (including Singapore) and in 1878 a Civil Law Ordinance would also import the application of English commercial law (Civil Law Ordinance [Ord No. 4, 1878] s.6). Under the Japanese occupation of Singapore in World War II, although civil courts would continue to function, criminal law was replaced by military law and the idea, influenced by the Chinese legalist school of some 2,500 years before, that law was to be the basis of government, that everyone must obey the law, and that penalties should be so harsh that no one dared break the law (Chan 2009: 4–5).

When the British and French returned to claim back their colonies after the war, their former legal orders were reinstated and Singapore became a separate Crown Colony and eventually a separate State with its own constitution before briefly merging with Malaya in the Federation of Malaysia in 1963. Singapore's constitution evolved throughout this period through acts of the National Assembly, not only to reflect its independence in 1965 after leaving the Federation, but also thereafter through a series of constitutional amendments (Tan 1989: 23–27). Upon independence, for example, Singapore found itself in a position of having its judicial system, which had been created under its state constitution, still tied to the Federation of Malaysia. In order to correct this problem, an amending act was passed to constitute the Singapore judiciary as well as to constitute the Judicial Committee of the Privy Council in London to act as Singapore's final court of appeal. Changes in the amendment process in 1965 had transformed the Singapore constitution into a very flexible one. This was necessary for the passing of wide-ranging legislation to effect the economic and political development of the country by the only party that has ruled Singapore since independence – the People's Action Party (PAP) (Tan 1989: 23). The Constitution of Singapore, therefore, while departing from the original Westminster model, continued to form the basic framework for social, economic, and political advancement as well as provide a springboard for government action (Tan 1989: 28).

These sentiments were echoed by Singapore's then Chief Justice Chan in 2009 in an address to the New York State Bar Association where he commented that although the English legal system was inherited from the British, it was also modified: "The fundamental principles are the same, but our public law is quite different since this body of law must reflect the political, social and cultural values of the people." Moreover, Chan believed that:

> If you study the Singapore statute book today, you will find MM Lee's [Lee Kuan Yew's] precepts and values reflected in all the laws. But pervading all of the laws is the rule of law: the idea that political authority must be exercised subject to and in accordance with the rule of law.
>
> (Chan 2009: 3)

Describing Lee Kuan Yew as a political and legal realist, Chan outlined Lee's vision of the rule of law by citing a speech delivered by then Prime Minister Lee to the University of Singapore Law Society in 1962:

> There is a gulf between the principles of the rule of law, distilled to its quintessence in the background of peaceful 19th century England, and its actual practice in contemporary Britain. The gulf is even wider between the principle and its practical application in the hard realities of the social and economic conditions of Malaya. You will have to bridge the gulf between the ideal principle and its practice in our given sociological and economic milieu. For if the forms are not adapted and principles not adjusted to meet our own circumstances but blindly applied, it may be to our undoing.... The rule of law talks of habeas corpus, freedom, the right of association and expression, of assembly, of peaceful demonstration, concepts which first stemmed from the French Revolution and were later refined in Victorian England. But nowhere in the world today are these rights allowed to practise without limitations, for blindly applied, these ideals can work towards the undoing of organised society. For the acid test of any legal system is not the greatness nor the grandeur of its ideal concepts, but whether in fact it is able to produce order and justice in the relationships between man and man and between man and the State.... Justice and fair play according to predetermined rules of law can be achieved within our situation if there is integrity of purpose and an intelligent search for forms which will work and which will meet the needs of our society. Reality is relatively more fixed than form. So if we allow form to become fixed because reality cannot be so easily varied, then calamity must ... befall us.[1]

The particular "form" of the rule of law that was adopted for Singapore on the basis of this search criteria, and which pervades the laws that reflect Lee Kuan Yew's precepts and values, was the thin version rather than the thick version. According to Chan, "the thick describes the rule of law in liberal democracies and the thin describes the rule of law in all other democracies." When Singapore is criticized for paying lip-service to the rule of law, Chan (2009: 7) believes, critics are referring to their own version of the rule of law and not to Singapore's. Singapore is a non-liberal democracy where a thin version of the "rule of law simply means the supremacy of the law, without reference to whether the law is just or unjust." Since the law also applies to the state, one of the judiciary's roles is to determine whether the limits of the law have been breached by the state – either by reviewing legislation or executive acts to determine whether they are unconstitutional. According to Chan, so long as this power of judicial review exists in Singapore, judicial independence and the rule of law exists (Chan 2009: 7–10). But this does not necessarily require that the courts be concerned with whether the laws passed by Parliament are fair, just, and reasonable. Detention orders made under the provisions of the Internal Security Act (ISA), for example, are subject to judicial review whereby the courts can determine if a detention order was made in accordance with the law (Chan 2009: 10).

The thin or narrow version of the rule of law was justified by Lee and subsequently by the judiciary as being the most fitting form for Singapore given its own political, social, economic, and cultural values. While jurisprudence theorists might tag this form as an example of legal positivism (Fuller 1958), critics often infer a wider concept of the rule of law when they cite undemocratic or illiberal laws and outcomes. It is not the purpose of this chapter to enter into the debate on the justice or fairness of these laws and outcomes, but rather to focus on the meaning of the rule of law as understood by the laws' founders and subsequent adjudicators. Within the context of this form of the rule of law, legislatures in Singapore have continued to amend the constitution and to pass laws which could otherwise be considered undemocratic or a restraint on civil liberties in the West. These include amendments to remove trial by jury in criminal cases and a whole range of legislation containing provisions which operate in conjunction with the ISA, such as the Public Entertainment and Meetings Act, the Societies Act, the Undesirable Publications Act, the Films Act, and the Newspaper and Printing Presses Act.

Furthermore, the trend since the mid-1970s has been to revise the civil and criminal law so as to remove judicial sentencing discretion from most legislation and to limit scope for judicial review. The executive thus shares the judicial function – the courts decide on the broad merits of a case and the executive does the sentencing via legislation. Much legislation contains mandated sentencing provisions for offenses, including the Criminal Code and the Acts cited above (Worthington 2001: 510). According to Chan (2009: 16), "efficiency and strict enforcement of the criminal law" are the strong points of the Crime Control Model in Singapore, along with practicality and pragmatism. If the judiciary in Singapore interprets law in such a way that counters the intention of the legislature, the legislature has the means to correct such a decision through further legislative or constitutional amendments. While some have described examples of this occurring in Singapore as legislative override of excessive judicial activism (with the effect of restricting judicial review), the Singaporean authorities would believe that this practice lies within their realms of constitutional power given the rule of law as understood in their own context.

Two important examples help illustrate this phenomenon. In 1988, the Singapore Court of Appeal held that persons detained under the ISA were entitled to judicial review of the constitutionality, legality, and reasonableness of their detention (*Chng Suan Tze and Ors* v. *Minister of Home Affairs and Ors*, 1988). In a separate case, the Judicial Committee of the Privy Council overturned a decision of a Singapore district court to expel J.B. Jeyaretnam (of the opposition's Workers Party) from the Singapore Bar Association after having "suffered a grievous injustice" being "fined, imprisoned and publicly disgraced by offences of which [he was] not guilty" and "in addition [he has] been deprived of his seat in Parliament and disqualified for a year from practicing his profession" (*Jeyaretnam* v. *Law Society of Singapore*, 1989). The legislature subsequently moved to correct these anomalies with retrospective amendments to the Constitution and the ISA,[2] thus nullifying the effect of the Court of Appeal's decision on judicial review and severely limiting appeals to the Privy Council – such appeals were later abolished altogether. Kirby notes that after these amendments, a government lawyer criticized the "foreign" judges of the Privy Council, dismissing their arguments about the rule of law being based on a "vague and indefinable concept" (Kirby 1989).

Hirschl (2008: 109) believes that "political power holders often possess some control over the personal composition of national high courts" and that "consequently, the demographic characteristics, cultural propensities, and ideological tilts of supreme court judges in most countries are likely to match the rest of the political elite in these countries." Worthington (2001: 493) notes that this is also the case in Singapore, just as it is in the United Kingdom and other Westminster systems, and few non-PAP-affiliated appointments are made to the bench. However, the political executive also needs a Supreme Court which is seen as, and is capable of, maintaining the confidence of the international business community and this provides the Court with some power vis-à-vis the executive, particularly on commercial matters. It is also true that not all judges wish to be involved in political trials, nor can their support for the executive be guaranteed.

## The Cambodian rule of law

A modern civil law-based legal system was introduced under French colonial rule in the late nineteenth century; this came to a halt in 1975, when Cambodia fell under the radical regime of Democratic Kampuchea (DK) which terminated the entire system (Amnesty International 2002). Almost all Cambodians with legal backgrounds were killed, while other resources such as law schools, books, court buildings, and legal texts were either destroyed or converted to other uses. Arrests and sentencings were arbitrarily ordered by DK cadres who acted in the name of *Angkar* (the organization), resulting in grave systematic violations of human rights, summary executions, and a death-toll of over 1.7 million people (Chandler 1991). Thus, when the People's Republic of Kampuchea (PRK) came into existence under Vietnamese occupation in 1979, there was no legal system in place. The PRK would slowly re-establish a formal court system by offering short-term training courses for would-be judges and prosecutors (Donovan 1993: 81–82). However, because the regime considered the legal system to be an integral part of the ruling party's apparatus, the training emphasized Marxist-Leninist doctrines over legal subjects. Prosecutors and judges were usually former schoolteachers and literate Cambodians with "good biography" – meaning they had no political connection to the previous regime.

As in other communist states, the PRK judicial system was subservient to the party and the government (Donovan 1993: 90; Gottesman 2003: 243–254). The ruling party's distrust in the courts opened the space for frequent interference in the judicial process by government officials at both the central and provincial levels.[3] Soon after the departure of Vietnamese troops in 1989, the government – having anticipated a future pluralist electoral contest, and wishing to distance itself from the past – adopted a new name for the country, the State of Cambodia (SOC). It in turn promulgated a new constitution emphasizing fundamental freedoms and the rule of law. However, under the SOC government the previous relationship between the judicial and executive branches persisted and the courts remained subordinate to the party.

Given Cambodia's violent history, a concern to prevent "a return to the policies and practices of the past" was central to the negotiations for the Paris Peace Agreement. The 1991 Agreement ensured that the protection of fundamental human rights contained in the Universal Declaration of Human Rights and other relevant international instruments, including the United Nations Basic Principles on the Independence of the Judiciary, were to be enshrined in the constitution of the new government to be formed after the UN-sponsored elections. These basic principles include "due process and equality before the law, protection from arbitrary deprivation of property or deprivation of private property without just compensation, and freedom from racial, ethnic, religious or sexual discrimination" (United Nations Department of Information 1996: 145).

After the 1993 democratic elections, Cambodia adopted a system of checks and balances wherein judicial independence was enshrined in the constitution. Article 128 of the constitution specifies that the judicial body "shall be an independent power and shall guarantee and uphold impartiality and protect the rights and freedoms of the citizens." Article 130 stipulates that "Judicial power shall not be granted to either the legislative or the executive branch." To safeguard the constitution and to protect citizens' fundamental rights, complex judicial institutions were established to review laws, to impartially adjudicate laws, and to enforce constitutional provisions for equal protection under the law and for the defense of civil and social rights. The regular courts would consist of three tiers: the courts of first instance, an Appeals Court, and the Supreme Court.[4] Situated atop this system was the Supreme Council of Magistracy (SCM) whose constitutional role is to assist the king to ensure the independence of the judiciary, and to recommend judges and prosecutors for royal appointment, dismissal, and discipline. Moreover, the Constitutional Council was also created to ensure the constitutionality of laws, rules, and regulations through review and veto power.

Over time, however, these judicial institutions failed to function appropriately, and many of the laws and regulations have not been systematically implemented. Part of the reason for this is that civil law countries are less likely to permit judicial review over the constitutionality of laws.[5] Further, the character of judicial review also corresponds to the nature of a country's political past, and its judicial and executive relations. Cambodia's civil law legal system is today a mixture of French-influenced codes from the United Nations Transitional

Authority (UNTAC) period from 1992 to 1993, along with royal decrees and acts of the legislature. The introduction of the new Criminal Code in Cambodia with detailed provisions for defamation and insult, along with other judicial reforms currently underway, signifies an effort on the part of the executive to move Cambodia's legal system toward the Singaporean "thin" rule of law model.[6] In addition, further legislation has been drafted (the Law on Associations and Non-Governmental Organizations and the Law on Trade Unions) that will affect the constitutional rights to freedom of association for non-government organizations and trade unions, including a requirement for the compulsory registration of all NGOs and vague provisions that could provide for the selective denial of registration applications.[7]

## Obstacles to Cambodia's transition towards the Singaporean-style rule of law

As in Singapore, Cambodian leaders believe that the concept of rule of law should reflect the country's cultural values and level of development (Ledgerwood and Un 2003). However, unlike Singapore, Cambodia's legal development has been closely intertwined with decades of social, political, and economic turmoil, and international leverage following the 1993 United Nations sponsored elections. The belief in contextual particularity is reflected in more than two decades of struggle between the Cambodian government and the international community over the issue of judicial reform. While significant amounts of financial assistance since 1993 have pressured the Cambodian government to initiate certain judicial and legal reforms, the judiciary continues to display a lack of professionalism. Institutional weaknesses include a severe shortage of resources, including trained personnel. Since 2002, as part of the judicial reform process, government training programs increased the number of judges and lawyers to 309 and 594 respectively by 2010 – which is a welcome rise; however, the figure remains miniscule for a population of 13.39 million as of the last national census taken in 2008.[8] Overall, limited legal experience and inadequate knowledge of the law and legal procedures, as well as the presence of corruption and political dependency, negatively affect the quality of legal representation.

Overwhelming caseloads produce delays and distortions, limiting access for the poor, and inevitably corruption. Although there have been some improvements in the physical infrastructure in recent years, this has also come at a high social cost. The Cambodian government, capitalizing on the recent rise in metropolitan real estate values, entered into non-transparent land-swapping arrangements wherein old court buildings were traded for newly constructed buildings in areas of lower real estate value. There is also a very low degree of intra-institutional cooperation. The judicial police are an auxiliary arm of the court assisting on judicial issues, including investigations and the execution of court warrants and rulings. By law, prosecutors have the responsibility to supervise the judicial police in the latter's working relationship with the court. However, the court and the judicial police are in constant confrontation with one another, a precedent that dates back to the socialist regime of the 1980s (Gottesman 2003: 252–253; Council on Legal and Judicial Reform 2002). Consequently, there have been numerous instances and allegations in which the judicial police refused to execute court warrants or rulings, often with the support of the executive branch (Angkear 2002).

In addition, compared to Singapore where court officials are relatively well paid and higher court justices are remunerated at rates comparable to senior legal positions in the private sector, Cambodian judges seem to be poor cousins. The median monthly gross wage for lawyers in Singapore was S$8,400 in 2011 – excluding bonuses or increments for seniority (Ministry of Manpower 2012). It is not uncommon for lawyers in Singapore to earn over S$250,000 annually; legal partners would earn considerably more. Indeed, in 2012 the Public Services Division of the Prime Minister's Office underwent a review of the salaries of Administrative Service officers, the Judiciary, and Statutory Appointment Holders to ensure that their salaries remained competitive relative to their market benchmarks. Court officials in Cambodia, on the other hand, including judges and prosecutors, commonly attribute the prevalence of corruption in the judiciary to low salaries. Before 2002, the average monthly salary for judges, prosecutors, and other court officials was around US$24 – an amount that was never anywhere near sufficient to support individual court officials, let alone their families. As part of judicial reform, the salaries of judges and prosecutors were substantially increased, starting from US$250 per month to over US$600 depending on seniority (World Bank 2003). However, this salary increase did not diminish corruption within the judiciary and the corresponding public perception of the judiciary continues to be negative.

The prevalence of high levels of corruption is contingent upon three factors: uncertainty over job security among judges and prosecutors, the absence of institutional restraint, and the patronage political system. Similar to situations in other developing countries, if judges, prosecutors, and clerks have to buy their positions and maintain kickbacks to retain them, they also have to recoup their investment (Pepys 2007: 4–5). Furthermore, judges and prosecutors are required to contribute to the ruling party's patronage-based development projects such as constructing schools, rural roads, and other gifts during the elections. The politicized nature of Cambodian governance makes it impossible for a neutral judicial system to emerge. Indeed, one prosecutor stated that "the characteristics of politics determine the peculiarity of the court system" in Cambodia.[9] Because judges and prosecutors owe their careers to their parties or their patrons, in making any decision they have to consider "who offered them the seat."[10] Consequently, in Cambodia "it is unavoidable that court officials serve the interests of political parties and that the judicial system serves politics."[11]

Cultural sentiments that characterize the patrimonial system also shape judges' perceptions of corruption, and their responses to executive interference. Experience from other countries indicates that when corrupt practices are considered to be the norm, as is the case in patrimonialist settings, even clean judges bear the pressure of political, cultural, and societal conditions. Pressure comes not only from politicians and political institutions, but also from members of groups with whom they are associated (Kurkchiyan 2007: 103). The absence of institutional constraints, coupled with a wider sociopolitical environment dominated by patronage and corruption, blurs judges' perceptions of what constitutes legality and illegality, morality and immorality. Strong empirical evidence reveals that while judges do not reject the allegation of court corruption they defended their actions forcefully, arguing that some acts of receiving money from litigants do not constitute corruption. Rather, these monetary transactions can rightfully be called "fees," and accepting such a fee is not wrong – if not legally, at least morally. In addition, when faced with intervention by high-ranking government officials, judges and prosecutors generally acquiesce. Such acquiescence results not only from fear but also from "affection." Affection is the product of reciprocal relationships whereby people return favors for what others did for them; such relationships are a standard practice that is difficult to avoid in the patronage-based society of Cambodia. It is this sense of a desire to maintain a personal relationship and the need to maintain backing from higher authorities in the long run that stands in contrast to how "corruption" is often perceived in the West – as a purely financial transaction.

The most recent interaction of Cambodian courts with Western legal codes and norms followed the establishment in 2001 of the Extraordinary Chambers in the Courts of Cambodia to try the former Khmer Rouge leaders. This has been a prolonged process which was expected to produce a more transparent, independent, and efficient judicial system. It has often been said that as court personnel received training and interacted with foreign judges and lawyers the Cambodian judiciary would become more impartial, professional, and gain a greater respect for the rule of law as understood in Western legal norms – Western legal codes and norms were theoretically grafted onto existing institutions. However, while it is true that judges, prosecutors, and clerks enjoyed some degree of independence at the tribunal, this should not be interpreted as increasing judicial independence in Cambodia. This is a narrow and unique case, the politics of which had been ironed out in advance during protracted negotiations between the Cambodian government and the United Nations. Judges, prosecutors, and others do have some freedom of maneuver, though it is within already established parameters, and this freedom from political or institutional influence is unlikely to continue in the national courts. Because of the Cambodian courts' embeddedness in the existing political system, the impact of the tribunal on the overall Cambodian judiciary is minimal and is not likely to bring any substantial change in the way the local courts operate (Un and Ledgerwood 2010).

## Conclusion

This chapter has shown that constitutional contestation has been relatively muted in two single-party dominant illiberal regimes in Southeast Asia, particularly with regard to the rule of law and the courts. While it is true that in Singapore close relations with political elites have led to active support for the state's communitarian values (political stability, interracial harmony, and economic development), it should not be inferred that the courts have largely failed to consistently uphold the rule of law and that justice mechanisms are absent. The latter observation would only be true if indeed the country's founders, and its political and legal elites, intended to create a Western liberal democratic version of the rule of law – an assumption which this chapter has found to be false. Comparing regimes to some ideal type of liberal democracy fails to adequately explain how the rule of law is intertwined with the social, political, and economic realities of many countries in Southeast Asia. Achieving a more nuanced understanding of Asian constitutional developments and the rule of law requires that one does not view current outcomes as lagging versions of Western models but rather as distinct outcomes reflecting unique sociopolitical circumstances and political cultures. That the particular kind of rule of law must be culturally acceptable in each country has also been argued by some Western scholars as well as by Singapore's legal elite (Fukuyama 2010: 42; Chan 2009).

The similarities to Cambodia outlined above also reveal a strategy that is politically useful elsewhere in the region. Having presided over sustained economic growth and maintained a dominant party system over the past decade, Cambodian political elites have aspired to develop the country along Singaporean lines, including following the Singaporean version of the rule of law. However, Cambodia also faces major impediments as it undergoes this transition – high levels of corruption, low levels of expertise, and an undeveloped legal system set it apart from Singapore. At the same time, Singapore has been able to maintain an efficient and credible legal system in protecting property rights and adjudicating commercial cases while Cambodia has not. Indeed, Haggard *et al.* (2008: 215–218) note that common and civil law traditions vary in their deference to the state, the respect they show toward private property, and the enforcement of private claims. Civil law systems like Cambodia's are less hospitable to private economic activity, and the French legal tradition has particularly deleterious effects. Moreover, civil law countries normally tie the hands of judges and are less flexible and adaptable to changing circumstances, since this usually requires the costly revision of statutes – as has occurred in Cambodia. By contrast, common law systems can evolve through continual litigation and relitigation, which improves the efficiency of the law. In Singapore, however, although the "Efficiency Model" is often heralded by the highest justices (Chan 2009: 16), its evolution has been realized through continual litigation on commercial matters. On politically sensitive cases, evolution occurs through constitutional amendments and, more than anything else, a narrow interpretation of the rule of law.

The relative lack of constitutional contestation in the rule of law and the courts in these countries does not mean that contestation is absent elsewhere. The political opposition, civil society groups, and the blogosphere in Singapore, and in Cambodia especially, struggle to be heard and in some cases reach bargains with the ruling elites. As the 2013 national elections showed, the Cambodian people are no longer satisfied with the CPP's justification for its continuing rule in the name of peace, stability, and economic growth. Since that time, societal pressure – generated through significant electoral gains made by the opposition party and witnessed through spontaneous protests over alleged electoral fraud – has ignited a sense of urgency for the CPP to initiate reforms. The CPP has carried out some reforms at the national level, most noticeably the Cabinet reshuffle (the replacement of some aging ministers with more dynamic and better educated ones); the appearance of an oversight role for the National Assembly, and the restructuring of the National Electoral Commission; and improvements made in revenue collection. However, whether these reforms will spill over into the judicial arena – as demanded by the opposition party and civil society – remains unlikely, given the ruling party's insistence on following other Asian models like Singapore. Since the 2013 elections, allegedly under pressure from the government, the courts have continued to imprison opposition activists including parliamentarians for leading "insurrection" and causing "social disorder" (Willemyns and Dara 2014). For their struggles and bargains to spill over into areas concerning the rule of law and the judiciary would require far broader societal pressure, or a willingness among the political elites to subordinate their power to a more liberal rule of law.

It is remarkable that despite each country's divergent political histories, legal systems, and development strategies since independence, they appear to be merging in terms of the form of rule of law practiced in both. As we have seen, the rule of law in Singapore evolved from the English common law and was modified (and justified) to suit the political, social, and cultural values of the people. Likewise, Singapore's own version of democracy emerged from within, evolving and being modified by legislators with the same justification. This form of democracy is clearly not meant to be a liberal one and the rule of law reflects this, while the highest justices openly state that any wider interpretations of the rule of law are not meant for Singapore. Cambodia, on the other hand, had a liberal form of democracy imposed upon the country by the drafters of its constitution following the framework of Western democratic principles.[12] In practice, however, these principles have been twisted to meet the interests of the Cambodian political elites. When the dust of democratic imposition settled, Cambodian leaders looked toward Singapore as a model of the rule of law.

## Notes

1 Chief Justice Chan Sek Keong, Keynote Address, New York State Bar Association Seasonal Meeting, Singapore, October 27, 2009, pp. 2–3.

2 See the Constitution of the Republic of Singapore (Amendment) Act 1989 (Singapore), assented January 26, 1989; Internal Security (Amendment) Act 1989 (Singapore), assented January 28, 1989.

3 Interviews with court officials revealed that such interference was extensive. These officials consistently used the phrase "they act like during the communist era" (Fieldnotes, September–December 2002). See also Gottesman (2003: 250–254).

4 The government under the Council for Legal and Judicial Reform has since drawn up a blueprint for the creation of specialized courts.

5 See La Porta *et al.* (2004).

6 It is widely recognized that Prime Minister Hun Sen has admired Lee Kuan Yew and Singapore's political system. Phnom Penh-based diplomats have noted that "he wants to leave a good legacy for future generations. He wants to be Cambodia's LKY (Lee Kuan Yew)." See Chongkittavor (2013).
7 See Cambodian Center for Human Rights (CCHR) and Article 19 (2011).
8 In real terms, this amounts to approximately one judge per 43,351 people, and one lawyer per 22,551 potential clients. The total population figure in 2016 was over 15 million. See National Institute of Statistics (2008), *General Population Census of Cambodia.*
9 Interview with Municipal Court judge, September 25, 2002. Subsequent research has revealed that such remarks, though made several years ago, remain relevant to present-day conditions.
10 Interview with Municipal Court clerk, November 20, 2001.
11 Interview with Municipal Court judge, October 2, 2002. Subsequent research proved that this statement remains true.
12 Constitution of Cambodia, Preamble and Article 1.

## References


Amnesty International (2002). "Kingdom of Cambodia: Urgent Need for Judicial Reform." Available at: www.amnesty.org/en/library/asset/ASA23/004/2002/en4, 2013>bb7350b9-d82c-11dd-9df8–936c90684588/asa230042002en.html (accessed January 4, 2014).

Angkear Heng (2002). "The President of Chilbo Industrial Co, LTD., Congratulates Mr. Heng Peou." *Rasmei Kampuchea Daily*, December 8, 2002.

Article 19 (2009). "Relevant Provisions in the Draft Penal Code That May Sffect the Free Speech" and "Comment on the Draft Cambodian Penal Code." Article 19, London, September, available at: www.article19.org/data/files/pdfs/laws/cambodia-draft-penal-code.pdf (accessed January 9, 2014).

Beeson, M. (2011). "Crisis Dynamics and Regionalism: East Asia in Comparative Perspective." *The Pacific Review*, 24(3): 357–374.

Buscaglia, E. (2007). "Judicial Corruption and the Broader Justice System." In *Transparency International, Global Corruption Report 2007: Corruption in Judicial Systems*, 68. Cambridge, Cambridge University Press.

Cambodian Center for Human Rights (CCHR) and ARTICLE 19, "Cambodia: Freedom of Expression and the Point of No Return" (2011). Press Release, February 14, available at: www.scoop.co.nz/stories/WO1102/S00488/cambodia-freedom-of-expression-and-the-point-of-no-return.htm (accessed January 9, 2014).

Chan Sek Keong (2009). Keynote Address, New York State Bar Association Seasonal Meeting, Singapore, October 27, 2009: 4–5, available at: http://app.supremecourt.gov.sg/data/doc/ManagePage/3021/CJ%20Keynote%20Address%20at%20NYSBA%20International%20Seasonal%20Meeting_27%20Oct%202009.pdf (accessed January 9, 2014).

Chandler, D. (1991). *The Tragedy of Cambodian History: Politics, War, and Revolution Since 1945.* New Haven, CT, Yale University Press.

*Chng Suan Tze and Ors* v. *Minister of Home Affairs and Ors* (1988). Court of Appeal of Singapore, December 8.

Chongkittavor Kavi (2013). "What is the Political Legacy of Cambodia's PM Hun Sen." *The Nation*, available at: www.nationmultimedia.com/home/2010/09/13/opinion/Hun-Sen-ponders-his-political-legacy-30137808.html (accessed January 4, 2014).

Civil Law Ordinance (1878). (Ord No. 4, 1878), s. 6.

Constitution of the Kingdom of Cambodia (1993). Available at: www.ccc.gov.kh/english/CONSTITUTIONEng.pdf (accessed January 4, 2014).

Constitution of the Republic of Singapore (1989). (Amendment) Act 1989 (Singapore), assented January 26, 1989.

Council on Legal and Judicial Reform (2002). *Report on the Situation of Courts*. Phnom Penh, Council of Ministers.

Diamond, L. (1999). *Developing Democracy: Towards Consolidation*. Baltimore, MD, Johns Hopkins University Press.

Donovan, D.A. (1993). "The Cambodian Legal System: An Overview." In *Rebuilding Cambodia: Human Resources, Human Rights, and Law*, ed. F. Brown. Washington, DC, Foreign Policy Institute, Paul H. Nitze School of Advanced International Studies, Johns Hopkins University, pp. 81–82.

Frankel, M.E. (1993). "Concerning the Role the Judiciary May Serve in the Proper Functioning of a Democracy." In *Transition to Democracy in Latin America: The Role of the Judiciary*, ed. I.P. Stotzky. Boulder, CO, Westview Press, pp. 23–31.

Fukuyama, F. (2010). "Transitions to the Rule of Law." *Journal of Democracy*, 21(1): 33–44.

Fukuyama, F. (2012). "China and East Asian Democracy: The Patterns of History." *Journal of Democracy*, 23(1): 14–26.

Fuller, L.L. (1958). "Positivism and Fidelity to Law: A Reply to Professor Hart." *Harvard Law Review*, 17(4): 630–672.

Gottesman, E. (2003). *Cambodia After the Khmer Rouge: Inside the Politics of Nation Building*. New Haven, CT, Yale University Press.

Gunther, R., Hans-Jurgen, P. and Nikiforos Diamandouros, P. (1995). "Introduction." In *The Politics of Democratic Consolidation: Southern Europe in Comparative Perspective*, eds R. Gunther *et al.* Baltimore, MD, Johns Hopkins University Press, pp. 1–32.

Haggard, S., MacIntyre, A. and Tiede, L. (2008). "The Rule of Law and Economic Development." *Annual Review of Political Science*, 11: 205–234.

Hirschl, R. (2008). "The Judicialization of Mega-politics and the Rise of Political Courts." *Annual Review of Political Science*, 11: 93–98.

Huber, E., Rueschemeyer, D., and Stephens, J.D. (1999). "The Paradoxes of Contemporary Democracy: Formal, Participatory, and Social Dimensions." In *Transitions to Democracy*, ed. L. Anderson. New York, Columbia University Press, pp. 168–192.

Internal Security (Amendment) Act (1989). (Singapore), assented January 28, 1989.

*Jeyaretnam* v. *Law Society of Singapore* (1989). 2 WLR 207 (PC).

Kirby, M. (1989). "Singapore: Detention of a Lawyer Leads to Limits on Privy Council Appeals." *Australian Law Journal* (speech), available at: www.michaelkirby.com.au/images/stories/speeches/1980s/vol. 21/793-ALJ_-_Singapore_Detention_of_a_Lawyer_Leads_to_Limits_on_Privy_Council_ Appeals.pdf (accessed January 9, 2014).

Kurkchiyan, M. (2007). "Judicial Corruption in the Context of Legal Culture." In *Transparency International, Global Corruption Report 2007: Corruption in Judicial Systems*. Cambridge, Cambridge University Press, pp. 99–106.

La Porta, R., Lopez-de-Silanes, F., Shleifer, A. and Vishny, R.W. (2004). "Judicial Checks and Balances." *Journal of Political Economy*, 112(2): 445–470.

Ledgerwood, J. and Un, K. (2003). "Global Concepts and Local Meaning: Human Rights and Buddhism in Cambodia." *Journal of Human Rights*, 2(4): 531–549.

Lee, K.T.Y. (1989). "The Evolution of Singapore's Modern Constitution: Developments from 1945 to the Present Day." *Singapore Academy of Law Journal*, 1(1): 23–27.

Levitsky, S. and Way, L. (2010). *Competitive Authoritarianism: Hybrid Regimes After the Cold War*. New York, Cambridge University Press.

Ministry of Manpower (2012). *Report on Wages in Singapore, 2011*. Singapore, Manpower Research and Statistics Department.

National Institute of Statistics (2008). *General Population Census of Cambodia 2008: Final Census Results*. Phnom Penh, National Institute of Statistics.

O'Donnell, G. (2004). "Why the Rules of Law Matters." *Journal of Democracy*, 15(2): 32–46.

Pepys, M.N. (2007). "Corruption within the Judiciary: Causes and Remedies." In *Transparency International, Global Corruption Report 2007: Corruption in Judicial Systems*. Cambridge, Cambridge University Press, pp. 3–10.

Schedler, A. (2006). *Electoral Authoritarianism: The Dynamics of Unfree Competition*. Boulder, CO: Lynne Rienner.

Silverstein, G. (2003). "Globalization and the Rule of Law: 'A Machine that Runs of Itself?'" *International Journal of Constitutional Law*, 3: 427–445.

Silverstein, G. (2007). "Singapore: The Exception that Proves Rules Matter." In *Rule by Law: The Politics of Courts in Authoritarian Regimes*, eds T. Ginsburg and T. Moustafa. Cambridge, Cambridge University Press, pp. 73–102.

Tan, K.Y.L. (1989). "The Evolution of Singapore's Modern Constitution: Developments from 1945 to the Present Day." *Singapore Academy of Law Journal*, 1(1): 23–28.

Un, K. and Ledgerwood, J. (2010). "Is the Trial of Duch a Catalyst for Change in Cambodia's Courts?" *Asia Pacific Issues*, 95: 1–12. Honolulu, East West Center.

United Nations Department of Information (1996). *The United Nations and Cambodia, 1991–1995*. New York, United Nations.

Willemyns, A. and Dara, M. (2014). "Parties to Meet for 'Final Talks' on Basis of 2018 Election." *The Cambodia Daily*, July 21, pp. 1–2.

World Bank (2003). *Cambodia: Legal and Judicial Sector Assessment*. Phnom Penh, Legal Vice Presidency, World Bank.

Worthington, R. (2001). "Between Hermes and Themis: An Empirical Study of the Contemporary Judiciary in Singapore." *Journal of Law and Society*, 8(4): 490–510.

# 16 Constitutionalism, the rule of law, and religious freedom in Malaysia

*Malik Imtiaz Sarwar*

## Introduction

In their insightful discussion of the evolution of constitutional politics in Southeast Asia, Björn Dressel and Marco Bünte (2014: 1–22) identify four areas which they consider primary causes of uneven constitutional practice: constitutional drafting and design; individual and religious rights; the role of the military in constitutional politics; and the rule of law, courts, and justice. The aim of this chapter is to further that discussion with reference to Malaysia. Since the military has not yet played a major role in shaping constitutional politics there, I will center this discussion on the first, second, and fourth areas. Malaysian constitutional practice had been fairly steady until 1987 and 1988, when controversial events undermined certain state institutions, especially the judiciary, and left them vulnerable to political attack. The result was the vesting in the executive of a degree of power and control that surpassed the limits envisaged by the Federal Constitution, leaving the freedoms the constitution guaranteed vulnerable to situational politics. These freedoms have since not been given due recognition. This is particularly true of the freedom of religion, given the undue emphasis on matters of race and religion in Malaysian politics.

## The historical backdrop

Until 1963, the peninsula was known as the Federation of Malaya, which had gained independence from Britain in 1957. In 1963, Malaysia was formed when the federation merged with Singapore and the Borneo territories of Sabah and Sarawak. A condensed history of the states of Malaya starts with the Anglo–Dutch treaty of 1824, when the Dutch withdrew from the Peninsula. By 1826, the British controlled Penang, Malacca, Singapore, and Labuan, an island off Borneo, which were integrated into a crown colony, the Straits Settlements. This was administered by the East India Company up until 1867, when control was ceded to the Colonial Office in London. In 1909, the Siamese Kingdom relinquished its claims to the states of Kedah, Kelantan, Perlis, and Terengganu. These states, whose rulers had taken on British advisers, came to be known, together with the southern kingdom of Johor, as the Unfederated Malay States

(UFMS). Before 1900 four other states – Pahang, Perak, Selangor, and Negri Sembilan – had taken on British Residents and were organized by the British into the Federated Malay States (FMS; Moustafa 2014: 157).

The British viewed the Peninsula as primarily an economic concern. To fuel industry and to ensure the profitability of its plantations, immigrant labor was encouraged, causing a significant increase in the population of non-Malays. Ethnic tensions increased during the Japanese Occupation of 1942 to 1945, energizing Malay nationalism and the Malayan Communist Party.[1] When the British returned to Malaya in 1945, they found that sentiment had shifted. In 1946 the Malayan Union was established, effectively uniting the Straits Settlements (except for Singapore and Labuan), the FMS, and the UFMS into a single crown colony. Although the intent was to prepare the colony for independence, the arrangement both undermined the sovereignty of the Malay rulers and established equality between Malays and non-Malays. One reaction was the formation of the United Malays National Organization (UMNO). In 1948, the Malayan Union was dismantled and the Federation of Malaya emerged. In 1955 elections were held for the Federal Legislative Council. A coalition of UMNO, the Malayan Indian Congress (MIC), and the Malayan Chinese Association (MCA) – the Alliance – secured 51 of the 52 seats, paving the way for a demand for independence (Khoo 2005: 12).

Up until independence, English law was applied. The Charter of Justice of 1807 had established Courts of Judicature in Penang. A second charter in 1826 permitted similar courts in Penang, Malacca, and Singapore. These charters brought English common law and equity into the Malay Peninsula (Omar 1987: 2). The practice of lay judges – the Governor and members of the Executive Council – ceased after the Colonial Office took control. By 1868, when the Supreme Court of the Straits Settlement was established, all judges were professionals (Omar 1987: 3). When the FMS was formed in 1895, in each state legislation established a common appeals court, the Court of the Judicial Commissioner, which was the highest court in the FMS until it was superseded by the Supreme Court in 1905 (Omar 1987: 3). Each state in the UFMS had its own judges and Supreme Court, though the court constitutions courts varied from state to state (Omar 1987: 3). When the Malayan Union was established, the three systems were fused, and a Supreme Court and Court of Appeal added.

In 1948 the new Federation of Malaya created a new structure of inferior courts, comprising the Sessions Court, the Magistrate's Court, and the Penghulus Courts, which complemented the Malayan Union superior courts (Omar 1987: 6). The state of Johor had adopted a constitution in 1895 and Terengganu in 1911; both were constitutional monarchies. The Federation of Malaya Agreement required each state to have a written constitution and throughout 1948, except for Penang, Malacca, and Negeri Sembilan, the states established constitutional monarchies.[2] Thus independent courts that applied English law and the written constitutions demonstrate that constitutional practice pre-dated Malayan independence.

## The written constitution

In January 1956, at a conference in London to determine the principles on which independence was to be granted, the Federation of Malaya Constitutional Commission (the Reid Commission) was appointed. Essentially, the Commission was to make recommendations providing for a Westminster-style parliamentary democracy with a bicameral legislature, a strong central government (though safeguarding the position of the rulers), and a common nationality which safeguarded the special position of the Malays but also the legitimate interests of other communities (Report of the Federation of Malaya Constitutional Commission 1957 [RFMCC 1957]; Faruqi 2008: 5–11). After holding public and private hearings in 1956, the Commission issued its recommendations in February 1957. The Alliance submitted a memorandum on what it considered to be critical, highlighting the need to deal with communal issues and the diversity of the population, which was influential in amendments to the draft.

Because of dissatisfaction with Commission recommendations, a Tripartite Working Party was established, comprising representatives of the colonial government, the rulers, and the Alliance. The rulers were thus involved in the design of the constitution. Amendments were ultimately accepted (Constitutional Proposals for the Federation of Malaya 1957 [CPFM 1957]), and the new constitution was ready when independence was declared on August 31, 1957. It has been in force ever since. The Federal Constitution provided for:

1. The legal supremacy of the constitution (Article 4(1))
2. Citizenship for all who had been citizens of the Federation of Malaya before independence and those born in the Federation on or after independence. Citizens of the United Kingdom and British colonies who had been born in the Federation before independence were entitled to claim citizenship within a year if they relinquished citizenship elsewhere. Citizenship by registration of persons aged 18 or older who were born in the Federation before independence but would not be citizens by operation of law was also allowed. Women married to a citizen and children born to citizens were entitled to seek citizenship by registration (CPFM 1957: 4, Articles 14, 15, and 16).
3. Islam as the religion of the Federation (Federal Constitution, Article 3(1)), though other religions "may be practised in peace and harmony in any part of the Federation" (Article 3(1)). The intent was made even clearer by a declaration that nothing in the article "derogates from any other provision of this Constitution" (Article 3(4)), and the Reid Commission also issued a clarification (RFMCC 1957: 20):

> This will in no way affect the present position of the Federation as a secular State, and every person will have the right to profess and practise his own religion and the right to propagate such religion, though this last right is subject to any restrictions imposed by State law relating to the propagation of any religious doctrine among persons professing the Muslim religion.

4 A guarantee of nondiscrimination on grounds of, among others, religion, race, or descent. Further, it was guaranteed that all persons were "equal before the law" and were "entitled to the equal protection of the law" (Article 8).
5 Freedom of expression (Article 10(1) (a)). Parliament could only limit this freedom by:

> such restrictions as it deems necessary or expedient in the interest of the security of the Federation or any part thereof, friendly relations with other countries, public order or morality and restrictions designed to protect the privileges of Parliament or of any Legislative Assembly or to provide against contempt of court, defamation, or incitement to any offence.
> (Article 10(2)(a))

6 Freedom of every person "to profess and practise his religion" (Article 11(1)).
7 An independent judiciary. The constitution vested judicial power in a Supreme Court and such inferior courts as Federal law provided for (Article 121).
8 Legislative powers, vested in Parliament (Article 74(1)) to enact laws in the Federal list, and the Legislative Assemblies of each state to enact laws in the State List (Article 74(2)). Either was able to enact laws in the Concurrent List.
9 Item 21 of the Federal List referred to "Newspapers; publications; publishers; printing and printing presses." Item 22 referred to "Censorship" (List 1, 9th Schedule).
10 Item 1 of the State List provided for laws related to the administration of Islam and allowed for Muslim courts to be established with jurisdiction over persons professing the religion of Islam. It also allowed for the creation of offenses against the precepts of Islam "except in regard to matters included in the Federal List" (List 2, 9th Schedule).

These features of the Federal Constitution are immediately relevant here. They were the product of an inclusive process of consultation and compromise between the primary stakeholders. They were also understood to reflect a constitutional arrangement that in many ways mirrored the arrangement in pre-independence Malaya. As the Reid Commission noted (RFMCC 1957: 7):

> In making our recommendations we have had constantly in mind two objectives: first that there must be the fullest opportunity for the growth of a united, free and democratic nation, and secondly that there must be every facility for the development of the resources of the country and the maintenance and improvement of the standard of living of the people. These objectives can only be achieved by the action of the people themselves: our task is to provide the framework most appropriate for their achievement.

> We must start from the present position as we find it, taking account not only of the history and tradition of Malaya but also of existing social and economic conditions. Much that is good has already been achieved and we would not seek to undo what has been done. But many existing arrangements are inappropriate for a self-governing and independent country, and ... we have borne in mind that the new provisions must be both practicable in existing circumstances and fair to all sections of the community.

## From 1957 to 1987

The Alliance was the predecessor to the National Front coalition currently in power.[3] The backbone of both were the three political parties: the UMNO, MIC, and MCA. From the outset the UMNO was dominant, characterizing itself as defender and protector of Malays. During the period leading to the declaration of independence and immediately after, the UMNO favored a secular system in which religion was less visible; it was for all intents and purposes a private matter (Wan 2007: 20). Having the political space, it sought to foster a secular nationalism to integrate a multi-ethnic and religiously diverse population (Wan 2007: 68–69).

At first there was little contestation about matters of faith and ethnicity, though the Islamist political party Parti Al-Islam Se-Malaysia (PAS) rebranded itself as such in 1973. As an Islamist party, its aim has consistently been a government that embraces Islamic values and approaches identity issues from an Islamic point of view (Hirschl 2013). Islam as a fundamental criterion for Malay-ness sets the PAS apart from the UMNO (Wan 2007: 24) and contrasts it with the UMNO's ethnic emphasis on identity (Harding 2002: 158). It has long been disdainful of the UMNO's seeming satisfaction with the status of Islam as a legitimizing instrument rather than as a living vital faith (Wan 2007: 27; Moustafa 2014: 161). However, for reasons beyond the scope of this chapter, the PAS did not gain much political traction in the three decades or so after independence (Noor 2004).

At the time, the nation was developing rapidly – a fact the National Front exploited. The race riots that erupted following the general election in 1969 (Khoo and Loh 2002: 4) left an indelible mark on the Malaysian consciousness. Alliance leaders were quick to blame the riots on disparities in the economic status of the Malays and the more successful Chinese and the insensitivity of non-Malays to matters at the heart of the Malay identity: the rulers, the national language, and the special privileges of Malays. This last was designed to undermine claims of opposition parties for greater equality between ethnic groups, something they had pursued in the general election of 1969. The course of the riots and the purported insensitivity of the non-Malays became a constant theme for the Alliance, and later the National Front, as a reminder not just of the need to co-exist with sensitivity but also of the ostensible value of the National Front taking the lead. It is not surprising that the opposition found it hard to retake the ground it had claimed during the 1969 election.[4]

During this phase, constitutional practice was fairly smooth. The judiciary was perceived as independent and competent. The constitution was unquestionably supreme. As Lord President Tun Suffian observed in *Ah Thian* v. *Government of Malaysia* [1976] 2 MLJ 112, 113:

> The doctrine of the supremacy of Parliament does not apply in Malaysia. Here we have a written constitution. The power of Parliament and of state legislatures in Malaysia is limited by the Constitution, and they cannot make any law they please.

Equally, there was no doubt about whether the doctrine of the separation of powers applied. As the Lord President pithily observed in *Merdeka University Berhad* v. *Government of Malaysia* [1982] 2 MLJ 243, 252 (Lee 2005):

> The fact that the Federal and High Courts are excluded from the definition of public authority does not affect the question before us. It is due to the need to maintain judicial independence and to make clear that these courts are not part of the Executive.

The judiciary appreciated, and proclaimed, its role as a bulwark against executive excesses. Chief Justice Raja Azlan Shah[5] famously proclaimed in *Pengarah Tanah dan Galian, Wilayah Persekutuan* v. *Sri Lempah Enterprise Sdn Bhd* [1979] 1 MLJ 135, 148 that:

> Every legal power must have legal limits, otherwise there is dictatorship. In particular, it is a stringent requirement that discretion should be exercised for a proper purpose, and that it should not be exercised unreasonably. In other words, every discretion cannot be free from legal restraint; where it is wrongly exercised, it becomes the duty of the courts to intervene.... In these days, when government departments and public authorities have such great powers and influence, this is a most important safeguard for the ordinary citizen: so that the courts can see that these great powers and influence are exercised in accordance with law. I would once again emphasise what has often been said before, that "public bodies must be compelled to observe the law and it is essential that bureaucracy should be kept in its place."
>
> (per Danckwerts L.J. in *Bradbury* v. *London Borough of Enfield* [1967] 3 All ER 434 442)

The judiciary was also unequivocal in its position that the public sphere of the country was secular, notwithstanding the declaration in Article 3(1) of the Federal Constitution that Islam was the religion of the Federation (Harding 2002: 166–167). In *Che Omar bin Che Soh* v. *Public Prosecutor* [1988] 2 MLJ 55, the Supreme Court[6] was confronted with the question of whether the mandatory death sentence meted out to the appellant, who had been convicted of drug trafficking, was constitutional. It was argued that the death sentence was contrary to

Article 3(1) as it was against the injunctions of Islam, Islamic law not recognizing such a sentence for such an offense. Speaking for a unanimous court, Lord President Salleh Abas dismissed the argument:

> During the British colonial period, through their system of indirect rule and establishment of secular institutions, Islamic law was rendered isolated in a narrow confinement of the law of marriage, divorce and inheritance only (see M.B. Hooker, *Islamic Law in South-east Asia*, 1984). In our view, it is in this sense of dichotomy that the framers of the Constitution understood the meaning of the word "Islam" in the context of Article 3. It if had been otherwise, there would have been another provision in the Constitution which would have the effect that any law contrary to the injunction of Islam will be void.... Article 162, on the other hand, purposely preserves the continuity of secular law prior to the Constitution, unless such law is contrary to the latter.

## The Islamic race

Dr. Mahathir Mohamad became Prime Minister in 1981 as the PAS was aligning itself with Islamist movements and political organizations elsewhere (Noor 2004: 33–36; Khoo 2004: 7–8).[7] Noor identified in this year two important developments within the party: the rise to prominence of the *ulama* (Islamic scholars), and the steady radicalization and "Arabization" of the party's political discourse. The party had evolved from critic of neo-colonialism to staunch defender of Malay rights to violent opponent of communalism, secularism, and the materialism of the capitalist development promoted by the UMNO (Noor 2004: 349–351). According to Noor, this threatened to give the PAS the upper hand in defining the meaning and content of Islam. The UMNO responded by positioning itself as protector of not only Malays but also Islam (Noor 2004: 371). It began to apply a state Islamization policy designed to promote its version of Islam as a modern way of life, culture, and government (Noor 2004: 371; Moustafa 2014: 161). In 1981, the UMNO General Assembly issued a resolution that state and federal Islamic councils should enforce and defend the purity of Islam (Noor 2004: 374).

Dr. Mahathir and the UMNO espoused a modernist and moderate Islam, rejecting the PAS version as obscurantist, extremist, fanatical, and intolerant (Noor 2004: 373). The machinery of the state was directed to eliminating different sites and sources of Islamic authority and outdoing the claims and promises of the PAS and other Islamist movements, esepecially Anwar Ibrahim's Islamic Youth Movement. Sects and groups were identified as deviationist: in 1982 the Ahmadis were stripped of their status as Malays, certain Sufi and Shia teachings were declared deviationist, and Islamic universities, think tanks, research institutes, and an Islamic Bank were launched (Noor 2004: 374–377; Moustafa 2014: 161). These policies persist today.

These efforts boosted Dr. Mahathir's image as a Muslim leader, internationally as well as domestically. After the UMNO defeated the PAS in all the 1982 and 1983 by-elections (Noor 2004: 378), the PAS stepped up its ideological offensive (Khoo 2004: 10). Its leaders denounced the UMNO-led effort as a charade to disguise as Islamic the entrenchment of the nation within the global liberal-capitalist system (Noor 2004: 379). Dr. Mahathir's government was aware that by raising the stakes in what had become an Islamization race, it was bound to antagonize other Islamist movements and parties (Moustafa 2014: 167). It had allowed debate about the correct interpretation and practice of Islam (Noor 2004: 381). Contestation had heightened, with the PAS effectively forcing a reframing of the political discourse about Islam (Khoo 2004: 9–10).

To preclude the possibility of further doctrinal conflict, the government empowered the religious arm of the bureaucracy. The notorious Internal Security Act was invoked to detain purported militant Islamic fundamentalists; clearly, the government was willing to use the machinery of state where matters of religion were concerned (Noor 2004: 383). The PAS was unrelenting, capitalizing on a series of controversies involving Dr. Mahathir and his government, and exploiting all opportunities to expose the UMNO. For instance, in 1983 there was a stand-off between the rulers and Dr. Mahathir when the latter sought to amend the Federal Constitution to make the discretionary power of the king (Federal Constitution, Article 66) to assent to a parliamentary bill a mere formality and to allow the prime minister to unilaterally declare a state of emergency (Article 159). The amendments were passed only after public controversy during which the PAS defended the rulers (Noor 2004: 388).[8] The PAS also exploited disclosures of wrongdoing related to the state-owned Bank Bumiputra and its investment arm, Bumiputra Malaysia Finance, which in 1982 lost RM2.5 billion. Irregular lending practices, indiscriminate investment, and the use of political connections to secure financing marked the scandal, the first of the Mahathir administration (Noor 2004: 391). This was followed by a scandal involving the Malaysian Mining Company – the Malaysian government's price support vehicle in the global tin market (Noor 2004: 391–392).

The PAS continued on the offensive, condemning government cronyism and misfeasance. In 1984, it criticized the government for not abandoning the Federal Constitution as a relic of colonial rule. It argued that if the government was serious about Islamization it should lay the foundation for a truly Islamic State (Noor 2004: 393). As Noor observed, the PAS was again raising the Islamization stakes, accusing the UMNO of betraying the interests of Malay Muslims. Several PAS leaders were detained under the Internal Security Act on the ground that their speeches and sermons were a threat to national security and harmony (Noor 2004: 393).When one of the *ulama* targeted for detention, Ibrahim Mahmood, escaped, he became the target of a raid by security forces in 1985 in which 15 people died, including Ibrahim himself. A force used in the raid on the village where he was living was hugely disproportionate; automatic rifles, tear gas, and an armored vehicle were employed. The nation was shocked, and the PAS was again able to denounce the UMNO as fundamentally opposed to Islam.

The situation confronting Dr. Mahathir and the UMNO was dire. In early 1986 the country entered its first recession since independence, caused in part by a transition from a commodity-based to an industrial-based economy. The public was increasingly frustrated because the government seemed unable to steer the country out of the recession. A UMNO leadership crisis was precipitated by the acrimonious resignation of Dr. Mahathir's deputy, Musa Hitam. Dr. Mahathir was increasingly viewed as authoritarian; banning the *Asian Wall Street Journal* for exposing two major bank scandals did not help (Noor 2004: 407–408).

## What happened in 1987?

Although the National Front won the general election in 1986, it became clear that Dr. Mahathir had to take drastic steps to secure his position. Musa Hitam, aligned with Razaleigh Hamzah, mounted a leadership challenge. When they lost, their faction was expelled. They took the matter to the High Court, arguing that certain delegates were not entitled to vote. Surprisingly, the High Court (*Mohd Noor Bin Othman and Ors* v. *Mohd Yusof Jaafar and Ors* [1988] 2 MLJ 129) declared the UMNO to be an unlawful society (Noor 2004: 420). Dr. Mahathir and his supporters then registered a new political party, the UMNO Baru (the new UMNO)[9] – a highly controversial move.[10] The dissident faction also established a new party, Semangat 46 (The Spirit of 46), recalling the UMNO's original rationale and denouncing Dr. Mahathir's leadership.

Meanwhile, the MCA was also having problems. Its president, Tan Koon Swan, had been imprisoned in Singapore for having abetted a criminal breach of trust. The MCA was in no position to support Dr. Mahathir, especially since public support was swinging to the predominantly Chinese opposition Democratic Action Party (DAP). Meanwhile, dissident elements within the parties began raising sensitive race-based issues to attract support. By mid-1987 both conservative Malay nationalists and Chinese community leaders were making inflammatory demands. In October 1987, the Mahathir government detained 119 persons under the Internal Security Act, many of them opposition politicians and Members of Parliament, and banned several mainstream newspapers (Noor 2004: 421–424). The internal National Front crisis had now become a national crisis.

## The judicial crisis

Meanwhile, in 1986, dissatisfied with several court decisions that he felt unfairly limited the powers of the executive,[11] Dr. Mahathir began a virulent campaign against the judiciary. In an interview in *Time* magazine (November 24, 1986), he said:

> The Judiciary says [to us], "Although you passed a law with a certain thing in mind, we think that your mind is wrong, and we want to give our interpretation." If we disagree, the Courts will say, "We will interpret your disagreement". If we go along, we are going to lose our power of legislation. We know exactly what we want to do, but once we do it, it is interpreted in

> a different way, and we have no means to reinterpret it our way. If we find out that a Court always … interprets contrary to why we made the law, we will have to find a way of producing a law that will have to be interpreted according to our wish.[12]

It is perhaps unfortunate that in this heightened atmosphere the power to review came to prominence before the Supreme Court in 1987 (*Public Prosecutor* v. *Dato' Yap Peng* [1987] CLJ Rep 284). The issue was the constitutionality of Section 418A of the Criminal Procedure Code which entitled the Public Prosecutor to require, by certificate, a subordinate court to transfer a pending criminal case to a High Court of the Public Prosecutor's choice. The power to transfer proceedings had historically been exclusive to the High Court. Not surprisingly, the High Court ([1987] 2 MLJ 311) struck down the section for having interfered with judicial power under Article 121(1) of the Malaysian Constitution as it then stood. A Supreme Court majority affirmed.[13] There followed the High Court decision in *Karpal Singh* v. *Menteri Hal Ehwal Dalam Negeri, Malaysia and Anor* [1988] 1 CLJ Rep 632, which granted *habeas corpus* to Karpal Singh, an opposition stalwart and long-Mahathir foe, who had been detained in the 1987 crackdown. On March 17, 1988, the government reacted with a bill to amend Article 121(1). Having passed both Houses of Parliament, the amendment came into force on June 10. Before amendment, the article read:

> Subject to Clause (2), the Judicial Power of the Federation shall be vested in two High Courts of co-ordinate jurisdiction and status, namely –
>
> (a) one in the States of Malaya, which shall be known as the High Court in Malaya and shall have its principal registry in Kuala Lumpur; and
> (b) one in the States of Sabah and Sarawak, which shall be known as the High Court in Borneo and shall have its principal registry at such place in the States of Sabah and Sarawak as the Yang di-Pertuan Agong may determine;
> (c) (Repealed)
>
> and in such inferior courts as may be provided by federal law.

As amended, the last line was expanded to read: "and such inferior courts as may be provided by federal law and the High Courts and inferior courts shall have such jurisdiction and powers as may be conferred by or under federal law." The amendment also introduced a provision that has since proven pivotal in efforts to recast the constitution. Article 121(1A) now provided: "The courts referred to in Clause (1) shall have no jurisdiction in respect of any matter within the jurisdiction of the Syariah courts."

After Mahathir's attacks the Superior Court judges decided that the Lord President would send a confidential letter to the Yang di-Pertuan Agong describing their unease at the state of affairs. It expressed the hope that "the unfounded accusations [by the Prime Minister] will be stopped." The Lord President was then charged with misconduct in office, and a tribunal removed him on July 7. His crime was to have acted as any reasonable Chief Justice would. Two other Supreme Court justices were removed for having defended the Lord President (Mohamed and Das 1989). These events were roundly condemned (Lee 2005, Lee 1995: 47). Dr. Mahathir's successor, Abdullah Badawi, issued an apology in his speech at the Malaysian Bar Council dinner at the J.W. Marriott Hotel, Kuala Lumpur on April 17, 2008.[14]

## Implications of the amendment

Dr. Mahathir delivered on his threats against the judiciary by sacking the Lord President and amending Article 121(1). He thus suborned the judiciary through intimidation and by fettering its power through, in my view, an unconstitutional legal contrivance. A former prime minister described the sacking of the Lord President as demonstrating "spiritual corruption," "cynicism," "viciousness," and "horrible ruthlessness" (Mohamed and Das 1989: Foreword). Michael Kirby, then president of the New South Wales Court of Appeal and a member of the International Commission of Jurists, observed that the events were so "unprecedented as to attract the anxiety of the world assembly of the Commission" (Mohamed and Das 1989: Foreword). As for the amendment, Sultan Azlan Shah, a former Lord President, stated (Lee 2005):

> With this amendment, it would appear that the judicial power is no longer vested in the courts, and more importantly the High Courts have been stripped of their inherent jurisdiction. Their powers are now only to be derived from any federal law that may be passed by Parliament. The effect of this change may have far-reaching consequences on the separation of powers doctrine under the Federal Constitution.

The International Commission noted that making High Court jurisdiction and powers dependent on federal law meant that there could be "no constitutionally entrenched original jurisdiction," which

> undermines the separation of powers and presents a subtle form of influence over the exercise of judicial power. This makes the operation of the High Court dependent on the legislature and is a threat to the structural independence of the judiciary.
>
> (Lee 2005: 7–9)

The Mahathir assault on the judiciary was clearly intended to undermine judicial independence. As Tun Suffian underscored a few years later (Wu 1999: 99):

> The judiciary in our country is supposed to be independent. Well, you know what the position is today regardless of what individual judges think and

> feel – and they are honest men. Public confidence in the judiciary has been seriously eroded and it will take a whole generation before the damage can be remedied.

Perhaps an indication of the extent of the damage, and its lasting effect, is that the judiciary has still not seized the chance to remedy it. In 2007, the Court of Appeal heard an appeal that presented a unique opportunity to find a way around the 1988 amendment. When the appellant was convicted of murder by the High Court, because he was a minor, Section 97(1) of the Child Act 2001 applied. This prohibited sentencing a child to death; instead, Section 92(2) provided for detention in prison during the pleasure of the Ruler of the State where the offense was committed (Child Act, Section 97). The High Court accordingly sent him to prison. The appeal argued that Section 97(2) violated the doctrine of separation of powers because it vested the judicial power of punishment in the executive. The Court of Appeal (*Kok Wah Kuan* v. *Public Prosecutor* [2007] 5 MLJ 174) allowed the appeal, holding that the section was unconstitutional because the 1988 amendment could not have had the effect of divesting judicial power from the judiciary. The Federal Court (*Public Prosecutor* v. *Kok Wah Kuan* [2008] 1 MLJ 1) disagreed, affirming the validity of the amendment and further expressing doubt that separation of powers was part of the constitutional arrangement.

Judicial acceptance of the stifling effect of the amendment was perhaps most clearly shown when the Federal Court thereafter endorsed a literal and formulaic application of ouster or privative provisions to preclude judicial review. In *Kerajaan Malaysia* v. *Nasharuddin Nasir* [2004] 1 CLJ 81, the Federal Court had before it Internal Security Act Section 8B, a privative clause. The police had detained the appellant under Section 73, which allowed for detention without trial for up to 60 days. *Habeas corpus* proceedings were commenced, in the course of which the Minister of Home Affairs issued a detention order under Section 8, which allowed for detention of up to two years. Section 8B applied to the second order. The High Court granted *habeas corpus*, but the Federal Court reversed, holding that the ouster provision had effect. Steve Shim, Chief Judge Sabah and Sarawak, said at p. 95:

> [A]n ouster clause may be effective in ousting the court's review jurisdiction if that is the clear effect that Parliament intended … if the intention of Parliament is expressed in words which are clear and explicit, then the court must give expression to that intention. Clearly, the intention of Parliament is to be garnered from the wording of the ouster clause.

## The impact of Article 121(1A)

Dr. Mahathir had made it clear that his word was law, and that he would brook no resistance to what he believed to be necessary. Although between 1987 and 1990 economic recovery brought growth, the National Front won the 1990 general election by a narrower margin, and a significant number of parliamentary seats went to the PAS and Semangat 46 (Harding 2002: 173–174; Khoo 2004: 2). The PAS also toppled the National Front in Kelantan to form the state government. This was a major blow to the party, and to Dr. Mahathir. Contestation intensified (Wan 2007: 106). Among other things, in 1993 the PAS passed a law endorsing Islamic *hudud* and *qisas* criminal law in Kelantan (Harding 2002: 174).[15] The UMNO-led government countered by declaring that the law was not appropriate for a multi-ethnic population, and the version the PAS proposed was in any case not consistent with Islam. The argument carried on into 1998, when Dr. Mahathir ousted Anwar Ibrahim from the Cabinet; Ibrahim was then prosecuted for abuse of power and sodomy. This allowed the PAS to frame and counter-frame political discourse so as to keep Islam at the forefront of the discussion (Wan 2007: 147–150). By 2001 Dr. Mahathir was pushed into declaring that Malaysia was an Islamic state.[16]

While many were quick to dismiss it as simply political posturing, the declaration was made at a point where the primary state institutions were all under the influence, direct or indirect, of the Mahathir government. It was widely believed, for instance, that the power to appoint and promote judges was entirely within the prerogative of the prime minister. This clearly affected how judges perceived their relationship with the executive (Report of the Royal Commission of Enquiry 2008). Significantly, soon after the Lord President was removed, the judiciary was plagued by corruption scandals that the government chose not to deal with (Report of the International Bar Association *et al.* 2000: 55–63, Harding 2012: ch. 6). The potential for executive influence had increased.

Moreover, following the judicial crisis, the number of judges appointed from the Bar dwindled almost to vanishing point; the vast majority were appointed from the Attorney General's Chambers. Never having been in private practice, many of these had no direct experience of the traditions of the Bar and were thus not able to fully appreciate the distinction between Bar and Bench. In some cases, the lack of experience may have blurred the lines defining judicial roles and encouraged a tendency to be more responsive to authority than was previously the case. That almost all such appointees were ethnically Malay is a fact that cannot be ignored, given the cultural context, the sentiments of the community, and the constitutional status of Malays.

Although the Federal government had acknowledged the need for better-qualified judges (Sarwar 2012) and had in 2009 set up a Judicial Appointments Commission, although this was a step in the right direction, the law governing that Commission leaves much to be desired. In fact, since 2008, more new High Court judges have been drawn from the Bar.

## Impact on constitutional practices

The trend of decisions pertaining to the administration of Islam since the mid-1990s illustrates the impact this state of affairs has had on constitutional practice. These cases reflect an approach that is wholly out of step with how the judiciary from independence to 1988 had understood its role and applied the Federal Constitution. Since the mid-1990s courts have been reluctant to address matters related to Islam on the even plane that the Federal Constitution requires and with regard to the equal protection it guarantees.

It may be that the judiciary, cowed by the assault on it in 1988 and completely at the mercy of the government, has over the years felt it necessary to secure its position by being as nonconfrontational as possible when it perceives matters to be particularly sensitive to the government. It may also be that the government's intensifying Islamization efforts have indirectly led Muslim judges to believe that they are expected, if not entitled, to defend their faith and interpret the Federal Constitution accordingly. Considering how many such cases come before the courts, judges are clearly not shielded from the contestation. The Federal Court has on more than one occasion been beseeched[17] to depart from *Che Omar bin Che Soh* v. *Public Prosecutor* [1988] 2 MLJ 55, and to interpret Article 3(1) as making Islamic law supreme.[18] As this chapter was written, two appeals were pending before the Federal Court in which the central issue is whether Islamic law must be consistent with fundamental constitutional guarantees. That the appellants were given leave to appeal is perhaps an indication of how the court may rule.

The Attorney General's Chambers has been harnessed to further the efforts to Islamize the legal system (Patail 2007). Indeed, in these matters Chambers officers advocate positions that are not easily reconciled with the Federal Constitution.[19]

Moreover, efforts at constitutional revisionism have continued (Lee 2010: 57–59; Sarwar 2008) – driven in part by the UMNO's highly divisive racial and religious rhetoric (Sarwar 2014). Not only did the trend survive Dr. Mahathir's retirement; his successors, Ahmad Badawi and Najib Razak, have made even greater efforts to position Islam in the public sphere.[20] Razak has even seemed to condone PAS efforts to enforce *hudud* and *qisas* law in Kelantan.

## The Islamic conversion cases

The approach taken to cases of conversion to and from Islam reflect how judicial attitudes have changed. No cases concerning apostasy came to the High Court until the early 1990s. Before that, there seem to have been no issues related to legal constraints on the right to renounce; rather, challenges would usually arise in one of two situations:

- Applications for declaratory relief to the effect that a deceased person had not died a Muslim – usually prompted by the Islamic authorities having laid claim to the deceased for Islamic burial rites. The cases of *Dalip Kaur* v. *Pegawai Polis Daerah, Balai Polis Daerah, Bukit Mertajam and Anor* [1992] 8 Jurnal Hukum 306 (High Court) and *Dalip Kaur* v. *Pegawai Polis Daerah, Balai Polis Daerah, Bukit Mertajam and Anor* [1992] 1 MLJ 1 (Supreme Court) are illustrative. Dalip Kaur petitioned the High Court for a declaration that her deceased son, who had early in life embraced Islam, had returned to Sikhism before he died. Treating the matter as a question of fact, the High Court assumed jurisdiction. This was, in my view, correct. Because the religious status of the deceased involved application of the constitutional guarantee of freedom of religion, it was a matter of public law. Moreover, the plaintiff, Dalip Kaur, had no standing in an Islamic court.

- Persons seeking declarations that they not be treated as Muslims for purposes of law. Muslims are subject to numerous Islamic laws and may not marry non-Muslims. Starting in the early 1990s, Islamic authorities were not accepting declarations by individuals that they no longer professed the religion and continued to treat them as Muslims for purposes of law. With Islamization efforts ramping up and PAS and UMNO at loggerheads, this became, as it still is, a thorny issue. One Muslim woman had retained a lawyer for advice on how to renounce Islam in favor of Christianity. The lawyer prepared a statutory declaration for her, and she affirmed it. Her parents confined her to the house but she escaped. The police were called in and the lawyer was arrested and remanded for refusing on grounds of professional privilege to divulge information that could lead to her whereabouts, though ultimately no charges were preferred (*In re Leonard Teoh* [1988] 1 CLJ 857).

The High Court was initially willing to deal with these situations, as was shown by its approach in the Dalip Kaur case. However, as Islamization efforts picked up, some stakeholders began to adopt the position that even where litigants were non-Muslims, Article 121(1A) obliged the Islamic courts to take jurisdiction – not the High Court.

Some judges rejected this view, concluding that where the relief sought was beyond the remedies available to an Islamic court, such cases were properly before the High Court (*Faridah Bte Dato Talib* v. *Mohamed Habibullah Bin Mahmood* [1990] 1 MLJ 174). Alternatively, they concluded, Islamic courts had only the jurisdiction conferred by written law; otherwise, Article 121(1A) does not apply (*Lim Chan Seng* v. *Pengarah Jabatan Agama Islam Pulau Pinang and Another Case* [1996] 3 CLJ 231).

Other judges, however, adopted the view that even where there was no such written law, the fact that the legislature was competent to enact such a law was sufficient to remove jurisdiction from the High Court (*Md Hakim Lee* v. *Majlis Agama Islam Wilayah Persekutuan, Kuala Lumpur* [1998] 1 MLJ 681). This conclusion is patently contrary not only to the actual wording of Article 121(1A) but also to constitutional guarantees of freedom of religion and equal protection before the law. Furthermore, High Courts are empowered to issue any order necessary to give effect to the fundamental liberties of an individual (Courts of Judicature Act 1964, Item 1 of the Schedule and Section 25).

Nevertheless, the Federal Court eventually endorsed the latter view *(Majlis Ugama Pulau Pinang* v. *Shaikh Zolkaffily* [2003] 3 CLJ 289, *Lina Joy* v. *Majlis Agama Islam Wilayah Persekutuan and Ors* [2007] 4 MLJ 585) – even though it leaves aggrieved litigants without a remedy.[21] Although the Federal Court did reaffirm the basis of the jurisdiction of Islamic courts, declaring in *Latifah bte Mat Zin* v. *Rosmawati bte Sharibun and Anor* [2007] 5 MLJ 101 that they had only such jurisdiction as was vested in them by written law, the situation is not yet resolved: in *Subashini a/p Rajasingam* v. *Saravanan a/l Thangathoray and other Appeals* [2008] 2 MLJ 147, the court questioned the correctness of that view.

Moreover, the Federal Court continues to hold that persons born into or converted to the Islamic religion must secure an order from an Islamic court declaring them to be apostate before they may assert for legal purposes that they are not Muslim. Its most recent pronouncement on the subject came in *Hj Raimi bin Abdullah* v. *Siti Hasnah Vangarama bt Abdullah and Another Appeal* [2014] 3 MLJ 757, where it reaffirmed its decision in *Soon Singh A/L Bikar Singh* v. *Pertubuhan Kebajikan Islam Malaysia (PERKIM) Kedah and Anor* [1999] 1 MLJ 489 that, since an Islamic court was vested with jurisdiction to deal with conversions to Islam, impliedly it had jurisdiction to deal with the renouncement of Islam.

This was not correct. Islamic courts did not have jurisdiction over conversions to Islam because that is an administrative matter not involving the courts – as the Federal Court had recognized in *Subashini a/p Rajasingam* v. *Saravanan a/l Thangathoray and other Appeals* (2008). The Hj Raimi bin Abdullah court did not take this into consideration, not even citing *Subashini a/p Rajasingam* v. *Saravanan a/l Thangathoray and other Appeals* (2008).

That the Federal Court has continued to apply its 1999 Soon Singh decision is regrettable. It has not been willing to address the constitutionality of the requirement of an "exit order" on the ground that the issue had not been raised in the High Court, even though it has been a practice to allow points of constitutionality to be raised at any stage.

Although the Federal Court did consider the constitutional argument in *Lina Joy* v. *Majlis Agama Islam Wilayah Persekutuan and Ors* (2007), the Court rejected it on the theory that the constitutional guarantee was to be read as subject to Islamic law where Muslims were concerned – even though the guarantee was framed as applying to all persons. The Court further read Item 1 of the State List as vesting legislative competence in state assemblies to enact laws on apostasy, again despite the fact that the item expressly provides that the jurisdiction of Islamic courts is limited to persons professing the religion of Islam. Apostates are by definition persons who do not profess a religion and Islamic court jurisdiction would thus not apply. It seems to me that how the Court implied terms into the constitution was not justified in law. The Court, however, did not address the argument that it was not entitled to do so.

## Limits on religious freedom

The judiciary has clearly been unwillingly to directly address the conflicts of jurisdiction between the Islamic courts and the High Court in a way that conforms to the constitutional guarantees. One result has been tremendous controversy.[22]

The implications are grave. The issue goes well beyond the apostasy and "body-snatching" cases. It arises also in cases involving the unilateral conversion of children of a marriage between non-Muslims to Islam when one spouse converts to Islam. This is particularly so when the new convert attempts to commence divorce and custody proceedings in an Islamic court. The High Court has not addressed the matter directly, which has understandably caused great frustration.[23] Although the High Court decision in *Indira Gandhi a/p Mutho* v. *Pengarah Jabatan Agama Islam Perak and Ors* [2013], 5 MLJ 552 was a welcome departure from the trend, that case is still subject to appeal.

Parallel proceedings have also not had satisfactory outcomes. The High Court in *Indira Gandhi a/p Mutho* v. *Patmanathan a/l Krishnan* (anyone having and control over Prasana Diksa) [2015] 7 MLJ 153) had found the husband to be in contempt of a custody order for refusing to hand over one of their three children to the wife; the court ruled that the husband could not rely on a prior Islamic court order granting him custody of the child. When the High Court granted a committal and recovery order, the Inspector General of Police refused to execute it. The High Court (*Indira Gandhi a/p Mutho* v. *Ketua Polis Negara* [2015] 9 MLJ 301) then granted a mandamus order to compel the Inspector General to execute the previous order. When the Court of Appeal overturned this decision in *Ketua Polis Negara* v. *Indira Gandhi a/p Mutho* [2015] 2 MLJ 149, the Federal Court granted Indira Gandhi leave to appeal.

Some insight into High Court thinking on matters related to the administration of Islam may be gleaned from its decisions on the Allah case. In granting the Catholic Church a permit to publish a Malay version of the *Herald* newspaper, the Ministry of Home Affairs had prohibited use in the publication of the word "Allah." However, the Church had in its congregations Malay-speaking believers who had long used the word to refer to God. The Church sought judicial review and won in the High Court (*Titular Roman Catholic Archbishop of Kuala Lumpur* v. *Menteri Dalam Negeri and Anor* [2010] 2 MLJ 78).

Malay right-wing groups then condemned the judge for having interfered with Islam, and the Church for interfering in matters concerning the Islamic religion (Neo 2014: 4). UMNO politicians expressed similar views, and the government appealed. The rhetoric transformed the dispute from one over the use of Allah in a newsletter to use of the word by non-Muslims in any way whatsoever. Ultimately, the Court of Appeal (*Menteri Dalam Negeri and Ors* v. *Titular Roman Catholic Archbishop of Kuala Lumpur* [2013] 6 MLJ 468) overturned the decision of the High Court, controversially declaring that because the word had no place in the Christian faith it could be proscribed in a judgment that, in my view, went much further than it should have. The dispute consequently became much larger than when it began (Sarwar 2013a, 2013b). When the Church sought leave to appeal to the Federal Court, the Attorney General's Chambers opposed the application and the court refused leave on a 4 to 3 vote (*Titular Roman Catholic Archbishop of Kuala Lumpur* v. *Menteri Dalam Negeri and Ors* [2014] 4 MLJ 765).

This was unfortunate, The issue had become extremely divisive and it was essential that the matter be put in its proper context by a reasoned judgment of the highest court. The issue had always been narrow, the court being asked only to determine whether there were reasons to quash the condition imposed by the Minister. The question before the courts was really whether the Minister had reasonable grounds for his belief that use of the word would lead to public disorder – not whether its use was integral to the Christian faith. The Federal Court should have taken the opportunity to state conclusively that it was not for the courts to define religion. Sadly, it did not. The unfortunate consequence was that it reinforced the impressions of Malays that Muslims are entitled to exclusive use of the word "Allah" (Zurairi 2015).

## The narrowing of the public space

Cases of this nature have increasingly become focal points for highly charged racial and religious posturing. As its public support faded, the National Front, in particular the UMNO, has resorted to ever-broader racial and religious appeals. When the National Front lost the popular vote in the thirteenth general election, it immediately accused the Chinese community of having betrayed its trust (Bakar 2013). The UMNO has since not only ratcheted up such rhetoric, it has caused the Federal government to more aggressively suppress dissent. The government has championed use of the Sedition Act in matters concerning the Malay rulers, the Malay race, and Islam; it is perhaps not coincidental that the Royal Malaysian Police and the Attorney General's Chambers have arrested, investigated, and charged a significant number of politicians and activists with sedition on similar grounds (Malaysian Bar 2014). The authorities have been accused of being selective in their use of the law, notably taking no action even when the president of a right-wing Malay organization, Persatuan Peribumi Perkasa, suggested that Bibles containing the word "Allah" be burnt (Tan 2014).

This has narrowed the already restricted public space for discussion of the issues considered here. The Islamic administration continues to widen its influence, unchecked by public sentiment. One of the more surprising concessions has been the ceding of legislative authority to *fatwa* committees. The statutes for Islamic administration provide for such committees in order that opinions (*fatwas*) may be sought as needed. Under classical Islamic law, *fatwas* are not binding until incorporated into binding edicts or laws made by an authority having the power to do so. However, *fatwas* are declared to be binding on Muslims and enforceable in Islamic courts once they are gazetted with the assent of the ruler. Because this bypasses legislative bodies, in effect *fatwa* committees are making law. The issue has been complicated even further by creation of the offense of acting contrary to *fatwa*, for which the elements of the offense were determined by a *fatwa* committee rather than by the legislative body.

This issue went before the Federal Court in *Sulaiman bin Takrib* v. *Kerajaan Negeri Terengganu* (Kerajaan Malaysia, intervener) and other applications [2009] 6 MLJ 354. Both the Federal government and the Terengganu state government opposed the petition on the theory footing that the framework allowing for issuance of binding *fatwas* was constitutional, notwithstanding that it in effect allowed *fatwa* committees to act as legislative bodies. They also argued for the validity of the offense. The Federal Court concluded that both framework and offense were constitutional.

It was to be expected that the boundaries would be tested by Islamic administrators. In 2014, the Selangor *Fatwa* Committee issued a *fatwa*, which was gazetted, declaring that any individual, institution, or organization holding to a liberal and pluralist religious understanding of Islam was to be considered misguided and deviationist. The *fatwa* singled out Sisters in Islam (SIS), an internationally acclaimed nongovernmental organization which promotes an understanding of Islam that gives due recognition and deference to the rights of women. The *fatwa* banned materials containing elements of liberalism and pluralism, and directed the Malaysian Communications and Multimedia Commission to block any websites containing such elements. It clearly transgressed every legal boundary: it sought to restrict free expression, even by persons not within the jurisdiction of the Islamic courts, non-Muslims and bodies corporate, and sought to direct agencies of the Federal government. SIS obtained leave to seek judicial review and the proceedings are now before the High Court.

Similarly, the Islamic prosecutors sought to charge the Muslim director of the publishing company that published the Malay translation of Irshad Manji's book, *Of Allah, Freedom and Love*, for publication of material contrary to Islamic law. It did not appear to matter that issues of publication and censorship were not within the purview of the Islamic authorities or the Islamic courts. Similarly, the prosecutors chose not to recognize that for legal purposes the publisher was the company, not the director, and the High Court had quashed a Federal government ban on distribution of the book. A challenge to the law that the prosecution relied on was taken up in the Federal Court, and once again the Federal and the Selangor state governments argued for the validity of the law. The Federal Court has not yet issued its decision.

## Conclusion

These examples are intended only as instances chosen to illuminate the points made. The subject is complex and nuanced, involving many different elements that are regrettably beyond the scope of this chapter.

The instances, however, demonstrate a clear departure from established constitutional practice since 1987 and 1988. The events removed judicial power from the judiciary – an essential feature of the constitution – and allowed Parliament, and by extension the executive, to suborn the courts. Draconian laws to reinforce the position of the executive and vest it with greater control, such as ouster clauses, further undermined the rule of law. The problem was exacerbated by a weakening of all the primary state institutions, not just the judiciary. Given the importance of race and religion in Malaysian politics, it was inevitable that eventually the rights of racial and religious minorities would be affected. These events created an environment in which how the constitution was applied would almost certainly be contested, with those holding power and influence ultimately shaping the outcome.

It must be recognized that the Federal Court recently seems to have embraced a more progressive approach toward constitutional guarantees, tentatively accepting application of the doctrine of proportionality when the state encroaches upon matters guaranteed by the constitution (*Sivarasa Rasiah* v. *Badan Peguam Malaysia* [2010] 2 MLJ 333, *Lee Kwan Woh* v. *Public Prosecutor* [2009] 5 MLJ 301). It is, however, too soon to say that a few instances will coalesce into a distinct trend, or that matters pertaining to religion would be integrated into it.

## Notes

1 The Malayan Communist Party (MCP) was formed in April 1930. When the Japanese invaded Malaysia in December 1941, the MCP worked with the British against the Japanese. Its original 1940 policy of "expulsion of British imperialism" was replaced in 1943 with a nine-point "Anti-Japanese Program." When the war ended in 1945, the MCP found itself for the first time de facto a legal organization. See Short (1975).

2 *Undang-Undang Tubuh Kerajaan Perak*, promulgated on January 2, 1948; *Undang-Undang Tubuh Kerajaan Selangor*, promulgated on January 2, 1948; *Undang-Undang Tubuh Kerajaan Pahang*, promulgated on January 2, 1948; *Undang-Undang Tubuh Kerajaan Perlis*, promulgated January 2, 1948; *Undang-Undang Tubuh Kerajaan Kelantan*, promulgated on January 2, 1948; *Undang-Undang Tubuh Kerajaan Kedah*, promulgated on January 2, 1948.

3 The National Front (*Barisan Nasional*) was registered in 1974 to succeed the Alliance and regain ground lost in the 1969 general election when the popular vote swung to the opposition. The successor coalition was broader, including political parties that were previously in the opposition and political parties from Sabah and Sarawak.

4 The Alliance, and later the National Front, had the benefit of innumerable laws that allowed for detention without trial, prosecution for sedition, and the regulation of societies and the press.

5 He was later installed as the thirty-fourth Sultan of Perak.

6 The Supreme Court, established at independence, was renamed the Federal Court in 1994.

7 Events in Iran were a major factor.

8 The amendments came into force on December 16, 1983.

9 The key events are set out in the decision of the High Court in *Tunku Abdul Rahman Putra Al-Haj and Ors* v. *Dato Seri Dr Mahathir Mohammad* [1989] 1 MLJ 48.

10 The Societies Act 1966 was amended to allow for the assets of the unlawful party to vest in the new party. Challenges in court were unavailing.

11 He was particularly incensed when the Supreme Court quashed his decision to cancel an employment pass issued to an *Asian Wall Street Journal* reporter (see *John Peter Berthelsen* v. *Director-General of Immigration, Malaysia and Ors* [1986] CLJ Rep 160.

12 This became the subject of contempt proceedings brought by Lim Kit Siang, an opposition stalwart, against Dr. Mahathir. The decision of the High Court refusing leave to commence committal proceedings is reported at [1986] CLJ Rep 462. The decision was affirmed by the Supreme Court in [1987] CLJ Rep 168.

13 The Lord President, Tun Salleh Abas, dissented, as did Hashim Yeop Sani SCJ.

14 See www.malaysianbar.org.my/speeches/prime_minister_delivering_justice_renewing_trust.html.

15 The Kelantan Shariah Criminal Code (II) Enactment 1993 could not be implemented without the cooperation of the Federal government; it required both a constitutional amendment and amendments to Federal laws vesting Islamic courts with sentencing powers.

16 At the opening of the Gerakan annual delegates' conference in September 2001. Gerakan is a component of the National Front.
17 Arguments to that effect were made in *Lina Joy* v. *Majlis Agama Islam Wilayah Persekutuan and Ors* [2007] 4 MLJ 585 and *Subashini a/p Rajasingam* v. *Saravanan a/l Thangathoray and other Appeals* [2008] 2 MLJ 147 (Federal Court).
18 See *Subashini a/p Rajasingam* v. *Saravanan a/l Thangathoray* [2007] 4 MLJ 97 (Court of Appeal) and *Subashini a/p Rajasingam* v. *Saravanan a/l Thangathoray and other Appeals* [2008] 2 MLJ 147 (Federal Court).
19 The Attorney General's Chambers has repeatedly called for highly restrictive interpretations of constitutional guarantees, not just in matters pertaining to Islam. See, for instance, *Muhammad Hilman bin Idham and Ors* v. *Kerajaan Malaysia and Ors* [2011] 6 MLJ 507, on whether university students could be prohibited from involving themselves in politics, *Malaysian Trade Union Congress and Ors* v. *Menteri Tenaga, Air dan Komunikasi and Anor* [2014] 3 MLJ 145, on disclosure of information, and *Dato' Seri Syed Hamid bin Syed Jaafar Albar (Menteri Dalam Negeri)* v. *SIS Forum (Malaysia)* [2012] 6 MLJ 340, on the banning of books.
20 Abdullah Badawi introduced Malaysians to Islam Hadhari, a governance framework informed by moderate Islam. In doing so, he unequivocally made Islam a consideration in public matters. Although Najib Razak's 1 Malaysia platform was initially promoted as inclusive and multicultural, his administration is now seen as having brought race relations to the brink. See speech by the Yang di-Pertuan Agong (the King), "Royal Address" (Opening of the … the thirteenth Kedah State Legislative Assembly, January 19, 2015) on how racial tensions have heightened to a worrying point.
21 See, for instance, *Shamala Sathiyaseelan* v. *Dr Jeyaganesh C Mogarajah and Anor* [2004] 2 MLJ 646. See also *Kamariah Ali and Ors* v. *Kelantan State Government and Anor* [2005] 1 MLJ 197, where the Federal Court declined to answer the questions posed to it on the ground that they were academic, even though the religious status of the appellants was a live issue. The appellants were later arrested again for deviationist practices even though they had renounced Islam. The validity of their renunciation was one of the issues before the Federal Court.
22 In 2004, civil society groups formed a coalition, "Article 11," to highlight the matter. Its 2005 roadshow, "Equal Protection For All," became controversial, condemned as a threat to racial and religious harmony by actors from both sides of the political divide. Abdullah Badawi directed that the coalition cease its efforts. See Lee (2010: 83–98, n. 97). In 2005, the Bar Council called a national conference to consider whether a non-adjudicatory Interfaith Commission should be established to address matters of infringement of religious harmony. This too was opposed. See Akbarzadeh and MacQueen (2008: 129–141).
23 The Federal Court had the opportunity to resolve the issue in *Subashini a/p Rajasingam* v. *Saravanan a/l Thangathoray and other Appeals* [2008] 2 MLJ 147 (Federal Court), but decided that the Muslim husband could commence proceedings in the Islamic court and the wife could seek relief in the High Court. The recent decision of the High Court in *Indira Gandhi a/p Mutho* v. *Patmanathan a/l Krishnan* [2015] 7 MLJ 153 may bring some resolution; the High Court concluded that even though the spouse had converted, it still had jurisdiction.

## Bibliography

Akbarzadeh, S. and MacQueen, B. (2008). *Islam and Human Rights in Practice: Perspective Across the Ummah*. London, Routledge.

Bakar, Z. (2013) "Apa lagi orang Cina mau?" Utusan Melayu, May 7, 2013, available at: http://ww1.utusan.com.my/utusan/Pilihan_Raya/20130507/px_03/Apa-lagi-orang-Cina-mahu (accessed August 5, 2015).

Constitutional Proposals for the Federation of Malaya (1957). London, Colonial Office, Her Majesty's Stationary Office, June.

Dressel, B. and Bünte, M. (2014). "Constitutional Politics in Southeast Asia: From Contestation to Constitutionalism?" *Contemporary Southeast Asia*, 36(1): 1–22.

Faruqi, S.S. (2008). *Document Of Destiny: The Constitution Of The Federation Of Malaysia*. Petaling Jaya, Star Publications.

Harding, A. (2002). "The Keris, The Crescent and the Blind Goddess: The State, Islam and the Constitution in Malaysia." *Singapore Journal of International and Comparative Law*, 6: 154–180.

Harding, A. (2012). *The Constitution of Malaysia: A Contextual Analysis*. London, Bloomsbury Publishing.

Hirschl, R. (2013). "Constitutional Courts as Bulwarks of Secularism." In *Consequential Courts: Judicial Role in Global Perspective*, eds D. Kapiszewski, G. Silverstein and R.A. Kagan. Cambridge, Cambridge University Press.

Justice in Jeopardy: Malaysia 2000 (2000). Report of a Mission on Behalf of The International Bar Association, The ICJ Center for the Independence of Judges and Lawyers, The Commonwealth Lawyer's Association and The Union Internationale Des Advocats.

Khoo, B.T. (2004). "Searching for Islam in Malaysian Politics: Confluences, Divisions and Governance." Working Paper Series No. 72. Southeast Asia Research Center.

Khoo, B.T. (2005). "Ethnic Structure, Inequality and Governance in the Public Sector: Malaysian Experiences." Democracy, Governance and Human Rights Program Paper No. 20. United Nations Research Institute for Social Development.

Khoo, B.T. and Loh, F.K.W. (2002). *Democracy in Malaysia: Discourses and Practices*. Surrey, Curzon Press.

Lee, H.P. (1995). *Constitutional Conflicts In Contemporary Malaysia*. Clarendon, Oxford University Press.

Lee, H.P. (2005). "Judicial Power and Constitutional Government: Convergence and Divergence in the Australian and Malaysian Experience." *Journal of Malaysian and Comparative Law*, 30(5): 45–57.

Lee, J.C.H. (2010). *Islamization and Activism in Malaysia*. Petaling Jaya, Strategic Information and Research Development Center.

Malaysian Bar (2014). Resolution against the Sedition Act, other laws and actions taken which stifle speech and expression, and matters in connection therewith. Kuala Lumpur, Extraordinary General Meeting of the Malaysian Bar, available at: www.malaysianbar.org.my/malaysian_bar_s_resolutions/resolution_adopted_at_the_extraordinary_general_meeting_of_the_malaysian_bar_held_at_wisma_mca_kuala_lumpur_friday_19_sept_2014.html (accessed August 5, 2015).

Mohamed, S. and Das, K. (1989). *Mayday for Justice: The Lord President's Version*. Kuala Lumpur, Magnus Books.

Moustafa, T. (2014). "Judging in God's Name: State Power, Secularism, and the Politics of Islamic Law in Malaysia." *Oxford Journal of Law and Religion*, 3(1): 152–167.

Nair, S. (1997): *Islam in Malaysian Foreign Policy*. London, Routledge.

Neo, J. (2014). "What's In a Name? Malaysia's 'Allah' Controversy and The Judicial Intertwining of Islam with Ethnic Identity." Working Paper No. 2014/008. National University of Singapore.

Noor, F.A. (2004). *Islam Embedded: The Historical Development of the Pan-Malaysian Islamic Party PAS (1951–2003)*. Kuala Lumpur, Malaysian Sociological Research Institute.

Omar, A.H. (1987). "Administration of Justice in Malaysia." *Denning Law Journal*, 2: 1–22.

Patail, A.G. (2007). "Harmonisation of Civil Laws and Shariah: Effective Strategies for Implementation." Speech presented at the third International Conference on Harmonisation of Civil Laws and Shariah, Kuala Lumpur, December 4.

Report of the Federation of Malaya Constitutional Commission (1957). London, Colonial No. 330, Her Majesty's Stationery Office.

Report of the Royal Commission of Enquiry into the Video Clip Recording of Images of a Person Purported to be an Advocate and Solicitor Speaking on the Telephone on Matters Regarding the Appointment of Judges (2008).

Sarwar, M.I. (2008). "The Politics of Race." The Malay Mail, July 29, available at: http://malikimtiaz.blogspot.com/2008/07/politics-of-race.html (accessed August 5, 2015).

Sarwar, M.I. (2012). "Pushing Ahead with Judicial Reforms." The Edge, October 23, available at: www.fz.com/content/pushing-ahead-judicial-reform (accessed August 5, 2015).

Sarwar, M.I. (2013a). "A Matter of Law, not Policy." The Edge, October 27, available at: www.fz.com/content/matter-law-not-policy (accessed August 5, 2015).

Sarwar, M.I. (2013b). "Of Allah and the State of Malaysia." Al-Jazeera, October 28, available at: www.aljazeera.com/indepth/opinion/2013/10/20131028444333318666.html (accessed August 5, 2015).

Sarwar, M.I. (2014). "Taking Liberties with the Fundamentals. The Edge, January 25, Available at: www.fz.com/content/taking-liberties-fundamentals (accessed August 5, 2015).

Short, A. (1975). *The Communist Insurrection in Malaya: 1948–1960*. London, Frederick Muller.

Tan, Y.L. (2014). "A-G: Ibrahim Ali's Bible Burning Remark not of 'Seditious Tendency'." The Star, October 27, available at: www.thestar.com.my/News/Nation/2014/10/27/attorney-general-ibrahim-ali-bible-burning-speech-not-seditious/ (accessed August 5, 2015).

Wan Napi, W.K. (2007). "The Islamization of Politics in Malaysia: How Religious Political Opportunities and Threats Influence Religious Framing and Counterframing." Dissertation submitted in partial fulfillment of the requirements for the Doctor of Philosophy Degree, Southern Illinois University.

Wu, M.A. (1999). *Public Law in Contemporary Malaysia*. Petaling Jaya, Longman.

Yang di-Pertuan Agong (the King) (2015). "Royal Address." Speech presented at the opening of the first meeting of the thirteenth Kedah State Legislative Assembly, January 19.

Zurairi, A.R. (2015). "After 'Allah' Case, Muslim Group Demands Herald Stop Using Malay." The Malay Mail, January 23, available at: www.themalaymailonline.com/malaysia/article/after-allah-case-muslim-group-demands-herald-stop-using-malay (accessed August 5, 2015).

# Index

Page numbers in *italics* denote tables.

For Product Safety Concerns and Information please contact our EU
representative GPSR@taylorandfrancis.com
Taylor & Francis Verlag GmbH, Kaufingerstraße 24, 80331 München, Germany

www.ingramcontent.com/pod-product-compliance
Ingram Content Group UK Ltd.
Pitfield, Milton Keynes, MK11 3LW, UK
UKHW020022200926
475702UK00014B/2006

*9780815356042*